Essentials of
Strategic Management

The Quest for Competitive Advantage

7e

JOHN E. GAMBLE
Texas A&M University-Corpus Christi

MARGARET A. PETERAF
Dartmouth College

ARTHUR A. THOMPSON, JR.
The University of Alabama

ESSENTIALS OF STRATEGIC MANAGEMENT: THE QUEST FOR COMPETITIVE ADVANTAGE, SEVENTH EDITION

Published by McGraw-Hill Education, 2 Penn Plaza, New York, NY 10121. Copyright © 2021 by McGraw-Hill Education. All rights reserved. Printed in the United States of America. Previous editions © 2019. No part of this publication may be reproduced or distributed in any form or by any means, or stored in a database or retrieval system, without the prior written consent of McGraw-Hill Education, including, but not limited to, in any network or other electronic storage or transmission, or broadcast for distance learning.

Some ancillaries, including electronic and print components, may not be available to customers outside the United States.

This book is printed on acid-free paper.

2 3 4 5 6 7 8 9 LWI 24 23 22 21 20

ISBN 978-1-260-26154-7 (bound edition)
MHID 1-260-26154-9 (bound edition)
ISBN 978-1-260-78584-5 (loose-leaf edition)
MHID 1-260-78584-x (loose-leaf edition)

Director: *Michael Ablassmeir*
Lead Product Developer: *Kelly Delso*
Product Developer: *Anne Ehrenworth*
Executive Marketing Manager: *Debbie Clare*
Content Project Managers: *Melissa M. Leick, Keri Johnson, Karen Jozefowicz*
Buyer: *Laura Fuller*
Design: *Matt Diamond*
Content Licensing Specialist: *Traci Vaske*
Compositor: *SPi Global*
Cover Image: *helloSG/Shutterstock*

All credits appearing on page or at the end of the book are considered to be an extension of the copyright page.

Library of Congress Cataloging-in-Publication Data

Names: Gamble, John (John E.) author. | Thompson, Arthur A., 1940- author.
 | Peteraf, Margaret Ann, author.
Title: Essentials of strategic management : the quest for competitive
 advantage / John Gamble, Texas A&M University-Corpus Christi, Margaret
 A. Peteraf, Dartmouth College, Arthur A. Thompson, Jr., The University
 of Alabama.
Description: Seventh Edition. | New York : McGraw-Hill Education, 2020. |
 Revised edition of the authors' Essentials of strategic management, 2019.
Identifiers: LCCN 2019047351 | ISBN 9781260261547 (hardcover)
Subjects: LCSH: Strategic planning. | Business planning. | Competition. |
 Strategic planning–Case studies.
Classification: LCC HD30.28 .G353 2020 | DDC 658.4/012–dc23
LC record available at https://lccn.loc.gov/2019047351

The Internet addresses listed in the text were accurate at the time of publication. The inclusion of a website does not indicate an endorsement by the authors or McGraw-Hill Education, and McGraw-Hill Education does not guarantee the accuracy of the information presented at these sites.

mheducation.com/highered

Dedication

To our families and especially our spouses:
Heather, Paul, and Hasseline.

About the Authors

John E. Gamble
Courtesy of John E. Gamble

John E. Gamble is a Professor of Management and Dean of the College of Business at Texas A&M University-Corpus Christi. His teaching and research have focused on strategic management at the undergraduate and graduate levels. He has conducted courses in strategic management in Germany since 2001, which have been sponsored by the University of Applied Sciences in Worms.

Dr. Gamble's research has been published in various scholarly journals, and he is the author or co-author of more than 75 case studies published in an assortment of strategic management and strategic marketing texts. He has done consulting on industry and market analysis for clients in a diverse mix of industries.

Professor Gamble received his PhD, Master of Arts, and Bachelor of Science degrees from the University of Alabama and was a faculty member in the Mitchell College of Business at the University of South Alabama before his appointment to the faculty at Texas A&M University-Corpus Christi.

Margaret A. Peteraf
Courtesy of Margaret A. Peteraf

Margaret A. Peteraf is the Leon E. Williams Professor of Management at the Tuck School of Business at Dartmouth College. She is an internationally recognized scholar of strategic management, with a long list of publications in top management journals. She has earned myriad honors and prizes for her contributions, including the 1999 Strategic Management Society Best Paper Award recognizing the deep influence of her work on the field of strategic management. Professor Peteraf is on the Board of Directors of the Strategic Management Society and has been elected as a Fellow of the Society. She served previously as a member of the Academy of Management's Board of Governors and as Chair of the Business Policy and Strategy Division of the Academy. She has also served in various editorial roles and is presently on nine editorial boards, including the *Strategic Management Journal,* the *Academy of Management Review,* and *Organization Science.* She has taught in Executive Education programs around the world and has won teaching awards at the MBA and Executive level.

Professor Peteraf earned her PhD, MA, and MPhil at Yale University and held previous faculty appointments at Northwestern University's Kellogg Graduate School of Management and at the University of Minnesota's Carlson School of Management.

Arthur A. Thompson, Jr. earned his BS and PhD degrees in economics from the University of Tennessee, spent three years on the economics faculty at Virginia Tech, and served on the faculty of the University of Alabama's College of Commerce and Business Administration for 25 years. In 1974 and again in 1982, Dr. Thompson spent semester-long sabbaticals as a visiting scholar at the Harvard Business School.

His areas of specialization are business strategy, competition and market analysis, and the economics of business enterprises. In addition to publishing over 30 articles in some 25 different professional and trade publications, he has authored or co-authored five textbooks and six computer-based simulation exercises that are used in colleges and universities worldwide.

Dr. Thompson spends much of his off-campus time giving presentations, putting on management development programs, working with companies, and helping operate a business simulation enterprise in which he is a major partner.

Dr. Thompson and his wife of 59 years have two daughters, two grandchildren, and a Yorkshire terrier.

Arthur A. Thompson, Jr.
Courtesy of Arthur A. Thompson, Jr.

Brief Contents

Preface

The standout features of this seventh edition of *Essentials of Strategic Management* are its concisely written and robust coverage of strategic management concepts and its compelling collection of cases. The text presents a conceptually strong treatment of strategic management principles and analytic approaches that features straight-to-the-point discussions, timely examples, and a writing style that captures the interest of students. While this edition retains the 10-chapter structure of the prior edition, every chapter has been reexamined, refined, and refreshed. New content has been added to keep the material in line with the latest developments in the theory and practice of strategic management. Also, scores of new examples have been added, along with fresh Concepts & Connections illustrations, to make the content come alive and to provide students with a ringside view of strategy in action. The fundamental character of the seventh edition of *Essentials of Strategic Management* is very much in step with the best academic thinking and contemporary management practice. The chapter content continues to be solidly mainstream and balanced, mirroring *both* the penetrating insight of academic thought and the pragmatism of real-world strategic management.

Complementing the text presentation is a truly appealing lineup of 12 diverse, timely, and thoughtfully crafted cases. All of the cases are tightly linked to the content of the 10 chapters, thus pushing students to apply the concepts and analytical tools they have read about. Six of the cases were written by the coauthors to illustrate specific tools of analysis or distinct strategic management theories. Cases not written by the coauthors were included because of their exceptional pedagogical value and linkage to strategic management concepts presented in the text. We are confident you will be impressed with how well each of the 12 cases in the collection will work in the classroom and the amount of student interest they will spark.

For some years now, growing numbers of strategy instructors at business schools worldwide have been transitioning from a purely text-cases course structure to a more robust and energizing text-cases-simulation course structure. Incorporating a competition-based strategy simulation has the strong appeal of providing class members with *an immediate and engaging opportunity to apply the concepts and analytical tools covered in the chapters in a head-to-head competition with companies run by other class members.* Two widely used and pedagogically effective online strategy simulations, *The Business Strategy Game* and *GLO-BUS,* are optional companions for this text. Both simulations, like the cases, are closely linked to the content of each chapter in the text. The Exercises for Simulation Participants, found at the end of each chapter and integrated into the *Connect*® package for the text, provide clear guidance to class members in applying the concepts and analytical tools covered in the chapters to the issues and decisions that they have to wrestle with in managing their simulation company.

Through our experiences as business school faculty members, we also fully understand the assessment demands on faculty teaching strategic management and business

policy courses. In many institutions, capstone courses have emerged as the logical home for assessing student achievement of program learning objectives. The seventh edition includes Assurance of Learning Exercises at the end of each chapter that link to the specific Learning Objectives appearing at the beginning of each chapter and are highlighted throughout the text. *An important instructional feature of this edition is the linkage of selected chapter-end Assurance of Learning Exercises and cases to* Connect®. Your students will be able to use *Connect* to (1) complete two of the Assurance of Learning Exercises appearing at the end of each of the 10 chapters, (2) complete Exercises for Simulation Participants, (3) complete chapter-end quizzes, and (4) complete case tutorials based upon the suggested assignment questions for all 12 cases in this edition. With the exception of some of the chapter-end Assurance of Learning Exercises and Exercises for Simulation Participants, all of the *Connect* exercises are automatically graded, thereby enabling you to easily assess the learning that has occurred.

In addition, both of the companion strategy simulations have a built-in Learning Assurance Report that quantifies how well each member of your class performed on nine skills/learning measures *versus tens of thousands of other students worldwide* who completed the simulation in the past 12 months. We believe the chapter-end Assurance of Learning Exercises, the online and automatically graded *Connect* exercises, and the Learning Assurance Report generated at the conclusion of *The Business Strategy Game* and *GLO-BUS* simulations provide you with easy-to-use, empirical measures of student learning in your course. All can be used in conjunction with other instructor-developed or school-developed scoring rubrics and assessment tools to comprehensively evaluate course or program learning outcomes.

Taken together, the various components of the seventh edition package and the supporting set of Instructor Resources available in *Connect* provide you with enormous course design flexibility and a powerful kit of teaching/learning tools. We've done our very best to ensure that the elements comprising this edition will work well for you in the classroom and help you economize on the time needed to be well prepared for each class; students will conclude that your course is one of the very best they have ever taken, from the standpoint of both enjoyment and learning.

Differentiation from Other Texts

Five noteworthy traits strongly differentiate this text and the accompanying instructional package from others in the field:

1. *Our integrated coverage of the two most popular perspectives on strategic management positioning theory and resource-based theory is unsurpassed by any other leading strategy text.* Principles and concepts from both the positioning perspective and the resource-based perspective are prominently and comprehensively integrated into our coverage of crafting both single-business and multibusiness strategies. By highlighting the relationship between a firm's resources and capabilities to the activities it conducts along its value chain, we show explicitly how these two perspectives relate to one another. Moreover, in Chapters 3 through 8, it is emphasized repeatedly that a company's strategy must be matched not only to its external market circumstances but also to its internal resources and competitive capabilities.

2. *Our coverage of business ethics, core values, social responsibility, and environmental sustainability is unsurpassed by any other leading strategy text.* Chapter 9, "Ethics, Corporate Social Responsibility, Environmental Sustainability, and Strategy," is embellished with fresh content so that it can better fulfill the important functions of (1) alerting students to the role and importance of ethical and socially responsible decision making and (2) addressing the accreditation requirements that business ethics be visibly and thoroughly embedded in the core curriculum. Moreover, discussions of the roles of values and ethics are integrated into portions of other chapters to further reinforce why and how considerations relating to ethics, values, social responsibility, and sustainability should figure prominently into the managerial task of crafting and executing company strategies.

3. *The caliber of the case collection in the seventh edition is truly unrivaled* from the standpoints of student appeal, teachability, and suitability for drilling students in the use of the concepts and analytical treatments in Chapters 1 through 10. The 12 cases included in this edition are the very latest, the best, and the most on-target that we could find. The ample information about the cases in the Instructor's Manual makes it effortless to select a set of cases each term that will capture the interest of students from start to finish.

4. *Connect* is tightly linked to the text chapters, business simulation, and case lineup. The *Connect* package for the seventh edition allows professors to assign autograded quizzes and select chapter-end Assurance of Learning Exercises to assess class members' understanding of chapter concepts. The *Connect* package for the seventh edition also includes open-ended and autograded Exercises for Simulation Users. In addition, our texts have pioneered the extension of *Connect* to case analysis. The autograded case exercises for each of the 12 cases in this edition are robust and extensive and will better enable students to make meaningful contributions to class discussions. The autograded *Connect* case exercises may also be used as graded assignments in the course.

5. The two cutting-edge and widely used strategy simulations—*The Business Strategy Game* and *GLO-BUS*—that are optional companions to the seventh edition give you unmatched capability to employ a text-case-simulation model of course delivery.

Organization, Content, and Features of the Seventh Edition Text Chapters

The following rundown summarizes the noteworthy features and topical emphasis in this new edition:

- Chapter 1 serves as an introduction to the topic of strategy, focusing on the managerial actions that will determine why a company matters in the marketplace. We introduce students to the primary approaches to building competitive advantage and the key elements of business-level strategy. Following Henry Mintzberg's pioneering research, we also stress why a company's strategy is partly planned and partly reactive and why this strategy tends to evolve. The chapter also discusses why it is important for a company to have a *viable business model* that outlines the company's customer value proposition and its profit formula. This brief chapter is the perfect accompaniment to your opening-day lecture on what the course is all about and why it matters.

- Chapter 2 delves more deeply into the managerial process of actually crafting and executing a strategy. It makes a great assignment for the second day of class and provides a smooth transition into the heart of the course. The focal point of the chapter is the five-stage managerial process of crafting and executing strategy: (1) forming a strategic vision of where the company is headed and why, (2) developing strategic as well as financial objectives with which to measure the company's progress, (3) crafting a strategy to achieve these targets and move the company toward its market destination, (4) implementing and executing the strategy, and (5) evaluating a company's situation and performance to identify corrective adjustments that are needed. Students are introduced to such core concepts as strategic visions, mission statements and core values, the balanced scorecard, and business-level versus corporate-level strategies. There's a robust discussion of why *all managers are on a company's strategy-making, strategy-executing team* and why a company's strategic plan is a collection of strategies devised by different managers at different levels in the organizational hierarchy. The chapter winds up with a section on how to exercise good corporate governance and examines the conditions that led to recent high-profile corporate governance failures.

- Chapter 3 sets forth the now-familiar analytical tools and concepts of industry and competitive analysis and demonstrates the importance of tailoring strategy to fit the circumstances of a company's industry and competitive environment. The standout feature of this chapter is a presentation of Michael Porter's "five forces model of competition" *that has long been the clearest, most straightforward discussion of any text in the field.* Chapter revisions include an improved discussion of the macro-environment, focusing on the use of the PESTEL analysis framework for assessing the *p*olitical, *e*conomic, *s*ocial, *t*echnological, *e*nvironmental, and *l*egal factors in a company's macro-environment. New to this edition is a discussion of Michael Porter's Framework for Competitor Analysis used for assessing a rival's likely strategic moves.

- Chapter 4 presents the resource-based view of the firm, showing why resource and capability analysis is such a powerful tool for sizing up a company's competitive assets. It offers a simple framework for identifying a company's resources and capabilities and explains how the VRIN framework can be used to determine whether they can provide the company with a sustainable competitive advantage over its competitors. Other topics covered in this chapter include dynamic capabilities, SWOT analysis, value chain analysis, benchmarking, and competitive strength assessments, thus enabling a solid appraisal of a company's relative cost position and customer value proposition vis-à-vis its rivals.

- Chapter 5 deals with the basic approaches used to compete successfully and gain a competitive advantage over market rivals. This discussion is framed around the five generic competitive strategies—low-cost leadership, differentiation, best-cost provider, focused differentiation, and focused low-cost. It describes when each of these approaches works best and what pitfalls to avoid. It explains the role of *cost drivers* and *value drivers* in reducing a company's costs and enhancing its differentiation, respectively.

- Chapter 6 deals with the *strategy options* available to complement a company's competitive approach and maximize the power of its overall strategy. These include a variety of offensive or defensive competitive moves, and their timing, such as blue ocean strategy and first-mover advantages and disadvantages. It also includes choices concerning the breadth of a company's activities (or its scope of operations along an industry's entire value chain), ranging from horizontal mergers and acquisitions, to vertical integration, outsourcing, and strategic alliances. This material serves to segue into that covered in the next two chapters on international and diversification strategies.

- Chapter 7 explores the full range of strategy options for competing in international markets: export strategies, licensing, franchising, establishing a subsidiary in a foreign market, and using strategic alliances and joint ventures to build competitive strength in foreign markets. There is also a discussion of how to best tailor a company's international strategy to cross-country differences in market conditions and buyer preferences; how to use international operations to improve overall competitiveness; the choice between multidomestic, global, and transnational strategies; and the unique characteristics of competing in emerging markets.

- Chapter 8 introduces the topic of corporate-level strategy—a topic of concern for multibusiness companies pursuing diversification. This chapter begins by explaining why successful diversification strategies must create shareholder value and lays out the three essential tests that a strategy must pass to achieve this goal (*the industry attractiveness, cost of entry, and better-off tests*). Corporate strategy topics covered in the chapter include methods of entering new businesses, related diversification, unrelated diversification, combined related and unrelated diversification approaches, and strategic options for improving the overall performance of an already diversified company. The chapter's analytical spotlight is trained on the techniques and procedures for assessing a diversified company's business portfolio—the relative attractiveness of the various businesses the company has diversified into, the company's competitive strength in each of its business lines, and the *strategic fit* and *resource fit* among a diversified company's different businesses. The chapter concludes with a brief survey of a company's four main post-diversification strategy alternatives: (1) sticking closely with the existing business lineup, (2) broadening the diversification base, (3) divesting some businesses and retrenching to a narrower diversification base, and (4) restructuring the makeup of the company's business lineup.

- Although the topic of ethics and values comes up at various points in this textbook, Chapter 9 brings more direct attention to such issues and may be used as a standalone assignment in either the early, middle, or late part of a course. It concerns the themes of ethical standards in business, approaches to ensuring consistent ethical standards for companies with international operations, corporate social responsibility, and environmental sustainability. The contents of this chapter are sure to give students some things to ponder, rouse lively discussion, and help to make students more ethically aware and conscious of *why all companies should conduct their business in a socially responsible and sustainable manner.*

- Chapter 10 is anchored around a pragmatic, compelling conceptual framework: (1) building dynamic capabilities, core competencies, resources, and structure necessary for proficient strategy execution; (2) allocating ample resources to strategy-critical activities; (3) ensuring that policies and procedures facilitate rather than impede strategy execution; (4) pushing for continuous improvement in how value chain activities are performed; (5) installing information and operating systems that enable company personnel to better carry out essential activities; (6) tying rewards and incentives directly to the achievement of performance targets and good strategy execution; (7) shaping the work environment and corporate culture to fit the strategy; and (8) exerting the internal leadership needed to drive execution forward. The recurring theme throughout the chapter is that implementing and executing strategy entails figuring out the specific actions, behaviors, and conditions that are needed for a smooth strategy-supportive operation—the goal here is to ensure that students understand that the strategy implementing/strategy executing phase is a make-it-happen-right kind of managerial exercise that leads to operating excellence and good performance.

In this latest edition, we have put our utmost effort into ensuring that the 10 chapters are consistent with the latest and best thinking of academics and practitioners in the field of strategic management and hit the bull's-eye in topical coverage for senior- and MBA-level strategy courses. The ultimate test of the text, of course, is the positive pedagogical impact it has in the classroom. If this edition sets a more effective stage for your lectures and does a better job of helping you persuade students that the discipline of strategy merits their rapt attention, then it will have fulfilled its purpose.

The Case Collection

The 12-case lineup in this edition is flush with interesting companies and valuable lessons for students in the art and science of crafting and executing strategy. There is a good blend of cases from a length perspective—about one-third are under 10 pages yet offer plenty for students to chew on; about a third are medium-length cases; and the remaining one-third are detail-rich cases that call for sweeping analysis.

At least 10 of the 12 cases involve companies, products, people, or activities that students will have heard of, know about from personal experience, or can easily identify with. The lineup includes at least four cases that will provide students with insight into the special demands of competing in industry environments where technological developments are an everyday event, product life cycles are short, and competitive maneuvering among rivals comes fast and furious. All of the cases involve situations where the role of company resources and competitive capabilities in the strategy formulation, strategy execution scheme is emphasized. Scattered throughout the lineup are eight cases concerning non-U.S. companies, globally competitive industries, and/or cross-cultural situations; these cases, in conjunction with the globalized content of the text chapters, provide abundant material for linking the study of strategic management tightly to the ongoing globalization of the world economy. You will also find two cases dealing with the strategic problems of family-owned or relatively small entrepreneurial businesses and 10 cases involving public companies and situations where students can do further research on the Internet. All cases have accompanying videotape segments.

The Two Strategy Simulation Supplements: *The Business Strategy Game* and *GLO-BUS*

The Business Strategy Game and *GLO-BUS: Developing Winning Competitive Strategies*—two competition-based strategy simulations that are delivered online and that feature automated processing and grading of performance—are being marketed by the publisher as companion supplements for use with the 7th edition.

- *The Business Strategy Game* is the world's most popular strategy simulation, having been used by nearly 3,500 different instructors for courses involving some 950,000 students at 1,270+ university campuses in 77 countries. It features global competition in the athletic footwear industry, a product/market setting familiar to students everywhere and one whose managerial challenges are easily grasped. A freshly updated and much-enhanced version of *The Business Strategy Game* was introduced in August 2018.

- *GLO-BUS,* a newer and somewhat simpler strategy simulation first introduced in 2004 and freshly revamped in 2016 to center on competition in two exciting product categories—wearable miniature action cameras and unmanned camera-equipped drones suitable for multiple commercial purposes—has been used by 1,800+ different instructors for courses involving over 330,000 students at 750+ university campuses in 53 countries.

How the Strategy Simulations Work

In both *The Business Strategy Game (BSG)* and *GLO-BUS,* class members are divided into teams of one to five persons and assigned to run a company that competes head-to-head against companies run by other class members. In both simulations, companies compete in a global market arena, selling their products in four geographic regions—Europe-Africa, North America, Asia-Pacific, and Latin America. Each management team is called upon to craft a strategy for their company and make decisions relating to production operations, workforce compensation, pricing and marketing, social responsibility/citizenship, and finance.

Company co-managers are held accountable for their decision making. Each company's performance is scored on the basis of earnings per share, return-on-equity investment, stock price, credit rating, and image rating. Rankings of company performance, along with a wealth of industry and company statistics, are available to company co-managers after each decision round to use in making strategy adjustments and operating decisions for the next competitive round. You can be certain that the market environment, strategic issues, and operating challenges that company co-managers must contend with are *very tightly linked* to what your class members will be reading about in the text chapters. The circumstances that co-managers face in running their simulation company embrace the very concepts, analytical tools, and strategy options they encounter in the text chapters (this is something you can quickly confirm by skimming through some of the Exercises for Simulation Participants that appear at the end of each chapter).

We suggest that you schedule 1 or 2 practice rounds and anywhere from 4 to 10 regular (scored) decision rounds (more rounds are better than fewer rounds). Each

decision round represents a year of company operations and will entail roughly two hours of time for company co-managers to complete. In traditional 13-week, semester-long courses, there is merit in scheduling one decision round per week. In courses that run 5 to 10 weeks, it is wise to schedule two decision rounds per week for the last several weeks of the term (sample course schedules are provided for courses of varying length and varying numbers of class meetings).

When the instructor-specified deadline for a decision round arrives, the simulation server automatically accesses the saved decision entries of each company, determines the competitiveness and buyer appeal of each company's product offering relative to the other companies being run by students in your class, and then awards sales and market shares to the competing companies, geographic region by geographic region. The unit sales volumes awarded to each company *are totally governed by:*

- How its prices compare against the prices of rival brands.
- How its product quality compares against the quality of rival brands.
- How its product line breadth and selection compare.
- How its advertising effort compares.
- And so on, for a total of 11 competitive factors that determine unit sales and market shares.

The competitiveness and overall buyer appeal of each company's product offering *in comparison to the product offerings of rival companies* is all-decisive—this algorithmic feature is what makes *BSG* and *GLO-BUS* "competition-based" strategy simulations. Once each company's sales and market shares are awarded based on the competitiveness and buyer appeal of its respective overall product offering vis-à-vis those of rival companies, the various company and industry reports detailing the outcomes of the decision round are then generated. Company co-managers can access the results of the decision round 15 to 20 minutes after the decision deadline.

The Compelling Case for Incorporating Use of a Strategy Simulation

There are *three exceptionally important benefits* associated with using a competition-based simulation in strategy courses taken by seniors and MBA students:

- *A three-pronged text-case-simulation course model delivers significantly more teaching-learning power than the traditional text-case model.* Using *both* cases and a strategy simulation to drill students in thinking strategically and applying what they read in the text chapters is a stronger, more effective means of helping them connect theory with practice and develop better business judgment. What cases do that a simulation cannot is give class members broad exposure to a variety of companies and industry situations and insight into the kinds of strategy-related problems managers face. But what a competition-based strategy simulation does far better than case analysis is thrust class members squarely into *an active, hands-on managerial role* where they are totally responsible for assessing market conditions, determining how to respond to the actions of competitors, forging a long-term direction and strategy for their company, and making all kinds of operating decisions. Because they are held fully accountable for their decisions and their company's performance, *co-managers are strongly motivated* to dig deeply into company operations, probe for ways to be more cost-efficient and competitive, and ferret out strategic moves and decisions calculated to boost company performance. *Consequently, incorporating both case assignments and a strategy simulation to develop the skills of class members in thinking strategically and applying the concepts and tools of strategic analysis turns out to be more pedagogically powerful than relying solely on case assignments—there's stronger retention of the lessons learned and better achievement of course learning objectives.*

To provide you with quantitative evidence of the learning that occurs with using *The Business Strategy Game* or *GLO-BUS,* there is a built-in Learning Assurance Report showing how well each class member performs on nine skills/learning measures versus tens of thousands of students worldwide who have completed the simulation in the past 12 months.

- *The competitive nature of a strategy simulation arouses positive energy and steps up the whole tempo of the course by a notch or two.* Nothing sparks class excitement quicker or better than the concerted efforts on the part of class members at each decision round to achieve a high industry ranking and avoid the perilous consequences of being outcompeted by other class members. Students really enjoy taking on the role of a manager, running their own company, crafting strategies, making all kinds of operating decisions, trying to outcompete rival companies, and getting immediate feedback on the resulting company performance. Lots of back-and-forth chatter occurs when the results of the latest simulation round become available and co-managers renew their quest for strategic moves and actions that will strengthen company performance. Co-managers become *emotionally invested* in running their company and figuring out what strategic moves to make to boost their company's performance. Interest levels climb. All this stimulates learning and causes students to see the practical relevance of the subject matter and the benefits of taking your course.

  As soon as your students start to say "Wow! Not only is this fun but I am learning a lot," *which they will,* you have won the battle of engaging students in the subject matter and moved the value of taking your course to a much higher plateau in the business school curriculum. This translates into *a livelier, richer learning experience from a student perspective and better instructor-course evaluations.*

- *Use of a fully automated online simulation reduces the time instructors spend on course preparation, course administration, and grading.* Since the simulation exercise involves a 20- to 30-hour workload for student teams (roughly 2 hours per decision round times 10 to 12 rounds, plus optional assignments), simulation adopters often compensate by trimming the number of assigned cases from, say, 10 to 12 to perhaps 4 to 6. This significantly reduces the time instructors spend reading cases, studying teaching notes, and otherwise getting ready to lead class discussion of a case or grade oral team presentations. Course preparation time is further cut because you can use several class days to have students meet in the computer lab to work on upcoming decision rounds or a three-year strategic plan (in lieu of lecturing on a chapter or covering an additional assigned case). Not only does use of a simulation permit assigning fewer cases, but it also permits you to eliminate

at least one assignment that entails considerable grading on your part. Grading one less written case or essay exam or other written assignment saves enormous time. With *BSG* and *GLO-BUS,* grading is effortless and takes only minutes; once you enter percentage weights for each assignment in your online grade book, a suggested overall grade is calculated for you. You'll be pleasantly surprised—and quite pleased—at how little time it takes to gear up for and administer *The Business Strategy Game* or *GLO-BUS.*

In sum, incorporating use of a strategy simulation turns out to be *a win–win proposition for both students and instructors.* Moreover, a very convincing argument made that a competition-based strategy simulation is *the single most effective teaching/learning tool that instructors can employ to teach the discipline of business and competitive strategy, to make learning more enjoyable, and to promote better achievement of course learning objectives.*

A Bird's-Eye View of *The Business Strategy Game*

The setting for *The Business Strategy Game (BSG)* is the global athletic footwear industry (there can be little doubt in today's world that a globally competitive strategy simulation is *vastly superior* to a simulation with a domestic-only setting). Global market demand for footwear grows at the rate of 7 to 9 percent annually for the first five years and 5 to 7 percent annually for the second five years. However, market growth rates vary by geographic region—North America, Latin America, Europe-Africa, and Asia-Pacific.

Companies begin the simulation producing branded and private-label footwear in two plants, one in North America and one in Asia. They have the option to establish production facilities in Latin America and Europe-Africa. Company co-managers exercise control over production costs on the basis of the styling and quality they opt to manufacture, plant location (wages, incentive compensation, and import tariffs vary from region to region), the use of best practices and Six Sigma programs to reduce the production of defective footwear and to boost worker productivity, and compensation practices.

All newly produced footwear is shipped in bulk containers to one of four geographic distribution centers. All sales in a geographic region are made from footwear inventories in that region's distribution center. Costs at the four regional distribution centers are a function of inventory storage costs, packing and shipping fees, import tariffs paid on incoming pairs shipped from foreign plants, and exchange rate impacts. At the start of the simulation, import tariffs average $4 per pair in North America, $6 in Europe-Africa, $8 per pair in Latin America, and $10 in the Asia-Pacific region. Instructors have the option to alter tariffs as the game progresses.

Companies market their brand of athletic footwear to footwear retailers worldwide and to individuals buying online at the company's website. Each company's sales and market share in the branded footwear segments hinge on its competitiveness on 13 factors: attractive pricing, footwear styling and quality, product line breadth, advertising, use of mail-in rebates, appeal of celebrities endorsing a company's brand, success in convincing footwear retailers to carry its brand, number of weeks it takes to fill retailer orders, effectiveness of a company's online sales effort at its website, and brand reputation. Sales of private-label footwear hinge solely on being the low-price bidder.

All told, company co-managers make as many as 57 types of decisions each period that cut across production operations (up to 11 decisions per plant, with a maximum of four plants), the addition of facility space, equipment, and production improvement options (up to 8 decisions per plant), worker compensation and training (up to 6 decisions per plant), shipping and distribution center operations (5 decisions per geographic region), pricing and marketing (up to 9 decisions in four geographic regions), bids to sign celebrities (2 decision entries per bid), financing of company operations (up to 8 decisions), and corporate social responsibility and environmental sustainability (up to 8 decisions). Plus, there are 10 entries for each region pertaining to assumptions about the upcoming-year actions and competitive efforts of rival companies that factor directly into the forecasts of a company's unit sales, revenues, and market share in each of the four geographic regions.

Each time company co-managers make a decision entry, an assortment of on-screen calculations instantly shows the projected effects on unit sales, revenues, market shares, unit costs, profit, earnings per share, ROE, and other operating statistics. The on-screen calculations help team members evaluate the relative merits of one decision entry versus another and put together a promising strategy.

Companies can employ any of the five generic competitive strategy options in selling branded footwear—low-cost leadership, differentiation, best-cost provider, focused low cost, and focused differentiation. They can pursue essentially the same strategy worldwide or craft slightly or very different strategies for the Europe-Africa, Asia-Pacific, Latin America, and North America markets. They can strive for competitive advantage based on more advertising, a wider selection of models, more appealing styling/quality, bigger rebates, and so on.

Any well-conceived, well-executed competitive approach is capable of succeeding, provided it is not overpowered by the strategies of competitors or defeated by the presence of too many copycat strategies that dilute its effectiveness. The challenge for each company's management team is to craft and execute a competitive strategy that produces good performance on five measures: earnings per share, return on equity investment, stock price appreciation, credit rating, and brand image.

All activity for *The Business Strategy Game* takes place at www.bsg-online.com.

A Bird's-Eye View of *GLO-BUS*

In *GLO-BUS,* class members run companies that are in a neck-and-neck race for global market leadership in two product categories: (1) wearable video cameras smaller than a teacup that deliver stunning video quality and have powerful photo capture capabilities (comparable to those designed and marketed by global industry leader GoPro and numerous others) and (2) sophisticated camera-equipped copter drones that incorporate a company designed and assembled action-capture camera and that are sold to commercial enterprises for prices in the $850 to $2,000+ range. Global market demand for action cameras grows at the rate of 6 to 8 percent annually for the first five years and 4 to 6 percent annually for the second five years. Global market demand for commercial drones grows briskly at rates averaging 20 percent for the first two years, then gradually slows over eight years to a rate of 4 to 6 percent.

Companies assemble action cameras and drones of varying designs and performance capabilities at a Taiwan facility and ship finished goods directly to buyers in North

America, Asia-Pacific, Europe-Africa, and Latin America. Both products are assembled usually within two weeks of being received and are then shipped to buyers no later than two to three days after assembly. Companies maintain no finished goods inventories and all parts and components are delivered by suppliers on a just-in-time basis (which eliminates the need to track inventories and simplifies the accounting for plant operations and costs).

Company co-managers determine the quality and performance features of the cameras and drones being assembled. They impact production costs by raising/lowering specifications for parts/components and expenditures for product R&D, adjusting work force compensation, spending more/less on worker training and productivity improvement, lengthening/shortening warranties offered (which affects warranty costs), and how cost-efficiently they manage assembly operations. They have options to manage/control selling and certain other costs as well.

Each decision round, company co-managers make some 50 types of decisions relating to the design and performance of the company's two products (21 decisions, 10 for cameras and 11 for drones), assembly operations and workforce compensation (up to 8 decision entries for each product), pricing and marketing (7 decisions for cameras and 5 for drones), corporate social responsibility and citizenship (up to 6 decisions), and the financing of company operations (up to 8 decisions). In addition, there are 10 entries for cameras and 7 entries for drones involving assumptions about the competitive actions of rivals; these entries help company co-managers to make more accurate forecasts of their company's unit sales (so they have a good idea of how many cameras and drones will need to be assembled each year to fill customer orders). Each time co-managers make a decision entry, an assortment of on-screen calculations instantly shows the projected effects on unit sales, revenues, market shares, total profit, earnings per share, ROE, costs, and other operating outcomes. All of these on-screen calculations help co-managers evaluate the relative merits of one decision entry versus another. Company managers can try out as many different decision combinations as they wish in stitching the separate decision entries into a cohesive whole that is projected to produce good company performance.

Competition in action cameras revolves around 11 factors that determine each company's unit sales/market share:

1. How each company's average wholesale price to retailers compares against the all-company average wholesale prices being charged in each geographic region.

2. How each company's camera performance and quality compare against industry-wide camera performance/quality.

3. How the number of week-long sales promotion campaigns a company has in each region compares against the regional average number of weekly promotions.

4. How the size of each company's discounts off the regular wholesale prices during sales promotion campaigns compares against the regional average promotional discount.

5. How each company's annual advertising expenditures compare against regional average advertising expenditures.

6. How the number of models in each company's camera line compares against the industry-wide average number of models.

7. The number of retailers stocking and merchandising a company's brand in each region.

8. Annual expenditures to support the merchandising efforts of retailers stocking a company's brand in each region.

9. The amount by which a company's expenditures for ongoing improvement and updating of its company's website in a region is above/below the all-company regional average expenditure.

10. How the length of each company's camera warranties compares against the warranty periods of rival companies.

11. How well a company's brand image/reputation compares against the brand images/reputations of rival companies.

Competition among rival makers of commercial copter drones is more narrowly focused on just nine sales-determining factors:

1. How a company's average retail price for drones at the company's website in each region compares against the all-company regional average website price.

2. How each company's drone performance and quality compare against the all-company average drone performance/quality.

3. How the number of models in each company's drone line compares against the industry-wide average number of models.

4. How each company's annual expenditures to recruit/support third-party online electronics retailers in merchandising its brand of drones in each region compare against the regional average.

5. The amount by which a company's price discount to third-party online retailers is above/below the regional average discounted price.

6. How well a company's expenditures for search engine advertising in a region compare against the regional average.

7. How well a company's expenditures for ongoing improvement and updating of its website in a region compare against the regional average.

8. How the length of each company's drone warranties in a region compares against the regional average warranty period.

9. How well a company's brand image/reputation compares against the brand images/reputations of rival companies.

Each company typically seeks to enhance its performance and build competitive advantage via its own custom-tailored competitive strategy based on more attractive pricing, greater advertising, a wider selection of models, more appealing performance/quality, longer warranties, a better image/reputation, and so on. The greater the differences in the overall competitiveness of the product offerings of rival companies, the bigger the differences in their resulting sales volumes and market shares. Conversely, the smaller the overall competitive differences in the product offerings of rival companies, the smaller the differences in sales volumes and market shares. This algorithmic approach is what makes *GLO-BUS* a "competition-based" strategy simulation and

accounts for why *the sales and market share outcomes for each decision round are always unique to the particular strategies and decision combinations employed by the competing companies.*

As with *BSG, all the various generic competitive strategy options*—low-cost leadership, differentiation, best-cost provider, focused low-cost, and focused differentiation—*are viable choices for pursuing competitive advantage and good company performance.* A company can have a strategy aimed at being the clear market leader in either action cameras or drones or both. It can focus its competitive efforts on one or two or three geographic regions or strive to build strong market positions in all four geographic regions. It can pursue essentially the same strategy worldwide or craft customized strategies for the Europe-Africa, Asia-Pacific, Latin America, and North America markets. Just as with *The Business Strategy Game, most any well-conceived, well-executed competitive approach is capable of succeeding, provided it is not overpowered by the strategies of competitors or defeated by the presence of too many copycat strategies that dilute its effectiveness.*

The challenge for each company's management team is to craft and execute a competitive strategy that produces good performance on five measures: earnings per share, return on equity investment, stock price appreciation, credit rating, and brand image.

All activity for *GLO-BUS* occurs at www.glo-bus.com.

Special Note: The time required of company co-managers to complete each decision round in *GLO-BUS* is typically about 15 to 30 minutes less than for *The Business Strategy Game* because

(a) there are only 8 market segments (versus 12 in *BSG*),

(b) co-managers have only one assembly site to operate (versus potentially as many as 4 plants in *BSG,* one in each geographic region), and

(c) newly assembled cameras and drones are shipped directly to buyers, eliminating the need to manage finished goods inventories and operate distribution centers.

Administration and Operating Features of the Two Simulations

The Internet delivery and user-friendly designs of both *BSG* and *GLO-BUS* make them incredibly easy to administer, even for first-time users. And the menus and controls are so similar that you can readily switch between the two simulations or use one in your undergraduate class and the other in a graduate class. If you have not yet used either of the two simulations, you may find the following of particular interest:

• Setting up the simulation for your course is done online and takes about 10 to 15 minutes. Once setup is completed, no other administrative actions are required beyond those of moving participants to a different team (should the need arise) and monitoring the progress of the simulation (to whatever extent desired).

• Participant's Guides are delivered electronically to class members at the website— students can read the guide on their monitors or print out a copy, as they prefer.

• There are two- to four-minute Video Tutorials scattered throughout the software (including each decision screen and each page of each report) that provide on-demand guidance to class members who may be uncertain about how to proceed.

- Complementing the Video Tutorials are detailed and clearly written Help sections explaining "all there is to know" about (a) each decision entry and the relevant cause-effect relationships, (b) the information on each page of the Industry Reports, and (c) the numbers presented in the Company Reports. *The Video Tutorials and the Help screens allow company co-managers to figure things out for themselves, thereby curbing the need for students to ask the instructor "how things work."*

- Team members running the same company who are logged in simultaneously on different computers at different locations can click a button to enter Collaboration Mode, enabling them to work collaboratively from the same screen in viewing reports and making decision entries, and click a second button to enter Audio Mode, letting them talk to one another.

  - When in "Collaboration Mode," each team member sees the same screen at the same time as all other team members who are logged in and have joined Collaboration Mode. If one team member chooses to view a particular decision screen, that same screen appears on the monitors for all team members in Collaboration Mode.

  - Each team member controls their own color-coded mouse pointer (with their first-name appearing in a color-coded box linked to their mouse pointer) and can make a decision entry or move the mouse to point to particular on-screen items.

  - A decision entry change made by one team member is seen by all, in real time, and all team members can immediately view the on-screen calculations that result from the new decision entry.

  - If one team member wishes to view a report page and clicks on the menu link to the desired report, that same report page will immediately appear for the other team members engaged in collaboration.

  - Use of Audio Mode capability requires that each team member work from a computer with a built-in microphone (if they want to be heard by their team members) and speakers (so they may hear their teammates) or else have a headset with a microphone that they can plug into their desktop or laptop. A headset is recommended for best results, but most laptops now are equipped with a built-in microphone and speakers that will support use of our new voice chat feature.

  - Real-time VoIP audio chat capability among team members who have entered both the Audio Mode and the Collaboration Mode is a tremendous boost in functionality that enables team members to go online simultaneously on computers at different locations and conveniently and effectively collaborate in running their simulation company.

    In addition, instructors have the capability to join the online session of any company and speak with team members, thus circumventing the need for team members to arrange for and attend a meeting in the instructor's office. Using the standard menu for administering a particular industry, instructors can connect with the company desirous of assistance. Instructors who wish not

only to talk but also to enter Collaboration (highly recommended because all attendees are then viewing the same screen) have a red-colored mouse pointer linked to a red box labeled Instructor.

Without a doubt, the Collaboration and Voice-Chat capabilities are hugely valuable for students enrolled in online and distance-learning courses where meeting face-to-face is impractical or time-consuming. Likewise, the instructors of online and distance-learning courses will appreciate having the capability to join the online meetings of particular company teams when their advice or assistance is requested.

- Both simulations are quite suitable for use in distance-learning or online courses (and are currently being used in such courses on numerous campuses).

- Participants and instructors are notified via e-mail when the results are ready (usually about 15 to 20 minutes after the decision round deadline specified by the instructor/game administrator).

- Following each decision round, participants are provided with a complete set of reports—a six-page Industry Report, a one-page Competitive Intelligence report for each geographic region that includes strategic group maps and a set of Company Reports (income statement, balance sheet, cash flow statement, and assorted production, marketing, and cost statistics).

- Two "open-book" multiple-choice tests of 20 questions are built into each simulation. The quizzes, which you can require or not as you see fit, are taken online and automatically graded, with scores reported instantaneously to participants and automatically recorded in the instructor's electronic grade book. Students are automatically provided with three sample questions for each test.

- Both simulations contain a three-year strategic plan option that you can assign. Scores on the plan are automatically recorded in the instructor's online grade book.

- At the end of the simulation, you can have students complete online peer evaluations (again, the scores are automatically recorded in your online grade book).

- Both simulations have a Company Presentation feature that enables each team of company co-managers to easily prepare PowerPoint slides for use in describing their strategy and summarizing their company's performance in a presentation to either the class, the instructor, or an "outside" board of directors.

- *A Learning Assurance Report provides you with hard data concerning how well your students performed vis-à-vis students playing the simulation worldwide over the past 12 months.* The report is based on nine measures of student proficiency, business know-how, and decision-making skill and can also be used in evaluating the extent to which your school's academic curriculum produces the desired degree of student learning insofar as accreditation standards are concerned.

For more details on either simulation, please consult Section 2 of the Instructor's Manual accompanying this text or register as an instructor at the simulation websites (www.bsg-online.com and www.glo-bus.com) to access even more comprehensive information. You should also consider signing up for one of the webinars that the simulation

authors conduct several times each month (sometimes several times weekly) to demonstrate how the software works, walk you through the various features and menu options, and answer any questions. You have an open invitation to call the senior author of this text at (205) 722-9145 to arrange a personal demonstration or talk about how one of the simulations might work in one of your courses. We think you'll be quite impressed with the cutting-edge capabilities that have been programmed into *The Business Strategy Game* and *GLO-BUS,* the simplicity with which both simulations can be administered, and their exceptionally tight connection to the text chapters, core concepts, and standard analytical tools.

Resources and Support Materials for the Seventh Edition for Students

Key Points Summaries

At the end of each chapter is a synopsis of the core concepts, analytical tools, and other key points discussed in the chapter. These chapter-end synopses, along with the core concept definitions and margin notes scattered throughout each chapter, help students focus on basic strategy principles, digest the messages of each chapter, and prepare for tests.

Two Sets of Chapter-End Exercises

Each chapter concludes with two sets of exercises. The Assurance of Learning Exercises can be used as the basis for class discussion, oral presentation assignments, short written reports, and substitutes for case assignments. The Exercises for Simulation Participants are designed expressly for use by adopters who have incorporated use of a simulation and wish to go a step further in tightly and explicitly connecting the chapter content to the simulation company their students are running. The questions in both sets of exercises (along with those Concepts & Connections illustrations that qualify as "mini cases") can be used to round out the rest of a 75-minute class period, should your lecture on a chapter only last for 50 minutes.

Connect

The seventh edition of *Essentials of Strategic Management* takes full advantage of the publisher's innovative *Connect* assignment and assessment platform. The *Connect* package for this edition includes several robust and valuable features that simplify the task of assigning and grading three types of exercises for students:

- Autograded chapter quizzes consisting of 20 multiple-choice questions that students can take to measure their grasp of the material presented in each of the 10 chapters.

- Interactive versions of two Assurance of Learning Exercises for each chapter that drill students in the use and application of the concepts and tools of strategic analysis. There is both an autograded and open-ended short-answer interactive exercise for each of the 10 chapters.

- New integration of Exercises for Simulation Participants into *Connect.* Students are required to apply concepts presented in all 10 chapters to business simulation participation in both autograded and open-ended assignment questions.

   The *Connect* package also includes fully autograded interactive application exercises for each of the 12 cases in this edition. The exercises require students to work through tutorials based upon the analysis set forth in the assignment questions for the case; these exercises have multiple components such as resource and capability analysis, financial ratio analysis, identification of a company's strategy, or analysis of the five competitive forces. The content of these case exercises is tailored to match the circumstances presented in each case, calling upon students to do whatever strategic thinking and strategic analysis is called for to arrive at pragmatic, analysis-based action recommendations for improving company performance. The entire exercise is autograded, allowing instructors to focus on grading only the students' strategic recommendations.

All of the *Connect* exercises are automatically graded (with the exception of a few exercise components that entail student entry of essay answers), thereby simplifying the task of evaluating each class member's performance and monitoring the learning outcomes. The progress-tracking function built into the *Connect* system enables you to:

- View scored work immediately and track individual or group performance with assignment and grade reports.

- Access an instant view of student or class performance relative to learning objectives.

- Collect data and generate reports required by many accreditation organizations, such as AACSB International.

For Instructors

Connect

Connect's Instructor Resources includes an Instructor's Manual, Test Bank, PowerPoint slides, and other support materials. Your McGraw-Hill representative can arrange delivery of instructor support materials in a format-ready Standard Cartridge for Blackboard, WebCT, and other web-based educational platforms.

Instructor's Manual

The accompanying IM contains:

- A section on suggestions for organizing and structuring your course.
- Sample syllabi and course outlines.
- A set of lecture notes on each chapter.
- Answers to the chapter-end Assurance of Learning Exercises.

- A comprehensive case teaching note for each of the 12 cases. These teaching notes are filled with suggestions for using the case effectively, have very thorough, analysis-based answers to the suggested assignment questions for the case, and contain an epilogue detailing any important developments since the case was written.

A Comprehensive Test Bank and Test Builder Software

There is a 600+ question test bank, consisting of both multiple-choice questions and short-answer/essay questions. All of the test bank questions are also accessible via Test Builder.

Available within *Connect*, Test Builder is a cloud-based tool that enables instructors to format tests that can be printed or administered within an LMS. Test Builder offers a modern, streamlined interface for easy content configuration that matches course needs, without requiring a download.

Test Builder allows you to:

- access all test bank content from this title.
- easily pinpoint the most relevant content through robust filtering options.
- manipulate the order of questions or scramble questions and/or answers.
- pin questions to a specific location within a test.
- determine your preferred treatment of algorithmic questions.
- choose the layout and spacing.
- add instructions and configure default settings.

Test Builder provides a secure interface for better protection of content and allows for just-in-time updates to flow directly into assessments.

PowerPoint Slides

To facilitate delivery preparation of your lectures and to serve as chapter outlines, you'll have access to approximately 350 colorful and professional-looking slides displaying core concepts, analytical procedures, key points, and all the figures in the text chapters.

The Business Strategy Game and GLO-BUS Online Simulations

Using one of the two companion simulations is a powerful and constructive way of emotionally connecting students to the subject matter of the course. We know of no more effective way to arouse the competitive energy of students and prepare them for the challenges of real-world business decision making than to have them match strategic wits with classmates in running a company in head-to-head competition for global market leadership.

Acknowledgments

We heartily acknowledge the contributions of the case researchers whose case-writing efforts appear herein and the companies whose cooperation made the cases possible. To each one goes a very special thank-you. We cannot overstate the importance of timely, carefully researched cases in contributing to a substantive study of strategic management issues and practices. From a research standpoint, strategy-related cases are invaluable in exposing the generic kinds of strategic issues that companies face in forming hypotheses about strategic behavior and in drawing experienced-based generalizations about the practice of strategic management. From an instructional standpoint, strategy cases give students essential practice in diagnosing and evaluating the strategic situations of companies and organizations, in applying the concepts and tools of strategic analysis, in weighing strategic options and crafting strategies, and in tackling the challenges of successful strategy execution. Without a continuing stream of fresh, well-researched, and well-conceived cases, the discipline of strategic management would lose its close ties to the very institutions whose strategic actions and behavior it is aimed at explaining. There's no question, therefore, that first-class case research constitutes a valuable scholarly contribution to the theory and practice of strategic management.

A great number of colleagues and students at various universities, business acquaintances, and people at McGraw-Hill provided inspiration, encouragement, and counsel during the course of this project. Like all text authors in the strategy field, we are intellectually indebted to the many academics whose research and writing have blazed new trails and advanced the discipline of strategic management.

We also express our thanks to Todd M. Alessandri, Michael Anderson, Alexander Assouad, Gerald D. Baumgardner, Edith C. Busija, Gerald E. Calvasina, Sam D. Cappel, Richard Churchman, John W. Collis, Connie Daniel, Christine DeLaTorre, Vickie Cox Edmondson, Diane D. Galbraith, Naomi A. Gardberg, Sanjay Goel, Darel Hargrove, Randall Harris, Les Jankovich, Jonatan Jelen, William Jiang, Bonnie Johnson, Roy Johnson, John J. Lawrence, Robert E. Ledman, Mark Lehrer, Joyce LeMay, Fred Maidment, David Marion, Frank Markham, Renata Mayrhofer, Simon Medcalfe, Elouise Mintz, Marcel Minutolo, Michael Monahan, Gerry Nkombo Muuka, Cori J. Myers, Jeryl L. Nelson, David Olson, John Perry, Krishnan Ramaya, L. Jeff Seaton, Charles F. Seifert, Eugene S. Simko, Karen J. Smith, Garrison Spencer, Susan Steiner, Troy V. Sullivan, Elisabeth J. Teal, Lori Tisher, Vincent Weaver, Jim Whitlock, and Beth Woodard. These reviewers provided valuable guidance in steering our efforts to improve this and earlier editions.

As always, we value your recommendations and thoughts about the book. Your comments regarding coverage and contents will be taken to heart, and we always are grateful for the time you take to call our attention to printing errors, deficiencies, and other shortcomings. Please e-mail us at john.gamble@tamucc.edu, or athompso@cba.ua.edu, or margaret.a.peteraf@tuck.dartmouth.edu.

John E. Gamble
Margaret A. Peteraf
Arthur A. Thompson

Table of Contents

Chapter 6   Strengthening a Company's Competitive Position: Strategic Moves, Timing, and Scope of Operations   110

Chapter 7   Strategies for Competing in International Markets   131

PART TWO CASES IN CRAFTING AND EXECUTING STRATEGY   231

Cases

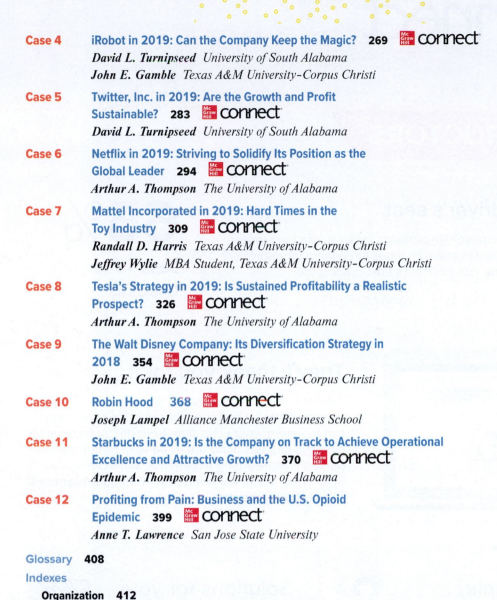

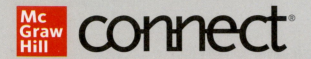

You're in the driver's seat.

Want to build your own course? No problem. Prefer to use our turnkey, prebuilt course? Easy. Want to make changes throughout the semester? Sure. And you'll save time with Connect's auto-grading too.

65%
Less Time Grading

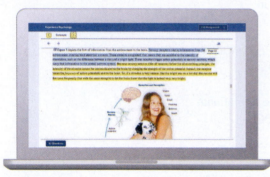

Laptop: McGraw-Hill; Woman/dog: George Doyle/Getty Images

They'll thank you for it.

Adaptive study resources like SmartBook® 2.0 help your students be better prepared in less time. You can transform your class time from dull definitions to dynamic debates. Find out more about the powerful personalized learning experience available in SmartBook 2.0 at **www.mheducation.com/highered/ connect/smartbook**

Make it simple, make it affordable.

Connect makes it easy with seamless integration using any of the major Learning Management Systems— Blackboard®, Canvas, and D2L, among others—to let you organize your course in one convenient location. Give your students access to digital materials at a discount with our inclusive access program. Ask your McGraw-Hill representative for more information.

Padlock: Jobalou/Getty Images

Solutions for your challenges.

A product isn't a solution. Real solutions are affordable, reliable, and come with training and ongoing support when you need it and how you want it. Our Customer Experience Group can also help you troubleshoot tech problems— although Connect's 99% uptime means you might not need to call them. See for yourself at **status. mheducation.com**

Checkmark: Jobalou/Getty Images

Effective, efficient studying.

Connect helps you be more productive with your study time and get better grades using tools like SmartBook 2.0, which highlights key concepts and creates a personalized study plan. Connect sets you up for success, so you walk into class with confidence and walk out with better grades.

Study anytime, anywhere.

Download the free ReadAnywhere app and access your online eBook or SmartBook 2.0 assignments when it's convenient, even if you're offline. And since the app automatically syncs with your eBook and SmartBook 2.0 assignments in Connect, all of your work is available every time you open it. Find out more at **www.mheducation.com/readanywhere**

> *"I really liked this app—it made it easy to study when you don't have your textbook in front of you."*
>
> - Jordan Cunningham, Eastern Washington University

Calendar: owattaphotos/Getty Images

No surprises.

The Connect Calendar and Reports tools keep you on track with the work you need to get done and your assignment scores. Life gets busy; Connect tools help you keep learning through it all.

Learning for everyone.

McGraw-Hill works directly with Accessibility Services Departments and faculty to meet the learning needs of all students. Please contact your Accessibility Services office and ask them to email accessibility@mheducation.com, or visit **www.mheducation.com/about/accessibility** for more information.

Top: Jenner Images/Getty Images, Left: Hero Images/Getty Images, Right: Hero Images/Getty Images

Course Design and Delivery

CREATE

 Instructors can now tailor their teaching resources to match the way they teach! With McGraw-Hill Create, www.mcgrawhillcreate.com, instructors can easily rearrange chapters, combine material from other content sources, and quickly upload and integrate their own content, such as course syllabi or teaching notes. Find the right content in Create by searching through thousands of leading McGraw-Hill textbooks. Arrange the material to fit your teaching style. Order a Create book and receive a complimentary print review copy in three to five business days or a complimentary electronic review copy via e-mail within one hour. Go to www.mcgrawhillcreate.com today and register.

TEGRITY: LECTURES 24/7

  Tegrity in *Connect* is a tool that makes class time available 24/7 by automatically capturing every lecture. With a simple one-click start-and-stop process, you capture all computer screens and corresponding audio in a format that is easy to search, frame by frame. Students can replay any part of any class with easy-to-use, browser-based viewing on a PC, Mac, iPod, or other mobile device.

Educators know that the more students can see, hear, and experience class resources, the better they learn. In fact, studies prove it. Tegrity's unique search feature helps students efficiently find what they need, when they need it, across an entire semester of class recordings. Help turn your students' study time into learning moments immediately supported by your lecture. With Tegrity, you also increase intent listening and class participation by easing students' concerns about note-taking. Using Tegrity in *Connect* will make it more likely you will see students' faces, not the tops of their heads.

Essentials of
Strategic
Management

7e

1 STRATEGY, BUSINESS MODELS, AND COMPETITIVE ADVANTAGE

LEARNING OBJECTIVES

After reading this chapter, you should be able to:

LO1-1 Understand what is meant by a company's strategy.

LO1-2 Explain why a company needs a creative, distinctive strategy that sets it apart from rivals.

LO1-3 Explain why it is important for a company to have a viable business model that outlines the company's customer value proposition and its profit formula.

LO1-4 Identify the five most dependable strategic approaches for setting a company apart from rivals and winning a sustainable competitive advantage.

LO1-5 Understand that a company's strategy tends to evolve over time because of changing circumstances and ongoing management efforts to improve the company's strategy.

LO1-6 Identify the three tests of a winning strategy.

According to *The Economist,* a leading publication on business, economics, and international affairs, "In business, strategy is king. Leadership and hard work are all very well and luck is mighty useful, but it is strategy that makes or breaks a firm."[1] Luck and circumstance can explain why some companies are blessed with initial, short-lived success. But only a well-crafted, well-executed, constantly evolving strategy can explain why an elite set of companies somehow manages to rise to the top and stay there, year after year, pleasing their customers, shareholders, and other stakeholders alike in the process. Companies such as Apple, Samsung, Disney, Emirates Airlines, Microsoft, Alphabet (formerly Google), Berkshire Hathaway, General Electric, and Southwest Airlines come to mind.

In this opening chapter, we define the concept of *strategy* and describe its many facets. We explain what is meant by a competitive advantage, discuss the relationship between a company's strategy and its business model, and introduce you to the kinds of competitive strategies that can give a company an advantage over rivals in attracting customers and earning above-average profits. We look at what sets a winning strategy apart from others and why the caliber of a company's strategy determines whether the company will enjoy a competitive advantage over other firms. By the end of this chapter, you will have a clear idea of why the tasks of crafting and executing strategy are core management functions and why excellent execution of an excellent strategy is the most reliable recipe for turning a company into a standout performer over the long term.

LO1-1   Understand what is meant by a company's strategy.

A company's **strategy** is the coordinated set of actions that its managers take to outperform the company's competitors and achieve superior profitability. The objective of a well-crafted strategy is not merely temporary competitive success and profits in the short run, but rather the sort of lasting success that can support growth and secure the company's future over the long term. Achieving this entails making a managerial commitment to a coherent array of well-considered choices about how to compete.[2] These include choices about:

> **CORE CONCEPT**
> A company's **strategy** is the coordinated set of actions that its managers take to outperform the company's competitors and achieve superior profitability.

- *How* to create products or services that attract and please customers.
- *How* to position the company in the industry.
- *How* to develop and deploy resources to build valuable competitive capabilities.
- *How* each functional piece of the business (R&D, supply chain activities, production, sales and marketing, distribution, finance, and human resources) will be operated.
- *How* to achieve the company's performance targets.

In most industries, companies have considerable freedom in choosing the *hows* of strategy. Thus some rivals strive to create superior value for customers by achieving lower costs than rivals, while others pursue product superiority or personalized customer service or the development of capabilities that rivals cannot match. Some competitors position themselves in only one part of the industry's chain of production/distribution activities, while others are partially or fully integrated, with operations ranging from components production to manufacturing and assembly to wholesale distribution or retailing. Some competitors deliberately confine their operations to local or regional markets; others opt to compete nationally, internationally (several countries), or globally. Some companies decide to operate in only one industry, while others diversify broadly or narrowly, into related or unrelated industries.

The Importance of a Distinctive Strategy and Competitive Approach

LO1-2 Explain why a company needs a creative, distinctive strategy that sets it apart from rivals.

For a company to matter in the minds of customers, its strategy needs a distinctive element that sets it apart from rivals and produces a competitive edge. A strategy must tightly fit a company's own particular situation, but there is no shortage of opportunity to fashion a strategy that is discernibly different from the strategies of rivals. In fact, competitive success requires a company's managers to make strategic choices about the key building blocks of its strategy that differ from the choices made by competitors—not 100 percent different but at least different in several important respects. A strategy stands a chance of succeeding only when it is predicated on actions, business approaches, and competitive moves aimed at appealing to buyers *in ways that set a company apart from rivals.* Simply trying to mimic the strategies of the industry's successful companies never works. Rather, every company's strategy needs to have some distinctive element that draws in customers and produces a competitive edge. Strategy, at its essence, is about competing differently—doing what rival firms *don't* do or, better yet, what rival firms *can't* do.[3]

Mimicking the strategies of successful industry rivals—with either copycat product offerings or efforts to stake out the same market position—rarely works. A creative, distinctive strategy that sets a company apart from rivals and yields a competitive advantage is a company's most reliable ticket for earning above-average profits.

The Relationship Between a Company's Strategy and Business Model

LO1-3 Explain why it is important for a company to have a viable business model that outlines the company's customer value proposition and its profit formula.

Closely related to the concept of strategy is the concept of a company's **business model.** While the company's strategy sets forth an approach to offering superior value, a company's business model is management's blueprint for delivering a valuable product or service to customers in a manner that will yield an attractive profit.[4] The two elements of a company's business model are (1) its *customer value proposition* and (2) its *profit formula.* The customer value proposition is established by the company's overall strategy and lays out the company's approach to satisfying buyer wants and needs at a price customers will consider a good

CORE CONCEPT

A company's **business model** sets forth how its strategy and operating approaches will create value for customers, while at the same time generating ample revenues to cover costs and realizing a profit. The two elements of a company's business model are its (1) customer value proposition and (2) its profit formula.

value. The greater the value provided and the lower the price, the more attractive the value proposition is to customers. The profit formula describes the company's approach to determining a cost structure that will allow for acceptable profits given the pricing tied to its customer value proposition. The lower the costs given the customer value proposition, the greater the ability of the business model to be a moneymaker. The nitty-gritty issue surrounding a company's business model is whether it can execute its customer value proposition profitably. Just because company managers have crafted a strategy for competing and running the business does not automatically mean the strategy will lead to profitability—it may or it may not.[5]

Cable television providers utilize a business model, keyed to delivering news and entertainment that viewers will find valuable, to secure sufficient revenues from subscriptions and advertising to cover operating expenses and allow for profits. Aircraft engine manufacturer Rolls-Royce employs a "power-by-the-hour" business model that charges airlines leasing fees for engine use, maintenance, and repairs based upon actual hours flown. The company retains ownership of the engines and is able to minimize engine maintenance costs through the use of sophisticated sensors that optimize maintenance and repair schedules. Gillette's business model in razor blades involves achieving economies of scale in the production of its shaving products, selling razors at an attractively low price, and then making money on repeat purchases of razor blades. Concepts & Connections 1.1 discusses three contrasting business models in radio broadcasting.

Strategy and the Quest for Competitive Advantage

LO1-4   Identify the five most dependable strategic approaches for setting a company apart from rivals and winning a sustainable competitive advantage.

The heart and soul of any strategy is the actions and moves in the marketplace that managers are taking to gain a competitive edge over rivals.[6] Five of the most frequently used and dependable strategic approaches to setting a company apart from rivals and winning a sustainable competitive advantage are:

1. *A low-cost provider strategy*—achieving a cost-based advantage over rivals. Walmart and Southwest Airlines have earned strong market positions because of the low-cost advantages they have achieved over their rivals. Low-cost provider strategies can produce a durable competitive edge when rivals find it hard to match the low-cost leader's approach to driving costs out of the business.

2. *A broad differentiation strategy*—seeking to differentiate the company's product or service from rivals' in ways that will appeal to a broad spectrum of buyers. Successful adopters of broad differentiation strategies include Johnson & Johnson in baby products (product reliability) and Apple (innovative products). Differentiation strategies can be powerful so long as a company is sufficiently innovative to thwart rivals' attempts to copy or closely imitate its product offering.

3. *A focused low-cost strategy*—concentrating on a narrow buyer segment (or market niche) and outcompeting rivals by having lower costs than rivals and thus being able to serve niche members at a lower price. Private-label manufacturers of food,

CONCEPTS & CONNECTIONS 1.1

PANDORA, SIRIUS XM, AND OVER-THE-AIR BROADCAST RADIO: THREE CONTRASTING BUSINESS MODELS

	Pandora	Sirius XM	Over-the-Air Radio Broadcasters
Customer value proposition	• Through free-of-charge Internet radio service, allowed PC, tablet computer, and smartphone users to create up to 100 personalized music and comedy stations • Utilized algorithms to generate playlists based on users' predicted music preferences • Offered programming interrupted by brief, occasional ads; eliminated advertising for Pandora One subscribers	• For a monthly subscription fee, provided satellite-based music, news, sports, national and regional weather, traffic reports in limited areas, and talk radio programming • Also offered subscribers streaming Internet channels and the ability to create personalized, commercial-free stations for online and mobile listening • Offered programming interrupted only by brief, occasional ads	• Provided free-of-charge music, national and local news, local traffic reports, national and local weather, and talk radio programming • Included frequent programming interruption for ads
Profit Formula	Revenue generation: Display, audio, and video ads targeted to different audiences and sold to local and national buyers; subscription revenues generated from an advertising-free option called Pandora One	Revenue generation: Monthly subscription fees, sales of satellite radio equipment, and advertising revenues	Revenue generation: Advertising sales to national and local businesses
	Cost structure: Fixed costs associated with developing software for computers, tablets, and smartphones	Cost structure: Fixed costs associated with operating a satellite-based music delivery service and streaming Internet service	Cost structure: Fixed costs associated with terrestrial broadcasting operations
	Fixed and variable costs related to operating data centers to support streaming network content royalties, marketing, and support activities	Fixed and variable costs related to programming and content royalties, marketing, and support activities	Fixed and variable costs related to local news reporting, advertising sales operations, network affiliate fees, programming and content royalties, commercial production activities, and support activities
	Profit margin: Profitability dependent on generating sufficient advertising revenues and subscription revenues to cover costs and provide attractive profits	Profit margin: Profitability dependent on attracting a sufficiently large number of subscribers to cover costs and provide attractive profits	Profit margin: Profitability dependent on generating sufficient advertising revenues to cover costs and provide attractive profits

Sources: Company documents, 10-Ks, and information posted on their websites.

health and beauty products, and nutritional supplements use their low-cost advantage to offer supermarket buyers lower prices than those demanded by producers of branded products.

4. *A focused differentiation strategy*—concentrating on a narrow buyer segment (or market niche) and outcompeting rivals by offering niche members customized attributes that meet their tastes and requirements better than rivals' products. Louis Vuitton and Rolex have sustained their advantage in the luxury goods industry through a focus on affluent consumers demanding luxury and prestige.

5. *A best-cost provider strategy*—giving customers more value for the money by satisfying buyers' expectations on key quality/features/performance/service attributes, while beating their price expectations. This approach is a hybrid strategy that blends elements of low-cost provider and differentiation strategies; the aim is to have the lowest (best) costs and prices among sellers offering products with comparable differentiating attributes. Target's best-cost advantage allows it to give discount store shoppers more value for the money by offering an attractive product lineup and an appealing shopping ambience at low prices.

In Concepts & Connections 1.2, it is evident that Apple has gained a competitive advantage through its strategy keyed to product innovation, brand image, and reputation for social responsibility. A creative, distinctive strategy such as that used by Apple is a company's most reliable ticket for developing a sustainable competitive advantage and earning above-average profits. A **sustainable competitive advantage** allows a company to attract sufficiently large numbers of buyers who have a lasting preference for its products or services over those offered by rivals, despite the efforts of competitors to offset that appeal and overcome the company's advantage. The bigger and more durable the competitive advantage, the better a company's prospects for winning in the marketplace and earning superior long-term profits relative to rivals.

> **CORE CONCEPT**
>
> A company achieves **sustainable competitive advantage** when an attractively large number of buyers develop a durable preference for its products or services over the offerings of competitors, despite the efforts of competitors to overcome or erode its advantage.

The Importance of Capabilities in Building and Sustaining Competitive Advantage

Winning a *sustainable* competitive edge over rivals with any of the previous five strategies generally hinges as much on building competitively valuable capabilities that rivals cannot readily match as it does on having a distinctive product offering. Clever rivals can nearly always copy the attributes of a popular product or service, but it is substantially more difficult for rivals to match the know-how and specialized capabilities a company has developed and perfected over a long period. FedEx, for example, has superior capabilities in next-day delivery of small packages. And Hyundai has become the world's fastest-growing automaker as a result of its advanced manufacturing processes and unparalleled quality control system. The capabilities of both of these companies have proven difficult for competitors to imitate or best and have allowed each to build and sustain competitive advantage.

CONCEPTS & CONNECTIONS 1.2

APPLE INC.'S STRATEGY AND SUCCESS IN THE MARKETPLACE

Apple Inc. is one of the most profitable companies in the world, with revenues of more than $265 billion and net income of nearly $60 billion in 2018. For more than 10 consecutive years, it has ranked number one on *Fortune*'s list of the "World's Most Admired Companies." Given the worldwide popularity of its products and services, along with its reputation for superior technological innovation and design capabilities, this is not surprising. The key elements of Apple's successful strategy include:

- **Designing and developing its own operating systems**, *hardware, application software, and services*. This allows Apple to bring the best user experience to its customers through products and solutions with innovative design, superior ease-of-use, and seamless integration across platforms. The ability to use services like iCloud across devices incentivizes users to join Apple's technological ecosystem and has been critical to fostering brand loyalty.

- **Continuously investing in research and development (R&D) and frequently introducing products.** Apple has invested heavily in R&D, spending upwards of $11 billion a year, to ensure a continual and timely injection of competitive products, services, and technologies into the marketplace. Its successful products and services include the Mac, iPod, iPhone, iPad, Apple Watch, Apple TV, and Apple Music. It is currently investing in an Apple electric car and Apple solar energy.

- **Strategically locating its stores and staffing them with knowledgeable personnel.** By operating its own Apple stores and positioning them in high-traffic locations, Apple is better equipped to provide its customers with the optimal buying experience. The stores' employees are well versed in the value of the hardware and software integration and demonstrate the unique solutions available on its products. This high-quality sale and after-sale support allows Apple to continuously attract new and retain existing customers.

- **Expanding Apple's reach domestically and internationally.** Apple operates globally in 500 retail stores across 18 countries. During fiscal year 2017, 63 percent of Apple's revenue came from international sales.

- **Maintaining a quality brand image, supported by premium pricing.** Although the computer industry is incredibly price competitive, Apple has managed to sustain a competitive edge by focusing on its inimitable value proposition and deliberately keeping a price premium—thus creating an aura of prestige around its products.

- **Committing to corporate social responsibility and sustainability through supplier relations.** Apple's strict Code of Conduct requires its suppliers to comply with several standards regarding safe working conditions, fair treatment of workers, and environmentally safe manufacturing.

- **Cultivating a diverse workforce rooted in transparency.** Apple believes that diverse teams make innovation possible and is dedicated to incorporating a broad range of perspectives in its workforce. Every year, Apple publishes data showing the representation of women and different race and ethnicity groups across functions.

Note: Developed with Shawnda Lee Duvigneaud.
Sources: Apple 10-K, Company website.

Why a Company's Strategy Evolves over Time

 LO1-5   Understand that a company's strategy tends to evolve over time because of changing circumstances and ongoing management efforts to improve the company's strategy.

The appeal of a strategy that yields a sustainable competitive advantage is that it offers the potential for an enduring edge over rivals. However, managers of every company must be willing and ready to modify the strategy in response to the unexpected moves of competitors, shifting buyer needs and preferences, emerging market opportunities, new ideas for improving the strategy, and mounting evidence that the strategy is not working well. Most of the time, a company's strategy evolves incrementally as management fine-tunes various pieces of the strategy and adjusts the strategy to respond to unfolding events. However, on occasion, major strategy shifts are called for, such as when the strategy is clearly failing or when industry conditions change in dramatic ways.

Regardless of whether a company's strategy changes gradually or swiftly, the important point is that the task of crafting strategy is not a one-time event but is always a work in progress.[7] The evolving nature of a company's strategy means the typical company strategy is a blend of (1) *proactive* moves to improve the company's financial performance and secure a competitive edge and (2) *adaptive* reactions to unanticipated developments and fresh market conditions—see Figure 1.1.[8] The biggest portion of a company's current strategy flows from ongoing actions that have proven themselves in the marketplace and newly launched initiatives aimed at building a larger lead over rivals and further boosting financial performance. This part of management's action plan for running the company is its proactive, **deliberate strategy.**

At times, certain components of a company's deliberate strategy will fail in the marketplace and become **abandoned strategy elements.** Also, managers must always be willing to supplement or modify planned, deliberate strategy elements with as-needed reactions to unanticipated developments. Inevitably, there will be occasions when market and competitive conditions take unexpected turns that call for some kind of strategic reaction. Novel strategic moves on the part of rival firms, unexpected shifts in customer preferences, fast-changing technological developments, and new market opportunities call for unplanned, reactive adjustments that form the company's **emergent strategy.** As shown in Figure 1.1, a company's **realized strategy** tends to be a *combination* of deliberate planned elements and unplanned, emergent elements.

> Changing circumstances and ongoing management efforts to improve the strategy cause a company's strategy to evolve over time—a condition that makes the task of crafting a strategy a work in progress, not a one-time event.

CORE CONCEPT

A company's **realized strategy** is a combination of *deliberate planned elements* and *unplanned emergent elements*. Some components of a company's deliberate strategy will fail in the marketplace and become *abandoned strategy elements*.

FIGURE 1.1

A Company's Strategy Is a Blend of Planned Initiatives and Unplanned Reactive Adjustments

Abandoned strategy elements

Deliberate Strategy Elements

Planned new initiatives plus ongoing strategies continued from prior periods

Unplanned reactive responses to changing circumstances by management

Emergent Strategy Elements

Realized Business Strategy

The Three Tests of a Winning Strategy

LO1-6   Identify the three tests of a winning strategy.

Three questions can be used to distinguish a winning strategy from a so-so or flawed strategy:

> A winning strategy must fit the company's external and internal situation, build sustainable competitive advantage, and improve company performance.

1. *How well does the strategy fit the company's situation?* To qualify as a winner, a strategy has to be well matched to the company's external and internal situations. The strategy must fit competitive conditions in the industry and other aspects of the enterprise's external environment. At the same time, it should be tailored to the company's collection of competitively important resources and capabilities. It's unwise to build a strategy upon the company's weaknesses or pursue a strategic approach that requires resources that are deficient in the company. Unless a strategy exhibits a tight fit with both the external and internal aspects of a company's overall situation, it is unlikely to produce respectable, first-rate business results.

2. *Is the strategy helping the company achieve a sustainable competitive advantage?* Strategies that fail to achieve a durable competitive advantage over rivals are unlikely to produce superior performance for more than a brief period of time. Winning strategies enable a company to achieve a competitive advantage over key rivals that is long lasting. The bigger and more durable the competitive edge that the strategy helps build, the more powerful it is.

3. *Is the strategy producing good company performance?* The mark of a winning strategy is strong company performance. Two kinds of performance improvements tell the most about the caliber of a company's strategy: (1) gains in profitability and financial strength and (2) advances in the company's competitive strength and market standing.

Strategies that come up short on one or more of these tests are plainly less appealing than strategies passing all three tests with flying colors. Managers should use the same questions when evaluating either proposed or existing strategies. New initiatives that don't seem to match the company's internal and external situation should be scrapped before they come to fruition, while existing strategies must be scrutinized on a regular basis to ensure they have a good fit, offer a competitive advantage, and have contributed to above-average performance or performance improvements.

Why Crafting and Executing Strategy Are Important Tasks

High-achieving enterprises are nearly always the product of astute, creative, and proactive strategy making. Companies don't get to the top of the industry rankings or stay there with illogical strategies, copycat strategies, or timid attempts to try to do better. Among all the things managers do, nothing affects a company's ultimate success or failure more fundamentally than how well its management team charts the company's direction, develops competitively effective strategic moves and business approaches, and pursues what needs to be done internally to produce good day-in, day-out strategy execution and operating excellence. Indeed, *good strategy and good strategy execution are the most telling signs of good management.* The rationale for using the twin standards of good strategy making and good strategy execution to determine whether a company is well managed is therefore compelling: *The better conceived a company's strategy and the more competently it is executed, the more likely that the company will be a standout performer in the marketplace.* In stark contrast, a company that lacks clear-cut direction, has a flawed strategy, or cannot execute its strategy competently is a company whose financial performance is probably suffering, whose business is at long-term risk, and whose management is sorely lacking.

> How well a company performs is directly attributable to the caliber of its strategy and the proficiency with which the strategy is executed.

The Road Ahead

Throughout the chapters to come and the accompanying case collection, the spotlight is trained on the foremost question in running a business enterprise: *What must managers do, and do well, to make a company a winner in the marketplace?* The answer that emerges is that doing a good job of managing inherently requires good strategic thinking and good management of the strategy-making, strategy-executing process.

The mission of this book is to provide a solid overview of what every business student and aspiring manager needs to know about crafting and executing strategy. We will explore what good strategic thinking entails, describe the core concepts and tools of strategic analysis, and examine the ins and outs of crafting and executing strategy. The accompanying cases will help build your skills in both diagnosing how well the strategy-making, strategy-executing task is being performed and prescribing actions for how the strategy in question or its execution can be improved. The strategic management course that you are enrolled in may also include a strategy simulation exercise where you will run a company in head-to-head competition with companies run by your classmates. Your mastery of the strategic management concepts presented in the following chapters will put you in a strong position to craft a winning strategy for your company and figure out how to execute it in a cost-effective and profitable manner. As you progress through the chapters of the text and the activities assigned during the term, we hope to convince you that first-rate capabilities in crafting and executing strategy are essential to good management.

KEY POINTS

1. A company's strategy is the coordinated set of actions that its managers take to outperform the company's competitors and achieve superior profitability.

2. Closely related to the concept of strategy is the concept of a company's business model. A company's business model is management's blueprint for delivering customer value in a manner that will generate revenues sufficient to cover costs and yield an attractive profit. The two elements of a company's business model are its (1) customer value proposition and (2) its profit formula.

3. The central thrust of a company's strategy is undertaking moves to build and strengthen the company's long-term competitive position and financial performance by competing differently from rivals and gaining a sustainable competitive advantage over them.

4. A company's strategy typically evolves over time, arising from a blend of (1) proactive and deliberate actions on the part of company managers and (2) adaptive emergent responses to unanticipated developments and fresh market conditions.

5. A winning strategy fits the circumstances of a company's external and internal situations, builds competitive advantage, and boosts company performance.

ASSURANCE OF LEARNING EXERCISES

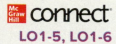

LO1-1, LO1-2, LO1-4

1. Based on your experiences as a computer, tablet, or smartphone user, does Apple, Inc.'s strategy as described in Concepts & Connections 1.2 seem to set it apart from rivals? Does the strategy seem to be keyed to a cost-based advantage, differentiating features, serving the unique needs of a niche, or some combination of these? What is there about Apple Inc.'s strategy that can lead to sustainable competitive advantage?

LO1-3

2. Go to investor.siriusxm.com and check whether SiriusXM's recent financial reports indicate that its business model is working. Are its subscription fees increasing or declining? Is its revenue stream from advertising and equipment sales growing or declining? Does its cost structure allow for acceptable profit margins?

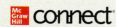

LO1-5, LO1-6

3. Elements of Amazon's strategy have evolved in meaningful ways since the company's founding in 1994. After reviewing the company's history of innovations at www.aboutamazon.com/innovation and all of the links at the company's investor relations site (ir.aboutamazon.com), prepare a one- to two-page report that discusses how its strategy has evolved. Your report should also assess how well Amazon's strategy passes the three tests of a winning strategy.

EXERCISES FOR SIMULATION PARTICIPANTS

After you have read the Participant's Guide or Player's Manual for the strategy simulation exercise that you will participate in during this academic term, you and your co-managers should come up with brief one- or two-paragraph answers to the questions that follow *before* entering your first set of decisions. While your answers to the first of the six questions can be developed from your reading of the manual, the remaining questions will require a collaborative discussion among the members of your company's management team about how you intend to manage the company you have been assigned to run.

LO1-1

1. Your company's strategy in the business simulation for this course should include choices about what types of issues?

LO1-6

2. What is your company's current situation? A substantive answer to this question should cover the following issues:

    •   Does your company appear to be in sound financial condition?

    •   What problems does your company have that need to be addressed?

LO1-4

3. Why will your company matter to customers? A complete answer to this question should say something about each of the following:

    •   How will you create customer value?

    •   What will be distinctive about the company's products or services?

    •   How will capabilities and resources be deployed to deliver customer value?

4. What are the primary elements of your company's business model?   **LO1-3**

   • Describe your customer value proposition.

   • Discuss the profit formula tied to your business model.

   • What level of revenues is required for your company's business model to become a moneymaker?

5. How will you build and sustain competitive advantage?   **LO1-6**

   • Which of the basic strategic and competitive approaches discussed in this chapter do you think makes the most sense to pursue?

   • What kind of competitive advantage over rivals will you try to achieve?

   • How do you envision that your strategy might evolve as you react to the competitive moves of rival firms?

   • Does your strategy have the ability to pass the three tests of a winning strategy? Explain.

6. Why will strategy execution be important to your company's success?   **LO1-6**

ENDNOTES

1. B. R., "An A-Z of Business Quotations: Strategy," *The Economist,* October 19, 2012, www.economist.com/blogs/schumpeter/2012/10/z-business-quotations-1 (accessed January 4, 2014).

2. Jan Rivkin, "An Alternative Approach to Making Strategic Choices," Harvard Business School case 9-702-433, 2001.

3. Michael E. Porter, "What Is Strategy?" *Harvard Business Review* 74, no. 6 (November–December 1996).

4. Mark W. Johnson, Clayton M. Christensen, and Henning Kagermann, "Reinventing Your Business Model," *Harvard Business Review* 86, no. 12 (December 2008); and Joan Magretta, "Why Business Models Matter," *Harvard Business Review* 80, no. 5 (May 2002).

5. W. Chan Kim and Renée Mauborgne, "How Strategy Shapes Structure," *Harvard Business Review* 87, no. 9 (September 2009).

6. Porter, "What Is Strategy?"

7. Cynthia A. Montgomery, "Putting Leadership Back Into Strategy," *Harvard Business Review* 86, no. 1 (January 2008).

8. Henry Mintzberg and Joseph Lampel, "Reflecting on the Strategy Process," *Sloan Management Review* 40, no. 3 (Spring 1999); Henry Mintzberg and J. A. Waters, "Of Strategies, Deliberate and Emergent," *Strategic Management Journal* 6 (1985); Costas Markides, "Strategy as Balance: From 'Either-Or' to 'And,'" *Business Strategy Review* 12, no. 3 (September 2001); Henry Mintzberg, Bruce Ahlstrand, and Joseph Lampel, *Strategy Safari: A Guided Tour through the Wilds of Strategic Management* (New York: Free Press, 1998); C. K. Prahalad and Gary Hamel, "The Core Competence of the Corporation," *Harvard Business Review* 70, no. 3 (May–June 1990).

2 STRATEGY FORMULATION, EXECUTION, AND GOVERNANCE

LEARNING OBJECTIVES

After reading this chapter, you should be able to:

LO2-1 Understand why it is critical for company managers to have a clear strategic vision of where a company needs to head and why.

LO2-2 Explain the importance of setting both strategic and financial objectives.

LO2-3 Explain why the strategic initiatives taken at various organizational levels must be tightly coordinated to achieve companywide performance targets.

LO2-4 Recognize what a company must do to achieve operating excellence and to execute its strategy proficiently.

LO2-5 Identify the role and responsibility of a company's board of directors in overseeing the strategic management process.

Crafting and executing strategy are the heart and soul of managing a business enterprise. But exactly what is involved in developing a strategy and executing it proficiently? What are the various components of the strategy formulation, strategy execution process, and to what extent are company personnel—aside from senior management—involved in the process? This chapter presents an overview of the ins and outs of crafting and executing company strategies. Special attention will be given to management's direction-setting responsibilities—charting a strategic course, setting performance targets, and choosing a strategy capable of producing the desired outcomes. We will also explain why strategy formulation is a task for a company's entire management team and discuss which kinds of strategic decisions tend to be made at which levels of management. The chapter concludes with a look at the roles and responsibilities of a company's board of directors and how good corporate governance protects shareholder interests and promotes good management.

The Strategy Formulation, Strategy Execution Process

The managerial process of crafting and executing a company's strategy is an ongoing, continuous process consisting of five integrated stages:

1. *Developing a strategic vision* that charts the company's long-term direction, a *mission statement* that describes the company's business, and a set of *core values* to guide the pursuit of the strategic vision and mission.

2. *Setting objectives* for measuring the company's performance and tracking its progress in moving in the intended long-term direction.

3. *Crafting a strategy* for advancing the company along the path to management's envisioned future and achieving its performance objectives.

4. *Implementing and executing the chosen strategy* efficiently and effectively.

5. *Evaluating and analyzing the external environment and the company's internal situation and performance* to identify corrective adjustments that are needed in the company's long-term direction, objectives, strategy, or approach to strategy execution.

Figure 2.1 displays this five-stage process. The model illustrates the need for management to evaluate a number of external and internal factors in deciding upon a strategic direction, appropriate objectives, and approaches to crafting and executing strategy (see Table 2.1). Management's decisions that are made in the strategic management process must be shaped by the prevailing economic conditions and competitive environment and the company's own internal resources and competitive capabilities. These strategy-shaping conditions will be the focus of Chapters 3 and 4.

The model shown in Figure 2.1 also illustrates the need for management to evaluate the company's performance on an ongoing basis. Any indication that the company is failing to achieve its objectives calls for corrective adjustments in one of the first four stages of the process. The company's implementation efforts might have fallen short, and new tactics must be devised to fully exploit the potential of the company's strategy. If management determines that the company's execution efforts are sufficient, it should challenge the assumptions underlying the company's business model and strategy and make alterations to better fit competitive conditions and the company's internal capabilities. If the

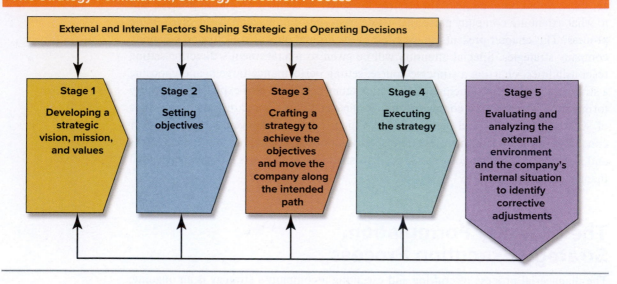

FIGURE 2.1

The Strategy Formulation, Strategy Execution Process

External and Internal Factors Shaping Strategic and Operating Decisions

Stage 1
Developing a strategic vision, mission, and values

Stage 2
Setting objectives

Stage 3
Crafting a strategy to achieve the objectives and move the company along the intended path

Stage 4
Executing the strategy

Stage 5
Evaluating and analyzing the external environment and the company's internal situation to identify corrective adjustments

company's strategic approach to competition is rated as sound, then perhaps management set overly ambitious targets for the company's performance.

The evaluation stage of the strategic management process shown in Figure 2.1 also allows for a change in the company's vision, but this should be necessary only when it becomes evident to management that the industry has changed in a

TABLE 2.1

Factors Shaping Decisions in the Strategy Formulation, Strategy Execution Process

External Considerations
- Does sticking with the company's present strategic course present attractive opportunities for growth and profitability?
- What kind of competitive forces are industry members facing, and are they acting to enhance or weaken the company's prospects for growth and profitability?
- What factors are driving industry change, and what impact on the company's prospects will they have?
- How are industry rivals positioned, and what strategic moves are they likely to make next?
- What are the key factors of future competitive success, and does the industry offer good prospects for attractive profits for companies possessing those capabilities?

Internal Considerations
- Does the company have an appealing customer value proposition?
- What are the company's competitively important resources and capabilities, and are they potent enough to produce a sustainable competitive advantage?
- Does the company have sufficient business and competitive strength to seize market opportunities and nullify external threats?
- Are the company's costs competitive with those of key rivals?
- Is the company competitively stronger or weaker than key rivals?

significant way that renders the vision obsolete. Such occasions can be referred to as **strategic inflection points.** When a company reaches a strategic inflection point, management has tough decisions to make about the company's direction because abandoning an established course carries considerable risk. However, responding to unfolding changes in the marketplace in a timely fashion lessens a company's chances of becoming trapped in a stagnant or declining business or letting attractive new growth opportunities slip away.

The first three stages of the strategic management process make up a strategic plan. A **strategic plan** maps out where a company is headed, establishes strategic and financial targets, and outlines the competitive moves and approaches to be used in achieving the desired business results.[1]

Stage 1: Developing a Strategic Vision, a Mission, and Core Values

LO2-1   Understand why it is critical for company managers to have a clear strategic vision of where a company needs to head and why.

At the outset of the strategy formulation, strategy execution process, a company's senior managers must wrestle with the issue of what directional path the company should take and whether its market positioning and future performance prospects could be improved by changing the company's product offerings and/or the markets in which it participates and/or the customers it caters to and/or the technologies it employs. Top management's views about the company's direction and future product-customer-market-technology focus constitute a **strategic vision** for the company. A clearly articulated strategic vision communicates management's aspirations to stakeholders about "where we are going" and helps steer the energies of company personnel in a common direction. For instance, the vision of Google's co-founders Larry Page and Sergey Brin "to organize the world's information and make it universally accessible and useful"[2] captured the imagination of Google employees, served as the basis for crafting the company's strategic actions, and aided internal efforts to mobilize and direct the company's resources.

> **CORE CONCEPT**
>
> A **strategic vision** describes "where we are going"— the course and direction management has charted and the company's future product-customer-market-technology focus.

Well-conceived visions are *distinctive* and *specific* to a particular organization; they avoid generic, feel-good statements such as "We will become a global leader and the first choice of customers in every market we choose to serve"[3]—which could apply to any of hundreds of organizations.[4] And they are not the product of a committee charged with coming up with an innocuous but well-meaning one-sentence vision that wins consensus approval from various stakeholders. Nicely worded vision statements with no specifics about the company's product-market-customer-technology focus fall well short of what it takes for a vision to measure up.

For a strategic vision to function as a valuable managerial tool, it must provide understanding of what management wants its business to look like and provide managers with a reference point in making strategic decisions. It must say something definitive about how the company's leaders intend to position the company beyond where it is today. Table 2.2 lists some characteristics of effective vision statements.

A surprising number of the vision statements found on company websites and in annual reports are vague and unrevealing, saying very little about the company's future product-market-customer-technology focus. Some could apply to most any company in any industry. Many read like a public relations statement—lofty words that someone came up with because it is fashionable for companies to have an official vision statement.[5] Table 2.3 provides a list of the most common shortcomings in company vision statements. Like any tool, vision statements can be used properly or improperly, either clearly conveying a company's strategic course or not. Concepts & Connections 2.1 provides a critique of the strategic visions of several prominent companies.

TABLE 2.2

Characteristics of Effectively Worded Vision Statements

Graphic—Paints a picture of the kind of company that management is trying to create and the market position(s) the company is striving to stake out.

Directional—Is forward-looking; describes the strategic course that management has charted and the kinds of product-market-customer-technology changes that will help the company prepare for the future.

Focused—Is specific enough to provide managers with guidance in making decisions and allocating resources.

Flexible—Is not so focused that it makes it difficult for management to adjust to changing circumstances in markets, customer preferences, or technology.

Feasible—Is within the realm of what the company can reasonably expect to achieve.

Desirable—Indicates why the directional path makes good business sense.

Easy to communicate—Is explainable in 5 to 10 minutes and, ideally, can be reduced to a simple, memorable "slogan" (like Henry Ford's famous vision of "a car in every garage").

Source: Based partly on John P. Kotter, *Leading Change* (Harvard Business School Press, 1996).

TABLE 2.3

Common Shortcomings in Company Vision Statements

Vague or incomplete—Short on specifics about where the company is headed or what the company is doing to prepare for the future.

Not forward-looking—Does not indicate whether or how management intends to alter the company's current product-market-customer-technology focus.

Too broad—So all-inclusive that the company could head in most any direction, pursue most any opportunity, or enter most any business.

Bland or uninspiring—Lacks the power to motivate company personnel or inspire shareholder confidence about the company's direction.

Not distinctive—Provides no unique company identity; could apply to companies in any of several industries (including rivals operating in the same market arena).

Too reliant on superlatives—Does not say anything specific about the company's strategic course beyond the pursuit of such distinctions as being a recognized leader, a global or worldwide leader, or the first choice of customers.

Source: Based on information in Hugh Davidson, *The Committed Enterprise* (Oxford: Butterworth Heinemann, 2002), chap. 2; and Michel Robert, *Strategy Pure and Simple II* (New York: McGraw-Hill, 1998), chaps. 2, 3, and 6.

CONCEPTS & CONNECTIONS 2.1

EXAMPLES OF STRATEGIC VISIONS—HOW WELL DO THEY MEASURE UP?

Vision Statement	Effective Elements	Shortcomings
Whole Foods Whole Foods Market is a dynamic leader in the quality food business. We are a mission-driven company that aims to set the standards of excellence for food retailers. We are building a business in which high standards permeate all aspects of our company. Quality is a state of mind at Whole Foods Market. Our motto—Whole Foods, Whole People, Whole Planet—emphasizes that our vision reaches far beyond just being a food retailer. Our success in fulfilling our vision is measured by customer satisfaction, team member happiness and excellence, return on capital investment, improvement in the state of the environment and local and larger community support. Our ability to instill a clear sense of interdependence among our various stakeholders (the people who are interested and benefit from the success of our company) is contingent upon our efforts to communicate more often, more openly, and more compassionately. Better communication equals better understanding and more trust.	• Forward-looking • Graphic • Focused • Desirable	• Long • Not memorable
Keurig Dr Pepper A leading producer and distributor of hot and cold beverages to satisfy every consumer need, anytime and anywhere.	• Focused • Desirable • Easy to communicate	• Not graphic • Not distinctive
Caterpillar Our vision is a world in which all people's basic needs—such as shelter, clean water, sanitation, food and reliable power—are fulfilled in an environmentally sustainable way and a company that improves the quality of the environment and the communities where we live and work.	• Graphic • Desirable	• Too broad • Too reliant on superlatives • Not distinctive
Nike NIKE, Inc., fosters a culture of invention. We create products, services and experiences for today's athlete* while solving problems for the next generation.	• Forward-looking • Flexible	• Vague • Not focused • Too reliant on superlatives

* "If you have a body, you are an athlete."

Source: Company documents and websites.

The Importance of Communicating the Strategic Vision

A strategic vision has little value to the organization unless it's effectively communicated down the line to lower-level managers and employees. It would be difficult for a vision statement to provide direction to decision makers and energize employees toward achieving long-term strategic intent unless they know of the vision and observe management's commitment to that vision. Communicating the vision to organization members nearly always means putting "where we are going and why" in writing, distributing the statement organizationwide, and having executives personally explain the vision and its rationale to as many people as feasible. Ideally, executives should present their vision for the company in a manner that reaches out and grabs people's attention. An engaging and convincing strategic vision has enormous motivational value—for the same reason that a stonemason is inspired by building a great cathedral for the ages. Therefore, an executive's ability to paint a convincing and inspiring picture of a company's journey to a future destination is an important element of effective strategic leadership.[6]

Expressing the Essence of the Vision in a Slogan   The task of effectively conveying the vision to company personnel is assisted when management can capture the vision of where to head in a catchy or easily remembered slogan. A number of organizations have summed up their vision in a brief phrase. Disney's overarching vision for its five business groups—theme parks, movie studios, television channels, consumer products, and interactive media entertainment—is to "create happiness by providing the finest in entertainment for people of all ages, everywhere."[7] The Mayo Clinic's vision is to provide "The best care to every patient every day,"[8] while Greenpeace's envisioned future is "To halt environmental abuse and promote environmental solutions."[9] Creating a short slogan to illuminate an organization's direction and then using it repeatedly as a reminder of "where we are headed and why" helps rally organization members to hurdle whatever obstacles lie in the company's path and maintain their focus.

> An effectively communicated vision is a valuable management tool for enlisting the commitment of company personnel to engage in actions that move the company in the intended direction.

Why a Sound, Well-Communicated Strategic Vision Matters   A well-thought-out, forcefully communicated strategic vision pays off in several respects: (1) it crystallizes senior executives' own views about the firm's long-term direction; (2) it reduces the risk of rudderless decision making by management at all levels; (3) it is a tool for winning the support of employees to help make the vision a reality; (4) it provides a beacon for lower-level managers in forming departmental missions; and (5) it helps an organization prepare for the future.

> The distinction between a **strategic vision** and a **mission statement** is fairly clear-cut: A strategic vision portrays a company's *future business scope* ("where we are going"), whereas a company's mission statement typically describes its *present business and purpose* ("who we are, what we do, and why we are here").

> **CORE CONCEPT**
>
> A well-conceived **mission statement** conveys a company's purpose in language specific enough to give the company its own identity.

Developing a Company Mission Statement

The defining characteristic of a well-conceived **strategic vision** is what it says about the company's *future strategic course*—"where we are headed and what our future product-customer-market-technology focus will be." In contrast, a **mission statement** describes the enterprise's *present business scope and purpose*—"who we are, what we do, and why we are here." It is purely descriptive. Ideally, a company mission statement (1) identifies the company's products and/or services, (2) specifies the buyer needs that the company seeks to satisfy and the customer groups or markets that it serves, and (3) gives the company its own identity. Consider, for example, the mission statement of

Singapore Airlines, which is consistently rated among the world's best airlines in terms of passenger safety and comfort:

> Singapore Airlines is a global company dedicated to providing air transportation services of the highest quality and to maximizing returns for the benefit of its shareholders and employees.[10]

Note that Singapore Airlines' mission statement does a good job of conveying "who we are, what we do, and why we are here," but it provides no sense of "where we are headed."

An example of a well-stated mission statement with ample specifics about what the organization does is that of St. Jude Children's Research Hospital: "To advance cures, and means of prevention, for pediatric catastrophic diseases through research and treatment. Consistent with the vision of our founder Danny Thomas, no child is denied treatment based on race, religion or a family's ability to pay."[11] Twitter's mission statement, while short, still captures the essence of what the company is about: "To give everyone the power to create and share ideas and information instantly, without barriers."[12] An example of a not-so-revealing mission statement is that of Microsoft: "To empower every person and every organization on the planet to achieve more"[13] says nothing about its products or business and does not give the company its own identity. A mission statement that provides scant indication of "who we are and what we do" has no apparent value.

Occasionally, companies state that their mission is to simply earn a profit. This is misguided. Profit is more correctly an *objective* and a *result* of what a company does. Moreover, earning a profit is the obvious intent of every commercial enterprise. Such companies as BMW, Netflix, Shell Oil, Procter & Gamble, and Citigroup are each striving to earn a profit for shareholders, but the fundamentals of their businesses are substantially different when it comes to "who we are and what we do." It is management's answer to "make a profit doing what and for whom?" that reveals the substance of a company's true mission and business purpose.

Linking the Strategic Vision and Mission with Company Values

Many companies have developed a statement of **values** (sometimes called *core values*) to guide the actions and behavior of company personnel in conducting the company's business and pursuing its strategic vision and mission. These values are the designated beliefs and desired ways of doing things at the company and frequently relate to such things as fair treatment, honor and integrity, ethical behavior, innovativeness, teamwork, a passion for excellence, social responsibility, and community citizenship.

> **CORE CONCEPT**
>
> A company's **values** are the beliefs, traits, and behavioral norms that company personnel are expected to display in conducting the company's business and pursuing its strategic vision and mission.

Most companies normally have four to eight core values. At Samsung, five core values are linked to its philosophy of devoting its talent and technology to create superior products and services that contribute to a better global society: (1) giving people opportunities to reach their full potential, (2) developing the best products and services on the market, (3) embracing change, (4) operating in an ethical way, and (5) dedication to social and environmental responsibility. L. L. Bean's two core values are encompassed in a quote from founder Leon Leonwood Bean—"Sell good merchandise at a reasonable profit, treat your customers like human beings, and they will always come back for more."[14]

Do companies practice what they preach when it comes to their professed values? Sometimes no, sometimes yes—it runs the gamut. At one extreme are companies with window-dressing values; the professed values are given lip service by top executives but have little discernible impact on either how company personnel behave or how the company operates. At the other extreme are companies whose executives are committed to grounding company operations on sound values and principled ways of doing business. Executives at these companies deliberately seek to ingrain the designated core values into the corporate culture—the core values thus become an integral part of the company's DNA and what makes it tick. At such values-driven companies, executives "walk the talk" and company personnel are held accountable for displaying the stated values. Concepts & Connections 2.2 describes how core values drive the company's mission and business model at TOMS Shoes.

CONCEPTS & CONNECTIONS 2.2

TOMS SHOES: ITS MISSION-DRIVEN BUSINESS MODEL

TOMS Shoes was founded in 2006 by Blake Mycoskie after a trip to Argentina where he witnessed many children with no access to shoes in areas of extreme poverty. Mycoskie returned to the United States and founded TOMS Shoes with the purpose of matching every pair of shoes purchased by customers with a new pair of shoes to give to a child in need, a model he called One for One®. In contrast to many companies that begin with a product and then articulate a mission, Mycoskie started with the mission to "help improve lives through business" and then built a company around it. Although the company has since expanded their product portfolio, its mission remains essentially the same:

"Improving Lives: With every product you purchase, TOMS will help a person in need. One for One.®" TOMS's mission is ingrained in their business model. While Mycoskie could have set up a non-profit organization to address the problem he witnessed, he was certain he didn't want to rely on donors to fund giving to the poor; he wanted to create a business that would fund the giving itself. With the one-for-one model, TOMS built the cost of giving away a pair of shoes into the price of each pair they sold, enabling the company to make a profit while still giving away shoes to the needy.

Much of TOMS's success (and ability to differentiate itself in a competitive marketplace) is attributable to the appeal of its mission and origin story. Mycoskie first got TOMS shoes into a trendy store in Los Angeles because he told them the story of why he founded the company, which got picked up by the *Los Angeles Times* and quickly spread. As the company has expanded communication channels, they continue to focus on leading with the story of their mission to ensure that customers know they are doing more than just buying a product.

As TOMS expanded to other products, they stayed true to the One-for-One business model, adapting it to each new product category. In 2011, the company launched TOMS Eyewear, where every purchase of glasses helps restore sight to an individual. They've since launched TOMS Roasting Co. that helps support access to safe water with every purchase of coffee, TOMS Bags where purchases fund resources for safe birth, and TOMS High Road Backpack Collection where purchases provide training for bullying prevention.

By ingraining the mission in the company's business model, TOMS has been able to truly live up to Mycoskie's aspiration of improving lives through business. TOMS even ensured that the business model will never change; when Mycoskie sold 50 percent of the company to Bain Capital in 2014, part of the transaction protected the One-for-One business model forever. TOMS is a successful example of a company that proves a commitment to core values can spur both revenue growth and giving back.

Note: Developed with Carry S. Resor.

Sources: TOMS Shoes website, accessed February 2018, http://www.toms.com/about-toms; Shana Lebowitz, "TOMS Blake Mycoskie Talks Growing a Business While Balancing Profit with Purpose," *Business Insider,* June 15, 2016, http://www.businessinsider.com/ toms-blake-mycoskie-talks-growing-a-business-while-balancing-profit-with-purpose-2016-6; Blake Mycoskie, "The Founder of TOMS on Reimaging the Company's Mission," *Harvard Business Review,* January–February 2016, https://hbr.org/2016/01/the-founder-of-toms-on-reimagining-the-companys-mission.

Stage 2: Setting Objectives

 LO2-2   Explain the importance of setting both strategic and financial objectives.

The managerial purpose of setting **objectives** is to convert the strategic vision into specific performance targets. Objectives reflect management's aspirations for company performance in light of the industry's prevailing economic and competitive conditions and the company's internal capabilities. Well-stated objectives are *quantifiable,* or *measurable,* and contain a *deadline for achievement.* Concrete, measurable objectives are managerially valuable for three reasons: (1) They focus organizational attention and align actions throughout the organization, (2) they serve as yardsticks for tracking a company's performance and progress, and (3) they motivate employees to expend greater effort and perform at a high level.

The Imperative of Setting Stretch Objectives

The experiences of countless companies teach that one of the best ways to promote outstanding company performance is for managers to deliberately set performance targets high enough to stretch an organization to perform at its full potential. Challenging company personnel to go all out and deliver "stretch" gains in performance pushes an enterprise to be more inventive and to exhibit more urgency in improving its financial performance and business position. Stretch objectives spur exceptional performance and help build a firewall against contentment with modest gains in organizational performance.

A company exhibits *strategic intent* when it relentlessly pursues an ambitious strategic objective, concentrating the full force of its resources and competitive actions on achieving that objective. Both Google (now Alphabet) and Amazon have had the strategic intent of developing drones, Amazon's for delivery and Google's for both delivery and high-speed Internet delivery from the skies. Stretch goals have mobilized employees at companies such as Southwest Airlines, 3M, and General Electric to produce best-in-industry performance. However, radical objectives that are not achieved can erode employee confidence and ultimately damage company performance. Stretch objectives are most likely to produce desired results when the company is building upon strong recent performance and when ample resources are available to support growth aspirations.[15]

What Kinds of Objectives to Set

Two very distinct types of performance yardsticks are required: those relating to financial performance and those relating to strategic performance. **Financial objectives** communicate management's targets for financial performance. Common financial objectives relate to revenue growth, profitability, and return on investment. **Strategic objectives** are related to a company's marketing standing and competitive vitality. The importance of attaining financial objectives is intuitive. Without adequate profitability and financial strength, a company's long-term health and ultimate survival is jeopardized.

> **CORE CONCEPT**
>
> **Objectives** are an organization's performance targets—the results management wants to achieve.
>
> **Strategic objectives** set performance targets high enough to stretch an organization to perform at its full potential and deliver the best possible results.
>
> A company exhibits **strategic intent** when it relentlessly pursues an ambitious strategic objective, concentrating the full force of its resources and competitive actions on achieving that objective.

CORE CONCEPT

Financial objectives relate to the financial performance targets management has established for the organization to achieve.

Strategic objectives relate to target outcomes that indicate a company is strengthening its market standing, competitive vitality, and future business prospects.

Furthermore, subpar earnings and a weak balance sheet alarm shareholders and creditors and put the jobs of senior executives at risk. However, good financial performance, by itself, is not enough.

A company's financial objectives are really *lagging indicators* that reflect the results of past decisions and organizational activities.[16] The results of past decisions and organizational activities are not reliable indicators of a company's future prospects. Companies that have been poor financial performers are sometimes able to turn things around, and good financial performers on occasion fall upon hard times. Hence, the best and most reliable predictors of a company's success in the marketplace and future financial performance are strategic objectives. Strategic outcomes are *leading indicators* of a company's future financial performance and business prospects. The accomplishment of strategic objectives signals the company is well positioned to sustain or improve its performance. For instance, if a company is achieving ambitious strategic objectives, then there's reason to expect that its *future* financial performance will be better than its current or past performance. If a company begins to lose competitive strength and fails to achieve important strategic objectives, then its ability to maintain its present profitability is highly suspect.

Consequently, utilizing a performance measurement system that strikes a *balance* between financial objectives and strategic objectives is optimal.[17] Just tracking a company's financial performance overlooks the fact that what ultimately enables a company to deliver better financial results is the achievement of strategic objectives that improve its competitiveness and market strength. Representative examples of financial and strategic objectives that companies often include in a **balanced scorecard** approach to measuring their performance are displayed in Table 2.4.[18]

CORE CONCEPT

The **balanced scorecard** is a widely used method for combining the use of both strategic and financial objectives, tracking their achievement, and giving management a more complete and balanced view of how well an organization is performing.

In 2015, nearly 50 percent of global companies used a balanced scorecard approach to measuring strategic and financial performance.[19] Examples of organizations that have adopted a balanced scorecard approach to setting objectives and measuring performance include Siemens AG, Wells Fargo Bank, Ann Taylor Stores, Ford Motor Company, Hilton Hotels, and over 30 colleges and universities.[20] Concepts & Connections 2.3 provides selected strategic and financial objectives of three prominent companies.

Short-Term and Long-Term Objectives

A company's set of financial and strategic objectives should include both near-term and long-term performance targets. Short-term objectives focus attention on delivering performance improvements in the current period, whereas long-term targets force the organization to consider how actions currently under way will affect the company later. Specifically, long-term objectives stand as a barrier to an undue focus on short-term results by nearsighted management. When trade-offs have to be made between achieving long-run and short-run objectives, long-run objectives should take precedence (unless the achievement of one or more short-run performance targets has unique importance).

The Need for Objectives at All Organizational Levels

Objective setting should not stop with the establishment of companywide performance targets. Company objectives need to be broken into performance targets for each of the organization's

CONCEPTS & CONNECTIONS 2.3

EXAMPLES OF COMPANY OBJECTIVES

JetBlue

Increase EPS by $0.65–$0.95 in 2020; further develop fare options, a co-branded credit card, and the Mint franchise; commit to achieving total cost savings of $250 to $300 million by 2020; kickoff multi-year cabin restyling program; convert all core A321 aircraft from 190 to 200 seats; target growth in key cities like Boston, plan to grow 150 flights a day to 200 over the coming years; grow toward becoming the carrier of choice in South Florida; organically grow west coast presence by expanding Mint offering to more transcontinental routes; optimize fare mix to increase overall average fare.

General Mills

Generate low single-digit organic net sales growth and high single-digit growth in earnings per share; deliver double-digit returns to shareholders over the long term; to drive future growth, focus on Consumer First strategy to gain a deep understanding of consumer needs and respond quickly to give them what they want; more specifically: (1) grow cereal globally with a strong line-up of new products, including new flavors of iconic Cheerios, (2) innovate in fast growing segments of the yogurt category to improve performance and expand the yogurt platform into new cities in China; (3) expand distribution and advertising for high performing brands, such as Häagen-Dazs and Old El Paso; (4) build a more agile organization by streamlining support functions, allowing for more fluid use of resources and idea sharing around the world; enhancing e-commerce know-how to capture more growth in this emerging channel; and investing in strategic revenue management tools to optimize promotions, prices and mix of products to drive sales growth.

YUM! Brands (KFC, Pizza Hut, Taco Bell)

Achieve same store sales growth of 2–3 percent annually; increase net new units by 3–4 percent annually; achieve system sales growth of mid to high single digit annually; achieve EPS growth in low double-digits annually; add 1,250 net new KFC units annually; reduce Pizza Hut dine-in assets from 42 percent in 2018 to 25 percent of assets by 2021–2023; 90 percent of net new Pizza Hut units will be small format assets; double telepizza footprint in Latin America by 2,500 net new units by 2038; open 100 new Taco Bell units in India by 2021; increase Taco Bell global system sales from $10.8 billion in 2018 to $15 billion by 2021.

Source: Information posted on company websites.

TABLE 2.4		
The Balanced Scorecard Approach to Performance Measurement		

Financial Objectives

- An x percent increase in annual revenues
- Annual increases in earnings per share of x percent
- An x percent return on capital employed (ROCE) or shareholder investment (ROE)
- Bond and credit ratings of x
- Internal cash flows of x to fund new capital investment

Strategic Objectives

- Win an x percent market share
- Achieve customer satisfaction rates of x percent
- Achieve a customer retention rate of x percent
- Acquire x number of new customers
- Introduce x number of new products in the next three years
- Reduce product development times to x months
- Increase percentage of sales coming from new products to x percent
- Improve information systems capabilities to give frontline managers defect information in x minutes
- Improve teamwork by increasing the number of projects involving more than one business unit to x

separate businesses, product lines, functional departments, and individual work units. Employees within various functional areas and operating levels will be guided much better by narrow objectives relating directly to their departmental activities than broad organizational-level goals. Objective setting is thus a top-down process that must extend to the lowest organizational levels. And it means that each organizational unit must take care to set performance targets that support—rather than conflict with or negate—the achievement of companywide strategic and financial objectives.

Stage 3: Crafting a Strategy

 LO2-3   Explain why the strategic initiatives taken at various organizational levels must be tightly coordinated to achieve companywide performance targets.

As indicated earlier, the task of stitching a strategy together entails addressing a series of *hows: how* to attract and please customers, *how* to compete against rivals, *how* to position the company in the marketplace and capitalize on attractive opportunities to grow the business, *how* best to respond to changing economic and market conditions, *how* to manage each functional piece of the business, and *how* to achieve the company's performance targets. It also means choosing among the various strategic alternatives and proactively searching for opportunities to do new things or to do existing things in new or better ways.[21]

In choosing among opportunities and addressing the *hows* of strategy, strategists must embrace the risks of uncertainty and the discomfort that naturally accompanies such risks. Bold strategies involve making difficult choices and placing bets on the future. Good strategic planning is not about eliminating risks, but increasing the odds of success. In sorting through the possibilities of what the company should and should not do, managers may conclude some opportunities are unrealistic or not sufficiently attractive to pursue. However, innovative strategy making that results in a powerful customer value proposition or pushes the company into new markets will likely require the development of new resources and capabilities and force the company outside its comfort zone.[22] Such a quest for continuous improvement in the competitive approach helps generate business model innovations and is essential to sustaining competitive advantage.

> Management must be alert to changes in the marketplace that call for an alteration of its competitive approach or revisions to its business model.

Strategy Formulation Involves Managers at All Organizational Levels

In some enterprises, the CEO or owner functions as strategic visionary and chief architect of the strategy, personally deciding what the key elements of the company's strategy will be, although the CEO may seek the advice of key subordinates in fashioning an overall strategy and deciding on important strategic moves. However, it is a mistake to view strategy making as a *top* management function—the exclusive province of owner-entrepreneurs, CEOs, high-ranking executives, and board members. The more a company's operations cut across different products, industries, and geographical areas, the more that headquarters executives have little option but to delegate considerable strategy-making authority to down-the-line managers. On-the-scene managers who

> In most companies, crafting strategy is a *collaborative team effort* that includes managers in various positions and at various organizational levels. Crafting strategy is rarely something only high-level executives do.

oversee specific operating units are likely to have a more detailed command of the strategic issues and choices for the particular operating unit under their supervision—knowing the prevailing market and competitive conditions, customer requirements and expectations, and all the other relevant aspects affecting the several strategic options available.

A Company's Strategy-Making Hierarchy

The larger and more diverse the operations of an enterprise, the more points of strategic initiative it will have and the more managers at different organizational levels will have a relevant strategy-making role. In diversified companies, where multiple and sometimes strikingly different businesses have to be managed, crafting a full-fledged strategy involves four distinct types of strategic actions and initiatives, each undertaken at different levels of the organization and partially or wholly crafted by managers at different organizational levels, as shown in Figure 2.2. A company's overall strategy is therefore *a collection of strategic initiatives and actions* devised by managers up and down the whole organizational hierarchy. Ideally, the pieces of a company's strategy up and down the strategy hierarchy should be cohesive and mutually reinforcing, fitting together like a jigsaw puzzle.

> **Corporate strategy** establishes an overall game plan for managing a *set of businesses* in a diversified, multibusiness company.
>
> **Business strategy** is primarily concerned with strengthening the company's market position and building competitive advantage in a single-business company or a single business unit of a diversified multibusiness corporation.

As shown in Figure 2.2, **corporate strategy** is orchestrated by the CEO and other senior executives and establishes an overall game plan for managing a *set of businesses* in a diversified, multibusiness company. Corporate strategy addresses the questions of how to capture cross-business synergies, what businesses to hold or divest, which new markets to enter, and how to best enter new markets—by acquisition, by creation of a strategic alliance, or through internal development. Corporate strategy and business diversification are the subject of Chapter 8, where they are discussed in detail.

Business strategy is primarily concerned with building competitive advantage in a single business unit of a diversified company or strengthening the market position of a nondiversified single business company. Business strategy is also the responsibility of the CEO and other senior executives, but key business-unit heads may also be influential, especially in strategic decisions affecting the businesses they lead. *In single-business companies, the corporate and business levels of the strategy-making hierarchy merge into a single level—business strategy—*because the strategy for the entire enterprise involves only one distinct business. So, a single-business company has three levels of strategy: business strategy, functional-area strategies, and operating strategies.

Functional-area strategies concern the actions related to particular functions or processes within a business. A company's product development strategy, for example, represents the managerial game plan for creating new products that are in tune with what buyers are looking for. Lead responsibility for functional strategies within a business is normally delegated to the heads of the respective functions, with the general manager of the business having final approval over functional strategies. For the overall business strategy to have maximum impact, a company's marketing strategy, production strategy, finance strategy, customer service strategy, product development strategy, and human resources strategy should be compatible and mutually reinforcing rather than each serving its own narrower purpose.

FIGURE 2.2

A Company's Strategy-Making Hierarchy

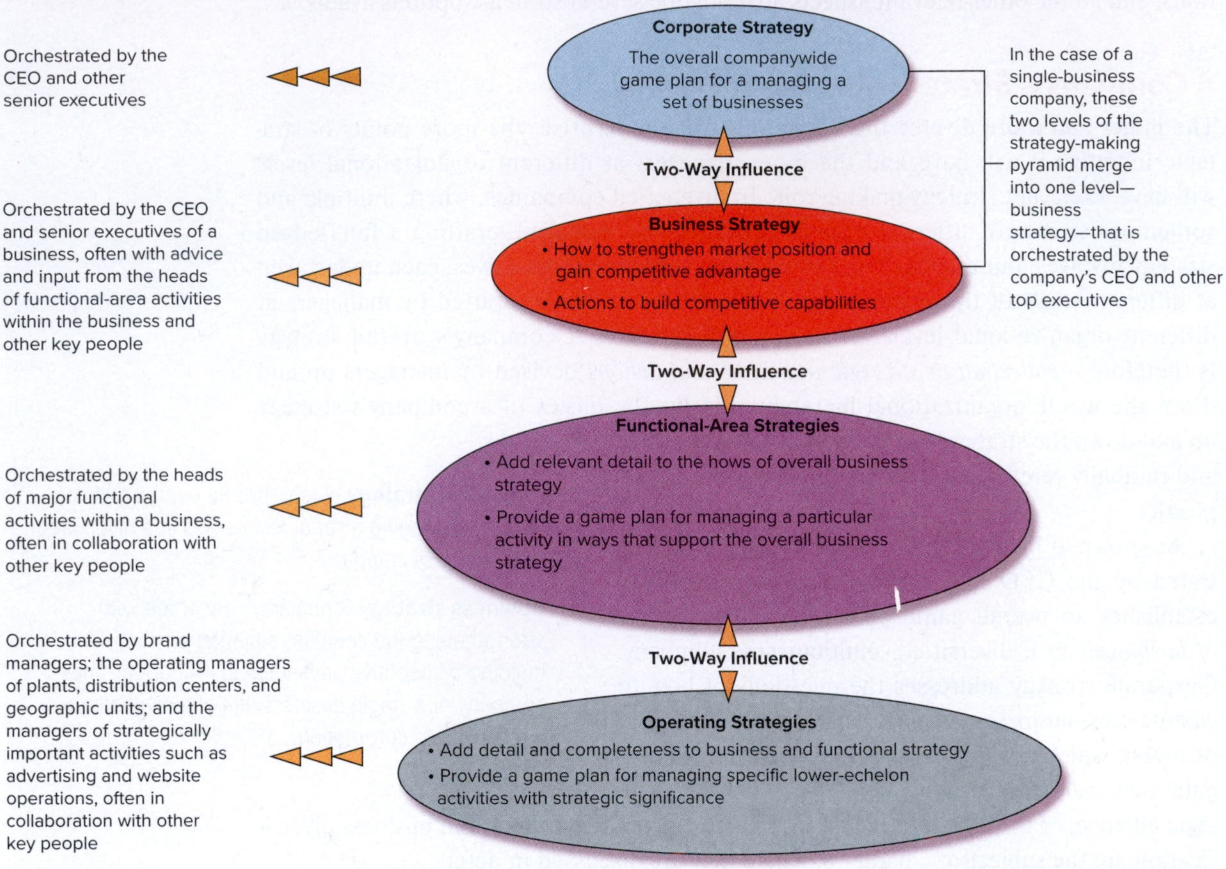

Orchestrated by the CEO and other senior executives

Corporate Strategy
The overall companywide game plan for a managing a set of businesses

In the case of a single-business company, these two levels of the strategy-making pyramid merge into one level—business strategy—that is orchestrated by the company's CEO and other top executives

Two-Way Influence

Orchestrated by the CEO and senior executives of a business, often with advice and input from the heads of functional-area activities within the business and other key people

Business Strategy
- How to strengthen market position and gain competitive advantage
- Actions to build competitive capabilities

Two-Way Influence

Orchestrated by the heads of major functional activities within a business, often in collaboration with other key people

Functional-Area Strategies
- Add relevant detail to the hows of overall business strategy
- Provide a game plan for managing a particular activity in ways that support the overall business strategy

Two-Way Influence

Orchestrated by brand managers; the operating managers of plants, distribution centers, and geographic units; and the managers of strategically important activities such as advertising and website operations, often in collaboration with other key people

Operating Strategies
- Add detail and completeness to business and functional strategy
- Provide a game plan for managing specific lower-echelon activities with strategic significance

Operating strategies concern the relatively narrow strategic initiatives and approaches for managing key operating units (plants, distribution centers, geographic units) and specific operating activities such as materials purchasing or Internet sales. Operating strategies are limited in scope but add further detail to functional-area strategies and the overall business strategy. Lead responsibility for operating strategies is usually delegated to front-line managers, subject to review and approval by higher-ranking managers.

Stage 4: Implementing and Executing the Chosen Strategy

LO2-4   Recognize what a company must do to achieve operating excellence and to execute its strategy proficiently.

Managing the implementation and execution of strategy is easily the most demanding and time-consuming part of the strategic management process. Good strategy execution entails that managers pay careful attention to how key internal business processes are performed and see to it that employees' efforts are directed toward the accomplishment of desired operational outcomes. The task of implementing and executing the strategy also necessitates an ongoing analysis of the efficiency and effectiveness of a company's internal activities and a managerial awareness of new technological developments that might improve business processes. In most situations, managing the strategy execution process includes the following principal aspects:

- Staffing the organization to provide needed skills and expertise.
- Allocating ample resources to activities critical to good strategy execution.
- Ensuring that policies and procedures facilitate rather than impede effective execution.
- Installing information and operating systems that enable company personnel to perform essential activities.
- Pushing for continuous improvement in how value chain activities are performed.
- Tying rewards and incentives directly to the achievement of performance objectives.
- Creating a company culture and work climate conducive to successful strategy execution.
- Exerting the internal leadership needed to propel implementation forward.

Stage 5: Evaluating Performance and Initiating Corrective Adjustments

The fifth stage of the strategy management process—evaluating and analyzing the external environment and the company's internal situation and performance to identify needed corrective adjustments—is the trigger point for deciding whether to continue or change the company's vision, objectives, business model or strategy, and/or strategy execution methods. So long as the company's direction and strategy seem well matched to industry and competitive conditions and performance targets are being met, company executives may well decide to stay the course. Simply fine-tuning the strategic plan and continuing with efforts to improve strategy execution are sufficient.

> A company's vision, objectives, strategy, and approach to strategy execution are never final; managing strategy is an ongoing process, not an every-now-and-then task.

But whenever a company encounters disruptive changes in its environment, questions need to be raised about the appropriateness of its direction and strategy. If a company experiences a downturn in its market position or persistent shortfalls in performance, then company managers are obligated to ferret out the causes—do they relate to an obsolete business model, poor strategy, poor strategy execution, or a combination of all?—and take timely corrective action. A company's direction, objectives, and business model have to be revisited any time external or internal conditions warrant.

Also, it is not unusual for a company to find that one or more aspects of its strategy implementation and execution are not going as well as intended. Proficient strategy execution is always the product of much organizational learning. It is achieved unevenly—coming quickly in some areas and proving nettlesome in others. Successful strategy execution entails vigilantly searching for ways to improve and then making corrective adjustments whenever and wherever it is useful to do so.

Corporate Governance: The Role of the Board of Directors in the Strategy Formulation, Strategy Execution Process

LO2-5 Identify the role and responsibility of a company's board of directors in overseeing the strategic management process.

Although senior managers have *lead responsibility* for crafting and executing a company's strategy, it is the duty of the board of directors to exercise strong oversight and see that the five tasks of strategic management are done in a manner that benefits shareholders (in the case of investor-owned enterprises) or stakeholders (in the case of not-for-profit organizations). In watching over management's strategy formulation, strategy execution actions, a company's board of directors has four important corporate governance obligations to fulfill:

1. *Oversee the company's financial accounting and financial reporting practices.* While top management, particularly the company's CEO and CFO (chief financial officer), is primarily responsible for seeing that the company's financial statements accurately report the results of the company's operations, board members have a fiduciary duty to protect shareholders by exercising oversight of the company's financial practices. In addition, corporate boards must ensure that generally acceptable accounting principles (GAAP) are properly used in preparing the company's financial statements and determine whether proper financial controls are in place to prevent fraud and misuse of funds. Virtually all boards of directors monitor the financial reporting activities by appointing an audit committee, always composed entirely of *outside directors* (*inside directors* hold management positions in the company and either directly or indirectly report to the CEO). The members of the audit committee have lead responsibility for overseeing the decisions of the company's financial officers and consulting with both internal and external auditors to ensure that financial reports are accurate and adequate financial controls are in place.

2. *Diligently critique and oversee the company's direction, strategy, and business approaches.* Even though board members have a legal obligation to warrant the accuracy of the company's financial reports, directors must set aside time to guide management in choosing a strategic direction and to make independent judgments about the validity and wisdom of management's proposed strategic actions. Many boards have found that meeting agendas become consumed by compliance matters and little time is left to discuss matters of strategic importance. The board of directors and management at Philips Electronics hold annual two- to three-day retreats devoted to evaluating the company's long-term direction and various strategic proposals. The company's exit from the semiconductor business and its increased focus on medical technology and home health care resulted from management–board discussions during such retreats.[23]

3. *Evaluate the caliber of senior executives' strategy formulation and strategy execution skills.* The board is always responsible for determining whether the current CEO

is doing a good job of strategic leadership and whether senior management is actively creating a pool of potential successors to the CEO and other top executives.[24] Evaluation of senior executives' strategy formulation and strategy execution skills is enhanced when outside directors go into the field to personally evaluate how well the strategy is being executed. Independent board members at GE visit operating executives at each major business unit once per year to assess the company's talent pool and stay abreast of emerging strategic and operating issues affecting the company's divisions. Home Depot board members visit a store once per quarter to determine the health of the company's operations.[25]

4. *Institute a compensation plan for top executives that rewards them for actions and results that serve shareholder interests.* A basic principle of corporate governance is that the owners of a corporation delegate operating authority and managerial control to top management in return for compensation. In their role as an *agent* of shareholders, top executives have a clear and unequivocal duty to make decisions and operate the company in accord with shareholder interests (but this does not mean disregarding the interests of other stakeholders, particularly those of employees, with whom they also have an agency relationship). Most boards of directors have a compensation committee, composed entirely of directors from outside the company, to develop a salary and incentive compensation plan that rewards senior executives for boosting the company's *long-term performance* and growing the economic value of the enterprise on behalf of shareholders; the compensation committee's recommendations are presented to the full board for approval.

But during the past 10 to 15 years, many boards of directors have done a poor job of ensuring that executive salary increases, bonuses, and stock option awards are tied tightly to performance measures that are truly in the long-term interests of shareholders. Rather, compensation packages at many companies have rewarded executives for *short-term performance* improvements—most notably, achieving quarterly and annual earnings targets and boosting the stock price by specified percentages. This has had the perverse effect of causing company managers to become preoccupied with actions to improve a company's near-term performance, even if excessively risky and damaging to long-term company performance. As a consequence, the need to overhaul and reform executive compensation has become a hot topic in both public circles and corporate boardrooms. Concepts & Connections 2.4 discusses how weak governance at Volkswagen contributed to the 2015 emissions cheating scandal, which cost the company billions of dollars and the trust of its stakeholders.

Every corporation should have a strong, independent board of directors that (1) is well informed about the company's performance, (2) guides and judges the CEO and other top executives, (3) has the courage to curb management actions it believes are inappropriate or unduly risky, (4) certifies to shareholders that the CEO is doing what the board expects, (5) provides insight and advice to management, and (6) is intensely involved in debating the pros and cons of key decisions and actions.[26] Boards of directors that lack the backbone to challenge a strong-willed or "imperial" CEO or that rubber-stamp most anything the CEO recommends without probing inquiry and debate abandon their duty to represent and protect shareholder interests.

CONCEPTS & CONNECTIONS 2.4

CORPORATE GOVERNANCE FAILURES AT VOLKSWAGEN

In 2015, Volkswagen admitted to installing "defeat devices" on at least 11 million vehicles with diesel engines. These devices enabled the cars to pass emission tests, even though the engines actually emitted pollutants up to 40 times above what is allowed in the United States. Current estimates are that it will cost the company at least €7 billion to cover the cost of repairs and lawsuits. Although management must have been involved in approving the use of cheating devices, the Volkswagen supervisory board has been unwilling to accept any responsibility. Some board members even questioned whether it was the board's responsibility to be aware of such problems, stating "matters of technical expertise were not for us" and "the scandal had nothing, not one iota, to do with the advisory board." Yet governing boards do have a responsibility to be well informed, to provide oversight, and to become involved in key decisions and actions. So what caused this corporate governance failure? Why is this the third time in the past 20 years that Volkswagen has been embroiled in scandal?

The key feature of Volkswagen's board that appears to have led to these issues is a lack of independent directors. However, before explaining this in more detail it is important to understand the German governance model. German corporations operate two-tier governance structures, with a management board and a separate supervisory board that does not contain any current

executives. In addition, German law requires large companies to have at least 50 percent supervisory board representation from workers. This structure is meant to provide more oversight by independent board members and greater involvement by a wider set of stakeholders.

In Volkswagen's case, these objectives have been effectively circumvented. Although Volkswagen's supervisory board does not include any current management, the chairmanship appears to be a revolving door of former senior executives. Ferdinand Piëch, the chair during the scandal, was CEO for nine years prior to becoming chair in 2002. Martin Winterkorn, the recently ousted CEO, was expected to become supervisory board chair prior to the scandal. The company continues to elevate management to the supervisory board even though they have presided over past scandals. Hans Dieter Poetsch, the newly appointed chair, was part of the management team that did not inform the supervisory board of the EPA investigation for two weeks.

VW also has a unique ownership structure where a single family, Porsche, controls more than 50 percent of voting shares. Piëch, a family member and chair until 2015, forced out CEOs and installed unqualified family members on the board, such as his former nanny and current wife. He also pushed out independent-minded board members, such as Gerhard Cromme, author of Germany's corporate governance code. The company has lost numerous independent directors over the past 10 years, leaving it with only one non-shareholder, non-labor representative. Although Piëch has now been removed, it is unclear that Volkswagen's board has solved the underlying problem. Shareholders have seen billions of dollars wiped away and the Volkswagen brand tarnished. As long as the board continues to lack independent directors, change will likely be slow.

Note: Developed with Jacob M. Crandall.

Source: "Piëch under Fire," *The Economist,* December 8, 2005; Chris Bryant and Richard Milne, "Boardroom Politics at Heart of VW Scandal," *Financial Times,* 2014; Andreas Cremer and Jan Schwartz, "Volkswagen Mired in Crisis as Board Members Criticize Piëch," Reuters, 2015; and Richard Milne, "Volkswagen: System Failure,"*Financial Times,* 2015.

©AR Pictures/Shutterstock

KEY POINTS

The strategic management process consists of five interrelated and integrated stages:

1. Developing a *strategic vision* of the company's future, a *mission statement* that defines the company's current purpose, and a set of *core values* to guide the pursuit of the vision and mission. This stage of strategy making provides direction for the company, motivates and inspires company personnel, aligns and guides actions throughout the organization, and communicates to stakeholders management's aspirations for the company's future.

2. *Setting objectives* and using the targeted results as yardsticks for measuring the company's performance. Objectives need to spell out *how much* of *what kind* of performance *by when*. A *balanced scorecard* approach for measuring company performance entails setting both *financial objectives* and *strategic objectives*. *Stretch objectives* spur exceptional performance and help build a firewall against complacency and mediocre performance. A company exhibits *strategic intent* when it relentlessly pursues an ambitious strategic objective, concentrating the full force of its resources and competitive actions on achieving that objective.

3. *Crafting a strategy to achieve the objectives* and move the company along the strategic course that management has charted. The total strategy that emerges is really a collection of strategic actions and business approaches initiated partly by senior company executives, partly by the heads of major business divisions, partly by functional-area managers, and partly by operating managers on the front lines. A single business enterprise has three levels of strategy—*business strategy* for the company as a whole, *functional-area strategies* for each main area within the business, and *operating strategies* undertaken by lower-echelon managers. In diversified, multibusiness companies, the strategy-making task involves four distinct types or levels of strategy: *corporate strategy* for the company as a whole, *business strategy* (one for each business the company has diversified into), *functional-area strategies* within each business, and *operating strategies*. Typically, the strategy-making task is more top-down than bottom-up, with higher-level strategies serving as the guide for developing lower-level strategies.

4. *Implementing and executing the chosen strategy efficiently and effectively.* Managing the implementation and execution of strategy is an operations-oriented, make-things-happen activity aimed at shaping the performance of core business activities in a strategy supportive manner. Management's handling of the strategy implementation process can be considered successful if things go smoothly enough that the company meets or beats its strategic and financial performance targets and shows good progress in achieving management's strategic vision.

5. *Evaluating and analyzing the external environment and the company's internal situation and performance to identify corrective adjustments* in vision, objectives, business model or strategy, or execution. This stage of the strategy management process is the trigger point for deciding whether to continue or change the company's vision, objectives, strategy, and/or strategy execution methods. Changes in goals, business model, or approaches to execution are to be expected, but a change in the company's vision should be necessary only when it becomes evident to management that the industry has changed in a significant way that renders the vision obsolete. Such a change is referred to as a *strategic inflection point*.

The sum of a company's strategic vision, objectives, and strategy constitutes a *strategic plan*. Boards of directors have a duty to shareholders to play a vigilant role in overseeing management's handling of a company's strategy formulation, strategy execution process. A company's board is obligated to (1) ensure that the company issues accurate financial reports and has adequate financial controls, (2) critically appraise and ultimately approve strategic action plans,

(3) evaluate the strategic leadership skills of the CEO, and (4) institute a compensation plan for top executives that rewards them for actions and results that serve stakeholder interests, most especially those of shareholders.

ASSURANCE OF LEARNING EXERCISES

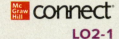

LO2-1

1. Using the information in Tables 2.2 and 2.3, critique the adequacy and merit of the following vision statements, listing effective elements and shortcomings. Rank the vision statements from best to worst once you complete your evaluation.

VISION STATEMENT	Effective Elements	Shortcomings
American Express		
We work hard every day to make American Express the world's most respected service brand.[27]		
Hilton Hotels Corporation		
Our vision is to be the first choice of the world's travelers. Hilton intends to build on the rich heritage and strength of our brands by: • Consistently delighting our customers • Investing in our team members • Delivering innovative products and services • Continuously improving performance • Increasing shareholder value • Creating a culture of pride • Strengthening the loyalty of our constituents[28]		
MasterCard		
A world beyond cash.[29]		
BASF		
We are "The Chemical Company" successfully operating in all major markets. • Our customers view BASF as their partner of choice. • Our innovative products, intelligent solutions and services make us the most competent worldwide supplier in the chemical industry. • We generate a high return on assets. • We strive for sustainable development. • We welcome change as an opportunity. • We, the employees of BASF, together ensure our success.[30]		

Source: Company websites and annual reports.

LO2-2

2. Go to the company investor relations websites for Starbucks (investor.starbucks.com), Pfizer (www.pfizer.com/investors), and Salesforce (investor.salesforce.com) to find examples of strategic and financial objectives. List four objectives for each company, and indicate which of these are strategic and which are financial.

LO2-3

3. Boeing has been recognized by *Forbes* and other business publications as one of the world's best managed companies. The company discusses how its people and organizational units bring to bear the "best of Boeing" to its customers in 150 countries at www.boeing.com/company. Prepare a one- to two-page report that suggests how design or software problems with the 737 MAX may have occurred despite Boeing's commitment to excellence at various organizational levels and functional areas.

4. Go to the investor relations website for Walmart (http://stock.walmart.com) and review past presentations it has made during various investor conferences by clicking on the Events option in the navigation bar. Prepare a one- to two-page report that outlines what Walmart has said to investors about its approach to strategy execution. Specifically, what has management discussed concerning staffing, resource allocation, policies and procedures, information and operating systems, continuous improvement, rewards and incentives, corporate culture, and internal leadership at the company?

LO2-4

5. Based on the information provided in Concepts & Connections 2.4, describe the ways in which Volkswagen did not fulfill the requirements of effective corporate governance. In what ways did the board of directors sidestep its obligations to protect shareholder interests? How could Volkswagen better select its board of directors to avoid mistakes such as the emissions scandal in 2015?

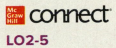

LO2-5

EXERCISES FOR SIMULATION PARTICIPANTS

1. Which of the four stages of the strategy formulation, strategy execution process apply to your company in the business simulation? Explain

LO2-4

2. Meet with your co-managers and prepare a strategic vision statement for your company. It should be at least one sentence long and no longer than a brief paragraph. When you are finished, check to see if your vision statement meets the conditions for an effectively worded strategic vision set forth in Table 2.2 and avoids the shortcomings set forth in Table 2.3. If not, then revise it accordingly. What would be a good slogan that captures the essence of your strategic vision and that could be used to help communicate the vision to company personnel, shareholders, and other stakeholders?

LO2-1

3. What are your company's financial objectives? What are your company's strategic objectives?

LO2-2

4. What are the three or four key elements of your company's strategy?

LO2-3

5. The strategy execution process for your company in the business simulation includes which principal aspects?

LO2-4

ENDNOTES

1. Gordon Shaw, Robert Brown, and Philip Bromiley, "Strategic Stories: How 3M Is Rewriting Business Planning," *Harvard Business Review* 76, no. 3 (May–June 1998); David J. Collins and Michael G. Rukstad, "Can You Say What Your Strategy Is?" *Harvard Business Review* 86, no. 4 (April 2008).

2. *Our Mission,* Google Inc.

3. Hugh Davidson, *The Committed Enterprise: How to Make Values and Visions Work* (Routledge, 2003).

4. Hugh Davidson, *The Committed Enterprise: How to Make Vision and Values Work* (Oxford: Butterworth

Heinemann, 2002); W. Chan Kim and Renée Mauborgne, "Charting Your Company's Future," *Harvard Business Review* 80, no. 6 (June 2002); James C. Collins and Jerry I. Porras, "Building Your Company's Vision," *Harvard Business Review* 74, no. 5 (September–October 1996); Jim Collins and Jerry Porras, *Built to Last: Successful Habits of Visionary Companies* (New York: HarperCollins, 1994); Michel Robert, *Strategy Pure and Simple II: How Winning Companies Dominate Their Competitors* (New York: McGraw-Hill, 1998).

5. Hugh Davidson, *The Committed Enterprise* (Oxford: Butterworth Heinemann, 2002).

6. Hugh Davidson, *The Committed Enterprise* (Oxford: Butterworth Heinemann, 2002).

7. Bruce Jones, *Customer Service 101: Happiness Is a Purple Balloon* (Disney Institute, 2017).

8. *Mayo Clinic Mission and Values*, Mayo Clinic, 2019.

9. *Our Vision*, Greenpeace.

10. *Sustainibility Report FY 2017/18*, Singapore Airlines, 2018.

11. St. Jude Children's Research Hospital.

12. *Our Services, and Corporate Affiliates*, Twitter, Inc., 2019.

13. *About*, Microsoft, 2019.

14. *Company Information*, L.L. Bean Inc., 2019.

15. S. Sitkin, C. Miller, and K. See, "The Stretch Goal Paradox," *Harvard Business Review*, 95, no. 1 (January–February 2017), pp. 92–99.

16. Robert S. Kaplan and David P. Norton, *The Strategy-Focused Organization* (Boston: Harvard Business School Press, 2001).

17. Robert S. Kaplan and David P. Norton, *The Strategy-Focused Organization* (Boston: Harvard Business School Press, 2001). Also, see Robert S. Kaplan and David P. Norton, *The Balanced Scorecard: Translating Strategy into Action* (Boston: Harvard Business School Press, 1996); Kevin B. Hendricks, Larry Menor, and Christine Wiedman, "The Balanced Scorecard: To Adopt or Not to Adopt," *Ivey Business Journal* 69, no. 2 (November–December 2004); Sandy Richardson, "The Key Elements of Balanced Scorecard Success," *Ivey Business Journal* 69, no. 2 (November–December 2004).

18. Kaplan and Norton, *The Balanced Scorecard: Translating Strategy into Action,* pp. 25–29. Kaplan and Norton classify strategic objectives under the categories of customer-related, business processes, and learning and growth. In practice, companies using the balanced scorecard may choose categories of strategic objectives that best reflect the organization's value-creating activities and processes.

19. Information posted on the website of Bain and Company, www.bain.com (accessed May 27, 2011).

20. Information posted on the website of Balanced Scorecard Institute (accessed May 27, 2011).

21. Henry Mintzberg, Bruce Ahlstrand, and Joseph Lampel, *Strategy Safari: A Guided Tour Through the Wilds of Strategic Management* (New York: Free Press, 1998); Bruce Barringer and Allen C. Bluedorn, "The Relationship Between Corporate Entrepreneurship and Strategic Management," *Strategic Management Journal* 20 (1999); Jeffrey G. Covin and Morgan P. Miles, "Corporate Entrepreneurship and the Pursuit of Competitive Advantage," *Entrepreneurship: Theory and Practice* 23, no. 3 (Spring 1999); David A. Garvin and Lynne C. Levesque, "Meeting the Challenge of Corporate Entrepreneurship," *Harvard Business Review* 84, no. 10 (October 2006).

22. Roger L. Martin, "The Big Lie of Strategic Planning," *Harvard Business Review* 92, no. 1/2 (January–February 2014), pp. 78–84.

23. Jay W. Lorsch and Robert C. Clark, "Leading from the Boardroom," *Harvard Business Review* 86, no. 4 (April 2008).

24. Jay W. Lorsch and Robert C. Clark, "Leading from the Boardroom," *Harvard Business Review* 86, no. 4 (April 2008), p. 110.

25. Stephen P. Kaufman, "Evaluating the CEO," *Harvard Business Review* 86, no. 10 (October 2008).

26. David A. Nadler, "Building Better Boards," *Harvard Business Review* 82, no. 5 (May 2004); Cynthia A. Montgomery and Rhonda Kaufman, "The Board's Missing Link," *Harvard Business Review* 81, no. 3 (March 2003); John Carver, "What Continues to Be Wrong with Corporate Governance and How to Fix It," *Ivey Business Journal* 68, no. 1 (September–October 2003); Gordon Donaldson, "A New Tool for Boards: The Strategic Audit," *Harvard Business Review* 73, no. 4 (July–August 1995).

27. American Express Company, 2019.

28. Hilton Worldwide.

29. *Vision,* MasterCard, 2019.

30. *Vision Values Principles*, BASF, 2004.

EVALUATING A COMPANY'S EXTERNAL ENVIRONMENT

LEARNING OBJECTIVES

After reading this chapter, you should be able to:

LO3-1 Identify factors in a company's broad macro-environment that may have strategic significance.

LO3-2 Recognize the factors that cause competition in an industry to be fierce, more or less normal, or relatively weak.

LO3-3 Map the market positions of key groups of industry rivals.

LO3-4 Determine whether an industry's outlook presents a company with sufficiently attractive opportunities for growth and profitability.

In Chapter 2, we learned that the strategy formulation, strategy execution process begins with an appraisal of the company's present situation. The company's situation includes two facets: (1) its external environment—most notably, the competitive conditions in the industry in which the company operates; and (2) its internal environment—particularly the company's resources and organizational capabilities.

Charting a company's long-term direction, conceiving its customer value proposition, setting objectives, or crafting a strategy without first gaining an understanding of the company's external and internal environments hamstrings attempts to build competitive advantage and boost company performance. Indeed, the first test of a winning strategy inquires, *"How well does the strategy fit the company's situation?"*

This chapter presents the concepts and analytical tools for zeroing in on a single-business company's external environment. Attention centers on the competitive arena in which the company operates, the drivers of market change, the market positions of rival companies, and the factors that determine competitive success. Chapter 4 explores the methods of evaluating a company's internal circumstances and competitiveness.

Assessing the Company's Industry and Competitive Environment

Thinking strategically about a company's industry and competitive environment entails using some well-validated concepts and analytical tools to get clear answers to seven questions:

1. Do macro-environmental factors and industry characteristics offer sellers opportunities for growth and attractive profits?

2. What kinds of competitive forces are industry members facing, and how strong is each force?

3. What forces are driving industry change, and what impact will these changes have on competitive intensity and industry profitability?

4. What market positions do industry rivals occupy—who is strongly positioned and who is not?

5. What strategic moves are rivals likely to make next?

6. What are the key factors of competitive success?

7. Does the industry outlook offer good prospects for profitability?

Analysis-based answers to these questions are prerequisites for a strategy offering good fit with the external situation. The remainder of this chapter is devoted to describing the methods of obtaining solid answers to these seven questions.

Question 1: What Are the Strategically Relevant Components of the Macro-Environment?

LO3-1   Identify factors in a company's broad macro-environment that may have strategic significance.

A company's external environment includes the immediate industry and competitive environment and broader macro-environmental factors such as general economic conditions, societal values and cultural norms, political factors, the legal and regulatory environment, ecological considerations, and technological factors. These two levels of a company's external environment—the broad outer ring macro-environment and immediate inner ring industry and competitive environment—are illustrated in Figure 3.1. Strictly speaking, the **macro-environment** encompasses all of the *relevant factors* making up the broad environmental context in which a company operates; by *relevant,* we mean the factors are important enough that they should shape management's decisions regarding the company's long-term direction, objectives, strategy, and business model. The relevance of macro-environmental factors can be evaluated using **PESTEL analysis,** an acronym for the six principal components of the macro-environment: political factors, economic conditions in the firm's general environment, sociocultural forces, technological factors, environmental forces, and legal/regulatory factors. Table 3.1 provides a description of each of the six PESTEL components of the macro-environment.

The impact of outer ring macro-environmental factors on a company's choice of strategy can be big or small. But even if the factors of the macro-environment change slowly or are likely to have a low impact on the company's business situation, they still merit a watchful eye. Changes in sociocultural forces and technological factors have begun to have strategy-shaping effects on companies competing in industries ranging from news and entertainment to taxi services. As company

> ### CORE CONCEPT
>
> The **macro-environment** encompasses the broad environmental context in which a company is situated and is comprised of six principal components: political factors, economic conditions, sociocultural forces, technological factors, environmental factors, and legal/regulatory conditions.
>
> **PESTEL analysis** can be used to assess the strategic relevance of the six principal components of the macro-environment: political, economic, sociocultural, technological, environmental, and legal forces.

FIGURE 3.1

The Components of a Company's External Environment

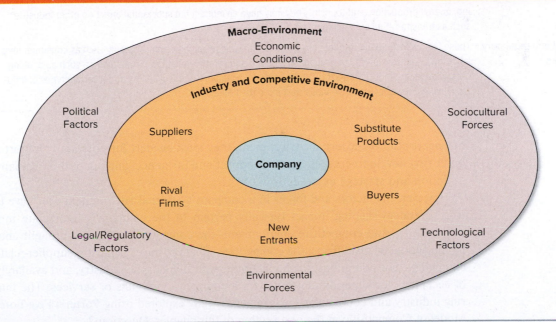

TABLE 3.1

The Six Components of the Macro-Environment Included in a PESTEL Analysis

Component	Description
Political factors	These factors include political policies and processes, including the extent to which a government intervenes in the economy. They include such matters as tax policy, fiscal policy, tariffs, the political climate, and the strength of institutions such as the federal banking system. Some political factors, such as bailouts, are industry-specific. Others, such as energy policy, affect certain types of industries (energy producers and heavy users of energy) more than others.
Economic conditions	Economic conditions include the general economic climate and specific factors such as interest rates, exchange rates, the inflation rate, the unemployment rate, the rate of economic growth, trade deficits or surpluses, savings rates, and per capita domestic product. Economic factors also include conditions in the markets for stocks and bonds, which can affect consumer confidence and discretionary income. Some industries, such as construction, are particularly vulnerable to economic downturns but are positively affected by factors such as low interest rates. Others, such as discount retailing, may benefit when general economic conditions weaken, as consumers become more price-conscious. Economic characteristics of the industry such as market size and growth rate are also important to evaluate when assessing an industry's prospects for growth and attractive profits.
Sociocultural forces	Sociocultural forces include the societal values, attitudes, cultural factors, and lifestyles that impact businesses, as well as demographic factors such as the population size, growth rate, and age distribution. Sociocultural forces vary by locale and change over time. An example is the trend toward healthier lifestyles, which can shift spending toward exercise equipment and health clubs and away from alcohol and snack foods. Population demographics can have large implications for industries such as health care, where costs and service needs vary with demographic factors such as age and income distribution.
Technological factors	Technological factors include the pace of technological change and technical developments that have the potential for wide-ranging effects on society, such as genetic engineering and nanotechnology. They include institutions involved in creating knowledge and controlling the use of technology, such as R&D consortia, university-sponsored technology incubators, patent and copyright laws, and government control over the Internet. Technological change can encourage the birth of new industries, such as those based on nanotechnology, and disrupt others, such as the recording industry.
Environmental forces	These include ecological and environmental forces such as weather, climate, climate change, and associated factors such as water shortages. These factors can directly impact industries such as insurance, farming, energy production, and tourism. They may have an indirect but substantial effect on other industries such as transportation and utilities.
Legal and regulatory factors	These factors include the regulations and laws with which companies must comply such as consumer laws, labor laws, antitrust laws, and occupational health and safety regulations. Some factors, such as banking deregulation, are industry-specific. Others, such as minimum wage legislation, affect certain types of industries (low-wage, labor-intensive industries) more than others.

managers scan the external environment, they must be alert for potentially important outer ring developments, assess their impact and influence, and adapt the company's direction and strategy as needed.

However, the factors and forces in a company's external environment that have the *biggest* strategy-shaping impact typically pertain to the company's immediate inner ring industry and competitive environment—the competitive pressures brought about by the actions of rival firms, the competitive effects of buyer behavior, supplier-related competitive considerations, the impact of new entrants to the industry, and availability of acceptable or superior substitutes for a company's products or services. The inner ring industry and competitive environment is fully explored using Porter's Five Forces Model of Competition in the next section of this chapter, Question 2.

Question 2: How Strong Are the Industry's Competitive Forces?

LO3-2 Recognize the factors that cause competition in an industry to be fierce, more or less normal, or relatively weak.

After an understanding of the industry's general economic characteristics is gained, industry and competitive analysis should focus on the competitive dynamics of the industry. The nature and subtleties of competitive forces are never the same from one industry to another and must be wholly understood to accurately assess the company's current situation. Far and away the most powerful and widely used tool for assessing the strength of the industry's competitive forces is the *five forces model of competition*.[1] This model, as depicted in Figure 3.2, holds that competitive forces affecting industry

FIGURE 3.2

The Five Forces Model of Competition

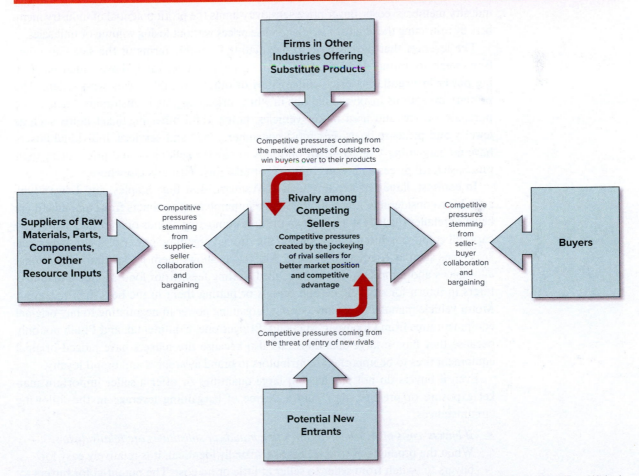

Sources: Based on Michael E. Porter, "How Competitive Forces Shape Strategy," *Harvard Business Review* 57, no. 2 (March–April 1979), pp. 137–145; and Michael E. Porter, "The Five Competitive Forces That Shape Strategy," *Harvard Business Review* 86, no. 1 (January 2008), pp. 80–86.

attractiveness go beyond rivalry among competing sellers and include pressures stemming from four coexisting sources. The five competitive forces affecting industry attractiveness are listed below.

1. Competitive pressures stemming from *buyer* bargaining power.
2. Competitive pressures coming from companies in other industries to win buyers over to *substitute products.*
3. Competitive pressures stemming from *supplier* bargaining power.
4. Competitive pressures associated with the threat of *new entrants* into the market.
5. Competitive pressures associated with *rivalry among competing sellers* to attract customers. This is usually the strongest of the five competitive forces.

The Competitive Force of Buyer Bargaining Power

Whether seller-buyer relationships represent a minor or significant competitive force depends on (1) whether some or many buyers have sufficient bargaining leverage to obtain price concessions and other favorable terms, and (2) the extent to which buyers are price sensitive. Buyers with strong bargaining power can limit industry profitability by demanding price concessions, better payment terms, or additional features and services that increase industry members' costs. Buyer price sensitivity limits the profit potential of industry members by restricting the ability of sellers to raise prices without losing volume or unit sales.

The leverage that buyers have in negotiating favorable terms of the sale can range from weak to strong. Individual consumers, for example, rarely have much bargaining power in negotiating price concessions or other favorable terms with sellers. The primary exceptions involve situations in which price haggling is customary, such as the purchase of new and used motor vehicles, homes, and other big-ticket items such as jewelry and pleasure boats. For most consumer goods and services, individual buyers have no bargaining leverage—their option is to pay the seller's posted price, delay their purchase until prices and terms improve, or take their business elsewhere.

In contrast, large retail chains such as Walmart, Best Buy, Staples, and Lowe's typically have considerable negotiating leverage in purchasing products from manufacturers because retailers usually stock just two or three competing brands of a product and rarely carry all competing brands. In addition, the strong bargaining power of major supermarket chains such as Kroger, Publix, and Albertsons allows them to demand promotional allowances and lump-sum payments (called slotting fees) from food products manufacturers in return for stocking certain brands or putting them in the best shelf locations. Motor vehicle manufacturers have strong bargaining power in negotiating to buy original equipment tires from Goodyear, Michelin, Bridgestone, Continental, and Pirelli not only because they buy in large quantities but also because tire makers have judged original equipment tires to be important contributors to brand awareness and brand loyalty.

Even if buyers do not purchase in large quantities or offer a seller important market exposure or prestige, they gain a degree of bargaining leverage in the following circumstances:

- *If buyers' costs of switching to competing brands or substitutes are relatively low.*
  When the products of rival sellers are virtually identical, it is relatively easy for buyers to switch from seller to seller at little or no cost. The potential for buyers to easily switch from one seller to another encourages sellers to make concessions to win or retain a buyer's business.

- *If the number of buyers is small or if a customer is particularly important to a seller.* The smaller the number of buyers, the less easy it is for sellers to find alternative buyers when a customer is lost to a competitor. The prospect of losing a customer who is not easily replaced often makes a seller more willing to grant concessions of one kind or another.

- *If buyer demand is weak.* Weak or declining demand creates a "buyers' market"; conversely, strong or rapidly growing demand creates a "sellers' market" and shifts bargaining power to sellers.

- *If buyers are well informed about sellers' products, prices, and costs.* The more information buyers have, the better bargaining position they are in. The mushrooming availability of product information on the Internet (and is readily available on smartphones) has given added bargaining power to consumers.

- *If buyers pose a credible threat of integrating backward into the business of sellers.* Anheuser-Busch InBev has integrated backward into metal can manufacturing to gain bargaining power in obtaining the balance of its can requirements from otherwise powerful metal can manufacturers.

Figure 3.3 summarizes factors causing buyer bargaining power to be strong or weak. It is important to recognize that *not all buyers of an industry's product have equal degrees of bargaining power with sellers,* and some may be less sensitive than others to price, quality, or service differences. For example, apparel manufacturers confront significant bargaining power when selling to big retailers such as Macy's, T. J. Maxx, or Kohl's, but they can command much better prices selling to small owner-managed apparel boutiques.

FIGURE 3.3
Factors Affecting the Strength of Buyer Bargaining Power

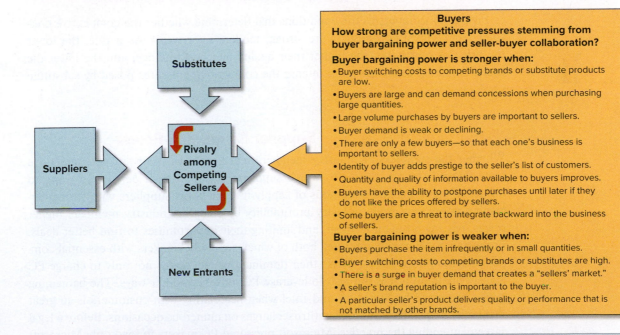

Buyers

How strong are competitive pressures stemming from buyer bargaining power and seller-buyer collaboration?

Buyer bargaining power is stronger when:
- Buyer switching costs to competing brands or substitute products are low.
- Buyers are large and can demand concessions when purchasing large quantities.
- Large volume purchases by buyers are important to sellers.
- Buyer demand is weak or declining.
- There are only a few buyers—so that each one's business is important to sellers.
- Identity of buyer adds prestige to the seller's list of customers.
- Quantity and quality of information available to buyers improves.
- Buyers have the ability to postpone purchases until later if they do not like the prices offered by sellers.
- Some buyers are a threat to integrate backward into the business of sellers.

Buyer bargaining power is weaker when:
- Buyers purchase the item infrequently or in small quantities.
- Buyer switching costs to competing brands or substitutes are high.
- There is a surge in buyer demand that creates a "sellers' market."
- A seller's brand reputation is important to the buyer.
- A particular seller's product delivers quality or performance that is not matched by other brands.

The Competitive Force of Substitute Products

Companies in one industry are vulnerable to competitive pressure from the actions of companies in another industry whenever buyers view the products of the two industries as good substitutes. For instance, the producers of sugar experience competitive pressures from the sales and marketing efforts of the makers of Splenda, Truvia, and Sweet'N Low. Similarly, cable television networks and providers are finding it more difficult to maintain their relevance to subscribers who find greater value in streaming devices and services.

Just how strong the competitive pressures are from the sellers of substitute products depends on three factors:

1. *Whether substitutes are readily available and attractively priced.* The presence of readily available and attractively priced substitutes creates competitive pressure by placing a ceiling on the prices industry members can charge. When substitutes are cheaper than an industry's product, industry members come under heavy competitive pressure to reduce their prices and find ways to absorb the price cuts with cost reductions.

2. *Whether buyers view the substitutes as comparable or better in terms of quality, performance, and other relevant attributes.* Customers are prone to compare performance and other attributes as well as price. For example, consumers have found smartphones to be a superior substitute to digital cameras because of constant availability of smartphones and superior ease of use in managing images.

3. *Whether the costs that buyers incur in switching to the substitutes are high or low.* High switching costs deter switching to substitutes, whereas low switching costs make it easier for the sellers of attractive substitutes to lure buyers to their products. Typical switching costs include the inconvenience of switching to a substitute, the costs of additional equipment, the psychological costs of severing old supplier relationships, and employee retraining costs.

Figure 3.4 summarizes the conditions that determine whether the competitive pressures from substitute products are strong, moderate, or weak. As a rule, the lower the price of substitutes, the higher their quality and performance, and the lower the user's switching costs, the more intense the competitive pressures posed by substitute products.

The Competitive Force of Supplier Bargaining Power

Whether the suppliers of industry members represent a weak or strong competitive force depends on the degree to which suppliers have sufficient *bargaining power* to influence the terms and conditions of supply in their favor. Suppliers with strong bargaining power can erode industry profitability by charging industry members higher prices, passing costs on to them, and limiting their opportunities to find better deals. For instance, Microsoft and Intel, both of which supply PC makers with essential components, have been known to use their dominant market status not only to charge PC makers premium prices but also to leverage PC makers in other ways. The bargaining power possessed by Microsoft and Intel when negotiating with customers is so great that both companies have faced antitrust charges on numerous occasions. Before a legal agreement ending the practice, Microsoft pressured PC makers to load only Microsoft

FIGURE 3.4

Factors Affecting Competition from Substitute Products

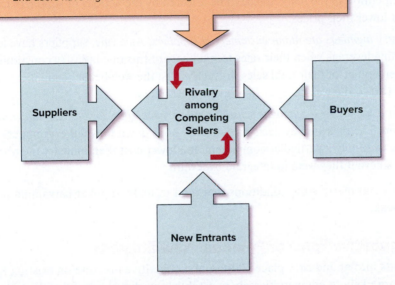

Firms in Other Industries Offering Substitute Products

How strong are competitive pressures coming from substitute products from outside the industry?

Competitive pressures from substitutes are stronger when:

- Good substitutes are readily available or new ones are emerging.
- Substitutes are attractively priced.
- Substitutes have comparable or better performance features.
- End users have low costs in switching to substitutes.
- End users grow more comfortable with using substitutes.

Competitive pressures from substitutes are weaker when:

- Good substitutes are not readily available or don't exist.
- Substitutes are higher priced relative to the performance they deliver.
- End users have high costs in switching to substitutes.

Signs That Competition from Substitutes Is Strong

- Sales of substitutes are growing faster than sales of the industry being analyzed (an indication that the sellers of substitutes are drawing customers away from the industry in question).
- Producers of substitutes are moving to add new capacity.
- Profits of the producers of substitutes are on the rise.

Suppliers

Rivalry among Competing Sellers

Buyers

New Entrants

---

products on the PCs they shipped. Intel has also defended against antitrust charges resulting from its bargaining strength but continues to give PC makers that use the biggest percentages of Intel chips in their PC models top priority in filling orders for newly introduced Intel chips. Being on Intel's list of preferred customers helps a PC maker get an early allocation of Intel's latest chips and thus allows a PC maker to get new models to market ahead of rivals.

The factors that determine whether any of the industry suppliers are in a position to exert substantial bargaining power or leverage are fairly clear-cut:

- *If the item being supplied is a commodity that is readily available from many suppliers.* Suppliers have little or no bargaining power or leverage whenever industry members have the ability to source from any of several alternative and eager suppliers.

- *The ability of industry members to switch their purchases from one supplier to another or to switch to attractive substitutes.* High switching costs increase supplier bargaining power, whereas low switching costs and the ready availability of good substitute inputs weaken supplier bargaining power.

- *If certain inputs are in short supply.* Suppliers of items in short supply have some degree of pricing power.

- *If certain suppliers provide a differentiated input that enhances the performance, quality, or image of the industry's product.* The greater the ability of a particular input to enhance a product's performance, quality, or image, the more bargaining leverage its suppliers are likely to possess.

- *Whether certain suppliers provide equipment or services that deliver cost savings to industry members in conducting their operations.* Suppliers who provide cost-saving equipment or services are likely to possess some degree of bargaining leverage.

- *The fraction of the costs of the industry's product accounted for by the cost of a particular input.* The bigger the cost of a specific part or component, the more opportunity for competition in the marketplace to be affected by the actions of suppliers to raise or lower their prices.

- *If industry members are major customers of suppliers.* As a rule, suppliers have less bargaining leverage when their sales to members of this one industry constitute a big percentage of their total sales. In such cases, the well-being of suppliers is closely tied to the well-being of their major customers.

- *Whether it makes good economic sense for industry members to vertically integrate backward.* The make-or-buy decision generally boils down to whether suppliers are able to supply a particular component at a lower cost than industry members could achieve if they were to integrate backward.

Figure 3.5 summarizes the conditions that tend to make supplier bargaining power strong or weak.

The Competitive Force of Potential New Entrants

New entrants into an industry place additional competitive pressure on existing firms since they are likely to compete fiercely to establish market share and will add to the industry's production capacity. But even the *threat* of new entry can be an important competitive force. This is because credible *threat* of entry often prompts industry members to lower their prices and initiate defensive actions in an attempt to deter new entrants. Just how serious the threat of entry is in a particular market depends on two classes of factors: (1) *the expected reaction of incumbent firms to new entry* and (2) *barriers to entry.* The threat of entry is low in industries where incumbent firms are likely to retaliate against new entrants with sharp price discounting and other moves designed to make entry unprofitable. The threat of entry is also low when entry barriers are high.

The most widely encountered barriers that entry candidates must hurdle include:[2]

- *The presence of sizable economies of scale in production or other areas of operation.* When incumbent companies enjoy cost advantages associated with large-scale operations, outsiders must either enter on a large scale (a costly and perhaps risky move) or accept a cost disadvantage and consequently lower profitability.

Factors Affecting the Strength of Supplier Bargaining Power

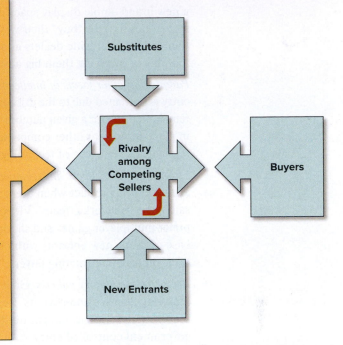

Suppliers of Resource Inputs

How strong are the competitive pressures stemming from supplier bargaining power and seller-supplier collaboration?

Supplier bargaining power is stronger when:

- Industry members incur high costs in switching their purchases to alternative suppliers.
- Needed inputs are in short supply (which gives suppliers more leverage in setting prices).
- A supplier has a differentiated input that enhances the quality, performance, or image of sellers' products or is a valuable or critical part of sellers' production processes.
- There are only a few suppliers of a particular input.

Supplier bargaining power is weaker when:

- The item being supplied is a "commodity" that is readily available from many suppliers at the going market price.
- Seller switching costs to alternative suppliers are low.
- Good substitute inputs exist or new ones emerge.
- There is a surge in the availability of supplies (thus greatly weakening supplier pricing power).
- Industry members account for a big fraction of suppliers' total sales and continued high-volume purchases are important to the well-being of suppliers.
- Industry members are a threat to integrate backward into the business of suppliers and to self-manufacture their own requirements.

- *Cost and resource disadvantages not related to scale of operation.* Aside from enjoying economies of scale, industry incumbents can have cost advantages that stem from the possession of proprietary technology, partnerships with the best and cheapest suppliers, low fixed costs (because they have older facilities that have been mostly depreciated), and experience/learning-curve effects. Manufacturing unit costs for microprocessors tend to decline about 20 percent each time *cumulative* production volume doubles. With a 20 percent experience-curve effect, if the first 1 million chips cost $100 each, once production volume reaches 2 million, the unit cost would fall to $80 (80 percent of $100), and by a production volume of 4 million, the unit cost would be $64 (80 percent of $80).[3] The bigger the learning- or experience-curve effect, the bigger the cost advantage of the company with the largest *cumulative* production volume.

- *Strong brand preferences and high degrees of customer loyalty.* The stronger the attachment of buyers to established brands, the harder it is for a newcomer to break into the marketplace.

- *High capital requirements.* The larger the total dollar investment needed to enter the market successfully, the more limited the pool of potential entrants. The most obvious capital requirements for new entrants relate to manufacturing facilities and equipment, introductory advertising and sales promotion campaigns, working capital to finance inventories and customer credit, and sufficient cash to cover start-up costs.

- *The difficulties of building a network of distributors-retailers and securing adequate space on retailers' shelves.* A potential entrant can face numerous distribution channel challenges. Wholesale distributors may be reluctant to take on a product that lacks buyer recognition. Retailers have to be recruited and convinced to give a new brand ample display space and an adequate trial period. Potential entrants sometimes have to "buy" their way into wholesale or retail channels by cutting their prices to provide dealers and distributors with higher markups and profit margins or by giving them big advertising and promotional allowances.

- *Patents and other forms of intellectual property protection.* In a number of industries, entry is prevented due to the existence of intellectual property protection laws that remain in place for a given number of years. Often, companies have a "wall of patents" in place to prevent other companies from entering with a "me too" strategy that replicates a key piece of technology.

- *Strong "network effects" in customer demand.* In industries where buyers are more attracted to a product when there are many other users of the product, there are said to be "network effects." Video game systems are an example, since many users prefer multiplayer games and sharing games. When incumbents have a large existing base of users, new entrants with otherwise comparable products face a serious disadvantage in attracting buyers.

- *Restrictive regulatory policies.* Government agencies can limit or even bar entry by requiring licenses and permits. Regulated industries such as cable TV, telecommunications, electric and gas utilities, and radio and television broadcasting entail government-controlled entry.

- *Tariffs and international trade restrictions.* National governments commonly use tariffs and trade restrictions (antidumping rules, local content requirements, local ownership requirements, quotas, etc.) to raise entry barriers for foreign firms and protect domestic producers from outside competition.

- *The ability and willingness of industry incumbents to launch vigorous initiatives to block a newcomer's successful entry.* Even if a potential entrant has or can acquire the needed competencies and resources to attempt entry, it must still worry about the reaction of existing firms.[4] Sometimes, there's little that incumbents can do to throw obstacles in an entrant's path. But there are times when incumbents use price cuts, increase advertising, introduce product improvements, and launch legal attacks to prevent the entrant from building a clientele. Taxicab companies across the world are aggressively lobbying local governments to impose regulations that would bar ride-sharing services such as Uber or Lyft.

Figure 3.6 summarizes conditions making the threat of entry strong or weak.

The Competitive Force of Rivalry among Competing Sellers

The strongest of the five competitive forces is nearly always the rivalry among competing sellers of a product or service. In effect, *a market is a competitive battlefield* where there's no end to the campaign for buyer patronage. Rival sellers are prone to employ whatever weapons they have in their business arsenal to improve their market positions, strengthen their market position with buyers, and earn good profits. The strategy formulation challenge is to craft a competitive strategy that, at the very least, allows a company to hold its own against rivals and that, ideally, *produces a competitive edge over rivals.* But competitive

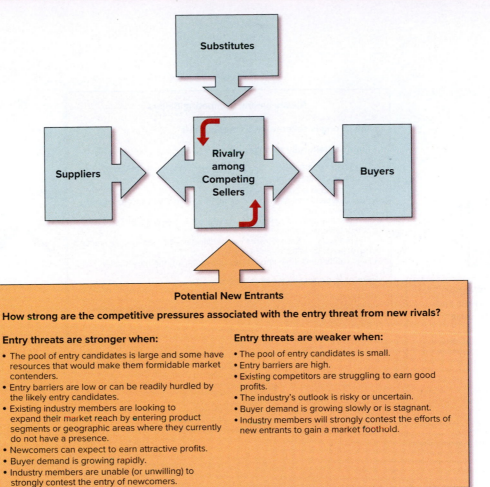

Factors Affecting the Threat of Entry

contests are ongoing and dynamic. When one firm makes a strategic move that produces good results, its rivals typically respond with offensive or defensive countermoves of their own. This pattern of action and reaction produces a continually evolving competitive land-scape in which the market battle ebbs and flows and produces winners and losers. But the current market leaders have no guarantees of continued leadership. In every industry, the ongoing jockeying of rivals leads to one or more companies gaining or losing momentum in the marketplace according to whether their latest strategic maneuvers succeed or fail.[5]

Figure 3.7 shows a sampling of competitive weapons that firms can deploy in battling rivals and indicates the factors that influence the intensity of their rivalry. Some factors that influence the tempo of rivalry among industry competitors include:

- *Rivalry is stronger in industries when the number of competitors increases and they become more equal in size and capability.* Competitive rivalry in the quick-service restaurant industry is particularly strong where there are numerous relatively equal-sized hamburger, deli sandwich, chicken, and taco chains. For the most part,

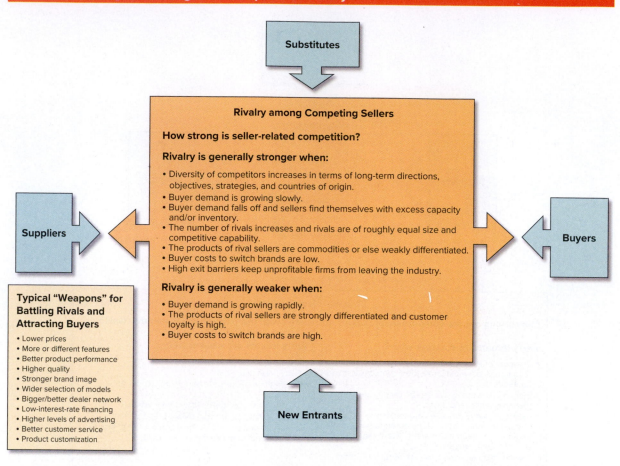

FIGURE 3.7

Factors Affecting the Strength of Competitive Rivalry

Substitutes

Rivalry among Competing Sellers

How strong is seller-related competition?

Rivalry is generally stronger when:

- Diversity of competitors increases in terms of long-term directions, objectives, strategies, and countries of origin.
- Buyer demand is growing slowly.
- Buyer demand falls off and sellers find themselves with excess capacity and/or inventory.
- The number of rivals increases and rivals are of roughly equal size and competitive capability.
- The products of rival sellers are commodities or else weakly differentiated.
- Buyer costs to switch brands are low.
- High exit barriers keep unprofitable firms from leaving the industry.

Rivalry is generally weaker when:

- Buyer demand is growing rapidly.
- The products of rival sellers are strongly differentiated and customer loyalty is high.
- Buyer costs to switch brands are high.

Suppliers

Buyers

Typical "Weapons" for Battling Rivals and Attracting Buyers

- Lower prices
- More or different features
- Better product performance
- Higher quality
- Stronger brand image
- Wider selection of models
- Bigger/better dealer network
- Low-interest-rate financing
- Higher levels of advertising
- Better customer service
- Product customization

New Entrants

McDonald's, Burger King, Taco Bell, Arby's, Chick-fil-A, and other national fast-food chains have comparable capabilities and are required to compete aggressively to hold their own in the industry.

- *Rivalry is usually stronger when demand is growing slowly or declining.* Rapidly expanding buyer demand produces enough new business for all industry members to grow. But in markets where growth is sluggish or where buyer demand drops off unexpectedly, it is not uncommon for competitive rivalry to intensify significantly as rivals battle for market share and volume gains.

- *Rivalry increases as it becomes less costly for buyers to switch brands.* The less costly it is for buyers to switch their purchases from one seller to another, the easier it is for sellers to steal customers away from rivals. Switching costs include not only monetary costs but also the time, inconvenience, and psychological costs involved in switching brands. For example, retailers may not switch to the brands of rival manufacturers because they are hesitant to sever long-standing supplier relationships or incur the additional expense of retraining employees, accessing technical support, or testing the quality and reliability of the new brand.

- *Rivalry increases when sellers find themselves with excess capacity and/or inventory.* Excess supply conditions create a "buyers' market," putting added competitive pressure on industry rivals to scramble for profitable sales levels (often by price discounting).

- *Rivalry increases as the products of rival sellers become less strongly differentiated.* When the offerings of rivals are identical or weakly differentiated, buyers have less reason to be brand loyal—a condition that makes it easier for rivals to persuade buyers to switch to their offering.

- *Rivalry becomes more intense as the diversity of competitors increases in terms of long-term directions, objectives, strategies, and countries of origin.* A diverse group of sellers often contains one or more mavericks willing to try novel or rule-breaking market approaches, thus generating a more volatile and less predictable competitive environment. Globally competitive markets are often more rivalrous, especially when aggressors have lower costs and are intent on gaining a strong foothold in new country markets.

- *Rivalry is stronger when high exit barriers keep unprofitable firms from leaving the industry.* In industries where the assets cannot easily be sold or transferred to other uses, where workers are entitled to job protection, or where owners are committed to remaining in business for personal reasons, failing firms tend to hold on longer than they might otherwise—even when they are bleeding red ink. Deep price discounting of this sort can destabilize an otherwise attractive industry.

Rivalry can be characterized as *cutthroat* or *brutal* when competitors engage in protracted price wars or habitually employ other aggressive tactics that are mutually destructive to profitability. Rivalry can be considered *fierce* to *strong* when the battle for market share is so vigorous that the profit margins of most industry members are squeezed to bare-bones levels. Rivalry can be characterized as *moderate* or *normal* when the maneuvering among industry members, while lively and healthy, still allows most industry members to earn acceptable profits. Rivalry is *weak* when most companies in the industry are relatively well satisfied with their sales growth and market share and rarely undertake offensives to steal customers away from one another.

The Collective Strengths of the Five Competitive Forces and Industry Profitability

Scrutinizing each of the five competitive forces one by one provides a powerful diagnosis of what competition is like in a given market. Once the strategist has gained an understanding of the competitive pressures associated with each of the five forces, the next step is to evaluate the collective strength of the five forces and determine if companies in this industry should reasonably expect to earn decent profits.

As a rule, the stronger the collective impact of the five competitive forces, the lower the combined profitability of industry participants. The most extreme case of a "competitively unattractive" industry is when all five forces are producing strong competitive pressures: Rivalry among sellers is vigorous, low entry barriers allow new rivals to gain a market foothold, competition from substitutes is intense, and both suppliers and customers are able to exercise considerable bargaining leverage. Fierce to strong competitive pressures coming from all five directions nearly always drive industry profitability to unacceptably low levels, frequently producing losses for many industry members and forcing some out of business. But an industry can be competitively unattractive without all five

> The stronger the forces of competition, the harder it becomes for industry members to earn attractive profits.

competitive forces being strong. Fierce competitive pressures from just one of the five forces, such as brutal price competition among rival sellers, may suffice to destroy the conditions for good profitability.

In contrast, when the collective impact of the five competitive forces is moderate to weak, an industry is competitively attractive in the sense that industry members can reasonably expect to earn good profits and a nice return on investment. The ideal competitive environment for earning superior profits is one in which both suppliers and customers are in weak bargaining positions, there are no good substitutes, high barriers block further entry, and rivalry among present sellers generates only moderate competitive pressures. Weak competition is the best of all possible worlds for companies with mediocre strategies and second-rate implementation because even they can expect a decent profit.

Question 3: What Are the Industry's Driving Forces of Change, and What Impact Will They Have?

The intensity of competitive forces and the level of industry attractiveness are almost always fluid and subject to change. It is essential for strategy makers to understand the current competitive dynamics of the industry, but it is equally important for strategy makers to consider how the industry is changing and the effect of industry changes that are under way. Any strategies devised by management will play out in a dynamic industry environment, so it's imperative that such plans consider what the industry environment might look like during the near term.

The Concept of Industry Driving Forces

Industry and competitive conditions change because forces are enticing or pressuring certain industry participants (competitors, customers, suppliers) to alter their actions in important ways. The most powerful of the change agents are called **driving forces** because they have the biggest influences in reshaping the industry landscape and altering competitive conditions. Some driving forces originate in the outer ring of the company's macro-environment (see Figure 3.1), but most originate in the company's more immediate industry and competitive environment.

> **CORE CONCEPT**
>
> **Driving forces** are the major underlying causes of change in industry and competitive conditions.

Driving forces analysis has three steps: (1) identifying what the driving forces are; (2) assessing whether the drivers of change are, individually or collectively, acting to make the industry more or less attractive; and (3) determining what strategy changes are needed to prepare for the impact of the driving forces.

Identifying an Industry's Driving Forces

Many developments can affect an industry powerfully enough to qualify as driving forces, but most drivers of industry and competitive change fall into one of the following categories:

- *Changes in an industry's long-term growth rate.* Shifts in industry growth have the potential to affect the balance between industry supply and buyer demand, entry and exit, and the character and strength of competition. An upsurge in buyer demand triggers a race among established firms and newcomers to capture the new sales opportunities. A slowdown in the growth of demand nearly always brings an increase in rivalry and increased efforts by some firms to maintain their high rates of growth by taking sales and market share away from rivals.

- *Increasing globalization.* Competition begins to shift from primarily a regional or national focus to an international or global focus when industry members begin seeking customers in foreign markets or when production activities begin to migrate to countries where costs are lowest. The forces of globalization are sometimes such a strong driver that companies find it highly advantageous, if not necessary, to spread their operating reach into more and more country markets. Globalization is very much a driver of industry change in such industries as energy, mobile phones, steel, social media, and pharmaceuticals.

- *Changes in who buys the product and how they use it.* Shifts in buyer demographics and the ways products are used can alter competition by affecting how customers perceive value, how customers make purchasing decisions, and where customers purchase the product. The burgeoning popularity of streaming video has affected broadband providers, wireless phone carriers, and television broadcasters, and created opportunities for such new entertainment businesses as Hulu and Netflix.

- *Product innovation.* An ongoing stream of product innovations tends to alter the pattern of competition in an industry by attracting more first-time buyers, rejuvenating industry growth, and/or creating wider or narrower product differentiation among rival sellers. Philips Lighting Hue bulbs allow homeowners to use a smartphone app to remotely turn lights on and off, blink if an intruder is detected, and create a wide range of white and color ambiances.

- *Technological change and manufacturing process innovation.* Advances in technology can cause disruptive change in an industry by lowering costs, introducing new substitutes, or opening new industry frontiers. For instance, revolutionary change in autonomous system technology has put Google, Tesla, Apple, and every major automobile manufacturer into a race to develop viable self-driving vehicles.

- *Marketing innovation.* When firms are successful in introducing *new ways* to market their products, they can spark a burst of buyer interest, widen industry demand, increase product differentiation, and lower unit costs—any or all of which can alter the competitive positions of rival firms and force strategy revisions.

- *Entry or exit of major firms.* The entry of one or more foreign companies into a geographic market once dominated by domestic firms nearly always shakes up competitive conditions. Likewise, when an established domestic firm from another industry attempts entry either by acquisition or by launching its own start-up venture, it usually pushes competition in new directions.

- *Diffusion of technical know-how across more companies and more countries.* As knowledge about how to perform a particular activity or execute a particular manufacturing technology spreads, the competitive advantage held by firms originally possessing this know-how erodes. Knowledge diffusion can occur through scientific journals, trade publications, onsite plant tours, word of mouth among suppliers and customers, employee migration, and Internet sources.

- *Changes in cost and efficiency.* Widening or shrinking differences in the costs among key competitors tend to dramatically alter the state of competition.

Declining costs to produce tablet computers have enabled price cuts and spurred tablet sales by making them more affordable to users.

- *Growing buyer preferences for differentiated products instead of a commodity product (or for a more standardized product instead of strongly differentiated products).* When a shift from standardized to differentiated products occurs, rivals must adopt strategies to outdifferentiate one another. However, buyers sometimes decide that a standardized, budget-priced product suits their requirements as well as a premium-priced product with lots of snappy features and personalized services.

- *Regulatory influences and government policy changes.* Government regulatory actions can often force significant changes in industry practices and strategic approaches. New rules and regulations pertaining to government-sponsored health insurance programs are driving changes in the health care industry. In international markets, host governments can drive competitive changes by opening their domestic markets to foreign participation or closing them.

- *Changing societal concerns, attitudes, and lifestyles.* Emerging social issues and changing attitudes and lifestyles can be powerful instigators of industry change. Consumer concerns about the use of chemical additives and the nutritional content of food products have forced food producers to revamp food-processing techniques, redirect R&D efforts into the use of healthier ingredients, and compete in developing nutritious, good-tasting products.

While many forces of change may be at work in a given industry, *no more than three or four* are likely to be true driving forces powerful enough to qualify as the *major determinants* of why and how the industry is changing. Thus, company strategists must resist the temptation to label every change they see as a driving force. Table 3.2 lists the most common driving forces.

Assessing the Impact of the Industry Driving Forces

The second step in driving forces analysis is to determine whether the prevailing driving forces are acting to make the industry environment more or less attractive. Getting a handle on

TABLE 3.2

Common Driving Forces

1. Changes in the long-term industry growth rate
2. Increasing globalization
3. Emerging new Internet capabilities and applications
4. Changes in who buys the product and how they use it
5. Product innovation
6. Technological change and manufacturing process innovation
7. Marketing innovation
8. Entry or exit of major firms
9. Diffusion of technical know-how across more companies and more countries
10. Changes in cost and efficiency
11. Growing buyer preferences for differentiated products instead of a standardized commodity product (or for a more standardized product instead of strongly differentiated products)
12. Regulatory influences and government policy changes
13. Changing societal concerns, attitudes, and lifestyles

the collective impact of the driving forces usually requires looking at the likely effects of each force separately, because the driving forces may not all be pushing change in the same direction. For example, two driving forces may be acting to spur demand for the industry's product, while one driving force may be working to curtail demand. Whether the net effect on industry demand is up or down hinges on which driving forces are the more powerful.

> An important part of driving forces analysis is to determine whether the individual or collective impact of the driving forces will be to increase or decrease market demand, make competition more or less intense, and lead to higher or lower industry profitability.

Determining Strategy Changes Needed to Prepare for the Impact of Driving Forces

The third step of driving forces analysis—where the real payoff for strategy making comes—is for managers to draw some conclusions about what strategy adjustments will be needed to deal with the impact of the driving forces. Without understanding the forces driving industry change and the impacts these forces will have on the industry environment over the next one to three years, managers are ill prepared to craft a strategy tightly matched to emerging conditions. Similarly, if managers are uncertain about the implications of one or more driving forces, or if their views are off-base, it will be difficult for them to craft a strategy that is responsive to the consequences of driving forces. So driving forces analysis is not something to take lightly; it has practical value and is basic to the task of thinking strategically about where the industry is headed and how to prepare for the changes ahead.

> The real payoff of driving forces analysis is to help managers understand what strategy changes are needed to prepare for the impacts of the driving forces.

Question 4: How Are Industry Rivals Positioned?

LO3-3 Map the market positions of key groups of industry rivals.

The nature of competitive strategy inherently positions companies competing in an industry into strategic groups with diverse price/quality ranges, different distribution channels, varying product features, and different geographic coverages. The best technique for revealing the market positions of industry competitors is **strategic group mapping.** This analytical tool is useful for comparing the market positions of industry competitors or for grouping industry combatants into like positions.

CORE CONCEPT
Strategic group mapping is a technique for displaying the different market or competitive positions that rival firms occupy in the industry.

Using Strategic Group Maps to Assess the Positioning of Key Competitors

A **strategic group** consists of those industry members with similar competitive approaches and positions in the market. Companies in the same strategic group can resemble one another in any of several ways: They may have comparable product-line breadth, sell in the same price/quality range, emphasize the

CORE CONCEPT
A **strategic group** is a cluster of industry rivals that have similar competitive approaches and market positions.

same distribution channels, use essentially the same product attributes to appeal to similar types of buyers, depend on identical technological approaches, or offer buyers similar services and technical assistance.[6] An industry with a commodity-like product may contain only one strategic group whereby all sellers pursue essentially identical strategies and have comparable market positions. But even with commodity products, there is likely some attempt at differentiation occurring in the form of varying delivery times, financing terms, or levels of customer service. Most industries offer a host of competitive approaches that allow companies to find unique industry positioning and avoid fierce competition in a crowded strategic group. Evaluating strategy options entails examining what strategic groups exist, identifying which companies exist within each group, and determining if a competitive "white space" exists where industry competitors are able to create and capture altogether new demand.

The procedure for constructing a *strategic group map* is straightforward:

- Identify the competitive characteristics that delineate strategic approaches used in the industry. Typical variables used in creating strategic group maps are the price/quality range (high, medium, low), geographic coverage (local, regional, national, global), degree of vertical integration (none, partial, full), product-line breadth (wide, narrow), choice of distribution channels (retail, wholesale, Internet, multiple channels), and degree of service offered (no-frills, limited, full).

- Plot firms on a two-variable map based upon their strategic approaches.

- Assign firms occupying the same map location to a common strategic group.

- Draw circles around each strategic group, making the circles proportional to the size of the group's share of total industry sales revenues.

This produces a two-dimensional diagram like the one for selected pizza chains in Concepts & Connections 3.1.

Several guidelines need to be observed in creating strategic group maps. First, the two variables selected as axes for the map should *not* be highly correlated; if they are, the circles on the map will fall along a diagonal and strategy makers will learn nothing more about the relative positions of competitors than they would by considering just one of the variables. For instance, if companies with broad product lines use multiple distribution channels, while companies with narrow lines use a single distribution channel, then looking at product line-breadth reveals just as much about industry positioning as looking at the two competitive variables. Second, the variables chosen as axes for the map should reflect key approaches to offering value to customers and expose big differences in how rivals position themselves in the marketplace. Third, the variables used as axes do not have to be either quantitative or continuous; rather, they can be discrete variables or defined in terms of distinct classes and combinations. Fourth, drawing the sizes of the circles on the map proportional to the combined sales of the firms in each strategic group allows the map to reflect the relative sizes of each strategic group. Fifth, if more than two good competitive variables can be used as axes for the map, multiple maps can be drawn to give different exposures to the competitive positioning in the industry. Because there is not necessarily one best map for portraying how competing firms are positioned in the market, it is advisable to experiment with different pairs of competitive variables.

CONCEPTS & CONNECTIONS 3.1

COMPARATIVE MARKET POSITIONS OF SELECTED PIZZA CHAINS: A STRATEGIC GROUP MAP EXAMPLE

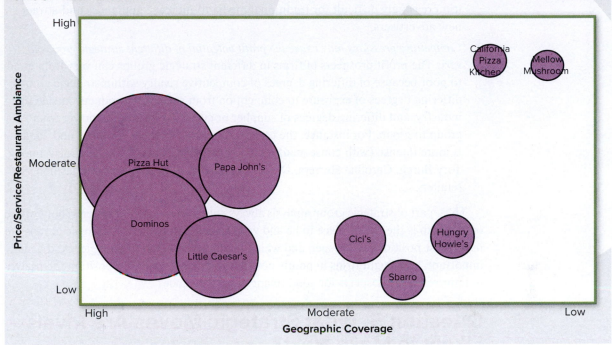

The Value of Strategic Group Maps

Strategic group maps are revealing in several respects. The most important has to do with identifying which rivals are similarly positioned and are thus close rivals and which are distant rivals. Generally, *the closer strategic groups are to each other on the map, the stronger the cross-group competitive rivalry tends to be.* Although firms in the same strategic group are the closest rivals, the next closest rivals are in the immediately adjacent groups.[7] Often, firms in strategic groups that are far apart on the map hardly compete. For instance, Walmart's clientele, merchandise selection, and pricing points are much too different to justify calling Walmart a close competitor of Neiman Marcus or Saks Fifth Avenue in retailing. For the same reason, Timex is not a meaningful competitive rival of Rolex, and Kia is not a close competitor of Porsche or BMW.

The second thing to be gleaned from strategic group mapping is that *not all positions on the map are equally attractive.* Two reasons account for why some positions can be more attractive than others:

> Some strategic groups are more favorably positioned than others because they confront weaker competitive forces and/or because they are more favorably impacted by industry driving forces.

1. *Industry driving forces may favor some strategic groups and hurt others.* Driving forces in an industry may be acting to grow the demand for the products of

firms in some strategic groups and shrink the demand for the products of firms in other strategic groups—as is the case in the news industry where Internet news services and cable news networks are gaining ground at the expense of newspapers and network television. The industry driving forces of emerging Internet capabilities and applications, changes in who buys the product and how they use it, and changing societal concerns, attitudes, and lifestyles are making it increasingly difficult for traditional media to increase audiences and attract new advertisers.

2. *Competitive pressures may cause the profit potential of different strategic groups to vary.* The profit prospects of firms in different strategic groups can vary from good to poor because of differing degrees of competitive rivalry within strategic groups, differing degrees of exposure to competition from substitute products outside the industry, and differing degrees of supplier or customer bargaining power from group to group. For instance, the competitive battle between Walmart and Target is more intense (with consequently smaller profit margins) than the rivalry among Tory Burch, Carolina Herrera, Dolce & Gabbana, and other high-end fashion retailers.

Thus, part of strategic group analysis always entails drawing conclusions about where on the map is the "best" place to be and why. Which companies or strategic groups are in the best positions to prosper, and which might be expected to struggle? And equally important, how might firms in poorly positioned strategic groups reposition themselves to improve their prospects for good financial performance?

Question 5: What Strategic Moves Are Rivals Likely to Make Next?

Unless a company pays attention to the strategies and situations of competitors and has some inkling of what moves they will be making, it ends up flying blind into competitive battle. As in sports, scouting the business opposition is an essential part of game plan development. Having good information about the strategic direction and likely moves of key competitors allows a company to prepare defensive countermoves, to craft its own strategic moves with some confidence about what market maneuvers to expect from rivals in response, and to exploit any openings that arise from competitors' missteps. The question is where to look for such information, since rivals rarely reveal their strategic intentions openly. If information is not directly available, what are the best indicators?

Michael Porter's Framework for Competitor Analysis points to four indicators of a rival's likely strategic moves. These include a rival's *current strategy, objectives, capabilities,* and *assumptions* about itself and the industry. A strategic profile of a rival that provides good clues to its behavioral proclivities can be constructed by characterizing the rival along these four dimensions.

Current Strategy   To succeed in predicting a competitor's next moves, company strategists need to have a good understanding of each rival's current strategy. Questions to consider include: How is the competitor positioned in the market? What is the basis for its competitive advantage? What kinds of investments in infrastructure, technology, or other resources is it making?

Objectives   An appraisal of a rival's objectives should include not only its financial objectives but strategic objectives as well. What is even more important is to consider the extent to which the rival is meeting these objectives and if its management is under pressure to improve. Rivals with good financial performance are likely to continue their present strategy with only minor fine-tuning. Poorly performing rivals are virtually certain to make fresh strategic moves.

Capabilities   A rival's strategic moves and countermoves are both enabled and constrained by the set of capabilities it has at hand. Thus a rival's capabilities (and efforts to acquire new capabilities) serve as a strong signal of future strategic actions.

Assumptions   How a rival's top managers think about their strategic situation can have a big impact on how they behave. Managers of casual dining chains convinced that sociocultural forces and economic conditions will drive industry growth may turn to franchising to vastly expand a chain's footprint and number of units. Assessing a rival's assumptions entails considering their assumptions about itself as well as the industry it participates in.

> Studying competitors' past behavior and preferences provides a valuable assist in anticipating what moves rivals are likely to make next and outmaneuvering them in the marketplace.

Information regarding these four analytical components can often be gleaned from company press releases, information posted on the company's website (especially investor presentations), and such public documents as annual reports and 10-K filings. Many companies also have a competitive intelligence unit that sifts through the available information to construct up-to-date strategic profiles of rivals.

Doing the necessary detective work can be time-consuming, but scouting competitors well enough to anticipate their next moves allows managers to prepare effective countermoves and to take rivals' probable actions into account in crafting their own strategic offensives.

Question 6: What Are the Industry Key Success Factors?

An industry's **key success factors** (KSFs) are those competitive factors that most affect industry members' ability to prosper in the marketplace. Key success factors may include particular strategy elements, product attributes, resources, competitive capabilities, or intangible assets. KSFs by their very nature are so important to future competitive success that *all firms* in the industry must pay close attention to them or risk an eventual exit from the industry.

> **CORE CONCEPT**
>
> **Key success factors** are the strategy elements, product attributes, competitive capabilities, or intangible assets with the greatest impact on future success in the marketplace.

In the ready-to-wear apparel industry, the KSFs are appealing designs and color combinations, low-cost manufacturing, a strong network of retailers or company-owned stores, distribution capabilities that allow stores to keep the best-selling items in stock, and advertisements that effectively convey the brand's image. These attributes and capabilities apply to all brands of apparel ranging from private-label brands sold by discounters to premium-priced ready-to-wear brands sold by upscale department stores. Table 3.3 lists the most common types of industry key success factors.

TABLE 3.3	
Common Types of Industry Key Success Factors	
Technology-related KSFs	• Expertise in a particular technology or in scientific research (important in pharmaceuticals, Internet applications, mobile communications, and most high-tech industries) • Proven ability to improve production processes (important in industries where advancing technology opens the way for higher manufacturing efficiency and lower production costs)
Manufacturing-related KSFs	• Ability to achieve scale economies and/or capture experience curve effects (important to achieving low production costs) • Quality control know-how (important in industries where customers insist on product reliability) • High utilization of fixed assets (important in capital-intensive/high-fixed-cost industries) • Access to attractive supplies of skilled labor • High labor productivity (important for items with high labor content) • Low-cost product design and engineering (reduces manufacturing costs) • Ability to manufacture or assemble products that are customized to buyer specifications
Distribution-related KSFs	• A strong network of wholesale distributors/dealers • Strong direct sales capabilities via the Internet and/or having company-owned retail outlets • Ability to secure favorable display space on retailer shelves
Marketing-related KSFs	• Breadth of product line and product selection • A well-known and well-respected brand name • Fast, accurate technical assistance • Courteous, personalized customer service • Accurate filling of buyer orders (few back orders or mistakes) • Customer guarantees and warranties (important in mail-order and online retailing, big-ticket purchases, and new-product introductions) • Clever advertising
Skills- and capability-related KSFs	• A talented workforce (superior talent is important in professional services such as accounting and investment banking) • National or global distribution capabilities • Product innovation capabilities (important in industries where rivals are racing to be first to market with new product attributes or performance features) • Design expertise (important in fashion and apparel industries) • Short delivery time capability • Supply chain management capabilities • Strong e-commerce capabilities—a user-friendly website and/or skills in using Internet technology applications to streamline internal operations
Other types of KSFs	• Overall low costs (not just in manufacturing) to be able to meet low-price expectations of customers • Convenient locations (important in many retailing businesses) • Ability to provide fast, convenient, after-the-sale repairs and service • A strong balance sheet and access to financial capital (important in newly emerging industries with high degrees of business risk and in capital-intensive industries) • Patent protection

An industry's key success factors can usually be deduced through identifying the industry's dominant characteristics, assessing the five competitive forces, considering the impacts of the driving forces, comparing the market positions of industry members, and forecasting the likely next moves of key rivals. In addition, the answers to three questions help identify an industry's key success factors. Those questions are:

1. On what basis do buyers of the industry's product choose between the competing brands of sellers? That is, what product attributes are crucial?

2. Given the nature of the competitive forces prevailing in the marketplace, what resources and competitive capabilities does a company need to have to be competitively successful?

3. What shortcomings are almost certain to put a company at a significant competitive disadvantage?

Only rarely are there more than five or six key factors for future competitive success. Managers should therefore resist the temptation to label a factor that has only minor importance as a KSF. To compile a list of every factor that matters even a little bit defeats the purpose of concentrating management attention on the factors truly critical to long-term competitive success.

Question 7: Does the Industry Offer Good Prospects for Attractive Profits?

 LO3-4 Determine whether an industry's outlook presents a company with sufficiently attractive opportunities for growth and profitability.

The final step in evaluating the industry and competitive environment is boiling down the results of the analyses performed in Questions 1 through 6 to determine if the industry offers a company strong prospects for attractive profits.

The important factors on which to base such a conclusion include:

*   The industry's growth potential.

*   Whether powerful competitive forces are squeezing industry profitability to subpar levels and whether competition appears destined to grow stronger or weaker.

*   Whether industry profitability will be favorably or unfavorably affected by the prevailing driving forces.

*   The company's competitive position in the industry vis-à-vis rivals. (Well-entrenched leaders or strongly positioned contenders have a much better chance of earning attractive margins than those fighting a steep uphill battle.)

*   How competently the company performs industry key success factors.

It is a mistake to think of a particular industry as being equally attractive or unattractive to all industry participants and all potential entrants. Conclusions have to be drawn from the perspective of a particular company. Industries attractive to insiders may be unattractive to outsiders. Industry environments unattractive to weak competitors may be attractive to strong competitors. A favorably positioned company may survey a business environment and see a host of opportunities that weak competitors cannot capture.

When a company decides an industry is fundamentally attractive, a strong case can be made that it should invest aggressively to capture the opportunities it sees. When a strong competitor concludes an industry is relatively unattractive, it may elect to simply protect its present position, investing cautiously, if at all, and begin looking for opportunities in other industries. A competitively weak company in an unattractive industry may see its best option as finding a buyer, perhaps a rival, to acquire its business.

The degree to which an industry is attractive or unattractive is not the same for all industry participants and potential new entrants. The attractiveness of an industry depends on the degree of fit between a company's competitive capabilities and industry key success factors.

KEY POINTS

Thinking strategically about a company's external situation involves probing for answers to seven questions:

1. *What are the strategically relevant components of the macro-environment?* Industries differ as to how they are affected by conditions in the broad macro-environment. PESTEL analysis of the political, economic, sociocultural, technological, environmental/ecological, and legal/regulatory factors provides a framework for approaching this issue systematically.

2. *What kinds of competitive forces are industry members facing, and how strong is each force?* The strength of competition is a composite of five forces: (1) competitive pressures stemming from buyer bargaining power and seller-buyer collaboration, (2) competitive pressures associated with the sellers of substitutes, (3) competitive pressures stemming from supplier bargaining power and supplier-seller collaboration, (4) competitive pressures associated with the threat of new entrants into the market, and (5) competitive pressures stemming from the competitive jockeying among industry rivals.

3. *What forces are driving changes in the industry, and what impact will these changes have on competitive intensity and industry profitability?* Industry and competitive conditions change because forces are in motion that create incentives or pressures for change. The first phase is to identify the forces that are driving industry change. The second phase of driving forces analysis is to determine whether the driving forces, taken together, are acting to make the industry environment more or less attractive.

4. *What market positions do industry rivals occupy—who is strongly positioned and who is not?* Strategic group mapping is a valuable tool for understanding the similarities and differences inherent in the market positions of rival companies. Rivals in the same or nearby strategic groups are close competitors, whereas companies in distant strategic groups usually pose little or no immediate threat. Some strategic groups are more favorable than others. The profit potential of different strategic groups may not be the same because industry driving forces and competitive forces likely have varying effects on the industry's distinct strategic groups.

5. *What strategic moves are rivals likely to make next?* Scouting competitors well enough to anticipate their actions can help a company prepare effective countermoves and allows managers to take rivals' probable actions into account in designing their own company's best course of action. Using a Framework for Competitor Analysis that considers rivals' current strategy, objectives, resources and capabilities, and assumptions can be helpful in this regard.

6. *What are the key factors for competitive success?* An industry's key success factors (KSFs) are the particular product attributes, competitive capabilities, and intangible assets that spell the difference between being a strong competitor and a weak competitor—and sometimes between profit and loss. KSFs by their very nature are so important to competitive success that *all firms* in the industry must pay close attention to them or risk being driven out of the industry.

7. *Does the outlook for the industry present the company with sufficiently attractive prospects for profitability?* Conclusions regarding industry attractiveness are a major driver of company strategy. When a company decides an industry is fundamentally attractive and presents good opportunities, a strong case can be made that it should invest aggressively to capture the opportunities it sees. When a strong competitor concludes an industry is relatively unattractive and lacking in opportunity, it may elect to simply protect its present position, investing cautiously, if at all, and looking for opportunities in other industries. A competitively weak company in an unattractive industry may see its best option as finding a buyer,

perhaps a rival, to acquire its business. On occasion, an industry that is unattractive overall is still very attractive to a favorably situated company with the skills and resources to take business away from weaker rivals.

ASSURANCE OF LEARNING EXERCISES

1. Prepare a brief analysis of the organic food industry using the information provided by the Organic Trade Association (www.ota.com). Based upon information provided in *Organic Report* magazine (theorganicreport.com), draw a five-forces diagram for the organic food industry and briefly discuss the nature and strength of each of the five competitive forces.

   Mc Graw Hill **connect**
   LO3-2

2. Based on the strategic group map in Concepts & Connections 3.1, which pizza chains are Hungry Howie's closest competitors? With which strategic group does California Pizza Kitchen compete the least, according to this map? Why do you think no pizza chains are positioned in the area above Pizza Hut?

   LO3-3

3. The National Restaurant Association publishes an annual industry fact book that can be found at www.restaurant.org. Based on information in the latest report, does it appear that macro-environmental factors and the economic characteristics of the industry will present industry participants with attractive opportunities for growth and profitability? Explain.

   Mc Graw Hill **connect**
   LO3-1
   LO3-4

EXERCISES FOR SIMULATION PARTICIPANTS

1. Which of the five competitive forces is creating the strongest competitive pressures for your company?

   Mc Graw Hill **connect**
   LO3-1, LO3-2
   LO3-3, LO3-4

2. What are the "weapons of competition" that rival companies in your industry can use to gain sales and market share? See Figure 3.7 to help you identify the various competitive factors.

3. What are the factors affecting the intensity of rivalry in the industry in which your company is competing? Use Figure 3.7 and the accompanying discussion to help you in pinpointing the specific factors most affecting competitive intensity. Would you characterize the rivalry and jockeying for better market position, increased sales, and market share among the companies in your industry as fierce, very strong, strong, moderate, or relatively weak? Why?

4. Are there any driving forces in the industry in which your company is competing? What impact will these driving forces have? Will they cause competition to be more or less intense? Will they act to boost or squeeze profit margins? List at least two actions your company should consider taking to combat any negative impacts of the driving forces.

5. Draw a strategic group map showing the market positions of the companies in your industry. Which companies do you believe are in the most attractive position on the map? Which companies are the most weakly positioned? Which companies do you believe are likely to try to move to a different position on the strategic group map?

6. What do you see as the key factors for being a successful competitor in your industry? List at least three.

7. Does your overall assessment of the industry suggest that industry rivals have sufficiently attractive opportunities for growth and profitability? Explain.

ENDNOTES

1. Michael E. Porter, *Competitive Strategy: Techniques for Analyzing Industries and Competitors* (New York: Free Press, 1980), chapter 1; Michael E. Porter, "The Five Competitive Forces That Shape Strategy," *Harvard Business Review* 86, no. 1 (January 2008).

2. J. S. Bain, *Barriers to New Competition* (Cambridge, MA: Harvard University Press, 1956); F. M. Scherer, *Industrial Market Structure and Economic Performance* (Chicago: Rand McNally & Co., 1971).

3. Pankaj Ghemawat, "Building Strategy on the Experience Curve," *Harvard Business Review* 64, no. 2 (March–April 1985).

4. Michael E. Porter, "How Competitive Forces Shape Strategy," *Harvard Business Review* 57, no. 2 (March–April 1979).

5. Pamela J. Derfus, Patrick G. Maggitti, Curtis M. Grimm, and Ken G. Smith, "The Red Queen Effect: Competitive Actions and Firm Performance," *Academy of Management Journal* 51, no. 1 (February 2008).

6. Mary Ellen Gordon and George R. Milne, "Selecting the Dimensions That Define Strategic Groups: A Novel Market-Driven Approach," *Journal of Managerial Issues* 11, no. 2 (Summer 1999).

7. Avi Fiegenbaum and Howard Thomas, "Strategic Groups as Reference Groups: Theory, Modeling and Empirical Examination of Industry and Competitive Strategy," *Strategic Management Journal* 16 (1995); S. Ade Olusoga, Michael P. Mokwa, and Charles H. Noble, "Strategic Groups, Mobility Barriers, and Competitive Advantage," *Journal of Business Research* 33 (1995).

EVALUATING A COMPANY'S RESOURCES, CAPABILITIES, AND COMPETITIVENESS

4

LEARNING OBJECTIVES

After reading this chapter, you should be able to:

LO4-1   Assess how well a company's strategy is working.

LO4-2   Understand why a company's resources and capabilities are centrally important in giving the company a competitive edge over rivals.

LO4-3   Grasp how a company's value chain activities can affect the company's cost structure and customer value proposition.

LO4-4   Evaluate a company's competitive strength relative to key rivals.

LO4-5   Understand how a comprehensive evaluation of a company's external and internal situations can assist managers in making critical decisions about their next strategic moves.

Chapter 3 described how to use the tools of industry and competitive analysis to assess a company's external environment and lay the groundwork for matching a company's strategy to its external situation. This chapter discusses the techniques of evaluating a company's internal situation, including its collection of resources and capabilities, its cost structure and customer value proposition, and its competitive strength versus that of its rivals. The analytical spotlight will be trained on five questions:

1. How well is the company's strategy working?
2. What are the company's competitively important resources and capabilities?
3. Are the company's cost structure and customer value proposition competitive?
4. Is the company competitively stronger or weaker than key rivals?
5. What strategic issues and problems merit front-burner managerial attention?

The answers to these five questions complete management's understanding of the company's overall situation and position the company for a good strategy-situation fit required by the "The Three Tests of a Winning Strategy" (see Chapter 1).

Question 1: How Well Is the Company's Strategy Working?

 LO4-1   Assess how well a company's strategy is working.

The two best indicators of how well a company's strategy is working are (1) whether the company is recording gains in financial strength and profitability, and (2) whether the company's competitive strength and market standing are improving. Persistent shortfalls in meeting company financial performance targets and weak performance relative to rivals are reliable warning signs that the company suffers from poor strategy making, less-than-competent strategy execution, or both. Other indicators of how well a company's strategy is working include:

• Trends in the company's sales and earnings growth.
• Trends in the company's stock price.
• The company's overall financial strength.
• The company's customer retention rate.
• The rate at which new customers are acquired.
• Changes in the company's image and reputation with customers.
• Evidence of improvement in internal processes such as defect rate, order fulfillment, delivery times, days of inventory, and employee productivity.

The stronger a company's current overall performance, the less likely the need for radical changes in strategy. The weaker a company's financial performance and market standing, the more its current strategy must be questioned. (A compilation of financial ratios most commonly used to evaluate a company's financial performance and balance sheet strength is presented in the Appendix.)

Question 2: What Are the Company's Competitively Important Resources and Capabilities?

LO4-2 Understand why a company's resources and capabilities are centrally important in giving the company a competitive edge over rivals.

As discussed in Chapter 1, a company's business model and strategy must be well matched to its collection of resources and capabilities. An attempt to create and deliver customer value in a manner that depends on resources or capabilities that are deficient and cannot be readily acquired or developed is unwise and positions the company for failure. A company's competitive approach requires a tight fit with a company's internal situation and is strengthened when it exploits resources that are competitively valuable, rare, hard to copy, and not easily trumped by rivals' substitute resources. In addition, long-term competitive advantage requires the ongoing development and expansion of resources and capabilities to pursue emerging market opportunities and defend against future threats to its market standing and profitability.[1]

Sizing up the company's collection of resources and capabilities and determining whether they can provide the foundation for competitive success can be achieved through **resource and capability analysis.** This is a two-step process: (1) Identify the company's resources and capabilities, and (2) examine them more closely to ascertain which are the most competitively important and whether they can support a sustainable competitive advantage over rival firms.[2] This second step involves applying the *four tests of a resource's competitive power.*

Identifying Competitively Important Resources and Capabilities

A company's **resources** are competitive assets that are owned or controlled by the company and may either be *tangible resources* such as plants, distribution centers, manufacturing equipment, patents, information systems, and capital reserves or creditworthiness, or *intangible assets* such as a well-known brand or a results-oriented organizational culture. Table 4.1 lists the common types of tangible and intangible resources that a company may possess.

A **capability** is the capacity of a firm to competently perform some internal activity. A capability may also be referred to as a **competence.** Capabilities or competencies also vary in form, quality, and competitive importance, with some being more competitively valuable than others. Proficiently performed internal capabilities that also rank high in competitive importance are referred to as core competencies. *Organizational capabilities are developed and enabled through the deployment of a company's resources or some combination of its resources.*[3] Some capabilities rely heavily on a company's intangible resources such as human assets and intellectual capital. For example, Nestlé's brand management capabilities for its 2,000+ food, beverage, and pet care brands draw upon the knowledge of the company's brand managers, the expertise of its marketing department, and the company's relationships with retailers in nearly 200 countries. W. L. Gore's product innovation capabilities in its fabrics,

> **CORE CONCEPT**
>
> A **resource** is a competitive asset that is owned or controlled by a company; a **capability** is the capacity of a company to competently perform some internal activity. Capabilities are developed and enabled through the deployment of a company's resources.

> **CORE CONCEPT**
>
> A **competence** is an activity that a company has learned to perform with proficiency. A core competence is an activity that a company performs proficiently and that is central to its strategy and competitive success.

> **TABLE 41**
>
> **Common Types of Tangible and Intangible Resources**
>
> **Tangible Resources**
> - *Physical resources*—state-of-the-art manufacturing plants and equipment, efficient distribution facilities, attractive real estate locations, or ownership of valuable natural resource deposits
> - *Financial resources*—cash and cash equivalents, marketable securities, and other financial assets such as a company's credit rating and borrowing capacity
> - *Technological assets*—patents, copyrights, superior production technology, and technologies that enable activities
> - *Organizational resources*—information and communication systems (servers, workstations, etc.), proven quality control systems, and a strong network of distributors or retail dealers
>
> **Intangible Resources**
> - *Human assets and intellectual capital*—an experienced and capable workforce, talented employees in key areas, collective learning embedded in the organization, or proven managerial know-how
> - *Brand, image, and reputational assets*—brand names, trademarks, product or company image, buyer loyalty, reputation for quality, superior service
> - *Relationships*—alliances or joint ventures that provide access to technologies, specialized know-how, or geographic markets, and trust established with various partners
> - *Company culture*—the norms of behavior, business principles, and ingrained beliefs within the company

medical, and industrial products businesses result from the personal initiative, creative talents, and technological expertise of its associates and the company's culture that encourages accountability and creative thinking.

Determining the Competitive Power of a Company's Resources and Capabilities

> **CORE CONCEPT**
>
> The **VRIN tests for sustainable competitive advantage** ask if a resource or capability is *valuable, rare, inimitable,* and *nonsubstitutable.*

What is most telling about a company's aggregation of resources and capabilities is how powerful they are in the marketplace. The competitive power of a resource or capability is measured by how many of four tests for sustainable competitive advantage it can pass.[4]

The tests are often referred to as the **VRIN tests for sustainable competitive advantage**—an acronym for *valuable, rare, inimitable,* and *nonsubstitutable.* The first two tests determine whether the resource or capability may contribute to a competitive advantage. The last two determine the degree to which the competitive advantage potential can be sustained.

1. *Is the resource or capability competitively **valuable?*** All companies possess a collection of resources and capabilities—some have the potential to contribute to a competitive advantage, while others may not. Google failed in converting its technological resources and software innovation capabilities into success for Google Wallet, which incurred losses of more than $300 million before being abandoned in 2016. While these resources and capabilities have made Google the world's number-one search engine, they proved to be less valuable in the mobile payments industry.

2. *Is the resource or capability **rare**—is it something rivals lack?* Resources and capabilities that are common among firms and widely available cannot be a source of competitive advantage. All makers of branded cookies and sweet snacks have valuable

marketing capabilities and brands. Therefore, these skills are not rare or unique in the industry. However, the brand strength of Oreo is uncommon and has provided Kraft Foods with greater market share as well as the opportunity to benefit from brand extensions such as Golden Oreo cookies, Oreo Thins, and Mini Oreo cookies.

3. *Is the resource or capability **inimitable** or hard to copy?* The more difficult and more expensive it is to imitate a company's resource or capability, the more likely that it can also provide a *sustainable* competitive advantage. Resources tend to be difficult to copy when they are unique (a fantastic real estate location, patent protection), when they must be built over time (a brand name, a strategy-supportive organizational culture), and when they carry big capital requirements (a cost-effective plant to manufacture cutting-edge microprocessors). Imitation by rivals is most challenging when capabilities reflect a high level of *social complexity* (for example, a stellar team-oriented culture or unique trust-based relationships with employees, suppliers, or customers) and *causal ambiguity,* a term that signifies the hard-to-disentangle nature of complex processes such as the web of intricate activities enabling a new drug discovery.

4. *Is the resource or capability **nonsubstitutable** or is it vulnerable to the threat of substitution from different types of resources and capabilities?* Resources that are competitively valuable, rare, and costly to imitate may lose much of their ability to offer competitive advantage if rivals possess equivalent substitute resources. For example, manufacturers relying on automation to gain a cost-based advantage in production activities may find their technology-based advantage nullified by rivals' use of low-wage offshore manufacturing. Resources can contribute to a competitive advantage only when resource substitutes do not exist.

Very few firms have resources and capabilities that can pass all four tests, but those that do enjoy a sustainable competitive advantage with far greater profit potential. Costco is a notable example, with strong employee incentive programs and capabilities in supply chain management that have surpassed those of its warehouse club competitors for over 35 years. Lincoln Electric Company, less well known but no less notable in its achievements, has been the world leader in welding products for over 100 years as a result of its unique piecework incentive system for compensating production workers and the unsurpassed worker productivity and product quality that this system has fostered.[5]

If management determines that the company does not possess a resource that independently passes all four tests with high marks, it may have a bundle of resources that can pass the tests. Although PetSmart's supply chain and marketing capabilities are matched well by rival Petco, the company has outperformed and continues to outperform competitors through its customer service capabilities (including animal grooming, veterinary, and day care services). Nike's bundle of styling expertise, marketing research skills, professional endorsements, brand name, and managerial know-how has allowed it to remain number one in the athletic footwear and apparel industry for more than 20 years.

> **CORE CONCEPT**
>
> **Social complexity** and **causal ambiguity** are two factors that inhibit the ability of rivals to imitate a firm's most valuable resources and capabilities. Causal ambiguity makes it very hard to figure out how a complex resource contributes to competitive advantage and therefore exactly what to imitate.

> **CORE CONCEPT**
>
> Companies that lack a standalone resource that is competitively powerful may nonetheless develop a competitive advantage through **resource bundles** that enable the superior performance of important cross-functional capabilities.

The Importance of Dynamic Capabilities in Sustaining Competitive Advantage

Resources and capabilities must be continually strengthened and nurtured to sustain their competitive power and, at times, may need to be broadened and deepened to allow the company to position itself to pursue emerging market opportunities.[6] Organizational resources and capabilities that grow stale can impair competitiveness unless they are refreshed, modified, or even phased out and replaced in response to ongoing market changes and shifts in company strategy. In addition, disruptive environmental change may destroy the value of key strategic assets, turning *static* resources and capabilities "from diamonds to rust."[7]

Management's organization-building challenge has two elements: (1) attending to ongoing recalibration of existing capabilities and resources, and (2) casting a watchful eye for opportunities to develop totally new capabilities for delivering better customer value and/or outcompeting rivals. Companies that know the importance of recalibrating and upgrading resources and capabilities make it a routine management function to build new resource configurations and capabilities. Such a managerial approach allows a company to prepare for market changes and pursue emerging opportunities. This ability to build and integrate new competitive assets becomes a capability in itself—a **dynamic capability.** A dynamic capability is the ability to modify, deepen, or reconfigure the company's existing resources and capabilities in response to its changing environment or market opportunities.[8]

Management at Toyota has aggressively upgraded the company's capabilities in fuel-efficient hybrid engine technology and constantly fine-tuned the famed Toyota Production System to enhance the company's already proficient capabilities in manufacturing top-quality vehicles at relatively low costs. Likewise, management at BMW developed new organizational capabilities in hybrid engine design that allowed the company to launch its highly touted i3 and i8 plug-in hybrids. Resources and capabilities can also be built and augmented through alliances and acquisitions.[9] Bristol-Myers Squibb's famed "string of pearls" acquisition strategy has enabled it to replace degraded resources such as expiring patents with new patents and newly acquired capabilities in drug discovery for new disease domains.

> **CORE CONCEPT**
>
> A **dynamic capability** is the ability to modify, deepen, or reconfigure the company's existing resources and capabilities in response to its changing environment or market opportunities.

> A company requires a dynamically evolving portfolio of resources and capabilities in order to sustain its competitiveness and position itself to pursue future market opportunities.

> **CORE CONCEPT**
>
> **SWOT analysis** is a simple but powerful tool for sizing up a company's internal strengths and competitive deficiencies, its market opportunities, and the external threats to its future well-being.

Is the Company Able to Seize Market Opportunities and Nullify External Threats?

An essential element in evaluating a company's overall situation entails examining the company's resources and competitive capabilities in terms of the degree to which they enable it to pursue its best market opportunities and defend against the external threats to its future well-being. The simplest and most easily applied tool for conducting this examination is widely known as **SWOT analysis,** so named because it zeros in on a company's internal **S**trengths and **W**eaknesses, market **O**pportunities, and external **T**hreats. *A company's internal strengths should always serve as the basis of its strategy—placing heavy reliance on a company's best* *competitive assets is the soundest route to attracting customers and competing successfully against rivals.*[10]

As a rule, strategies that place heavy demands on areas where the company is weakest or has unproven competencies should be avoided. Plainly, managers must look toward correcting competitive weaknesses that make the company vulnerable, hold down profitability, or disqualify it from pursuing an attractive opportunity. Furthermore, a company's strategy should be aimed squarely at capturing those market opportunities that are most attractive and suited to the company's collection of capabilities. How much attention to devote to defending against external threats to the company's future performance hinges on how vulnerable the company is, whether defensive moves can be taken to lessen their impact, and whether the costs of undertaking such moves represent the best use of company resources. A first-rate SWOT analysis provides the basis for crafting a strategy that capitalizes on the company's strengths, aims squarely at capturing the company's best opportunities, and defends against the threats to its well-being. Table 4.2 lists the kinds of factors to consider in compiling a company's resource strengths and weaknesses.

> Basing a company's strategy on its strengths resulting from most competitively valuable resources and capabilities gives the company its best chance for market success.

The Value of a SWOT Analysis

A SWOT analysis involves more than making four lists. The most important parts of SWOT analysis are:

> Simply listing a company's strengths, weaknesses, opportunities, and threats is not enough; the payoff from SWOT analysis comes from the conclusions about a company's situation and the implications for strategy improvement that flow from the four lists.

1. Drawing conclusions from the SWOT listings about the company's overall situation.

2. Translating these conclusions into strategic actions to better match the company's strategy to its strengths and market opportunities, correcting problematic weaknesses, and defending against worrisome external threats.

Question 3: Are the Company's Cost Structure and Customer Value Proposition Competitive?

LO4-3 Grasp how a company's value chain activities can affect the company's cost structure and customer value proposition.

Company managers are often stunned when a competitor cuts its prices to "unbelievably low" levels or when a new market entrant comes on strong with a great new product offered at a surprisingly low price. Such competitors may not, however, be buying market positions with prices that are below costs. They may simply have substantially lower costs and therefore are able to offer prices that result in more appealing customer value propositions. One of the most telling signs of whether a company's business position is strong or precarious is whether its cost structure and customer value proposition are competitive with those of industry rivals.

Cost comparisons are especially critical in industries where price competition is typically the ruling market force. But even in industries where products are differentiated, rival companies have to keep their costs in line with rivals offering value propositions based upon a similar mix of differentiating features. A company must also remain competitive in terms of its customer value proposition. Patagonia's value

TABLE 4.2

Factors to Consider When Identifying a Company's Strengths, Weaknesses, Opportunities, and Threats

Potential Internal Strengths and Competitive Capabilities

- Core competencies
- A strong financial condition; ample financial resources to grow the business
- Strong brand-name image/company reputation
- Economies of scale and/or learning and experience curve advantages over rivals
- Proprietary technology/superior technological skills/important patents
- Cost advantages over rivals
- Product innovation capabilities
- Proven capabilities in improving production processes
- Good supply chain management capabilities
- Good customer service capabilities
- Better product quality relative to rivals
- Wide geographic coverage and/or strong global distribution capability
- Alliances/joint ventures with other firms that provide access to valuable technology, competencies, and/or attractive geographic markets

Potential Internal Weaknesses and Competitive Deficiencies

- No clear strategic direction
- No well-developed or proven core competencies
- A weak balance sheet; burdened with too much debt
- Higher overall unit costs relative to key competitors
- A product/service with features and attributes that are inferior to those of rivals
- Too narrow a product line relative to rivals
- Weak brand image or reputation
- Weaker dealer network than key rivals
- Behind on product quality, R&D, and/or technological know-how
- Lack of management depth
- Short on financial resources to grow the business and pursue promising initiatives

Potential Market Opportunities

- Serving additional customer groups or market segments
- Expanding into new geographic markets
- Expanding the company's product line to meet a broader range of customer needs
- Utilizing existing company skills or technological know-how to enter new product lines or new businesses
- Falling trade barriers in attractive foreign markets
- Acquiring rival firms or companies with attractive technological expertise or capabilities

Potential External Threats to a Company's Future Prospects

- Increasing intensity of competition among industry rivals—may squeeze profit margins
- Slowdowns in market growth
- Likely entry of potent new competitors
- Growing bargaining power of customers or suppliers
- A shift in buyer needs and tastes away from the industry's product
- Adverse demographic changes that threaten to curtail demand for the industry's product
- Vulnerability to unfavorable industry driving forces
- Restrictive trade policies on the part of foreign governments
- Costly new regulatory requirements

proposition, for example, remains attractive to customers who value quality, wide selection, and corporate environmental responsibility over cheaper outerwear alternatives. Target's customer value proposition has withstood the Walmart low-price juggernaut by attention to product design, image, and attractive store layouts in addition to efficiency. The key for managers is to keep close track of how *cost-effectively* the company can deliver value to customers relative to its competitors. *If the company can deliver the same amount of value with lower expenditures (or more value at a similar cost), it will maintain a competitive edge.* Two analytical tools are particularly useful in determining whether a company's value proposition and costs are competitive: value chain analysis and benchmarking.

> Competitive advantage hinges on how cost-effectively a company can execute its customer value proposition.

Company Value Chains

Every company's business consists of a collection of activities undertaken in the course of designing, producing, marketing, delivering, and supporting its product or service. All of the various activities that a company performs internally combine to form a **value chain,** so called because the underlying intent of a company's activities is to do things that ultimately *create value for buyers.*

> **CORE CONCEPT**
>
> A company's **value chain** identifies the primary activities that create customer value and related support activities.

As shown in Figure 4.1, a company's value chain consists of two broad categories of activities that drive costs and create customer value: the *primary activities* that are foremost in creating value for customers and the requisite *support activities* that facilitate and enhance the performance of the primary activities.[11] For example, the primary activities and cost drivers for a department store retailer such as Nordstrom include merchandise selection and buying, store layout and product display, advertising, and customer service; its support activities that affect customer value and costs include hiring and training, store maintenance, plus the usual assortment of administrative activities. The primary value chain activities and costs of a hotel operator like Marriott International are mainly comprised of reservations and hotel operations (check-in and check-out, maintenance and housekeeping, dining and room service, and conventions and meetings); principal support activities that drive costs and impact customer value include accounting, hiring and training hotel staff, and general administration. Supply chain management is a crucial activity for Boeing and Amazon.com but is not a value chain component at LinkedIn or DirectTV. Sales and marketing are dominant activities at Ford Motor Company and J. Crew but have minor roles at oil and gas drilling and exploration companies and pipeline companies. With its focus on value-creating activities, the value chain is an ideal tool for examining how a company delivers on its customer value proposition. It permits a deep look at the company's cost structure and ability to offer low prices. It reveals the emphasis that a company places on activities that enhance differentiation and support higher prices, such as service and marketing.

The value chain also includes a profit margin component; profits are necessary to compensate the company's owners/shareholders and investors, who bear risks and provide capital. Tracking the profit margin along with the value-creating activities is critical because unless an enterprise succeeds in delivering customer value profitably (with a sufficient return on invested capital), it cannot survive for long. Attention to a company's profit formula in addition to its customer value proposition is the essence of a sound business model, as described in Chapter 1. Concepts & Connections 4.1 shows representative costs for various activities performed by Boll & Branch, a maker of luxury linens and bedding sold directly to consumers online.

FIGURE 4.1

A Representative Company Value Chain

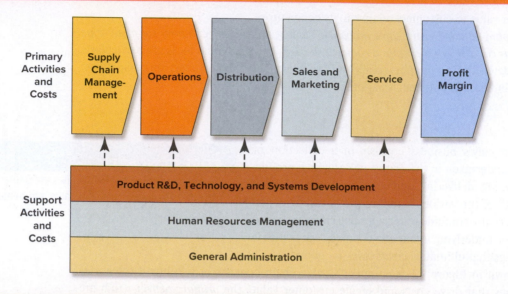

PRIMARY ACTIVITIES

- **Supply Chain Management**—Activities, costs, and assets associated with purchasing fuel, energy, raw materials, parts and components, merchandise, and consumable items from vendors; receiving, storing, and disseminating inputs from suppliers; inspection; and inventory management.

- **Operations**—Activities, costs, and assets associated with converting inputs into final product form (production, assembly, packaging, equipment maintenance, facilities, operations, quality assurance, environmental protection).

- **Distribution**—Activities, costs, and assets dealing with physically distributing the product to buyers (finished goods warehousing, order processing, order picking and packing, shipping, delivery vehicle operations, establishing and maintaining a network of dealers and distributors).

- **Sales and Marketing**—Activities, costs, and assets related to sales force efforts, advertising and promotion, market research and planning, and dealer/distributor support.

- **Service**—Activities, costs, and assets associated with providing assistance to buyers, such as installation, spare parts delivery, maintenance and repair, technical assistance, buyer inquiries, and complaints.

SUPPORT ACTIVITIES

- **Product R&D, Technology, and Systems Development**—Activities, costs, and assets relating to product R&D, process R&D, process design improvement, equipment design, computer software development, telecommunications systems, computer-assisted design and engineering, database capabilities, and development of computerized support systems.

- **Human Resources Management**—Activities, costs, and assets associated with the recruitment, hiring, training, development, and compensation of all types of personnel; labor relations activities; and development of knowledge-based skills and core competencies.

- **General Administration**—Activities, costs, and assets relating to general management, accounting and finance, legal and regulatory affairs, safety and security, management information systems, forming strategic alliances and collaborating with strategic partners, and other "overhead" functions.

Source: Based on the discussion in Michael E. Porter, *Competitive Advantage* (New York: Free Press, 1985), pp. 37–43.

CONCEPTS & CONNECTIONS 4.1

THE VALUE CHAIN FOR BOLL & BRANCH

Bohbeh/Shutterstock

A KING-SIZE SET OF SHEETS FROM BOLL & BRANCH IS MADE FROM 6 METERS OF FABRIC, REQUIRING 11 KILOGRAMS OF RAW COTTON.

Raw Cotton	**$ 28.16**
Spinning/Weaving/Dyeing	12.00
Cutting/Sewing/Finishing	9.50
Material Transportation	3.00
Factory Fee	15.80
Cost of Goods	**$ 68.46**
Inspection Fees	5.48
Ocean Freight/Insurance	4.55
Import Duties	8.22
Warehouse/Packing	8.50
Packaging	15.15
Customer Shipping	14.00
Promotions/Donations*	30.00
Total Cost	**$154.38**
Boll & Brand Markup	About 60%
Boll & Brand Retail Price	**$250.00**
Gross Margin**	**$ 95.62**

* A $5 donation for every set of sheets sold is paid to an anti–human-trafficking organization.

**Gross margin covers overhead, advertising costs, and profit.

Source: Adapted from Christina Brinkley, "What Goes into the Price of Luxury Sheets?" *The Wall Street Journal.*

Benchmarking: A Tool for Assessing Whether a Company's Value Chain Activities Are Competitive

Benchmarking entails comparing how different companies perform various value chain activities—how materials are purchased, how inventories are managed, how products are assembled, how customer orders are filled and shipped, and how maintenance is performed—and then making cross-company comparisons of the costs and effectiveness of these activities.[12] The objectives of benchmarking are to identify the best practices in performing an activity and to emulate those best practices when they are possessed by others.

A **best practice** is a method of performing an activity or business process that consistently delivers superior results compared to other approaches.[13] To qualify as a legitimate best practice, the method must have been employed

> **CORE CONCEPT**
>
> **Benchmarking** is a potent tool for learning which companies are best at performing particular activities and then using their techniques (or "best practices") to improve the cost and effectiveness of a company's own internal activities.

> **CORE CONCEPT**
>
> A **best practice** is a method of performing an activity that consistently delivers superior results compared to other approaches.

by at least one enterprise and shown to be consistently more effective in lowering costs, improving quality or performance, shortening time requirements, enhancing safety, or achieving some other highly positive operating outcome. Best practices thus identify a path to operating excellence with respect to value chain activities.

Xerox led the way in the use of benchmarking to become more cost-competitive by deciding not to restrict its benchmarking efforts to its office equipment rivals, but by comparing itself to *any company* regarded as "world class" in performing activities relevant to Xerox's business. Other companies quickly picked up on Xerox's approach. Toyota managers got their idea for just-in-time inventory deliveries by studying how U.S. supermarkets replenished their shelves. Southwest Airlines reduced the turnaround time of its aircraft at each scheduled stop by studying pit crews on the auto-racing circuit. More than 80 percent of Fortune 500 companies reportedly use benchmarking for comparing themselves against rivals on cost and other competitively important measures.

The tough part of benchmarking is not whether to do it, but rather how to gain access to information about other companies' practices and costs. Sometimes benchmarking can be accomplished by collecting information from published reports, trade groups, and industry research firms and by talking to knowledgeable industry analysts, customers, and suppliers. Sometimes field trips to the facilities of competing or noncompeting companies can be arranged to observe how things are done, compare practices and processes, and perhaps exchange data on productivity and other cost components. However, such companies, even if they agree to host facilities tours and answer questions, are unlikely to share competitively sensitive cost information. Furthermore, comparing two companies' costs may not involve comparing apples to apples if the two companies employ different cost accounting principles to calculate the costs of particular activities.

However, a fairly reliable source of benchmarking information has emerged. The explosive interest of companies in benchmarking costs and identifying best practices has prompted consulting organizations (e.g., Accenture, A. T. Kearney, Benchnet—The Benchmarking Exchange, and Best Practices, LLC) and several councils and associations (e.g., the Qualserve Benchmarking Clearinghouse and the Strategic Planning Institute's Council on Benchmarking) to gather benchmarking data, distribute information about best practices, and provide comparative cost data without identifying the names of particular companies. Having an independent group gather the information and report it in a manner that disguises the names of individual companies avoids the disclosure of competitively sensitive data and lessens the potential for unethical behavior on the part of company personnel in gathering their own data about competitors.

The Value Chain System for an Entire Industry

A company's value chain is embedded in a larger system of activities that includes the value chains of its suppliers and the value chains of whatever distribution channel allies it utilizes in getting its product or service to end users. The value chains of forward channel partners are relevant because (1) the costs and margins of a company's distributors and retail dealers are part of the price the consumer ultimately pays, and (2) the activities that distribution allies perform affect the company's customer value proposition. For these reasons, companies normally work closely with their suppliers and forward channel allies to perform value chain activities in mutually beneficial ways. For instance, motor vehicle manufacturers work closely with their forward channel allies (local automobile dealers) to ensure that owners are satisfied with dealers' repair and maintenance services.[14] Also, many automotive parts suppliers have built plants near the auto assembly plants they supply to facilitate just-in-time deliveries, reduce warehousing and shipping costs, and promote close collaboration on parts design and production scheduling. Irrigation equipment companies, suppliers of grape-harvesting and winemaking equipment, and firms making barrels, wine bottles, caps, corks, and labels all have facilities in the California wine country to be close to the nearly 700 winemakers they supply.[15] The lesson here is that a company's value chain activities are often closely linked to the value chains of its suppliers and the forward allies.

> A company's customer value proposition and cost competitiveness depend not only on internally performed activities (its own company value chain), but also on the value chain activities of its suppliers and forward channel allies.

As a consequence, *accurately assessing the competitiveness of a company's cost structure and customer value proposition requires that company managers understand an industry's entire value chain system for delivering a product or service to customers, not just the company's own value chain.* A typical industry value chain that incorporates the value-creating activities, costs, and margins of suppliers and forward channel allies, if any, is shown in Figure 4.2. However, industry value chains vary significantly by industry. For example, the primary value chain activities in the pulp and paper industry (timber farming, logging, pulp mills, and papermaking) differ from those for the home appliance industry (parts and components manufacture, assembly, wholesale distribution, retail sales) and yet again from the cloud computing industry (IT hardware infrastructure, systems software infrastructure, application development, and application hosting, management, and security services).

Strategic Options for Remedying a Cost or Value Disadvantage

The results of value chain analysis and benchmarking may disclose cost or value disadvantages relative to key rivals. These competitive disadvantages are likely to lower a company's relative profit margin or weaken its customer value proposition. In such instances, actions to improve a company's value chain are called for to boost profitability

FIGURE 4.2
Representative Value Chain for an Entire Industry

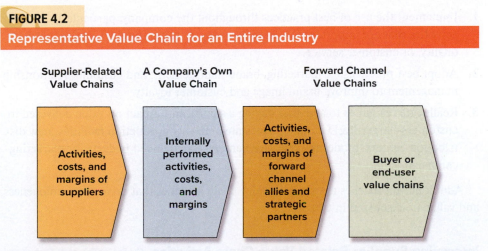

Source: Based in part on the single-industry value chain displayed in Michael E. Porter, *Competitive Advantage* (New York: Free Press, 1985), p. 35.

or to allow for the addition of new features that drive customer value. There are three main areas in a company's overall value chain where important differences between firms in costs and value can occur: a company's own internal activities, the suppliers' part of the industry value chain, and the forward channel portion of the industry chain.

Improving Internally Performed Value Chain Activities   Managers can pursue any of several strategic approaches to reduce the costs of internally performed value chain activities and improve a company's cost competitiveness.

1. *Implement the use of best practices* throughout the company, particularly for high-cost activities.

2. *Try to eliminate some cost-producing activities* by revamping the value chain. Many retailers have found that donating returned items to charitable organizations and taking the appropriate tax deduction results in a smaller loss than incurring the costs of the value chain activities involved in reverse logistics.

3. *Relocate high-cost activities* (such as manufacturing) to geographic areas such as China, Latin America, or Eastern Europe where they can be performed more cheaply.

4. *Outsource certain internally performed activities* to vendors or contractors if they can perform them more cheaply than can be done in-house.

5. *Invest in productivity-enhancing, cost-saving technological improvements* (robotics, flexible manufacturing techniques, state-of-the-art electronic networking).

6. *Find ways to detour around the activities or items where costs are high.* Computer chip makers regularly design around the patents held by others to avoid paying royalties; automakers have substituted lower-cost plastic for metal at many exterior body locations.

7. *Redesign the product* and/or some of its components to facilitate speedier and more economical manufacture or assembly.

8. *Try to make up the internal cost disadvantage* by reducing costs in the supplier or forward channel portions of the industry value chain—usually a last resort.

Rectifying a weakness in a company's customer value proposition can be accomplished by applying one or more of the following approaches:

1. Implement the use of best practices throughout the company, particularly for activities that are important for creating customer value—product design, product quality, or customer service.

2. Adopt best practices for marketing, brand management, and customer relationship management to improve brand image and customer loyalty.

3. Reallocate resources to activities having a significant impact on value delivered to customers—larger R&D budgets, new state-of-the-art production facilities, new distribution centers, modernized service centers, or enhanced budgets for marketing campaigns.

Additional approaches to managing value chain activities that drive costs, uniqueness, and value are discussed in Chapter 5.

Improving Supplier-Related Value Chain Activities   Supplier-related cost disadvantages can be attacked by pressuring suppliers for lower prices, switching to lower-priced substitute inputs, and collaborating closely with suppliers to identify mutual cost-saving opportunities.[16] For example, just-in-time deliveries from suppliers can lower a company's inventory and internal logistics costs, eliminate capital expenditures for additional warehouse space, and improve cash flow and financial ratios by reducing accounts payable. In a few instances, companies may find that it is cheaper to integrate backward into the business of high-cost suppliers and make the item in-house instead of buying it from outsiders.

Similarly, a company can enhance its customer value proposition through its supplier relationships. Some approaches include selecting and retaining suppliers that meet higher-quality standards, providing quality-based incentives to suppliers, and integrating suppliers into the design process. When fewer defects exist in components provided by suppliers, this not only improves product quality and reliability, but can also lower costs because there is less disruption to production processes and lower warranty expenses.

Improving Value Chain Activities of Forward Channel Allies There are three main ways to combat a cost disadvantage in the forward portion of the industry value chain: (1) Pressure dealers-distributors and other forward channel allies to reduce their costs and markups; (2) work closely with forward channel allies to identify win-win opportunities to reduce costs—for example, Walmart and Target require suppliers to meet a two-day shipping arrival window, which not only improves distribution center operating efficiency but also reduces costly unloading wait times for the shipper; and (3) change to a more economical distribution strategy or perhaps integrate forward into company-owned retail outlets.

A company can improve its customer value proposition through the activities of forward channel partners by the use of (1) cooperative advertising and promotions with forward channel allies; (2) training programs for dealers, distributors, or retailers to improve the purchasing experience or customer service; and (3) creating and enforcing operating standards for resellers or franchisees to ensure consistent store operations. Papa John's International, for example, is consistently rated highly by customers for its pizza quality, convenient ordering systems, and responsive customer service across its 5,100 company-owned and franchised units. The company's marketing campaigns and extensive employee training and development programs enhance its value proposition and the unit sales and operating profit for its franchisees in all 50 states and 45 countries.

How Value Chain Activities Relate to Resources and Capabilities

A close relationship exists between the value-creating activities that a company performs and its resources and capabilities. When companies engage in a value-creating activity, they do so by drawing on specific company resources and capabilities that underlie and enable the activity. For example, brand-building activities that enhance a company's customer value proposition can depend on human resources, such as experienced brand managers, as well as organizational capabilities related to developing and executing effective marketing campaigns. Distribution activities that lower costs may derive from organizational capabilities in inventory management and resources such as cutting-edge inventory tracking systems.

Because of the linkage between activities and enabling resources and capabilities, value chain analysis complements resource and capability analysis as another tool for assessing a company's competitive advantage. Resources and capabilities that are *both valuable and rare* provide a company with the *necessary preconditions* for competitive advantage. When these assets are deployed in the form of a value-creating activity, *that potential is realized.* Resource analysis is a valuable tool for assessing the competitive advantage potential of resources and capabilities. But the actual competitive benefit provided by resources and capabilities can only be assessed objectively after they are deployed in the form of activities.

Question 4: What Is the Company's Competitive Strength Relative to Key Rivals?

 LO4-4   Evaluate a company's competitive strength relative to key rivals.

An additional component of evaluating a company's situation is developing a comprehensive assessment of the company's overall competitive strength. Making this determination requires answers to two questions:

1. How does the company rank relative to competitors on each of the important factors that determine market success?

2. All things considered, does the company have a net competitive advantage or disadvantage versus major competitors?

Step 1 in doing a competitive strength assessment is to list the industry's key success factors and other telling measures of competitive strength or weakness (6 to 10 measures usually suffice). Step 2 is to assign a weight to each measure of competitive strength based on its perceived importance in shaping competitive success. (The sum of the weights for each measure must add up to 1.0.) Step 3 is to calculate weighted strength ratings by scoring each competitor on each strength measure (using a 1-to-10 rating scale where 1 is very weak and 10 is very strong) and multiplying the assigned rating by the assigned weight. Step 4 is to sum the weighted strength ratings on each factor to get an overall measure of competitive strength for each company being rated. Step 5 is to use the overall strength ratings to draw conclusions about the size and extent of the company's net competitive advantage or disadvantage and to take specific note of areas of strength and weakness. Table 4.3 provides an example of a competitive strength assessment using the hypothetical ABC Company against four rivals. ABC's total score of 5.95 signals a net competitive advantage over Rival 3 (with a score of 2.10) and Rival 4 (with a score of 3.70) but indicates a net competitive disadvantage against Rival 1 (with a score of 7.70) and Rival 2 (with an overall score of 6.85).

Interpreting the Competitive Strength Assessments

Competitive strength assessments provide useful conclusions about a company's competitive situation. The ratings show how a company compares against rivals, factor by factor or capability by capability, thus revealing where it is strongest and weakest. Moreover, the overall competitive strength scores indicate whether the company is at a net competitive advantage or disadvantage against each rival.

A company's competitive strength scores pinpoint its strengths and weaknesses against rivals and point to offensive and defensive strategies capable of producing first-rate results.

In addition, the strength ratings provide guidelines for designing wise offensive and defensive strategies. For example, consider the ratings and weighted scores in Table 4.3. If ABC Co. wants to go on the offensive to win additional sales and market share, such an offensive probably needs to be aimed directly at winning customers

TABLE 4.3

Illustration of a Competitive Strength Assessment

Key Success Factor/ Strength Measure	Importance Weight	ABC CO.		RIVAL 1		RIVAL 2		RIVAL 3		RIVAL 4	
		Strength Rating	Score	Strength Rating	Score	Strength Rating	Score	Strength Rating	Score	Strength Rating	Score
Quality/product performance	0.10	8	0.80	5	0.50	10	1.00	1	0.10	6	0.60
Reputation/image	0.10	8	0.80	7	0.70	10	1.00	1	0.10	6	0.60
Manufacturing capability	0.10	2	0.20	10	1.00	4	0.40	5	0.50	1	0.10
Technological skills	0.05	10	0.50	1	0.05	7	0.35	3	0.15	8	0.40
Dealer network/distribution capability	0.05	9	0.45	4	0.20	10	0.50	5	0.25	1	0.05
New product innovation capability	0.05	9	0.45	4	0.20	10	0.50	5	0.25	1	0.05
Financial resources	0.10	5	0.50	10	1.00	7	0.70	3	0.30	1	0.10
Relative cost position	0.30	5	1.50	10	3.00	3	0.90	1	0.30	4	1.20
Customer service capabilities	0.15	5	0.75	7	1.05	10	1.50	1	0.15	4	0.60
Sum of importance weights	1.00										
Weighted overall strength rating			**5.95**		**7.70**		**6.85**		**2.10**		**3.70**

(Rating scale: 1 = very weak; 10 = very strong)

away from Rivals 3 and 4 (which have lower overall strength scores) rather than Rivals 1 and 2 (which have higher overall strength scores). ABC's advantages over Rival 4 tend to be in areas that are moderately important to competitive success in the industry, but ABC outclasses Rival 3 on the two most heavily weighted strength factors—relative cost position and customer service capabilities. Therefore, Rival 3 should be viewed as the primary target of ABC's offensive strategies, with Rival 4 being a secondary target.

A competitively astute company should utilize the strength scores in deciding what strategic moves to make. When a company has important competitive strengths in areas where one or more rivals are weak, it makes sense to consider offensive moves to exploit rivals' competitive weaknesses. When a company has competitive weaknesses in important areas where one or more rivals are strong, it makes sense to consider defensive moves to curtail its vulnerability.

Question 5: What Strategic Issues and Problems Must Be Addressed by Management?

LO4-5 Understand how a comprehensive evaluation of a company's external and internal situations can assist managers in making critical decisions about their next strategic moves.

The final and most important analytical step is to zero in on exactly what strategic issues company managers need to address. This step involves drawing on the results of both industry and competitive analysis and the evaluations of the company's internal situation. The task here is to get a clear fix on exactly what industry and competitive challenges confront the company, which of the company's internal weaknesses need fixing, and what specific problems merit front-burner attention by company managers. *Pinpointing the precise things that management needs to worry about sets the agenda for deciding what actions to take next to improve the company's performance and business outlook.*

If the items on management's "worry list" are relatively minor, which suggests the company's strategy is mostly on track and reasonably well matched to the company's overall situation, company managers seldom need to go much beyond fine-tuning the present strategy. If, however, the issues and problems confronting the company are serious and indicate the present strategy is not well suited for the road ahead, the task of crafting a better strategy has got to go to the top of management's action agenda.

> Compiling a "worry list" of problems and issues creates an agenda for managerial strategy making.

KEY POINTS

In analyzing a company's own particular competitive circumstances and its competitive position vis-à-vis key rivals, consider five key questions:

1. *How well is the present strategy working?* This involves evaluating the strategy in terms of the company's financial performance and competitive strength and market standing. The stronger a company's current overall performance, the less likely the need for radical strategy changes. The weaker a company's performance and/or the faster the changes in its external

situation (which can be gleaned from industry and competitive analysis), the more its current strategy must be questioned.

2. *Do the company's resources and capabilities have sufficient competitive power to give it a sustainable advantage over competitors?* The answer to this question comes from conducting the four tests of a resource's competitive power—the VRIN tests. If a company has resources and capabilities that are competitively *valuable* and *rare,* the firm will have the potential for a competitive advantage over market rivals. If its resources and capabilities are also hard to copy (*inimitable*) with no good substitutes (*nonsubstitutable*), then the firm may be able to sustain this advantage even in the face of active efforts by rivals to overcome it.

    SWOT analysis can be used to assess if a company's resources and capabilities are sufficient to seize market opportunities and overcome external threats to its future well-being. The two most important parts of SWOT analysis are (1) drawing conclusions about what story the compilation of strengths, weaknesses, opportunities, and threats tells about the company's overall situation, and (2) acting on the conclusions to better match the company's strategy to its internal strengths and market opportunities, to correct the important internal weaknesses, and to defend against external threats. A company's strengths and competitive assets are strategically relevant because they are the most logical and appealing building blocks for strategy; internal weaknesses are important because they may represent vulnerabilities that need correction. External opportunities and threats come into play because a good strategy necessarily aims at capturing a company's most attractive opportunities and at defending against threats to its well-being.

3. *Are the company's cost structure and customer value proposition competitive?* One telling sign of whether a company's situation is strong or precarious is whether its costs are competitive with those of industry rivals. Another sign is how it compares with rivals in terms of its customer value proposition. Value chain analysis and benchmarking are essential tools in determining whether the company is performing particular functions and activities well, whether its costs are in line with competitors, whether it is able to offer an attractive value proposition to customers, and whether particular internal activities and business processes need improvement. Value chain analysis complements resource and capability analysis because of the tight linkage between activities and enabling resources and capabilities.

4. *Is the company competitively stronger or weaker than key rivals?* The key appraisals here involve how the company matches up against key rivals on industry key success factors and other chief determinants of competitive success and whether and why the company has a competitive advantage or disadvantage. Quantitative competitive strength assessments, using the method presented in Table 4.3, indicate where a company is competitively strong and weak and provide insight into the company's ability to defend or enhance its market position. As a rule, a company's competitive strategy should be built around its competitive strengths and should aim at shoring up areas where it is competitively vulnerable. When a company has important competitive strengths in areas where one or more rivals are weak, it makes sense to consider offensive moves to exploit rivals' competitive weaknesses. When a company has important competitive weaknesses in areas where one or more rivals are strong, it makes sense to consider defensive moves to curtail its vulnerability.

5. *What strategic issues and problems merit front-burner managerial attention?* This analytical step zeros in on the strategic issues and problems that stand in the way of the company's success. It involves using the results of both industry and competitive analysis and company situation analysis to identify a "worry list" of issues to be resolved for the company to be financially and competitively successful in the years ahead. Actually deciding upon a strategy and what specific actions to take comes after the list of strategic issues and problems that merit front-burner management attention has been developed.

Good company situation analysis, like good industry and competitive analysis, is a valuable precondition for good strategy making.

ASSURANCE OF LEARNING EXERCISES

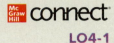

LO4-1

1. Using the financial ratios provided in the Appendix and the following financial statement information for Macy's, Inc., calculate the following ratios for Macy's for both 2017 and 2018.

    1. Gross profit margin
    2. Operating profit margin
    3. Net profit margin
    4. Times interest earned coverage
    5. Return on shareholders' equity
    6. Return on assets
    7. Long-term debt-to-equity ratio
    8. Days of inventory
    9. Inventory turnover ratio
    10. Average collection period

    Based on these ratios, did Macy's financial performance improve, weaken, or remain about the same from 2015 to 2016?

Consolidated Statements of Income for Macy's, Inc., 2017–2018 (in millions, except per share amounts)

	2018	2017
Net sales	$24,971	$ 24,939
Credit Card Revenues, Net	768	702
Cost of sales	(15,215)	(15,181)
Selling, general and administrative expenses	(9,039)	(8,954)
Gains on sale of real estate	389	544
Restructuring, impairment, store closing and other costs	(136)	(186)
Operating income (loss)	1,738	1,864
Benefit plan income, net	39	57
Settlement charges	(88)	(105)
Interest expense	(261)	(321)
Gains (losses) on early retirement of debt	(33)	10
Interest income	25	11
Income (loss) before income taxes	1,420	1,516
Federal, state and local income tax benefit (expense)	(322)	39
Net income (loss)	1,098	1,555
Net loss attributable to noncontrolling interest	10	11
Net income attributable to Macy's, Inc. shareholders	$ 1,108	$ 1,566
Basic earnings per share attributable to Macy's, Inc. shareholders	$3.60	$5.13
Diluted earnings per share attributable to Macy's, Inc. shareholders	$3.56	$5.10

Macy's Inc., 2018 Annual Report, February 26, 2019, https://www.macysinc.com/news-media/press-releases/detail/1548/macys-inc-reports-fourth-quarter-and-fiscal-year-2018.

Consolidated Balance Sheets for Macy's, Inc., 2017–2018 (in millions)		
	2018	2017
ASSETS		
Current Assets:		
Cash and cash equivalents	$ 1,162	$ 1,455
Receivables	400	363
Merchandise Inventories	5,263	5,178
Prepaid expenses and other current assets	620	650
Total Current Assets	7,445	7,646
Property and Equipment – net	6,637	6,672
Goodwill	3,908	3,897
Other Intangible Assets – net	478	488
Other Assets	726	880
Total Assets	19,194	9,583
LIABILITIES AND SHAREHOLDERS' EQUITY		
Current Liabilties:		
Short-term debt	43	22
Merchandise accounts payable	1,655	1,590
Accounts payable and accrued liabilities	3,366	3,271
Income taxes	168	296
Total Current Liabilities	5,232	5,179
Long-Term Debt	4,708	5,861
Deferred Income Taxes	1,238	1,148
Other Liabilities	1,580	1,662
Shareholders' Equity:		
Common stock (307.5 and 304.8 shares outstanding)	3	3
Additional paid-in capital	652	676
Accumulated equity	8,050	7,246
Treasury stock	(1,318)	(1,456)
Accumulated other comprehensive loss	(951)	(724)
Total Macy's, Inc., Shareholders' Equity	6,436	5,745
Noncontrolling interest	0	(21)
Total Shareholders' Equity	6,436	5,733
Total Liabilities and Shareholders' Equity	$19,194	$19,583

Macy's Inc., 2018 Annual Report, February 26, 2019, https://www.macysinc.com/news-media/press-releases/detail/1548/macys-inc-reports-fourth-quarter-and-fiscal-year-2018.

2. REI operates more than 140 sporting goods and outdoor recreation stores in 36 states. How many of the four tests of the competitive power of a resource does the retail store network pass? Explain your answer. **LO4-2**

3. Review the information in Concepts & Connections 4.1 concerning Boll & Branch's average costs of producing and selling a king-sized sheet set, and compare this with the representative value chain depicted in Figure 4.1. Then answer the following questions: **LO4-3**

   (a) Which of the company's costs correspond to the primary value chain activities depicted in Figure 4.1?

   (b) Which of the company's costs correspond to the support activities described in Figure 4.1?

   (c) What value chain activities might be important in securing or maintaining Boll & Branch's competitive advantage? Explain your answer.

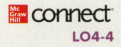

LO4-4

4. Using the methodology illustrated in Table 4.3 and your knowledge as an automobile owner, prepare a competitive strength assessment for General Motors and its rivals Ford, Chrysler, Toyota, and Honda. Each of the five automobile manufacturers should be evaluated on the key success factors/strength measures of cost competitiveness, product-line breadth, product quality and reliability, financial resources and profitability, and customer service. What does your competitive strength assessment disclose about the overall competitiveness of each automobile manufacturer? What factors account most for Toyota's competitive success? Does Toyota have competitive weaknesses that were disclosed by your analysis? Explain.

EXERCISES FOR SIMULATION PARTICIPANTS

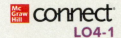

LO4-1

1. Using the formulas in the Appendix and the data in your company's latest financial statements, calculate the following measures of financial performance for your company:

   1. Operating profit margin
   2. Return on total assets
   3. Current ratio
   4. Working capital
   5. Long-term debt-to-capital ratio
   6. Price-earnings ratio

LO4-1

2. Based on your company's latest financial statements and all of the other available data regarding your company's performance that appear in the Industry Report, list the three measures of financial performance on which your company did "best" and the three measures on which your company's financial performance was "worst."

LO4-1

3. What hard evidence can you cite that indicates your company's strategy is working fairly well (or perhaps not working so well, if your company's performance is lagging that of rival companies)?

LO4-2

4. What internal strengths and weaknesses does your company have? What external market opportunities for growth and increased profitability exist for your company? What external threats to your company's future well-being and profitability do you and your co-managers see? What does the SWOT analysis indicate about your company's present situation and future prospects—where on the scale from "exceptionally strong" to "alarmingly weak" does the attractiveness of your company's situation rank?

LO4-2

5. Does your company have any core competencies? If so, what are they?

LO4-3

6. What are the key elements of your company's value chain? Refer to Figure 4.1 in developing your answer.

LO4-4

7. Using the methodology illustrated in Table 4.3, do a weighted competitive strength assessment for your company and two other companies that you and your co-managers consider to be very close competitors.

ENDNOTES

1. Birger Wernerfelt, "A Resource-Based View of the Firm," *Strategic Management Journal* 5, no. 5 (September–October 1984); Jay Barney, "Firm Resources and Sustained Competitive Advantage," *Journal of Management* 17, no. 1 (1991); Margaret A. Peteraf, "The Cornerstones of Competitive Advantage: A Resource-Based View," *Strategic Management Journal* 14, no. 3 (March 1993).

2. Birger Wernerfelt, "A Resource-Based View of the Firm," *Strategic Management Journal* 5, no. 5 (September–October 1984), pp. 171–180; Jay Barney, "Firm Resources and Sustained Competitive Advantage," *Journal of Management* 17, no. 1 (1991); Margaret A. Peteraf, "The Cornerstones of Competitive Advantage: A Resource-Based View," *Strategic Management Journal* 14, no. 3 (March 1993).

3. R. Amit and P. Schoemaker, "Strategic Assets and Organizational Rent," *Strategic Management Journal* 14, no. 1 (1993).

4. David J. Collis and Cynthia A. Montgomery, "Competing on Resources: Strategy in the 1990s," *Harvard Business Review* 73, no. 4 (July–August 1995).

5. Margaret A. Peteraf and Mark E. Bergen, "Scanning Dynamic Competitive Landscapes: A Market-Based and Resource-Based Framework," *Strategic Management Journal* 24 (2003), pp. 1027–1042.

6. David J. Teece, Gary Pisano, and Amy Shuen, "Dynamic Capabilities and Strategic Management," *Strategic Management Journal* 18, no. 7 (1997); Constance E. Helfat and Margaret A. Peteraf, "The Dynamic Resource-Based View: Capability Lifecycles," *Strategic Management Journal* 24, no. 10 (2003).

7. C. Montgomery, "Of Diamonds and Rust: A New Look at Resources," in *Resource-Based and Evolutionary Theories of the Firm,* ed. C. Montgomery (Boston: Kluwer Academic Publishers, 1995), pp. 251–268.

8. D. Teece, G. Pisano, and A. Shuen, "Dynamic Capabilities and Strategic Management," *Strategic Management Journal* 18, no. 7 (1997); K. Eisenhardt and J. Martin, "Dynamic Capabilities: What Are They?" *Strategic Management Journal* 21, nos. 10–11 (2000); M. Zollo and S. Winter, "Deliberate Learning and the Evolution of Dynamic Capabilities," *Organization Science* 13 (2002); C. Helfat et al., *Dynamic Capabilities: Understanding Strategic Change in Organizations* (Malden, MA: Blackwell, 2007).

9. W. Powell, K. Koput, and L. Smith-Doerr, "Interorganizational Collaboration and the Locus of Innovation," *Administrative Science Quarterly* 41, no. 1 (1996).

10. M. Peteraf, "The Cornerstones of Competitive Advantage: A Resource-Based View," *Strategic Management Journal,* March 1993, pp. 179–191.

11. Michael E. Porter, *Competitive Advantage* (New York: Free Press, 1985).

12. Gregory H. Watson, *Strategic Benchmarking: How to Rate Your Company's Performance Against the World's Best* (New York: John Wiley & Sons, 1993); Robert C. Camp, *Benchmarking: The Search for Industry Best Practices That Lead to Superior Performance* (Milwaukee: ASQC Quality Press, 1989); Christopher E. Bogan and Michael J. English, *Benchmarking for Best Practices: Winning through Innovative Adaptation* (New York: McGraw-Hill, 1994); Dawn Iacobucci and Christie Nordhielm, "Creative Benchmarking," *Harvard Business Review* 78, no. 6 (November–December 2000).

13. www.businessdictionary.com/definition/best-practice.html (accessed June 5, 2017).

14. M. Hegert and D. Morris, "Accounting Data for Value Chain Analysis," *Strategic Management Journal* 10 (1989); Robin Cooper and Robert S. Kaplan, "Measure Costs Right: Make the Right Decisions," *Harvard Business Review* 66, no. 5 (September–October 1988); John K. Shank and Vijay Govindarajan, *Strategic Cost Management* (New York: Free Press, 1993).

15. Michael E. Porter, "Clusters and the New Economics of Competition," *Harvard Business Review* 76, no. 6 (November–December 1998).

16. Reuben E. Stone, "Leading a Supply Chain Turnaround," *Harvard Business Review* 82, no. 10 (October 2004).

5

THE FIVE GENERIC COMPETITIVE STRATEGIES

LEARNING OBJECTIVES

After reading this chapter, you should be able to:

LO5-1 Understand what distinguishes each of the five generic strategies and why some of these strategies work better in certain kinds of industry and competitive conditions than in others.

LO5-2 Explain the major avenues for achieving a competitive advantage based on lower costs.

LO5-3 Explain the major avenues for developing a competitive advantage based on differentiating a company's product or service offering from the offerings of rivals.

LO5-4 Recognize the attributes of a best-cost provider strategy—a hybrid of low-cost provider and differentiation strategies.

A company can employ any of several basic approaches to competing successfully and gaining a competitive advantage, but they all involve giving buyers what they perceive as superior value compared to the offerings of rival sellers. A superior value proposition can be based on offering a good product at a lower price, a superior product that is worth paying more for, or a best-value offering that represents an attractive combination of price, features, quality, service, and other appealing attributes.

This chapter describes the *five generic competitive strategy options* for building competitive advantage and delivering superior value to customers. Which of the five to employ is a company's first and foremost choice in crafting an overall strategy and beginning its quest for competitive advantage.

The Five Generic Competitive Strategies

LO5-1   Understand what distinguishes each of the five generic strategies and why some of these strategies work better in certain kinds of industry and competitive conditions than in others.

A company's **competitive strategy** *deals exclusively with the specifics of management's game plan for competing successfully*—its specific efforts to please customers, strengthen its market position, counter the maneuvers of rivals, respond to shifting market conditions, and achieve a particular competitive advantage. The chances are remote that any two companies—even companies in the same industry—will employ competitive strategies that are exactly alike. However, when one strips away the details to get at the real substance, the two biggest factors that distinguish

> **CORE CONCEPT**
>
> A **competitive strategy** concerns the specifics of management's game plan for competing successfully and securing a competitive advantage over rivals in the marketplace.

one competitive strategy from another boil down to (1) whether a company's market target is broad or narrow, and (2) whether the company is pursuing a competitive advantage linked to lower costs or differentiation. These two factors give rise to the five competitive strategy options shown below and in Figure 5.1.[1]

1. *A low-cost provider strategy*—striving to achieve lower overall costs than rivals and appealing to a broad spectrum of customers, usually by underpricing rivals

2. *A broad differentiation strategy*—seeking to differentiate the company's product or service from rivals' in ways that will appeal to a broad spectrum of buyers

3. *A focused low-cost strategy*—concentrating on a narrow buyer segment (or market niche) and outcompeting rivals by having lower costs than rivals and thus being able to serve niche members at a lower price

4. *A focused differentiation strategy*—concentrating on a narrow buyer segment (or market niche) and outcompeting rivals by offering niche members customized attributes that meet their tastes and requirements better than rivals' products

5. *A best-cost provider strategy*—giving customers more value for the money by satisfying buyers' expectations on key quality/features/performance/service attributes while beating their price expectations. This option is a *hybrid* strategy that blends elements of low-cost provider and differentiation strategies; the aim is to have the lowest (best) costs and prices among sellers offering products with comparable differentiating attributes.

The remainder of this chapter explores the ins and outs of the five generic competitive strategies and how they differ.

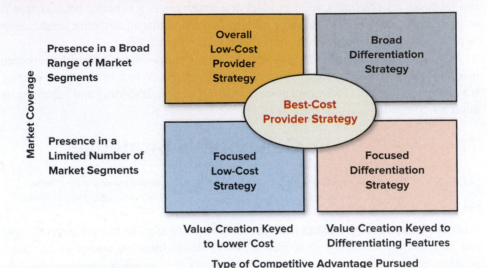

FIGURE 5.1

The Five Generic Competitive Strategies

Source: This is an author-expanded version of a three-strategy classification discussed in Michael E. Porter, *Competitive Strategy* (New York: Free Press, 1980), pp. 35–40.

Low-Cost Provider Strategies

 Explain the major avenues for achieving a competitive advantage based on lower costs.

Striving to be the industry's overall low-cost provider is a powerful competitive approach in markets with many price-sensitive buyers. A company achieves low-cost leadership when it becomes the industry's lowest-cost provider rather than just being one of perhaps several competitors with low costs. Successful low-cost providers boast meaningfully lower costs than rivals, but not necessarily the absolutely lowest possible cost. In striving for a cost advantage over rivals, managers must include features and services that buyers consider essential. A product offering that is too frills-free can be viewed by consumers as offering little value, regardless of its pricing.

> **CORE CONCEPT**
>
> A **low-cost leader**'s basis for competitive advantage is lower overall costs than competitors'. Success in achieving a low-cost edge over rivals comes from eliminating and/or curbing "nonessential" activities and/or outmanaging rivals in performing essential activities.

A company has two options for translating a low-cost advantage over rivals into attractive profit performance. Option 1 is to use the lower-cost edge to underprice competitors and attract price-sensitive buyers in great enough numbers to increase total profits. Option 2 is to maintain the present price, be content with the present market share, and use the lower-cost edge to earn a higher profit margin on each unit sold, thereby raising the firm's total profits and overall return on investment.

The Two Major Avenues for Achieving Low-Cost Leadership

To achieve a low-cost edge over rivals, a firm's cumulative costs across its overall value chain must be lower than competitors' cumulative costs. There are two major avenues for accomplishing this:[2]

1. Performing essential value chain activities more cost-effectively than rivals.
2. Revamping the firm's overall value chain to eliminate or bypass some cost-producing activities.

Cost-Efficient Management of Value Chain Activities For a company to do a more cost-efficient job of managing its value chain than rivals, managers must launch a concerted, ongoing effort to ferret out cost-saving opportunities in every part of the value chain. No activity can escape cost-saving scrutiny, and all company personnel must be expected to use their talents and ingenuity to come up with innovative and effective ways to keep costs down. Particular attention needs to be paid to **cost drivers,** which are factors that have an especially strong effect on the costs of a company's value chain activities. The number of products in a company's product line, its capacity utilization, the type of components used in the assembly of its products, and the extent of its employee benefits package are all factors affecting the company's overall cost position. Figure 5.2 shows the most important cost drivers. Cost-saving approaches that demonstrate effective management of the cost drivers in a company's value chain include:

> **CORE CONCEPT**
>
> A **cost driver** is a factor having a strong effect on the cost of a company's value chain activities and cost structure.

- *Striving to capture all available economies of scale.* Economies of scale stem from an ability to lower unit costs by increasing the scale of operation. For example, Anheuser-Busch InBev SA/NA was able to capture scale economies with its $5 million SuperBowl ad in 2019 because the cost could be distributed over the millions of cases of Budweiser and Bud Light sold that year.

- *Taking full advantage of experience and learning-curve effects.* The cost of performing an activity can decline over time as the learning and experience of company personnel build.

- *Trying to operate facilities at full capacity.* Whether a company is able to operate at or near full capacity has a big impact on unit costs when its value chain contains activities associated with substantial fixed costs. Higher rates of capacity utilization allow depreciation and other fixed costs to be spread over a larger unit volume, thereby lowering fixed costs per unit.

- *Substituting lower-cost inputs whenever there is little or no sacrifice in product quality or product performance.* If the costs of certain raw materials and parts are "too high," a company can switch to using lower-cost alternatives when they exist.

- *Employing advanced production technology and process design to improve overall efficiency.* Often production costs can be cut by utilizing design for manufacture (DFM) procedures and computer-assisted design (CAD) techniques that enable more integrated and efficient production methods, investing in highly automated robotic production technology, and shifting to production processes that enable manufacturing multiple versions of a product as cost efficiently as mass producing a single version.

Important Cost Drivers in a Company's Value Chain

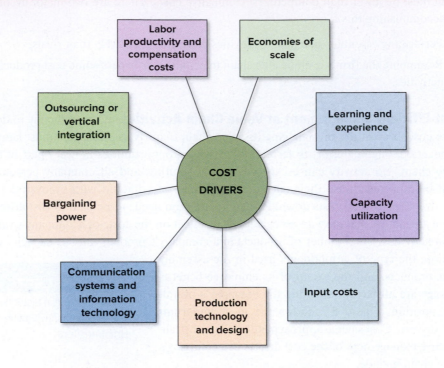

Source: Adapted from M. Porter, *The Competitive Advantage: Creating and Sustaining Superior Performance* (New York: Free Press, 1985).

A number of companies are ardent users of total quality management systems, business process reengineering, Six Sigma methodology, and other business process management techniques that aim at boosting efficiency and reducing costs.

- *Using communication systems and information technology to achieve operating efficiencies.* For example, sharing data and production schedules with suppliers, coupled with the use of enterprise resource planning (ERP) and manufacturing execution system (MES) software, can reduce parts inventories, trim production times, and lower labor requirements.

- *Using the company's bargaining power vis-à-vis suppliers to gain concessions.* A company may have sufficient bargaining clout with suppliers to win price discounts on large-volume purchases or realize other cost savings.

- *Being alert to the cost advantages of outsourcing and vertical integration.* Outsourcing the performance of certain value chain activities can be more economical than performing them in-house if outside specialists, by virtue of their expertise and volume, can perform the activities at lower cost.

- *Pursuing ways to boost labor productivity and lower overall compensation costs.* A company can economize on labor costs by using incentive compensation systems that promote high productivity, installing labor-saving equipment, shifting production from geographic areas where pay scales are high to geographic areas where pay scales are low, and avoiding the use of union labor where possible (because costly work rules can stifle productivity and because of union demands for above-market pay scales and costly fringe benefits).

Revamping the Value Chain   Dramatic cost advantages can often emerge from reengineering the company's value chain in ways that eliminate costly work steps and bypass certain cost-producing value chain activities. Such value chain revamping can include:

- *Selling directly to consumers and cutting out the activities and costs of distributors and dealers.* To circumvent the need for distributors–dealers, a company can (1) create its own direct sales force (which adds the costs of maintaining and supporting a sales force but may be cheaper than utilizing independent distributors and dealers to access buyers), and/or (2) conduct sales operations at the company's website (costs for website operations and shipping may be a substantially cheaper way to make sales to customers than going through distributor–dealer channels). Costs in the wholesale/retail portions of the value chain frequently represent 35 to 50 percent of the price final consumers pay, so establishing a direct sales force or selling online may offer big cost savings.

- *Streamlining operations by eliminating low-value-added or unnecessary work steps and activities.* Southwest Airlines has achieved considerable cost savings by reconfiguring the traditional value chain of commercial airlines to eliminate low-value-added activities and work steps. Southwest does not offer assigned seating, baggage transfer to connecting airlines, or first-class seating and service, thereby eliminating all the cost-producing activities associated with these features. Also, the company's carefully designed point-to-point route system minimizes connections, delays, and total trip time for passengers, allowing about 75 percent of Southwest passengers to fly nonstop to their destinations and at the same time helping reduce Southwest's costs for flight operations.

- *Improving supply chain efficiency to reduce materials handling and shipping costs.* Collaborating with suppliers to streamline the ordering and purchasing process, to reduce inventory carrying costs via just-in-time inventory practices, to economize on shipping and materials handling, and to ferret out other cost-saving opportunities is a much-used approach to cost reduction. A company with a distinctive competence in cost-efficient supply chain management, such as BASF (the world's leading chemical company), can sometimes achieve a sizable cost advantage over less adept rivals.

Concepts & Connections 5.1 describes the path that Vanguard has followed in achieving its position as the low-cost leader in the investment management industry.

When a Low-Cost Provider Strategy Works Best

A competitive strategy predicated on low-cost leadership is particularly powerful when:

1. *Price competition among rival sellers is especially vigorous.* Low-cost providers are in the best position to compete offensively on the basis of price and to survive price wars.

2. *The products of rival sellers are essentially identical and are readily available from several sellers.* Commoditylike products and/or ample supplies set the stage for lively price competition; in such markets, it is the less efficient, higher-cost companies that are most vulnerable.

CONCEPTS & CONNECTIONS 5.1

VANGUARD'S PATH TO BECOMING THE LOW-COST LEADER IN INVESTMENT MANAGEMENT

Vanguard is now one of the world's largest investment management companies. It became an industry giant by leading the way in low-cost passive index investing. In active trading, an investment manager is compensated for making an educated decision on which stocks to sell and which to buy. This incurs both transactional and management fees. In contrast, passive index portfolios aim to mirror the movements of a major market index like the S&P 500, Dow Jones Industrial Average, or NASDAQ. Passive portfolios incur fewer fees and can be managed with lower operating costs. A measure used to compare operating costs in this industry is known as the expense ratio, which is the percentage of an investment that goes toward expenses. In 2018, Vanguard's expense ratio was less than 18 percent of the industry's average expense ratio. Vanguard was the first to capitalize on what was at the time an underappreciated fact: Over long horizons, well-managed index funds, with their lower costs and fees, typically outperform their actively trading competitors.

Vanguard provides low-cost investment options for its clients in several ways. By creating funds that track index(es) over a long horizon, the client does not incur transaction and management fees normally charged in actively managed funds. Possibly more important, Vanguard was created with a unique client-owner structure. When you invest with Vanguard you become an owner of Vanguard. This structure effectively cuts out traditional shareholders who seek to share in profits. Under client ownership, any returns in excess of operating costs are returned to the clients/investors.

Vanguard keeps its costs low in several other ways. One notable way is its focus on its employees and organizational structure. The company prides itself on low turnover rates (8 percent) and very flat organizational structure. In several instances Vanguard has been able to capitalize on being a fast follower. They launched several product lines after their competitors introduced those products. Being a fast follower allowed them to develop superior products and reach scale more quickly—both further lowering their cost structure.

The low-cost structure has not come at the expense of performance. Vanguard now has 370 funds, over 20 million investors, has surpassed $4.5 trillion in AUM (assets under management), and is growing faster than all its competitors combined. When *Money* published its January 2018 list of recommended investment funds, 42 out of 100 products listed were Vanguard funds.

Vanguard's low-cost strategy has been so successful that industry experts now refer to The Vanguard Effect. This refers to the pressure that this investment management giant has put on competitors to lower their fees in order to compete with Vanguard's low-cost value proposition.

Note: Developed with Vedrana B. Greatorex.

Sources: https://www.nytimes.com/2017/04/14/business/mutfund/vanguard-mutual-index-funds-growth.html; https://investor.vanguard.com; and A. Sunderam, L. Viceira, and A. Ciechanover, *The Vanguard Group, Inc. in 2015: Celebrating 40*, HBS No. 9-216-026 (Boston, MA: Harvard Business School Publishing, 2016).

Kristoffer Tripplaar/Alamy Stock Photo

3. *There are few ways to achieve product differentiation that have value to buyers.* When the product or service differences between brands do not matter much to buyers, buyers nearly always shop the market for the best price.

4. *Buyers incur low costs in switching their purchases from one seller to another.* Low switching costs give buyers the flexibility to shift purchases to lower-priced sellers having equally good products. A low-cost leader is well positioned to use low price to induce its customers not to switch to rival brands.

As a rule, the more price-sensitive buyers are, the more appealing a low-cost strategy becomes. A low-cost company's ability to set the industry's price floor and still earn a profit erects protective barriers around its market position.

Pitfalls to Avoid in Pursuing a Low-Cost Provider Strategy

Perhaps the biggest pitfall of a low-cost provider strategy is getting carried away with *overly aggressive price cutting* and ending up with lower, rather than higher, profitability. A low-cost/low-price advantage results in superior profitability only if (1) prices are cut by less than the size of the cost advantage or (2) the added volume is large enough to bring in a bigger total profit despite lower margins per unit sold. Thus, a company with a 5 percent cost advantage cannot cut prices 20 percent, end up with a volume gain of only 10 percent, and still expect to earn higher profits!

A second big pitfall is *relying on an approach to reduce costs that can be easily copied by rivals.* The value of a cost advantage depends on its sustainability. Sustainability, in turn, hinges on whether the company achieves its cost advantage in ways difficult for rivals to replicate or match. If rivals find it relatively easy or inexpensive to imitate the leader's low-cost methods, then the leader's advantage will be too short-lived to yield a valuable edge in the marketplace.

A third pitfall is becoming *too fixated on cost reduction.* Low costs cannot be pursued so zealously that a firm's offering ends up being too features-poor to gain the interest of buyers. Furthermore, a company driving hard to push its costs down has to guard against misreading or ignoring increased buyer preferences for added features or declining buyer price sensitivity. Even if these mistakes are avoided, a low-cost competitive approach still carries risk. Cost-saving technological breakthroughs or process improvements by rival firms can nullify a low-cost leader's hard-won position.

Broad Differentiation Strategies

Differentiation strategies are attractive whenever buyers' needs and preferences are too diverse to be fully satisfied by a standardized product or service. A company attempting to succeed through differentiation must study buyers' needs and behavior carefully to learn what buyers think has value and what they are willing to pay for. Then the company must include these desirable features to clearly set itself apart from rivals lacking such product or service attributes.

> **CORE CONCEPT**
>
> The essence of a **broad differentiation strategy** is to offer unique product or service attributes that a wide range of buyers find appealing and worth paying for.

Successful differentiation allows a firm to:

- Command a premium price, and/or
- Increase unit sales (because additional buyers are won over by the differentiating features), and/or
- Gain buyer loyalty to its brand (because some buyers are strongly attracted to the differentiating features and bond with the company and its products).

Differentiation enhances profitability whenever the extra price the product commands outweighs the added costs of achieving the differentiation. Company differentiation strategies fail when buyers do not value the brand's uniqueness and/or when a company's approach to differentiation is easily copied or matched by its rivals.

Approaches to Differentiation

LO5-3   Explain the major avenues for developing a competitive advantage based on differentiating a company's product or service offering from the offerings of rivals.

Companies can pursue differentiation from many angles: a unique taste (Red Bull, Doritos), multiple features (Microsoft Office, Apple Watch), wide selection and one-stop shopping (Home Depot, Amazon.com), superior service (Ritz-Carlton, Nordstrom), spare parts availability (Caterpillar guarantees 48-hour spare parts delivery to any customer anywhere in the world or else the part is furnished free), engineering design and performance (Mercedes-Benz, BMW), luxury and prestige (Rolex, Gucci, Chanel), product reliability (Whirlpool and Bosch in large home appliances), quality manufacturing (Michelin in tires, Toyota and Honda in automobiles), technological leadership (3M Corporation in bonding and coating products), a full range of services (Charles Schwab in stock brokerage), and a complete line of products (Campbell soups, Frito-Lay snack foods).

The most appealing approaches to differentiation are those that are hard or expensive for rivals to duplicate. Resourceful competitors can, in time, clone almost any product or feature or attribute. If Toyota introduces lane departure warning or adaptive cruise control features, so can Ford and Honda. Socially complex intangible attributes, such as company reputation, long-standing relationships with buyers, and image are much harder to imitate.

Differentiation that creates switching costs that lock in buyers also provides a route to sustainable advantage. For example, if a buyer makes a substantial investment in mastering usage of a product, that buyer is less likely to switch to a competitor's system. This has kept many users from switching away from Microsoft Office products, despite the efforts of rivals to develop and market superior performing software applications. As a rule, differentiation yields a longer-lasting and more profitable competitive edge when it is based on product innovation, technical superiority, product quality and reliability, comprehensive customer service, and unique competitive capabilities. Such differentiating attributes tend to be tough for rivals to copy or offset profitably, and buyers widely perceive them as having value.

> Easy-to-copy differentiating features cannot produce sustainable competitive advantage; differentiation based on hard-to-copy competencies and capabilities tends to be more sustainable.

Managing the Value Chain in Ways That Enhance Differentiation

Success in employing a differentiation strategy results from management's ability to offer superior customer value through the addition of product/service attributes and features that differentiate a company's offering from the offerings of rivals. Differentiation opportunities can exist in activities all along an industry's value chain and particularly in activities and factors that meaningfully impact customer value. Such activities are referred to as **value drivers**—analogous to cost drivers—but have a high impact on differentiation rather than on a company's overall cost position. Figure 5.3 lists important uniqueness drivers found in a company's value chain. Ways that managers can enhance differentiation through the systematic management of uniqueness drivers include the following:

CORE CONCEPT

A **value driver** is a value chain activity or factor that can have a strong effect on customer value and creating differentiation.

FIGURE 5.3

FIGURE 5.3

Important Value Drivers Creating a Differentiation Advantage

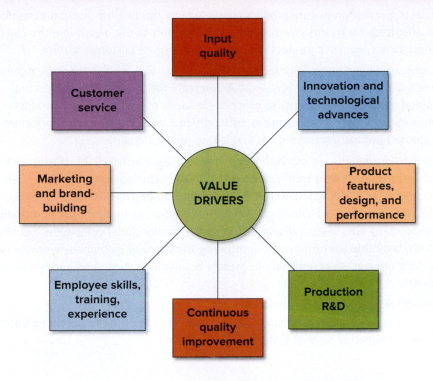

Source: Adapted from M. Porter, *The Competitive Advantage: Creating and Sustaining Superior Performance* (New York: Free Press, 1985).

- *Seeking out high-quality inputs.* Input quality can ultimately spill over to affect the performance or quality of the company's end product. Starbucks, for example, gets high ratings on its coffees partly because of its very strict specifications for coffee beans purchased from suppliers.

- *Striving for innovation and technological advances.* Successful innovation is the route to more frequent first-on-the-market victories and is a powerful differentiator. If the innovation proves hard to replicate, through patent protection or other means, it can provide a company with a first-mover advantage that is sustainable.

- *Creating superior product features, design, and performance.* The physical and functional features of a product have a big influence on differentiation. Styling and appearance are big differentiating factors in the apparel and motor vehicle industries. Graphics resolution and processing speed matter in video game consoles. Most companies employing broad differentiation strategies make a point of incorporating innovative and novel features in their product/service offering, especially those that improve performance.

- *Investing in production-related R&D activities.* Engaging in production R&D may permit custom-order manufacture at an efficient cost, provide wider product variety and selection, or improve product quality. Many manufacturers have developed flexible manufacturing systems that allow different models and product versions to be made on the same assembly line. Being able to provide buyers with made-to-order products can be a potent differentiating capability.

- *Pursuing continuous quality improvement.* Quality control processes reduce product defects, prevent premature product failure, extend product life, make it economical to offer longer warranty coverage, improve economy of use, result in more end-user convenience, enhance product appearance, or improve customer service.

- *Emphasizing human resource management activities that improve the skills, expertise, and knowledge of company personnel.* A company with high-caliber intellectual capital often has the capacity to generate the kinds of ideas that drive product innovation, technological advances, better product design and product performance, improved production techniques, and higher product quality.

- *Increasing emphasis on marketing and brand-building activities.* Marketing and advertising can have a tremendous effect on the value perceived by buyers and therefore their willingness to pay more for the company's offerings. A highly skilled and competent sales force, effectively communicated product information, eye-catching ads, in-store displays, and special promotional campaigns can all cast a favorable light on the differentiating attributes of a company's product/service offering and contribute to greater brand-name awareness and brand-name power.

- *Improving customer service or adding additional services.* Better customer service, in areas such as delivery, returns, and repair, can be as important in creating differentiation as superior product features.

Revamping the Value Chain System to Increase Differentiation Just as pursuing a cost advantage can involve the entire value chain system, the same is true for a differentiation advantage. As was discussed in Chapter 4, activities performed upstream by suppliers or downstream by distributors and retailers can have a meaningful effect on customers' perceptions of a company's offerings and its value proposition. Approaches to enhancing differentiation through changes in the value chain system include:

- *Coordinating with channel allies to enhance customer value.* Coordinating with downstream partners such as distributors, dealers, brokers, and retailers can contribute to differentiation in a variety of ways. Many manufacturers work directly with retailers on in-store displays and signage, joint advertising campaigns, and providing sales clerks with product knowledge and tips on sales techniques—all to enhance customer buying experiences. Companies can work with distributors and shippers to ensure fewer "out-of-stock" annoyances, quicker delivery to customers, more-accurate order filling, lower shipping costs, and a variety of shipping choices to customers.

- *Coordinating with suppliers to better address customer needs.* Collaborating with suppliers can also be a powerful route to a more effective differentiation strategy. This is particularly true for companies that engage only in assembly operations, such as Dell in PCs and Ducati in motorcycles. Close coordination with suppliers can also enhance differentiation by speeding up new product development cycles or speeding delivery to end customers. Strong relationships with suppliers can also mean that the company's supply requirements are prioritized when industry supply is insufficient to meet overall demand.

Delivering Superior Value via a Differentiation Strategy

While it is easy enough to grasp that a successful differentiation strategy must offer value in ways unmatched by rivals, a big issue in crafting a differentiation strategy is deciding what is valuable to customers. Typically, value can be delivered to customers in three basic ways.

1. *Include product attributes and user features that lower the buyer's costs.* Commercial buyers value products that can reduce their cost of doing business. For example, making a company's product more economical for a buyer to use can be done by reducing the buyer's raw materials waste (providing cut-to-size components), reducing a buyer's inventory requirements (providing just-in-time deliveries), increasing product reliability to lower a buyer's repair and maintenance costs, and providing free technical support. Similarly, consumers find value in differentiating features that will reduce their expenses. Rising costs for gasoline prices have spurred the efforts of motor vehicle manufacturers worldwide to introduce models with better fuel economy.

2. *Incorporate tangible features that improve product performance.* Commercial buyers and consumers alike value higher levels of performance in many types of products. Product reliability, output, durability, convenience, and ease of use are aspects of product performance that differentiate products offered to buyers. Tablet computer manufacturers are currently in a race to develop next-generation tablets with the functionality and processing power to capture market share from rivals and cannibalize the laptop computer market.

3. *Incorporate intangible features that enhance buyer satisfaction in noneconomic ways.* Toyota's Prius appeals to environmentally conscious motorists who wish to help reduce global carbon dioxide emissions. Bentley, Ralph Lauren, Louis Vuitton, Tiffany, Cartier, and Rolex have differentiation-based competitive advantages linked to buyer desires for status, image, prestige, upscale fashion, superior craftsmanship, and the finer things in life.

> Differentiation can be based on *tangible* or *intangible* features and attributes.

Perceived Value and the Importance of Signaling Value

The price premium commanded by a differentiation strategy reflects *the value actually delivered* to the buyer and *the value perceived* by the buyer. The value of certain differentiating features is rather easy for buyers to detect, but in some instances, buyers may have trouble assessing what their experience with the product will be. Successful differentiators go to great lengths to make buyers knowledgeable about a product's value and incorporate signals of value such as attractive packaging, extensive ad campaigns, the quality of brochures and sales presentations, the seller's list of customers, the length of time the firm has been in business, and the professionalism, appearance, and personality of the seller's employees. Such signals of value may be as important as actual value (1) when the nature of differentiation is subjective or hard to quantify, (2) when buyers are making a first-time purchase, (3) when repurchase is infrequent, and (4) when buyers are unsophisticated.

When a Differentiation Strategy Works Best

Differentiation strategies tend to work best in market circumstances where:

1. *Buyer needs and uses of the product are diverse.* Diverse buyer preferences allow industry rivals to set themselves apart with product attributes that appeal to particular buyers.

For instance, the diversity of consumer preferences for menu selection, ambience, pricing, and customer service gives restaurants exceptionally wide latitude in creating differentiated concepts. Other industries offering opportunities for differentiation based upon diverse buyer needs and uses include magazine publishing, automobile manufacturing, footwear, kitchen appliances, and computers.

2. *There are many ways to differentiate the product or service that have value to buyers.* Industries that allow competitors to add features to product attributes are well suited to differentiation strategies. For example, hotel chains can differentiate on such features as location, size of room, range of guest services, in-hotel dining, and the quality and luxuriousness of bedding and furnishings. Similarly, cosmetics producers are able to differentiate based upon prestige and image, formulations that fight the signs of aging, UV light protection, exclusivity of retail locations, the inclusion of antioxidants and natural ingredients, or prohibitions against animal testing.

3. *Few rival firms are following a similar differentiation approach.* The best differentiation approaches involve trying to appeal to buyers on the basis of attributes that rivals are not emphasizing. A differentiator encounters less head-to-head rivalry when it goes its own separate way to create uniqueness and does not try to outdifferentiate rivals on the very same attributes.

4. *Technological change is fast-paced and competition revolves around rapidly evolving product features.* Rapid product innovation and frequent introductions of next-version products heighten buyer interest and provide space for companies to pursue distinct differentiating paths. In smartphones, wearable devices, and commercial and hobby drones, competitors are locked into an ongoing battle to set themselves apart by introducing the best next-generation products; companies that fail to come up with new and improved products and distinctive performance features quickly lose out in the marketplace.

Pitfalls to Avoid in Pursuing a Differentiation Strategy

Differentiation strategies can fail for any of several reasons. *A differentiation strategy keyed to product or service attributes that are easily and quickly copied is always suspect.* Rapid imitation means that no rival achieves meaningful differentiation, because whatever new feature one firm introduces that strikes the fancy of buyers is almost immediately added by rivals. This is why a firm must search out sources of uniqueness that are time-consuming or burdensome for rivals to match if it hopes to use differentiation to win a sustainable competitive edge over rivals.

Differentiation strategies can also falter when buyers see little value in the unique attributes of a company's product. Thus, even if a company sets the attributes of its brand apart from its rivals' brands, its strategy can fail because of trying to differentiate on the basis of something that does not deliver adequate value to buyers. Any time many potential buyers look at a company's differentiated product offering and conclude "so what," the company's differentiation strategy is in deep trouble; buyers will likely decide the product is not worth the extra price, and sales will be disappointingly low.

Overspending on efforts to differentiate is a strategy flaw that can erode profitability. Company efforts to achieve differentiation nearly always raise costs. The trick to profitable differentiation is either to keep the costs of achieving differentiation below the price premium the differentiating attributes can command in the marketplace or to offset thinner profit margins by selling enough additional units to increase total profits. If a company goes overboard in pursuing costly differentiation, it could be saddled with unacceptably thin profit margins or even losses. The need to contain differentiation costs is why many companies add little touches of differentiation that add to buyer satisfaction but are inexpensive to institute.

Other common pitfalls and mistakes in crafting a differentiation strategy include:

- *Failing to open up meaningful gaps in quality or service or performance features vis-à-vis the products of rivals.* Trivial differences between rivals' product offerings may not be visible or important to buyers. In markets where differentiators achieve only weak differentiation, customer loyalty is weak, the costs of brand switching are low, and competitors end up chasing the same buyers with much the same product offerings.

- *Over-differentiating so that product quality or service levels exceed buyers' needs.* A dazzling array of features and options not only drives up product price but also runs the risk that many buyers will conclude that a less deluxe and lower-priced brand is a better value since they have little occasion to use the deluxe attributes.

- *Trying to charge too high a price premium.* Even if buyers view certain extras or deluxe features as "nice to have," they may still conclude that the added benefit or luxury is not worth the price differential over that of lesser differentiated products.

A low-cost provider strategy can always defeat a differentiation strategy when buyers are satisfied with a basic product and do not think "extra" attributes are worth a higher price.

Focused (or Market Niche) Strategies

What sets focused strategies apart from low-cost leadership or broad differentiation strategies is a concentration on a narrow piece of the total market. The targeted segment, or niche, can be defined by geographic uniqueness or by special product attributes that appeal only to niche members. The advantages of focusing a company's entire competitive effort on a single market niche are considerable, especially for smaller and medium-sized companies that may lack the breadth and depth of resources to tackle going after a national customer base with a "something for everyone" lineup of models, styles, and product selection.

Community Coffee, the largest family-owned specialty coffee retailer in the United States, has a geographic focus on the state of Louisiana and communities across the Gulf of Mexico. Community holds only a small share of the national coffee market but has recorded sales in excess of $100 million and has won a strong following in the 20-state region where its coffee is distributed. Examples of firms that concentrate on a well-defined market niche keyed to a particular product or buyer segment include Zipcar (hourly and daily car rental in urban areas), Airbnb and HomeAway (by owner lodging rental), Fox News Channel and HGTV (cable TV), Blue Nile (online jewelry), Tesla Motors (electric cars), and CGA, Inc. (a specialist in providing insurance to cover the cost of lucrative hole-in-one prizes at golf tournaments). Microbreweries, local bakeries, bed-and-breakfast inns, and retail boutiques have also scaled their operations to serve narrow or local customer segments.

A Focused Low-Cost Strategy

A focused strategy based on low cost aims at securing a competitive advantage by serving buyers in the target market niche at a lower cost and a lower price than rival competitors. This strategy has considerable attraction when a firm can lower costs significantly by limiting its customer base to a well-defined buyer segment. The avenues to achieving a cost advantage over rivals also serving the target market niche are the same as for low-cost leadership—outmanage rivals in keeping the costs to a bare minimum and searching for innovative ways to bypass or reduce nonessential activities. The only real difference between a low-cost provider strategy and a focused low-cost strategy is the size of the buyer group to which a company is appealing.

Focused low-cost strategies are fairly common. Producers of private-label goods are able to achieve low costs in product development, marketing, distribution, and advertising by concentrating on making generic items similar to name-brand merchandise and selling directly to retail chains wanting a low-priced store brand. The Perrigo Company has become a leading manufacturer of over-the-counter health care and self-care products with 2018 sales of more than $4.7 billion by focusing on producing private-label brands for retailers such as Walmart, CVS, Walgreens, Rite Aid, and Safeway. Even though Perrigo does not make branded products, a focused low-cost strategy is appropriate for the makers of branded products as well. Budget motel chains, like Motel 6, Sleep Inn, and Super 8, cater to price-conscious travelers who just want to pay for a clean, no-frills place to spend the night. Concepts & Connections 5.2 describes how Clinícas del Azúcar's focus on lowering the costs of diabetes care is allowing it to address a major health issue in Mexico.

A Focused Differentiation Strategy

Focused differentiation strategies are keyed to offering carefully designed products or services to appeal to the unique preferences and needs of a narrow, well-defined group of buyers (as opposed to a broad differentiation strategy aimed at many buyer groups and market segments). Companies such as Four Seasons Hotels and Resorts in lodging; Molton Brown in bath, body, and beauty products; and Louis Vuitton in leather goods employ successful differentiation-based focused strategies targeted at buyers seeking products and services with world-class attributes. Indeed, most markets contain a buyer segment willing to pay a price premium for the very finest items available, thus opening the strategic window for some competitors to pursue differentiation-based focused strategies aimed at the very top of the market pyramid.

Another successful focused differentiator is "fashion food retailer" Trader Joe's, a 474-store, 43-state chain that is a combination gourmet deli and food warehouse. Customers shop Trader Joe's as much for entertainment as for conventional grocery items; the store stocks out-of-the-ordinary culinary treats such as raspberry salsa, salmon burgers, and jasmine fried rice, as well as the standard goods normally found in supermarkets. What sets Trader Joe's apart is not just its unique combination of food novelties and competitively priced grocery items but also its capability to turn an otherwise mundane grocery excursion into a whimsical treasure hunt that is just plain fun. Concepts & Connections 5.3 describes how Canada Goose has become a popular winter apparel brand with revenues of nearly $300 million in 2016 through its focused differentiation strategy.

When a Focused Low-Cost or Focused Differentiation Strategy Is Viable

A focused strategy aimed at securing a competitive edge based on either low cost or differentiation becomes increasingly attractive as more of the following conditions are met:

- The target market niche is big enough to be profitable and offers good growth potential.

- Industry leaders have chosen not to compete in the niche—focusers can avoid battling head-to-head against the industry's biggest and strongest competitors.

CONCEPTS & CONNECTIONS 5.2

CLINÍCAS DEL AZÚCAR'S FOCUSED LOW-COST STRATEGY

Though diabetes is a manageable condition, it is the leading cause of death in Mexico. Over 14 million adults (14 percent of all adults) suffer from diabetes, 3.5 million cases remain undiagnosed, and more than 80,000 die due to related complications each year. The key driver behind this public health crisis is limited access to affordable, high-quality care. Approximately 90 percent of the population cannot access diabetes care due to financial and time constraints; private care can cost upwards of $1,000 USD per year (approximately 45 percent of Mexico's population has an annual income less than $2,000 USD) while average wait times alone at public clinics surpass five hours. Clinícas del Azúcar (CDA), however, is quickly scaling a solution that uses a focused low-cost strategy to provide affordable and convenient care to low-income patients.

By relentlessly focusing only on the needs of its target population, CDA has reduced the cost of diabetes care by more than 70 percent and clinic visit times by over 80 percent. The key has been the use of proprietary technology and a streamlined care

Rob Marmion/Shutterstock

system. First, CDA leverages evidence-based algorithms to diagnose patients for a fraction of the costs of traditional diagnostic tests. Similarly, its mobile outreach significantly reduces the costs of supporting patients in managing their diabetes after leaving CDA facilities. Second, CDA has redesigned the care process to implement a streamlined "patient process flow" that eliminates the need for multiple referrals to other care providers and brings together the necessary professionals and equipment into one facility. Consequently, CDA has become a one-stop shop for diabetes care, providing every aspect of diabetes treatment under one roof.

The bottom line: CDA's cost structure allows it to keep its prices for diabetes treatment very low, saving patients both time and money. Patients choose from three different care packages, ranging from preventive to comprehensive care, paying an annual fee that runs between approximately $70 and $200 USD. Given this increase in affordability and convenience, CDA estimates that it has saved its patients over $2 million USD in medical costs and will soon increase access to affordable, high-quality care for 10 to 80 percent of the population. These results have attracted investment from major funders including Endeavor, Echoing Green, and the Clinton Global Initiative. As a result, CDA and others expect CDA to grow from 5 clinics serving approximately 5,000 patients to more than 50 clinics serving over 100,000 patients throughout Mexico by 2020.

Note: Developed with David B. Washer.

Sources: www.clinicasdelazucar.com; "Funding Social Enterprises Report," Echoing Green, June 2014; Jude Webber, "Mexico Sees Poverty Climb Despite Rise in Incomes," *Financial Times,* July 2015, www.ft.com/intl/cms/s/3/98460bbc-31e1-11e5-8873775ba7c2ea3d.html#axzz3zz8grtec; and "Javier Lozano," Schwab Foundation for Social Entrepreneurship, 2016, www.schwabfound.org/content/javier-lozano.

- It is costly or difficult for multisegment competitors to meet the specialized needs of niche buyers and at the same time satisfy the expectations of mainstream customers.

- The industry has many different niches and segments, thereby allowing a focuser to pick a niche suited to its resource strengths and capabilities.

- Few, if any, rivals are attempting to specialize in the same target segment.

The Risks of a Focused Low-Cost or Focused Differentiation Strategy

Focusing carries several risks. The *first major risk* is the chance that competitors will find effective ways to match the focused firm's capabilities in serving the target niche. In the lodging business, large chains such as Marriott and Hilton have launched

CONCEPTS & CONNECTIONS 5.3

CANADA GOOSE'S FOCUSED DIFFERENTIATION STRATEGY

Open up a winter edition of *People* and you will probably see photos of a celebrity sporting a Canada Goose parka. Recognizable by a distinctive red, white, and blue arm patch, the brand's parkas have been spotted on movie stars like Emma Stone and Bradley Cooper, on New York City streets, and on the cover of *Sports Illustrated*. Lately, Canada Goose has become extremely successful thanks to a focused differentiation strategy that enables it to thrive within its niche in the $1.2 trillion fashion industry. By targeting upscale buyers and providing a uniquely functional and stylish jacket, Canada Goose can charge nearly $1,000 per jacket and never need to put its products on sale.

While Canada Goose was founded in 1957, its recent transition to a focused differentiation strategy allowed it to rise to the top of the luxury parka market. In 2001, CEO Dani Reiss took control of the company and made two key decisions. First, he cut private-label and non-outerwear production in order to focus

on the branded outerwear portion of Canada Goose's business. Second, Reiss decided to remain in Canada despite many North American competitors moving production to Asia to increase profit margins. Fortunately for him, these two strategy decisions have led directly to the company's current success. While other luxury brands, like Moncler, are priced similarly, no competitor's products fulfill the promise of handling harsh winter weather quite like a Canada Goose "Made in Canada" parka. The Canadian heritage, use of down sourced from rural Canada, real coyote fur (humanely trapped), and promise to provide warmth in minus 25°F temperatures have let Canada Goose break away from the pack when it comes to selling parkas. The company's distinctly Canadian product has made it a hit among buyers, which is reflected in the willingness to pay a steep premium for extremely high-quality and warm winter outerwear.

Since Canada Goose's shift to a focused differentiation strategy, the company has seen a boom in revenue and appeal across the globe. Prior to Reiss's strategic decisions in 2001, Canada Goose had annual revenue of about $3 million. By 2018, the company's revenues had grown to more than $600 million with sales in 50 countries. The strength of the company's strategy allowed it to raise $255 million through a successful IPO in 2017.

Rblfmr/Shutterstock

Note: Developed with Arthur J. Santry.

Sources: Matthew Zeitlin, "Here Are 7 Things We Learned about Canada Goose from Its IPO Filing," *BuzzFeed News,* February 16, 2017, www.cnbc.com; Drake Bennett, "How Canada Goose Parkas Migrated South," *Bloomberg Businessweek,* March 13, 2015, www.bloomberg.com; Hollie Shaw, "Canada Goose's Made-in-Canada Marketing Strategy Translates into Success," *Financial Post,* May 18, 2012, www.financialpost.com; and "The Economic Impact of the Fashion Industry," *The Economist,* June 13, 2015, www.maloney.house.gov; and company website (accessed February 21, 2016).

multibrand strategies that allow them to compete effectively in several lodging segments simultaneously. Hilton has flagship hotels with a full complement of services and amenities that allow it to attract travelers and vacationers going to major resorts; it has Waldorf Astoria, Conrad Hotels & Resorts, Hilton Hotels & Resorts, and DoubleTree hotels that provide deluxe comfort and service to business and leisure travelers; it has Homewood Suites, Embassy Suites, and Home2 Suites designed as a "home away from home" for travelers staying five or more nights; and it has nearly 700 Hilton Garden Inn and 2,100 Hampton by Hilton locations that cater to travelers looking for quality lodging at an "affordable" price. Tru by Hilton is the company's newly introduced brand focused on value-conscious travelers seeking basic accommodations. Hilton has also added Curio Collection, Tapestry Collection, and Canopy by Hilton hotels that offer stylish, distinctive decors and personalized services that appeal to young professionals seeking distinctive lodging alternatives. Multibrand strategies are attractive to large companies such as Hilton precisely because they enable a company to enter a market niche and siphon business away from companies that employ a focus strategy.

A *second risk* of employing a focus strategy is the potential for the preferences and needs of niche members to shift over time toward the product attributes desired by the majority of buyers. An erosion of the differences across buyer segments lowers entry barriers into a focuser's market niche and provides an open invitation for rivals in adjacent segments to begin competing for the focuser's customers. A *third risk* is that the segment may become so attractive it is soon inundated with competitors, intensifying rivalry and splintering segment profits.

Best-Cost Provider Strategies

LO5-4   Recognize the attributes of a best-cost provider strategy—a hybrid of low-cost provider and differentiation strategies.

As Figure 5.1 indicates, **best-cost provider strategies** are a *hybrid* of low-cost provider and differentiation strategies that aim at satisfying buyer expectations on key quality/features/performance/service attributes and beating customer expectations on price. Companies pursuing best-cost strategies aim squarely at the sometimes great mass of value-conscious buyers looking for a good-to-very-good product or service at an economical price. The essence

> **CORE CONCEPT**
>
> **Best-cost provider strategies** are a *hybrid* of low-cost provider and differentiation strategies that aim at satisfying buyer expectations on key quality/features/performance/service attributes and beating customer expectations on price.

of a best-cost provider strategy is giving customers *more value for the money* by satisfying buyer desires for appealing features/performance/quality/service and charging a lower price for these attributes compared to that of rivals with similar-caliber product offerings.[3]

To profitably employ a best-cost provider strategy, a company *must have the capability to incorporate attractive or upscale attributes at a lower cost than rivals.* This capability is contingent on (1) a superior value chain configuration that eliminates or minimizes activities that do not add value, (2) unmatched efficiency in managing essential value chain activities, and (3) core competencies that allow differentiating attributes to be incorporated at a low cost. When a company can incorporate appealing features, good-to-excellent product performance or quality, or more satisfying customer service into its product offering *at a lower cost than that of rivals,* then it enjoys "best-cost" status—it is the low-cost provider of a product or service with *upscale attributes.* A best-cost provider can use its low-cost advantage to underprice rivals whose products or services have similar upscale attributes and still earn attractive profits.

Concepts & Connections 5.4 describes how American Giant has applied the principles of a best-cost provider strategy in producing and marketing its hoodie sweatshirts.

When a Best-Cost Provider Strategy Works Best

A best-cost provider strategy works best in markets where product differentiation is the norm and attractively large numbers of value-conscious buyers can be induced to purchase midrange products rather than the basic products of low-cost producers or the expensive products of top-of-the-line differentiators. A best-cost provider usually needs to position itself near the middle of the market with either a medium-quality product

CONCEPTS & CONNECTIONS 5.4

AMERICAN GIANT'S BEST-COST PROVIDER STRATEGY

Bayard Winthrop, founder and owner of American Giant, set out to make a hoodie like the soft, ultra-thick Navy sweatshirts his dad used to wear in the 1950s. But he also had two other aims: He wanted it to have a more updated look with a tailored fit, and he wanted it produced cost-effectively so that it could be sold at a great price. To accomplish these aims, he designed the sweatshirt with the help of a former industrial engineer from Apple and an internationally renowned pattern maker, rethinking every aspect of sweatshirt design and production along the way. The result was a hoodie differentiated from others on the basis of extreme attention to fabric, fit, construction, and durability. The hoodie is made from heavy-duty cotton that is run through a machine that carefully picks loops of thread out of the fabric to create a thick, combed, ring-spun fleece fabric that feels three times thicker than most sweatshirts. A small amount of spandex paneling along the shoulders and sides creates the fitted look and maintains the shape, keeping the sweatshirt from looking slouchy or sloppy. It has double stitching with strong thread on critical seams to avoid deterioration

David Paul Morris/Bloomberg/Getty Images

and boost durability. The zippers and draw cord are customized to match the sweatshirt's color—an uncommon practice in the business.

American Giant sources yarn from Parkdale, South Carolina, and turns it into cloth at the nearby Carolina Cotton Works. This reduces transport costs, creates a more dependable, durable product that American Giant can easily quality-check, and shortens product turnaround to about a month, lowering inventory costs. This process also enables the company to use a genuine "Made in the USA" label, a perceived quality driver.

American Giant disrupts the traditional, expensive distribution models by having no stores or resellers. Instead, it sells directly to customers from its website, with free two-day shipping and returns. Much of the company's growth comes from word of mouth and a strong public relations effort that promotes the brand in magazines, newspapers, and key business-oriented television programs. American Giant has a robust refer-a-friend program that offers a discount to friends of, and a credit to, current owners. Articles in popular media proclaiming its product "the greatest hoodie ever made" have made demand for its sweatshirts skyrocket.

At $104 for the men's classic pullover, American Giant is not cheap but offers customers value in terms of both price and quality. The price is higher than what one would pay at The Gap or American Apparel and comparable to Levi's, J.Crew, or Banana Republic. But its quality is more on par with high-priced designer brands, while its price is far more affordable.

Note: Developed with Sarah Boole.

Sources: www.nytimes.com/2013/09/20/business/us-textile-factories-return.html?emc=eta1&_r=0; www.american-giant.com; www.slate.com/articles/technology/technology/2012/12/american_giant_hoodie_this_is_the_greatest_sweatshirt_known_to_man.html; and www.businessinsider.com/this-hoodie-is-so-insanely-popular-you-have-to-wait-months-to-get-it-2013-12.

at a below-average price or a high-quality product at an average or slightly higher-than-average price. Best-cost provider strategies also work well in recessionary times when great masses of buyers become value-conscious and are attracted to economically priced products and services with especially appealing attributes.

The Danger of an Unsound Best-Cost Provider Strategy

A company's biggest vulnerability in employing a best-cost provider strategy is not having the requisite core competencies and efficiencies in managing value chain activities to support the addition of differentiating features without significantly increasing costs.

A company with a modest degree of differentiation and no real cost advantage will most likely find itself squeezed between the firms using low-cost strategies and those using differentiation strategies. Low-cost providers may be able to siphon customers away with the appeal of a lower price (despite having marginally less appealing product attributes). High-end differentiators may be able to steal customers away with the appeal of appreciably better product attributes (even though their products carry a somewhat higher price tag). Thus, a successful best-cost provider must offer buyers *significantly* better product attributes to justify a price above what low-cost leaders are charging. Likewise, it has to achieve significantly lower costs in providing upscale features so that it can outcompete high-end differentiators on the basis of a *significantly* lower price.

Successful Competitive Strategies Are Resource Based

For a company's competitive strategy to succeed in delivering good performance and the intended competitive edge over rivals, it has to be well matched to a company's internal situation and underpinned by an appropriate set of resources, know-how, and competitive capabilities. To succeed in employing a low-cost provider strategy, a company has to have the resources and capabilities to keep its costs below those of its competitors; this means having the expertise to cost-effectively manage value chain activities better than rivals and/or the innovative capability to bypass certain value chain activities being performed by rivals. To succeed in strongly differentiating its product in ways that are appealing to buyers, a company must have the resources and capabilities (such as better technology, strong skills in product innovation, expertise in customer service) to incorporate unique attributes into its product offering that a broad range of buyers will find appealing and worth paying for.

Strategies focusing on a narrow segment of the market require the capability to do an outstanding job of satisfying the needs and expectations of niche buyers. Success in employing a strategy keyed to a best-value offering requires the resources and capabilities to incorporate upscale product or service attributes at a lower cost than that of rivals.

> A company's competitive strategy should be well matched to its internal situation and predicated on leveraging its collection of competitively valuable resources and competencies.

KEY POINTS

1. Early in the process of crafting a strategy, company managers have to decide which of the five basic competitive strategies to employ: overall low-cost, broad differentiation, focused low-cost, focused differentiation, or best-cost provider.

2. In employing a low-cost provider strategy, a company must do a better job than rivals of cost-effectively managing internal activities, and/or it must find innovative ways to eliminate or bypass cost-producing activities. Particular attention should be paid to cost drivers, which are factors having a strong effect on the cost of a company's value chain activities and cost structure. Low-cost provider strategies work particularly well when price competition is strong and the products of rival sellers are very weakly differentiated. Other conditions favoring a low-cost provider strategy are when supplies are readily available from eager

sellers, when there are not many ways to differentiate that have value to buyers, and when buyer switching costs are low.

3.   Broad differentiation strategies seek to produce a competitive edge by incorporating attributes and features that set a company's product/service offering apart from rivals in ways that buyers consider valuable and worth paying for. Such features and attributes are best integrated through the systematic management of value drivers—value chain activities or factors that can have a strong effect on customer value and creating differentiation. Successful differentiation allows a firm to (1) command a premium price for its product, (2) increase unit sales (because additional buyers are won over by the differentiating features), and/or (3) gain buyer loyalty to its brand (because some buyers are strongly attracted to the differentiating features and bond with the company and its products). Differentiation strategies work best in markets with diverse buyer preferences where there are big windows of opportunity to strongly differentiate a company's product offering from those of rival brands, in situations where few other rivals are pursuing a similar differentiation approach, and in circumstances where technological change is fast-paced and competition centers on rapidly evolving product features. A differentiation strategy is doomed when competitors are able to quickly copy most or all of the appealing product attributes a company comes up with, when a company's differentiation efforts meet with a ho-hum or so-what market reception, or when a company erodes profitability by overspending on efforts to differentiate its product offering.

4.   A focused strategy delivers competitive advantage either by achieving lower costs than rivals in serving buyers comprising the target market niche or by offering niche buyers an appealingly differentiated product or service that meets their needs better than rival brands. A focused strategy becomes increasingly attractive when the target market niche is big enough to be profitable and offers good growth potential, when it is costly or difficult for multisegment competitors to put capabilities in place to meet the specialized needs of the target market niche and at the same time satisfy the expectations of their mainstream customers, when there are one or more niches that present a good match with a focuser's resource strengths and capabilities, and when few other rivals are attempting to specialize in the same target segment.

5.   Best-cost provider strategies stake out a middle ground between pursuing a low-cost advantage and a differentiation-based advantage and between appealing to the broad market as a whole and a narrow market niche. The aim is to create competitive advantage by giving buyers more value for the money—satisfying buyer expectations on key quality/features/performance/ service attributes while beating customer expectations on price. To profitably employ a best-cost provider strategy, a company *must have the capability to incorporate attractive or upscale attributes at a lower cost than that of rivals.* This capability is contingent on (1) a superior value chain configuration, (2) unmatched efficiency in managing essential value chain activities, and (3) resource strengths and core competencies that allow differentiating attributes to be incorporated at a low cost. A best-cost provider strategy works best in markets where opportunities to differentiate exist and where many buyers are sensitive to price and value.

6.   Deciding which generic strategy to employ is perhaps the most important strategic commitment a company makes—it tends to drive the rest of the strategic actions a company decides to undertake, and it sets the whole tone for the pursuit of a competitive advantage over rivals.

ASSURANCE OF LEARNING EXERCISES

LO5-1, LO5-2, LO5-3, LO5-4

1.   Best Buy is the largest consumer electronics retailer in the United States with fiscal 2019 sales of nearly $43 billion. The company competes aggressively on price with rivals such as Costco Wholesale, Sam's Club, Walmart, and Target but is also known by consumers for its first-rate customer service. Best Buy customers have commented that the retailer's

sales staff is exceptionally knowledgeable about products and can direct them to the exact location of difficult-to-find items. Best Buy customers also appreciate that demonstration models of PC monitors, digital media players, and other electronics are fully powered and ready for in-store use. Best Buy's Geek Squad tech support and installation services are additional customer service features valued by many customers.

How would you characterize Best Buy's competitive strategy? Should it be classified as a low-cost provider strategy? A differentiation strategy? A best-cost strategy? Explain your answer.

2. Concepts & Connections 5.1 discusses Vanguard's low-cost position in the investment management industry. Based on information provided in the capsule, explain how Vanguard has built its low-cost advantage in the industry and why a low-cost provider strategy is well suited to the industry.

LO5-2

3. USAA is a Fortune 500 insurance and financial services company with 2018 annual revenues exceeding $30 billion. The company was founded in 1922 by 25 Army officers who decided to insure each other's vehicles and continues to limit its membership to active-duty and retired military members, officer candidates, and adult children and spouses of military-affiliated USAA members. The company has received countless awards, including being listed among *Fortune*'s World's Most Admired Companies in 2014 through 2019 and 100 Best Companies to Work For in 2010 through 2019. You can read more about the company's history and strategy at www.usaa.com. How would you characterize USAA's competitive strategy? Should it be classified as a low-cost provider strategy? A differentiation strategy? A best-cost strategy? Also, has the company chosen to focus on a narrow piece of the market, or does it appear to pursue a broad market approach? Explain your answer.

LO5-1, LO5-2, LO5-3, LO5-4

4. Explore Kendra Scott's website at www.kendrascott.com and see if you can identify at least three ways in which the company seeks to differentiate itself from rival jewelry firms. Is there reason to believe that Kendra Scott's differentiation strategy has been successful in producing a competitive advantage? Why or why not?

LO5-3

EXERCISES FOR SIMULATION PARTICIPANTS

1. Which one of the five generic competitive strategies can be utilized to compete successfully in the business simulation?

2. Which rival companies appear to be employing a low-cost provider strategy?

3. Which rival companies appear to be employing a broad differentiation strategy?

4. Which rival companies appear to be employing a best-cost provider strategy?

5. Which cost drivers and value drivers are important in creating superior customer value in the business simulation?

6. What is your company's action plan to achieve a sustainable competitive advantage over rival companies? List at least three (preferably, more than three) specific kinds of decision entries on specific decision screens that your company has made or intends to make to win this kind of competitive edge over rivals.

LO5-1, LO5-2, LO5-3, LO5-4

ENDNOTES

1. Michael E. Porter, *Competitive Strategy: Techniques for Analyzing Industries and Competitors* (New York: Free Press, 1980), chapter 2; Michael E. Porter, "What Is Strategy?" *Harvard Business Review* 74, no. 6 (November–December 1996).

2. Michael E. Porter, *Competitive Advantage* (New York: Free Press, 1985).

3. Peter J. Williamson and Ming Zeng, "Value-for-Money Strategies for Recessionary Times," *Harvard Business Review* 87, no. 3 (March 2009).

6

STRENGTHENING A COMPANY'S COMPETITIVE POSITION: STRATEGIC MOVES, TIMING, AND SCOPE OF OPERATIONS

LEARNING OBJECTIVES

After reading this chapter, you should be able to:

LO6-1 Understand whether and when to pursue offensive or defensive strategic moves to improve a company's market position.

LO6-2 Recognize when being a first mover or a fast follower or a late mover can lead to competitive advantage.

LO6-3 Identify the strategic benefits and risks of expanding a company's horizontal scope through mergers and acquisitions.

LO6-4 Explain the advantages and disadvantages of extending a company's scope of operations via vertical integration.

LO6-5 Describe the conditions that favor farming out certain value chain activities to outside parties.

LO6-6 Explain how strategic alliances and collaborative partnerships can bolster a company's collection of resources and capabilities.

Once a company has settled on which of the five generic competitive strategies to employ, attention turns to what *other strategic actions* it can take to complement its competitive approach and maximize the power of its overall strategy. As illustrated in Figure 6.1, several decisions regarding the company's operating scope and how to best strengthen its market standing must be made:

- When to undertake strategic moves based upon whether it is advantageous to be a first mover or a fast follower or a late mover

- Whether and when to go on the offensive and initiate aggressive strategic moves to improve the company's market position

- Whether and when to employ defensive strategies to protect the company's market position

FIGURE 6.1

Strategies to Strengthen a Company's Competitive Approaches

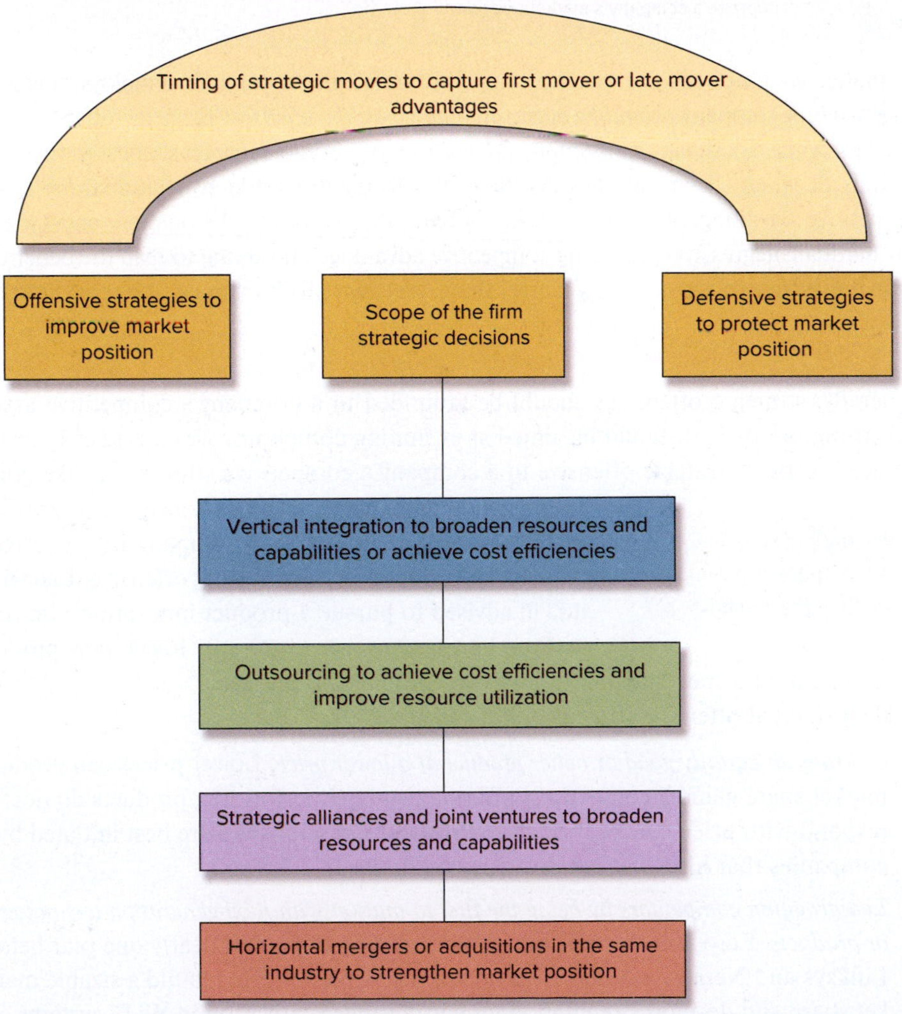

Timing of strategic moves to capture first mover or late mover advantages

Offensive strategies to improve market position

Scope of the firm strategic decisions

Defensive strategies to protect market position

Vertical integration to broaden resources and capabilities or achieve cost efficiencies

Outsourcing to achieve cost efficiencies and improve resource utilization

Strategic alliances and joint ventures to broaden resources and capabilities

Horizontal mergers or acquisitions in the same industry to strengthen market position

- Scope of the firm decisions to broaden resources and capabilities, achieve cost efficiencies, or strengthen market position
  - Whether to integrate backward or forward into more stages of the industry value chain
  - Which value chain activities, if any, should be outsourced
  - Whether to enter into strategic alliances or partnership arrangements with other enterprises
  - Whether to bolster the company's market position by merging with or acquiring another company in the same industry

This chapter presents the pros and cons of each of these measures that round out a company's overall strategy.

Launching Strategic Offensives to Improve a Company's Market Position

 LO6-1 Understand whether and when to pursue offensive or defensive strategic moves to improve a company's market position.

No matter which of the five generic competitive strategies a company employs, there are times when a company *should be aggressive and go on the offensive*. Strategic offensives are called for when a company spots opportunities to gain profitable market share at the expense of rivals or when a company has no choice but to try to whittle away at a strong rival's competitive advantage. Companies such as Samsung, Amazon, Autonation, and Google play hardball, aggressively pursuing competitive advantage and trying to reap the benefits a competitive edge offers—a leading market share, excellent profit margins, and rapid growth.[1]

Choosing the Basis for Competitive Attack

Generally, strategic offensives should be grounded in a company's competitive assets and strong points and should be aimed at exploiting competitor weaknesses.[2] Ignoring the need to tie a strategic offensive to a company's competitive strengths is like going to war with a popgun—the prospects for success are dim. For instance, it is foolish for a company with relatively high costs to employ a price-cutting offensive. Likewise, it is ill advised to pursue a product innovation offensive without having proven expertise in R&D, new product development, and speeding new or improved products to market.

> The best offensives use a company's most competitively potent resources to attack rivals in those competitive areas where they are weakest.

The principal offensive strategy options include:

1. *Offering an equally good or better product at a lower price.* Lower prices can produce market share gains if competitors offering similarly performing products do not respond with price cuts of their own. Price-cutting offensives are best initiated by companies that have *first achieved a cost advantage.*[3]

2. *Leapfrogging competitors by being the first to market with next-generation technology or products.* Eero got its whole home Wi-Fi system to market nearly one year before Linksys and Netgear developed competing systems, helping it build a sizable market share and develop a reputation for cutting-edge innovation in Wi-Fi systems.

3. *Pursuing continuous product innovation to draw sales and market share away from less innovative rivals.* Ongoing introductions of new or improved products can put rivals under tremendous competitive pressure, especially when rivals' new product development capabilities are weak.

4. *Pursuing disruptive product innovations to create new markets.* While this strategy can be riskier and more costly than a strategy of continuous innovation, it can be a game changer if successful. Disruptive innovation involves perfecting new products or services that offer an altogether new and better value proposition. Examples include Netflix, Venmo, Twitter, and Waymo.

5. *Adopting and improving on the good ideas of other companies (rivals or otherwise).* The idea of warehouse-type home improvement centers did not originate with Home Depot co-founders Arthur Blank and Bernie Marcus; they got the "big box" concept from their former employer, Handy Dan Home Improvement. But they were quick to improve on Handy Dan's business model and strategy and take Home Depot to a higher plateau in terms of product-line breadth and customer service.

6. *Using hit-and-run or guerrilla warfare tactics to grab sales and market share from complacent or distracted rivals.* Options for "guerrilla offensives" include occasional lowballing on price (to win a big order or steal a key account from a rival) or surprising key rivals with sporadic but intense bursts of promotional activity (offering a 20 percent discount for one week to draw customers away from rival brands).[4] Guerrilla offensives are particularly well suited to small challengers who have neither the resources nor the market visibility to mount a full-fledged attack on industry leaders.

7. *Launching a preemptive strike to capture a rare opportunity or secure an industry's limited resources.*[5] What makes a move preemptive is its one-of-a-kind nature—whoever strikes first stands to acquire competitive assets that rivals cannot readily match. Examples of preemptive moves include (1) securing the best distributors in a particular geographic region or country; (2) moving to obtain the most favorable site at a new interchange or intersection, in a new shopping mall, and so on; and (3) tying up the most reliable, high-quality suppliers via exclusive partnerships, long-term contracts, or even acquisition. To be successful, a preemptive move doesn't have to totally block rivals from following or copying; it merely needs to give a firm a prime position that is not easily circumvented.

Choosing Which Rivals to Attack

Offensive-minded firms need to analyze which of their rivals to challenge as well as how to mount that challenge. The best targets for offensive attacks are:

- *Market leaders that are vulnerable.* Offensive attacks make good sense when a company that leads in terms of size and market share is not a true leader in terms of serving the market well. Signs of leader vulnerability include unhappy buyers, an inferior product line, a weak competitive strategy with regard to low-cost leadership or differentiation, a preoccupation with diversification into other industries, and mediocre or declining profitability.

- *Runner-up firms with weaknesses in areas where the challenger is strong.* Runner-up firms are an especially attractive target when a challenger's resource strengths and competitive capabilities are well suited to exploiting their weaknesses.

- *Struggling enterprises that are on the verge of going under.* Challenging a hard-pressed rival in ways that further sap its financial strength and competitive position can hasten its exit from the market.

- *Small local and regional firms with limited capabilities.* Because small firms typically have limited expertise and resources, a challenger with broader capabilities is well positioned to raid their biggest and best customers.

Blue Ocean Strategy—A Special Kind of Offensive

A **blue ocean strategy** seeks to gain a dramatic and durable competitive advantage *by abandoning efforts to beat out competitors in existing markets and, instead, inventing a new industry or distinctive market segment that renders existing competitors largely irrelevant and allows a company to create and capture altogether new demand.*[6] This strategy views the business universe as consisting of two distinct types of market space. One is where industry boundaries are defined and accepted, the competitive rules of the game are well understood by all industry members, and companies try to outperform rivals by capturing a bigger share of existing demand; in such markets, lively competition constrains a company's prospects for rapid growth and superior profitability since rivals move quickly to either imitate or counter the successes of competitors. The second type of market space is a "blue ocean" where the industry does not really exist yet, is untainted by competition, and offers wide-open opportunity for profitable and rapid growth if a company can come up with a product offering and strategy that allows it to create new demand rather than fight over existing demand. A terrific example of such wide-open or blue ocean market space is the online auction industry that eBay created and now dominates.

> **CORE CONCEPT**
>
> **Blue ocean strategies** offer growth in revenues and profits by discovering or inventing new industry segments that create altogether new demand.

Other examples of companies that have achieved competitive advantages by creating blue ocean market spaces include Drybar in hair blowouts, FedEx in overnight package delivery, Uber in ride-sharing services, and Cirque du Soleil in live entertainment. Cirque du Soleil "reinvented the circus" by creating a distinctively different market space for its performances (Las Vegas nightclubs and theater-type settings) and pulling in a whole new group of customers—adults and corporate clients—who were willing to pay several times more than the price of a conventional circus ticket to have an "entertainment experience" featuring sophisticated clowns and star-quality acrobatic acts in a comfortable atmosphere.

Blue ocean strategies provide a company with a great opportunity in the short run. But they do not guarantee a company's long-term success, which depends more on whether a company can protect the market position it opened up. Concepts & Connections 6.1 discusses how Etsy used a blue ocean strategy to open a new competitive space in online retailing.

Using Defensive Strategies to Protect a Company's Market Position and Competitive Advantage

In a competitive market, all firms are subject to offensive challenges from rivals. The purposes of defensive strategies are to lower the risk of being attacked, weaken the impact of any attack that occurs, and influence challengers to aim their efforts at other rivals. While defensive strategies usually do not enhance a firm's competitive

CONCEPTS & CONNECTIONS 6.1

ETSY'S BLUE OCEAN STRATEGY IN ONLINE RETAILING OF HOMEMADE CRAFTS

Etsy was a market discovery of three New York entrepreneurs who saw that eBay had become too large and ineffective for craftspeople and artisans who wished to sell their one-of-a-kind products online. While eBay's timed auction format made for an exciting marketplace for bargain-hunting consumers, Etsy promoted its ability to connect thoughtful consumers with artisans selling unique hand-crafted items. Typical Etsy buyers valued craftsmanship and wanted to know how items were made and who made them. The ability to develop a direct relationship with the seller was important to many Etsy buyers who enjoyed a personalized shopping experience. Purchases made by Etsy buyers ranged from $5 ornaments to $50 hand-made clothing items to $2,000 custom-made coffee tables.

In 2018, approximately 39 million buyers had purchased merchandise offered by 2.1 million crafters and artisans. The company's gross merchandise sales totaled more than $3.9 billion in 2018. Etsy charged sellers a 3.5 percent transaction fee and a 20-cent listing fee and generated additional revenue from payment processing fees and the sales of shipping labels. The company's revenues had grown from $74.6 million in 2012 to $603.7 million in 2018.

The success of the company's Blue Ocean Strategy had not gone unnoticed, with Amazon announcing in May 2016 that it would launch a site featuring artisan goods named Handmade. Amazon believed that its free 2-day shipping to Prime members would give it an advantage over Etsy. In June 2019, the company's stock traded at nearly three times its IPO first-day closing price of $22.24 in April 2015. The strength of its strategy and the quality of its execution would determine if Etsy would be able to defend against well-funded new entrants into its specialty online retailing sector.

Note: Developed with Rochelle R. Brunson and Marlene M. Reed.

advantage, they can definitely help fortify its competitive position. Defensive strategies can take either of two forms: actions to block challengers and actions signaling the likelihood of strong retaliation.

> Good defensive strategies can help protect competitive advantage but rarely are the basis for creating it.

Blocking the Avenues Open to Challengers

The most frequently employed approach to defending a company's present position involves actions to restrict a competitive attack by a challenger. A number of obstacles can be put in the path of would-be challengers.[7] A defender can introduce new features, add new models, or broaden its product line to close vacant niches to opportunity-seeking challengers. It can thwart the efforts of rivals to attack with a lower price by maintaining economy-priced options of its own. It can try to discourage buyers from trying competitors' brands by making early announcements about upcoming new products or planned price changes. Finally, a defender can grant volume discounts or better financing terms to dealers and distributors to discourage them from experimenting with other suppliers.

Signaling Challengers That Retaliation Is Likely

The goal of signaling challengers that strong retaliation is likely in the event of an attack is either to dissuade challengers from attacking or to divert them to less threatening options. Either goal can be achieved by letting challengers know the battle will cost more than it is worth. Would-be challengers can be signaled by:

- Publicly announcing management's commitment to maintain the firm's present market share.

- Publicly committing the company to a policy of matching competitors' terms or prices.
- Maintaining a war chest of cash and marketable securities.
- Making an occasional strong counterresponse to the moves of weak competitors to enhance the firm's image as a tough defender.

Timing a Company's Offensive and Defensive Strategic Moves

LO6-2 Recognize when being a first mover or a fast follower or a late mover can lead to competitive advantage.

When to make a strategic move is often as crucial as *what* move to make. Timing is especially important when **first-mover advantages or disadvantages** exist. Under certain conditions, being first to initiate a strategic move can have a high payoff in the form of a competitive advantage that later movers cannot dislodge. Moving first is no guarantee of success, however, since first movers also face some significant disadvantages. Indeed, there are circumstances in which it is more advantageous to be a fast follower or even a late mover. Because the timing of strategic moves can be consequential, it is important for company strategists to be aware of the nature of first-mover advantages and disadvantages and the conditions favoring each type of move.[8]

> **CORE CONCEPT**
>
> Because of **first-mover advantages and disadvantages,** competitive advantage can spring from *when* a move is made as well as from *what* move is made.

Sometimes, though, markets are slow to accept the innovative product offering of a first mover, in which case a fast follower with substantial resources and marketing muscle can overtake a first mover. CNN had enjoyed a powerful first-mover advantage in cable news for more than 20 years, until it was surpassed by Fox News as the number-one cable news network. Fox has used innovative programming and intriguing hosts to expand its demographic appeal to retain its number-one ranking since 2002. Sometimes furious technological change or product innovation makes a first mover vulnerable to quickly appearing next-generation technology or products. For instance, former market leaders in mobile phones Nokia and BlackBerry have been victimized by far more innovative iPhone and Android models. Hence, there are no guarantees that a first mover will win sustainable competitive advantage.[9]

There are five conditions in which first-mover advantages are most likely to arise:

1. *When pioneering helps build a firm's reputation and creates strong brand loyalty.* Customer loyalty to an early mover's brand can create a tie that binds, limiting the success of later entrants' attempts to poach from the early mover's customer base and steal market share. For example, Open Table's early move as an online restaurant reservation service built a strong brand that has since fueled its expansion worldwide.

2. *When a first mover's customers will thereafter face significant switching costs.* Switching costs can protect first movers when consumers make large investments in learning how to use a specific company's product or in purchasing complementary products that are also brand-specific.

3. *When property rights protections thwart rapid imitation of the initial move.* In certain types of industries, property rights protections in the form of patents, copyrights, and trademarks prevent the ready imitation of an early mover's initial moves. First-mover advantages in pharmaceuticals, for example, are heavily dependent on patent protections, and patent races in this industry are common.

4. *When an early lead enables the first mover to move down the learning curve ahead of rivals.* When there is a steep learning curve and when learning can be kept proprietary, a first-mover advantage can be preserved over long periods of time. Intel's advantage in microprocessors has been attributed to such an effect.

5. *When a first mover can set the technical standard for the industry.* In many technology-based industries, the market will converge around a single technical standard. By establishing the industry standard, a first mover can gain a powerful advantage that, like experience-based advantages, builds over time. The keys to developing such an advantage are to enter early on the basis of strong fast-cycle product development capabilities, gain the support of key customers and suppliers, employ penetration pricing, and make allies of the producers of complementary products.

The Potential for Late-Mover Advantages or First-Mover Disadvantages

There are instances when there are actually *advantages* to being an adept follower rather than a first mover. Late-mover advantages (or *first-mover disadvantages*) arise in four instances:

- When pioneering leadership is more costly than followership and only negligible experience or learning-curve benefits accrue to the leader—a condition that allows a follower to end up with lower costs than the first mover.

- When the products of an innovator are somewhat primitive and do not live up to buyer expectations, thus allowing a clever follower to win disenchanted buyers away from the leader with better-performing products.

- When potential buyers are skeptical about the benefits of a new technology or product being pioneered by a first mover.

- When rapid market evolution (due to fast-paced changes in either technology or buyer needs and expectations) gives fast followers and maybe even cautious late movers the opening to leapfrog a first mover's products with more attractive next-version products.

Deciding Whether to Be an Early Mover or Late Mover

In weighing the pros and cons of being a first mover versus a fast follower versus a slow mover, it matters whether the race to market leadership in a particular industry is a marathon or a sprint. In marathons, a slow mover is not unduly penalized—first-mover advantages can be fleeting, and there's ample time for fast followers and sometimes even late movers to catch up.[10] Thus the speed at which the pioneering innovation is likely to catch on matters considerably as companies struggle with whether to pursue a particular emerging market opportunity aggressively or cautiously. For instance, it took 5.5 years for worldwide mobile phone use to grow from 10 million to 100 million worldwide and close to 10 years for the number of at-home broadband subscribers to grow to 100 million worldwide. The lesson here is that there is a market-penetration curve for every emerging opportunity; typically, the curve has an inflection point at which all the pieces of the business model fall into place, buyer demand explodes, and the market takes off. The inflection point can come early on a fast-rising curve (as with the use of e-mail) or farther on up a slow-rising curve (such as the use of broadband). Any company that seeks competitive advantage by being a first mover thus needs to ask some hard questions:

- Does market takeoff depend on the development of complementary products or services that currently are not available?

- Is new infrastructure required before buyer demand can surge?

- Will buyers need to learn new skills or adopt new behaviors? Will buyers encounter high switching costs?

- Are there influential competitors in a position to delay or derail the efforts of a first mover?

When the answers to any of these questions are yes, then a company must be careful not to pour too many resources into getting ahead of the market opportunity—the race is likely going to be more of a 10-year marathon than a 2-year sprint.

Strengthening a Company's Market Position via Its Scope of Operations

LO6-3 Identify the strategic benefits and risks of expanding a company's horizontal scope through mergers and acquisitions.

CORE CONCEPT

The **scope of the firm** refers to the range of activities the firm performs internally, the breadth of its product and service offerings, the extent of its geographic market presence, and its mix of businesses.

Apart from considerations of offensive and defensive competitive moves and their timing, another set of managerial decisions can affect the strength of a company's market position. These decisions concern the **scope of the firm**—the breadth of a company's activities and the extent of its market reach. For example, Ralph Lauren Corporation designs, markets, and distributes fashionable apparel and other merchandise to more than 22,000 major department stores and specialty retailers around the world, plus it also operates over 110 Ralph Lauren retail stores, 290 factory stores, and 10 e-commerce sites. Scope decisions also concern which segments of the market to serve—decisions that can include geographic market segments as well as product and service segments. Almost 50 percent of Ralph Lauren's sales are made outside the United States, and its product line includes apparel, fragrances, home furnishings, eyewear, watches and jewelry, and handbags and other leather goods. The company has also expanded its brand lineup through the acquisitions of Chaps menswear and casual retailer Club Monaco.

Four dimensions of firm scope have the capacity to strengthen a company's position in a given market: the breadth of its product and service offerings, the range of activities the firm performs internally, the extent of its geographic market presence, and its mix of businesses. In this chapter, we discuss horizontal and vertical scope decisions in relation to its breadth of offerings and range of internally performed activities. A company's

horizontal scope, which is the range of product and service segments that it serves, can be expanded through new-business development or mergers and acquisitions of other companies in the marketplace. The company's **vertical scope** is the extent to which it engages in the various activities that make up the industry's entire value chain system—from raw-material or component production all the way to retailing and after-sales service. Expanding a company's vertical scope by means of vertical integration can also affect the strength of a company's market position.

Additional dimensions of a firm's scope are discussed in Chapter 7, which focuses on the company's geographic scope and expansion into foreign markets, and Chapter 8, which takes up the topic of business diversification and corporate strategy.

> **CORE CONCEPT**
>
> **Horizontal scope** is the range of product and service segments that a firm serves within its focal market.

> **CORE CONCEPT**
>
> **Vertical scope** is the extent to which a firm's internal activities encompass one, some, many, or all of the activities that make up an industry's entire value chain system, ranging from raw-material production to final sales and service activities.

Horizontal Merger and Acquisition Strategies

Mergers and acquisitions are much-used strategic options to strengthen a company's market position. A *merger* is the combining of two or more companies into a single corporate entity, with the newly created company often taking on a new name. An *acquisition* is a combination in which one company, the acquirer, purchases and absorbs the operations of another, the acquired. The difference between a merger and an acquisition relates more to the details of ownership, management control, and financial arrangements than to strategy and competitive advantage. The resources and competitive capabilities of the newly created enterprise end up much the same whether the combination is the result of an acquisition or merger.

Horizontal mergers and acquisitions, which involve combining the operations of companies within the same product or service market, allow companies to rapidly increase scale and horizontal scope. For example, the merger of AMR Corporation (parent of American Airlines) with US Airways has increased the airlines' scale of operations and their reach geographically to create the world's largest airline.

> Combining the operations of two companies, via merger or acquisition, is an attractive strategic option for achieving operating economies, strengthening the resulting company's competencies and competitiveness, and opening avenues of new market opportunity.

Merger and acquisition strategies typically set sights on achieving any of five objectives:[11]

1. *Extending the company's business into new product categories.* Many times a company has gaps in its product line that need to be filled. Acquisition can be a quicker and more potent way to broaden a company's product line than going through the exercise of introducing a company's own new product to fill the gap. Coca-Cola's strategy to expand beyond carbonated soft drinks has been supported by acquisitions of producers of fruit juices, soy-based beverages, and bottled water.

2. *Creating a more cost-efficient operation out of the combined companies.* When a company acquires another company in the same industry, there's usually enough overlap in operations that certain inefficient plants can be closed or distribution and sales

activities can be partly combined and downsized. The combined companies may also be able to reduce supply chain costs through buying in greater volume from common suppliers. Likewise, it is usually feasible to squeeze out cost savings in administrative activities, again by combining and downsizing such activities as finance and accounting, information technology, human resources, and so on.

3. *Expanding a company's geographic coverage.* One of the best and quickest ways to expand a company's geographic coverage is to acquire rivals with operations in the desired locations. Food products companies such as Nestlé, Kraft, Unilever, and Procter & Gamble have made acquisitions an integral part of their strategies to expand internationally.

4. *Gaining quick access to new technologies or complementary resources and capabilities.* Making acquisitions to bolster a company's technological know-how or to expand its skills and capabilities allows a company to bypass a time-consuming and expensive internal effort to build desirable new resources and capabilities. From 2000 through June 2019, Cisco Systems purchased 152 companies to give it more technological reach and product breadth, thereby enhancing its standing as the world's largest provider of hardware, software, and services for building and operating Internet networks.

5. *Leading the convergence of industries whose boundaries are being blurred by changing technologies and new market opportunities.* Such acquisitions are the result of a company's management betting that two or more distinct industries are converging into one and deciding to establish a strong position in the consolidating markets by bringing together the resources and products of several different companies. The convergence of the pharmacy industry with health insurers and benefits management led to both the mergers between Cigna and Express Scripts and between CVS and Aetna in 2018.

Concepts & Connections 6.2 describes how Walmart employed a horizontal acquisition strategy to expand into the e-commerce domain.

Why Mergers and Acquisitions Sometimes Fail to Produce Anticipated Results

Despite many successes, mergers and acquisitions do not always produce the hoped-for outcomes.[12] Cost savings may prove smaller than expected. Gains in competitive capabilities may take substantially longer to realize or, worse, may never materialize. Efforts to mesh the corporate cultures can stall due to formidable resistance from organization members. Key employees at the acquired company can quickly become disenchanted and leave; the morale of company personnel who remain can drop to disturbingly low levels because they disagree with newly instituted changes. Differences in management styles and operating procedures can prove hard to resolve. In addition, the managers appointed to oversee the integration of a newly acquired company can make mistakes in deciding which activities to leave alone and which activities to meld into their own operations and systems.

A number of mergers/acquisitions have been notably unsuccessful. Google's $12.5 billion acquisition of struggling smartphone manufacturer Motorola Mobility in 2012 turned out to be minimally beneficial in helping to "supercharge Google's Android ecosystem"

CONCEPTS & CONNECTIONS 6.2

WALMART'S EXPANSION INTO E-COMMERCE VIA HORIZONTAL ACQUISITION

As the boundaries between traditional retailing and online retailing have begun to blur, Walmart has responded by expanding its presence in e-commerce via horizontal acquisition. In 2016, Walmart acquired Jet.com, an innovative U.S. e-commerce startup that was designed to compete with Amazon. Jet.com rewards customers for ordering multiple items, using a debit card instead of a credit card, or choosing a no-returns option; it passes its cost savings on to customers in the form of lower prices. The low-price approach of Jet.com fit well with Walmart's low-price strategy. In addition, Walmart hoped that the acquisition would help it to accelerate its growth in e-commerce, provide quick access to some valuable e-commerce knowledge and capabilities, increase its breadth of online product offerings, and attract new customer segments.

Walmart, like other brick and mortar retailers, was facing a myriad of issues caused by changing customer expectations. Consumers increasingly valued large assortments of products, a convenient shopping experience, and low prices. Price sensitivity was increasing due to the ease of comparing prices online. As a traditional retailer, Walmart was facing stiff competition from Amazon, the world's largest and fastest growing e-commerce company. Amazon's seemingly endless inventory of goods, excellent customer service, expertise in search engine marketing, and appeal to a wide consumer demographic added pressure on the overall global retail industry.

Sundry Photography/Shutterstock

The acquisition of Jet built on the foundation already in place for Walmart to respond to the external pressure and continue growing as an omni-channel retailer (i.e., bricks and mortar, online, or mobile). After investing heavily in their own online channel, Walmart.com, the company was looking for other ways to attract customers by lowering prices, broadening their product assortment, and offering the simplest, most convenient shopping experience. Jet's breadth of products, access to millennial and higher income customer segments, and best-in-class pricing algorithms would accelerate Walmart's progress across all of these priorities.

Jet sells everything from household goods and electronics to beauty products, apparel, and toys from more than 2,400 retailer and brand partners. Jet has also continued to expand its own offerings with private-label groceries, further increasing competition with Amazon's AmazonFresh grocery business. In 2017, Walmart made several other acquisitions of online apparel companies, thereby strengthening Jet's apparel offerings and further expanding Walmart's presence in e-commerce. These include ShoeBuy (a competitor of Amazon-owned Zappos), Bonobos in menswear, Moosejaw in outdoor gear and apparel, and Modcloth in vintage and indie womenswear.

One year later, Jet is averaging 25,000 daily processed orders and is continuing to act as an innovation pilot for Walmart. Over the same period, Walmart's U.S. e-commerce sales had risen, climbing 63 percent in its most recent quarter, and the stock had gained 10 percent over the last year. While Walmart's e-commerce sales still pale in comparison to Amazon, this was significantly better than the broader retail industry and represents a promising start for Walmart, as the retail industry continues to transform.

Note: Developed with Dipti Badrinath.

Sources: http://www.businessinsider.com/jet-walmart-weapon-vs-amazon-2017-9; https://news.walmart.com/2016/08/08/walmart-agrees-to-acquire-jetcom-one-of-the-fastest-growing-e-commerce-companies-in-the-us; https://www.fool.com/investing/2017/10/03/1-year-later-wal-marts-jetcom-acquisition-is-an-un.aspx; and https://blog.walmart.com/business/20160919/five-big-reasons-walmart-bought-jetcom.

(Google's stated reason for making the acquisition). Google invested over $1.3 billion to rejuvenate Motorola's smartphone lineup but failed to boost sales and incurred substantial operating losses. Google sold Motorola Mobility to China-based PC maker Lenovo for $2.9 billion in 2014. The jury is still out on whether Lenovo's acquisition of Motorola will prove to be a moneymaker.

Vertical Integration Strategies

LO6-4   Explain the advantages and disadvantages of extending a company's scope of operations via vertical integration.

Vertical integration extends a firm's competitive and operating scope within the same industry. It involves expanding the firm's range of value chain activities backward into sources of supply and/or forward toward end users. Thus, if a manufacturer invests in facilities to produce certain component parts that it formerly purchased from outside suppliers or if it opens its own chain of retail stores to market its products to consumers, it is engaging in vertical integration. For example, paint manufacturer Sherwin-Williams remains in the paint business even though it has integrated forward into retailing by operating more than 4,000 retail stores that market its paint products directly to consumers.

A firm can pursue vertical integration by starting its own operations in other stages of the vertical activity chain, by acquiring a company already performing the activities it wants to bring in-house, or by means of a strategic alliance or joint venture. Vertical integration strategies can aim at *full integration* (participating in all stages of the vertical chain) or *partial integration* (building positions in selected stages of the vertical chain). Companies may choose to pursue *tapered integration,* a strategy that involves both outsourcing and performing the activity internally. Oil companies' practice of supplying their refineries with both crude oil produced from their own wells and crude oil supplied by third-party operators and well owners is an example of tapered backward integration. Coach, Inc., the maker of Coach handbags and accessories, engages in tapered forward integration since it operates full-price and factory outlet stores but also sells its products through third-party department store outlets.

The Advantages of a Vertical Integration Strategy

The two best reasons for investing company resources in vertical integration are to strengthen the firm's competitive position and/or to boost its profitability.[13] Vertical integration has no real payoff unless it produces sufficient cost savings to justify the extra investment, adds materially to a company's technological and competitive strengths, and/or helps differentiate the company's product offering.

Integrating Backward to Achieve Greater Competitiveness   It is harder than one might think to generate cost savings or boost profitability by integrating backward into activities such as parts and components manufacture. For backward integration to be a viable and profitable strategy, a company must be able to (1) achieve the same scale economies as outside suppliers and (2) match or beat suppliers' production efficiency with no decline in quality. Neither outcome is easily achieved. To begin with, a company's in-house requirements are often too small to reach the optimum size for low-cost operation; for instance, if it takes a minimum production volume of 1 million units to achieve scale economies and a company's in-house requirements are just 250,000 units, then it falls way short of being able to match the costs of outside suppliers (who may readily find buyers for 1 million or more units).

But that said, there are still occasions when a company can improve its cost position and competitiveness by performing a broader range of value chain activities in-house rather than having these activities performed by outside suppliers. The best potential for being able to reduce costs via a backward integration strategy exists in situations where suppliers have very large profit margins, where the item being supplied is a major cost component, and where the requisite technological skills are easily mastered or acquired. Backward vertical integration can produce a differentiation-based competitive advantage when performing activities internally contributes to a better-quality product/service offering, improves the caliber of customer service, or in other ways enhances the performance of a final product. Other potential advantages of backward integration include sparing a company the uncertainty of being dependent on suppliers for crucial components or support services and lessening a company's vulnerability to powerful suppliers inclined to raise prices at every opportunity. Spanish clothing maker Inditex has backward integrated into fabric making, as well as garment design and manufacture, for its successful Zara chain of clothing stores. By tightly controlling the design and production processes, it can quickly respond to changes in fashion trends to keep its stores stocked with the hottest new items and lines.

Integrating Forward to Enhance Competitiveness   Vertical integration into forward stages of the industry value chain allows manufacturers to gain better access to end users, improve market visibility, and include the end user's purchasing experience as a differentiating feature. For example, Harley-Davidson's company-owned retail stores bolster the company's image and appeal through personalized selling, attractive displays, and riding classes that create new motorcycle riders and build brand loyalty. Insurance companies and brokerages such as Allstate and Edward Jones have the ability to make consumers' interactions with local agents and office personnel a differentiating feature by focusing on building relationships.

Most consumer goods companies have opted to integrate forward into retailing by selling direct to consumers via their websites. Bypassing regular wholesale/retail channels in favor of direct sales and Internet retailing can have appeal if it lowers distribution costs, produces a relative cost advantage over certain rivals, offers higher margins, or results in lower selling prices to end users. In addition, sellers are compelled to include the Internet as a retail channel when a sufficiently large number of buyers in an industry prefer to make purchases online. However, a company that is vigorously pursuing online sales to consumers at the same time that it is also heavily promoting sales to consumers through its network of wholesalers and retailers *is competing directly against its distribution allies.* Such actions constitute *channel conflict* and create a tricky route to negotiate. A company that is actively trying to grow online sales to consumers is signaling *a weak strategic commitment to its dealers* and *a willingness to cannibalize dealers' sales and growth potential.* The likely result is angry dealers and loss of dealer goodwill. Quite possibly, a company may stand to lose more sales by offending its dealers than it gains from its own online sales effort. Consequently, in industries where the strong support and goodwill of dealer networks are essential, companies may conclude that it is important to avoid channel conflict and that *their website should be designed to partner with dealers rather than compete with them.*

The Disadvantages of a Vertical Integration Strategy

Vertical integration has some substantial drawbacks beyond the potential for channel conflict.[14] The most serious drawbacks to vertical integration include:

- Vertical integration *increases a firm's capital investment* in the industry.

- Integrating into more industry value chain segments *increases business risk* if industry growth and profitability sour.

- Vertically integrated companies are often *slow to embrace technological advances* or more-efficient production methods when they are saddled with older technology or facilities.

- Integrating backward potentially results in less flexibility in accommodating shifting buyer preferences when a new product design does not include parts and components that the company makes in-house.

- Vertical integration poses all kinds of *capacity matching problems.* In motor vehicle manufacturing, for example, the most efficient scale of operation for making axles is different from the most economic volume for radiators and different yet again for both engines and transmissions. Consequently, integrating across several production stages in ways that achieve the lowest feasible costs can be a monumental challenge.

- Integration forward or backward often requires the *development of new skills and business capabilities.* Parts and components manufacturing, assembly operations, wholesale distribution and retailing, and direct sales via the Internet are different businesses with different key success factors.

> A vertical integration strategy has appeal *only* if it significantly strengthens a firm's competitive position and/or boosts its profitability.

Electric automobile maker Tesla, Inc. has made vertical integration a central part of its strategy, as described in Concepts & Connections 6.3.

Outsourcing Strategies: Narrowing the Scope of Operations

 LO6-5   Describe the conditions that favor farming out certain value chain activities to outside parties.

CORE CONCEPT

Outsourcing involves contracting out certain value chain activities to outside specialists and strategic allies.

Outsourcing forgoes attempts to perform certain value chain activities internally and instead farms them out to outside specialists and strategic allies. Outsourcing makes strategic sense whenever:

- *An activity can be performed better or more cheaply by outside specialists.* A company should generally *not* perform any value chain activity internally that can be performed more efficiently or effectively by outsiders. The chief exception is when a particular activity is strategically crucial and internal control over that activity is deemed essential.

CONCEPTS & CONNECTIONS 6.3

TESLA'S VERTICAL INTEGRATION STRATEGY

Unlike many vehicle manufacturers, Tesla embraces vertical integration from component manufacturing all the way through vehicle sales and servicing. The majority of the company's $22.6 billion in 2019 revenue came from electric vehicle sales and leasing, with the remainder coming from servicing those vehicles and selling residential battery packs and solar energy systems.

At its core an electric vehicle manufacturer, Tesla uses both backward and forward vertical integration to achieve multiple strategic goals. In order to drive innovation in a critical part of its supply chain, Tesla has invested in a "gigafactory" that manufactures the batteries that are essential for a long-lasting electric vehicle. According to Tesla's former VP of Production, in-house manufacturing of key components and new parts that require frequent updates has enabled the company to learn quickly and launch new versions faster. Moreover, having closer relationships between engineering and manufacturing gives Tesla greater control over product design. Tesla uses forward vertical integration to improve the customer experience by owning the distribution and servicing of the vehicles it builds. Their network of dealerships allows Tesla to sell directly to consumers and handle maintenance needs without relying on third parties that sometimes have competing priorities.

Beyond vertically integrating the manufacture and distribution of their electric vehicles, Tesla uses the strategy to build the ecosystem that is necessary to support further adoption of their vehicles. As many consumers perceive electric cars to have limited range and long charging times that prevent long-distance travel, Tesla is building a network of Supercharger stations to overcome this pain point. By investing in this development themselves, Tesla does not need to wait for another company to deliver the critical infrastructure that drivers demand before they switch from traditional gasoline-powered cars. Similarly, Tesla sells solar power generation and storage products that make it easier for customers to make the switch to transportation powered by sustainable energy.

While Tesla's mission to accelerate the world's transition to sustainable energy has required large investments throughout the value chain, this strategy has not been without challenges. Unlike batteries, seats are of limited strategic importance, yet Tesla decided to manufacture their Model 3 seats in house. While there is no indication that the seats were the source of major production delays in 2017, diverting resources to develop new manufacturing capabilities could have added to the problem. Although Tesla's vertical integration strategy is not without downsides, it has enabled the firm to quickly roll out innovative new products and launch the network that is required for widespread vehicle adoption. Investors have rewarded Tesla for this bold strategy by valuing it at almost $51 billion, higher than the other major American automakers.

Hadrian/Shutterstock

Note: Developed with Edward J. Silberman.

Sources: Tesla 2017 Annual Report; G. Reichow, "Tesla's Secret Second Floor," *Wired*, October 18, 2017, https://www.wired.com/story/teslas-secret-second-floor/; and A. Sage, "Tesla's Seat Strategy Goes Against the Grain . . . For Now," Reuters, October 26, 2017, https://www.reuters.com/article/us-tesla-seats/teslas-seat-strategy-goes-against-the-grain-for-now-idUSKBN1CV0DS; Yahoo Finance.

- *The activity is not crucial to the firm's ability to achieve sustainable competitive advantage and will not hollow out its capabilities, core competencies, or technical know-how.* Outsourcing of support activities such as maintenance services, data processing and data storage, fringe benefit management, and website operations has become common. Colgate-Palmolive, for instance, has been able to reduce its information technology operational costs by more than 10 percent per year through an outsourcing agreement with IBM.

- *It improves organizational flexibility and speeds time to market.* Outsourcing gives a company the flexibility to switch suppliers in the event that its present supplier falls behind competing suppliers. Also, to the extent that its suppliers can speedily get next-generation parts and components into production, a company can get its own next-generation product offerings into the marketplace quicker.

- *It reduces the company's risk exposure to changing technology and/or buyer preferences.* When a company outsources certain parts, components, and services, its suppliers must bear the burden of incorporating state-of-the-art technologies and/or undertaking redesigns and upgrades to accommodate a company's plans to introduce next-generation products.

- *It allows a company to concentrate on its core business, leverage its key resources and core competencies, and do even better what it already does best.* A company is better able to build and develop its own competitively valuable competencies and capabilities when it concentrates its full resources and energies on performing those activities. Apple outsources production of its iPod, iPhone, and iPad models to Chinese contract manufacturer Foxconn. Hewlett-Packard and others have sold some of their manufacturing plants to outsiders and contracted to repurchase the output from the new owners.

> A company should guard against outsourcing activities that hollow out the resources and capabilities that it needs to be a master of its own destiny.

The Big Risk of an Outsourcing Strategy   The biggest danger of outsourcing is that a company will farm out the wrong types of activities and thereby hollow out its own capabilities.[15] In such cases, a company loses touch with the very activities and expertise that over the long run determine its success. But most companies are alert to this danger and take actions to protect against being held hostage by outside suppliers. Cisco Systems guards against loss of control and protects its manufacturing expertise by designing the production methods that its contract manufacturers must use. Cisco keeps the source code for its designs proprietary, thereby controlling the initiation of all improvements and safeguarding its innovations from imitation. Further, Cisco uses the Internet to monitor the factory operations of contract manufacturers around the clock and can know immediately when problems arise and decide whether to get involved.

Strategic Alliances and Partnerships

LO6-6   Explain how strategic alliances and collaborative partnerships can bolster a company's collection of resources and capabilities.

Companies in all types of industries have elected to form strategic alliances and partnerships to complement their accumulation of resources and capabilities and strengthen their competitiveness in domestic and international markets. A **strategic alliance** is a formal agreement between two or more separate companies in which there is strategically relevant collaboration of some sort, joint contribution of resources, shared risk, shared control, and mutual dependence. Collaborative relationships between partners may entail a contractual agreement, but they commonly stop short of formal ownership ties between the partners (although there are a few

CORE CONCEPT

A **strategic alliance** is a formal agreement between two or more companies to work cooperatively toward some common objective.

strategic alliances where one or more allies have minority ownership in certain of the other alliance members). Collaborative arrangements involving shared ownership are called joint ventures. A **joint venture** is a partnership involving the establishment of an independent corporate entity that is jointly owned and controlled by two or more companies. Since joint ventures involve setting up a mutually owned business, they tend to be more durable but also riskier than other arrangements.

> **CORE CONCEPT**
>
> A **joint venture** is a type of strategic alliance that involves the establishment of an independent corporate entity that is jointly owned and controlled by the two partners.

The most common reasons companies enter into strategic alliances are to expedite the development of promising new technologies or products, to overcome deficits in their own technical and manufacturing expertise, to bring together the personnel and expertise needed to create desirable new skill sets and capabilities, to improve supply chain efficiency, to gain economies of scale in production and/or marketing, and to acquire or improve market access through joint marketing agreements.[16] Arabian Chemical Insulation Company (ACIC) is a joint venture established in 1976 between Dow Chemical Company and E.A. Juffali & Brothers to manufacture and sell polystyrene insulation products throughout the Middle East. ACIC continued to be one of the leading producers of insulation in the Middle East in 2017 and was Dow Chemical's longest-running joint venture in the region. Volkswagen established a joint venture with China-based Anhui Jianghuai Automobile Company in 2017 to develop and produce electric and plug-in hybrid vehicles for sale in China. The two partners expected the joint venture would sell 400,000 vehicles by 2020 and 1.5 million electric cars by 2025.

Because of the varied benefits of strategic alliances, many large corporations have become involved in 30 to 50 alliances, and a number have formed hundreds of alliances. Roche, a leader in pharmaceuticals and diagnostics, has formed R&D alliances with over 160 companies to boost its prospects for developing new cures for various diseases. In 2016, more than one-third of its pharmaceutical sales came from partnered products. Companies that have formed a host of alliances need to manage their alliances like a portfolio—terminating those that no longer serve a useful purpose or that have produced meager results, forming promising new alliances, and restructuring existing alliances to correct performance problems and/or redirect the collaborative effort.

Failed Strategic Alliances and Cooperative Partnerships

Most alliances with an objective of technology sharing or providing market access turn out to be temporary, fulfilling their purpose after a few years because the benefits of mutual learning have occurred. Although long-term alliances sometimes prove mutually beneficial, most partners do not hesitate to terminate the alliance and go it alone when the payoffs run out. Alliances are more likely to be long lasting when (1) they involve collaboration with partners that do not compete directly, (2) a trusting relationship has been established, and (3) both parties conclude that continued collaboration is in their mutual interest, perhaps because new opportunities for learning are emerging.

A surprisingly large number of alliances never live up to expectations, with estimates that as many as 60 to 70 percent of alliances fail each year. The high "divorce rate" among strategic allies has several causes, the most common of which are:[17]

- Diverging objectives and priorities.
- An inability to work well together.
- Changing conditions that make the purpose of the alliance obsolete.

- The emergence of more attractive technological paths.
- Marketplace rivalry between one or more allies.

Experience indicates that *alliances stand a reasonable chance of helping a company reduce competitive disadvantage, but very rarely have they proved a strategic option for gaining a durable competitive edge over rivals.*

The Strategic Dangers of Relying on Alliances for Essential Resources and Capabilities

The Achilles' heel of alliances and cooperative strategies is becoming dependent on other companies for *essential* expertise and capabilities. To be a market leader (and perhaps even a serious market contender), a company must ultimately develop its own resources and capabilities in areas where internal strategic control is pivotal to protecting its competitiveness and building competitive advantage. Moreover, some alliances hold only limited potential because the partner guards its most valuable skills and expertise; in such instances, acquiring or merging with a company possessing the desired know-how and resources is a better solution.

KEY POINTS

Once a company has selected which of the five basic competitive strategies to employ in its quest for competitive advantage, then it must decide whether and how to supplement its choice of a basic competitive strategy approach.

1. Companies have a number of offensive strategy options for improving their market positions and trying to secure a competitive advantage: (1) attacking competitors' weaknesses, (2) offering an equal or better product at a lower price, (3) pursuing sustained product innovation, (4) leapfrogging competitors by being first to adopt next-generation technologies or the first to introduce next-generation products, (5) adopting and improving on the good ideas of other companies, (6) deliberately attacking those market segments where key rivals make big profits, (7) going after less contested or unoccupied market territory, (8) using hit-and-run tactics to steal sales away from unsuspecting rivals, and (9) launching preemptive strikes. A blue ocean offensive strategy seeks to gain a dramatic and durable competitive advantage by abandoning efforts to beat out competitors in existing markets and, instead, inventing a new industry or distinctive market segment that renders existing competitors largely irrelevant and allows a company to create and capture altogether new demand.

2. Defensive strategies to protect a company's position usually take the form of making moves that put obstacles in the path of would-be challengers and fortify the company's present position while undertaking actions to dissuade rivals from even trying to attack (by signaling that the resulting battle will be more costly to the challenger than it is worth).

3. The timing of strategic moves also has relevance in the quest for competitive advantage. Company managers are obligated to carefully consider the advantages or disadvantages that attach to being a first mover versus a fast follower versus a wait-and-see late mover.

4. Decisions concerning the scope of a company's operations can also affect the strength of a company's market position. The scope of the firm refers to the range of its activities, the breadth of its product and service offerings, the extent of its geographic market presence,

and its mix of businesses. Companies can expand their scope horizontally (more broadly within their focal market) or vertically (up or down the industry value chain system that starts with raw-materials production and ends with sales and service to the end consumer). Horizontal mergers and acquisitions (combinations of market rivals) provide a means for a company to expand its horizontal scope. Vertical integration expands a firm's vertical scope.

5. Horizontal mergers and acquisitions can be an attractive strategic option for strengthening a firm's competitiveness. When the operations of two companies are combined via merger or acquisition, the new company's competitiveness can be enhanced in any of several ways—lower costs; stronger technological skills; more or better competitive capabilities; a more attractive lineup of products and services; wider geographic coverage; and/or greater financial resources with which to invest in R&D, add capacity, or expand into new areas.

6. Vertically integrating forward or backward makes strategic sense only if it strengthens a company's position via either cost reduction or creation of a differentiation-based advantage. Otherwise, the drawbacks of vertical integration (increased investment, greater business risk, increased vulnerability to technological changes, and less flexibility in making product changes) are likely to outweigh any advantages.

7. Outsourcing pieces of the value chain formerly performed in-house can enhance a company's competitiveness whenever (1) an activity can be performed better or more cheaply by outside specialists; (2) the activity is not crucial to the firm's ability to achieve sustainable competitive advantage and will not hollow out its core competencies, capabilities, or technical know-how; (3) it improves a company's ability to innovate; and/or (4) it allows a company to concentrate on its core business and do what it does best.

8. Many companies are using strategic alliances and collaborative partnerships to help them in the race to build a global market presence or be a leader in the industries of the future. Strategic alliances are an attractive, flexible, and often cost-effective means by which companies can gain access to missing technology, expertise, and business capabilities.

ASSURANCE OF LEARNING EXERCISES

1. Live Nation operates music venues, provides management services to music artists, and promotes more than 35,000 shows and 100 festivals in 40 countries annually. The company acquired House of Blues, merged with Ticketmaster, and has also acquired concert and festival promoters in the United States, Australia, and Great Britain. How has the company used horizontal mergers and acquisitions to strengthen its competitive position? Are these moves primarily offensive or defensive? Has either Live Nation or Ticketmaster achieved any type of advantage based on the timing of its strategic moves?

LO6-1, LO6-2, LO6-3

2. Tesla, Inc., has rapidly become a stand-out among American car companies. Concepts & Connections 6.3 describes how Tesla has made vertical integration a central part of its strategy. What value chain segments has Tesla chosen to enter and perform internally? How has vertical integration of its ecosystem aided the organization in building competitive advantage? Has vertical integration strengthened its market position? Explain why or why not.

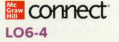

LO6-4

3. Perform an Internet search to identify at least two companies in different industries that have entered into outsourcing agreements with firms with specialized services. In addition, describe what value chain activities the companies have chosen to outsource. Do any of these outsourcing agreements seem likely to threaten any of the companies' competitive capabilities?

LO6-5

4. Using your university library's business research resources, find two examples of how companies have relied on strategic alliances or joint ventures to substitute for horizontal or vertical integration.

LO6-6

McGraw Hill connect

EXERCISES FOR SIMULATION PARTICIPANTS

LO6-1, LO6-2   1.   Has your company relied more on offensive or defensive strategies to achieve your rank in the industry? What options for being a first mover does your company have? Do any of these first-mover options hold competitive advantage potential?

LO6-3   2.   What would be an advantage of a horizontal merger within the industry?

LO6-4   3.   What are the pros and cons of vertical integration in the industry?

LO6-5   4.   What do you see as pros and cons of outsourcing in the business simulation?

ENDNOTES

1. George Stalk, Jr., and Rob Lachenauer, "Hardball: Five Killer Strategies for Trouncing the Competition," *Harvard Business Review* 82, no. 4 (April 2004); Richard D'Aveni, "The Empire Strikes Back: Counterrevolutionary Strategies for Industry Leaders," *Harvard Business Review* 80, no. 11 (November 2002); David J. Bryce and Jeffrey H. Dyer, "Strategies to Crack Well-Guarded Markets," *Harvard Business Review* 85, no. 5 (May 2007).

2. David B. Yoffie and Mary Kwak, "Mastering Balance: How to Meet and Beat a Stronger Opponent," *California Management Review* 44, no. 2 (Winter 2002).

3. Ian C. MacMillan, Alexander B. van Putten, and Rita Gunther McGrath, "Global Gamesmanship," *Harvard Business Review* 81, no. 5 (May 2003); Askay R. Rao, Mark E. Bergen, and Scott Davis, "How to Fight a Price War," *Harvard Business Review* 78, no. 2 (March–April 2000).

4. Ming-Jer Chen and Donald C. Hambrick, "Speed, Stealth, and Selective Attack: How Small Firms Differ from Large Firms in Competitive Behavior," *Academy of Management Journal* 38, no. 2 (April 1995); Ian MacMillan, "How Business Strategists Can Use Guerrilla Warfare Tactics," *Journal of Business Strategy* 1, no. 2 (Fall 1980); William E. Rothschild, "Surprise and the Competitive Advantage," *Journal of Business Strategy* 4, no. 3 (Winter 1984); Kathryn R. Harrigan, *Strategic Flexibility* (Lexington, MA: Lexington Books, 1985); Liam Fahey, "Guerrilla Strategy: The Hit-and-Run Attack," in *The Strategic Management Planning Reader*, ed. Liam Fahey (Englewood Cliffs, NJ: Prentice Hall, 1989).

5. Ian MacMillan, "Preemptive Strategies," *Journal of Business Strategy* 14, no. 2 (Fall 1983).

6. W. Chan, Kim, and Renee Mauborgne. "Blue Ocean Strategy." Strategy (2004). *Harvard Business Review*.

7. Michael E. Porter, *Competitive Advantage* (New York: Free Press, 1985).

8. Jeffrey G. Covin, Dennis P. Slevin, and Michael B. Heeley, "Pioneers and Followers: Competitive Tactics, Environment, and Growth," *Journal of Business Venturing* 15, no. 2 (March 1999); Christopher A. Bartlett and Sumantra Ghoshal, "Going Global: Lessons from Late-Movers," *Harvard Business Review* 78, no. 2 (March–April 2000).

9. Fernando Suarez and Gianvito Lanzolla, "The Half-Truth of First-Mover Advantage," *Harvard Business Review* 83 no. 4 (April 2005).

10. Costas Markides and Paul A. Geroski, "Racing to Be 2nd: Conquering the Industries of the Future," *Business Strategy Review* 15, no. 4 (Winter 2004).

11. Joseph L. Bower, "Not All M&As Are Alike—and That Matters," *Harvard Business Review* 79, no. 3 (March 2001); O. Chatain and P. Zemsky, "The Horizontal Scope of the Firm: Organizational Tradeoffs vs. Buyer-Supplier Relationships," *Management Science* 53, no. 4 (April 2007), pp. 550–565.

12. Jeffrey H. Dyer, Prashant Kale, and Harbir Singh, "When to Ally and When to Acquire," *Harvard Business Review* 82, no. 4 (July–August 2004), pp. 109–110.

13. Kathryn R. Harrigan, "Matching Vertical Integration Strategies to Competitive Conditions," *Strategic Management Journal* 7, no. 6 (November–December 1986); John Stuckey and David White, "When and When Not to Vertically Integrate," *Sloan Management Review*, Spring 1993.

14. Thomas Osegowitsch and Anoop Madhok, "Vertical Integration Is Dead, or Is It?" *Business Horizons* 46, no. 2 (March–April 2003).

15. Jérôme Barthélemy, "The Seven Deadly Sins of Outsourcing," *Academy of Management Executive* 17, no. 2 (May 2003); Gary P. Pisano and Willy C. Shih, "Restoring American Competitiveness," *Harvard Business Review* 87, no. 7/8 (July–August 2009); Ronan McIvor, "What Is the Right Outsourcing Strategy for Your Process?" *European Management Journal* 26, no. 1 (February 2008).

16. Michael E. Porter, *The Competitive Advantage of Nations* (New York: Free Press, 1990); K. M. Eisenhardt and C. B. Schoonhoven, "Resource-Based View of Strategic Alliance Formation: Strategic and Social Effects in Entrepreneurial Firms," *Organization Science* 7, no. 2 (March–April 1996); Nancy J. Kaplan and Jonathan Hurd, "Realizing the Promise of Partnerships," *Journal of Business Strategy* 23, no. 3 (May–June 2002); Salvatore Parise and Lisa Sasson, "Leveraging Knowledge Management across Strategic Alliances," *Ivey Business Journal* 66, no. 4 (March–April 2002); David Ernst and James Bamford, "Your Alliances Are Too Stable," *Harvard Business Review* 83, no. 6 (June 2005).

17. Yves L. Doz and Gary Hamel, *Alliance Advantage: The Art of Creating Value Through Partnering* (Boston: Harvard Business School Press, 1998).

STRATEGIES FOR COMPETING IN INTERNATIONAL MARKETS

LEARNING OBJECTIVES

After reading this chapter, you should be able to:

LO7-1 Identify the primary reasons companies choose to compete in international markets.

LO7-2 Understand why and how differing market conditions across countries influence a company's strategy choices in international markets.

LO7-3 Identify the five general modes of entry into foreign markets.

LO7-4 Identify the three main options for tailoring a company's international strategy to cross-country differences in market conditions and buyer preferences.

LO7-5 Explain how multinational companies are able to use international operations to improve overall competitiveness.

LO7-6 Recognize the unique characteristics of competing in developing-country markets.

Any company that aspires to industry leadership in the 21st century must think in terms of global, not domestic, market leadership. The world economy is globalizing at an accelerating pace as countries previously closed to foreign companies open their markets, as countries with previously planned economies embrace market or mixed economies, as information technology shrinks the importance of geographic distance, and as ambitious, growth-minded companies race to build stronger competitive positions in the markets of more and more countries. The forces of globalization are changing the competitive landscape in many industries, offering companies attractive new opportunities but at the same time introducing new competitive threats. Companies in industries where these forces are greatest are under considerable pressure to develop strategies for competing successfully in international markets.

This chapter focuses on strategy options for expanding beyond domestic boundaries and competing in the markets of either a few or many countries. We will discuss the factors that shape the choice of strategy in international markets and the specific market circumstances that support the adoption of multidomestic, transnational, and global strategies. The chapter also includes sections on strategy options for entering foreign markets; how international operations may be used to improve overall competitiveness; and the special circumstances of competing in such emerging markets as China, India, Brazil, Russia, and Eastern Europe.

Why Companies Expand into International Markets

 LO7-1   Identify the primary reasons companies choose to compete in international markets.

A company may opt to expand outside its domestic market for any of five major reasons:

1. *To gain access to new customers.* Expanding into foreign markets offers potential for increased revenues, profits, and long-term growth, and becomes an especially attractive option when a company's home markets are mature. Honda has done this with its classic 50-cc motorcycle, the Honda Cub, which is still selling well in developing markets, more than 50 years after it was introduced in Japan.

2. *To achieve lower costs through economies of scale, experience, and increased purchasing power.* Many companies are driven to sell in more than one country because domestic sales volume alone is not large enough to capture fully economies of scale in product development, manufacturing, or marketing. Similarly, firms expand internationally to increase the rate at which they accumulate experience and move down the learning curve. International expansion can also lower a company's input costs through greater pooled purchasing power. The relatively small size of country markets in Europe and limited domestic volume explains why companies like Michelin, BMW, and Nestlé long ago began selling their products all across Europe and then moved into markets in North America and Latin America.

3. *To gain access to low-cost inputs of production.* Companies in industries based on natural resources (e.g., oil and gas, minerals, rubber, and lumber) often find it necessary to operate in the international arena since raw-material supplies are located in different parts of the world and can be accessed more cost-effectively at the source. Other companies enter foreign markets to access low-cost human

resources; this is particularly true of industries in which labor costs make up a high proportion of total production costs.

4. *To further exploit its core competencies.* A company may be able to extend a market-leading position in its domestic market into a position of regional or global market leadership by leveraging its core competencies further. H&M is capitalizing on its considerable expertise in online retailing to expand its reach internationally. By bringing its easy-to-use and mobile-friendly online shopping to 43 different countries, the company hopes to pave the way for setting up physical stores in these countries. Companies can often leverage their resources internationally by replicating a successful business model, using it as a basic blueprint for international operations, as Starbucks and McDonald's have done.

5. *To gain access to resources and capabilities located in foreign markets.* An increasingly important motive for entering foreign markets is to acquire resources and capabilities that cannot be accessed as readily in a company's home market. Companies often enter into cross-border alliances, make acquisitions abroad, or establish operations in foreign countries to access local resources such as distribution networks, low-cost labor, natural resources, or specialized technical knowledge.[1]

In addition, companies that are the suppliers of other companies often expand internationally when their major customers do so, to meet their customers' needs abroad and retain their position as a key supply chain partner. For example, when motor vehicle companies have opened new plants in foreign locations, big automotive parts suppliers have frequently opened new facilities nearby to permit timely delivery of their parts and components to the plant.

Factors That Shape Strategy Choices in International Markets

 LO7-2 Understand why and how differing market conditions across countries influence a company's strategy choices in international markets.

Four important factors shape a company's strategic approach to competing in foreign markets: (1) the degree to which there are important cross-country differences in demographic, cultural, and market conditions; (2) whether opportunities exist to gain a location-based advantage based on wage rates, worker productivity, inflation rates, energy costs, tax rates, and other factors that impact cost structure; (3) the risks of adverse shifts in currency exchange rates; and (4) the extent to which governmental policies affect the local business climate.

Cross-Country Differences in Demographic, Cultural, and Market Conditions

Buyer tastes for a particular product or service sometimes differ substantially from country to country. For example, ice cream flavors such as eel, shark fin, and dried shrimp appeal to Japanese customers, whereas fruit-based flavors have more appeal in the United States and Europe. In France, top-loading washing machines are very popular with consumers, whereas in most other European countries, consumers prefer front-loading machines. Consequently, companies operating in a global marketplace must wrestle with *whether and how much to customize their offerings in each different country market to match the tastes and preferences of local buyers or whether to pursue a strategy of offering a mostly standardized product worldwide.* While making products that are closely matched to local tastes makes them more appealing to local buyers, customizing a company's products country by country may raise production and distribution costs. Greater standardization of a global company's product offering, on the other hand, can lead to scale economies and learning curve effects, thus contributing to the achievement of a low-cost advantage. *The tension between the market pressures to localize a company's product offerings country by country and the competitive pressures to lower costs is one of the big strategic issues that participants in foreign markets have to resolve.*

Understandably, differing population sizes, income levels, and other demographic factors give rise to considerable differences in market size and growth rates from country to country. In emerging markets such as India, China, Brazil, and Malaysia, market growth potential is far higher for such products as mobile phones, steel, credit cards, and electric energy than in the more mature economies of Britain, Canada, and Japan. The potential for market growth in automobiles is explosive in China, where 2016 sales of new vehicles amounted to 28 million, surpassing U.S. sales of 17 million and making China the world's largest market for the seventh year in a row.[2] Owing to widely differing population demographics and income levels, there is a far bigger market for luxury automobiles in the United States and Germany than in Argentina, India, Mexico, and Thailand. Cultural influences can also affect consumer demand for a product. For instance, in China, many parents are reluctant to purchase PCs even when they can afford them because of concerns that their children will be distracted from their schoolwork by surfing the web, playing PC-based video games, and downloading and listening to pop music.

Market growth can be limited by the lack of infrastructure or established distribution and retail networks in emerging markets. India has well-developed national channels for distribution of goods to the nation's 3 million retailers, whereas in China distribution is primarily local. Also, the competitive rivalry in some country marketplaces is only moderate, whereas others are characterized by strong or fierce competition. The managerial challenge at companies with international or global operations is how best to tailor a company's strategy to take all these cross-country differences into account.

Opportunities for Location-Based Cost Advantages

Differences from country to country in wage rates, worker productivity, energy costs, environmental regulations, tax rates, inflation rates, and the like are often so big that *a company's operating costs and profitability are significantly impacted by where its production, distribution, and customer service activities are located.* Wage rates, in particular, vary enormously from country to country. For example, in 2016, hourly compensation for manufacturing workers averaged about $1.60 in India, $4.11 in China, $3.91 in Mexico, $9.82 in Taiwan, $8.60 in Hungary, $7.98 in Brazil, $10.96 in Portugal, $22.98 in South Korea, $26.46 in Japan, $30.08 in Canada, $39.03 in the United States, $43.18 in Germany, and $48.62 in Norway.[3] Not surprisingly, China has emerged as the manufacturing capital of the world—virtually all of the world's major manufacturing companies now have facilities in China. This in turn has driven up manufacturing wages in China by more than double the average hourly compensation cost of $1.98 in 2010.

For other types of value chain activities, input quality or availability are more important considerations. Tiffany entered the mining industry in Canada to access diamonds that could be certified as "conflict free" and not associated with either the funding of African wars or unethical mining conditions. Many U.S. companies locate call centers in countries such as India and Ireland, where English is spoken and the workforce is well educated. Other companies locate R&D activities in countries where there are prestigious research institutions and well-trained scientists and engineers. Likewise, concerns about short delivery times and low shipping costs make some countries better locations than others for establishing distribution centers.

Industry Cluster Knowledge Sharing Opportunities

There are advantages available to companies operating in a location containing a cluster of related industries, including others within the same value chain system (e.g., suppliers of components and equipment, distributors) and the makers of complementary products or those that are technologically related. The sports car makers Ferrari and Maserati, for example, are located in an area of Italy known as the "engine technological district," which includes other firms involved in racing, such as Ducati Motorcycles, along with hundreds of small suppliers. The advantage to firms that develop as part of a related-industry cluster comes from the close collaboration with key suppliers and the greater knowledge sharing throughout the cluster, resulting in greater efficiency and innovativeness.

The Risks of Adverse Exchange Rate Shifts

When companies produce and market their products and services in many different countries, they are subject to the impacts of sometimes favorable and sometimes unfavorable changes in currency exchange rates. The rates of exchange between different currencies can vary by as much as 20 to 40 percent annually, with the changes occurring sometimes gradually and sometimes swiftly. Sizable shifts in exchange rates, which tend to be hard to predict because of the variety of factors involved and the uncertainties surrounding when and by how much these factors will change, *shuffle the global cards of which countries represent the low-cost manufacturing location* and *which rivals have the upper hand in the marketplace.*

To illustrate the competitive risks associated with fluctuating exchange rates, consider the case of a U.S. company that has located manufacturing facilities in Brazil (where the currency is reals—pronounced *ray-alls*) and that exports most of its Brazilian-made goods to markets in the European Union (where the currency is euros). To keep the numbers simple, assume the exchange rate is 4 Brazilian reals for 1 euro and that the product being made in Brazil has a manufacturing cost of 4 Brazilian reals (or 1 euro). Now suppose that for some reason the exchange rate shifts from 4 reals per euro to 5 reals per euro (meaning the real has declined in value and the euro is stronger). Making the product in Brazil is now more cost-competitive because a Brazilian good costing 4 reals to produce has fallen to only 0.8 euro at the new exchange rate (4 reals divided by 5 reals per euro = 0.8 euro). On the other hand, should the value of the Brazilian real grow stronger in relation to the euro—resulting in an exchange rate of 3 reals to 1 euro—the same Brazilian-made good formerly costing 4 reals to produce now has a cost of 1.33 euros (4 reals divided by 3 reals per euro = 1.33). This increase in the value of the real has eroded the cost advantage of the Brazilian manufacturing facility for goods shipped to Europe and affects the ability of the U.S. company to underprice European producers of similar goods. Thus, *the lesson of fluctuating exchange rates is that companies that export goods to foreign countries always gain in competitiveness when the currency of the country in which the goods are manufactured is weak. Exporters are disadvantaged when the currency of the country where goods are being manufactured grows stronger.*

The Impact of Government Policies on the Business Climate in Host Countries

National governments enact all kinds of measures affecting business conditions and the operation of foreign companies in their markets. It matters whether these measures create a favorable or unfavorable business climate. Governments of countries eager to spur economic growth, create more jobs, and raise living standards for their citizens usually make a special effort to create a business climate that outsiders will view favorably. They may provide such incentives as reduced taxes, low-cost loans, and site-development assistance to companies agreeing to construct or expand production and distribution facilities in the host country.

On the other hand, governments sometimes enact policies that, from a business perspective, make locating facilities within a country's borders less attractive. For example, the nature of a company's operations may make it particularly costly to achieve compliance with environmental regulations in certain countries. Some governments, wishing to discourage foreign imports, may enact deliberately burdensome customs procedures and requirements or impose tariffs or quotas on imported goods. Host-country governments may also specify that products contain a certain percentage of locally produced parts and components, require prior approval of capital spending projects, limit withdrawal of funds from the country, and require local ownership stakes in foreign-company operations in the host country. Such governmental actions make a country's business climate unattractive and in some cases may be sufficiently onerous as to discourage a company from locating facilities in that country or selling its products there.

A country's business climate is also a function of the political and economic risks associated with operating within its borders. **Political risks** have to do with the instability of weak governments, the likelihood of new onerous legislation or regulations on foreign-owned businesses, or the potential for future elections to produce government leaders hostile to foreign-owned businesses. In a growing number of emerging markets, governments are pursuing state capitalism in industries deemed to be of national importance. Financial services, information technology, telecommunications, and food sectors have become politicized in some emerging markets and are tightly controlled by government. In 2017, for example, Venezuela nationalized a General Motors plant in Valencia employing nearly 2,700 workers. China has established very low price ceilings on as many as 500 prescription drugs, which helps boost the profitability of its state-owned hospitals but makes it challenging for global pharmaceutical companies to do business in China.

> ### CORE CONCEPT
>
> **Political risks** stem from instability or weakness in national governments and hostility to foreign business; **economic risks** stem from the stability of a country's monetary system, economic and regulatory policies, and the lack of property rights protections.

Economic risks have to do with the threat of piracy and lack of protection for the company's intellectual property and the stability of a country's economy—whether inflation rates might skyrocket or whether uncontrolled deficit spending on the part of government could lead to a breakdown of the country's monetary system and prolonged economic distress.

Strategy Options for Entering Foreign Markets

 LO7-3 Identify the five general modes of entry into foreign markets.

A company choosing to expand outside its domestic market may elect one of the following five general modes of entry into a foreign market:

1. Maintain a national (one-country) production base and export goods to foreign markets.
2. License foreign firms to produce and distribute the company's products abroad.
3. Employ a franchising strategy.
4. Establish a subsidiary in a foreign market via acquisition or internal development.
5. Rely on strategic alliances or joint ventures with foreign partners to enter new country markets.

This section of the chapter discusses the five general options in more detail.

Export Strategies

Using domestic plants as a production base for exporting goods to foreign markets is an excellent initial strategy for pursuing international sales. It is a conservative way to test the international waters. The amount of capital needed to begin exporting is often quite minimal, and existing production capacity may be sufficient to make goods for export. With an export-based entry strategy, a manufacturer can limit its involvement in foreign markets by contracting with foreign wholesalers experienced in importing to handle the entire distribution and marketing function in their countries or regions of the world. If it is more advantageous to maintain control over these functions, however, a manufacturer can establish its own distribution and sales organizations in some or all of the target foreign markets. Either way, a home-based production and export strategy helps the firm minimize its direct investments in foreign countries.

An export strategy is vulnerable when (1) manufacturing costs in the home country are substantially higher than in foreign countries where rivals have plants, (2) the costs of shipping the product to distant foreign markets are relatively high, or (3) adverse shifts occur in currency exchange rates. Unless an exporter can both keep its production and shipping costs competitive with rivals and successfully hedge against unfavorable changes in currency exchange rates, its success will be limited.

Licensing Strategies

Licensing as an entry strategy makes sense when a firm with valuable technical know-how or a unique patented product has neither the internal organizational capability nor the resources to enter foreign markets. Licensing also has the advantage of avoiding the risks of committing resources to country markets that are unfamiliar, politically volatile, economically unstable, or otherwise risky. By licensing the technology or the production rights to foreign-based firms, the firm does not have to bear the costs and risks of entering foreign markets on its own, yet it is able to generate income from royalties. The big disadvantage of licensing is the risk of providing valuable technological know-how to foreign companies and thereby losing some degree of control over its use. Also, monitoring licensees and safeguarding the company's proprietary know-how can prove quite difficult in some circumstances. But if the royalty potential is considerable and the companies to which the licenses are being granted are both trustworthy and reputable, then licensing can be a very attractive option. Many software and pharmaceutical companies use licensing strategies.

Franchising Strategies

While licensing works well for manufacturers and owners of proprietary technology, franchising is often better suited to the global expansion efforts of service and retailing enterprises. McDonald's, Yum! Brands (the parent of Pizza Hut, KFC, and Taco Bell), the UPS Store, 7-Eleven, and Hilton Hotels have all used franchising to build a presence in international markets. Franchising has much the same advantages as licensing. The franchisee bears most of the costs and risks of establishing foreign locations, so a franchisor has to expend only the resources to recruit, train, support, and monitor franchisees. The big problem a franchisor faces is maintaining quality control. In many cases, foreign franchisees do not always exhibit strong commitment to consistency and standardization, especially when the local culture does not stress the same kinds of quality concerns. Another problem that can arise is whether to allow foreign franchisees to modify the franchisor's product offering to better satisfy the tastes and expectations of local buyers. Should McDonald's allow its franchised units in Japan to modify Big Macs slightly to suit Japanese tastes? Should the franchised KFC units in China be permitted to substitute spices that appeal to Chinese consumers? Or should the same menu offerings be rigorously and unvaryingly required of all franchisees worldwide?

Foreign Subsidiary Strategies

While exporting, licensing, and franchising rely upon the resources and capabilities of allies in international markets to deliver goods or services to buyers, companies pursuing international expansion may elect to take responsibility for the performance of all essential value chain activities in foreign markets. Companies that prefer direct control over all aspects of operating in a foreign market can establish a wholly owned subsidiary, either by acquiring a foreign company or by establishing operations from the ground up via internal development.

Acquisition is the quicker of the two options, and it may be the least risky and most cost-efficient means of hurdling such entry barriers as gaining access to local distribution channels, building supplier relationships, and establishing working relationships with key government officials and other constituencies. Buying an ongoing operation allows the acquirer to move directly to the tasks of transferring resources and personnel to the newly acquired business, integrating and redirecting the activities of the acquired business into its own operation, putting its own strategy into place, and accelerating efforts to build a strong market position.[4]

The big issue an acquisition-minded firm must consider is whether to pay a premium price for a successful local company or to buy a struggling competitor at a bargain price. If the buying firm has little knowledge of the local market but ample capital, it is often better off purchasing a capable, strongly positioned firm—unless the acquisition price is prohibitive. However, when the acquirer sees promising ways to transform a weak firm into a strong one and has the resources and managerial know-how to do it, a struggling company can be the better long-term investment.

Entering a new foreign country via internal development and building a foreign subsidiary from scratch makes sense when a company already operates in a number of countries, has experience in getting new subsidiaries up and running and overseeing their operations, and has a sufficiently large pool of resources and competencies to rapidly equip a new subsidiary with the personnel and capabilities it needs to compete successfully and profitably. Four other conditions make an internal startup strategy appealing:

- When creating an internal startup is cheaper than making an acquisition.
- When adding new production capacity will not adversely impact the supply–demand balance in the local market.
- When a startup subsidiary has the ability to gain good distribution access (perhaps because of the company's recognized brand name).
- When a startup subsidiary will have the size, cost structure, and resources to compete head-to-head against local rivals.

Alliance and Joint Venture Strategies

Strategic alliances, joint ventures, and other cooperative agreements with foreign companies are a favorite and potentially fruitful means for entering a foreign market or strengthening a firm's competitiveness in world markets.[5] Historically, export-minded firms in industrialized nations sought alliances with firms in less-developed countries to import and market their products locally; such arrangements were often necessary to win approval for entry from the host country's government. Both Japanese and American companies are actively forming alliances with European companies to strengthen their ability to compete in the 28-nation European Union (and the five countries that are candidates to become EU members) and to capitalize on the opening of Eastern European markets. Many U.S. and European companies are allying with Asian companies in their efforts to enter markets in China, India, Malaysia, Thailand, and other Asian countries. Many foreign companies, of course, are particularly interested in strategic partnerships that will strengthen their ability to gain a foothold in the U.S. market.

However, cooperative arrangements between domestic and foreign companies have strategic appeal for reasons besides gaining better access to attractive country markets.[6] A second big appeal of cross-border alliances is to capture economies of scale in production and/or marketing. By joining forces in producing components, assembling models, and marketing their products, companies can realize cost savings not achievable with their own small volumes. A third motivation for entering into a cross-border alliance is to fill gaps in technical expertise and/or knowledge of local markets (buying habits and product preferences of consumers, local customs, and so on). A fourth motivation for cross-border alliances is to share distribution facilities and dealer networks, and to mutually strengthen each partner's access to buyers.

A fifth benefit is that cross-border allies can direct their competitive energies more toward mutual rivals and less toward one another; teaming up may help them close the gap on leading companies. A sixth driver of cross-border alliances comes into play when companies wanting to enter a new foreign market conclude that alliances with local companies are an effective way to establish working relationships with key officials in the host-country government.[7] And, finally, alliances can be a particularly useful way for companies across the world to gain agreement on important technical standards—they have been used to arrive at standards for assorted PC devices, Internet-related technologies, high-definition televisions, and mobile phones.

What makes cross-border alliances an attractive strategic means of gaining the aforementioned types of benefits (as compared to acquiring or merging with foreign-based companies) is that entering into alliances and strategic partnerships allows a company to preserve its independence and avoid using perhaps scarce financial resources to fund acquisitions. Furthermore, an alliance offers the flexibility to readily disengage once its purpose has been served or if the benefits prove elusive, whereas an acquisition is a more permanent sort of arrangement.[8] Concepts & Connections 7.1 discusses how Walgreens has expanded internationally through an alliance followed by merger with U.K.-based Alliance Boots.

The Risks of Strategic Alliances with Foreign Partners   Alliances and joint ventures with foreign partners have their pitfalls, however. Cross-border allies typically have to overcome language and cultural barriers and figure out how to deal with diverse

CONCEPTS & CONNECTIONS 7.1

WALGREENS BOOTS ALLIANCE, INC.: ENTERING FOREIGN MARKETS VIA ALLIANCE FOLLOWED BY MERGER

Walgreens pharmacy began in 1901 as a single store on the South Side of Chicago, and grew to become the largest chain of pharmacy retailers in America. Walgreens was an early pioneer of the "self-service" pharmacy and found success by moving quickly to build a vast domestic network of stores after World War II. This growth-focused strategy served Walgreens well until the beginning of the 21st century, by which time it had nearly saturated the U.S. market. By 2014, 75 percent of Americans lived within five miles of a Walgreens. The company was also facing threats to its core business model. Walgreens relies heavily on pharmacy sales, which generally are paid for by someone other than the patient—usually the government or an insurance company. As the government and insurers started to make a more sustained effort to cut costs, Walgreens's core profit center was at risk. To mitigate these threats, Walgreens looked to enter foreign markets.

Walgreens found an ideal international partner in Alliance Boots. Based in the United Kingdom, Alliance Boots had a global footprint with 3,300 stores across 10 countries. A partnership with Alliance Boots had several strategic advantages,

allowing Walgreens to gain swift entry into foreign markets as well as complementary assets and expertise. First, it gave Walgreens access to new markets beyond the saturated United States for its retail pharmacies. Second, it provided Walgreens with a new revenue stream in wholesale drugs. Alliance Boots held a vast European distribution network for wholesale drug sales; Walgreens could leverage that network and expertise to build a similar model in the United States. Finally, a merger with Alliance Boots would strengthen Walgreens's existing business by increasing the company's market position and therefore bargaining power with drug companies. In light of these advantages, Walgreens moved quickly to partner with and later acquire Alliance Boots and merged both companies in 2014 to become Walgreens Boots Alliance. Walgreens Boots Alliance, Inc., is now one of the world's largest drug purchasers, able to negotiate from a strong position with drug companies and other suppliers to realize economies of scale in its current businesses.

The market has thus far responded favorably to the merger. Walgreens Boots Alliance's stock has more than doubled in value since the first news of the partnership in 2012. However, the company is still struggling to integrate and faces new risks such as currency fluctuation in its new combined position. Yet as the pharmaceutical industry continues to consolidate, Walgreens is in an undoubtedly stronger position to continue to grow in the future thanks to its strategic international acquisition.

Johndavidphoto/123RF

Note: Developed with Katherine Coster.

Sources: Company 10-K Form, 2015, investor.walgreensbootsalliance .com/secfiling.cfm?filingID=1140361-15-38791&CIK=1618921; L. Capron and W. Mitchell, "When to Change a Winning Strategy," *Harvard Business Review,* July 25, 2012, hbr.org/2012/07/when-to-change-a-winning-strat; and T. Martin and R. Dezember, "Walgreens Spends $6.7 Billion on Alliance Boots Stake," *The Wall Street Journal,* June 20, 2012.

(or perhaps conflicting) operating practices. The communication, trust-building, and coordination costs are high in terms of management time.[9] It is not unusual for partners to discover they have conflicting objectives and strategies, deep differences of opinion about how to proceed, or important differences in corporate values and ethical standards. Tensions build, working relationships cool, and the hoped-for benefits never materialize. The recipe for successful alliances requires many meetings of many people working in good faith over a period of time to iron out what is to be shared, what is to remain proprietary, and how the cooperative arrangements will work.[10]

Even if the alliance becomes a win-win proposition for both parties, there is the danger of becoming overly dependent on foreign partners for essential expertise and competitive capabilities. If a company is aiming for global market leadership and needs to develop capabilities of its own, then at some juncture cross-border merger or acquisition may have to be substituted for cross-border alliances and joint ventures. One of the lessons about cross-border alliances is that they are more effective in helping a company establish a beachhead of new opportunity in world markets than they are in enabling a company to achieve and sustain global market leadership.

International Strategy: The Three Principal Options

LO7-4 Identify the three main options for tailoring a company's international strategy to cross-country differences in market conditions and buyer preferences.

Broadly speaking, a company's **international strategy** is simply its strategy for competing in two or more countries simultaneously. Typically, a company will start to compete internationally by entering just one or perhaps a select few foreign markets, selling its products or services in countries where there is a ready market for them. But as it expands further internationally, it will have to confront head-on the conflicting pressures of local responsiveness versus efficiency gains from standardizing its product offering globally. As discussed earlier in the chapter, deciding upon the degree to vary its competitive approach to fit the specific market conditions and buyer preferences in each host country is perhaps the foremost strategic issue that must be addressed when operating in two or more foreign markets.[11] Figure 7.1 shows a company's three strategic approaches for competing internationally and resolving this issue.

> **CORE CONCEPT**
> A company's **international strategy** is its strategy for competing in two or more countries simultaneously.

Multidomestic Strategy—A Think Local, Act Local Approach to Strategy Making

A **multidomestic strategy** or **think local, act local** approach to strategy making is essential when there are significant country-to-country differences in customer preferences and buying habits, when there are significant cross-country differences in distribution channels and marketing methods, when host governments enact regulations requiring that products sold locally

> **CORE CONCEPT**
> A **multidomestic strategy** calls for varying a company's product offering and competitive approach from country to country in an effort to be responsive to significant cross-country differences in customer preferences, buyer purchasing habits, distribution channels, or marketing methods. **Think local, act local** strategy-making approaches are also essential when host-government regulations or trade policies preclude a uniform, coordinated worldwide market approach.

FIGURE 7.1

A Company's Three Principal Strategic Options for Competing Internationally

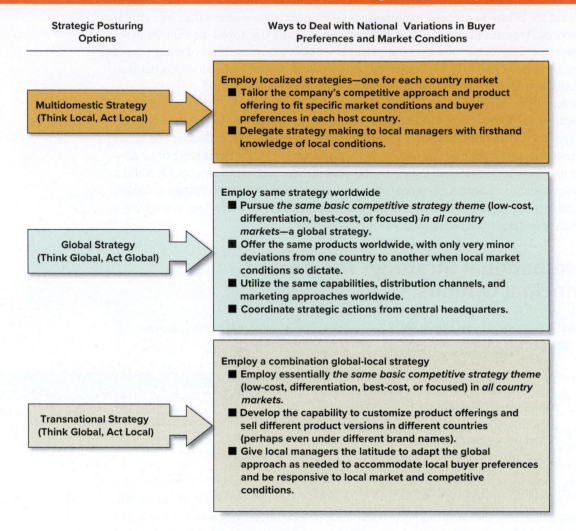

Strategic Posturing Options | Ways to Deal with National Variations in Buyer Preferences and Market Conditions

Multidomestic Strategy (Think Local, Act Local)

Employ localized strategies—one for each country market
- Tailor the company's competitive approach and product offering to fit specific market conditions and buyer preferences in each host country.
- Delegate strategy making to local managers with firsthand knowledge of local conditions.

Global Strategy (Think Global, Act Global)

Employ same strategy worldwide
- Pursue *the same basic competitive strategy theme* (low-cost, differentiation, best-cost, or focused) *in all country markets*—a global strategy.
- Offer the same products worldwide, with only very minor deviations from one country to another when local market conditions so dictate.
- Utilize the same capabilities, distribution channels, and marketing approaches worldwide.
- Coordinate strategic actions from central headquarters.

Transnational Strategy (Think Global, Act Local)

Employ a combination global-local strategy
- Employ essentially *the same basic competitive strategy theme* (low-cost, differentiation, best-cost, or focused) in *all country markets*.
- Develop the capability to customize product offerings and sell different product versions in different countries (perhaps even under different brand names).
- Give local managers the latitude to adapt the global approach as needed to accommodate local buyer preferences and be responsive to local market and competitive conditions.

meet strict manufacturing specifications or performance standards, and when the trade restrictions of host governments are so diverse and complicated that they preclude a uniform, coordinated worldwide market approach. With localized strategies, a company often has different product versions for different countries and sometimes sells the products under different brand names. Government requirements for gasoline additives that help reduce carbon monoxide, smog, and other emissions are almost never the same from country to country. BP utilizes localized strategies in its gasoline and service station business segment because of these cross-country formulation differences and because of customer familiarity with local brand names. For example, the company markets gasoline in the United States under its BP and Arco brands, but markets gasoline in Germany, Belgium, Poland, Hungary, and the Czech Republic under the Aral brand. Companies in the food products industry often vary the ingredients in their products and sell the localized versions under local brand names to cater to country-specific tastes and eating preferences. The strength of employing a set of localized or multidomestic strategies is that the company's actions and business approaches are deliberately crafted to appeal to the tastes and expectations of buyers in each country and to stake out the most attractive market positions vis-à-vis local competitors.[12]

However, think local, act local strategies have two big drawbacks: (1) They hinder transfer of a company's competencies and resources across country boundaries because the strategies in different host countries can be grounded in varying competencies and capabilities; and (2) they do not promote building a single, unified competitive advantage, especially one based on low cost. Companies employing highly localized or multidomestic strategies face big hurdles in achieving low-cost leadership *unless* they find ways to customize their products and *still* be in a position to capture scale economies and learning-curve effects. Toyota's unique mass customization production capability has been key to its ability to effectively adapt product offerings to local buyer tastes, while maintaining low-cost leadership.

Global Strategy—A Think Global, Act Global Approach to Strategy Making

While multidomestic strategies are best suited for industries where a fairly high degree of local responsiveness is important, global strategies are best suited for globally standardized industries. A **global strategy** is one in which the company's approach is predominantly the same in all countries: It sells the same products under the same brand names everywhere, utilizes much the same distribution channels in all countries, and competes on the basis of the same capabilities and marketing approaches worldwide. Although the company's strategy or product offering may be adapted in very minor ways to accommodate specific situations in a few host countries, the company's fundamental competitive approach (low-cost, differentiation, or focused) remains very much intact worldwide, and local managers stick close to the global strategy. A **think global, act global** strategic theme prompts company managers to integrate and coordinate the company's strategic moves worldwide and to expand into most, if not all, nations where there is significant buyer demand. It puts considerable strategic emphasis on building a *global* brand name and aggressively pursuing opportunities to transfer ideas, new products, and capabilities from one country to another.

> **CORE CONCEPT**
>
> **Global strategies** employ the same basic competitive approach in all countries where a company operates and are best suited to industries that are globally standardized in terms of customer preferences, buyer purchasing habits, distribution channels, or marketing methods. This is the **think global, act global** strategic theme.

Ford's global design strategy is a move toward a think global, act global strategy by the company and involves the development and production of standardized models with country-specific modifications limited primarily to what is required to meet local country emission and safety standards. The 2010 Ford Fiesta and 2011 Ford Focus were the company's first global design models to be marketed in Europe, North America, Asia, and Australia. In 2014, Ford added the Edge utility vehicle as a global model that would be sold in more than 60 countries. Whenever country-to-country differences are small enough to be accommodated within the framework of a global strategy, a global strategy is preferable to localized strategies because a company can more readily unify its operations and focus on establishing a brand image and reputation that is uniform from country to country. Moreover, with a global strategy, a company is better able to focus its full resources on securing a sustainable low-cost or differentiation-based competitive advantage over both domestic rivals and global rivals.

Transnational Strategy—A Think Global, Act Local Approach to Strategy Making

A **transnational strategy** is a **think global, act local** approach to developing strategy that accommodates cross-country variations in buyer tastes, local customs, and market conditions while also striving for the benefits of standardization. This middle-ground approach entails utilizing the same basic competitive theme (low-cost, differentiation, or focused) in each country but allows local managers the latitude to (1) incorporate whatever country-specific variations in product attributes are needed to best satisfy local buyers and (2) make whatever adjustments in production, distribution, and marketing are needed to respond to local market conditions and compete successfully against local rivals. Both McDonald's and KFC have discovered ways to customize their menu offerings in various countries without compromising costs, product quality, and operating effectiveness. Otis Elevator found that a transnational strategy delivers better results than a global strategy when competing in countries such as China where local needs are highly differentiated. By switching from its customary single-brand approach to a multibrand strategy aimed at serving different segments of the market, Otis was able to double its market share in China and increased its revenues sixfold over a nine-year period.[13]

> **CORE CONCEPT**
>
> A **transnational strategy** is a **think global, act local** approach to strategy making that involves employing essentially the same strategic theme (low-cost, differentiation, focused, best-cost) in all country markets, while allowing some country-to-country customization to fit local market conditions.

Concepts & Connections 7.2 explains how Four Seasons Hotels has been able to compete successfully on the basis of a transnational strategy.

As a rule, most companies that operate multinationally endeavor to employ as global a strategy as customer needs and market conditions permit. Electronic Arts has two major design studios—one in Vancouver, British Columbia, and one in Los Angeles—and smaller design studios in San Francisco, Orlando, London, and Tokyo. This dispersion of design studios helps EA to design games that are specific to different cultures: For example, the London studio took the lead in designing the popular FIFA Soccer game to suit European tastes and to replicate the stadiums, signage, and team rosters; the U.S. studio took the lead in designing games involving NFL football, NBA basketball, and NASCAR racing.

Using International Operations to Improve Overall Competitiveness

 LO7-5 Explain how multinational companies are able to use international operations to improve overall competitiveness.

A firm can gain competitive advantage by expanding outside its domestic market in two important ways. One, it can use location to lower costs or help achieve greater product differentiation. And two, it can use cross-border coordination in ways that a domestic-only competitor cannot.

CONCEPTS & CONNECTIONS 7.2

FOUR SEASONS HOTELS: LOCAL CHARACTER, GLOBAL SERVICE

Four Seasons Hotels is a Toronto, Canada–based manager of luxury hotel properties. With nearly 100 properties located in many of the world's most popular tourist destinations and business centers, Four Seasons commands a following of many of the world's most discerning travelers. In contrast to its key competitor, Ritz-Carlton, which strives to create one uniform experience globally, Four Seasons Hotels has gained market share by deftly combining local architectural and cultural experiences with globally consistent luxury service.

When moving into a new market, Four Seasons always seeks out a local capital partner. The understanding of local custom and business relationships this financier brings is critical to the process of developing a new Four Seasons hotel. Four Seasons also insists on hiring a local architect and design consultant for each property, as opposed to using architects or designers it has worked with in other locations. While this can be a challenge, particularly in emerging markets, Four Seasons has found it is worth it in the long run to have a truly local team.

The specific layout and programming of each hotel are also unique. For instance, when Four Seasons opened its hotel in

Mumbai, India, it prioritized space for large banquet halls to target the Indian wedding market. In India, weddings often draw guests numbering in the thousands. When moving into the Middle East, Four Seasons designed its hotels with separate prayer rooms for men and women. In Bali, where destination weddings are common, the hotel employs a "weather shaman" who, for some guests, provides reassurance that the weather will cooperate for their special day. In all cases, the objective is to provide a truly local experience.

When staffing its hotels, Four Seasons seeks to strike a fine balance between employing locals who have an innate understanding of the local culture alongside expatriate staff or "culture carriers" who understand the DNA of Four Seasons. It also uses global systems to track customer preferences and employs globally consistent service standards. Four Seasons claims that its guests experience the same high level of service globally but that no two experiences are the same.

While it is much more expensive and time-consuming to design unique architectural and programming experiences, doing so is a strategic trade-off Four Seasons has made to achieve the local experience demanded by its high-level clientele. Likewise, it has recognized that maintaining globally consistent operation processes and service standards is important too. Four Seasons has struck the right balance between thinking globally and acting locally—the marker of a truly transnational strategy. As a result, the company has been rewarded with an international reputation for superior service and a leading market share in the luxury hospitality segment.

Note: Developed with Brian R. McKenzie.

Sources: Four Seasons annual report and corporate website; and interview with Scott Woroch, Executive Vice President of Development, Four Seasons Hotels, February 22, 2014.

Viacheslav Lopatin/Shutterstock

Using Location to Build Competitive Advantage

To use location to build competitive advantage, a company must consider two issues: (1) whether to concentrate each internal process in a few countries or to disperse performance of each process to many nations, and (2) in which countries to locate particular activities.

When to Concentrate Internal Processes in a Few Locations Companies tend to concentrate their activities in a limited number of locations in the following circumstances:

- *When the costs of manufacturing or other activities are significantly lower in some geographic locations than in others.* For example, much of the world's athletic footwear is manufactured in Asia (China and Korea) because of low labor costs; much of the production of circuit boards for PCs is located in Taiwan because of both low costs and the high-caliber technical skills of the Taiwanese labor force.

- *When there are significant scale economies.* The presence of significant economies of scale in components production or final assembly means a company can gain major cost savings from operating a few superefficient plants as opposed to a host of small plants scattered across the world. Makers of digital cameras and LED TVs located in Japan, South Korea, and Taiwan have used their scale economies to establish a low-cost advantage.

- *When there is a steep learning curve associated with performing an activity.* In some industries, learning-curve effects in parts manufacture or assembly are so great that a company establishes one or two large plants from which it serves the world market. The key to riding down the learning curve is to concentrate production in a few locations to increase the accumulated volume at a plant (and thus the experience of the plant's workforce) as rapidly as possible.

- *When certain locations have superior resources, allow better coordination of related activities, or offer other valuable advantages.* A research unit or a sophisticated production facility may be situated in a particular nation because of its pool of technically trained personnel. Samsung became a leader in memory chip technology by establishing a major R&D facility in Silicon Valley and transferring the know-how it gained back to headquarters and its plants in South Korea.

> Companies that compete multinationally can pursue competitive advantage in world markets by locating their value chain activities in whichever nations prove most advantageous.

When to Disperse Internal Processes Across Many Locations There are several instances when dispersing a process is more advantageous than concentrating it in a single location. Buyer-related activities, such as distribution to dealers, sales and advertising, and after-sale service, usually must take place close to buyers. This makes it necessary to physically locate the capability to perform such activities in every country market where a global firm has major customers. For example, large public accounting firms have numerous international offices to service the foreign operations of their multinational corporate clients. Dispersing activities to many locations is also competitively important when high transportation costs, diseconomies of large size, and trade barriers make it too expensive to operate from a central location. In addition, it is strategically advantageous to disperse activities to hedge against the risks of fluctuating exchange rates and adverse political developments.

Using Cross-Border Coordination to Build Competitive Advantage

Multinational and global competitors are able to coordinate activities across different countries to build competitive advantage.[14] If a firm learns how to assemble its product more efficiently at, say, its Brazilian plant, the accumulated expertise and knowledge can be shared with assembly plants in other world locations. Also, knowledge gained in marketing a company's product in Great Britain, for instance, can readily be exchanged with company personnel in New Zealand or Australia. Other examples of cross-border coordination include shifting production from a plant in one country to a plant in another to take advantage of exchange rate fluctuations and to respond to changing wage rates, energy costs, or changes in tariffs and quotas.

Efficiencies can also be achieved by shifting workloads from where they are unusually heavy to locations where personnel are underutilized. Whirlpool's efforts to link its product R&D and manufacturing operations in North America, Latin America, Europe, and Asia allowed it to accelerate the discovery of innovative appliance features, coordinate the introduction of these features in the appliance products marketed in different countries, and create a cost-efficient worldwide supply chain. Whirlpool's conscious efforts to integrate and coordinate its various operations around the world have helped it achieve operational excellence and speed product innovations to market.

Strategies for Competing in the Markets of Developing Countries

LO7-6 Recognize the unique characteristics of competing in developing-country markets.

Companies racing for global leadership have to consider competing in developing-economy markets such as China, India, Brazil, Indonesia, Thailand, Poland, Russia, and Mexico—countries where the business risks are considerable but where the opportunities for growth are huge, especially as their economies develop and living standards climb toward levels in the industrialized world.[15] For example, in 2017 China was the world's second-largest economy (behind the United States) based upon purchasing power, and its population of 1.4 billion people made it the world's largest market for many commodities and types of consumer goods. China's growth in demand for consumer goods has made it the fifth-largest market for luxury goods, with sales greater than those in developed markets such as Germany, Spain, and the United Kingdom.[16] Thus, no company pursuing global market leadership can afford to ignore the strategic importance of establishing competitive market positions in China, India, other parts of the Asian-Pacific region, Latin America, and Eastern Europe.

Tailoring products to fit conditions in an emerging country market such as China, however, often involves more than making minor product changes and becoming more familiar with local cultures. McDonald's has had to offer vegetable burgers in parts of Asia and to rethink its prices, which are often high by local standards and affordable only by the well-to-do. Kellogg has struggled to introduce its cereals successfully because consumers in many less-developed countries do not eat cereal for breakfast—changing habits is difficult and expensive. Single-serving packages of detergents, shampoos, pickles, cough syrup, and cooking oils are very popular in India because they allow buyers to conserve cash by purchasing only what they need immediately. Thus, many companies find that trying to employ a strategy akin to that used in the markets of developed countries is hazardous.[17] Experimenting with some, perhaps many, local twists is usually necessary to find a strategy combination that works.

Strategy Options for Competing in Developing-Country Markets

Several strategy options for tailoring a company's strategy to fit the sometimes unusual or challenging circumstances presented in developing-country markets include:

- *Prepare to compete on the basis of low price.* Consumers in emerging markets are often highly focused on price, which can give low-cost local competitors the edge unless a company can find ways to attract buyers with bargain prices as well as better products. For example, when Unilever entered the market for laundry detergents in India, it developed a low-cost detergent (named Wheel) that was not harsh to the skin, constructed new superefficient production facilities, distributed the product to local merchants by handcarts, and crafted an economical marketing campaign that included painted signs on buildings and demonstrations near stores. The new brand quickly captured $100 million in sales and was the top detergent brand in India in 2014 based on dollar sales. Unilever later replicated the strategy with low-price shampoos and deodorants in India and in South America with a detergent brand named Ala.

- *Modify aspects of the company's business model or strategy to accommodate local circumstances (but not so much that the company loses the advantage of global scale and global branding).* For instance, Honeywell had sold industrial products and services for more than 100 years outside the United States and Europe using a foreign subsidiary model that focused international activities on sales only. When Honeywell entered China, it discovered that industrial customers in that country considered how many key jobs foreign companies created in China in addition to the quality and price of the product or service when making purchasing decisions. Honeywell added about 150 engineers, strategists, and marketers in China to demonstrate its commitment to bolstering the Chinese economy. Honeywell replicated its "East for East" strategy when it entered the market for industrial products and services in India. Within 10 years of Honeywell establishing operations in China and three years of expanding into India, the two emerging markets accounted for 30 percent of the firm's worldwide growth.

- *Try to change the local market to better match the way the company does business elsewhere.* A multinational company often has enough market clout to drive major changes in the way a local country market operates. When Japan's Suzuki entered India, it triggered a quality revolution among Indian auto parts manufacturers. Local parts and components suppliers teamed up with Suzuki's vendors in Japan and worked with Japanese experts to produce higher-quality products. Over the next two decades, Indian companies became very proficient in making top-notch parts and components for vehicles, won more prizes for quality than companies in any country other than Japan, and broke into the global market as suppliers to many automakers in Asia and other parts of the world. Mahindra and Mahindra, one of India's premier automobile manufacturers, has been recognized by a number of organizations for its product quality. Among its most noteworthy awards was its number-one ranking by J. D. Power Asia Pacific for new-vehicle overall quality.

- *Stay away from those emerging markets where it is impractical or uneconomical to modify the company's business model to accommodate local circumstances.* Home Depot expanded successfully into Mexico but has avoided entry into other emerging countries because its value proposition of good quality, low prices, and attentive customer service relies on (1) good highways and logistical systems to minimize store inventory costs, (2) employee stock ownership to help motivate store personnel to provide good customer service, and (3) high labor costs for housing construction and home repairs to encourage homeowners to engage in do-it-yourself projects. Relying on these factors in the U.S. and Canadian markets has worked spectacularly for Home Depot, but Home Depot has found that it cannot count on these factors in China, from which it withdrew in 2012.

Company experiences in entering developing markets such as China, India, Russia, and Brazil indicate that profitability seldom comes quickly or easily. Building a market for the company's products can often turn into a long-term process that involves reeducation of consumers, sizable investments in advertising and promotion to alter tastes and buying habits, and upgrades of the local infrastructure (the supplier base, transportation systems, distribution channels, labor markets, and capital markets). In such cases, a company must be patient, work within the system to improve the infrastructure, and lay the foundation for generating sizable revenues and profits once conditions are ripe for market takeoff.

> Profitability in emerging markets rarely comes quickly or easily. New entrants have to adapt their business models and strategies to local conditions and be patient in earning a profit.

KEY POINTS

1. Competing in international markets allows multinational companies to (1) gain access to new customers, (2) achieve lower costs and enhance the firm's competitiveness by more easily capturing scale economies or learning-curve effects, (3) leverage core competencies refined domestically in additional country markets, (4) gain access to resources and capabilities located in foreign markets, and (5) spread business risk across a wider market base.

2. Companies electing to expand into international markets must consider cross-country differences in buyer tastes, market sizes, and growth potential; location-based cost drivers; adverse exchange rates; and host-government policies when evaluating strategy options.

3. Options for entering foreign markets include maintaining a national (one-country) production base and exporting goods to foreign markets, licensing foreign firms to use the company's technology or produce and distribute the company's products, employing a franchising strategy, establishing a foreign subsidiary, and using strategic alliances or other collaborative partnerships.

4. In posturing to compete in foreign markets, a company has three basic options: (1) a multidomestic or think local, act local approach to crafting a strategy, (2) a global or think global, act global approach to crafting a strategy, and (3) a transnational strategy or combination think global, act local approach. A "think local, act local" or multicountry strategy is appropriate for industries or companies that must vary their product offerings and competitive approaches from country to country to accommodate differing buyer preferences and market conditions. A "think global, act global" approach (or global strategy) works best in markets that support employing the same basic competitive approach (low-cost, differentiation, focused) in all country markets and marketing essentially the same products under the same brand names in all countries where the company operates. A "think global, act local" approach can be used when it is feasible for a company to employ essentially the same basic competitive strategy in all markets but still customize its product offering and some aspect of its operations to fit local market circumstances.

5. There are two general ways in which a firm can gain competitive advantage (or offset domestic disadvantages) in global markets. One way involves locating various value chain activities among nations in a manner that lowers costs or achieves greater product differentiation. A second way draws on a multinational or global competitor's ability to deepen or broaden its resources and capabilities and to coordinate its dispersed activities in ways that a domestic-only competitor cannot.

6.   Companies racing for global leadership have to consider competing in emerging markets such as China, India, Brazil, Indonesia, and Mexico—countries where the business risks are considerable but the opportunities for growth are huge. To succeed in these markets, companies often have to (1) compete on the basis of low price, (2) be prepared to modify aspects of the company's business model or strategy to accommodate local circumstances (but not so much that the company loses the advantage of global scale and global branding), and/or (3) try to change the local market to better match the way the company does business elsewhere. Profitability is unlikely to come quickly or easily in emerging markets, typically because of the investments needed to alter buying habits and tastes and/or the need for infrastructure upgrades. And there may be times when a company should simply stay away from certain emerging markets until conditions for entry are better suited to its business model and strategy.

ASSURANCE OF LEARNING EXERCISES

LO7-1, LO7-3   1.   L'Oréal markets 34 brands of cosmetics, fragrances, and hair care products in 130 countries. The company's international strategy involves manufacturing these products in 42 plants located around the world. L'Oréal's international strategy is discussed in its operations section of the company's website (http://www.loreal.com/careers/who-you-can-be/operations) and in its press releases, annual reports, and presentations. Why has the company chosen to pursue a foreign subsidiary strategy? Are there strategic advantages to global sourcing and production in the cosmetics, fragrances, and hair care products industry relative to an export strategy?

LO7-1, LO7-3   2.   Alliances, joint ventures, and mergers with foreign companies are widely used as a means of entering foreign markets. Such arrangements have many purposes, including learning about unfamiliar environments, and the opportunity to access the complementary resources and capabilities of a foreign partner. Concepts & Connections 7.1 provides an example of how Walgreens used a strategy of entering foreign markets via alliance, followed by a merger with the same entity. What was this entry strategy designed to achieve, and why would this make sense for a company like Walgreens?

LO7-2, LO7-3   3.   Assume you are in charge of developing the strategy for a multinational company selling products in some 50 countries around the world. One of the issues you face is whether to employ a multidomestic, transnational, or global strategy.

   a.   If your company's product is mobile phones, do you think it would make better strategic sense to employ a multidomestic strategy, a transnational strategy, or a global strategy? Why?

   b.   If your company's product is dry soup mixes and canned soups, would a multidomestic strategy seem to be more advisable than a transnational or global strategy? Why or why not?

   c.   If your company's product is large home appliances such as washing machines, ranges, ovens, and refrigerators, would it seem to make more sense to pursue a multidomestic strategy or a transnational strategy or a global strategy? Why?

LO7-5, LO7-6   4.   Using your university library's business research resources and Internet sources, identify and discuss three key strategies that Volkswagen is using to compete in China.

EXERCISES FOR SIMULATION PARTICIPANTS

The following questions are for simulation participants whose companies operate in an international market arena. If your company competes only in a single country, then skip the questions in this section.

LO7-2   1.   To what extent, if any, have you and your co-managers adapted your company's strategy to take shifting exchange rates into account? In other words, have you undertaken any actions to try to minimize the impact of adverse shifts in exchange rates?

2. To what extent, if any, have you and your co-managers adapted your company's strategy to consider geographic differences in import tariffs or import duties? **LO7-2**

3. What are the attributes of each of the following approaches to competing in international markets? **LO7-4**

   • Multidomestic or think local, act local approach
   • Global or think global, act global approach
   • Transnational or think global, act local approach

Explain your answer and indicate two or three chief elements of your company's strategy for competing in two or more different geographic regions.

ENDNOTES

1. A. C. Inkpen and A. Dinur, "Knowledge Management Processes and International Joint Ventures," *Organization Science* 9, no. 4 (July–August 1998); P. Dussauge, B. Garrette, and W. Mitchell, "Learning from Competing Partners: Outcomes and Durations of Scale and Link Alliances in Europe, North America and Asia," *Strategic Management Journal* 21, no. 2 (February 2000); C. Dhanaraj, M. A. Lyles, H. K. Steensma, et al., "Managing Tacit and Explicit Knowledge Transfer in IJVS: The Role of Relational Embeddedness and the Impact on Performance," *Journal of International Business Studies* 35, no. 5 (September 2004); K. W. Glaister and P. J. Buckley, "Strategic Motives for International Alliance Formation," *Journal of Management Studies* 33, no. 3 (May 1996); J. Anand and B. Kogut, "Technological Capabilities of Countries, Firm Rivalry and Foreign Direct Investment," *Journal of International Business Studies* 28, no. 3 (1997); J. Anand and A. Delios, "Absolute and Relative Resources as Determinants of International Acquisitions," *Strategic Management Journal* 23, no. 2 (February 2002); A. Seth, K. Song, and A. Pettit, "Value Creation and Destruction in Cross-Border Acquisitions: An Empirical Analysis of Foreign Acquisitions of U.S. Firms," *Strategic Management Journal* 23, no. 10 (October 2002); J. Anand, L. Capron, and W. Mitchell, "Using Acquisitions to Access Multinational Diversity: Thinking Beyond the Domestic Versus Cross-Border M&A Comparison," *Industrial & Corporate Change* 14, no. 2 (April 2005).

2. Robert Ferris, "China Annual Auto Sales Fall for First Time in About Two Decades with More Pain on the Way," CNBC News, January 3, 2019, https://www.cnbc.com/2019/01/03/china-annual-auto-sales-fall-for-first-time-in-about-two-decades.html.

3. Actual and estimated rates reported by The Conference Board, "International Comparisons of Hourly Compensation Costs in Manufacturing, 2016," February 18, 2016. (Rates for India and China based upon 2013 estimates, respectively.)

4. E. Pablo, "Determinants of Cross-Border M&As in Latin America," *Journal of Business Research* 62, no. 9 (2009); R. Olie, "Shades of Culture and Institutions in International Mergers," *Organization Studies* 15, no. 3 (1994); K. E. Meyer, M. Wright, and S. Pruthi, "Institutions, Resources, and Entry Strategies in Emerging Economies," *Strategic Management Journal* 30, no. 5 (2009).

5. Joel Bleeke and David Ernst, "The Way to Win in Cross-Border Alliances," *Harvard Business Review* 69, no. 6 (November–December 1991); Gary Hamel, Yves L. Doz, and C. K. Prahalad, "Collaborate with Your Competitors—and Win," *Harvard Business Review* 67, no. 1 (January–February 1989).

6. Yves L. Doz and Gary Hamel, *Alliance Advantage* (Boston: Harvard Business School Press, 1998); Bleeke and Ernst, "The Way to Win in Cross-Border Alliances"; Hamel, Doz, and Prahalad, "Collaborate with Your Competitors—and Win"; Michael Porter, *The Competitive Advantage of Nations* (New York: Free Press, 1990).

7. H. Kurt Christensen, "Corporate Strategy: Managing a Set of Businesses," in *The Portable MBA in Strategy*, ed. Liam Fahey and Robert M. Randall (New York: John Wiley & Sons, 2001).

8. Jeffrey H. Dyer, Prashant Kale, and Harbir Singh, "When to Ally and When to Acquire," *Harvard Business Review* 82, no. 7/8 (July–August 2004).

9. Rosabeth Moss Kanter, "Collaborative Advantage: The Art of the Alliance," *Harvard Business Review* 72, no. 4 (July–August 1994).

10. Jeremy Main, "Making Global Alliances Work," *Fortune*, December 19, 1990, p. 125.

11. Pankaj Ghemawat, "Managing Differences: The Central Challenge of Global Strategy," *Harvard Business Review* 85, no. 3 (March 2007).

12. C. A. Bartlett and S. Ghoshal, *Managing Across Borders: The Transnational Solution*, 2nd ed. (Boston: Harvard Business School Press, 1998).

13. Lynn S. Paine, "The China Rules," *Harvard Business Review* 88, no. 6 (June 2010), pp. 103–108.

14. C. K. Prahalad and Yves L. Doz, *The Multinational Mission* (New York: Free Press, 1987), pp. 58–60.

15. David J. Arnold and John A. Quelch, "New Strategies in Emerging Markets," *Sloan Management Review* 40, no. 1 (Fall 1998); and C. K. Prahalad, *The Fortune at the Bottom of the Pyramid: Eradicating Poverty Through Profits* (Upper Saddle River, NJ: Wharton, 2005).

16. *Global Powers of Luxury Goods*, Deloitte Touche Tohmatsu Limited, 2017.

17. Tarun Khanna, Krishna G. Palepu, and Jayant Sinha, "Strategies That Fit Emerging Markets," *Harvard Business Review* 83, no. 6 (June 2005); Arindam K. Bhattacharya and David C. Michael, "How Local Companies Keep Multinationals at Bay," *Harvard Business Review* 86, no. 3 (March 2008).

8 CORPORATE STRATEGY: DIVERSIFICATION AND THE MULTIBUSINESS COMPANY

LEARNING OBJECTIVES

After reading this chapter, you should be able to:

LO8-1 Understand when and how business diversification can enhance shareholder value.

LO8-2 Explain how related diversification strategies can produce cross-business strategic fit capable of delivering competitive advantage.

LO8-3 Recognize the merits and risks of corporate strategies keyed to unrelated diversification.

LO8-4 Evaluate a company's diversification strategy.

LO8-5 Identify a diversified company's four main corporate strategy options for solidifying its diversification strategy and improving company performance.

This chapter moves up one level in the strategy-making hierarchy, from strategy making in a single-business enterprise to strategy making in a diversified enterprise. Because a diversified company is a collection of individual businesses, the strategy-making task is more complicated. In a one-business company, managers have to come up with a plan for competing successfully in only a single industry environment—the result is what Chapter 2 labeled as *business strategy* (or *business-level strategy*). But in a diversified company, the strategy-making challenge involves assessing multiple industry environments and developing a *set* of business strategies, one for each industry arena in which the diversified company operates. And top executives at a diversified company must still go one step further and devise a companywide or *corporate strategy* for improving the attractiveness and performance of the company's overall business lineup and for making a rational whole out of its diversified collection of individual businesses.

In most diversified companies, corporate-level executives delegate considerable strategy-making authority to the heads of each business, usually giving them the latitude to craft a business strategy suited to their particular industry and competitive circumstances and holding them accountable for producing good results. But the task of crafting a diversified company's overall corporate strategy falls squarely in the lap of top-level executives and involves four distinct facets:

1. *Picking new industries to enter and deciding on the means of entry.* The decision to pursue business diversification requires that management decide what new industries offer the best growth prospects and whether to enter by starting a new business from the ground up, acquiring a company already in the target industry, or forming a joint venture or strategic alliance with another company.

2. *Pursuing opportunities to leverage cross-business value chain relationships into competitive advantage.* Companies that diversify into businesses with strategic fit across the value chains of their business units have a much better chance of gaining a $1 + 1 = 3$ effect than do multibusiness companies lacking strategic fit.

3. *Establishing investment priorities and steering corporate resources into the most attractive business units.* A diversified company's business units are usually not equally attractive, and it is incumbent on corporate management to channel resources into areas where earnings potentials are higher.

4. *Initiating actions to boost the combined performance of the corporation's collection of businesses.* Corporate strategists must craft moves to improve the overall performance of the corporation's business lineup and sustain increases in shareholder value. Strategic options for diversified corporations include *(a)* sticking closely with the existing business lineup and pursuing opportunities presented by these businesses, *(b)* broadening the scope of diversification by entering additional industries, *(c)* retrenching to a narrower scope of diversification by divesting poorly performing businesses, and *(d)* broadly restructuring the business lineup with multiple divestitures and/or acquisitions.

The first portion of this chapter describes the various means a company can use to diversify and explores the pros and cons of related versus unrelated diversification strategies. The second part of the chapter looks at how to evaluate the attractiveness of a diversified company's business lineup, decide whether it has a good diversification strategy, and identify ways to improve its future performance.

When Business Diversification Becomes a Consideration

LO8-1   Understand when and how business diversification can enhance shareholder value.

As long as a single-business company can achieve profitable growth opportunities in its present industry, there is no urgency to pursue diversification. However, a company's opportunities for growth can become limited if the industry becomes competitively unattractive. Consider, for example, what mobile phone companies and marketers of Voice over Internet Protocol (VoIP) have done to the revenues of long-distance providers such as AT&T, British Telecommunications, and NTT in Japan. Thus, *diversifying into new industries always merits strong consideration whenever a single-business company encounters diminishing market opportunities and stagnating sales in its principal business.*[1]

Building Shareholder Value: The Ultimate Justification for Business Diversification

Diversification must do more for a company than simply spread its business risk across various industries. In principle, diversification cannot be considered a success unless it results in *added shareholder value*—value that shareholders cannot capture on their own by spreading their investments across the stocks of companies in different industries.

Business diversification stands little chance of building shareholder value without passing the following three tests:[2]

1. *The industry attractiveness test.* The industry to be entered through diversification must offer an opportunity for profits and return on investment that is equal to or better than that of the company's present business(es).

2. *The cost-of-entry test.* The cost to enter the target industry must not be so high as to erode the potential for good profitability. A catch-22 can prevail here, however. The more attractive an industry's prospects are for growth and good long-term profitability, the more expensive it can be to enter. It's easy for acquisitions of companies in highly attractive industries to fail the cost-of-entry test.

3. *The better-off test.* Diversifying into a new business must offer potential for the company's existing businesses and the new business to perform better together under a single corporate umbrella than they would perform operating as independent, standalone businesses. For example, let's say company A diversifies by purchasing company B in another industry. If A and B's consolidated profits in the years to come prove no greater than what each could have earned on its own, then A's diversification will not provide its shareholders with added value. Company A's shareholders could have achieved the same $1 + 1 = 2$ result by merely purchasing stock in company B. Shareholder value is not created by diversification unless it produces a $1 + 1 = 3$ effect.

> Creating added value for shareholders via diversification requires building a multibusiness company in which the whole is greater than the sum of its parts.

Diversification moves that satisfy all three tests have the greatest potential to grow shareholder value over the long term. Diversification moves that can pass only one or two tests are suspect.

Approaches to Diversifying the Business Lineup

The means of entering new industries and lines of business can take any of three forms: acquisition, internal development, or joint ventures with other companies.

Diversification by Acquisition of an Existing Business

Acquisition is a popular means of diversifying into another industry. Not only is it quicker than trying to launch a new operation, but it also offers an effective way to hurdle such entry barriers as acquiring technological know-how, establishing supplier relationships, achieving scale economies, building brand awareness, and securing adequate distribution. Buying an ongoing operation allows the acquirer to move directly to the task of building a strong market position in the target industry, rather than getting bogged down in the fine points of launching a startup.

The big dilemma an acquisition-minded firm faces is whether to pay a premium price for a successful company or to buy a struggling company at a bargain price.[3] If the buying firm has little knowledge of the industry but has ample capital, it is often better off purchasing a capable, strongly positioned firm—unless the price of such an acquisition is prohibitive and flunks the cost-of-entry test. However, when the acquirer sees promising ways to transform a weak firm into a strong one, a struggling company can be the better long-term investment.

Entering a New Line of Business Through Internal Development

Achieving diversification through *internal development* involves starting a new business subsidiary from scratch. Generally, forming a startup subsidiary to enter a new business has appeal only when (1) the parent company already has in-house most or all of the skills and resources needed to compete effectively; (2) there is ample time to launch the business; (3) internal entry has lower costs than entry via acquisition; (4) the targeted industry is populated with many relatively small firms such that the new startup does not have to compete against large, powerful rivals; (5) adding new production capacity will not adversely impact the supply–demand balance in the industry; and (6) incumbent firms are likely to be slow or ineffective in responding to a new entrant's efforts to crack the market.

Using Joint Ventures to Achieve Diversification

A joint venture to enter a new business can be useful in at least two types of situations.[4] First, a joint venture is a good vehicle for pursuing an opportunity that is too complex, uneconomical, or risky for one company to pursue alone. Second, joint ventures make sense when the opportunities in a new industry require a broader range of competencies and know-how than an expansion-minded company can marshal. Many of the opportunities in biotechnology call for the coordinated development of complementary innovations and tackling an intricate web of technical, political, and regulatory factors simultaneously. In such cases, pooling the resources and competencies of two or more companies is a wiser and less risky way to proceed.

However, as discussed in Chapters 6 and 7, partnering with another company—in the form of either a joint venture or a collaborative alliance—has significant drawbacks due to the potential for conflicting objectives, disagreements over how to best operate the venture, culture clashes, and so on. Joint ventures are generally the least durable of the entry options, usually lasting only until the partners decide to go their own ways.

Choosing the Diversification Path: Related Versus Unrelated Businesses

Once a company decides to diversify, its first big corporate strategy decision is whether to diversify into **related businesses, unrelated businesses,** or some mix of both (see Figure 8.1). *Businesses are said to be related when their value chains possess competitively valuable cross-business relationships.* These value chain matchups present opportunities for the businesses to perform better under the same corporate umbrella than they could by operating as stand-alone entities. *Businesses are said to be unrelated when the activities comprising their respective value chains and resource requirements are so dissimilar that no competitively valuable cross-business relationships are present.*

The next two sections explore the ins and outs of related and unrelated diversification.

CORE CONCEPT

Related businesses possess competitively valuable cross-business value chain and resource matchups; **unrelated businesses** have dissimilar value chains and resources requirements, with no competitively important cross-business value chain relationships.

FIGURE 8.1

Strategic Themes of Multibusiness Corporation

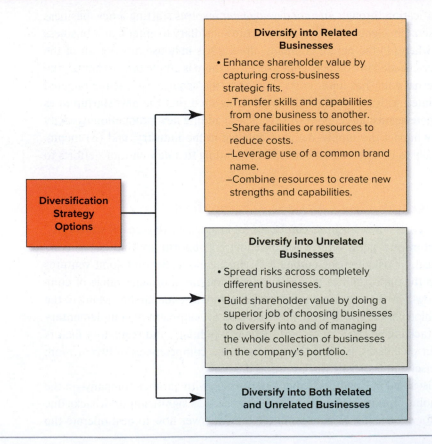

Diversification Strategy Options

Diversify into Related Businesses

- Enhance shareholder value by capturing cross-business strategic fits.
  - Transfer skills and capabilities from one business to another.
  - Share facilities or resources to reduce costs.
  - Leverage use of a common brand name.
  - Combine resources to create new strengths and capabilities.

Diversify into Unrelated Businesses

- Spread risks across completely different businesses.
- Build shareholder value by doing a superior job of choosing businesses to diversify into and of managing the whole collection of businesses in the company's portfolio.

Diversify into Both Related and Unrelated Businesses

Diversifying into Related Businesses

LO8-2   Explain how related diversification strategies can produce cross-business strategic fit capable of delivering competitive advantage.

A related diversification strategy involves building the company around businesses whose value chains possess competitively valuable strategic fit, as shown in Figure 8.2. **Strategic fit** exists whenever one or more activities comprising the value chains of different businesses are sufficiently similar to present opportunities for:[5]

> **CORE CONCEPT**
>
> **Strategic fit** exists when value chains of different businesses present opportunities for cross-business skills transfer, cost sharing, or brand sharing.

- *Transferring competitively valuable resources, expertise, technological know-how, or other capabilities from one business to another.* Google's technological know-how and innovation capabilities refined in its Internet search business have aided considerably in the development of its Android mobile operating system and Chrome operating system for computers. After acquiring Marvel Comics in 2009 and Lucasfilm in 2012, Walt Disney Company integrated Marvel's iconic characters such as Spider-Man and Iron Man and Lucasfilm's Star Wars and Indiana Jones

FIGURE 8.2

Related Diversification Is Built upon Competitively Valuable Strategic Fit in Value Chain Activities

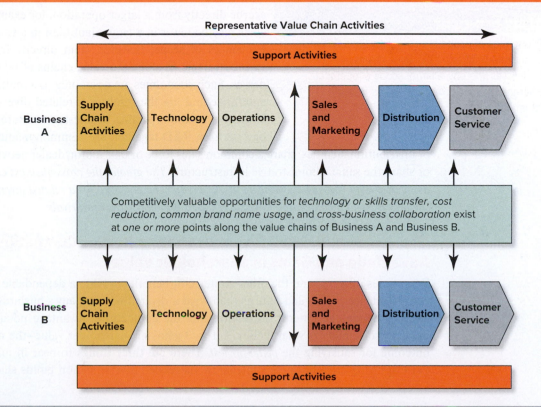

franchises into other Disney businesses, including its theme parks, retail stores, motion picture division, and video game business.

- *Cost sharing between separate businesses where value chain activities can be combined.* For instance, it is often feasible to manufacture the products of different businesses in a single plant or have a single sales force for the products of different businesses if they are marketed to the same types of customers.

- *Brand sharing between business units that have common customers or that draw upon common core competencies.* For example, Apple's reputation for producing easy-to-operate computers and stylish designs were competitive assets that facilitated the company's diversification into smartphones, tablet computers, and wearable technology.

Cross-business strategic fit can exist anywhere along the value chain: in R&D and technology activities, in supply chain activities, in manufacturing, in sales and marketing, or in distribution activities. Likewise, different businesses can often use the same administrative and customer service infrastructure. For instance, a cable operator that diversifies as a broadband provider can use the same customer data network, the same customer call centers and local offices, the same billing and customer accounting systems, and the same customer service infrastructure to support all its products and services.[6]

Strategic Fit and Economies of Scope

Strategic fit in the value chain activities of a diversified corporation's different businesses opens up opportunities for *economies of scope*—a concept distinct from *economies of scale*. Economies of *scale* are cost savings that accrue directly from a larger operation; for example, unit costs may be lower in a large plant than in a small plant. **Economies of scope,** however, stem directly from cost-saving strategic fit along the value chains of related businesses. Such economies are open only to a multibusiness enterprise and are the result of a related diversification strategy that allows sibling businesses to share technology, perform R&D together, use common manufacturing or distribution facilities, share a common sales force or distributor/dealer network, and/or share the same administrative infrastructure. *The greater the cross-business economies associated with cost-saving strategic fit, the greater the potential for a related diversification strategy to yield a competitive advantage based on lower costs than rivals.*

> **CORE CONCEPT**
>
> **Economies of scope** are cost reductions stemming from strategic fit along the value chains of related businesses (thereby, a larger scope of operations), whereas *economies of scale* accrue from a larger operation.

The Ability of Related Diversification to Deliver Competitive Advantage and Gains in Shareholder Value

Economies of scope and the other strategic-fit benefits provide a dependable basis for earning higher profits and returns than what a diversified company's businesses could earn as standalone enterprises. Converting the competitive advantage potential into greater profitability is what fuels $1 + 1 = 3$ gains in shareholder value—the necessary outcome for satisfying the *better-off test.* There are three things to bear in mind here: (1) Capturing cross-business strategic fit via related diversification builds shareholder value in ways that shareholders cannot replicate by simply owning a diversified portfolio of stocks; (2) the capture of cross-business strategic-fit benefits is possible only through related diversification; and (3) the benefits of cross-business strategic fit are not automatically realized—*the benefits materialize only after management has successfully pursued internal actions to capture them.*[7]

Concepts & Connections 8.1 describes the merger of Kraft Foods Group, Inc., with the H. J. Heinz Holding Corporation, in pursuit of the strategic fit benefits of a related diversification strategy.

CONCEPTS & CONNECTIONS 8.1

THE KRAFT–HEINZ MERGER: PURSUING THE BENEFITS OF CROSS-BUSINESS STRATEGIC FIT

Pranav Kukreja/Shutterstock

The $62.6 billion merger between Kraft and Heinz that was finalized in 2015 created the third-largest food and beverage company in North America and the fifth-largest in the world. It was a merger predicated on the idea that the strategic fit between these two companies was such that they could create more value as a combined enterprise than they could as two separate companies. As a combined enterprise, Kraft Heinz would be able to exploit its cross-business value chain activities and resource similarities to more efficiently produce, distribute, and sell profitable processed food products.

Kraft and Heinz products share many of the same raw materials (milk, sugar, salt, wheat, etc.), which allows the new company to leverage its increased bargaining power as a larger business to get better deals with suppliers, using strategic fit in supply chain activities to achieve lower input costs and greater inbound efficiencies. Moreover, because both of these brands specialize in prepackaged foods, there is ample manufacturing-related strategic fit in production processes and packaging technologies that allow the new company to trim and streamline manufacturing operations.

Their distribution-related strategic fit will allow for the complete integration of distribution channels and transportation networks, resulting in greater outbound efficiencies and a reduction in travel time for products moving from factories to stores. The Kraft Heinz Company is currently looking to leverage Heinz's global platform to expand Kraft's products internationally. By utilizing Heinz's already highly developed global distribution network and brand familiarity (key specialized resources), Kraft can more easily expand into the global market of prepackaged and processed food. Because these two brands are sold at similar types of retail stores (supermarket chains, wholesale retailers, and local grocery stores), they are now able to claim even more shelf space with the increased bargaining power of the combined company.

Strategic fit in sales and marketing activities will allow the company to develop coordinated and more effective advertising campaigns. Toward this aim, the Kraft Heinz Company is moving to consolidate its marketing capabilities under one marketing firm. Also, by combining R&D teams, the Kraft Heinz Company could come out with innovative products that may appeal more to the growing number of on-the-go and health-conscious buyers in the market. Many of these potential and predicted synergies for the Kraft Heinz Company have yet to be realized, since merger integration activities always take time.

Note: Developed with Maria Hart.

Sources: www.forbes.com/sites/paulmartyn/2015/03/31/heinz-and-kraft-merger-makes-supply-management-sense/; fortune.com/2015/03/25/kraft-mess-how-heinz-deal-helps/; and www.nytimes.com/2015/03/26/business/dealbook/kraft-and-heinz-to-merge.html?_r=2; company websites (accessed December 3, 2015).

Diversifying into Unrelated Businesses

LO8-3 Recognize the merits and risks of corporate strategies keyed to unrelated diversification.

An unrelated diversification strategy discounts the importance of pursuing cross-business strategic fit and, instead, focuses squarely on entering and operating businesses in industries that allow the company as a whole to increase its earnings. Companies that pursue a strategy of unrelated diversification generally exhibit a willingness to diversify into *any industry* where senior managers see opportunity to realize improved financial results. Such companies are frequently labeled *conglomerates* because their business interests range broadly across diverse industries.

Companies that pursue unrelated diversification nearly always enter new businesses by acquiring an established company rather than by internal development. The premise of acquisition-minded corporations is that growth by acquisition can deliver enhanced shareholder value through upward-trending corporate revenues and earnings and a stock price that *on average* rises enough year after year to amply reward and please shareholders. Three types of acquisition candidates are usually of particular interest: (1) businesses that have bright growth prospects but are short on investment capital, (2) undervalued companies that can be acquired at a bargain price, and (3) struggling companies whose operations can be turned around with the aid of the parent company's financial resources and managerial know-how.

Building Shareholder Value Through Unrelated Diversification

Given the absence of cross-business strategic fit with which to capture added competitive advantage, the task of building shareholder value via unrelated diversification ultimately hinges on the ability of the parent company to improve its businesses via other means. To succeed with a corporate strategy keyed to unrelated diversification, corporate executives must:

- Do a superior job of identifying and acquiring new businesses that can produce consistently good earnings and returns on investment.
- Do an excellent job of negotiating favorable acquisition prices.
- Do such a good job *overseeing* and *parenting* the firm's businesses that they perform at a higher level than they would otherwise be able to do through their own efforts alone. The parenting activities of corporate executives can take the form of providing expert problem-solving skills, creative strategy suggestions, and first-rate advice and guidance on how to improve competitiveness and financial performance to the heads of the various business subsidiaries.[8] Royal Little, the founder of Textron, was a major reason that the company became an exemplar of the unrelated diversification strategy while he was CEO. Little's bold moves transformed the company from its origins as a small textile manufacturer into a global powerhouse known for its Bell helicopters, Cessna aircraft, and a host of other strong brands in an array of industries.

The Pitfalls of Unrelated Diversification

Unrelated diversification strategies have two important negatives that undercut the pluses: very demanding managerial requirements and limited competitive advantage potential.

Demanding Managerial Requirements Successfully managing a set of fundamentally different businesses operating in fundamentally different industry and competitive environments is an exceptionally difficult proposition for corporate-level managers. The greater the number of businesses a company is in and the more diverse they are, the more difficult it is for corporate managers to:

1. Stay abreast of what's happening in each industry and each subsidiary.

2. Pick business-unit heads having the requisite combination of managerial skills and know-how to drive gains in performance.

3. Tell the difference between those strategic proposals of business-unit managers that are prudent and those that are risky or unlikely to succeed.

4. Know what to do if a business unit stumbles and its results suddenly head downhill.[9]

As a rule, the more unrelated businesses that a company has diversified into, the more corporate executives are forced to "manage by the numbers"—that is, keep a close track on the financial and operating results of each subsidiary and assume that the heads of the various subsidiaries have most everything under control so long as the latest key financial and operating measures look good. Managing by the numbers works if the heads of the various business units are quite capable and consistently meet their numbers. But problems arise when things start to go awry and corporate management has to get deeply involved in turning around a business it does not know much about.

> Unrelated diversification requires that corporate executives rely on the skills and expertise of business-level managers to build competitive advantage and boost the performance of individual businesses.

Limited Competitive Advantage Potential The second big negative associated with unrelated diversification is that such a strategy *offers limited potential for competitive advantage beyond what each individual business can generate on its own.* Unlike a related diversification strategy, there is no cross-business strategic fit to draw on for reducing costs; transferring capabilities, skills, and technology; or leveraging use of a powerful brand name and thereby adding to the competitive advantage possessed by individual businesses. *Without the competitive advantage potential of strategic fit, consolidated performance of an unrelated group of businesses is unlikely to be better than the sum of what the individual business units could achieve independently in most instances.*

Misguided Reasons for Pursuing Unrelated Diversification

Competently overseeing a set of widely diverse businesses can turn out to be much harder than it sounds. In practice, comparatively few companies have proved that they have top management capabilities that are up to the task. Far more corporate executives have failed than have been successful at delivering consistently good financial results with an unrelated diversification strategy.[10] Odds are that the result of unrelated diversification will be $1 + 1 = 2$ or less. In addition, management sometimes undertakes a strategy of unrelated diversification for the wrong reasons.

- *Risk reduction.* Managers sometimes pursue unrelated diversification to reduce risk by spreading the company's investments over a set of diverse industries. But this cannot create long-term shareholder value alone since the company's shareholders can more efficiently reduce their exposure to risk by investing in a diversified portfolio of stocks and bonds.

- *Growth.* While unrelated diversification may enable a company to achieve rapid or continuous growth in revenues, only profitable growth can bring about increases in shareholder value and justify a strategy of unrelated diversification.

- *Earnings stabilization.* In a broadly diversified company, there's a chance that market downtrends in some of the company's businesses will be partially offset by cyclical upswings in its other businesses, thus producing somewhat less earnings volatility. In actual practice, however, there's no convincing evidence that the consolidated profits of firms with unrelated diversification strategies are more stable than the profits of firms with related diversification strategies.

- *Managerial motives.* Unrelated diversification can provide benefits to managers such as higher compensation, which tends to increase with firm size and degree of diversification. Diversification for this reason alone is far more likely to reduce shareholder value than to increase it.

Diversifying into Both Related and Unrelated Businesses

There's nothing to preclude a company from diversifying into both related and unrelated businesses. Indeed, the business makeup of diversified companies varies considerably. Some diversified companies are really *dominant-business enterprises*—one major "core" business accounts for 50 to 80 percent of total revenues, and a collection of small related or unrelated businesses accounts for the remainder. Some diversified companies are *narrowly diversified* around a few (two to five) related or unrelated businesses. Others are *broadly diversified* around a wide-ranging collection of related businesses, unrelated businesses, or a mixture of both. And a number of multibusiness enterprises have diversified into *several unrelated groups of related businesses.* There's ample room for companies to customize their diversification strategies to incorporate elements of both related and unrelated diversification.

Evaluating the Strategy of a Diversified Company

LO8-4 Evaluate a company's diversification strategy.

Strategic analysis of diversified companies builds on the methodology used for single-business companies discussed in Chapters 3 and 4 but utilizes tools that streamline the overall process. The procedure for evaluating the pluses and minuses of a diversified company's strategy and deciding what actions to take to improve the company's performance involves six steps:

1. Assessing the attractiveness of the industries the company has diversified into.

2. Assessing the competitive strength of the company's business units.

3. Evaluating the extent of cross-business strategic fit along the value chains of the company's various business units.

4. Checking whether the firm's resources fit the requirements of its present business lineup.

5. Ranking the performance prospects of the businesses from best to worst and determining a priority for allocating resources.

6. Crafting new strategic moves to improve overall corporate performance.

The core concepts and analytical techniques underlying each of these steps are discussed further in this section of the chapter.

Step 1: Evaluating Industry Attractiveness

A principal consideration in evaluating the caliber of a diversified company's strategy is the attractiveness of the industries in which it has business operations. The more attractive the industries (both individually and as a group) a diversified company is in, the better its prospects for good long-term performance. A simple and reliable analytical tool for gauging industry attractiveness involves calculating quantitative industry attractiveness scores based upon the following measures:

- *Market size and projected growth rate.* Big industries are more attractive than small industries, and fast-growing industries tend to be more attractive than slow-growing industries, other things being equal.

- *The intensity of competition.* Industries in which competitive pressures are relatively weak are more attractive than industries with strong competitive pressures.

- *Emerging opportunities and threats.* Industries with promising opportunities and minimal threats on the near horizon are more attractive than industries with modest opportunities and imposing threats.

- *The presence of cross-industry strategic fit.* The more the industry's value chain and resource requirements match up well with the value chain activities of other industries in which the company has operations, the more attractive the industry is to a firm pursuing related diversification. However, cross-industry strategic fit may be of no consequence to a company committed to a strategy of unrelated diversification.

- *Resource requirements.* Industries having resource requirements within the company's reach are more attractive than industries where capital and other resource requirements could strain corporate financial resources and organizational capabilities.

- *Seasonal and cyclical factors.* Industries where buyer demand is relatively steady year-round and not unduly vulnerable to economic ups and downs tend to be more attractive than industries with wide seasonal or cyclical swings in buyer demand.

- *Social, political, regulatory, and environmental factors.* Industries with significant problems in such areas as consumer health, safety, or environmental pollution or that are subject to intense regulation are less attractive than industries where such problems are not burning issues.

- *Industry profitability.* Industries with healthy profit margins are generally more attractive than industries where profits have historically been low or unstable.

- *Industry uncertainty and business risk.* Industries with less uncertainty on the horizon and lower overall business risk are more attractive than industries whose prospects for one reason or another are quite uncertain.

Each attractiveness measure should be assigned a weight reflecting its relative importance in determining an industry's attractiveness; it is weak methodology to assume that the various attractiveness measures are equally important. The intensity of competition in an industry should nearly always carry a high weight (say, 0.20 to 0.30). Strategic-fit considerations should be assigned a high weight in the case of companies with related diversification strategies; but for companies with an unrelated diversification strategy, strategic fit with other industries may be given a low weight or even dropped from the list of attractiveness measures. Seasonal and cyclical factors generally are assigned a low weight (or maybe even eliminated from the analysis) unless a company has diversified into industries strongly characterized by seasonal demand and/or heavy vulnerability to cyclical upswings and downswings. The importance weights must add up to 1.0.

Next, each industry is rated on each of the chosen industry attractiveness measures, using a rating scale of 1 to 10 (where 10 signifies *high* attractiveness and 1 signifies *low* attractiveness). Weighted attractiveness scores are then calculated by multiplying the industry's rating on each measure by the corresponding weight. For example, a rating of 8 times a weight of 0.25 gives a weighted attractiveness score of 2.00. The sum of the weighted scores for all the attractiveness measures provides an overall industry attractiveness score. This procedure is illustrated in Table 8.1.

Calculating Industry Attractiveness Scores Two conditions are necessary for producing valid industry attractiveness scores using this method. One is deciding on appropriate weights for the industry attractiveness measures. This is not always easy because different analysts have different views about which weights are most appropriate. Also, different weightings may be appropriate for different companies—based on their

TABLE 8.1

Calculating Weighted Industry Attractiveness Scores

Industry Attractiveness Measure	Importance/ Weight	Industry A Rating/Score	Industry B Rating/Score	Industry C Rating/Score	Industry D Rating/Score
Market size and projected growth rate	0.10	8/0.80	5/0.50	2/0.20	3/0.30
Intensity of competition	0.25	8/2.00	7/1.75	3/0.75	2/0.50
Emerging opportunities and threats	0.10	2/0.20	9/0.90	4/0.40	5/0.50
Cross-industry strategic fit	0.20	8/1.60	4/0.80	8/1.60	2/0.40
Resource requirements	0.10	9/0.90	7/0.70	5/0.50	5/0.50
Seasonal and cyclical influences	0.05	9/0.45	8/0.40	10/0.50	5/0.25
Societal, political, regulatory, and environmental factors	0.05	10/0.50	7/0.35	7/0.35	3/0.15
Industry profitability	0.10	5/0.50	10/1.00	3/0.30	3/0.30
Industry uncertainty and business risk	0.05	5/0.25	7/0.35	10/0.50	1/0.05
Sum of the assigned weights	1.00				
Overall weighted industry attractiveness scores		**7.20**	**6.75**	**5.10**	**2.95**

Rating scale: 1 = Very unattractive to company; 10 = Very attractive to company

strategies, performance targets, and financial circumstances. For instance, placing a low weight on financial resource requirements may be justifiable for a cash-rich company, whereas a high weight may be more appropriate for a financially strapped company.

The second requirement for creating accurate attractiveness scores is to have sufficient knowledge to rate the industry on each attractiveness measure. It's usually rather easy to locate statistical data needed to compare industries on market size, growth rate, seasonal and cyclical influences, and industry profitability. Cross-industry fit and resource requirements are also fairly easy to judge. But the attractiveness measure that is toughest to rate is that of intensity of competition. It is not always easy to conclude whether competition in one industry is stronger or weaker than in another industry. In the event that the available information is too skimpy to confidently assign a rating value to an industry on a particular attractiveness measure, then it is usually best to use a score of 5, which avoids biasing the overall attractiveness score either up or down.

Despite the hurdles, calculating industry attractiveness scores is a systematic and reasonably reliable method for ranking a diversified company's industries from most to least attractive.

Step 2: Evaluating Business-Unit Competitive Strength

The second step in evaluating a diversified company is to determine how strongly positioned its business units are in their respective industries. Doing an appraisal of each business unit's strength and competitive position in its industry not only reveals its chances for industry success but also provides a basis for ranking the units from competitively strongest to weakest. Quantitative measures of each business unit's competitive strength can be calculated using a procedure similar to that for measuring industry attractiveness. The following factors may be used in quantifying the competitive strengths of a diversified company's business subsidiaries:

- *Relative market share.* A business unit's *relative market share* is defined as the ratio of its market share to the market share held by the largest rival firm in the industry, with market share measured in unit volume, not dollars. For instance, if business A has a market-leading share of 40 percent and its largest rival has 30 percent, A's relative market share is 1.33. If business B has a 15 percent market share and B's largest rival has 30 percent, B's relative market share is 0.5.

- *Costs relative to competitors' costs.* There's reason to expect that business units with higher relative market shares have lower unit costs than competitors with lower relative market shares because of the possibility of scale economies and experience or learning-curve effects. Another indicator of low cost can be a business unit's supply chain management capabilities.

- *Products or services that satisfy buyer expectations.* A company's competitiveness depends in part on being able to offer buyers appealing features, performance, reliability, and service attributes.

- *Ability to benefit from strategic fit with sibling businesses.* Strategic fit with other businesses within the company enhances a business unit's competitive strength and may provide a competitive edge.

- *Number and caliber of strategic alliances and collaborative partnerships.* Well-functioning alliances and partnerships may be a source of potential competitive advantage and thus add to a business's competitive strength.

- *Brand image and reputation.* A strong brand name is a valuable competitive asset in most industries.

- *Competitively valuable capabilities.* All industries contain a variety of important competitive capabilities related to product innovation, production capabilities, distribution capabilities, or marketing prowess.

- *Profitability relative to competitors.* Above-average returns on investment and large profit margins relative to rivals are usually accurate indicators of competitive advantage.

After settling on a set of competitive strength measures that are well matched to the circumstances of the various business units, weights indicating each measure's importance need to be assigned. As in the assignment of weights to industry attractiveness measures, the importance weights must add up to 1.0. Each business unit is then rated on each of the chosen strength measures, using a rating scale of 1 to 10 (where 10 signifies competitive *strength* and a rating of 1 signifies competitive *weakness*). If the available information is too skimpy to confidently assign a rating value to a business unit on a particular strength measure, then it is usually best to use a score of 5. Weighted strength ratings are calculated by multiplying the business unit's rating on each strength measure by the assigned weight. For example, a strength score of 6 times a weight of 0.15 gives a weighted strength rating of 0.90. The sum of weighted ratings across all the strength measures provides a quantitative measure of a business unit's overall market strength and competitive standing. Table 8.2 provides sample calculations of competitive strength ratings for four businesses.

Using a Nine-Cell Matrix to Evaluate the Strength of a Diversified Company's Business Lineup

The industry attractiveness and business strength scores can be used to portray the strategic positions of each business in a diversified company. Industry attractiveness is plotted on the vertical axis and competitive strength on the horizontal axis. A nine-cell grid emerges from dividing the vertical axis into three regions (high, medium, and low attractiveness) and the horizontal axis into three regions (strong, average, and weak competitive strength). As shown in Figure 8.3, high attractiveness is associated with scores of 6.7 or greater on a rating scale of 1 to 10, medium attractiveness with scores of 3.3 to 6.7, and low attractiveness with scores below 3.3. Likewise, high competitive strength is defined as a score greater than 6.7, average strength as scores of 3.3 to 6.7, and low strength as scores below 3.3. *Each business unit is plotted on the nine-cell matrix according to its overall attractiveness and strength scores, and then shown as a "bubble."* The size of each bubble is scaled to what percentage of revenues the business generates relative to total corporate revenues. The bubbles in Figure 8.3 were located on the grid using the four industry attractiveness scores from Table 8.1 and the strength scores for the four business units in Table 8.2.

The locations of the business units on the attractiveness–competitive strength matrix provide valuable guidance in deploying corporate resources. In general, *a diversified company's best prospects for good overall performance involve concentrating corporate resources on business units having the greatest competitive strength and industry attractiveness.* Businesses plotted in the three cells in the upper left portion of the attractiveness–competitive strength matrix have both favorable industry attractiveness and competitive

TABLE 8.2

Calculating Weighted Competitive Strength Scores for a Diversified Company's Business Units

Competitive Strength Measure	Importance/ Weight	Business A in Industry A Rating/Score	Business B in Industry B Rating/Score	Business C in Industry C Rating/Score	Business D in Industry D Rating/Score
Relative market share	0.15	10/1.50	1/0.15	6/0.90	2/0.30
Costs relative to competitors' costs	0.20	7/1.40	2/0.40	5/1.00	3/0.60
Ability to match or beat rivals on key product attributes	0.05	9/0.45	4/0.20	8/0.40	4/0.20
Ability to benefit from strategic fit with sister businesses	0.20	8/1.60	4/0.80	4/0.80	2/0.60
Bargaining leverage with suppliers/ buyers; caliber of alliances	0.05	9/0.45	3/0.15	6/0.30	2/0.10
Brand image and reputation	0.10	9/0.90	2/0.20	7/0.70	5/0.50
Competitively valuable capabilities	0.15	7/1.05	2/0.30	5/0.75	3/0.45
Profitability relative to competitors	0.10	5/0.50	1/0.10	4/0.40	4/0.40
Sum of the assigned weights	1.00				
Overall weighted competitive strength scores		**7.85**	**2.30**	**5.25**	**3.15**

Rating scale: 1 = Very weak; 10 = Very strong

strength and should receive a high investment priority. Business units plotted in these three cells (such as business A in Figure 8.3) are referred to as "grow and build" businesses because of their capability to drive future increases in shareholder value.

Next in priority come businesses positioned in the three diagonal cells stretching from the lower left to the upper right (businesses B and C in Figure 8.3). Such businesses usually merit medium or intermediate priority in the parent's resource allocation ranking. However, some businesses in the medium-priority diagonal cells may have brighter or dimmer prospects than others. For example, a small business in the upper right cell of the matrix (like business B), despite being in a highly attractive industry, may occupy too weak a competitive position in its industry to justify the investment and resources needed to turn it into a strong market contender. If, however, a business in the upper right cell has attractive opportunities for rapid growth and a good potential for winning a much stronger market position over time, management may designate it as a grow and build business—the strategic objective here would be to move the business leftward in the attractiveness–competitive strength matrix over time.

Businesses in the three cells in the lower right corner of the matrix (business D in Figure 8.3) typically are weak performers and have the lowest claim on corporate resources. Such businesses are typically good candidates for being divested or else managed in a manner calculated to squeeze out the maximum cash flows from operations. The cash flows from low-performing/low-potential businesses can then be diverted to financing expansion of business units with greater market opportunities. In exceptional cases where a business located in the three lower right cells is nonetheless fairly profitable or has the potential for good earnings and return on investment, the business merits retention and the allocation of sufficient resources to achieve better performance.

A Nine-Cell Industry Attractiveness–Competitive Strength Matrix

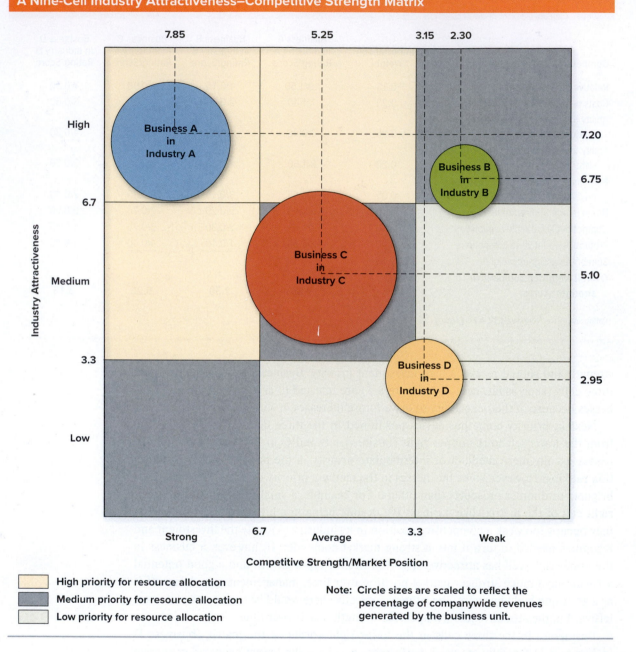

The nine-cell attractiveness–competitive strength matrix provides clear, strong logic for why a diversified company needs to consider both industry attractiveness and business strength in allocating resources and investment capital to its different businesses. A good case can be made for concentrating resources in those businesses that enjoy higher degrees of attractiveness and competitive strength, being very selective in making investments in businesses with intermediate positions on the grid, and withdrawing resources from businesses that are lower in attractiveness and strength unless they offer exceptional profit or cash flow potential.

Step 3: Determining the Competitive Value of Strategic Fit in Multibusiness Companies

The potential for competitively important strategic fit is central to making conclusions about the effectiveness of a company's related diversification strategy. This step can be bypassed for diversified companies whose businesses are all unrelated (because, by design, no cross-business strategic fit is present). Checking the competitive advantage potential of cross-business strategic fit involves evaluating how much benefit a diversified company can gain from value chain matchups that present:

1. Opportunities to combine the performance of certain activities, thereby reducing costs and capturing economies of scope.

2. Opportunities to transfer skills, technology, or intellectual capital from one business to another.

3. Opportunities to share use of a well-respected brand name across multiple product and/or service categories.

But more than just strategic-fit identification is needed. The real test is what competitive value can be generated from this fit. To what extent can cost savings be realized? How much competitive value will come from cross-business transfer of skills, technology, or intellectual capital? Will transferring a potent brand name to the products of sibling businesses grow sales significantly? Absent significant strategic fit and dedicated company efforts to capture the benefits, one has to be skeptical about the potential for a diversified company's businesses to perform better together than apart.

> The greater the value of cross-business strategic fit in enhancing a company's performance in the marketplace or the bottom line, the more powerful is its strategy of related diversification.

Step 4: Evaluating Resource Fit

The businesses in a diversified company's lineup need to exhibit good resource fit. **Resource fit** exists when (1) businesses, individually, strengthen a company's overall mix of resources and capabilities and (2) the parent company has sufficient resources that add customer value to support its entire group of businesses without spreading itself too thin.

> **CORE CONCEPT**
>
> A diversified company exhibits **resource fit** when its businesses add to a company's overall mix of resources and capabilities and when the parent company has sufficient resources to support its entire group of businesses without spreading itself too thin.

Financial Resource Fit   One important dimension of resource fit concerns whether a diversified company can generate the internal cash flows sufficient to fund the capital requirements of its businesses, pay its dividends, meet its debt obligations, and otherwise remain financially healthy. While additional capital can usually be raised in financial markets, it is also important for a diversified firm to have a healthy **internal capital market** that can support the financial requirements of its business lineup. The greater the extent to which a diversified company is able to fund investment in its businesses through internally generated free cash flows rather than from equity issues or borrowing, the more powerful its financial resource fit and the less dependent the firm is on external financial resources.

> **CORE CONCEPT**
>
> A strong **internal capital market** allows a diversified company to add value by shifting capital from business units generating *free cash flow* to those needing additional capital to expand and realize their growth potential.

A *portfolio approach* to ensuring financial fit among the firm's businesses is based on the fact that different businesses have different cash flow and investment characteristics. For example, business units in rapidly growing industries are often **cash hogs**—so labeled because the cash flows they generate from internal operations are not big enough to fund their expansion. To keep pace with rising buyer demand, rapid-growth businesses frequently need sizable annual capital infusions—for new facilities and equipment, technology improvements, and additional working capital to support inventory expansion. Because a cash hog's financial resources must be provided by the corporate parent, corporate managers have to decide whether it makes good financial and strategic sense to keep pouring new money into a cash hog business.

In contrast, business units with leading market positions in mature industries may be **cash cows**—businesses that generate substantial cash surpluses over what is needed to adequately fund their operations. Market leaders in slow-growth industries often generate sizable positive cash flows *over and above what is needed for growth and reinvestment* because the slow-growth nature of their industry often entails relatively modest annual investment requirements. Cash cows, though not always attractive from a growth standpoint, are valuable businesses from a financial resource perspective. The surplus cash flows they generate can be used to pay corporate dividends, finance acquisitions, and provide funds for investing in the company's promising cash hogs. It makes good financial and strategic sense for diversified companies to keep cash cows in healthy condition, fortifying and defending their market position to preserve their cash-generating capability over the long term and thereby have an ongoing source of financial resources to deploy elsewhere.

A diversified company has good financial resource fit when the excess cash generated by its cash cow businesses is sufficient to fund the investment requirements of promising cash hog businesses. Ideally, investing in promising cash hog businesses over time results in growing the hogs into self-supporting *star businesses* that have strong or market-leading competitive positions in attractive, high-growth markets and high levels of profitability. Star businesses are often the cash cows of the future—when the markets of star businesses begin to mature and their growth slows, their competitive strength should produce self-generated cash flows more than sufficient to cover their investment needs. The "success sequence" is thus cash hog to young star (but perhaps still a cash hog) to self-supporting star to cash cow.

If, however, a cash hog has questionable promise (because of either low industry attractiveness or a weak competitive position), then it becomes a logical candidate for divestiture. Aggressively investing in a cash hog with an uncertain future seldom makes sense because it requires the corporate parent to keep pumping more capital into the business with only a dim hope of turning the cash hog into a future star. Such businesses are a financial drain and fail the resource-fit test because they strain the corporate parent's ability to adequately fund its other businesses. Divesting a less-attractive cash hog business is usually the best alternative unless (1) it has highly valuable strategic fit with other business units or (2) the capital infusions needed from the corporate parent are modest relative to the funds available, and (3) there is a decent chance of growing the business into a solid bottom-line contributor.

Aside from cash flow considerations, two other factors to consider in assessing the financial resource fit for businesses in a diversified firm's portfolio are:

- *Do individual businesses adequately contribute to achieving companywide performance targets?* A business exhibits poor financial fit if it soaks up a disproportionate share of the company's financial resources, while making subpar or insignificant contributions to the bottom line. Too many underperforming businesses reduce the company's overall performance and ultimately limit growth in shareholder value.

- *Does the corporation have adequate financial strength to fund its different businesses and maintain a healthy credit rating?* A diversified company's strategy fails the resource fit test when the resource needs of its portfolio unduly stretch the company's financial health and threaten to impair its credit rating. Many of the world's largest banks, including Royal Bank of Scotland, Citigroup, and HSBC, recently found themselves so undercapitalized and financially overextended that they were forced to sell some of their business assets to meet regulatory requirements and restore public confidence in their solvency.

Examining a Diversified Company's Nonfinancial Resource Fit A diversified company must also ensure that the nonfinancial resource needs of its portfolio of businesses are met by its corporate capabilities. Just as a diversified company must avoid allowing an excessive number of cash-hungry businesses to jeopardize its financial stability, it should also avoid adding to the business lineup in ways that overly stretch such nonfinancial resources as managerial talent, technology and information systems, and marketing support.

- *Does the company have or can it develop the specific resources and competitive capabilities needed to be successful in each of its businesses?*[11] Sometimes the resources a company has accumulated in its core business prove to be a poor match with the competitive capabilities needed to succeed in businesses into which it has diversified. For instance, BTR, a multibusiness company in Great Britain, discovered that the company's resources and managerial skills were quite well suited for parenting industrial manufacturing businesses but not for parenting its distribution businesses (National Tyre Services and Texas-based Summers Group). As a result, BTR decided to divest its distribution businesses and focus exclusively on diversifying around small industrial manufacturing.

> Resource fit extends beyond financial resources to include a good fit between the company's resources and core competencies and the key success factors of each industry it has diversified into.

- *Are the company's resources being stretched too thinly by the resource requirements of one or more of its businesses?* A diversified company has to guard against overtaxing its resources, a condition that can arise when (1) it goes on an acquisition spree and management is called upon to assimilate and oversee many new businesses very quickly or (2) when it lacks sufficient resource depth to do a creditable job of transferring skills and competencies from one of its businesses to another.

Step 5: Ranking Business Units and Setting a Priority for Resource Allocation

Once a diversified company's businesses have been evaluated from the standpoints of industry attractiveness, competitive strength, strategic fit, and resource fit, the next step is to use this information to rank the performance prospects of the businesses from best to worst. Such rankings help top-level executives assign each business a priority for corporate resource support and new capital investment.

The locations of the different businesses in the nine-cell industry attractiveness–competitive strength matrix provide a solid basis for identifying high-opportunity businesses and low-opportunity businesses. Normally, competitively strong businesses in attractive industries have significantly better performance prospects than competitively weak businesses in unattractive industries. Also, normally, the revenue and earnings outlook for businesses in fast-growing industries is better than for businesses in slow-growing industries. As a rule, *business subsidiaries with the brightest profit and growth prospects, attractive positions in the nine-cell matrix, and solid strategic and resource fit should receive top priority for allocation of corporate resources.* However, in ranking the prospects of the different businesses from best to worst, it is usually wise to also consider each business's past performance as concerns sales growth, profit growth, contribution to company earnings, return on capital invested in the business, and cash flow from operations. While past performance is not always a reliable predictor of future performance, it does signal whether a business already has good to excellent performance or has problems to overcome.

Allocating Financial Resources   Figure 8.4 shows the chief strategic and financial options for allocating a diversified company's financial resources. Divesting businesses with the weakest future prospects and businesses that lack adequate strategic fit and/or resource fit is one of the best ways of generating additional funds for

FIGURE 8.4

The Chief Strategic and Financial Options for Allocating a Diversified Company's Financial Resources

Strategic Options for Allocating Company Financial Resources	Financial Options for Allocating Company Financial Resources
Invest in ways to strengthen or grow existing business	Pay off existing long-term or short-term debt
Make acquisitions to establish positions in new industries or to complement existing businesses	Increase dividend payments to shareholders
	Repurchase shares of the company's common stock
Fund long-range R&D ventures aimed at opening market opportunities in new or existing businesses	Build cash reserves; invest in short-term securities

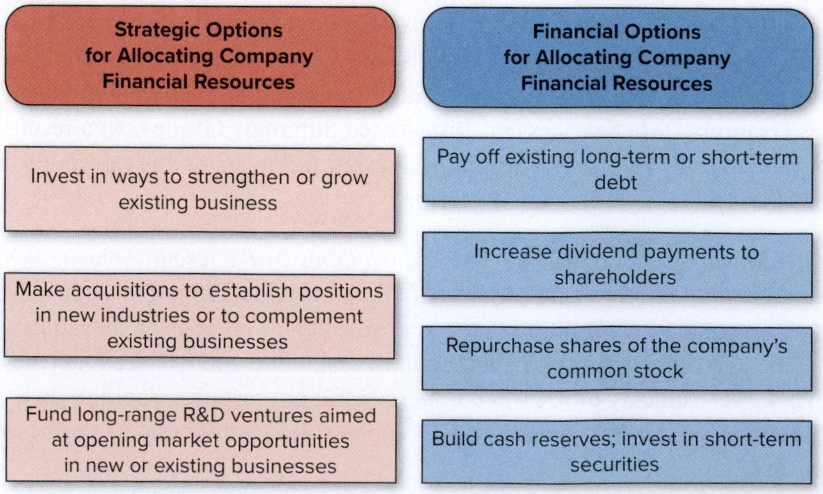

redeployment to businesses with better opportunities and better strategic and resource fit. Free cash flows from cash cow businesses also add to the pool of funds that can be usefully redeployed. *Ideally,* a diversified company will have sufficient financial resources to strengthen or grow its existing businesses, make any new acquisitions that are desirable, fund other promising business opportunities, pay off existing debt, and periodically increase dividend payments to shareholders and/or repurchase shares of stock. But, as a practical matter, a company's financial resources are limited. Thus, for top executives to make the best use of the available funds, they must steer resources to those businesses with the best opportunities and performance prospects and allocate little, if any, resources to businesses with marginal or dim prospects—this is why ranking the performance prospects of the various businesses from best to worst is so crucial. Strategic uses of corporate financial resources (see Figure 8.4) should usually take precedence unless there is a compelling reason to strengthen the firm's balance sheet or better reward shareholders.

Step 6: Crafting New Strategic Moves to Improve the Overall Corporate Performance

LO8-5 Identify a diversified company's four main corporate strategy options for solidifying its diversification strategy and improving company performance.

The conclusions flowing from the five preceding analytical steps set the agenda for crafting strategic moves to improve a diversified company's overall performance. The strategic options boil down to four broad categories of actions:

1. Sticking closely with the existing business lineup and pursuing the opportunities these businesses present

2. Broadening the company's business scope by making new acquisitions in new industries

3. Divesting some businesses and retrenching to a narrower base of business operations

4. Restructuring the company's business lineup and putting a whole new face on the company's business makeup

Sticking Closely with the Existing Business Lineup The option of sticking with the current business lineup makes sense when the company's present businesses offer attractive growth opportunities and can be counted on to generate good earnings and cash flows. As long as the company's set of existing businesses puts it in a good position for the future and these businesses have good strategic and/or resource fit, then rocking the boat with major changes in the company's business mix is usually unnecessary. Corporate executives can concentrate their attention on getting the best performance from each of the businesses, steering corporate resources into those areas of greatest potential and profitability. However, in the event that corporate executives are not entirely satisfied with the opportunities they see in the company's present set of businesses, they can opt for any of the three strategic alternatives listed in the remainder of this section.

Broadening the Diversification Base Diversified companies sometimes find it desirable to add to the diversification base for any one of the same reasons a single-business company might pursue initial diversification. Sluggish growth in revenues or profits, vulnerability to seasonality or recessionary influences, potential for transferring resources and capabilities to other related businesses, or unfavorable driving forces facing core businesses are all reasons management of a diversified company might choose to broaden diversification. An additional, and often very important, motivating factor for adding new businesses is to complement and strengthen the market position and competitive capabilities of one or more of its present businesses. Procter & Gamble's acquisition of Gillette strengthened and extended P&G's reach into personal care and household products—Gillette's businesses included Oral-B toothbrushes, Gillette razors and razor blades, Duracell batteries, Braun shavers and small appliances (coffeemakers, mixers, hair dryers, and electric toothbrushes), and toiletries (Right Guard, Foamy, Soft & Dry, White Rain, and Dry Idea).

Divesting Some Businesses and Retrenching to a Narrower Diversification Base A number of diversified firms have had difficulty managing a diverse group of businesses and have elected to get out of some of them. Selling a business outright to another company is far and away the most frequently used option for divesting a business. In 2012, Sara Lee Corporation sold its International Coffee and Tea business to J.M. Smucker and Nike sold its Umbro and Cole Haan brands to focus on the Jordan brand and Converse that are more complementary to the Nike brand. But sometimes a business selected for divestiture has ample resources and capabilities to compete successfully on its own. In such cases, a corporate parent may elect to **spin off** the unwanted business as a financially and managerially independent company, either by selling shares to the public via an initial public offering or by distributing shares in the new company to shareholders of the corporate parent. eBay spun off PayPal in 2015 at a valuation of $45 billion—a value 30 times more than what eBay paid for the company in a 2002 acquisition.

Retrenching to a narrower diversification base is usually undertaken when top management concludes that its diversification strategy has ranged too far afield and that the company can improve long-term performance by concentrating on building stronger positions in a smaller number of core businesses and industries. But there are other important reasons for divesting one or more of a company's present businesses. Sometimes divesting a business has to be considered because market conditions in a once-attractive industry have badly deteriorated. A business can become a prime candidate for divestiture because it lacks adequate strategic or resource fit, because it is a cash hog with questionable long-term potential, or because it is weakly positioned in its industry with little prospect of earning a decent return on investment. Sometimes a company acquires businesses that, down the road, just do not work out as expected, even though management has tried all it can think of to make them profitable. On occasion, a diversification move that seems sensible from a strategic fit standpoint turns out to be a poor cultural fit.[12]

Evidence indicates that pruning businesses and narrowing a firm's diversification base improves corporate performance.[13] Corporate parents often end up selling businesses too late and at too low a price, sacrificing shareholder value.[14] A useful guide to determine whether or when to divest a business subsidiary is to ask, "If we were not in this business today, would we want to get into it now?"[15] When the answer is no or probably not, divestiture should be considered. Another signal that a business should become a divestiture candidate is whether it is worth more to another company than to the present parent; in such cases, shareholders would be well served if the company were to sell the business and collect a premium price from the buyer for whom the business is a valuable fit.[16]

Broadly Restructuring the Business Lineup Through a Mix of Divestitures and New Acquisitions Corporate restructuring strategies involve divesting some businesses and acquiring others so as to put a new face on the company's business lineup. Performing radical surgery on a company's group of businesses is an appealing corporate strategy when its financial performance is squeezed or eroded by:

- A serious mismatch between the company's resources and capabilities and the type of diversification that it has pursued.
- Too many businesses in slow-growth, declining, low-margin, or otherwise unattractive industries.
- Too many competitively weak businesses.
- The emergence of new technologies that threaten the survival of one or more important businesses.
- Ongoing declines in the market shares of one or more major business units that are falling prey to more market-savvy competitors.
- An excessive debt burden with interest costs that eat deeply into profitability.
- Ill-chosen acquisitions that have not lived up to expectations.

Candidates for divestiture in a corporate restructuring effort typically include not only weak or up-and-down performers or those in unattractive industries but also business units that lack strategic fit with the businesses to be retained, businesses that are cash hogs or that lack other types of resource fit, and businesses incompatible with the company's revised diversification strategy (even though they may be profitable or in an attractive industry). As businesses are divested, corporate restructuring generally involves aligning the remaining business units into groups with the best strategic fit and then redeploying the cash flows from the divested business to either pay down debt or make new acquisitions.

> **CORE CONCEPT**
>
> **Corporate restructuring** involves radically altering the business lineup by divesting businesses that lack strategic fit or are poor performers and acquiring new businesses that offer better promise for enhancing shareholder value.

Over the past decade, corporate restructuring has become a popular strategy at many diversified companies, especially those that had diversified broadly into many different industries and lines of business. VF Corporation, maker of North Face and other popular "lifestyle" apparel brands, has used a restructuring strategy to provide its shareholders with returns that are more than five times greater than shareholder returns for competing apparel makers. Since its acquisition and turnaround of North Face in 2000, VF has spent nearly $5 billion to acquire 20 additional businesses, including about $2 billion in 2011 for Timberland. New apparel brands acquired by VF Corporation include Eastpak, Vans, Napapijri backpacks, 7 for All Mankind, Eagle Creek travel bags, Ella Moss, Dickies, Icebreaker Merino wood clothing and accessories, and Altra footwear. By 2018, VF Corporation had become a $12 billion powerhouse—one of the largest and most profitable apparel and footwear companies in the world.

KEY POINTS

1. The purpose of diversification is to build shareholder value. Diversification builds share-holder value when a diversified group of businesses can perform better under the auspices of a single corporate parent than they would as independent, standalone businesses—the goal is to achieve not just a $1 + 1 = 2$ result but rather to realize important $1 + 1 = 3$ performance benefits. Whether getting into a new business has potential to enhance share-holder value hinges on whether a company's entry into that business can pass the attractiveness test, the cost-of-entry test, and the better-off test.

2. Entry into new businesses can take any of three forms: acquisition, internal development, or joint venture/strategic partnership. Each has its pros and cons, but acquisition usually provides the quickest entry into a new business; internal development takes the longest to produce home-run results; and joint venture/strategic partnership tends to be the least durable.

3. There are two fundamental approaches to diversification: into related businesses and into unrelated businesses. The rationale for *related* diversification is based on cross-business *strategic fit:* Diversify into businesses with strategic fit along their respective value chains, capitalize on strategic-fit relationships to gain competitive advantage, and then use competitive advantage to achieve the desired $1 + 1 = 3$ impact on shareholder value.

4. *Unrelated diversification* strategies surrender the competitive advantage potential of strategic fit. Given the absence of cross-business strategic fit, the task of building shareholder value through a strategy of unrelated diversification hinges on the ability of the parent company to (1) do a superior job of identifying and acquiring new businesses that can produce consistently good earnings and returns on investment; (2) do an excellent job of negotiating favorable acquisition prices; and (3) do such a good job of overseeing and parenting the collection of businesses that they perform at a higher level than they would on their own efforts. The greater the number of businesses a company has diversified into and the more diverse these businesses are, the harder it is for corporate executives to select capable managers to run each business, know when the major strategic propos-als of business units are sound, or decide on a wise course of recovery when a business unit stumbles.

5. Evaluating a company's diversification strategy is a six-step process:

   - Step 1: *Evaluate the long-term attractiveness of the industries into which the firm has diversified.* Determining industry attractiveness involves developing a list of industry attractiveness measures, each of which might have a different importance weight.
   - Step 2: *Evaluate the relative competitive strength of each of the company's business units.* The purpose of rating each business's competitive strength is to gain clear understanding of which businesses are strong contenders in their industries, which are weak

contenders, and the underlying reasons for their strength or weakness. The conclusions about industry attractiveness can be joined with the conclusions about competitive strength by drawing an industry attractiveness–competitive strength matrix that helps identify the prospects of each business and what priority each business should be given in allocating corporate resources and investment capital.

- Step 3: *Check for cross-business strategic fit.* A business is more attractive strategically when it has value chain relationships with sibling business units that offer the potential to (1) realize economies of scope or cost-saving efficiencies; (2) transfer technology, skills, know-how, or other resources and capabilities from one business to another; and/or (3) leverage use of a well-known and trusted brand name. Cross-business strategic fit represents a significant avenue for producing competitive advantage beyond what any one business can achieve on its own.

- Step 4: *Check whether the firm's resources fit the requirements of its present business lineup.* Resource fit exists when (1) businesses, individually, strengthen a company's overall mix of resources and capabilities and (2) a company has sufficient resources to support its entire group of businesses without spreading itself too thin. One important test of financial resource fit involves determining whether a company has ample cash cows and not too many cash hogs.

- Step 5: *Rank the performance prospects of the businesses from best to worst, and determine what the corporate parent's priority should be in allocating resources to its various businesses.* The most important considerations in judging business-unit performance are sales growth, profit growth, contribution to company earnings, cash flow characteristics, and the return on capital invested in the business. Normally, strong business units in attractive industries should head the list for corporate resource support.

- Step 6: *Crafting new strategic moves to improve overall corporate performance.* This step entails using the results of the preceding analysis as the basis for selecting one of four different strategic paths for improving a diversified company's performance: *(a)* Stick closely with the existing business lineup and pursue opportunities presented by these businesses, *(b)* broaden the scope of diversification by entering additional industries, *(c)* retrench to a narrower scope of diversification by divesting poorly performing businesses, and *(d)* broadly restructure the business lineup with multiple divestitures and/or acquisitions.

ASSURANCE OF LEARNING EXERCISES

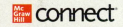

1. See if you can identify the value chain relationships that make the businesses of the following companies related in competitively relevant ways. In particular, you should consider whether there are cross-business opportunities for *(a)* transferring competitively valuable resources, expertise, technological know-how, and other capabilities, *(b)* cost sharing where value chain activities can be combined, and/or *(c)* leveraging use of a well-respected brand name.

LO8-1, LO8-2, LO8-3, LO8-4

Bloomin' Brands
- Outback Steakhouse
- Carrabba's Italian Grill
- Bonefish Grill (market-fresh fine seafood)
- Fleming's Prime Steakhouse & Wine Bar

L'Oréal

- Maybelline, Lancôme, Helena Rubinstein, Kiehl's, Garner, and Shu Uemura cosmetics
- L'Oréal and Soft Sheen/Carson hair care products
- Redken, Matrix, L'Oréal Professional, and Kerastase Paris professional hair care and skin care products
- Ralph Lauren and Giorgio Armani fragrances
- Biotherm skin care products
- La Roche–Posay and Vichy Laboratories dermo-cosmetics

Johnson & Johnson

- Baby products (powder, shampoo, oil, lotion)
- Band-Aids and other first-aid products
- Women's health and personal care products (Stayfree, Carefree, Sure & Natural)
- Neutrogena and Aveeno skin care products
- Nonprescription drugs (Tylenol, Motrin, Pepcid AC, Mylanta, Monistat)
- Prescription drugs
- Prosthetic and other medical devices
- Surgical and hospital products
- Acuvue contact lenses

LO8-1, LO8-2, LO8-3, LO8-4

2. Peruse the business group listings for 3M Company shown as follows and listed at its website (company.ingersollrand.com). How would you characterize the company's corporate strategy? Related diversification, unrelated diversification, or a combination related-unrelated diversification strategy? Explain your answer.

Consumer Products—for the home and office including Post-it (R) and Scotch (R)

Electronics and Energy—technology solutions for customers in electronics and energy markets

Health Care—products for health care professionals

Industrial—abrasives, adhesives, specialty materials, and filtration systems

Safety and Graphics—safety and security products; graphic solutions

LO8-1, LO8-2, LO8-3, LO8-4, LO8-5

3. ITT is a technology-oriented engineering and manufacturing company with the following business divisions and products:

Industrial Process Division—industrial pumps, valves, and monitoring and control systems; aftermarket services for the chemical, oil and gas, mining, pulp and paper, power, and biopharmaceutical markets

Motion Technologies Division—durable brake pads, shock absorbers, and damping technologies for the automotive and rail markets

Interconnect Solutions—connectors and fittings for the production of automobiles, aircraft, railcars and locomotives, oil field equipment, medical equipment, and industrial equipment

Control Technologies—energy absorption and vibration dampening equipment, transducers and regulators, and motion controls used in the production of robotics, medical equipment, automobiles, subsea equipment, industrial equipment, aircraft, and military vehicles

Based on this listing, would you say that ITT's business lineup reflects a strategy of related diversification, unrelated diversification, or a combination of related and unrelated diversification? What benefits are generated from any strategic fit existing between ITT's businesses? Also, what types of companies should ITT consider acquiring that might improve shareholder value? Justify your answer.

EXERCISES FOR SIMULATION PARTICIPANTS

1. In the event that your company had the opportunity to diversify into other products or businesses of your choosing, what would be the advantages of opting to pursue related diversification, unrelated diversification, or a combination of both? Explain why.

   LO8-1, LO8-2, LO8-3

2. What strategic-fit benefits might be captured by transferring resources and competitive capabilities to newly acquired related businesses?

   LO8-1, LO8-2

3. If your company opted to pursue a strategy of related diversification, what industries or product categories could your company diversify into that would allow it to achieve economies of scope? Name at least two or three such industries/product categories, and indicate the specific kinds of cost savings that might accrue from entry into each of these businesses/product categories.

   LO8-1, LO8-2

4. If your company opted to pursue a strategy of related diversification, what industries or product categories could your company diversify into that would allow your company to capitalize on using your company's present brand name and corporate image to good advantage in these newly entered businesses or product categories? Name at least two or three such industries or product categories, and indicate *the specific benefits* that might be captured by transferring your company's brand name to each of these other businesses/product categories.

   LO8-1, LO8-2, LO8-3, LO8-4, LO8-5

   Would you prefer to pursue a strategy of related or unrelated diversification? Why?

ENDNOTES

1. Constantinos C. Markides, "To Diversify or Not to Diversify," *Harvard Business Review* 75, no. 6 (November–December 1997).

2. Michael E. Porter, "From Competitive Advantage to Corporate Strategy," *Harvard Business Review* 45, no. 3 (May–June 1987).

3. Michael E. Porter, *Competitive Strategy: Techniques for Analyzing Industries and Competitors* (New York: Free Press, 1980).

4. Yves L. Doz and Gary Hamel, *Alliance Advantage: The Art of Creating Value Through Partnering* (Boston: Harvard Business School Press, 1998).

5. Michael E. Porter, *Competitive Advantage* (New York: Free Press, 1985); Constantinos C. Markides and Peter J. Williamson, "Corporate Diversification and Organization Structure: A Resource-Based View," *Academy of Management Journal* 39, no. 2 (April 1996).

6. Jeanne M. Liedtka, "Collaboration Across Lines of Business for Competitive Advantage," *Academy of Management Executive* 10, no. 2 (May 1996).

7. Kathleen M. Eisenhardt and D. Charles Galunic, "Coevolving: At Last, a Way to Make Synergies Work," *Harvard Business Review* 78, no. 1 (January–February 2000); Constantinos C. Markides and Peter J. Williamson, "Related Diversification, Core Competencies and Corporate Performance," *Strategic Management Journal* 15 (Summer 1994).

8. A. Campbell, M. Goold, and M. Alexander, "Corporate Strategy: The Quest for Parenting Advantage," *Harvard Business Review* 73, no. 2 (March–April 1995); Cynthia A. Montgomery and Birger Wernerfelt, "Diversification, Ricardian Rents, and Tobin-Q," *RAND Journal of Economics* 19, no. 4 (1988).

9. Patricia L. Anslinger and Thomas E. Copeland, "Growth Through Acquisitions: A Fresh Look," *Harvard Business Review* 74, no. 1 (January–February 1996).

10. Lawrence G. Franko, "The Death of Diversification? The Focusing of the World's Industrial Firms, 1980–2000," *Business Horizons* 47, no. 4 (July–August 2004).

11. Andrew Campbell, Michael Gould, and Marcus Alexander, "Corporate Strategy: The Quest for Parenting Advantage," *Harvard Business Review* 73, no. 2 (March–April 1995).

12. Peter F. Drucker, *Management: Tasks, Responsibilities, Practices* (New York: Harper & Row, 1974), p. 709.

13. Constantinos C. Markides, "Diversification, Restructuring, and Economic Performance," *Strategic Management Journal* 16 (February 1995).

14. Lee Dranikoff, Tim Koller, and Antoon Schneider, "Divestiture: Strategy's Missing Link," *Harvard Business Review* 80, no. 5 (May 2002).

15. Peter F. Drucker, *Management: Tasks, Responsibilities, Practices* (New York: Harper & Row, 1974).

16. David J. Collis and Cynthia A. Montgomery, "Creating Corporate Advantage," *Harvard Business Review* 76, no. 3 (May–June 1998).

9

ETHICS, CORPORATE SOCIAL RESPONSIBILITY, ENVIRONMENTAL SUSTAINABILITY, AND STRATEGY

LEARNING OBJECTIVES

After reading this chapter, you should be able to:

LO9-1   Understand why the standards of ethical behavior in business are no different from ethical standards in general.

LO9-2   Recognize conditions that give rise to unethical business strategies and behavior.

LO9-3   Identify the costs of business ethics failures.

LO9-4   Understand the concepts of corporate social responsibility and environmental sustainability and how companies balance these duties with economic responsibilities to shareholders.

Clearly, a company has a responsibility to make a profit and grow the business, but just as clearly, a company and its personnel also have a duty to obey the law and play by the rules of fair competition. But does a company have a duty to go beyond legal requirements and operate according to the ethical norms of the societies in which it operates? And does it have a duty or obligation to contribute to the betterment of society independent of the needs and preferences of the customers it serves? Should a company display a social conscience and devote a portion of its resources to bettering society? Should its strategic initiatives be screened for possible negative effects on future generations of the world's population?

This chapter focuses on whether a company, in the course of trying to craft and execute a strategy that delivers value to both customers and shareholders, also has a duty to (1) act in an ethical manner, (2) demonstrate socially responsible behavior by being a committed corporate citizen, and (3) adopt business practices that conserve natural resources, protect the interest of future generations, and preserve the well-being of the planet.

What Do We Mean by Business Ethics?

LO9-1   Understand why the standards of ethical behavior in business are no different from ethical standards in general.

Business ethics is the application of ethical principles and standards to the actions and decisions of business organizations and the conduct of their personnel.[1] Ethical principles in business are not materially different from ethical principles in general because business actions have to be judged in the context of society's standards of right and wrong. There is not a special set of rules that businesspeople decide to apply to their own conduct. If dishonesty is considered unethical and immoral, then dishonest behavior in business—whether it relates to customers, suppliers, employees, or shareholders—qualifies as equally unethical and immoral. If being ethical entails adhering to generally accepted norms about conduct concerning what is right and wrong, then managers must consider such norms when crafting and executing strategy.

CORE CONCEPT

Business ethics involves the application of general ethical principles to the actions and decisions of businesses and the conduct of their personnel.

While most company managers are careful to ensure that a company's strategy is within the bounds of what is legal, evidence indicates they are not always so careful to ensure that their strategies are within the bounds of what is considered ethical. In recent years, there have been revelations of ethical misconduct on the part of managers at such organizations as Volkswagen, FIFA, Wells Fargo, several leading investment banking firms, and a host of mortgage lenders. The consequences of crafting strategies that cannot pass the test of moral scrutiny are manifested in sharp drops in stock price that cost shareholders billions of dollars, devastating public relations hits, sizable fines, and criminal indictments and convictions of company executives.

Drivers of Unethical Strategies and Business Behavior

LO9-2   Recognize conditions that give rise to unethical business strategies and behavior.

Apart from "the business of business is business, not ethics" kind of thinking apparent in recent high-profile business scandals, three other main drivers of unethical business behavior also stand out:[2]

- *Faulty oversight, enabling the unscrupulous pursuit of personal gain and other selfish interests.* People who are obsessed with wealth accumulation, greed, power, status, and other selfish interests often push ethical principles aside in their quest for self-gain. Driven by their ambitions, they exhibit few qualms in skirting the rules or doing whatever is necessary to achieve their goals. A general disregard for business ethics can prompt all kinds of unethical strategic maneuvers and behaviors at companies. The numerous scandals that have tarnished the reputation of ridesharing company Uber and forced the resignation of its CEO are a case in point, as described in Concepts & Connections 9.1.

CORE CONCEPT

Self-dealing occurs when managers take advantage of their position to further their own private interests rather than those of the company.

Responsible corporate governance and oversight by the company's corporate board is necessary to guard against self-dealing and the manipulation of information to disguise such actions by a company's managers. **Self-dealing** occurs when managers take advantage of their position to further their own private interests rather than those of the firm.

- *Heavy pressures on company managers to meet or beat performance targets.* When key personnel find themselves scrambling to meet the quarterly and annual sales and profit expectations of investors and financial analysts or to hit other ambitious performance targets, they often feel enormous pressure to *do whatever it takes* to protect their reputation for delivering good results. As the pressure builds, they start stretching the rules further and further, until the limits of ethical conduct are overlooked.[3] Once people cross ethical boundaries to "meet or beat their numbers," the threshold for making more extreme ethical compromises becomes lower.

  To meet its demanding profit target, Wells Fargo put such pressure on its employees to hit sales quotas that many employees responded by fraudulently opening customer accounts. In 2017, after the practices came to light, the bank was forced to return $2.6 million to customers and pay $186 million in fines to the government. Wells Fargo's reputation took a big hit, its stock priced plummeted, and its CEO lost his job.[4]

- *A company culture that puts profitability and good business performance ahead of ethical behavior.* When a company's culture spawns an ethically corrupt or amoral work climate, people have a company-approved license to ignore "what's right" and engage in most any behavior or employ most any strategy they think they can get away with. Such cultural norms as "everyone else does it" and "it is OK to bend the rules to get the job done" permeate the work environment. At such

CONCEPTS & CONNECTIONS 9.1

ETHICAL VIOLATIONS AT UBER AND THEIR CONSEQUENCES

The peer-to-peer ridesharing company Uber has been credited with transforming the transportation industry, upending the taxi market, and changing the way consumers travel from place to place. But its lack of attention to ethics has resulted in numerous scandals, a tarnished reputation, a loss of market share to rival companies, and the ouster of its co-founder Travis Kalanick from his position as the company's CEO. The ethical lapses for which Uber has been criticized include the following:

- **Sexual harassment and a toxic workplace culture.** In June 2017, Uber fired over 20 employees as a result of an investigation that uncovered widespread sexual harassment that had been going on for years at the company. Female employees who had reported incidents of sexual harassment were subjected to retaliation by their managers, and reports of the incidents to senior executives resulted in inaction.

- **Price gouging during crises.** During emergencies such as Hurricane Sandy and the 2017 London Bridge attack, Uber added high surcharges to the cost of their services. This drew much censure, particularly since its competitors offered free or reduced cost rides during those same times.

- **Data breaches and violations of user privacy.** Since 2014, the names, e-mail addresses, and license information of over 700,000 drivers and the personal information of over 65 million users have been disclosed as a result

of data breaches. Moreover, in 2016 the company paid a hacker $100,000 in ransom to prevent the dissemination of personal driver and user data that had been breached, but it failed to publicly disclose the situation for over six months.

- **Inadequate attention to consumer safety.** Substandard vetting practices at Uber came to light after one of its drivers was arrested as the primary suspect in a mass shooting in Kalamazoo, Michigan, and after a series of reports alleging sexual assault and misconduct by its drivers. Uber's concern for safety was further questioned when a pedestrian was tragically struck and killed by one of its self-driving vehicles in 2018.

- **Unfair competitive practices.** When nascent competitor Gett launched in New York City, Uber employees ordered and canceled hundreds of rides to waste drivers' time and then offered the drivers cash to drop Gett and join Uber. Uber has been accused of employing similar practices against Lyft.

The ethical violations at Uber have not been without economic consequence. They contributed to a significant market share loss to Lyft, Uber's closest competitor in the United States. In January 2017, when Uber was thought to have engaged in price-gouging during protests against legislation banning immigrants from specific countries, its market share dropped 5 percentage points in a week. While Uber's ethical dilemmas are not the sole contributor to Lyft's increase in market share and expansion rate, the negative perceptions of Uber's brand from its unethical actions has afforded its competitors significant opportunities for brand and market share growth. And without a real change in Uber's culture and corporate governance practices, there is a strong likelihood that ethical scandals involving Uber will continue to surface.

Note: Developed with Alen A. Amini.

Sources: https://www.recode.net/2017/8/31/16227670/uber-lyft-market-share-deleteuber-decline-users; https://www.inc.com/associated-press/lyft-thrives-while-rival-uber-tries-to-stabilize-regain-control-2017.html; and https://www.entrepreneur.com/ article/300789.

Mr.Whiskey/Shutterstock

companies, ethically immoral or amoral people are certain to play down observance of ethical strategic actions and business conduct. Moreover, cultural pressures to utilize unethical means if circumstances become challenging can prompt otherwise honorable people to behave unethically. Enron's leaders created a culture that pressured company personnel to be innovative and aggressive in figuring out how to grow current earnings—regardless of the methods. Enron's annual "rank and yank" performance evaluation process, in which the lowest-ranking 15 to 20 percent of employees were let go, made it abundantly clear that bottom-line results were what mattered most. The name of the game at Enron became devising clever ways to boost revenues and earnings, even if this sometimes meant operating outside established policies. In fact, outside-the-lines behavior was celebrated if it generated profitable new business.

The Business Case for Ethical Strategies

 LO9-3 Identify the costs of business ethics failures.

While it is inarguable that there is a *moral case for an ethical business strategy* that reflects well on the character of the company and its personnel, it is also true that *an ethical strategy is good business and serves the self-interest of shareholders.* Pursuing unethical strategies and tolerating unethical conduct will in time damage a company's reputation and result in a wide-ranging set of other costly consequences. Figure 9.1

FIGURE 9.1

The Costs Companies Incur When Ethical Wrongdoing Is Discovered and Punished

Visible Costs	Internal Administrative Costs	Intangible or Less Visible Costs
• Government fines and penalties • Civil penalties arising from class-action lawsuits and other litigation aimed at punishing the company for its offense and the harm done to others • The costs to shareholders in the form of a lower stock price (and possibly lower dividends)	• Legal and investigative costs incurred by the company • The costs of providing remedial education and ethics training to company personnel • Costs of taking corrective actions • Administration costs associated with ensuring future compliance	• Customer defections • Loss of reputation • Lost employee morale and higher degrees of employee cynicism • Higher employee turnover • Higher recruiting costs and difficulty in attracting employees • Adverse effects on employee productivity • The costs of complying with often harsher government regulation

Source: Adapted from Thomas, Terry, John R. Schermerhorn, and John W. Dienhart, "Strategic Leadership of Ethical Behavior," *Academy of Management Executive* 18, no. 2 (May 2004), p. 58.

shows the wide-ranging costs a company can incur when unethical behavior is discovered and it is forced to make amends for its behavior. The more egregious a company's ethical violations, the higher are the costs and the bigger the damage to its reputation (and to the reputations of the company personnel involved). In high-profile instances, the costs of ethical misconduct can easily run into the hundreds of millions and even billions of dollars, especially if they provoke widespread public outrage and many people were harmed.

The fallout of ethical misconduct on the part of a company goes well beyond just the costs of making amends for the misdeeds. Buyers shun companies known for their shady behavior. Companies known to have engaged in unethical conduct have difficulty recruiting and retaining talented employees.[5] Most ethically upstanding people do not want to get entrapped in a compromising situation, nor do they want their personal reputations tarnished by the actions of an unsavory employer. A company's unethical behavior risks considerable damage to shareholders in the form of lost revenues, higher costs, lower profits, lower stock prices, and a diminished business reputation. To a significant degree, therefore, ethical strategies and ethical conduct are *good business.*

> Shareholders suffer major damage when a company's unethical behavior is discovered and punished. Making amends for unethical business conduct is costly, and it takes years to rehabilitate a tarnished company reputation.

Ensuring a Strong Commitment to Business Ethics in Companies with International Operations

Notions of right and wrong, fair and unfair, moral and immoral, ethical and unethical are present in all societies, organizations, and individuals. But there are three schools of thought about the extent to which the ethical standards travel across cultures and whether multinational companies can apply the same set of ethical standards in all of the locations where they operate.

The School of Ethical Universalism

According to the school of **ethical universalism,** some concepts of what is right and what is wrong are *universal* and transcend most all cultures, societies, and religions.[6] For instance, being truthful strikes a chord of what is right in the peoples of all nations. Ethical norms considered universal by many ethicists include honesty, trustworthiness, respecting the rights of others, practicing the Golden Rule, and avoiding unnecessary harm to workers or to the users of the company's product or service.[7] *To the extent there is common moral agreement about right and wrong actions and behaviors across multiple cultures and countries, there exists a set of universal ethical standards to which all societies, companies, and individuals can be held accountable.* The strength of ethical universalism is that it draws upon the collective views of multiple societies and cultures to put some clear boundaries on what constitutes ethical business behavior no matter what country market its personnel are operating in. This means that in those instances in which basic moral standards really

> **CORE CONCEPT**
>
> According to the school of **ethical universalism,** the same standards of what is ethical and what is unethical resonate with peoples of most societies, regardless of local traditions and cultural norms; hence, common ethical standards can be used to judge employee conduct in a variety of country markets and cultural circumstances.

do not vary significantly according to local cultural beliefs, traditions, or religious convictions, a multinational company can develop a code of ethics that it applies more or less evenly across its worldwide operations.

The School of Ethical Relativism

Beyond widely accepted ethical norms, many ethical standards likely vary from one country to another because of divergent religious beliefs, social customs, and prevailing political and economic doctrines (whether a country leans more toward a capitalistic market economy or one heavily dominated by socialistic or state-directed capitalism principles). The school of **ethical relativism** holds that when there are national or cross-cultural differences in what is deemed an ethical or unethical business situation, it is appropriate for local moral standards to take precedence over what the ethical standards may be in a company's home market. The thesis is that whatever a culture thinks is right or wrong really is right or wrong for that culture.[8]

> **CORE CONCEPT**
>
> According to the school of **ethical relativism,** different societal cultures and customs create divergent standards of right and wrong; thus, what is ethical or unethical must be judged in the light of local customs and social mores, and can vary from one culture or nation to another.

A company that adopts the principle of ethical relativism and holds company personnel to local ethical standards necessarily assumes that what prevails as local morality is an adequate guide to ethical behavior. This can be ethically dangerous; it leads to the conclusion that if a country's culture generally accepts bribery or environmental degradation or exposing workers to dangerous conditions, then managers working in that country are free to engage in such activities. Adopting such a position places a company in a perilous position if it is required to defend these activities to its stakeholders in countries with higher ethical expectations. Moreover, from a global markets perspective, ethical relativism results in a maze of conflicting ethical standards for multinational companies. Imagine, for example, that a multinational company in the name of ethical relativism takes the position that it is acceptable for company personnel to pay bribes and kickbacks in countries where such payments are customary but forbids company personnel from making such payments in those countries where bribes and kickbacks are considered unethical or illegal. Having thus adopted conflicting ethical standards for operating in different countries, company managers have little moral basis for enforcing ethical standards companywide. Rather, the clear message to employees would be that the company has no ethical standards or principles of its own, preferring to let its practices be governed by the countries in which it operates.

> Codes of conduct based upon ethical relativism can be *ethically dangerous* by creating a maze of conflicting ethical standards for multinational companies.

Integrative Social Contracts Theory

Integrative social contracts theory provides a middle position between the opposing views of universalism and relativism.[9] According to **integrative social contracts theory,** the ethical standards a company should try to uphold are governed both by (1) a limited

> **CORE CONCEPT**
>
> According to **integrative social contracts theory,** universal ethical principles based on collective views of multiple cultures combine to form a "social contract" that all employees in all country markets have a duty to observe. Within the boundaries of this social contract, there is room for host-country cultures to exert *some* influence in setting their own moral and ethical standards. However, *"first-order"* universal ethical norms always take precedence over *"second-order"* local ethical norms in circumstances in which local ethical norms are more permissive.

number of universal ethical principles that are widely recognized as putting legitimate ethical boundaries on actions and behavior in *all* situations and (2) the circumstances of local cultures, traditions, and shared values that further prescribe what constitutes ethically permissible behavior and what does not. This "social contract" by which managers in all situations have a duty to serve provides that *"first-order" universal ethical norms always take precedence over "second-order" local ethical norms in circumstances in which local ethical norms are more permissive.* Integrative social contracts theory offers managers in multinational companies clear guidance in resolving cross-country ethical differences: Those parts of the company's code of ethics that involve universal ethical norms must be enforced worldwide, but within these boundaries, there is room for ethical diversity and opportunity for host-country cultures to exert *some* influence in setting their own moral and ethical standards.

A good example of the application of integrative social contracts theory involves the payment of bribes and kickbacks. Bribes and kickbacks seem to be common in some countries, but does this justify paying them? Just because bribery flourishes in a country does not mean that it is an authentic or legitimate ethical norm. Virtually all of the world's major religions (Buddhism, Christianity, Confucianism, Hinduism, Islam, Judaism, Sikhism, and Taoism) and all moral schools of thought condemn bribery and corruption.[10] Therefore, a multinational company might reasonably conclude that the right ethical standard is one of refusing to condone bribery and kickbacks on the part of company personnel no matter what the second-order local norm is and no matter what the sales consequences are.

Strategy, Corporate Social Responsibility, and Environmental Sustainability

LO9-4 Understand the concepts of corporate social responsibility and environmental sustainability and how companies balance these duties with economic responsibilities to shareholders.

The idea that businesses have an obligation to foster social betterment, a much-debated topic in the past 50 years, took root in the 19th century when progressive companies in the aftermath of the industrial revolution began to provide workers with housing and other amenities. The notion that corporate executives should balance the interests of all stakeholders—shareholders, employees, customers, suppliers, the communities in which they operated, and society at large—began to blossom in the 1960s.

What Do We Mean by Corporate Social Responsibility?

The essence of socially responsible business behavior is that a company should balance strategic actions to benefit shareholders against the *duty* to be a good corporate citizen. The underlying thesis is that company managers should display a *social conscience* in operating the business and specifically consider how management decisions and company actions affect the well-being of employees, local communities, the environment, and society at large.[11] Acting in a socially responsible manner thus encompasses more than just participating in community service projects and donating monies to charities and other worthy social causes. Demonstrating **corporate social responsibility (CSR)** also entails undertaking actions that earn trust and respect from all stakeholders—operating in an honorable and ethical manner, striving to make the company a great place to work, demonstrating genuine respect for the environment, and trying to make a difference in bettering society. Corporate social responsibility programs commonly involve:

- *Efforts to employ an ethical strategy and observe ethical principles in operating the business.* A sincere commitment to observing ethical principles is a necessary component of a CSR strategy simply because unethical conduct is incompatible with the concept of good corporate citizenship and socially responsible business behavior.

- *Making charitable contributions, supporting community service endeavors, engaging in broader philanthropic initiatives, and reaching out to make a difference in the lives of the disadvantaged.* Some companies fulfill their philanthropic obligations by spreading their efforts over a multitude of charitable and community activities; for instance, Microsoft and Johnson & Johnson support a broad variety of community, art, and social welfare programs. Others prefer to focus their energies more narrowly. McDonald's, for example, concentrates on sponsoring the Ronald McDonald House program (which provides a home away from home for the families of seriously ill children receiving treatment at nearby hospitals). Leading prescription drug maker GlaxoSmithKline and other pharmaceutical companies either donate or heavily discount medicines for distribution in the least-developed nations. Companies frequently reinforce their philanthropic efforts by encouraging employees to support charitable causes and participate in community affairs, often through programs that match employee contributions.

- *Actions to protect the environment and, in particular, to minimize or eliminate any adverse impact on the environment stemming from the company's own business activities.* Corporate social responsibility as it applies to environmental protection entails actively striving to be good stewards of the environment. This means using the best available science and technology to reduce environmentally harmful aspects of its operations *below the levels required by prevailing environmental regulations.* It also means putting time and money into improving the environment in ways that extend past a company's own industry boundaries—such as participating in recycling projects, adopting energy conservation practices, and supporting efforts to clean up local water supplies.

- *Actions to create a work environment that enhances the quality of life for employees.* Numerous companies exert extra effort to enhance the quality of life for their employees, both at work and at home. This can include onsite day care, flexible work schedules, workplace exercise facilities, special leaves to care for sick family members, work-at-home opportunities, career development programs and education opportunities, special safety programs, and the like.

- *Actions to build a workforce that is diverse with respect to gender, race, national origin, and other aspects that different people bring to the workplace.* Most large companies in the United States have established workforce diversity programs, and some go the extra mile to ensure that their workplaces are attractive to ethnic minorities and inclusive of all groups and perspectives.

The particular combination of socially responsible endeavors a company elects to pursue defines its **corporate social responsibility strategy.** The specific components emphasized in a CSR strategy vary from company to company and are typically linked to a company's core values. Concepts & Connections 9.2 describes Warby Parker's approach to corporate social responsibility. General Mills builds its CSR strategy around the

theme of "nourishing lives" to emphasize its commitment to good nutrition as well as philanthropy, community building, and environmental protection.[12] Starbucks' CSR strategy includes four main elements (ethical sourcing, community service, environmental stewardship, and farmer support), all of which have touch points with the way that the company procures its coffee—a key aspect of its product differentiation strategy.[13]

Corporate Social Responsibility and the Triple Bottom Line   CSR initiatives undertaken by companies are frequently directed at improving the company's "triple bottom line"—a reference to three types of performance metrics: *economic, social, environmental.* The goal is for a company to succeed simultaneously in all three dimensions, as illustrated in Figure 9.2.[14] The three dimensions of performance are often referred to in terms of the three pillars of "people, planet, and profit." The term *people* refers to the various social initiatives that make up CSR strategies, such as corporate giving and community involvement. *Planet* refers to a firm's ecological impact and environmental practices. The term *profit* has a broader meaning with respect to the triple

FIGURE 9.2

The Triple Bottom Line: Excelling on Three Measures of Company Performance

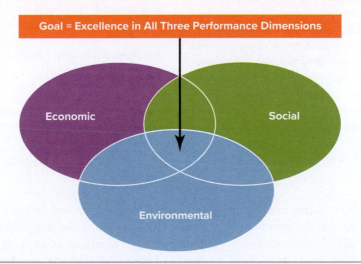

Goal = Excellence in All Three Performance Dimensions

Economic

Social

Environmental

CONCEPTS & CONNECTIONS 9.2

WARBY PARKER: COMBINING CORPORATE SOCIAL RESPONSIBILITY WITH AFFORDABLE FASHION

Michael Buckner/Getty Images

Since its founding in 2010, Warby Parker has succeeded in selling over one million pairs of high-fashion glasses at a discounted price of $95—roughly 80 percent below the average $500 price tag on a comparable pair of eyeglasses from another producer. With more than 70 stores in the United States, the company has built a brand recognized universally as one of the strongest in the world; it consistently posts a net promoter score (a measure of how likely someone would be to recommend the product) of close to 90—higher than companies like Zappos and Apple.

Corporate responsibility is at Warby Parker's core. For each pair of glasses sold, the company provides international non-profit partners like VisionSpring with a monthly donation of glasses; with Warby Parker's support, these partners provide basic eye exams and teach community members how to manufacture and sell glasses at very low prices to amplify beneficial effects in their communities. By 2019, the company had distributed more than 5 million pairs of glasses to people in more than 50 countries. The average impact on a recipient of a pair of donated glasses was a 20 percent increase in personal income and a 35 percent increase in productivity.

Efforts to be a responsible company expand beyond Warby Parker's international partnerships. The company voluntarily evaluates itself against benchmarks in the fields of "environment," "workers," "customers," "community," and "governance," demonstrating a nearly unparalleled dedication to outcomes outside of profit. The company is widely seen as an employer of choice and regularly attracts top talent for all roles across the organization. It holds to an extremely high environmental standard, running an entirely carbon neutral operation.

While socially impactful actions matter at Warby Parker, the company is mindful of the critical role of its customers as well. Both founders spent countless hours coordinating partnerships with dedicated suppliers to ensure quality, invested deeply in building a lean manufacturing operation to minimize cost, and sought to build an organization that would keep buyers happy. The net effect is a very economically healthy company—they post around $3,000 in sales per square foot, in line with Tiffany & Co.—with financial stability to pursue responsibilities outside of customer satisfaction.

The strong fundamentals put in place by the firm's founders blend responsibility into its DNA and attach each piece of commercial success to positive outcomes in the world. The company was recently recognized as number one on *Fast Company*'s "Most Innovative Companies" list and continues to build loyal followers—both of its products and its CSR efforts—as it expands.

Note: Developed with Jeremy P. Reich .

Sources: Warby Parker and "B Corp" websites; Max Chafkin, "Warby Parker Sees the Future of Retail," *Fast Company,* February 17, 2015, www.fastcompany.com/3041334/warby-parker-sees-the-future-of-retail (accessed February 22, 2016); and Jenni Avins, "Warby Parker Proves Customers Don't Have to Care about Your Social Mission," *Quartz,* December 29, 2014, https://qz.com/318499/warby-parker-proves-customers-dont-have-to-care-about-your-social-mission/ (accessed February 14, 2016); www.warbyparker.com.

bottom line than it does otherwise. It encompasses not only the profit a firm earns for its shareholders but also the economic impact the company has on society more generally. Triple-bottom-line (TBL) reporting is emerging as an increasingly important way for companies to make the results of their CSR strategies apparent to stakeholders.

What Do We Mean by Sustainability and Sustainable Business Practices?

The term *sustainability* is used in a variety of ways. In many firms, it is synonymous with corporate social responsibility; it is seen by some as a term that is gradually replacing CSR in the business lexicon. Indeed, sustainability reporting and TBL reporting are often one and the same. More often, however, the term takes on a more focused meaning, concerned with the relationship of a company to its *environment* and its use of *natural resources,* including land, water, air, minerals, and fossil fuels. Since corporations are the biggest users of finite natural resources, managing and maintaining these resources is critical for the long-term economic interests of corporations.

For some companies, this issue has direct and obvious implications for the continued viability of their business model and strategy. Pacific Gas and Electric has begun measuring the full carbon footprint of its supply chain to become not only "greener" but also a more efficient energy producer.[15] For other companies, the connection is less direct, but all companies are part of a business ecosystem whose economic health depends on the availability of natural resources. In response, most major companies have begun to change *how* they do business, emphasizing the use of **sustainable business practices,** defined as those capable of meeting the needs of the present without compromising the ability to meet the needs of the future.[16] Many have also begun to incorporate a consideration of environmental sustainability into their strategy-making activities.

Environmental sustainability strategies entail deliberate and concerted actions to operate businesses in a manner that protects and maybe even enhances natural resources and ecological support systems, guards against outcomes that will ultimately endanger the planet, and is therefore sustainable for centuries.[17] Sustainability initiatives undertaken by companies are directed at improving the company's triple bottom line—

> **CORE CONCEPT**
>
> **Sustainable business practices** are those that meet the needs of the present without compromising the ability to meet the needs of the future.

> **CORE CONCEPT**
>
> **Environmental sustainability** involves deliberate actions to protect the environment, provide for the longevity of natural resources, maintain ecological support systems for future generations, and guard against the ultimate endangerment of the planet.

its performance on economic, environment, and social metrics.[18] Unilever, a diversified producer of processed foods, personal care, and home cleaning products, is among the most committed corporations pursuing environmentally sustainable business practices. The company tracks 11 sustainable agricultural indicators in its processed-foods business and has launched a variety of programs to improve the environmental performance of its suppliers. Examples of such programs include special low-rate financing for tomato suppliers choosing to switch to water-conserving irrigation systems and training programs in India that have allowed contract cucumber growers to reduce pesticide use by 90 percent, while improving yields by 78 percent.

Unilever has also reengineered many internal processes to improve the company's overall performance on sustainability measures. For example, the company's factories have reduced water usage by 50 percent and manufacturing waste by 14 percent through the implementation of sustainability initiatives. Unilever has also redesigned packaging for many of its products to conserve natural resources and reduce the volume of consumer waste. The company's Suave shampoo bottles in the United States were reshaped to save almost 150 tons of plastic resin per year, which is the equivalent of

15 million fewer empty bottles. As the producer of Lipton Tea, Unilever is the world's largest purchaser of tea leaves; the company has committed to sourcing all of its tea from Rainforest Alliance Certified farms by 2015, due to Unilever's comprehensive triple-bottom-line approach toward sustainable farm management. Because 40 percent of Unilever's sales are made to consumers in developing countries, the company also is committed to addressing societal needs of consumers in those countries. Examples of the company's social performance include free laundries in poor neighborhoods in developing countries, startup assistance for women-owned micro businesses in India, and free drinking water provided to villages in Ghana.

Sometimes cost savings and improved profitability are drivers of corporate sustainability strategies. Nike's sustainability initiatives have reduced energy consumption by 24 percent, emissions by 21 percent, water consumption by 13 percent, waste by 35 percent, and chemical usage by 20 percent between 2010 and 2015. Procter & Gamble's Swiffer cleaning system, one of the company's best-selling products, was developed as a sustainable product; not only does the Swiffer system have an earth-friendly design, but it also outperforms less ecologically friendly alternatives. Although most consumers probably aren't aware that the Swiffer mop reduces demands on municipal water sources, saves electricity that would be needed to heat water, and does not add to the amount of detergent making its way into waterways and waste treatment facilities, they are attracted to purchasing Swiffer mops because they prefer Swiffer's disposable cleaning sheets to filling and refilling a mop bucket and wringing out a wet mop until the floor is clean.

Crafting Corporate Social Responsibility and Sustainability Strategies

While striving to be socially responsible and to engage in environmentally sustainable business practices, there's plenty of room for every company to make its own statement about what charitable contributions to make, what kinds of community service projects to emphasize, what environmental actions to support, how to make the company a good place to work, where and how workforce diversity fits into the picture, and what else it will do to support worthy causes and projects that benefit society. A company may choose to focus its social responsibility strategy on generic social issues, but social responsibility strategies linked to its customer value proposition or key value chain activities may also help build competitive advantage.[19]

Ford's sustainability strategy for reducing carbon emissions has contributed to competitive advantage and produced environmental benefits. Its Ford Fusion hybrid is among the least polluting automobiles on the road and ranks first among hybrid cars in terms of fuel economy and cabin size. The Ford Explorer plug-in hybrid SUV launched in Europe in 2019 provides 7-passenger seating capacity and has a 40-kilometer zero-emission city driving range. The development of hybrid models like the Fusion and Explorer have helped Ford gain the loyalty of fuel-conscious buyers and given the company a new green image.

CSR strategies that have the effect of both providing valuable social benefits and fulfilling customer needs in a superior fashion can lead to competitive advantage. Corporate social agendas that address generic social issues may help boost a company's reputation but are unlikely to improve its competitive strength in the marketplace.

Whole Foods Market's environmental sustainability strategy is evident throughout its company value chain and is a big part of its differentiation strategy. The company's procurement policies encourage stores to purchase fresh vegetables from local farmers and screen processed food items for ingredients that the company considers unhealthy or environmentally unsound. The company also has created the Animal Compassion Foundation to develop natural and humane ways of raising farm animals and has converted its vehicles to run on biofuels.

The Business Case for Socially Responsible Behavior

The moral case for why businesses should act in a manner that benefits all of the company's stakeholders—not just shareholders—boils down to "It's the right thing to do." In today's social climate, most business leaders can be expected to acknowledge that socially responsible actions are important and that businesses have a duty to be good corporate citizens. But there is a complementary school of thought that business operates on the basis of an implied social contract with the members of society. According to this contract, society grants a business the right to conduct its business affairs and agrees not to unreasonably restrain its pursuit of a fair profit for the goods or services it sells. In return for this "license to operate," a business is obligated to act as a responsible citizen, do its fair share to promote the general welfare, and avoid doing any harm. Such a view clearly puts a moral burden on a company to operate honorably, provide good working conditions to employees, be a good environmental steward, and display good corporate citizenship.

Whatever the moral arguments for socially responsible business behavior and environmentally sustainable business practices, there are definitely good business reasons why companies should devote time and resources to social responsibility initiatives, environmental sustainability, and good corporate citizenship:

- *Such actions can lead to increased buyer patronage.* A strong, visible social responsibility strategy gives a company an edge in differentiating itself from rivals and in appealing to those consumers who prefer to do business with companies that are good corporate citizens. Whole Foods Market, TOMS, Green Mountain Coffee Roasters, and Patagonia have definitely expanded their customer bases because of their visible and well-publicized activities as socially conscious companies.

- *A strong commitment to socially responsible behavior reduces the risk of reputation-damaging incidents.* Companies that place little importance on operating in a socially responsible manner are more prone to scandal and embarrassment. Consumer, environmental, and human rights activist groups are quick to criticize businesses whose behavior they consider to be out of line, and they are adept at getting their message into the media and onto the Internet. For many years, Nike received stinging criticism for not policing sweatshop conditions in the Asian factories that produced Nike footwear, causing Nike co-founder and former CEO Phil Knight to observe, "Nike has become synonymous with slave wages, forced overtime, and arbitrary abuse."[20] Nike began an extensive effort to monitor conditions in the 800 factories of the contract manufacturers that produced Nike shoes. Nonetheless, Nike has continually been plagued by complaints from human rights activists that its monitoring procedures are flawed and that it is not doing enough to correct the plight of factory workers.

- *Socially responsible actions and sustainable business practices can lower costs and enhance employee recruiting and workforce retention.* Companies with deservedly good reputations for contributing time and money to the betterment of society are better able to attract and retain employees compared to companies with tarnished reputations. Some employees just feel better about working for a company committed to improving society.[21] This can contribute to lower turnover and better worker productivity. Other direct and indirect economic benefits include lower costs for staff recruitment and training. For example, Starbucks is said to enjoy much lower rates of employee turnover because of its full benefits package for both full-time and part-time employees, management efforts to make Starbucks a great place to work, and the company's socially responsible practices. When a U.S. manufacturer of recycled paper, taking eco-efficiency to heart, discovered how to increase its fiber recovery rate, it saved the equivalent of 20,000 tons of waste paper—a factor that helped the company become the industry's lowest-cost producer. By helping two-thirds of its employees stop smoking and investing in a number of wellness programs for employees, Johnson & Johnson has saved $250 million on its health care costs over a 10-year period.[22]

- *Opportunities for revenue enhancement may also come from CSR and environmental sustainability strategies.* The drive for sustainability and social responsibility can spur innovative efforts that in turn lead to new products and opportunities for revenue enhancement. Electric cars such as the BMW i3 and the Nissan Leaf are one example. In many cases, the revenue opportunities are tied to a company's core products. PepsiCo and Coca-Cola, for example, have expanded into the juice business to offer a healthier alternative to their carbonated beverages. In other cases, revenue enhancement opportunities come from innovative ways to reduce waste and use the by-products of a company's production. Staples has become one of the largest non-utility corporate producers of renewable energy in the United States due to its installation of solar power panels in all of its outlets (and the sale of what it does not consume in renewable energy credit markets).

- *Well-conceived social responsibility strategies work to the advantage of shareholders.* A two-year study of leading companies found that improving environmental compliance and developing environmentally friendly products can enhance earnings per share, profitability, and the likelihood of winning contracts. The stock prices of companies that rate high on social and environmental performance criteria have been found to perform 35 to 45 percent better than the average of the 2,500 companies comprising the Dow Jones Global Index.[23] A review of some 135 studies indicated there is a positive, but small, correlation between good corporate behavior and good financial performance; only 2 percent of the studies showed that dedicating corporate resources to social responsibility harmed the interests of shareholders.[24]

In sum, companies that take social responsibility seriously can improve their business reputations and operational efficiency while also reducing their risk exposure and encouraging loyalty and innovation. Overall, companies that take special pains to protect the environment (beyond what is required by law), are active in community affairs, and are generous supporters of charitable causes and projects that benefit society are more likely to be seen as good investments and as good companies to work for or do business with. Shareholders are likely to view the business case for social responsibility as a strong one, even though they certainly have a right to be concerned about whether the time and money their company spends to carry out its social responsibility strategy outweigh the benefits and reduce the bottom line by an unjustified amount.

KEY POINTS

1. Business ethics concerns the application of ethical principles and standards to the actions and decisions of business organizations and the conduct of their personnel. Ethical principles in business are not materially different from ethical principles in general.

2. The three main drivers of unethical business behavior stand out:
   - Overzealous or obsessive pursuit of personal gain, wealth, and other selfish interests
   - Heavy pressures on company managers to meet or beat earnings targets
   - A company culture that puts profitability and good business performance ahead of ethical behavior

3. Business ethics failures can result in visible costs (fines, penalties, civil penalties arising from lawsuits, stock price declines), the internal administrative or "cleanup" costs, and intangible or less visible costs (customer defections, loss of reputation, higher turnover, harsher government regulations).

4. There are three schools of thought about ethical standards for companies with international operations:
   - According to the *school of ethical universalism,* the same standards of what is ethical and unethical resonate with peoples of most societies, regardless of local traditions and cultural norms; hence, common ethical standards can be used to judge the conduct of personnel at companies operating in a variety of international markets and cultural circumstances.
   - According to the *school of ethical relativism,* different societal cultures and customs have divergent values and standards of right and wrong; thus, what is ethical or unethical must be judged in the light of local customs and social mores and can vary from one culture or nation to another.
   - According to *integrative social contracts theory,* universal ethical principles or norms based on the collective views of multiple cultures and societies combine to form a "social contract" that all individuals in all situations have a duty to observe. Within the boundaries of this social contract, local cultures can specify other impermissible actions; however, universal ethical norms always take precedence over local ethical norms.

5. The term *corporate social responsibility* concerns a company's *duty* to operate in an honorable manner, provide good working conditions for employees, encourage workforce diversity, be a good steward of the environment, and support philanthropic endeavors in local communities in which it operates and in society at large. The particular combination of socially responsible endeavors a company elects to pursue defines its corporate social responsibility (CSR) strategy.

6. The triple bottom line refers to company performance in three realms: economic, social, environmental. Increasingly, companies are reporting their performance with respect to all three performance dimensions.

7. *Sustainability* is a term that is used variously, but most often, it concerns a firm's relationship to the environment and its use of natural resources. Environmentally sustainable business practices are those capable of meeting the needs of the present without compromising the world's ability to meet future needs. A company's environmental sustainability strategy consists of its deliberate actions to protect the environment, provide for the longevity of natural resources, maintain ecological support systems for future generations, and guard against ultimate endangerment of the planet.

8. There are also solid reasons CSR and environmental sustainability strategies may be good business: They can be conducive to greater buyer patronage, reduce the risk of reputation-damaging incidents, lower costs and enhance employee recruitment and retention, and provide opportunities for revenue enhancement. Well-crafted CSR and environmental sustainability strategies are in the best long-term interest of shareholders for the reasons above and because they can avoid or preempt costly legal or regulatory actions.

ASSURANCE OF LEARNING EXERCISES

LO9-1, LO9-4

1. Dell is widely known as an ethical company and has recently committed itself to becoming a more environmentally sustainable business. After reviewing the Corporate Social Responsibility section of Dell's website (www.dell.com/learn/us/en/uscorp1/cr?~ck=mn), prepare a list of 8 specific policies and programs that help the company bring about social and environmental change while still remaining innovative and profitable.

LO9-2, LO9-3

2. Prepare a one- to two-page analysis of a recent ethics scandal using your university library's resources. Your report should *(a)* discuss the conditions that gave rise to unethical business strategies and behavior and *(b)* provide an overview of the costs resulting from the company's business ethics failure.

LO9-4

3. Based on the information provided in Concepts & Connections 9.2, explain how Warby Parker's CSR strategy has contributed to its success in the marketplace. How are the company's various stakeholder groups affected by its commitment to social responsibility? How would you evaluate its triple-bottom-line performance?

LO9-4

4. The British outdoor clothing company, Páramo, was a Guardian Sustainable Business Award winner in 2016. The company's fabric technology and use of chemicals is discussed at https://www.theguardian.com/sustainable-business/2016/may/27/outdoor-clothing-paramo-toxic-pfc-greenpeace-fabric-technology. Describe how Páramo's business practices allowed it to become recognized for its bold moves. How do these initiatives help build competitive advantage?

EXERCISES FOR SIMULATION PARTICIPANTS

LO9-1

1. What factors build the business case for operating your company in an ethical manner?

LO9-4

2. In what ways, if any, is your company exercising corporate social responsibility? What are the elements of your company's CSR strategy? What changes to this strategy would you suggest?

LO9-3, LO9-4

3. If some shareholders complained that you and your co-managers have been spending too little or too much on corporate social responsibility, what would you tell them?

LO9-4

4. Is your company striving to conduct its business in an environmentally sustainable manner? What specific *additional* actions could your company take that would make an even greater contribution to environmental sustainability?

LO9-4

5. In what ways is your company's environmental sustainability strategy in the best long-term interest of shareholders? Does it contribute to your company's competitive advantage or profitability?

ENDNOTES

1. James E. Post, Anne T. Lawrence, and James Weber, *Business and Society: Corporate Strategy, Public Policy, Ethics,* 10th ed. (New York: McGraw-Hill Irwin, 2002).

2. John F. Veiga, Timothy D. Golden, and Kathleen Dechant, "Why Managers Bend Company Rules," *Academy of Management Executive* 18, no. 2 (May 2004).

3. Ronald R. Sims and Johannes Brinkmann, "Enron Ethics (Or: Culture Matters More Than Codes)," *Journal of Business Ethics* 45, no. 3 (July 2003).

4. Wilfred Frost, "Wells Fargo Board Slams Former CEO Stumpf and Tolstedt, Claws Back $75 million," *CNBC.com,* April 10, 2017, https://www.cnbc.com/2017/04/10/wells-fargo-board-slams-stumpf-and-tolstedt-claws-back-millions.html (accessed August 16, 2019).

5. Archie B. Carroll, "The Four Faces of Corporate Citizenship," *Business and Society Review* 100/101 (September 1998).

6. Mark S. Schwartz, "Universal Moral Values for Corporate Codes of Ethics," *Journal of Business Ethics* 59, no. 1 (June 2005).

7. Mark S. Schwartz, "A Code of Ethics for Corporate Codes of Ethics," *Journal of Business Ethics* 41, nos. 1–2 (November–December 2002).

8. T. L. Beauchamp and N. E. Bowie, *Ethical Theory and Business* (Upper Saddle River, NJ: Prentice Hall, 2001).

9. Thomas Donaldson and Thomas W. Dunfee, "Towards a Unified Conception of Business Ethics: Integrative Social Contracts Theory," *Academy of Management Review* 19, no. 2 (April 1994); Thomas Donaldson and Thomas W. Dunfee, *Ties That Bind: A Social Contracts Approach to Business Ethics* (Boston: Harvard Business School Press, 1999); Andrew Spicer, Thomas W. Dunfee, and Wendy J. Bailey, "Does National Context Matter in Ethical Decision Making? An Empirical Test of Integrative Social Contracts Theory," *Academy of Management Journal* 47, no. 4 (August 2004).

10. P. M. Nichols, "Outlawing Transnational Bribery Through the World Trade Organization," *Law and Policy in International Business* 28, no. 2 (1997).

11. Timothy M. Devinney, "Is the Socially Responsible Corporation a Myth? The Good, the Bad, and the Ugly of Corporate Social Responsibility," *Academy of Management Perspectives* 23, no. 2 (May 2009).

12. "General Mills' 2010 Corporate Social Responsibility Report Highlights New and Longstanding Achievements in the Areas of Health, Community, and Environment," *CSRwire,* April 15, 2010, www.csrwire.com/press_releases/29347-General-Mills-2010-Corporate-Social-Responsibility-report-now-available.html.

13. Arthur A. Thompson and Amit J. Shah, "Starbucks' Strategy and Internal Initiatives to Return to Profitable Growth," *Crafting & Executing Strategy: The Quest for Competitive Advantage,* 18th ed. (New York: McGraw-Hill Irwin, 2012).

14. Gerald I. J. M. Zwetsloot and Marcel N. A. van Marrewijk, "From Quality to Sustainability," *Journal of Business Ethics* 55 (December 2004), pp. 79–82.

15. Tilde Herrera, "PG&E Claims Industry First with Supply Chain Footprint Project," *GreenBiz.com,* June 30, 2010, www.greenbiz.com/news/2010/06/30/pge-claims-industry-first-supply-chain-carbon-footprint-project.

16. This definition is based on the Brundtland Commission's report, which described sustainable development in a like manner: United Nations General Assembly, "Report of the World Commission on Environment and Development: Our Common Future," 1987, www.un-documents.net/wced-ocf.htm, transmitted to the General Assembly as an annex to document A/42/427—"Development and International Co-operation: Environment" (accessed February 15, 2009).

17. Robert Goodland, "The Concept of Environmental Sustainability," *Annual Review of Ecology and Systematics* 26 (1995); J. G. Speth, *The Bridge at the End of the World: Capitalism, the Environment, and Crossing from Crisis to Sustainability* (New Haven, CT: Yale University Press, 2008).

18. Gerald I. J. M. Zwetsloot and Marcel N. A. van Marrewijk, "From Quality to Sustainability," *Journal of Business Ethics* 55 (December 2004); John B. Elkington, *Cannibals with Forks: The Triple Bottom Line of 21st Century Business* (Oxford: Capstone Publishing, 1997).

19. Michael E. Porter and Mark R. Kramer, "Strategy & Society: The Link Between Competitive Advantage and Corporate Social Responsibility," *Harvard Business Review* 84, no. 12 (December 2006).

20. Tom McCawley, "Racing to Improve Its Reputation: Nike Has Fought to Shed Its Image as an Exploiter of Third-World Labor Yet It Is Still a Target of Activists," *Financial Times,* December 2000.

21. E. J. Dionne, Jr., "Bad for Business," *The Washington Post,* May 15, 1998, https://www.washingtonpost.com/archive/opinions/1998/05/15/bad-for-business/112d99ce-a98c-479a-8b4e-9c371c786f36/?noredirect=on&utm_term=.2148b40aa0b8

22. Michael E. Porter and Mark Kramer, "Creating Shared Value," *Harvard Business Review* 89, nos. 1–2 (January–February 2011).

23. James C. Collins and Jerry I. Porras, *Built to Last: Successful Habits of Visionary Companies,* 3rd ed. (London: HarperBusiness, 2002).

24. Joshua D. Margolis and Hillary A. Elfenbein, "Doing Well by Doing Good: Don't Count on It," *Harvard Business Review* 86, no. 1 (January 2008); Lee E. Preston and Douglas P. O'Bannon, "The Corporate Social-Financial Performance Relationship," *Business and Society* 36, no. 4 (December 1997); Ronald M. Roman, Sefa Hayibor, and Bradley R. Agle, "The Relationship Between Social and Financial Performance: Repainting a Portrait," *Business and Society* 38, no. 1 (March 1999); Joshua D. Margolis and James P. Walsh, *People and Profits* (Mahwah, NJ: Lawrence Erlbaum, 2001).

10

SUPERIOR STRATEGY EXECUTION—ANOTHER PATH TO COMPETITIVE ADVANTAGE

LEARNING OBJECTIVES

After reading this chapter, you should be able to:

LO10-1 Recognize what managers must do to build an organization capable of good strategy execution.

LO10-2 Explain why resource allocation should always be based on strategic priorities.

LO10-3 Understand why policies and procedures should be designed to facilitate good strategy execution.

LO10-4 Understand how process management programs that drive continuous improvement help an organization achieve operating excellence.

LO10-5 Recognize the role of information and operating systems in enabling company personnel to carry out their strategic roles proficiently.

LO10-6 Explain how and why the use of well-designed incentives and rewards can be management's single most powerful tool for promoting operating excellence.

LO10-7 Explain how and why a company's culture can aid the drive for proficient strategy execution.

LO10-8 Recognize what constitutes effective managerial leadership in achieving superior strategy execution.

Once managers have decided on a strategy, the emphasis turns to converting it into actions and good results. Putting the strategy into place and getting the organization to execute it well call for different sets of managerial skills. Whereas crafting strategy is largely a market-driven and resource-driven activity, strategy implementation is an operations-driven activity primarily involving the management of people and business processes. Successful strategy execution depends on management's ability to direct organizational change and do a good job of allocating resources, building and strengthening competitive capabilities, instituting strategy-supportive policies, improving processes and systems, motivating and rewarding people, creating and nurturing a strategy-supportive culture, and consistently meeting or beating performance targets. While an organization's chief executive officer and other senior managers are ultimately responsible for ensuring that the strategy is executed successfully, it is middle and lower-level managers who must see to it that frontline employees and work groups competently perform the strategy-critical activities that allow companywide performance targets to be met. *Hence, strategy execution requires every manager to think through the answer to the question "What does my area have to do to implement its part of the strategic plan, and what should I do to get these things accomplished effectively and efficiently?"*

> **CORE CONCEPT**
>
> Good strategy execution requires a *team effort*. All managers have strategy execution responsibility in their areas of authority, and all employees are active participants in the strategy execution.

The Principal Managerial Components of Strategy Execution

Executing strategy entails figuring out the specific techniques, actions, and behaviors that are needed to get things done and deliver results. The exact items that need to be placed on management's action agenda always have to be customized to fit the particulars of a company's situation. The hot buttons for successfully executing a low-cost provider strategy are different from those in executing a differentiation strategy. Implementing a new strategy for a struggling company in the midst of a financial crisis is different from improving strategy execution in a company where the execution is already pretty good. While there's no definitive managerial recipe for successful strategy execution that cuts across all company situations and all types of strategies, certain managerial bases have to be covered no matter what the circumstances. Eight managerial tasks crop up repeatedly in company efforts to execute strategy (see Figure 10.1).

1. Building an organization with the capabilities, people, and structure needed to execute the strategy successfully

2. Allocating ample resources to strategy-critical activities

3. Ensuring that policies and procedures facilitate rather than impede effective strategy execution

4. Adopting process management programs that drive continuous improvement in how strategy execution activities are performed

5. Installing information and operating systems that enable company personnel to perform essential activities

6. Tying rewards directly to the achievement of performance objectives

7. Fostering a corporate culture that promotes good strategy execution

8. Exerting the internal leadership needed to propel implementation forward

FIGURE 10.1

The Eight Components of Strategy Execution

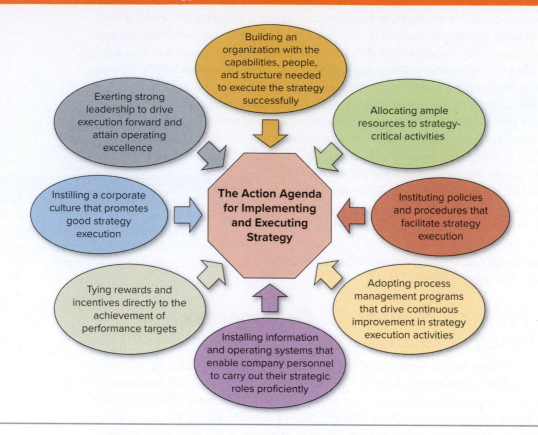

How well managers perform these eight tasks has a decisive impact on whether the outcome is a spectacular success, a colossal failure, or something in between. In the remainder of this chapter, we will discuss what is involved in performing the eight key managerial tasks that shape the process of implementing and executing strategy.

Building an Organization Capable of Good Strategy Execution: Three Key Actions

LO10-1 Recognize what managers must do to build an organization capable of good strategy execution.

Proficient strategy execution depends heavily on competent personnel, better-than-adequate competitive capabilities, and an effective internal organization. Building a capable organization is thus always a top priority in strategy execution. Three types of organization building actions are paramount:

1. *Staffing the organization*—putting together a strong management team, and recruiting and retaining employees with the needed experience, technical skills, and intellectual capital

2. *Acquiring, developing, and strengthening strategy-supportive resources and capabilities*—accumulating the required resources, developing proficiencies in performing strategy-critical value chain activities, and updating them to match changing market conditions and customer expectations

3. *Structuring the organization and work effort*—organizing value chain activities and business processes, establishing lines of authority and reporting relationships, and deciding how much decision-making authority to push down to lower-level managers and frontline employees

Staffing the Organization

No company can hope to perform the activities required for successful strategy execution without attracting and retaining talented managers and employees with suitable skills and intellectual capital.

Building Managerial Talent   Assembling a capable management team is a cornerstone of the organization-building task.[1] While company circumstances sometimes call for different mixes of backgrounds, experiences, management styles, and know-how, *the most important consideration is to fill key managerial slots with people who are good at figuring out what needs to be done and skilled in "making it happen" and delivering good results.*[2] Without a capable, results-oriented management team, the implementation–execution process ends up being hampered by missed deadlines, misdirected or wasteful efforts, and/or managerial ineptness.[3] Weak executives are serious impediments to getting optimal results because they are unable to differentiate between ideas that have merit and those that are misguided. In contrast, managers with strong strategy-implementing capabilities have a talent for asking tough, incisive questions. They know enough about the details of the business to be able to challenge and ensure the soundness of the approaches of the people around them, and they can discern whether the resources people are asking for make sense strategically. They are good at getting things done through others, typically by making sure they have the right people under them and that these people are put in the right jobs. They consistently follow through on issues and do not let important details slip through the cracks.

Sometimes a company's existing management team is suitable; at other times, it may need to be strengthened or expanded by promoting qualified people from within or by bringing in outsiders. The overriding aim in building a management team should be to assemble a critical mass of talented managers who can function as agents of change and further the cause of first-rate strategy execution. When a first-rate manager enjoys the help and support of other first-rate managers, it's possible to create a managerial whole that is greater than the sum of individual efforts: Talented managers who work well together as a team can produce organizational results that are dramatically better than what one- or two-star managers acting individually can achieve.[4] Concepts & Connections 10.1 describes Deloitte's highly effective approach to developing employee talent and a top-caliber management team.

Recruiting and Retaining a Capable Workforce   Assembling a capable management team is not enough. Staffing the organization with the right kinds of people must go much deeper than managerial jobs in order for value chain activities to be performed competently. *The quality of an organization's people is always an essential*

CONCEPTS & CONNECTIONS 10.1

MANAGEMENT DEVELOPMENT AT DELOITTE TOUCHE TOHMATSU LIMITED

Ken Wolter/Shutterstock

Hiring, retaining, and cultivating talent are critical activities at Deloitte, the world's largest professional services firm. By offering robust learning and development programs, Deloitte has been able to create a strong talent pipeline to the firm's partnership. Deloitte's emphasis on learning and development, across all stages of the employee life cycle, has led to recognitions such as being ranked number one on *Chief Executives*' list of "Best Private Companies for Leaders" and being listed among *Fortune*'s "100 Best Companies to Work For." The following programs contribute to Deloitte's successful execution of its talent strategy:

- *Clear path to partnership.* During the initial recruiting phase and then throughout an employee's tenure at the firm, Deloitte lays out a clear career path. The path indicates the expected timeline for promotion to each of the firm's hierarchy levels, along with the competencies and experience required. Deloitte's transparency on career paths, coupled with its in-depth performance management process, helps employees clearly understand their performance. This serves as a motivational tool for top performers, often leading to career acceleration.

- *Formal training programs.* Like other leading organizations, Deloitte has a program to ensure that recent college graduates are equipped with the necessary training and tools for succeeding on the job. Yet Deloitte's commitment to formal training is evident at all levels within the organization. Each time an employee is promoted, he or she attends "milestone" school, a week-long simulation that replicates true business situations employees would face as they transition to new stages of career development. In addition, Deloitte institutes mandatory training hours for all of its employees to ensure that individuals continue to further their professional development.

- *Special programs for high performers.* Deloitte also offers fellowships and programs to help employees acquire new skills and enhance their leadership development. For example, the Global Fellows program helps top performers work with senior leaders in the organization to focus on the realities of delivering client service across borders. Deloitte has also established the Emerging Leaders Development program, which utilizes skill building, 360-degree feedback, and one-on-one executive coaching to help top-performing managers and senior managers prepare for partnership.

- *Sponsorship, not mentorship.* To train the next generation of leaders, Deloitte has implemented formal mentorship programs to provide leadership development support. Deloitte, however, uses the term *sponsorship* to describe this initiative. A sponsor is tasked with taking a vested interest in an individual and advocating on his or her behalf. Sponsors help rising leaders navigate the firm, develop new competencies, expand their network, and hone the skills needed to accelerate their career.

Note: Developed with Heather Levy.

Sources: Company websites; www.accountingweb.com/article /leadership-development-community-service-integral-deloitte-university/220845 (accessed February 2014).

ingredient of successful strategy execution—knowledgeable, engaged employees are a company's best source of creative ideas for the nuts-and-bolts operating improvements that lead to operating excellence. Companies such as Mercedes-Benz, Google, Boston Consulting Group, and Procter & Gamble make a concerted effort to recruit the best and brightest people they can find and then retain them with excellent compensation packages, opportunities for rapid advancement and professional growth, and challenging and interesting assignments. Having a pool of "A players" with strong skill sets and lots of brainpower is essential to their business. Facebook makes a point of hiring the very brightest and most talented programmers it can find and motivating them with both good monetary incentives and the challenge of working on cutting-edge technology projects. The leading global accounting firms screen candidates not only on the basis of their accounting expertise but also on whether they possess the people skills needed to relate well with clients and colleagues. Southwest Airlines goes to considerable lengths to hire people who can have fun and be fun on the job; it uses special interviewing and screening methods to gauge whether applicants for customer-contact jobs have outgoing personality traits that match its strategy of creating a high-spirited, fun-loving, in-flight atmosphere for passengers. Southwest Airlines is so selective that only about 3 percent of the people who apply are offered jobs.

The tactics listed here are common among companies dedicated to staffing jobs with the best people they can find:

1. Putting forth considerable effort in screening and evaluating job applicants—selecting only those with suitable skill sets, energy, initiative, judgment, aptitudes for learning, and adaptability to the company's culture

2. Investing in training programs that continue throughout employees' careers

3. Providing promising employees with challenging, interesting, and skill-stretching assignments

4. Rotating people through jobs that span functional and geographic boundaries

5. Striving to retain talented, high-performing employees via promotions, salary increases, performance bonuses, stock options and equity ownership, fringe benefit packages, and other perks

6. Coaching average performers to improve their skills and capabilities, while weeding out underperformers and benchwarmers

Acquiring, Developing, and Strengthening Key Resources and Capabilities

High among the organization-building priorities in the strategy execution process is the need to build and strengthen competitively valuable resources and capabilities. As explained in Chapter 1, a company's ability to perform value-creating activities and realize its strategic objectives depends upon its resources and capabilities. In the course of crafting strategy, it is important for managers to identify the resources and capabilities that will enable the firm's strategy to succeed. Good strategy execution requires putting those resources and capabilities into place, refreshing and strengthening them as needed, and then modifying them as market conditions evolve. "Fast fashion" retailer Zara has developed valuable resources and capabilities that allow it to execute its strategy with great proficiency; see Concepts & Connections 10.2.

Three Approaches to Building and Strengthening Capabilities Building core competencies and competitive capabilities is a time-consuming, managerially challenging exercise. But with deliberate effort and continued practice, it is possible for a firm to become proficient at capability building. Indeed, by making capability-building activities a routine part of their strategy execution, some firms are able to develop *dynamic capabilities* that assist them in managing resource and capability change, as

CONCEPTS & CONNECTIONS 10.2

ZARA'S STRATEGY EXECUTION CAPABILITIES

jordi2r/123RF

Zara, a member of Inditex Group, is a "fast fashion" retailer. As soon as designs are seen in high-end fashion houses such as Prada, Zara's design team sets to work altering the clothing designs so that they can produce high fashion at mass-retailing prices. Zara's strategy is clever but by no means unique. The company's competitive advantage is in strategy execution. Every step of Zara's value chain execution is geared toward putting fashionable clothes in stores quickly, realizing high turnover, and strategically driving traffic.

The first key lever is a quick production process. Zara's design team uses inspiration from high fashion and nearly real-time feedback from stores to create up-to-the-minute pieces. Manufacturing largely occurs in factories close to headquarters in Spain, northern Africa, and Turkey, all areas considered to have a high cost of labor. Placing the factories strategically close allows for more flexibility and greater responsiveness to market needs, thereby outweighing the additional labor costs. The entire production process, from design to arrival at stores, takes only two weeks, while other retailers take six months. While traditional retailers commit up to 80 percent of their lines by the start of the season, Zara commits only 50 to 60 percent, meaning that up to half of the merchandise to hit stores is designed and manufactured during the season. Zara purposefully manufactures in small lot sizes to avoid discounting later on and also to encourage impulse shopping, as a particular item could be gone in a few days. From start to finish, Zara has engineered its production process to maximize turnover and turnaround time, creating a true advantage in this step of strategy execution.

Zara also excels at driving traffic to stores. First, the small lot sizes and frequent shipments (up to twice a week per store) drive customers to visit often and purchase quickly. Zara shoppers average 17 visits per year, versus 4 to 5 for The Gap. On average, items stay in a Zara store only 11 days. Second, Zara spends no money on advertising, but it occupies some of the most expensive retail space in town, always near the high-fashion houses it imitates. Proximity reinforces the high-fashion association, while the busy street drives significant foot traffic. Overall, Zara has managed to create competitive advantage in every level of strategy execution by tightly aligning design, production, advertising, and real estate with the overall strategy of fast fashion: extremely fast and extremely flexible.

Note: Developed with Sara Paccamonti.

Sources: Suzy Hansen, "How Zara Grew into the World's Largest Fashion Retailer," *New York Times,* November 9, 2012, www.nytimes.com/2012/11/11/magazine/how-zara-grew-into-the-worlds-largest-fashion-retailer.html?pagewanted=all (accessed February 5, 2014); and Seth Stevenson, "Polka Dots Are In? Polka Dots It Is!" *Slate,* June 21, 2012, www.slate.com/articles/arts/operations/l2012/06/zara_s_fast_fashion_how_the_company_gets_new_styles_to_stores_so_quickly_.html (accessed February 5, 2014).

> Building new competencies and capabilities is a multistage process that occurs over a period of months and years. It is not something that is accomplished overnight.

discussed in Chapter 4. The most common approaches to capability building include (1) internal development, (2) acquiring capabilities through mergers and acquisitions, and (3) accessing capabilities via collaborative partnerships.[5]

Developing Capabilities Internally Capabilities develop incrementally along an evolutionary path as organizations search for solutions to their problems. The process is complex because capabilities are the product of bundles of skills and know-how. In addition, capabilities tend to require the combined efforts of teams that are often cross-functional in nature, spanning a variety of departments and locations. For instance, the capability of speeding new products to market involves the collaborative efforts of personnel in R&D, engineering and design, purchasing, production, marketing, and distribution.

Because the process is incremental, the first step is to develop the *ability* to do something, however imperfectly or inefficiently. This entails selecting people with the requisite skills and experience, upgrading or expanding individual abilities as needed, and then molding the efforts of individuals into a collaborative effort to create an organizational ability. At this stage, progress can be fitful since it depends on experimentation, active search for alternative solutions, and learning through trial and error.[6] As experience grows and company personnel learn how to perform the activities consistently well and at an acceptable cost, the ability evolves into a tried-and-true competence.

> A company's capabilities must be continually refreshed and renewed to remain aligned with changing customer expectations, altered competitive conditions, and new strategic initiatives.

It is generally much easier and less time-consuming to update and remodel a company's existing capabilities as external conditions and company strategy change than it is to create them from scratch. Maintaining capabilities in top form may simply require exercising them continually and fine-tuning them as necessary. Similarly, augmenting a capability may require less effort if it involves the recombination of well-established company capabilities and draws on existing company resources.[7] For example, Williams-Sonoma first developed the capability to expand sales beyond its brick-and-mortar location in 1970, when it launched a catalog that was sent to customers throughout the United States. The company extended its mail-order business with the acquisitions of Hold Everything, a garden products catalog, and Pottery Barn, and entered online retailing in 2000 when it launched e-commerce sites for Pottery Barn and Williams-Sonoma. The ongoing renewal of these capabilities has allowed Williams-Sonoma to generate revenues of $5.7 billion in 2018 and be named to the Fortune 500 list of largest U.S. companies for a first time in 2019.

Acquiring Capabilities Through Mergers and Acquisitions Sometimes a company can build and refresh its competencies by acquiring another company with attractive resources and capabilities.[8] An acquisition aimed at building a stronger portfolio of resources and capabilities can be every bit as valuable as an acquisition aimed at adding new products or services to the company's lineup of offerings. The advantage of this mode of acquiring new capabilities is primarily one of speed, since developing new capabilities internally can take many years. Capabilities-motivated acquisitions are essential (1) when a market opportunity can slip by faster than a needed capability can be created internally and (2) when industry conditions, technology, or competitors are moving at such a rapid clip that time is of the essence.

At the same time, acquiring capabilities in this way is not without difficulty. Capabilities tend to involve tacit knowledge and complex routines that cannot be transferred readily from one organizational unit to another. This may limit the extent to which the new capability can be utilized by the acquiring organization. For example, since 2005 Facebook has spent more than $23 billion to acquire producers of augmented reality, voice recognition, image filters, language translation, face recognition, and other technologies to add capabilities that might enhance the social media experience. Transferring and integrating these capabilities to other parts of the Facebook organization prove easier said than done, however, as many technology acquisitions fail to yield the hoped-for benefits.

Accessing Capabilities Through Collaborative Partnerships Another method of acquiring capabilities from an external source is to access them via collaborative partnerships with suppliers, competitors, or other companies having the cutting-edge expertise. There are three basic ways to pursue this course of action:

1. *Outsource the function or activity requiring new capabilities to an outside provider.* As discussed in Chapter 6, outsourcing has the advantage of conserving resources so the firm can focus its energies on those activities most central to its strategy. It may be a good choice for firms that are too small and resource-constrained to execute all the parts of their strategy internally.

2. *Collaborate with a firm that has complementary resources and capabilities in a joint venture, strategic alliance, or other type of partnership to achieve a shared strategic objective.* Since the success of the venture will depend on how well the partners work together, potential partners should be selected as much for their management style, culture, and goals as for their resources and capabilities.

3. *Engage in a collaborative partnership for the purpose of learning how the partner performs activities, internalizing its methods and thereby acquiring its capabilities.* This may be a viable method when each partner has something to learn from the other. But in other cases, it involves an abuse of trust and puts the cooperative venture at risk.

Matching Organizational Structure to the Strategy

Building an organization capable of good strategy execution also relies on an organizational structure that lays out lines of authority and reporting relationships in a manner that supports the company's key strategic initiatives. The best approach to settling on an organizational structure is to first consider the key value chain activities that deliver value to the customer. In any business, some activities in the value chain are always more critical than others. For instance, hotel/motel enterprises have to be good at fast check-in/check-out, housekeeping, food service, and creating a pleasant ambience. In specialty chemicals, the strategy-critical activities include R&D, product innovation, getting new products onto the market quickly, effective marketing, and expertise in assisting customers. It is important for management to build its organization structure around proficient performance of these activities, making them the centerpieces or main building blocks on the organization chart.

The rationale for making strategy-critical activities the main building blocks in structuring a business is compelling: If activities crucial to strategic success are to have the resources, decision-making influence, and organizational impact they need, they have to be centerpieces in the organizational scheme. In addition, a new or changed strategy is likely to entail new or different key activities or capabilities and therefore to require a new or different organizational structure.[9] Attempting to carry out a new strategy with an old organizational structure is usually unwise.

Types of Organizational Structures It is common for companies engaged in a single line of business to utilize a **functional (or departmental) organizational structure** that organizes strategy-critical activities into distinct *functional, product, geographic, process,* or *customer* groups. For instance, a technical instruments manufacturer may be organized around research and development, engineering, supply chain management, assembly, quality control, marketing technical services, and corporate administration. A company with operations scattered across a large geographic area or many countries may organize activities and reporting relationships by geography.

> A functional structure organizes strategy-critical activities into distinct functional, product, geographic, process, or customer groups.

Many diversified companies utilize a **multidivisional (or divisional) organizational structure** consisting of a set of operating divisions organized along market, customer, product, or geographic lines, along with a central corporate headquarters, which monitors divisional activities, allocates resources, and exercises overall control. A multidivisional structure is appropriate for a diversified building materials company that designs, produces, and markets cabinets, plumbing fixtures, windows, and paints and stains. The divisional structure organizes all of the value chain activities involved with making each type of home construction product available to home builders and do-it-yourselfers into a common division and makes each division an independent profit center. Therefore the paint division, plumbing products division, cabinets division, and windows division all operate separately and report to a central corporate headquarters.

> A multidivisional structure consists of a set of operating divisions organized along market, customer, product, or geographic lines, along with a central corporate headquarters that monitors divisional activities, allocates resources, and exercises overall control.

Matrix organizational structures is a combination structure in which the organization is organized along two or more dimensions at once (e.g., business, geographic region, value chain function) for the purpose of enhancing cross-unit communication, collaboration, and coordination. In essence, it overlays one type of structure onto another type. Matrix structures are managed through multiple reporting relationships, so a middle manager may report to several bosses. For example, in a matrix structure based on product line, region, and function, a sales manager for plastic containers in Georgia might report to the manager of the plastics division, the head of the southeast sales region, and the head of marketing.

Organizational Structure and Authority in Decision Making Responsibility for results of decisions made throughout the organization ultimately lies with managers at the top of the organizational structure, but in practice, lower-level managers might possess a great deal of authority in decision making. Companies vary in the degree of authority delegated to managers of each organization unit and how much decision-making latitude is given to individual employees in performing their jobs. The two extremes are to *centralize decision making* at the top (the CEO and a few close lieutenants) or to *decentralize decision making* by giving managers and employees considerable decision-making latitude in their areas of responsibility. The two approaches are based on sharply different underlying principles and beliefs, with each having its pros and cons. *In a highly decentralized organization, decision-making authority is pushed down to the lowest organizational level capable of making timely, informed, competent decisions.* The objective is to put adequate decision-making authority in the hands of the people closest to and most familiar with the situation and train them

> A matrix structure is a combination structure that overlays one type of structure onto another type, with multiple reporting relationships. It is used to foster cross-unit collaboration and communication.

to weigh all the factors and exercise good judgment. Decentralized decision making means that the managers of each organizational unit are delegated lead responsibility for deciding how best to execute strategy.

The case for empowering down-the-line managers and employees to make decisions related to daily operations and executing the strategy is based on the belief that a company that draws on the combined intellectual capital of all its employees can outperform a command-and-control company.[10] Decentralized decision making means, for example, employees may be empowered to do what it takes to please customers and increase sales. At TJX, parent company of T. J. Maxx, Marshalls, and four other fashion and home decor retail store chains, buyers are encouraged to be intelligent risk takers in deciding what items to purchase for TJX stores—there is the story of a buyer for a seasonal product category who cut her own budget to have dollars allocated to other categories where sales were expected to be stronger. Another example of employee empowerment involves an employee at Starbucks who enthusiastically offered free coffee to waiting customers when a store's computerized cash register system went offline.

Pushing decision-making authority deep down into the organization structure and empowering employees presents its own organizing challenge: *how to exercise adequate control over the actions of empowered employees so that the business is not put at risk at the same time that the benefits of empowerment are realized.* Maintaining adequate organizational control over empowered employees is generally accomplished by placing limits on the authority that empowered personnel can exercise, holding people accountable for their decisions, instituting compensation incentives that reward people for doing their jobs in a manner that contributes to good company performance, and creating a corporate culture where there's strong peer pressure on individuals to act responsibly.

In a highly centralized organization structure, top executives retain authority for most strategic and operating decisions and keep a tight rein on business-unit heads, department heads, and the managers of key operating units; comparatively little discretionary authority is granted to frontline supervisors and rank-and-file employees. The command-and-control paradigm of centralized structures is based on the underlying assumptions that frontline personnel have neither the time nor the inclination to direct and properly control the work they are performing and that they lack the knowledge and judgment to make wise decisions about how best to do it.

The big advantage of an authoritarian structure is that it is easy to know who is accountable when things do not go well. But there are some serious disadvantages. Hierarchical command-and-control structures make an organization sluggish in responding to changing conditions because of the time it takes for the review/approval process to run up all the layers of the management bureaucracy. Also, centralized decision making is often impractical—the larger the company and the more scattered its operations, the more that decision-making authority has to be delegated to managers closer to the scene of the action.

Facilitating Collaboration with External Partners and Strategic Allies   Strategic alliances, outsourcing arrangements, joint ventures, and cooperative partnerships can contribute little of value without active management of the relationship. Building organizational bridges with external partners and strategic allies can be accomplished by appointing "relationship managers" with responsibility for fostering the success of strategic partnerships. Relationship managers have many roles and functions: getting the right people together, promoting good rapport, facilitating the flow of information, nurturing interpersonal communication and cooperation, and ensuring effective coordination.[11] Communication and coordination are particularly important since information sharing is required to make the relationship work and to address conflicts, trouble spots, and changing situations.

Communication and coordination are also aided by the adoption of a **network structure** that links independent organizations involved in cooperative arrangements to achieve some common undertaking. A well-managed network structure typically includes one firm in a more central role, with the responsibility of ensuring that the right partners are included and the activities across the network are coordinated. The high-end Italian motorcycle company Ducati operates in this manner, assembling its motorcycles from parts obtained from a hand-picked, integrated network of parts suppliers.

> **CORE CONCEPT**
>
> A **network structure** is the arrangement linking a number of independent organizations involved in some common undertaking.

> The ultimate goal of decentralized decision making is to put decision-making authority in the hands of those persons or teams closest to and most knowledgeable about the situation.

Allocating Resources to Strategy-Critical Activities

LO10-2   Explain why resource allocation should always be based on strategic priorities.

Early in the process of implementing and executing a new or different strategy, top management must determine what funding is needed to execute new strategic initiatives, to bolster value-creating processes, and to strengthen the company's capabilities and competencies. This includes careful screening of requests for more people and new facilities and equipment, approving those that hold promise for making a contribution to strategy execution, and turning down those that do not. Should internal cash flows prove insufficient to fund the planned strategic initiatives, then management must raise additional funds through borrowing or selling additional shares of stock to willing investors.

A company's ability to marshal the resources needed to support new strategic initiatives has a major impact on the strategy execution process. Too little funding slows progress and impedes the efforts of organizational units to execute their pieces of the strategic plan proficiently. Too much funding wastes organizational resources and reduces financial performance. Both outcomes argue for managers to be deeply involved in reviewing budget proposals and directing the proper amounts of resources to strategy-critical organization units.

A change in strategy nearly always calls for budget reallocations and resource shifting. Previously important units having a lesser role in the new strategy may need downsizing. Units that now have a bigger strategic role may need more people, new equipment, additional facilities, and above-average increases in their operating budgets. Strategy implementers have to exercise their power to put enough resources behind new strategic initiatives to make things happen, and they have to make the tough decisions to kill projects and activities that are no longer justified.

Google's strong support of R&D activities helped it to grow to a $527 billion giant in just 18 years. In 2013, however, Google decided to kill its 20 percent time policy, which allowed its staff to work on side projects of their choice one day a week. While this side project program gave rise to many innovations, such as Gmail and AdSense (a big contributor to Google's revenues), it also meant that fewer resources were available to projects that were deemed closer to the core of Google's mission. In the years since Google killed the 20 percent policy, the company has consistently topped *Fortune, Forbes,* and *Fast Company* magazines' "most innovative companies" list for ideas such as Google Chromebooks and its Waymo self-driving automobile project.

> A company's strategic priorities must drive how capital allocations are made and the size of each unit's operating budgets.

Instituting Strategy-Supportive Policies and Procedures

LO10-3 Understand why policies and procedures should be designed to facilitate good strategy execution.

A company's policies and procedures can either assist or become a barrier to good strategy execution. Anytime a company makes changes to its business strategy, managers are well advised to carefully review existing policies and procedures, and revise or discard those that are out of sync. Well-conceived policies and operating procedures act to facilitate organizational change and good strategy execution in three ways:

1. *Policies and procedures help enforce needed consistency in how particular strategy-critical activities are performed.* Standardization and strict conformity are sometimes desirable components of good strategy execution. Eliminating significant differences in the operating practices of different plants, sales regions, or customer service centers helps a company deliver consistent product quality and service to customers.

> Well-conceived policies and procedures aid strategy execution; out-of-sync ones are barriers to effective implementation.

2. *Policies and procedures support change programs by providing top-down guidance regarding how certain things now need to be done.* Asking people to alter established habits and procedures always upsets the internal order of things. It is normal for pockets of resistance to develop and for people to exhibit some degree of stress and anxiety about how the changes will affect them. Policies are a particularly useful way to counteract tendencies for some people to resist change—most people refrain from violating company policy or going against recommended practices and procedures without first gaining clearance or having strong justification.

3. *Well-conceived policies and procedures promote a work climate that facilitates good strategy execution.* Managers can use the policy-changing process as a powerful lever for changing the corporate culture in ways that produce a stronger fit with the new strategy.

McDonald's policy manual spells out detailed procedures that personnel in each McDonald's unit are expected to observe to ensure consistent quality across its 31,000 units. For example, "Cooks must turn, never flip, hamburgers. If they haven't been purchased, Big Macs must be discarded in 10 minutes after being cooked and French fries in 7 minutes." To get store personnel to dedicate themselves to outstanding customer service, Nordstrom has a policy of promoting only those people whose personnel records contain evidence of "heroic acts" to please customers, especially customers who may have made "unreasonable requests" that require special efforts.

One of the big policy-making issues concerns what activities need to be rigidly prescribed and what activities allow room for independent action on the part of empowered personnel. Few companies need thick policy manuals to prescribe exactly how daily operations are to be conducted. Too much policy can be confusing and erect obstacles to good strategy implementation. There is wisdom in a middle approach: *Prescribe enough policies to place boundaries on employees' actions; then empower them to act within these boundaries in whatever way they think makes sense.* Allowing company personnel to act anywhere between the "white lines" is especially appropriate when individual creativity and initiative are more essential to good strategy execution than standardization and strict conformity.

Striving for Continuous Improvement in Processes and Activities

 LO10-4 Understand how process management programs that drive continuous improvement help an organization achieve operating excellence.

Company managers can significantly advance the cause of superior strategy execution by pushing organization units and company personnel to strive for continuous improvement in how value chain activities are performed. In aiming for operating excellence, many companies have come to rely on three potent management tools: business process reengineering, total quality management (TQM) programs, and Six Sigma quality control techniques. *Business process reengineering* involves pulling the pieces of strategy-critical activities out of different departments and unifying their performance in a single department or cross-functional work group.[12] When done properly, business process reengineering can produce dramatic operating benefits. Hallmark reengineered its process for developing new greeting cards, creating teams of mixed-occupation personnel (artists, writers, lithographers, merchandisers, and administrators) to work on a single holiday or greeting card theme. The reengineered process speeded development times for new lines of greeting cards by up to 24 months, was more cost-efficient, and increased customer satisfaction.[13]

Total quality management (TQM) is a philosophy of managing a set of business practices that emphasizes continuous improvement in all phases of operations, 100 percent accuracy in performing tasks, involvement and empowerment of employees at all levels, team-based work design, benchmarking, and total customer satisfaction.[14] While TQM concentrates on the production of quality goods and fully satisfying customer expectations, it achieves its biggest successes when it is extended to employee efforts in *all departments*—human resources, billing, R&D, engineering, accounting and records, and information systems. It involves reforming the corporate culture and shifting to a total quality/continuous improvement business philosophy that permeates every facet of the organization.[15] TQM doctrine preaches that there is no such thing as "good enough" and that everyone has a responsibility to participate in continuous improvement. TQM is thus a race without a finish. Success comes from making little steps forward each day, a process that the Japanese call *kaizen.*

Six Sigma quality control consists of a disciplined, statistics-based system aimed at producing not more than 3.4 defects per million iterations for any business process—from manufacturing to customer transactions.[16] The Six Sigma process of define, measure, analyze, improve, and control (DMAIC, pronounced *dee-may-ic*) is an improvement system for existing processes falling below specification. The Six Sigma DMADV (define, measure, analyze, design, and verify) methodology is used to develop *new* processes or products at Six Sigma quality levels.[17] DMADV is sometimes referred to as Design for Six Sigma (DFSS). The statistical thinking underlying Six Sigma is based on the following three principles: All work is a process, all processes have variability, and all processes create data that explain variability.[18]

Since the programs were first introduced, thousands of companies and nonprofit organizations around the world have used Six Sigma to promote operating excellence. In the first five years of its adoption, Six Sigma at Bank of America helped the bank reap about $2 billion in revenue gains and cost savings. General Electric (GE), one of the most successful companies implementing Six Sigma training and pursuing Six Sigma perfection across the company's entire operations, estimated benefits of some $10 billion during the first five years of implementation—its Lighting division, for example, cut invoice defects and disputes by 98 percent.

While Six Sigma programs often improve the efficiency of many operating activities and processes, evidence shows that Six Sigma programs can stifle innovation. The essence of Six Sigma is to reduce variability in processes, but creative processes, by nature, include quite a bit of variability. In many instances, breakthrough innovations occur only after thousands of ideas have been abandoned and promising ideas have gone through multiple iterations and extensive prototyping. Alphabet Executive Chairman of the Board Eric Schmidt has commented that the innovation process is "anti–Six Sigma" and applying Six Sigma principles to those performing creative work at Google would choke off innovation at the company.[19]

A blended approach to Six Sigma implementation that is gaining in popularity pursues incremental improvements in operating efficiency, while R&D and other processes that allow the company to develop new ways of offering value to customers are given more free rein. Managers of these *ambidextrous organizations* are adept at employing continuous improvement in operating processes but allowing R&D to operate under a set of rules that allows for the development of breakthrough innovations. Ciba Vision, a global leader in contact lenses, dramatically reduced operating expenses through the use of continuous improvement programs, while simultaneously and harmoniously developing new series of contact lens products that grew its revenues by 300 percent over a 10-year period.[20]

The Difference Between Business Process Reengineering and Continuous Improvement Programs

Business process reengineering and continuous improvement efforts such as TQM and Six Sigma both aim at improved efficiency, better product quality, and greater customer satisfaction. The essential difference between business process reengineering and continuous improvement programs is that reengineering aims at *quantum gains* on the order of 30 to 50 percent or more, whereas total quality programs stress *incremental progress*—striving for inch-by-inch gains again and again in a never-ending stream. The two approaches to improved performance of value chain activities and operating excellence are not mutually exclusive; it makes sense to use them in tandem. Reengineering can be used first to produce a good basic design that yields quick, dramatic improvements in performing a business process. Total quality programs can then be used as a follow-up to deliver continuing improvements.

> The purpose of using benchmarking, best practices, business process reengineering, TQM, Six Sigma, or other operational improvement programs is to improve the performance of strategy-critical activities and promote superior strategy execution.

Installing Information and Operating Systems

LO10-5   Recognize the role of information and operating systems in enabling company personnel to carry out their strategic roles proficiently.

Company strategies and value-creating internal processes cannot be executed well without a number of internal operating systems. FedEx has internal communication systems that allow it to coordinate its more than 49,000 vehicles in handling a daily average of 11 million shipments to 220 countries. Its leading-edge flight operations systems allow a single controller to direct as many as 200 of FedEx's 650 aircraft simultaneously, overriding their flight plans should weather problems or other special circumstances arise. In addition, FedEx has created e-business tools for customers that allow them to track packages online, create address books, review shipping history, generate custom reports, simplify customer billing, reduce internal warehousing and inventory management costs, purchase goods and services from suppliers, and respond to quickly changing customer demands. All of FedEx's systems support the company's strategy of providing businesses and individuals with a broad array of package delivery services and enhancing its competitiveness against United Parcel Service, DHL, and the U.S. Postal Service.

Siemens Healthcare, one of the largest suppliers to the health care industry, uses a cloud-based business activity monitoring (BAM) system to continuously monitor and improve the company's processes across more than 190 countries. Customer satisfaction is one of Siemens's most important business objectives, so the reliability of its order management and services is crucial. Caesars Entertainment uses a sophisticated customer relationship database that records detailed information about its customers' gambling habits. When a member of the Caesars' Total Rewards program calls to make a reservation, the representative can review previous spending, including average bet size, to offer an upgrade or complimentary stay at Caesars Palace or one of the company's other properties. At Uber, there are systems for locating vehicles near a customer and real-time demand monitoring to price fares during high-demand periods.

> Having state-of-the-art operating systems, information systems, and real-time data is integral to competent strategy execution and operating excellence.

Information systems need to cover five broad areas: (1) customer data, (2) operations data, (3) employee data, (4) supplier/partner/collaborative ally data, and (5) financial performance data. All key strategic performance indicators must be tracked and reported in real time whenever possible. Real-time information systems permit company managers to stay on top of implementation initiatives and daily operations and to intervene if things seem to be drifting off course. Tracking key performance indicators, gathering information from operating personnel, quickly identifying and diagnosing problems, and taking corrective actions are all integral pieces of the process of managing strategy execution and overseeing operations.

Using Rewards and Incentives to Promote Better Strategy Execution

LO10-6   Explain how and why the use of well-designed incentives and rewards can be management's single most powerful tool for promoting operating excellence.

To create a strategy-supportive system of rewards and incentives, a company must emphasize rewarding people for accomplishing results related to creating value for customers, not for just dutifully performing assigned tasks. Focusing jobholders' attention and energy on what to *achieve* as opposed to what to *do* makes the work environment results-oriented. It is flawed management to tie incentives and rewards to satisfactory performance of duties and activities instead of desired business outcomes and company achievements.[21] In any job, performing assigned tasks is not equivalent to achieving intended outcomes. Diligently showing up for work and attending to job assignment does not, by itself, guarantee results. As any student knows, the fact that an instructor teaches and students go to class doesn't necessarily mean that the students are learning.

> A properly designed reward structure is management's most powerful tool for gaining employee commitment to superior strategy execution and excellent operating results.

Motivation and Reward Systems

It is important for both organization units and individuals to be properly aligned with strategic priorities and enthusiastically committed to executing strategy. *To get employees' sustained, energetic commitment, management has to be resourceful in designing and using motivational incentives—both monetary and nonmonetary.* The more a manager understands what motivates subordinates and is able to use appropriate motivational incentives, the greater will be employees' commitment to good day-in, day-out strategy execution and achievement of performance targets.

Guidelines for Designing Monetary Incentive Systems

Guidelines for creating incentive compensation systems that link employee behavior to organizational objectives include:

1. *Make the performance payoff a major, not a minor, piece of the total compensation package.* The payoff for high-performing individuals and teams must be meaningfully greater than the payoff for average performers, and the payoff for average performers meaningfully bigger than for below-average performers.

2. *Have incentives that extend to all managers and all workers, not just top management.* Lower-level managers and employees are just as likely as senior executives to be motivated by the possibility of lucrative rewards.

3. *Administer the reward system with scrupulous objectivity and fairness.* If performance standards are set unrealistically high or if individual/group performance evaluations are not accurate and well documented, dissatisfaction with the system will overcome any positive benefits.

4. *Tie incentives to performance outcomes directly linked to good strategy execution and financial performance.* Incentives should never be paid just because people

are thought to be "doing a good job" or because they "work hard." An argument can be presented that exceptions should be made in giving rewards to people who have come up short because of circumstances beyond their control. The problem with making exceptions for unknowable, uncontrollable, or unforeseeable circumstances is that once good excuses start to creep into justifying rewards for subpar results, the door is open for all kinds of reasons actual performance has failed to match targeted performance.

5. *Make sure the performance targets that each individual or team is expected to achieve involve outcomes that the individual or team can personally affect.* The role of incentives is to enhance individual commitment and channel behavior in beneficial directions.

6. *Keep the time between achieving the target performance outcome and the payment of the reward as short as possible.* Weekly or monthly payments for good performance work much better than annual payments for employees in most job categories. Annual bonus payouts work best for higher-level managers and for situations in which target outcome relates to overall company profitability or stock price performance.

Once the incentives are designed, they have to be communicated and explained. Everybody needs to understand how their incentive compensation is calculated and how individual/group performance targets contribute to organizational performance targets.

Nonmonetary Rewards

Financial incentives generally head the list of motivating tools for trying to gain whole-hearted employee commitment to good strategy execution and operating excellence. But most successful companies also make extensive use of nonmonetary incentives. Some of the most important nonmonetary approaches used to enhance motivation are listed here:[22]

- *Provide attractive perks and fringe benefits.* The various options include full coverage of health insurance premiums; college tuition reimbursement; paid vacation time; onsite child care; onsite fitness centers; telecommuting; and compressed workweeks (four 10-hour days instead of five 8-hour days).

- *Adopt promotion-from-within policies.* This practice helps bind workers to their employers and employers to their workers, plus it is an incentive for good performance.

- *Act on suggestions from employees.* Research indicates that the moves of many companies to push decision making down the line and empower employees increase employee motivation and satisfaction, as well as boost productivity.

- *Create a work atmosphere in which there is genuine sincerity, caring, and mutual respect among workers and between management and employees.* A "family" work environment in which people are on a first-name basis and there is strong camaraderie promotes teamwork and cross-unit collaboration.

- *Share information with employees about financial performance, strategy, operational measures, market conditions, and competitors' actions.* Broad disclosure and prompt communication send the message that managers trust their workers.

- *Have attractive office spaces and facilities.* A workplace environment with appealing features and amenities usually has decidedly positive effects on employee morale and productivity.

CONCEPTS & CONNECTIONS 10.3

HOW WEGMANS REWARDS AND MOTIVATES ITS EMPLOYEES

tarheel1776/Shutterstock

Companies use a variety of tools and strategies designed to motivate employees and engender superior strategy execution. In this respect, Wegmans Food Markets, Inc., serves as an exemplar. With approximately 48,000 employees spread across 96 stores across the Northeast and Mid-Atlantic, Wegmans stands out as an organization that delivers above average results in an industry known for its low margins, low wages, and challenging employee relationships. Guided by a philosophy of employees first, Wegmans employs an array of programs that enables the company to attract and retain the best people.

Since the creation of its broad benefits program for full-time employees in the 1950s, Wegmans has had a strong benefits philosophy. Today, flexible or compressed schedules are common, and policies extend to same-sex partners. Regarding financial compensation, wages are above average for the grocery

retail industry, which also has an added benefit of keeping its workforce nonunionized.

In addition to the traditional elements of compensation and benefits, Wegmans invests considerably in the training and education of its employees. Known for its strength in employee development, upwards of $50 million annually is spent on employee learning. Since 1984, the company has awarded nearly $110 million in tuition assistance, and over $50 million in scholarships.

Another crucial aspect of employee motivation is feeling heard. Employees see their ideas put into action through a series of programs designed to capture and implement their ideas. Wegmans deploys a series of programs, including open-door days, team huddles, focus groups, and two-way Q&As with senior management.

With the recognition that employees are critical to delivering a great customer experience, Wegmans directs a considerable amount of resources to its biggest asset, its people. Its suite of programs and benefits, along with a policy of filling at least half of its open opportunities internally, led to one of the lowest turnover rates in its industry. They have also resulted in Wegmans placing among the top five firms on *Fortune*'s list of the 100 Best Companies to Work For, year after year.

Note: Developed with Sadé M. Lawrence.

Sources: Company website; M. Boyle, "The Wegmans Way," January 24, 2005, http://archive.fortune.com/magazines/fortune/fortune_archive/2005/01/24/8234048/index.htm; and "Wegmans Food Markets, Inc.," *Great Place to Work*, February 14, 2018, http://reviews.greatplacetowork.com/wegmans-food-markets-inc.

Concepts & Connections 10.3 presents specific examples of the motivational tactics employed by Wegmans Food Markets—a consistently top-ranked company on *Fortune*'s list of the "100 Best Companies to Work For" in America.

Instilling a Corporate Culture That Promotes Good Strategy Execution

LO10-7   Explain how and why a company's culture can aid the drive for proficient strategy execution.

Every company has its own unique culture. The character of a company's culture or work climate defines "how we do things around here," its approach to people management, and the "chemistry" that permeates its work environment. The meshing of

shared core values, beliefs, ingrained behaviors and attitudes, and business principles constitutes a company's
corporate culture. A company's culture is important
because it influences the organization's actions and
approaches to conducting business—in a very real sense,
the culture is the company's organizational DNA.[23]

The psyche of corporate cultures varies widely. For
instance, the bedrock of Walmart's culture is dedication

to customer satisfaction, zealous pursuit of low costs and frugal operating practices, a
strong work ethic, ritualistic Saturday-morning headquarters meetings to exchange ideas
and review problems, and company executives' commitment to visiting stores, listening
to customers, and soliciting suggestions from employees. At Nordstrom, the corporate
culture is centered on delivering exceptional service to customers, where the company's
motto is "Respond to unreasonable customer requests," and each out-of-the-ordinary
request is seen as an opportunity for a "heroic" act by an employee that can further the
company's reputation for unparalleled customer service. Nordstrom makes a point of
promoting employees noted for their heroic acts and dedication to outstanding service.
The company motivates its salespeople with a commission-based compensation system
that enables Nordstrom's best salespeople to earn more than double what other department stores pay.

High-Performance Cultures

Some companies have so-called "high-performance" cultures in which the standout
cultural traits are a "can-do" spirit, pride in doing things right, no-excuses accountability, and a pervasive results-oriented work climate in which people go the extra mile to
meet or beat stretch objectives. In high-performance cultures, there is a strong sense of
involvement on the part of company personnel and emphasis on individual initiative
and creativity. Performance expectations are clearly stated for the company as a whole,
for each organizational unit, and for each individual. Issues and problems are promptly
addressed—there's a razor-sharp focus on what needs to be done. A high-performance
culture in which there's constructive pressure to achieve good results is a valuable contributor to good strategy execution and operating excellence. Results-oriented cultures
are permeated with a spirit of achievement and have a good track record in meeting or
beating performance targets.[24]

The challenge in creating a high-performance culture is to inspire high loyalty and
dedication on the part of employees such that they are energized to put forth their
very best efforts to do things right. Managers have to take pains to reinforce constructive behavior, reward top performers, and purge habits and behaviors that stand in the
way of good results. They must work at knowing the strengths and weaknesses of their
subordinates so as to better match talent with task. In sum, there has to be an overall
disciplined, performance-focused approach to managing the organization.

Adaptive Cultures

In direct contrast to change-resistant cultures, **adaptive
cultures** are very supportive of managers and employees
at all ranks who propose or help initiate useful change.
The hallmark of adaptive cultures is a willingness on the

part of organizational members to accept change and take on the challenge of introducing and executing new strategies. Company personnel share a feeling of confidence that the organization can deal with whatever threats and opportunities arise; they are receptive to risk taking, innovation, and changing strategies and practices. Internal entrepreneurship on the part of individuals and groups is encouraged and rewarded. Senior executives seek out, support, and promote individuals who exercise initiative, spot opportunities for improvement, and display the skills to take advantage of them. As in high-performance cultures, the company exhibits a proactive approach to identifying issues, evaluating the implications and options, and quickly moving ahead with workable solutions.

Technology companies, software companies, and Internet-based companies are good illustrations of organizations with adaptive cultures. Such companies thrive on change—driving it, leading it, and capitalizing on it (but sometimes also succumbing to change when they make the wrong move or are swamped by better technologies or the superior business models of rivals). Companies such as Amazon, Groupon, Apple, Adobe, Google, and Intel cultivate the capability to act and react rapidly. They are avid practitioners of entrepreneurship and innovation, with a demonstrated willingness to take bold risks to create new products, new businesses, and new industries. To create and nurture a culture that can adapt rapidly to changing or shifting business conditions, they staff their organizations with people who are proactive, who rise to the challenge of change, and who have an aptitude for adapting.

In fast-changing business environments, a corporate culture that is receptive to altering organizational practices and behaviors is a virtual necessity. However, adaptive cultures work to the advantage of all companies, not just those in rapid-change environments. Every company operates in a market and business climate that is changing to one degree or another. *As a company's strategy evolves, an adaptive culture is a definite ally in the strategy implementation, strategy execution process as compared to cultures that have to be coaxed and cajoled to change.*

Unhealthy Corporate Cultures

The distinctive characteristic of an unhealthy corporate culture is the presence of counterproductive cultural traits that adversely impact the work climate and company performance.[25] Five particularly unhealthy cultural traits are a heavily politicized internal environment, hostility to change, an insular "not invented here" mindset, a disregard for high ethical standards, and the presence of incompatible, clashing subcultures.

Politicized Cultures A politicized internal environment is unhealthy because political infighting consumes a great deal of organizational energy and often results in the company's strategic agenda taking a backseat to political maneuvering. In companies in which internal politics pervades the work climate, empire-building managers pursue their own agendas, and the positions they take on issues are usually aimed at protecting or expanding their turf. The support or opposition of politically influential executives and/or coalitions among departments with vested interests in a particular outcome typically weighs heavily in deciding what actions the company takes. All this maneuvering detracts from efforts to execute strategy with real proficiency and frustrates company personnel who are less political and more inclined to do what is in the company's best interests.

Change-Resistant Cultures Change-resistant cultures encourage a number of undesirable or unhealthy behaviors—avoiding risks, hesitation in pursuing emerging opportunities, and widespread aversion to continuous improvement in performing value chain activities. Change-resistant companies have little appetite for being first movers or fast followers, believing that being in the forefront of change is too risky and that acting too quickly increases vulnerability to costly mistakes. They are more inclined to adopt a wait-and-see posture, learn from the missteps of early movers, and then move forward cautiously with initiatives that are deemed safe. Hostility to change is most often found in companies with multilayered management bureaucracies that have enjoyed considerable market success in years past and that are wedded to the "We have done it this way for years" syndrome.

General Motors, IBM, Sears, and Eastman Kodak are classic examples of companies whose change-resistant bureaucracies have damaged their market standings and financial performance; clinging to what made them successful, they were reluctant to alter operating practices and modify their business approaches when signals of market change first sounded. As strategies of gradual change won out over bold innovation, all four lost market share to rivals that quickly moved to institute changes more in tune with evolving market conditions and buyer preferences. While IBM and GM have made strides in building a culture needed for market success, Sears and Kodak are still struggling to recoup lost ground.

Insular, Inwardly Focused Cultures Sometimes a company reigns as an industry leader or enjoys great market success for so long that its personnel start to believe they have all the answers or can develop them on their own. Such confidence breeds arrogance—company personnel discount the merits of what outsiders are doing and what can be learned by studying best-in-class performers. Benchmarking and a search for the best practices of outsiders are seen as offering little payoff. The big risk of a must-be-invented-here mindset and insular cultural thinking is that the company can underestimate the competencies and accomplishments of rival companies and overestimate its own progress—with a resulting loss of competitive advantage over time.

Unethical and Greed-Driven Cultures Companies that have little regard for ethical standards or that are run by executives driven by greed and ego gratification are scandals waiting to happen. Executives exude the negatives of arrogance, ego, greed, and an "ends-justify-the-means" mentality in pursuing overambitious revenue and profitability targets.[26] Senior managers wink at unethical behavior and may cross the line to unethical (and sometimes criminal) behavior themselves. They are prone to adopt accounting principles that make financial performance look better than it really is. Legions of companies have fallen prey to unethical behavior and greed, most notably Enron, Countrywide Financial, World Savings Bank, JPMorgan Chase, and BP with executives being indicted and/or convicted of criminal behavior.

Incompatible Subcultures It is not unusual for companies to have multiple subcultures with values, beliefs, and ingrained behaviors and attitudes varying to some extent by department, geographic location, division, or business unit. These subcultures within a company don't pose a problem as long as the subcultures don't conflict with the overarching corporate work climate and are supportive of the strategy execution effort. Multiple subcultures become unhealthy when they are incompatible with each other or the overall corporate culture. The existence of conflicting business philosophies and values eventually leads to inconsistent strategy execution. Incompatible subcultures arise most commonly because of important cultural differences between a company's culture and those of a recently acquired company or because of a merger between companies with cultural differences. Cultural due diligence is often as important as financial due diligence in deciding whether to go forward on an acquisition or merger. On a number of occasions, companies have decided to pass on acquiring particular companies because of culture conflicts they believed would be hard to resolve.

Changing a Problem Culture

Changing a company culture that impedes proficient strategy execution is among the toughest management tasks. It is natural for company personnel to cling to familiar practices and to be wary, if not hostile, to new approaches toward how things are to be done. Consequently, it takes concerted management action over a period of time to root out certain unwanted behaviors and replace an out-of-sync culture with more effective ways of doing things. *The single most visible factor that distinguishes successful culture-change efforts from failed attempts is competent leadership at the top.* Great power is needed to force major cultural change and overcome the unremitting resistance of entrenched cultures—and great power is possessed only by the most senior executives, especially the CEO. However, while top management must lead the culture-change effort, instilling new cultural behaviors is a job for the whole management team. Middle managers and frontline supervisors play a key role in implementing the new work practices and operating approaches, helping win rank-and-file acceptance of and support for the changes, and instilling the desired behavioral norms.

As shown in Figure 10.2, the first step in fixing a problem culture is for top management to identify those facets of the present culture that pose obstacles to executing new

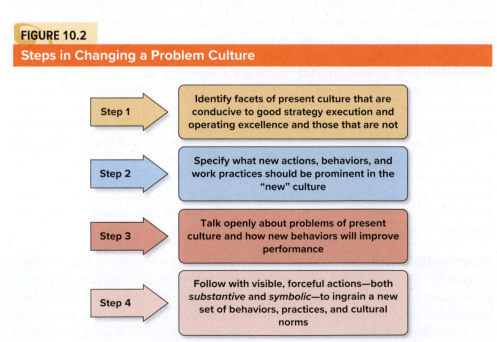

FIGURE 10.2

Steps in Changing a Problem Culture

Step 1 → Identify facets of present culture that are conducive to good strategy execution and operating excellence and those that are not

Step 2 → Specify what new actions, behaviors, and work practices should be prominent in the "new" culture

Step 3 → Talk openly about problems of present culture and how new behaviors will improve performance

Step 4 → Follow with visible, forceful actions—both *substantive* and *symbolic*—to ingrain a new set of behaviors, practices, and cultural norms

strategic initiatives. Second, managers have to clearly define the desired new behaviors and features of the culture they want to create. Third, managers have to convince company personnel why the present culture poses problems and why and how new behaviors and operating approaches will improve company performance. Finally, all the talk about remodeling the present culture has to be followed swiftly by visible, forceful actions on the part of management to promote the desired new behaviors and work practices.

Making a Compelling Case for a Culture Change   The place for management to begin a major remodeling of the corporate culture is by selling company personnel on the need for new-style behaviors and work practices. This means making a compelling case for why the company's new strategic direction and culture-remodeling efforts are in the organization's best interests and why company personnel should wholeheartedly join the effort to do things somewhat differently. This can be done by:

- Citing reasons the current strategy has to be modified and why new strategic initiatives are being undertaken. The case for altering the old strategy usually needs to be predicated on its shortcomings—why sales are growing slowly, why too many customers are opting to go with the products of rivals, why costs are too high, and so on. There may be merit in holding events where managers and other key personnel are forced to listen to dissatisfied customers or the complaints of strategic allies.

- Citing why and how certain behavioral norms and work practices in the current culture pose obstacles to good execution of new strategic initiatives.

- Explaining why new behaviors and work practices have important roles in the new culture and will produce better results.

Management's efforts to make a persuasive case for changing what is deemed to be a problem culture must be *quickly followed* by forceful, high-profile actions across several fronts. The actions to implant the new culture must be both substantive and symbolic.

Substantive Culture-Changing Actions   No culture-change effort can get very far when leaders merely talk about the need for different actions, behaviors, and work practices. Company executives have to give the culture-change effort some teeth by initiating *a series of actions* that company personnel will see as *unmistakable support* for the change program. The strongest signs that management is truly committed to instilling a new culture include:

1. Replacing key executives who stonewall needed organizational and cultural changes.

2. Promoting individuals who have stepped forward to advocate the shift to a different culture and who can serve as role models for the desired cultural behavior.

3. Appointing outsiders with the desired cultural attributes to high-profile positions—bringing in new-breed managers sends an unambiguous message that a new era is dawning.

4. Screening all candidates for new positions carefully, hiring only those who appear to fit in with the new culture.

5. Mandating that all company personnel attend culture-training programs to better understand the culture-related actions and behaviors that are expected.

6. Designing compensation incentives that boost the pay of teams and individuals who display the desired cultural behaviors, while hitting change-resisters in the pocketbook.

7. Revising policies and procedures in ways that will help drive cultural change.

Symbolic Culture-Changing Actions There is also an important place for symbolic managerial actions to alter a problem culture and tighten the strategy–culture fit. The most important symbolic actions are those that top executives take to *lead by example.* For instance, if the organization's strategy involves a drive to become the industry's low-cost producer, senior managers must display frugality in their own actions and decisions: inexpensive decorations in the executive suite, conservative expense accounts and entertainment allowances, a lean staff in the corporate office, few executive perks, and so on. At Walmart, all the executive offices are simply decorated; executives are habitually frugal in their own actions, and they are zealous in their own efforts to control costs and promote greater efficiency. At Nucor, one of the world's low-cost producers of steel products, executives fly coach class and use taxis at airports rather than limousines. Top executives must be alert to the fact that company personnel will be watching their actions and decisions to see if they are walking the talk.[27]

Another category of symbolic actions includes holding ceremonial events to single out and honor people whose actions and performance exemplify what is called for in the new culture. A point is made of holding events to celebrate each culture-change success. Executives sensitive to their role in promoting the strategy–culture fit make a habit of appearing at ceremonial functions to praise individuals and groups that get with the program. They show up at employee training programs to stress strategic priorities, values, ethical principles, and cultural norms. Every group gathering is seen as an opportunity to repeat and ingrain values, praise good deeds, and cite instances of how the new work practices and operating approaches have led to improved results. Concepts & Connections 10.4 discusses the approaches used at Goldman Sachs to change a culture that was impeding its efforts to recruit the best young talent.

Leading the Strategy Execution Process

LO10-8   Recognize what constitutes effective managerial leadership in achieving superior strategy execution.

For an enterprise to execute its strategy in truly proficient fashion and approach operating excellence, top executives have to take the lead in the implementation/execution process and personally drive the pace of progress. They have to be out in the field, seeing for themselves how well operations are going, gathering information firsthand, and gauging the progress being made. Proficient strategy execution requires company managers to be diligent and adept in spotting problems, learning what obstacles lie in the path of

CONCEPTS & CONNECTIONS 10.4

DRIVING CULTURAL CHANGE AT GOLDMAN SACHS

Goldman Sachs was long considered one of the best financial services companies to work for, due to its prestige, high salaries, bonuses, and perks. Yet by 2014, Goldman was beginning to have trouble recruiting the best and brightest MBAs at top business schools. Part of this was due to the banking crisis of 2008–2009 and the scandals that continued to plague the industry year after year, tarnishing the industry's reputation. But another reason was a change in the values and aspirations of the younger generation that made banking culture far less appealing than that of consulting, technology, and start-up companies. Newly minted MBAs were no longer as willing to accept the grueling hours and unpredictable schedules that were the norm in investment banking. They wanted to derive meaning and purpose from their work and prized work/life balance over monetary gain. The tech industry was known for fun, youth-oriented, and collaborative working environments, while the excitement and promise of entrepreneurial ventures offered much appeal. Goldman found itself competing with Amazon,

Omar Marques/SOPA Images/LightRocket/Getty Images

Google, Microsoft, and Facebook as well as with startups for the best young talent—and losing out.

Goldman's problem was compounded by the fact that its culture was regarded as stuffy and stodgy—qualities not likely to appeal to the young, particularly when contrasted with the hip cultures of tech and startup companies. Further, it had always been slow moving in terms of implementing organizational change. Recognizing the problem, the leadership at Goldman attempted to pivot sharply, asking its executives to think of Goldman as a tech company, complete with the associated values. The Chief Learning Office at Goldman Sachs was put in charge of the effort to transform its culture and began taking deliberate steps to enact changes. Buy-in was sought from the full C-suite—the leadership team at the very top of the firm. To foster a more familial atmosphere at work, the company began with small steps, such as setting up sports leagues and encouraging regular team happy hours. More significantly, they instituted more employee-friendly work schedules and policies, more accommodating of work/life balance. They liberalized their parental leave policies, provided greater flexibility in work schedules, and enacted protections for interns and junior bankers designed to limit their working hours. They also overhauled their performance review and promotion systems as well as their recruiting practices and policies regarding diversity. Although cultural change never comes swiftly, by 2017 results were apparent even to outside observers. That year, the career website Vault.com named Goldman Sachs as the best banking firm to work for, noting that when it came to workplace policies, Goldman led the industry.

Sources: http://www.goldmansachs.com/careers/blog/posts/goldman-sachs-vault-2017.html; and http://sps.columbia.edu/news/how-goldman-sachs-drives-culture-change-in-the-financial-industry.

good execution, and then clearing the way for progress: The goal must be to produce better results speedily and productively.[28] In general, leading the drive for good strategy execution and operating excellence calls for three actions on the part of the manager:

- Staying on top of what is happening and closely monitoring progress
- Putting constructive pressure on the organization to execute the strategy well and achieve operating excellence
- Initiating corrective actions to improve strategy execution and achieve the targeted performance results

Staying on Top of How Well Things Are Going

One of the best ways for executives to stay on top of strategy execution is by regularly visiting the field and talking with many different people at many different levels—a technique often labeled *managing by walking around* (MBWA). Walmart executives have had a long-standing practice of spending two to three days every week visiting stores and talking with store managers and employees. Jeff Bezos, Amazon.com's CEO, is noted for his frequent facilities visits and his insistence that other Amazon managers spend time in the trenches with their people to prevent overly abstract thinking and getting disconnected from the reality of what's happening.[29]

Most managers practice MBWA, attaching great importance to gathering information from people at different organizational levels about how well various aspects of the strategy execution are going. They believe facilities visits and face-to-face contacts give them a good feel for what progress is being made, what problems are being encountered, and whether additional resources or different approaches may be needed. Just as important, MBWA provides opportunities to give encouragement, lift spirits, shift attention from old to new priorities, and create excitement—all of which help mobilize organizational efforts behind strategy execution.

Putting Constructive Pressure on Organizational Units to Achieve Good Results and Operating Excellence

Managers have to be out front in mobilizing the effort for good strategy execution and operating excellence. Part of the leadership requirement here entails fostering a results-oriented work climate in which performance standards are high and a spirit of achievement is pervasive. Successfully leading the effort to foster a results-oriented, high-performance culture generally entails such leadership actions and managerial practices as:

- *Treating employees with dignity and respect.*
- *Encouraging employees to use initiative and creativity in performing their work.*
- *Setting stretch objectives and clearly communicating an expectation that company personnel are to give their best in achieving performance targets.*
- *Focusing attention on continuous improvement.*
- *Using the full range of motivational techniques and compensation incentives to reward high performance.*
- *Celebrating individual, group, and company successes.* Top management should miss no opportunity to express respect for individual employees and show appreciation of extraordinary individual and group effort.[30]

While leadership efforts to instill a spirit of high achievement into the culture usually accentuate the positive, there are negative reinforcers too. Low-performing workers and people who reject the results-oriented cultural emphasis have to be weeded out or at least moved to out-of-the-way positions. Average performers have to be candidly counseled that they have limited career potential unless they show more progress in the form of additional effort, better skills, and improved ability to deliver good results. In addition, managers whose units consistently perform poorly have to be replaced.

Initiating Corrective Actions to Improve Both the Company's Strategy and Its Execution

The leadership challenge of making corrective adjustments is twofold: deciding when adjustments are needed and deciding what adjustments to make. Both decisions are a normal and necessary part of managing the strategic management process, since no scheme for implementing and executing strategy can foresee all the events and problems that will arise.[31] There comes a time at every company when managers have to fine-tune or overhaul the company's strategy or its approaches to strategy execution and push for better results. Clearly, when a company's strategy or its execution efforts are not delivering good results, it is the leader's responsibility to step forward and push corrective actions.

KEY POINTS

Implementing and executing strategy is an operations-driven activity revolving around the management of people and business processes. The managerial emphasis is on converting strategic plans into actions and good results. *Management's handling of the process of implementing and executing the chosen strategy can be considered successful if and when the company achieves the targeted strategic and financial performance and shows good progress in making its strategic vision a reality.*

Like crafting strategy, executing strategy is a job for a company's whole management team, not just a few senior managers. Top-level managers have to rely on the active support and cooperation of middle and lower-level managers to push strategy changes into functional areas and operating units, and to see that the organization actually operates in accordance with the strategy on a daily basis.

Eight managerial tasks crop up repeatedly in company efforts to execute strategy:

1. *Building an organization capable of executing the strategy successfully.* Building an organization capable of good strategy execution entails three types of organization-building actions: *(a) staffing the organization*—assembling a talented, can-do management team, and recruiting and retaining employees with the needed experience, technical skills, and intellectual capital; *(b) acquiring, developing, and strengthening key resources and capabilities* that will enable good strategy execution; and *(c) structuring the organization and work effort*—organizing value chain activities and business processes and deciding how much decision-making authority to push down to lower-level managers and frontline employees.

2. *Allocating ample resources to strategy-critical activities.* Managers implementing and executing a new or different strategy must identify the resource requirements of each new strategic initiative and then consider whether the current pattern of resource allocation and the budgets of the various subunits are suitable.

3. *Ensuring that policies and procedures facilitate rather than impede effective strategy execution.* Anytime a company alters its strategy, managers should review existing policies and operating procedures, proactively revise or discard those that are out of sync, and formulate new ones to facilitate execution of new strategic initiatives.

4. *Adopting business processes that drive continuous improvement in how strategy execution activities are performed.* Reengineering core business processes and continuous improvement

initiatives such as total quality management (TQM) or Six Sigma programs all aim at improved efficiency, lower costs, better product quality, and greater customer satisfaction.

5. *Installing information and operating systems that enable company personnel to perform essential activities.* Well-conceived, state-of-the-art support systems not only facilitate better strategy execution but also strengthen organizational capabilities enough to provide a competitive edge over rivals.

6. *Tying rewards directly to the achievement of performance objectives.* For an incentive compensation system to work well, *(a)* the monetary payoff should be a major piece of the compensation package, *(b)* the use of incentives should extend to all managers and workers, *(c)* the system should be administered with care and fairness, *(d)* the incentives should be linked to performance targets spelled out in the strategic plan, *(e)* each individual's performance targets should involve outcomes the person can personally affect, *(f)* rewards should promptly follow the determination of good performance, and *(g)* monetary rewards should be supplemented with liberal use of nonmonetary rewards.

7. *Fostering a corporate culture that promotes good strategy execution.* The psyche of corporate cultures varies widely. There are five types of unhealthy cultures: *(a)* those that are highly political and characterized by empire-building, *(b)* those that are change resistant, *(c)* those that are insular and inwardly focused, *(d)* those that are ethically unprincipled and are driven by greed, and *(e)* those that possess clashing subcultures that prevent a company from coordinating its strategy execution efforts. High-performance cultures and adaptive cultures both have positive features that are conducive to good strategy execution.

8. *Exerting the internal leadership needed to propel implementation forward.* Leading the drive for good strategy execution and operating excellence calls for three actions on the part of the manager: *(a)* staying on top of what is happening, closely monitoring progress, and learning what obstacles lie in the path of good execution; *(b)* putting constructive pressure on the organization to achieve good results and operating excellence; and *(c)* pushing corrective actions to improve strategy execution and achieve the targeted results.

ASSURANCE OF LEARNING EXERCISES

LO10-1   1.   The heart of Zara's strategy in the apparel industry is to outcompete rivals by putting fashionable clothes in stores quickly and maximizing the frequency of customer visits. Concepts & Connections 10.2 discusses the capabilities that the company has developed in the execution of its strategy. How do its capabilities lead to a quick production process and new apparel introductions? How do these capabilities encourage customers to visit its stores every few weeks? Does the execution of the company's site selection capability also contribute to its competitive advantage? Explain.

LO10-2   2.   Implementing and executing a new or different strategy call for new resource allocations. Using your university's library resources, search for recent articles that discuss how a company has revised its pattern of resource allocation and divisional budgets to support new strategic initiatives.

LO10-3   3.   Netflix avoids the use of formal policies and procedures to better empower its employees to maximize innovation and productivity. The company goes to great lengths to hire, reward, and tolerate only what it considers mature, "A" player employees. How does the company's selection process affect its ability to operate without formal travel and expense policies, a fixed number of vacation days for employees, or a formal employee performance evaluation system?

LO10-4   4.   Explain how a blended approach to Six Sigma implementation produces advantages over more rigid statistical quality control programs.

5. Company strategies can't be implemented or executed well without a number of information systems to carry on business operations. Using your university's library resources, search for recent articles that discuss how a company has used real-time information systems and control systems to aid the cause of good strategy execution.

   LO10-5

6. Concepts & Connections 10.3 provides a description of the motivational practices employed by Wegmans Food Markets, a supermarket chain that is routinely listed among the top five companies to work for in the United States. Discuss how rewards and practices at Wegmans aid in the company's strategy execution efforts.

   LO10-6

7. Salesforce earned the top spot on *Fortune*'s list of the Best Companies to Work for in 2018, having been on the list for over 10 years. Use your university's library resources to see what are the key features of its culture. Do features of Salesforce's culture influence the company's ethical practices? If so, how?

   LO10-7

8. Leading the strategy execution process involves staying on top of the situation and monitoring progress, putting constructive pressure on the organization to achieve operating excellence, and initiating corrective actions to improve the execution effort. Using your university's library resources, discuss a recent example of how a company's managers have demonstrated the kind of effective internal leadership needed for superior strategy execution.

   LO10-8

EXERCISES FOR SIMULATION PARTICIPANTS

1. How would you describe the organization of your company's top management team? Is some decision making decentralized and delegated to individual managers? If so, explain how the decentralization works. Or are decisions made more by consensus, with all co-managers having input? What do you see as the advantages and disadvantages of the decision-making approach your company is employing?

   LO10-1

2. What are the ways that resource allocation contributes to good strategy execution and improved company performance?

   LO10-2

3. What are ways that incentive compensation can affect productivity gains and lower labor cost per unit?

   LO10-6

4. If you were making a speech to company personnel, what would you tell them about the kind of corporate culture you would like to have at your company? What specific cultural traits would you like your company to exhibit? Explain.

   LO10-7

5. Following each decision round, do you and your co-managers make corrective adjustments in either your company's strategy or how well the strategy is being executed? List at least three such adjustments you made in the most recent decision round. What hard evidence (in the form of results relating to your company's performance in the most recent year) can you cite that indicates the various corrective adjustments you made either succeeded or failed to improve your company's performance?

   LO10-8

ENDNOTES

1. Christopher A. Bartlett and Sumantra Ghoshal, "Building Competitive Advantage Through People," *MIT Sloan Management Review* 43, no. 2 (Winter 2002).

2. Justin Menkes, "Hiring for Smarts," *Harvard Business Review* 83, no. 11 (November 2005); Justin Menkes, *Executive Intelligence* (New York: HarperCollins, 2005).

3. Larry Bossidy and Ram Charan, *Execution: The Discipline of Getting Things Done* (New York: Crown Business, 2002).

4. Jim Collins, *Good to Great* (New York: HarperBusiness, 2001).

5. C. Helfat et al., *Dynamic Capabilities: Understanding Strategic Change in Organizations* (Malden, MA: Blackwell, 2007); R. Grant, *Contemporary Strategy*

Analysis, 6th ed. (Malden, MA: Blackwell, 2008).

6. G. Dosi, R. Nelson, and S. Winter, eds., *The Nature and Dynamics of Organizational Capabilities* (Oxford, England: Oxford University Press, 2001).

7. B. Kogut and U. Zander, "Knowledge of the Firm, Combinative Capabilities, and the Replication of Technology," *Organization Science* 3, no. 3 (August 1992), pp. 383–397.

8. S. Karim and W. Mitchell, "Path-Dependent and Path-Breaking Change: Reconfiguring Business Resources Following Business," *Strategic Management Journal* 21, nos. 10–11 (October–November 2000), pp. 1061–1082; L. Capron, P. Dussauge, and W. Mitchell, "Resource Redeployment Following Horizontal Acquisitions in Europe and North America, 1988–1992," *Strategic Management Journal* 19, no. 7 (July 1998), pp. 631–662.

9. Alfred Chandler, *Strategy and Structure* (Cambridge, MA: MIT Press, 1962).

10. Stanley E. Fawcett, Gary K. Rhoads, and Phillip Burnah, "People as the Bridge to Competitiveness: Benchmarking the 'ABCs' of an Empowered Workforce," *Benchmarking: An International Journal* 11, no. 4 (2004).

11. Rosabeth Moss Kanter, "Collaborative Advantage: The Art of the Alliance," *Harvard Business Review* 72, no. 4 (July–August 1994), pp. 96–108.

12. Michael Hammer and James Champy, *Reengineering the Corporation* (New York: HarperBusiness, 1993).

13. Charles A. O'Reilly and Michael L. Tushman, "The Ambidextrous Organization," *Harvard Business Review* 82, no. 4 (April 2004), pp. 74–81.

14. M. Walton, *The Deming Management Method* (New York: Pedigree, 1986); J. Juran, *Juran on Quality by Design* (New York: Free Press, 1992); Philip Crosby, *Quality Is Free: The Act of Making Quality Certain* (New York: McGraw-Hill, 1979); S. George, *The Baldrige Quality System* (New York: John Wiley & Sons, 1992); Mark J. Zbaracki, "The Rhetoric and Reality of Total Quality Management," *Administrative Science Quarterly* 43, no. 3 (September 1998).

15. Robert T. Amsden, Thomas W. Ferratt, and Davida M. Amsden, "TQM: Core Paradigm Changes," *Business Horizons* 39, no. 6 (November–December 1996).

16. Peter S. Pande and Larry Holpp, *What Is Six Sigma?* (New York: McGraw-Hill, 2002); Jiju Antony, "Some Pros and Cons of Six Sigma: An Academic Perspective," *The TQM Magazine* 16, no. 4 (2004); Peter S. Pande, Robert P. Neuman, and Roland R. Cavanagh, *The Six Sigma Way: How GE, Motorola and Other Top Companies Are Honing Their Performance* (New York: McGraw-Hill, 2000); Joseph Gordon and M. Joseph Gordon, Jr., *Six Sigma Quality for Business and Manufacture* (New York: Elsevier, 2002); Godecke Wessel and Peter Burcher, "Six Sigma for Small and Medium-Sized Enterprises," *The TQM Magazine* 16, no. 4 (2004).

17. Based on information posted at www.sixsigma.com, November 4, 2002.

18. Kennedy Smith, "Six Sigma for the Service Sector," *Quality Digest Magazine,* May 2003, www.qualitydigest.com (accessed September 28, 2003).

19. As quoted in "A Dark Art No More," *The Economist* 385, no. 8550 (October 13, 2007).

20. Charles A. O'Reilly and Michael L. Tushman, "The Ambidextrous Organization," *Harvard Business Review* 82, no. 4 (April 2004).

21. Steven Kerr, "On the Folly of Rewarding A while Hoping for B," *Academy of Management Executive* 9, no. 1 (February 1995); Steven Kerr, "Risky Business: The New Pay Game," *Fortune,* July 22, 1996; Doran Twer, "Linking Pay to Business Objectives," *Journal of Business Strategy* 15, no. 4 (July–August 1994).

22. Jeffrey Pfeffer and John F. Veiga, "Putting People First for Organizational Success," *Academy of Management Executive* 13, no. 2 (May 1999); Linda K. Stroh and Paula M. Caliguiri, "Increasing Global Competitiveness Through Effective People Management," *Journal of World Business* 33, no. 1 (Spring 1998); articles in *Fortune* on the 100 best companies to work for (various issues).

23. Joanne Reid and Victoria Hubbell, "Creating a Performance Culture," *Ivey Business Journal* 69, no. 4 (March–April 2005).

24. Jay B. Barney and Delwyn N. Clark, *Resource-Based Theory: Creating and Sustaining Competitive Advantage* (New York: Oxford University Press, 2007).

25. John P. Kotter and James L. Heskett, *Corporate Culture and Performance* (New York: Free Press, 1992).

26. Kurt Eichenwald, *Conspiracy of Fools: A True Story* (New York: Broadway Books, 2005).

27. Judy D. Olian and Sara L. Rynes, "Making Total Quality Work: Aligning Organizational Processes, Performance Measures, and Stakeholders," *Human Resource Management* 30, no. 3 (Fall 1991).

28. Larry Bossidy and Ram Charan, *Confronting Reality: Doing What Matters to Get Things Right* (New York: Crown Business, 2004); Larry Bossidy and Ram Charan, *Execution: The Discipline of Getting Things Done* (New York: Crown Business, 2002); John P. Kotter, "Leading Change: Why Transformation Efforts Fail," *Harvard Business Review* 73, no. 2 (March–April 1995); Thomas M. Hout and John C. Carter, "Getting It Done: New Roles for Senior Executives," *Harvard Business Review* 73, no. 6 (November–December 1995); Sumantra Ghoshal and Christopher A. Bartlett, "Changing the Role of Top Management: Beyond Structure to Processes," *Harvard Business Review* 73, no. 1 (January–February 1995).

29. Fred Vogelstein, "Winning the Amazon Way," *Fortune,* May 26, 2003.

30. Jeffrey Pfeffer, "Producing Sustainable Competitive Advantage Through the Effective Management of People," *Academy of Management Executive* 9, no. 1 (February 1995).

31. Cynthia A. Montgomery, "Putting Leadership Back into Strategy," *Harvard Business Review* 86, no. 1 (January 2008).

APPENDIX

Ratio	How Calculated	What It Shows
Profitability Ratios		
1. Gross profit margin	$\dfrac{\text{Sales revenues} - \text{Cost of goods sold}}{\text{Sales revenues}}$	Shows the percentage of revenues available to cover operating expenses and yield a profit. Higher is better, and the trend should be upward.
2. Operating profit margin (or return on sales)	$\dfrac{\text{Sales revenues} - \text{Operating expenses}}{\text{Sales revenues}}$ or $\dfrac{\text{Operating income}}{\text{Sales revenues}}$	Shows the profitability of current operations without regard to interest charges and income taxes. Higher is better, and the trend should be upward.
3. Net profit margin (or net return on sales)	$\dfrac{\text{Profits after taxes}}{\text{Sales revenues}}$	Shows after-tax profits per dollar of sales. Higher is better, and the trend should be upward.
4. Total return on assets	$\dfrac{\text{Profits after taxes} + \text{Interest}}{\text{Total assets}}$	A measure of the return on total monetary investment in the enterprise. Interest is added to after-tax profits to form the numerator since total assets are financed by creditors as well as by stockholders. Higher is better, and the trend should be upward.
5. Net return on total assets (ROA)	$\dfrac{\text{Profits after taxes}}{\text{Total assets}}$	A measure of the return earned by stockholders on the firm's total assets. Higher is better, and the trend should be upward.
6. Return on stockholders' equity	$\dfrac{\text{Profits after taxes}}{\text{Total stockholders' equity}}$	Shows the return stockholders are earning on their capital investment in the enterprise. A return in the 12–15% range is "average," and the trend should be upward.
7. Return on invested capital (ROIC); sometimes referred to as return on capital (ROCE)	$\dfrac{\text{Profits after taxes}}{\text{Long term debt} + \text{Total stockholders' equity}}$	A measure of the return shareholders are earning on the long-term monetary capital invested in the enterprise. Higher is better, and the trend should be upward.
8. Earnings per share (EPS)	$\dfrac{\text{Profits after taxes}}{\text{Number of shares of common stock outstanding}}$	Shows the earnings for each share of common stock outstanding. The trend should be upward, and the bigger the annual percentage gains, the better.
Liquidity Ratios		
1. Current ratio	$\dfrac{\text{Current assets}}{\text{Current liabilities}}$	Shows a firm's ability to pay current liabilities using assets that can be converted to cash in the near term. Ratio should definitely be higher than 1.0; ratios of 2 or higher are better still.
2. Working capital	$\text{Current assets} - \text{Current liabilities}$	Bigger amounts are better because the company has more internal funds available to (1) pay its current liabilities on a timely basis and (2) finance inventory expansion, additional accounts receivable, and a larger base of operations without resorting to borrowing or raising more equity capital.
Leverage Ratios		
1. Total debt-to-assets ratio	$\dfrac{\text{Total debt}}{\text{Total assets}}$	Measures the extent to which borrowed funds (both short-term loans and long-term debt) have been used to finance the firm's operations. A low fraction or ratio is better—a high fraction indicates overuse of debt and greater risk of bankruptcy.

Ratio	How Calculated	What It Shows
2. Long-term debt-to-capital ratio	$$\frac{\text{Long-term debt}}{\text{Long-term debt} + \text{Total stockholders' equity}}$$	An important measure of creditworthiness and balance sheet strength. It indicates the percentage of capital investment in the enterprise that has been financed by both long-term lenders and stockholders. A ratio below 0.25 is usually preferable since monies invested by stockholders account for 75% or more of the company's total capital. The lower the ratio, the greater the capacity to borrow additional funds. Debt-to-capital ratios above 0.50 and certainly above 0.75 indicate a heavy and perhaps excessive reliance on long-term borrowing, lower creditworthiness, and weak balance sheet strength.
3. Debt-to-equity ratio	$$\frac{\text{Total debt}}{\text{Total stockholders' equity}}$$	Shows the balance between debt (funds borrowed both short-term and long-term) and the amount that stockholders have invested in the enterprise. The farther the ratio is below 1.0, the greater the firm's ability to borrow additional funds. Ratios above 1.0 and definitely above 2.0 put creditors at greater risk, signal weaker balance sheet strength, and often result in lower credit ratings.
4. Long-term debt-to-equity ratio	$$\frac{\text{Long-term debt}}{\text{Total stockholders' equity}}$$	Shows the balance between long-term debt and stockholders' equity in the firm's *long-term* capital structure. Low ratios indicate greater capacity to borrow additional funds if needed.
5. Times-interest-earned (or coverage) ratio	$$\frac{\text{Operating income}}{\text{Interest expenses}}$$	Measures the ability to pay annual interest charges. Lenders usually insist on a minimum ratio of 2.0, but ratios progressively above 3.0 signal progressively better creditworthiness.

Activity Ratios

Ratio	How Calculated	What It Shows
1. Days of inventory	$$\frac{\text{Inventory}}{\text{Cost of goods sold} \div 365}$$	Measures inventory management efficiency. Fewer days of inventory are usually better.
2. Inventory turnover	$$\frac{\text{Cost of goods sold}}{\text{Inventory}}$$	Measures the number of inventory turns per year. Higher is better.
3. Average collection period	$$\frac{\text{Accounts receivable}}{\text{Total sales} \div 365}$$ or $$\frac{\text{Accounts receivable}}{\text{Average daily sales}}$$	Indicates the average length of time the firm must wait after making a sale to receive cash payment. A shorter collection time is better.

Other Important Measures of Financial Performance

Ratio	How Calculated	What It Shows
1. Dividend yield on common stock	$$\frac{\text{Annual dividends per share}}{\text{Current market price per share}}$$	A measure of the return that shareholders receive in the form of dividends. A "typical" dividend yield is 2–3%. The dividend yield for fast-growth companies is often below 1% (maybe even 0); the dividend yield for slow-growth companies can run 4–5%.
2. Price-earnings ratio	$$\frac{\text{Current market price per share}}{\text{Earnings per share}}$$	P-E ratios above 20 indicate strong investor confidence in a firm's outlook and earnings growth; firms whose future earnings are at risk or likely to grow slowly typically have ratios below 12.
3. Dividend payout ratio	$$\frac{\text{Annual dividends per share}}{\text{Earnings per share}}$$	Indicates the percentage of after-tax profits paid out as dividends.
4. Internal cash flow	After tax profits + Depreciation	A quick and rough estimate of the cash a company's business is generating after payment of operating expenses, interest, and taxes. Such amounts can be used for dividend payments or funding capital expenditures.
5. Free cash flow	After tax profits + Depreciation − Capital expenditures − Dividends	A quick and rough estimate of the cash a company's business is generating after payment of operating expenses, interest, taxes, dividends, and desirable reinvestments in the business. The larger a company's free cash flow, the greater is its ability to internally fund new strategic initiatives, repay debt, make new acquisitions, repurchase shares of stock, or increase dividend payments.

FIXER UPPER: EXPANDING THE MAGNOLIA BRAND

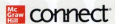

ROCHELLE R. BRUNSON *Baylor University*
MARLENE M. REED *Baylor University*

In the spring of 2018, Home and Garden Television (HGTV) aired the *Fixer Upper* season finale, closing five years on the network during which the series had become increasingly more popular. Not only had the program drawn attention to the other properties of Chip and Joanna Gaines, the stars of the show, but a spotlight had also been focused on the site of the show—Waco, Texas. With the end of *Fixer Upper,* people wondered what would happen to the various Magnolia businesses, as well as the host city whose prominence had grown along with the popularity of not only the *Fixer Upper* show, but also the Gaines family.

Background on Chip and Joanna Gaines

Both Chip and Joanna Gaines graduated from Baylor University, but they graduated three years apart and did not meet until after they left Baylor. Chip received a degree in marketing and started a few small businesses. He had hoped to play professional baseball until he was cut from the Baylor baseball team after his sophomore year. Joanna majored in communications and planned on becoming a broadcast journalist. Joanna's father owned an automobile shop—Jerry Stevens' Firestone—in Waco, Texas, and it was there that the couple met. Chip had come into the shop and noticed a picture of Joanna and immediately decided that was the girl he wanted to marry. Later when he brought his car in to have the brakes fixed, he met Joanna, and later asked her out on a date. That was in 2001, and in 2003 after many dates, the couple got married. Over the next several years, the couple began to establish a real estate business for themselves, invested in other ventures, and became the parents of five children. A timeline of the Gaineses' real estate investments is presented in Exhibit 1. The net worth each of Chip and Joanna Gaines was estimated at $9 million in 2018.

House Flipping

When Joanna married Chip, she decided to join him in his latest entrepreneurial venture of "flipping houses." This was the practice of buying a home as inexpensively as possible, renovating it, and then

EXHIBIT 1	
Timeline of the Gaineses' Properties	
Date	**Initiation of Property**
2003	House flipping Magnolia Market
2013	Pilot of *Fixer Upper*
2015	Silos opened (Magnolia Market at the Silos) Magnolia House
2016	The *Magnolia Journal*
2017	Hearth & Home for Target Hillcrest House
2018	*Fixer Upper* ends *Fixer Upper: Behind the Design* Magnolia Warehouse Shop (opens periodically for warehouse sales) Magnolia Table

attempting to sell the house at the highest possible margin. Then the entrepreneur normally takes the profits from the first home and invests in another home to start the process all over again. With the first home they flipped, the couple found they had much to learn about the practice. Joanna said of the experience,

> We painted over the wallpaper, left the popcorn ceilings intact, and spent most of our bathroom renovation budget on double shower heads.[1]

Magnolia Market

Soon after flipping their first house, the Gaineses borrowed $5,000 and opened their first retail store named Magnolia Market in 2003.[2] They privately called the operation the "Little Shop on Bosque." It was in this store, Joanna says, that she developed her design style and skills, grew as a business owner, and gained confidence in the store and herself. However, after their first two children were born, Chip and Joanna decided to close the store and concentrate on their Magnolia Homes real estate company. The store was reopened later for a couple of years and began to be used in March 2018 as a type of "outlet" for the Magnolia Market at the Silos. The shop featured last chance items and slightly damaged products at a discount. It was renamed the Magnolia Warehouse Shop and opened periodically for warehouse sales.[3]

Pilot of *Fixer Upper*

The show's pilot aired on April 23, 2013, on HGTV. The full season began on April 2, 2014. After five years of filming, the final season premiered on November 21, 2017. The thesis of the show was to showcase the work that Chip and Joanna Gaines had been doing in Waco, Texas, helping their clients to purchase and remodel homes. Normally, the buyers had an overall budget of under $200,000 with at least $30,000 to be invested in renovations. Viewers were often surprised to find that some of the homes selected for renovation sold for as little as $35,000. The Gaineses were paid a fee by the television production company plus an undisclosed fee by the people for whom the renovations had been performed. Exhibit 2 presents a summary of estimated revenues from *Fixer Upper*. The program was popular immediately, and the Season 4 finale attracted more than

---

EXHIBIT 2

Estimated Revenues from *Fixer Upper*

$30,000 per episode × 14 episodes = $420,000 each season
First 4 seasons = $1,680,000
Plus the last season =   540,000
Total for 5 seasons = $2,220,000

Note: Not included in these revenues are undisclosed fees from families helped with renovations. The Magnolia Brand was estimated to be worth more than $5 million in 2018.

Sources: "Here's How Much Chip and Joanna Gaines Are Really Making for the Last Season of *Fixer Upper*," https://www.cheatsheet.com/money-career/heres-much-chip-joanna-gaines-really-making-last-season-fixer-upper.html/?a=viewall; and Celebrity Net Worth, https://www.celebritynetworth.com/chip-and-joanna-gaines/.

5 million viewers. This made it the second most watched cable broadcast in the second quarter of 2017, behind only *The Walking Dead*.

Silos Opened

After the television program *Fixer Upper* began to take off, the Gaineses spent most of 2015 renovating and preparing to open their new Magnolia Market in two rusting silos near downtown Waco (see Exhibits 3 and 4). In order to avoid painting the massive silos, the couple had to get permission from the City of Waco to let them remain as they were—adding to the historic nature of the site. In addition to the silos, there was a 20,000-square-foot barn that now houses a marketplace full of decorating accessories.

EXHIBIT 3

The Silos

Magnolia Market, LLC

EXHIBIT 4
Outside of Magnolia Market

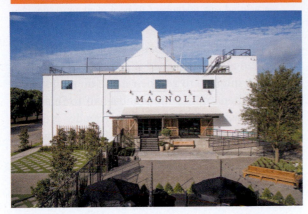

Magnolia Market, LLC

The market covers 2.5 acres and provides a large outside play area for children and a space for food trucks to park and deliver food to the store's patrons. At the far end of the property, Joanna established the Magnolia Seed & Supply store complete with flower beds filled with seasonal herbs and flowers.

In 2016, not long after the silos became operational, Chip and Joanna secured a small building on the corner of their property that had previously housed a floral shop and converted it into the Silos Baking Co. The shop serves a variety of cupcakes and breads whose names are associated with *Fixer Upper* such as "The Silo's Cookie" and the "Shiplap" cupcake as well as the classic cinnamon roll and the "Prize Pig" biscuit.

Magnolia Journal

Building on the success of the Magnolia brand, Chip and Joanna launched the *Magnolia Journal* as a quarterly lifestyle publication in 2016. Joanna said of the magazine:

> My goal in creating this magazine was to connect with readers from all walks of life, to share content so valuable and so meaningful that you hold on to each issue and return to them again and again.[4]

The journal contains Joanna's personal reflections and design tips with a focus on entertaining and seasonal celebrations. Exhibit 5 presents a review of the brand footprint, which describes the typical *Magnolia Journal* reader.

EXHIBIT 5
Magnolia Journal Typical Reader

Media income	$92,540
Home ownership	81%
Married	83%
Millennials	36%
Parents	44%
Median age	50

Hines, Emilie, "The *Magnolia Journal*: An Extension of the Chip and Jo Empire," *Magnolia*, 2019, https://dhlclass.wordpress.com/magnolia/.

Hearth & Hand with Magnolia

On November 5, 2017, Target released an exclusive home brand line of home goods in collaboration with Magnolia. The Hearth & Hand collection includes 300 items that range from home décor to gifts. Most of the items are priced under $30. Gaines said of the collaboration:

> Just as we've never created an exclusive line of product for a retailer before, Target has never done anything like this before either. Let me try to give you a visual; it's like a little shop inside of Target. Jo keeps calling the look "modern farmhouse," whatever that means. All I know is she's so excited about this collection that she wants to register for our wedding all over again.[5]

Fixer Upper Concludes

In fall 2017, Chip and Joanna announced to the public that their *Fixer Upper* television program would be coming to an end in the spring of 2018 (end of Season 5). The couple said they had mixed emotions about the closure, but that the taping schedule was beginning to wear upon them. Initially, they had anticipated that they would be filming about eight hours a day, but they soon found that was not to be. They discovered that to put together a season of programs, they had to film 11 months out of the year. They decided to spend more time with their family and have time to welcome a new baby to the family in the summer of 2018. However, a source told *Vanity Fair* magazine that Chip and Joanna clashed with HGTV executives over not being able to showcase their furniture line on the show.[6] The *New York Post* reported that Chip and Joanna were unhappy with their contract because it was so restrictive. The source reported in the *Post* suggested that their present contract would have prevented them from taking advantage of some lucrative deals.[7]

Fixer Upper: Behind the Design

The Gaineses' brand would not be separated from television for long. On April 10, 2018, Joanna launched a *Fixer Upper* spinoff series entitled "Behind the Design." In this series, Joanna plans to share details on her design strategies, decorating, and staging a home. The program will cover all the elements that go into home makeovers. The format of the program takes the viewer through the designs in the original *Fixer Upper* series room-by-room offering design secrets, insights, recommendations, and tips.

Magnolia Table

In February 2016, a Waco landmark, the Elite Café, was closed due to lack of profitability. The café had been opened 97 years earlier at a busy traffic circle in Waco and had served as a meeting place for local customers as well as tourists traveling between Dallas and Austin. One of the favorite stories about the restaurant concerned a young soldier stationed at nearby Fort Hood name Elvis Presley who had eaten at the Elite. The café had also become a favorite gathering place for Baylor University football fans in the fall of the year.

After the closing of the Elite, the Gaineses acquired the 8,356-square-foot facility, renovated it, and opened it under the name "Magnolia Table" in early 2018. Some history buffs in the city complained that the name "Elite" should have been retained since the café's history had been so intertwined with that of the town. However, Chip and Joanna Gaines realized that the success of the renovated restaurant depended upon the Magnolia brand.

> The Elite Café is a big part of Waco's history, and we wanted to honor that legacy, so we really, really struggled with whether to keep the original name or not. We knew that changing it could be an unpopular decision here in town, and we nearly kept it for that reason alone. But as we considered all that we hoped for this place—what we wanted this new iteration of the old restaurant to be—we quickly realized that the new hope

and old name were diametrically opposed. After much deliberation, we decided to name the café Magnolia Table. We chose this new name because we wanted our restaurant to be a clear representation of a place where *all* were welcome.[8]

Shortly after the opening of Magnolia Table, customers had already resigned themselves to waiting in line for 30 minutes to get their name on the list for a table and then another hour-and-a-half to finally get seated. However, because of the friendly greetings and accommodations of the staff who invited waiting customers to have a seat in a pavilion outside where they could purchase hot or cold beverages as well as some pastries, customers appeared to take the wait in stride. Some have even waited as long as two-and-a-half hours to be seated with no complaints. Magnolia Table is only open from 6 am until 3 pm Monday through Saturday. They do have a Take-Away area and gift store.

Magnolia Stay

During the taping of the *Fixer Upper* show, Chip and Joanna Gaines were able to secure a property in McGregor, Texas, 20 minutes outside of Waco known as the "Magnolia House." The renovation was featured on the show and it was available to reserve with a two-night minimum at $695/night (sleeps 8 people). They also purchased and renovated "Hillcrest Estate" in Waco, Texas, which was built in 1903. This home can be reserved as well with a two-night minimum at $995/night (sleeps 12 people). These two properties at Magnolia Stay are another part of the Magnolia/Gaines properties (businesses).[9]

The Effect on Waco

Rarely has a business had the kind of impact on a city that *Fixer Upper* and its brand extensions have had on Waco, Texas. The impact on the city of Waco was a realization of the company's mission to "Do good work that matters." Chip commented on the selection of the city for their television program:

> People typically reacted to the news of my being from Waco with sympathy or disdain. After the Branch Davidian incident, the name of our town even became part of popular culture. Considering Waco's reputation and small size, it was hard to convince HGTV to believe that

basing our show solely in Waco, Texas, would be a recipe for success. . . . The network tried to talk us into doing just the first few homes in Waco and then branching out into neighboring cities like Austin or Dallas. . . . After some discussion, the network understood that if they wanted us, a show based in Waco, Texas, had to be enough for them.[10]

The Waco Convention Center and Visitors' Bureau reported that the Magnolia Market at the Silos attracts a minimum of 30,000 visitors a week to the city. Parking had become a major challenge near the Silos, and some organizations are charging up to $10 a car for a favorable place to park. The Convention Center predicted that the Silos attraction could potentially draw 1.6 million visitors annually with roughly 50 percent of those visitors from outside of Texas. Local hotels and restaurants have been the recipients of increased traffic since the opening of the Silos; however, some locals have complained about the increased traffic, which makes it harder to maneuver downtown Waco. In March 2015,

properties in Waco on Realtor.com were reported to be viewed at four times the national average. There had been speculation about whether the Silos would be able to maintain its popularity after the demise of the popular television program *Fixer Upper.*

Future of the Magnolia Brand

By 2018, the Magnolia brand had been leveraged into such undertakings as a real estate company, television program, bed and breakfast, retail store, magazine, and restaurant. Magnolia now had 200 employees at Magnolia Table and approximately 800 employees companywide. The sky seemed to be the limit for the company and the city in which it was located. However, skeptics speculated about how sustainable the brand would be in the future with its primary driver—*Fixer Upper*—now canceled.

ENDNOTES

[1] Joanna Gaines, Instagram.

[2] Joanna Gaines, Instagram.

[3] *Magnolia,* https://twitter.com/magnolia/status/975453791188340736/.

[4] Joanna Gaines, Our Story, https://magnolia.com/about/.

[5] Chip Gaines, "An Exciting Announcement: Hearth & Hand with Magnolia," *Magnolia,* September 12, 2017. https://magnolia.com/hearth-hand-with-magnolia/.

[6] *New York Post,* https://pagesix. com/2017/10/09/the-real-reason-chip-andjoanna-gaines-quit-hgtv/.

[7] *New York Post,* https://pagesix.com/2017/10/09/ the-real-reason-chip-andjoanna-gaines-quit-hgtv/.

[8] Chip Gaines, *Capital Gaines: Smart Things I Learned Doing Stupid Stuff.* (Nashville,TN: Thomas Nelson, 2017).

[9] https://magnolia.com/stay.

[10] Chip Gaines, *Capital Gaines: Smart Things I Learned Doing Stupid Stuff.* (Nashville,TN: Thomas Nelson, 2017).

LOLA'S MARKET: CAPTURING A NEW GENERATION

KATHRINE GONZALEZ *MBA Student, Sonoma State University*
SERGIO CANAVATI *Sonoma State University*
ARMAND GILINSKY *Sonoma State University*

Our core is Latinos, try to trigger them, try to get every single Latino in our store . . . what's hard are the young ones; they are more focused with what is on their phone.

David Ortega, Owner, Lola's Market

"Before I used to tell them, 'Put those phones away,' now I just let it go, it happens so much . . . they do not listen."[1] As David Ortega, owner of Lola's Market, takes a break from replacing wallpaper and making repairs to his long-standing business in Santa Rosa, California, he surveys his store and watches as his millennial employees are fully invested in the tweets[2] and hashtags[3] that flood their notification screens. David contemplates on how he can engage these employees, and even further, how he can engage this generation. David is a man rooted in tradition and he believes that the traditions of good business and good customer service need to be passed down to the new generation, but how? Situated in Sonoma County, California, Lola's Market has five locations, each targeting the Latino consumer, each filled with generations of customers who have shopped at their various locations since their doors first opened in Santa Rosa. David is inspired to make changes for his business and knows that engaging the younger generation—the millennials[4]—will strengthen Lola's future business for years to come. David is at risk of losing this new coveted consumer base to retailers that "speak" to the millennials in their language—businesses that utilize social media and online shopping experiences to appease the tech savvy culture. Regardless of where he stands among

his competitors, David's outlook on the possibilities Lola's has is inspiring and will facilitate Lola's capacity to gain this new generation: "Never say you can't, you always have to be positive."[5] With this mindset, it is no surprise that David Ortega has been recognized by the *North Bay Business Journal* as one of the first honorees of the Latino Business Leadership Awards for outstanding leadership throughout the North Bay.[6] With this type of leadership, Lola's can potentially reposition itself as the sought-out center for the Latino millennial consumer and workforce.

Industry Overview

When looking at the Supermarket Industry as a whole—including markets who offer specialty services, such as Lola's bakery and restaurant—there are key success factors that will give a particular organization a competitive advantage. These key factors include proximity to key markets, access to a multiskilled and flexible workforce, the ability to control stock on hand, close monitoring of competition, and access to the latest available and most efficient technology and techniques.[7] Alongside these key success factors is evolution with the consumer: The new target consumer among industries is the millennial consumer—the millennial generation interests marketers due to its size and growing market influence.[8] This generation is one of the largest generations in history and is about to move into its prime spending years—millennials are positioned to reshape the economy.[9] Millennial consumers want to engage with brands on social media; about 62 percent of millennials say that if a brand engages with them on social networks, they are likely to become a loyal customer. With 87 percent of millennials using between two and three tech devices on a daily basis, brands must stay relevant by appealing to and engaging millennials on these tech platforms.[10]

In 2017, Amazon's acquisition of Whole Foods took the online retailer into the brick and mortar setting and Amazon is now driving down Whole Foods' prices across the board—this is causing supermarket competitors to raise the stakes.[11] Amazon is also implementing an additional shipping option utilizing its Prime delivery service for customers who choose to shop with Whole Foods.[12] Amazon is a company that has already created a strong relationship with the millennial generation, as a majority of Amazon Prime users are a part of this generation (see Exhibit 1). Since millennials already have ties with Amazon, which has the strong online presence and convenience that this customer base prefers, it will be even more difficult for smaller, family-owned businesses like Lola's to attain this consumer base.

When it comes to supermarkets in California, specifically the North Bay, there are various competitors who have their own takes on how to generate this technological change and brand advancement. Sonoma County is one of the most competitive food markets in the country, thanks to an array of strong local and national grocery businesses vying for customers' time and money.[13] In 2016, Oliver's Market, one of the largest competitors in the North Bay market, expanded its doors and rebranded itself with a more modern appeal even including the addition of instore Wi-Fi available to its customers.[14] To capture the millennial generation, specifically in the supermarket sector of the retail industry, companies need to take advantage of the latest technology and implement it within in-store and online (if applicable) IT systems, such as their points of sale processing. This will lead to increased productivity and higher profit margins.[15]

Lola's Story

> I'd go over to look at the bakery and think, one day I am going to open up something like this.
>
> "About: Lola's Market." Lola's Market., https://www.lolasmarkets.com/about.html.

As a 15-year-old young man working at Perez Family Restaurant in Santa Rosa, California, David Ortega had vast aspirations for his future and the future of his family. David recalls countlessly seeing the bakery next door from the restaurant in which he worked and dreaming that one day he would have a business of his own—a business that provided quality products, produced with the love and attention that the bakery he gazed upon provided. Along with having quality products, David wanted to offer the Latino consumer a taste of home by offering authentic Mexican bread and ready-to-eat food. In addition to authentic Mexican food, David paid tribute to his mother Dolores by naming his dream business after her. From a cost-effective play on her name (Lola for Dolores),[16] Lola's Market was born.

On February 8, 1992, with his mother Dolores and father at his side, David achieved his dream. With the smell of fresh *Pan Dulce*[17] in the air, the first Lola's opened on Dutton Avenue in Santa Rosa. It stood at about 1,000 square feet, filled with the promise of growing tradition and quality goods and services. Today, Lola's Market has expanded to five stores; each Lola's store still has its famous fresh bakery and restaurant, as well as a produce department and deli section. Lola's Market has two locations in Santa Rosa, one in Napa, one in Healdsburg, and its newest location in Petaluma, which opened in 2013. Lola's believes they can "compete with anybody"[18]

EXHIBIT 1

Amazon Prime User Demographics

Share of online consumers in the United States who are Amazon Prime members as of August 2016, by generation

	Share of Respondents
Millennial	71%
Generation X	54%
Boomers	34%
Retirees	31%
Total	47%

"Share of online consumers in the United States who are Amazon Prime members as of August 2016, by generation," Statista, https://www.statista.com/statistics/609991/amazon-prime-reach-usa-generation/.

and with the quality of goods and services they provide, they do have the potential to outgrow and stand ahead of their local competitors. David believes that Lola's is known for its service, quality meats and produce, and the comfort that the markets provide for its Spanish-speaking customers: "Hispanics like to communicate in their own language, that's probably why they shop here."[19]

Lola's Market is operated with David Ortega as President; General Manager, Mario Lozano; and Controller, Carlos Salvatierra, directly under him. The General Manager, Mario Lozano, oversees the chain's POS Supervisor, Safety Coordinator, and HR Coordinator, as well as all managers at the five store locations. Mario is the eyes and ears of Lola's on the employee level—he is key to helping David understand what the needs are from the employee–management perspective, as well as consumer needs. In doing so, Mario is able to provide the most insight as to what works within the store structure and what ultimately drives same-store sales. When David first opened Lola's his marketing tactics included creating promotional flyers that he would place on windshields in local church parking lots on Sunday mornings. This worked for him initially as it did bring in new Hispanic customers looking to enjoying traditional Mexican food after a Sunday service, or buy fresh produce and tortillas[20] to cook Sunday dinner for their family.

In 2016, 24 years after its first doors opened in Santa Rosa, Lola's was performing overall at a 30 percent gross margin, which was a 0.7 percent increase from the previous year. Even with the improvement in performance, Lola's was still experiencing a decrease in profitability of (0.8 percent). Lola's decrease in cost of goods sold from 71 percent in 2015 to 70 percent in 2016 demonstrated that Lola's had the potential to boost its profitability for the coming year if it continued to trend with a decrease in its cost of goods sold ratio—as a decrease in this ratio identifies improvements in Lola's cost controls. The implementation of new technology and possibly new marketing methods that had the potential to boost Lola's customer base might also decrease this ratio and result in an increase in gross profit (see Exhibit 2). Along with tactics toward technological improvement, David believes Lola's commitment to freshness and

EXHIBIT 2

Lola's Combined Statement of Income

Lola's Market, Inc. and Affiliates combined statement of income years ended December 31, 2016, and December 31, 2015

Profitability		
	2016	**2015**
Net Sales	100%	100%
COGS	69.97%	71%
Gross Margin	30.03%	29.31%
Direct Store Expenses	20.43%	18.75%
Administrative Expenses	4.43%	4.09%
Income from Operations	5.17%	6.47%
Total Other Income (Expenses)	−0.67%	−0.72%
Net Income Before Income Taxes	4.50%	5.75%
Liquidity		
Working Capital $000	$2,337	$2,389
Current Ratio	1.98	2.01
Quick Ratio	1.43	1.46
Year-on-Year Growth Rates, %		
Total Revenue	−0.76%	
Gross Margin	0.72%	
Operating Expenses	8.14%	

Source: Lola's Market, Inc. and Affiliates.

tradition will continue to boost sales and create high levels of customer satisfaction. "People know our commitment to freshness is the key. The secret is to stay true to your roots and serve everything fresh."[21]

Alternatives for Lola's

David Ortega is a man rooted in tradition and quality, but he is also a creative business man who has plans to remodel Lola's Dutton Ave location in Santa Rosa. This remodel is intended to fit consumer needs as it will offer a buffet style, self-serve setting similar to what is seen at large competitors such as Whole Foods. With this remodel, Lola's will have freshly prepared, authentic Mexican food with a breakfast, lunch, and dinner menu. Customers can serve themselves and will be charged based on the weight of their meal. David understands the need to capture the interest of the younger market base; on a global level the millennial consumer is seeking a fast meal that does not sacrifice health.[22] Implementing this self-serve option will offer the young Latino consumer the access to authentic meals that are healthy and require little-to-no excess effort on their part. The millennial consumer is already shopping within the specialty food store industry that Lola's is a part of, accounting for about 37.3 percent of this market (see Exhibit 3), so to differentiate itself from its competitors Lola's can align remodeling with a repositioning effort to be an engaging brand on social networks. Globally, millennials are considered to be the "first digital natives"[23] and as consumers they offer the potential of long-term customers.

A company's strategy rests on its unique activities,[24] and David Ortega's plans for remodeling are distinguished from his competitors by their offering—traditional, nostalgic, homemade food. What will further distinguish this strategy are the marketing activities taken to promote the new changes in the store. Also, David is hoping that the remodels at Lola's will set them apart from other Hispanic markets, so that everything is not so jam-packed.

David sees too many of his competitors put too much out on the floor and it is not shoppable. He understands one of the key metrics of the industry is dollars earned per square foot, and agrees it is better to have a smaller space bringing in more money (the Trader Joe's model) than to have a large store bringing in less money per square foot.

Millennials are interested in specialty food stores as they have an adequate source of living and are likely to use a significant share of their income for discretionary spending.[25] Millennials keep up with current health and diet trends; in order to retain this demographic, Lola's must show the consumer that despite the stigma that authentic Mexican food is inherently unhealthy, Lola's offers healthy options—even options for the vegetarian consumer. As leaders, David Ortega and his management team must ensure that all the changes and efforts toward rebranding are met with support and understanding by Lola's employees at all levels. When Lola's does launch their new remodeling at their Dutton Ave. location, employees must understand and adhere to the new store dynamic. All new roles and responsibilities that may be placed upon employees need to be addressed clearly and implemented with proper training.

To tighten its fit and truly target the millennial Latino consumer there are some additional resources Lola's may need. Though there are employees at Lola's who are part of the millennial generation, none of them currently possess experience in social media marketing. No one on Lola's team has a background in this type of promotional marketing tactic, as the most current marketing methods include monthly radio sound bites and weekly flyers distributed to neighborhoods near all five store locations. To be strategic in its industry Lola's must take advantage of the new industry change and utilize that to its benefit—social media allows for direct access to customers and direct access to customer feedback through applications such as Yelp. Instead of taking on the cost of hiring someone as a social media marketing specialist, Lola's can create a position for a college intern who would handle social media marketing in exchange for school credit. This type of relationship would give Lola's access to someone with insights to the platform and accountability for the work he or she is producing. As another

EXHIBIT 3

Specialty Food Stores: Consumer Base

Major market segmentation (2017)

- Millennials 37.3%
- Generation X 29.2%
- Baby boomers 21.1%
- Swing generation 12.4%

Total $9.5bn

Source: "Specialty Food Stores in New York: Industry Market Research Report," IBISWorld, February 2019, https://www.ibisworld.com/industry-trends/market-research-reports/new-york/retail-trade/specialty-food-stores-in-new-york.html.

alternative, David can implement HootSuite into his stores and train store managers on running this software. HootSuite is free, easy-to-use software that allows content management across all social media platforms and using this type of software will create a congruency and consistency among Lola's social media pages. Consistency among the platforms is key as all the content being pushed must be in alignment with Lola's mission statement and company culture. Overall, utilizing social media can potentially eliminate the number of flyers distributed weekly and some excessive marketing costs, while allowing Lola's to give its customers real-time updates on its new services, products, and promotions.

Future Directions

The focus on the millennial consumer is exciting as it will bring in a new market; but Lola's must not forget about its original consumer and employees who are part of the earlier generations. Companywide Lola's must ensure that the implementation of social media coincides with Lola's value on quality,

customer service, and authentic Mexican food. Only then will it distinguish itself from every other company marketing themselves on these platforms. By implementing social media into their brand dynamic, Lola's is taking a risk faced by many businesses in their situation—the potential loss of integrity a brand can face when implementing the new platforms. The Internet creates an unknown space where users have the option to freely voice their opinions, both good and bad, behind an anonymous mask. If Lola's is going to place itself in a position to be promoted for the better, it also needs to be prepared to expose itself to the potential of critique and various feedback from its customers. If Lola's actively chooses to listen to constructive criticism and reviews that its consumers offer, it can positively manipulate any negative side effects and utilize that data to its benefit—in fact, it will be receiving up-to-date consumer feedback at no financial cost. In every respect, Lola's must focus on keeping its integrity in light of new changes and challenges it may face with its coming business efforts.

ENDNOTES

[1] D. Ortega, personal communication, October 03, 2017.

[2] Tweets: On the social media platform Twitter, a "tweet" is when a user creates a new posting on their page.

[3] Hashtag: Utilized on all social media platforms including—but not limited to—Facebook, Instagram, and Twitter, a hashtag is a word or phrase that is preceded by a pound sign (#) and signifies that the content adheres to a specific topic or event.

[4] The Millennial generation is comprised of individuals born between the years of 1980 and 2000.

[5] D. Ortega, personal communication, November 21, 2017.

[6] "17 North Bay Latino Business Leaders," *North Bay Business Journal*, September 9, 2016, http://www.northbaybusinessjournal.com/events/6057702-181/north-bay-latino-business-leadership-awards-named?artslide=10.

[7] M. Guattery, *Industry Report 44511, Supermarkets and Grocery Stores in the U.S.*, IBISWorld, retrieved October 31, 2017, from IBISWorld database.

[8] M. Moore, "Interactive Media Usage Among Millennial Consumers," *Journal of Consumer Marketing*, 29, no. 6 (2012), pp. 436–444.

[9] D. Schawbel, "10 New Findings About the Millennial Consumer," *Forbes*, January 20, 2015, https://www.forbes.com/sites/danschawbel/2015/01/20/10-new-findings-about-the-millennial-consumer/#1db62f776c8f.

[10] D. Schawbel, "10 New Findings About the Millennial Consumer," *Forbes*, January 20, 2015, https://www.forbes.com/sites/danschawbel/2015/01/20/10-new-findings-about-the-millennialconsumer/# 1db62f776c8f.

[11] J. D. Rey, "Amazon and Walmart Are in an All-Out Price War That Is Terrifying America's Biggest Brands," *Recode*, March 30, 2017, https://www.recode.net/2017/3/30/14831602/amazon-walmart-cpg-grocery-price-war.

[12] J. D. Rey, "Amazon and Walmart Are in an All-Out Price War That Is Terrifying America's Biggest Brands," *Recode*, March 30, 2017, https://www.recode.net/2017/3/30/14831602/amazon-walmart-cpg-grocery-price-war.

[13] B. Swindell, "Oliver's Debuts Store of the Future in Windsor," *North Bay Business Journal*, May 17, 2016, http://www.northbaybusinessjournal.com/opinion/5627170-186/olivers-markets-new-windsor-store?gallery=5627183&artslide=0.

[14] B. Swindell, "Oliver's Debuts Store of the Future in Windsor," *North Bay Business Journal*, May 17, 2016, http://www.northbaybusinessjournal.com/opinion/5627170-186/olivers-markets-new-windsor-store?gallery=5627183&artslide=0.

[15] M. Guattery, *Industry Report 44511, Supermarkets and Grocery Stores in the U.S.*, IBISWorld, retrieved October 31, 2017 from IBISWorld database.

[16] Originally when David opened Lola's, the cost for the signage above the store was about $125/per letter. To save some money David shortened his mother's name from Dolores to her nickname "Lola."

[17] *Pan Dulce*—translated into "Sweet Bread." This term encompasses many rolls, cookies, and Mexican pastries.

[18] Lola's Market Home Site, *Lola's Market*, 2017, https://www.lolasmarkets.com/.

[19] J. Fletcher, "Mexican Food Flourishes in Sonoma County," *SFGATE,* April 24, 2002, http://www.sfgate.com/bayarea/article/Mexican-food-flourishes-in-Sonoma-County-2846114.php.

[20] Tortilla: (In Mexican cooking) a very thin, flat pancake of cornmeal or flour; sometimes with added spices or flavoring ingredients.

[21] D. Ortega, personal communication, October 3, 2017.

[22] Health & Wellness, *Food Marketing Institute,* 2017, https://www.fmi.org/GroceryRevolution/health-wellness/.

[23] Millennials Infographic, Goldman Sachs, n.d., http://www.goldmansachs.com/our-thinking/pages/millennials/.

[24] M. E. Porter, "What Is Strategy?" *Harvard Business Review,* 74, no.6 (1996), pp. 61–78.

[25] M. Guattery, *IBISWorld Industry Report 44529, Specialty Food Stores in the U.S.,* 2017, retrieved from the IBISWorld database.

UNDER ARMOUR'S STRATEGY IN 2019: ITS STRUGGLE TO REVIVE NORTH AMERICAN SALES AND PROFITABILITY

ARTHUR A. THOMPSON *The University of Alabama*

Founded in 1996 by former University of Maryland football player Kevin Plank, Under Armour was the originator of sports apparel made with performance-enhancing fabrics—gear engineered to wick moisture from the body, regulate body temperature, and enhance comfort regardless of weather conditions and activity levels. It started with a simple plan to make a T-shirt that provided compression and wicked perspiration off the wearer's skin, thereby avoiding the discomfort of sweat-absorbed apparel.

Plank formed KP Sports as a subchapter S corporation in Maryland in 1996 and commenced selling a performance fabric T-shirt to athletes and sports teams. He worked the phone and, with a trunk full of shirts in the back of his car, visited schools and training camps in person to show his products. Plank's sales successes were soon good enough that he convinced Kip Fulks, who played lacrosse at Maryland, to become a partner in his enterprise. Operations were conducted on a shoestring budget out of the basement of Plank's grandmother's house in Georgetown, a Washington, D.C., suburb. In 1998, the company's sales revenues and growth prospects were sufficient to secure a $250,000 small-business loan, enabling the company to move operations to a facility in Baltimore. Ryan Wood, one of Plank's acquaintances from high school, joined the company in 1999 and became a partner.

KP Sports' sales grew briskly as it expanded its product line to include high-tech undergarments tailored for athletes in different sports and for cold as well as hot temperatures, plus jerseys, team uniforms, socks, and other accessories. Increasingly, the company was able to secure deals not just to provide gear for a particular team but for most or all of a school's sports teams. However, the company's partners came to recognize the merits of tapping the retail market for high-performance apparel and began making sales calls on sports apparel retailers. In 2000, Scott Plank, Kevin's older brother, joined the company as Vice President of Finance and certain other operational and strategic responsibilities. When Galyan's, a large retail chain since acquired by Dick's Sporting Goods, signed on to carry KP Sports' expanding line of performance apparel for men, women, and youth in 2000, sales to other sports apparel retailers began to explode. By the end of 2000, the company's products were available in some 500 retail locations.

Prompted by growing operational complexity, increased financial requirements, and plans for further geographic expansion, KP Sports revoked its "S" corporation status and became a "C" corporation on

January 1, 2002. The company opened a Canadian sales office in 2003 and began selling its products in the United Kingdom in 2005. At year-end 2005, about 90 percent of the company's revenues came from sales to some 6,000 retail stores in the United States and 2,000 stores in Canada, Japan, and the United Kingdom. In addition, sales were being made to high-profile athletes and teams, most notably in the National Football League, Major League Baseball, the National Hockey League, and some 400 men's and women's sports teams at NCAA Division 1-A colleges and universities.

In late 2005, KP Sports changed its name to Under Armour and became a public company with an initial public offering of common stock that generated net proceeds of nearly $115 million. Under Armour immediately began pursuing a long-term strategy to grow its product line, establish a market presence in a growing number of countries across the world, and build public awareness of the Under Armour brand and its interlocking "U" and "A" logo.

Under Armour quickly earned a reputation as an up-and-coming company in the sports apparel business, achieving sales of $1 billion in 2010 and $3 billion in 2014. Starting in the second-quarter of 2010 and

continuing through the third-quarter of 2016, Under Armour cemented its status as a growth company by achieving revenue growth of 20+ percent for 26 consecutive quarters (see Exhibit 1). In announcing the company's 2016 third-quarter financial results, chairman and chief executive officer (CEO) Kevin Plank said:

> Over the past 20 years, we have established ourselves as a premium global brand with a track record of strong financial results. Looking back over the past nine months, it has never been more evident that we are at a pivotal moment in time, where the investments we are making today will fuel our growth and drive our industry leadership position for years to come. As a growth company with an expanding global footprint and businesses like footwear and women's each approaching a billion dollars this year, we have never been more focused on the long-term success of our Brand.[1]

But despite Plank's optimism about Under Armour's future prospects, management announced a reduced sales and earnings outlook for the fourth quarter of 2016 and weakening demand for Under Armour products in North America. The company's sales growth in North America during the first nine

Growth in Under Armour's Quarterly Revenues, 2010 – 2019 (in millions)

	QUARTER 1 (JAN.–MARCH)		QUARTER 2 (APRIL–JUNE)		QUARTER 3 (JULY–SEPT.)		QUARTER 4 (OCT.–DEC.)	
	Revenues	Percent Change from Prior Year's Quarter 1	Revenues	Percent Change from Prior Year's Quarter 2	Revenues	Percent Change from Prior Year's Quarter 3	Revenues	Percent Change from Prior Year's Quarter 4
2010	$ 229.4	14.7%	$ 204.8	24.4%	$ 328.6	21.9%	$ 301.2	35.5%
2011	312.7	36.3%	291.3	42.3%	465.5	41.7%	403.1	33.9%
2012	384.4	23.0%	369.5	26.8%	575.2	23.6%	505.9	25.5%
2013	471.6	22.7%	454.5	23.0%	723.1	25.7%	682.8	35.0%
2014	641.6	36.0%	609.7	34.1%	937.9	29.7%	895.2	31.1%
2015	804.9	25.5%	783.6	28.5%	1,204.1	28.4%	1,170.7	30.8%
2016	1,047.8	30.2%	1,000.8	27.7%	1,471.6	22.4%	1,305.3	11.5%
2017	1,119.8	6.9%	1,091.2	9.0%	1,409.0	(4.3)%	1,369.2	4.9%
2018	1,185.4	5.9%	1,174.9	7.7%	1,443.0	2.4%	1,390.0	1.5%
2019	1,204.7	1.6%	1,191.7	1.4%	N.A.	N.A.	N.A.	N.A.

Note: N.A. = Not applicable.

Sources: Company 10-K reports, 2018, 2017, 2016, 2015, 2013, 2012, and 2010, company press release May 2, 2019 and company press release, July 30, 2019.

months of 2016 dropped from 25.7 percent in Q1 to 21.5 percent in Q2 to 15.6 percent in Q3. The prices of Under Armour's Class A shares (trading under the symbol UAA) and Class C shares (trading under the symbol UA) dropped nearly 30 percent in the next three trading days, not only because of the weak outlook, but also because of investor concerns about reports of a slowdown in retail sales of sports apparel products in the United States.

The 2017–2018 Collapse in Under Armour's Financial Performance

Under Armour's report of its 2016 fourth-quarter and full-year results in January 2017 rang alarm bells. Total fourth-quarter revenues rose 11.7 percent; revenues in North America were up only 5.9 percent; income from operations dropped 6.1 percent companywide and 15.0 percent in North America. To make matters worse, the company's outlook for full-year 2017 was gloomy—expected revenue growth of 11 to 12 percent (the lowest annual growth rate since the company became a "C" corporation in 2002) and a decline in operating income to approximately $320 million, partly because of "strategic investments in the company's fastest growing businesses."[2] Nonetheless, Kevin Plank believed the company's resources and capabilities would enable it to cope with the challenges ahead:

> We are incredibly proud that in 2016, we once again posted record revenue and earnings; however, numerous challenges and disruptions in North American retail tempered our fourth quarter results. The strength of our Brand, an unparalleled connection with our consumers, and the continuation of investments in our fastest growing businesses—footwear, international and direct-to-consumer—give us great confidence in our ability to navigate the current retail environment, execute against our long-term growth strategy, and create value to our shareholders.[3]

In the days following the full-year 2016 earnings release and the 2017 outlook presented by management, the prices of the company's Class A shares and Class C shares—which were already trading about 30 percent below their highs earlier in 2016—dropped another 28 percent.

Under Armour's Financial Performance in 2017 Turned Out to Be Worse Than Expected

In its core North American market, Under Armour found itself on the defensive throughout 2017. A year after growing North American sales from almost $1.0 billion in 2012 to $4.0 billion in 2016 (a compound growth rate of 41.4 percent), Under Armour's 2017 sales in North America dropped $200 million (5.1 percent) to $3.8 billion. Total revenues worldwide were up a meager 3.1 percent—from $4.83 billion to $4.99 billion, after growing at a compound rate of 27.3 percent from 2012 to 2016. Operating income dropped from $417.5 million in 2016 to $27.8 million in 2017. Net income fell from a record high of $257.0 million to a net loss of $48.3 million. These big drops in Under Armour's operating income and the net loss of $48.3 million were largely due to management's announcement in August 2017 that it would pursue a $140 to $150 million restructuring plan to address operating inefficiencies, transition to a product category management structure, and reengineer the company's go-to-market process (product innovation and design, vendor relationships, delivery times of seasonal products, inventory management, profit margin control, and speed of response to shifting consumer preferences and market conditions). In addition, the plan called for a global workforce reduction of about 300 people, inventory reductions and write-downs, and charges for asset impairments, facility and lease terminations, and contract terminations.

The prices of the company's Class A shares and Class C shares, which began 2017 trading at $29.34 and $25.49, respectively, closed at $14.43 and $13.32 on the last trading day of December 2017. These declines in Under Armour's stock prices were all the more disheartening to the company's shareholders because the value of stocks listed on the NYSE and Nasdaq stock exchanges had climbed by more than $7 trillion in the 16 months since the 2016 presidential election. But the stock price declines were also a reflection of investor concerns about whether the Under Armour brand was in trouble in North America—the experiences of other troubled brands had demonstrated it was extremely difficult to rebuild a brand once it had fallen out of favor with the public. Investors had also been unnerved in November 2017 when analysts at 24/7 Wall St. had ranked Kevin Plank as No. 4 on its list of "20 Worst CEOs in America 2017."[4] Plank had been under the microscope since a controversial split of the company's stock in April 2016 into Class A (vote-entitled), Class B, and Class C (no voting power) shares, where Kevin Plank was granted Class B shares equal to his Class A shareholdings; each Class B share owned by Plank entitled him to 10 votes for every Class A share he owned. Since he owned about 15.8 percent of the Class A shares (as of April 2017), his super-vote Class B shares gave him about 65 percent of the total shareholder voting power on every shareholder vote taken.

Since the stock split, Plank had sold some of his Class C shares to fund the creation of Plank Industries, a privately held investment company with ownership interests in commercial real estate, hospitality, food and beverage, venture capital, and thoroughbred horse racing. Plank's critics had claimed the new venture was absorbing too much of his time. Plank's time in dealing with UA's operating issues and sales slowdown had also been constrained by his involvement in helping spearhead a 25-year, $5.5 billion project (being partially financed with bonds issued by the City of Baltimore's Baltimore Development Corp.) to develop waterfront property in South Baltimore into a mini-city called Port Covington that would create thousands of jobs and drive demand for office buildings, houses, shops, and restaurants. Plank Industries' Sycamore Development Co. was the lead private developer of the Port Covington project. So far, Sycamore had completed a number of properties in the project, including a $24 million renovation of a former Sam's Club into a 170,000 square-foot facility for Under Armour, tentatively named Building 37 (Plank's number on his University of Maryland football jersey was 37). Building 37 was on acreage Under Armour had purchased for $70.3 million in 2014 and was being leased by Sycamore to Under Armour for $1.1 million annually. Building 37 was the first phase of Under Armour's plan to create a 50-acre global headquarters campus that would include a new headquarters building on the site of Building 37, additional Under Armour facilities and manufacturing space, a man-made lake, and a small stadium—a layout designed to house as many as 10,000 Under Armour employees (UA employed approximately 2,100 people in Baltimore in early 2018, some 600 of which were housed in Building 37).

To compensate for the time he was spending on outside interests, Plank engineered the appointment of Patrik Frisk, formerly CEO of the ALDO Group, a global footwear and accessories company, as President and Chief Operating Officer (COO) of Under Armour in June 2017. Frisk had 30 years of experience in the apparel, footwear, and retail industry, holding top management positions with responsibility for such brands as The North Face®, Timberland®, JanSport®, lucy®, and SmartWool®. As president and COO, Frisk was assigned responsibility for Under Armour's go-to-market strategy and the successful execution of its long-term growth plan. Kevin Plank's titles were Chairman of the Board and CEO.

In 2008, Plank voluntarily reduced his salary from $500,000 to $26,000, which was his approximate salary when he founded Under Armour. As UA's largest stockholder, Plank believed he should be compensated for his services based primarily on the company's annual incentive plan tied to the company's performance and on annual performance-based equity awards. Plank's $26,000 salary remained in place in 2019.

Under Armour's 2017 Sales Performance in North America Was Worse Than Its Two Biggest Competitors

Under Armour's 5.1 percent decline in 2017 sales in North America compared unfavorably with long-time industry leader Nike, whose sales of $15.2 billion in North America from December 1, 2016, through November 30, 2017, were essentially unchanged from the $15.1 billion in sales Nike reported for December 1, 2015, through November 30, 2016.[5] While in 2015 Under Armour had overtaken Germany-based The adidas Group—the industry's second-ranking company in terms of *global* revenues in sports apparel, athletic footwear, and sports equipment and accessories—to become the second largest seller of sports apparel, active wear, and athletic footwear in North America in 2015, the situation changed dramatically in 2017.[6] Top executives at adidas (pronounced ah-di-dah) launched an unusually strong series of strategic initiatives at the beginning of 2017 to increase the company's share of the sports apparel, active wear, and athletic footwear market in North America from an estimated 10 percent to around 15 to 20 percent. The results were impressive, given the stagnant market demand for sports apparel and products in North America. Sales of adidas-branded products in North America grew by a resounding 25 percent in 2017, allowing adidas to reclaim second place in the overall North American sportwear market and dropping Under Armour back into third place.

Under Armour's 2018 Financial Performance Gets Even Worse

Despite the sizable restructuring efforts undertaken at Under Armour in the last four months of 2017 and continuing through 2018, Under Armour executives did not foresee a quick turnaround in North America. Their 2018 outlook for North American revenues was a mid-single-digit decline, although international sales were expected to grow 25 percent. Operating income was projected to be $20 million to $30 million (versus $28.7 million in 2017). Management explained the projections of operating income were low because, after additional review, a decision had been made to pursue a second restructuring plan in 2018 to further optimize operations. This plan entailed:

- Up to $105 million in cash-related charges, consisting of up to $55 million in facility and lease terminations and up to $50 million in contract termination and other restructuring charges; and

- Up to $25 million in non-cash charges, comprised of up to $10 million of inventory related charges and up to $15 million of asset-related impairments.

Management said it expected the 2017 and 2018 restructuring efforts to produce a minimum of $75 million in savings annually in 2019 and beyond.

As things turned out, North American sales declined less than 2 percent and international sales rose 23.2 percent; total net revenues rose 4.1 percent to nearly $5.2 billion. But operating income plummeted from $27.8 million in 2017 to an operating loss of

$25.0 million in 2018; net income was essentially flat—a net loss of $46.3 million in 2018 versus a net loss of $48.3 in 2017.

Under Armour's Outlook for 2019

In May 2019, Under Armour reported its results for the first quarter of 2019; highlights included the following:

- Net revenues of $1.2 billion, up 2 percent over the first quarter of 2018.

- A decline of 3 percent in sales revenues in North America.

- An increase of 12 percent in international revenues.

- Increases of 1 percent in apparel revenues and 8 percent in footwear revenues.

- Operating income of $35 million and net income of $22 million.

- Earnings per share of $0.05.

For full-year 2019, management's outlook was for net revenue gains of 3 to 4 percent, reflecting flat sales in North America and a low double-digit increase in international revenues. Full-year operating income was expected to be in the $220 to $230 million range, resulting in earnings per share of about $0.33. On May 6, 2019, Under Armour's vote-entitled Class A shares closed at $22.33, up from a closing price of $17.81 on January 2, 2019.

Exhibit 2 shows selected financial statement data for Under Armour for 2014 through 2018.

Under Armour's Strategy in 2019

Until 2018, Under Armour's mission was "to make all athletes better through passion, design, and the relentless pursuit of innovation."[7] A reworded mission—"Under Armour Makes You Better"—was publicly announced in early 2018. Kevin Plank said the new wording was meant to better convey that "in every way we connect, through the products we create, the experience we deliver and the inspiration we provide, we simply make you better."[8] In late 2018, Kevin Plank told a gathering of investors and Wall Street analysts that Under Armour's vision was "to inspire you with performance solutions you

EXHIBIT 2

Selected Financial Data for Under Armour, Inc., 2014–2018 (in millions)

	2018	2017	2016	2015	2014
Selected Income Statement Data					
Net revenues	$5,193.2	$4,989.2	$4,833.3	$3,963.3	$3,084.4
Cost of goods sold	2,852.7	2,737.8	2,584.7	2,057.8	1,152.2
Gross profit	2,340.5	2,251.4	2,248.6	1,905.5	1,512.2
Selling, general and administrative expenses	2,182.3	2,099.5	1831.1	1,497.0	1,158.3
Restructuring and impairment charges	183.1	124.0	–	–	–
Income from operations	(25.0)	27.8	417.5	408.5	354.0
Interest expense, net	(33.6)	(34.5)	(26.4)	(14.6)	(5.3)
Other expense, net	(9.2)	(3.6)	(2.8)	(7.2)	(6.4)
Income (loss) before income taxes	(67.8)	(10.3)	388.3	386.7	342.2
Provision for income taxes	(20.6)	38.0	131.3	154.1	134.2
Net income (loss)	$(46.3)	$(48.3)	$257.0	$232.6	$208.0
Selected Balance Sheet Data					
Cash and cash equivalents	$557.4	$312.5	$250.5	$129.9	$593.2
Working capital*	1,277.6	1,277.3	1,279.3	1,020.0	1,127.8
Inventories at year-end	1,019.5	1,158.5	917.5	783.0	536.7
Total assets	4,245.0	4,006.4	3,644.3	2,866.0	2,092.4
Long-term debt, including current maturities	728.8	792.0	817.4	666.1	281.5
Total stockholders' equity	2,016.9	2,018.6	2,030.9	1,668.2	1,350.3
Selected Cash Flow Data					
Net cash provided by operating activities	$628.2	$237.5	$366.6	($14.5)	$219.0

*Working capital is defined as current assets minus current liabilities.
Note: Some totals may not add up due to rounding.
Source: Company 10-K reports for 2018 and 2016.

never knew you needed and can't imagine living without."

The company's principal business activities in 2019 were the development, marketing, and distribution of branded performance apparel, footwear, and related sports accessories for men, women, and youth. The brand's moisture-wicking apparel products were engineered in many designs and styles for wear in nearly every climate to provide a performance alternative to traditional products. Under Armour sports apparel was worn by athletes at all levels, from youth to professional, and by consumers with active lifestyles. Sales of these products were made through two primary channels—wholesale sales to retailers and direct-to-consumer sales (sales at the company's websites in various

geographic regions and at its rapidly growing number of company-owned brick-and-mortar Brand Houses and factory outlet stores). In the company's earlier years, revenue growth was achieved primarily by growing wholesale sales to retailers of sports apparel, athletic footwear, and sports equipment and accessories. More recently, however, sales at the company's websites and company-owned retail stores had become the company's biggest growth engine in North America. Starting in 2010, Under Armour had steadily mounted greater efforts to increase its global footprint and increase its wholesale and online sales outside North America, most especially in countries in Europe, the Middle East, and Africa (EMEA), the Asia-Pacific, and Latin America.

In 2013, Under Armour acquired MapMyFitness, a provider of website services and mobile apps to fitness-minded consumers across the world; Under Armour used this acquisition, along with several follow-on acquisitions in 2014 and 2015, to create what it termed a "connected fitness" business offering digital fitness subscriptions and licenses, mobile apps, and other fitness-tracking and nutritional-tracking solutions to athletes and fitness-conscious individuals across the world. Kevin Plank expected the company's connected fitness strategic initiative to become a major revenue driver in the years to come.

Under Armour divided its sales into five product categories and also reported its sales and operating income by geographic segment. These are displayed in Exhibit 3 for the years 2015 through 2018.

Growth Strategy

Under Armour's growth strategy in 2018–2019 was centered on six strategic initiatives:

- Continuing to broaden the company's product offerings to men, women, and youth for wear in a widening variety of sports and recreational activities and to increase their appeal to buyers. Special emphasis was being placed on expanding Under Armour's line of women's products to better capitalize on the growth opportunities in the women's segment.

- Increasing its sales and market share in the athletic footwear segment.

- Securing additional distribution of Under Armour products in the retail marketplace by (1) opening greater numbers of Under Armour Brand House stores and factory outlet stores and (2) capitalizing on growing consumer preferences to shop online. UA management had recently concluded the company's profit opportunities were often better selling its products direct to consumers at retail prices than they were selling to retail stores at wholesale prices sufficiently low to be competitive with the wholesale prices being offered by Nike and adidas.

- Growing Under Armour's global footprint by expanding its sales in foreign countries and becoming an ever-stronger global competitor in the world market for sports apparel, athletic footwear, and related sports products.

- Growing global awareness of the Under Armour brand name and strengthening the connection between consumers and Under Armour branded products worldwide.

- Growing the company's connected fitness business and making it profitable.

EXHIBIT 3

Under Armour's Revenues and Operating Income, by Product Category and Geographic Region, 2015–2018

A. NET REVENUES BY PRODUCT CATEGORY (IN MILLIONS OF $)

	2018		2017		2016		2015	
	Dollars	Percent	Dollars	Percent	Dollars	Percent	Dollars	Percent
Apparel	$3,462.4	66.7%	$3,287.1	65.9%	$3,229.1	66.9%	$2,801.1	70.7%
Footwear	1,063.2	20.5%	1,037.8	20.8%	1,010.7	20.9%	677.7	17.1%
Accessories	422.5	8.1%	445.8	8.9%	406.6	8.4%	346.9	8.8%
Total net sales	4,948.0	95.3%	4,770.8	95.6%	4,646.4	96.3%	3,825.7	96.6%
License revenues	124.8	2.4%	116.6	2.3%	99.8	2.1%	84.2	2.1%
Connected fitness	120.4	2.3%	101.9	2.0%	88.5	1.7%	53.4	1.3%
Total net revenues	$5,193.2	100.0%	$4,989.2	99.9%	$4,833.3	100.0%	$3,963.3	100.0%

Note: Under Armour, Inc., 2018 Annual Report, accessed August 2, 2019, https://about.underarmour.com/sites/default/files/2019-03/Under%20Armour%202018%20Annual%20Report.pdf.

B. NET REVENUES BY GEOGRAPHIC REGION (IN MILLIONS OF $)

	2018	2017	2016	2015
North America	$3,735.3	$3,802.4	$4,005.3	$3,455.8
EMEA*	588.6	470.0	330.6	203.1
Asia-Pacific	558.2	433.6	268.6	144.9
Latin America	190.8	181.3	141.8	106.2
Connected fitness	120.4	101.9	88.5	53.4
Total net revenues	$5,193.2	$4,989.2	$4,833.3	$3,963.3

*Europe–Middle East–Africa

C. OPERATING INCOME (LOSS) BY GEOGRAPHIC REGION (IN MILLIONS OF $)

	2018	2017	2016	2015
North America	$ (66.3)	$ 20.2	$408.4	$461.0
EMEA*	(9.4)	18.0	11.4	3.1
Asia-Pacific	95.1	82.0	68.3	36.4
Latin America	(48.5)	(37.1)	(33.9)	(30.6)
Connected fitness	4.0	(55.3)	(36.8)	(61.3)
Total operating income	$ (25.0)	$ 27.8	$417.5	$408.5

*Europe–Middle East–Africa

Source: Company 10-K reports, 2018 and 2016.

Most pressing, of course, was the strategic urgency to revive the company's sales growth, particularly in North America, and return the company to attractive profitability.

Product Line Strategy

For a number of years, expanding the company's product offerings and marketing them at multiple price points had been a key element of Under Armour's strategy. The goal for each new item added to the lineup of offerings was to provide consumers with a product that was a *superior* alternative to the traditional products of rivals—striving to always introduce a superior product would, management believed, help foster and nourish a culture of innovation among all company personnel. According to Kevin Plank, "we focus on creating products you don't know you need yet, but once you have them, you won't remember how you lived without them."[9]

Apparel   The company designed and merchandised two lines of apparel gear intended to regulate body temperature and enhance comfort, mobility, and performance regardless of weather conditions: HEATGEAR® for hot weather conditions and COLDGEAR® for cold weather conditions.

HeatGear. HeatGear was designed to be worn in warm to hot temperatures under equipment or as a single layer. The company's first compression T-shirt was the original HeatGear product and was still one of the company's signature styles in 2015. In sharp contrast to a sweat-soaked cotton T-shirt that could weigh two to three pounds, HeatGear was engineered with a microfiber blend designed to wick moisture from the body to help the body stay cool, dry, and light. HeatGear was offered in a variety of tops and bottoms in a broad array of colors and styles for wear in the gym or outside in warm or hot weather.

ColdGear. Under Armour high-performance fabrics were appealing to people participating in cold-weather sports and vigorous recreational activities like snow skiing who needed both warmth and moisture-wicking protection from becoming overheated. ColdGear was designed to wick moisture from the body while circulating body heat from hotspots to maintain core body temperature. All ColdGear apparel provided dryness and warmth in a single light layer that could be worn beneath a jersey, uniform, protective gear or ski-vest, or other cold weather outerwear. ColdGear products generally were sold at higher price points than other Under Armour gear lines.

Products within each gear line were offered in three fit types: compression (tight fit), fitted (athletic fit), and loose (relaxed). In 2016, Under Armour introduced apparel items containing MicroThread, a fabric technology that used elastomeric (stretchable) thread to create a cool moisture-wicking microclimate, prevented clinging and chafing, allowed garments to dry 30 percent faster and be 70 percent more breathable than similar Lycra construction, and were so lightweight as to "feel like nothing." It also began using a newly developed insulation called Reactor in selected ColdGear items and introduced a new apparel collection with an exclusive CoolSwitch coating on the inside of the fabric that pulled heat away from the skin, allowing the wearer to feel cooler and perform longer.

Footwear Under Armour began marketing athletic footwear for men, women, and youth in 2006 and had expanded its footwear line every year since. Its 2019 offerings included footwear models specifically designed for performance training, running, footwear, basketball, golf, and outdoor wear, plus football, baseball, lacrosse, softball, and soccer cleats. Under Armour's footwear models were light, breathable, and built with performance attributes specific to their intended use. Over the past five years, a stream of innovative technologies had been incorporated in the ongoing generations of footwear models/styles to improve stabilization, cushioning, moisture management, comfort, directional control, and performance.

New footwear collections for men, women, and youth were introduced annually, sometimes seasonally. Most new models and styles incorporated fresh technological features of one kind or another. Since 2012, Under Armour had more than tripled the number of footwear styles/models priced above $100 per pair. Its best-selling offerings were in the basketball and running shoe categories.

To capitalize on a recently signed long-term endorsement contract with pro basketball superstar Stephen Curry, Under Armour began marketing a Stephen Curry Signature line of basketball shoes in 2014; the so-called Curry One models had a price point of $120. This was followed by a Curry Two collection in 2015 at a price point of $130, a Curry 2.5 collection at a price point of $135 during the NBA playoffs in May and June 2016, a Curry Three collection at a price point of $135 in Fall 2016, a Curry 4 collection at a price point of $130 in Fall 2017, a Curry 5 collection at a price point of $130 at the start of the NBA playoffs in May 2018, and a Curry 6 collection at a price point of $130 in December 2018.

After signing pro golfer Jordan Spieth to a 10-year endorsement contract in early 2015—Spieth had a spectacular year on the Professional Golf Association (PGA) tour in 2015 and was named 2015 PGA Tour Player of the Year—Under Armour promptly sought to leverage the signing by introducing an all-new 2016 golf shoe collection in April 2016. The collection had three styles, ranging in price from $160 to $220. A new Spieth One Signature collection was introduced in early 2017 with much the same price points, followed by a Spieth Two collection in early 2018, which was accompanied by a Spieth Tour™ golf glove, and a Spieth 3 collection in early 2019.

Under Armour debuted its first "smart shoe" (called the SpeedForm Gemini 2 Record Equipped) at a price point of $150 in 2016; smart shoe models were equipped with the capability to connect automatically to UA's connected fitness website and record certain activities in the wearer's fitness tracking account.

In 2018, using freshly developed connected fitness technologies and several other innovations, Under Armour debuted a new, multifeatured HOVR™ running shoe, which Kevin Plank hailed as a new product that hit what the company called "the trifecta—style, performance, and fit." HOVR models were priced from $100 to $140; all models used compression mesh and a special molded foam that provided a "zero gravity feel," gave the runner return energy with each step to reduce impact, and claimed to deliver "unmatched comfort." The higher-priced "Connected" HOVR models had built-in Under Armour Record Sensor™ technology that could be paired with a mobile phone and used to track, analyze, and store most every known running metric, enabling runners to know what they needed to do to get better. Plank believed the HOVR was "a home run" and a reflection of the company's growing capabilities to churn out innovative products. In 2019, HOVR models were available for running, basketball, golf, and casual wear; a number of the HOVR models for running had connected technology features.

Growing numbers of Under Armour's footwear models in 2019 featured such recently developed technologies as Anafoam, UA Clutch Fit®, and Charged Cushioning®, which provided stabilization, directional cushioning, and moisture management engineered to maximize comfort and control. Shoppers could also design their own customized footwear, using uploaded images, customizable patterns, an assortment of styles and technologies, and a giant array of color options.

Accessories   Under Armour's accessory line in 2019 included gloves, socks, hats and headwear, belts, backpacks and bags, eyewear, protective gear, headphones, phone cases and mounts, water bottles and coolers, and an assortment of sports equipment. All of these accessories featured performance advantages and functionality similar to other Under Armour products. For instance, the company's baseball batting, football, golf, and running gloves included HEATGEAR® and COLDGEAR® technologies and were designed with advanced fabrics to provide various high-performance attributes that differentiated Under Armour gloves from those of rival brands.

Connected Fitness   In December 2013, Under Armour acquired MapMyFitness, which served one of the largest fitness communities in the world at its website and offered a diverse suite of websites and mobile applications under its flagship brands, MapMyRun and MapMyRide. Utilizing GPS and other advanced technologies, MapMyFitness provided users with the ability to map, record, and share their workouts. Under Armour acquired European fitness app Endomondo and food-logging app MyFitnessPal in 2015, enabling UA to create a multifaceted connected fitness dashboard that used four independently functioning apps (MapMyFitness, MyFitnessPal, Endomondo, and UA Record™) to enable subscribers to log workouts, runs, and foods

eaten, and to use a digital dashboard to review measures relating to their sleep, fitness, activity, and nutrition. Next, UA introduced a Connected Fitness System called Under Armour HealthBox™ that consisted of a multifunctional wristband (that measured sleep, resting heart rate, steps taken, and workout intensity), heart rate strap, and a smart scale (that tracked body weight, body fat percentage, and progress toward a weight goal); the wristband was water resistant, could be worn 24/7, and had Bluetooth connectivity with UA Record.

Kevin Plank was so enthusiastic about the long-term potential of Under Armour's Connected Fitness business that he had boosted the company's team of engineers and software developers from 20 to over 350 during 2014 and 2015. In 2016, Under Armour organized all of its digital and fitness technologies and products into a new business division called Connected Fitness, under the leadership of a senior vice president of digital revenue. As of December 2018, Under Armour believed it had created the world's largest digital health and fitness community. More than 250 million people had downloaded one of the company's digital fitness apps. Many users were quite active, with more than 2 million workouts and 30 million foods being logged daily across the world. Under Armour had learned that members of its digital ecosystem purchased 36 percent more Under Armour products than other consumers and that their brand preference for Under Armour products was significantly higher.[10]

While Connected Fitness sales grew rapidly, the business lost millions of dollars annually—see Exhibits 3B and 3C. As part of the 2017 restructuring program, Under Armour merged its core connect fitness digital products, digital engineering, and digital media under the direction of a chief technology officer; this management arrangement evolved further in early 2018 with the appointment of a new senior vice president, digital product, who reported to the chief technology officer and had responsibility for leading the strategy for all digital product development in collaboration with executive management, product category heads, marketing, and creative/design. In Under Armour's February 2018 earnings announcement, the Connected Fitness business reported its first-ever positive operating income (almost

$800,000) for the fourth quarter of 2017; for full-year 2018, the Connected Fitness business reported operating income of $4 million. Under Armour reported that premium subscription revenue for its Connected Fitness business grew about 56 percent during 2018. UA's MyFitnessPal was the number one grossing health and fitness app in the Apple App Store; in 2018, users of this app had over 9 billion foods and burned more than 440 billion calories. Users of various Connected Fitness apps participated in social media communities on Instagram, WeChat, Snap, YouTube, Facebook, and other platforms.

Licensing   Under Armour had licensing agreements with a number of firms to produce and market Under Armour apparel, accessories, and equipment. Under Armour product, marketing, and sales teams were actively involved in all steps of the design process for licensed products in order to maintain brand standards and consistency. During 2018, licensees sold UA-branded collegiate, National Football League, and National Basketball Association apparel and accessories, baby and kids' apparel, team uniforms, socks, water bottles, eyewear, and other hard goods equipment that featured performance advantages and functionality similar to Under Armour's other product offerings.

Marketing, Promotion, and Brand Management Strategies

Under Armour had an in-house marketing and promotions department that designed and produced most of its advertising campaigns to drive consumer demand for its products and build awareness of Under Armour as a leading performance athletic brand. The company's total marketing expenses were $543.8 million in 2018, $565.1 million in 2017, $477.5 million in 2016, $417.8 million in 2015, and $333.0 million in 2014. These totals included the costs of sponsoring events and various sports teams, the costs of athlete endorsements, and ads placed in a variety of television, print, radio, and social media outlets. All were included as part of selling, general, and administrative expenses shown in Exhibit 1.

Sports Marketing   Under Armour's sports marketing and promotion strategy began with promoting the sales and use of its products to high-performing athletes and teams on the high school, collegiate, and professional levels. This strategy was executed by entering into outfitting agreements with a variety of collegiate and professional sports teams, sponsoring an assortment of collegiate and professional sports events, entering into endorsement agreements with individual athletes, and selling Under Armour products directly to team equipment managers and to individual athletes. As a result, UA products were seen on the playing field (typically with the Under Armour logo prominently displayed), giving them exposure to various consumer audiences attending live sports events or watching these events on television and through other media (pictures and videos accessed via the Internet and social media, magazines, and print). Management believed such exposure helped the company establish the on-field authenticity of the Under Armour brand with consumers. In addition, UA hosted combines, camps, and clinics for athletes in many sports at regional sites across the United States and was the title sponsor of a collection of high school All-America Games that created significant on-field and media exposure of its products and brand.

Going into 2019, Under Armour was the official outfitter of men's and women's athletic teams at such collegiate institutions as Notre Dame, UCLA, Boston College, Northwestern, Texas Tech, Maryland, South Carolina, the U.S. Naval Academy, Wisconsin, Indiana, Missouri, California, Utah, and Auburn. All told, it was the official outfitter of close to 100 men's and women's collegiate athletic teams, and growing numbers of high school athletic teams, and it supplied sideline apparel and fan gear for many collegiate teams as well. Under Armour had been the official supplier of competition suits, uniforms, and training resources for a number of U.S. teams in the 2014 Winter Olympics, 2016 Summer Olympics, and 2018 Winter Olympics.

Under Armour was equally active in negotiating agreements to supply products to high-profile professional athletes and professional sports teams, most notably in the National Football League (NFL), Major League Baseball (MLB), the National Hockey League (NHL), and the National Basketball Association (NBA). Under Armour had been an official supplier of football cleats to all NFL teams since 2006, the official supplier of gloves to NFL teams beginning in 2011, and a supplier of training apparel for athletes attending NFL tryout camps beginning in 2012. In 2011 Under Armour became the official supplier of performance footwear to all 30 MLB teams; in 2016, Under Armour signed a 10-year deal with MLB to extend its role as official supplier for all 30 teams from just footwear to include uniforms, performance apparel, and connected fitness products and to also be an official sponsor of Major League Baseball. However, in 2018 UA exited its agreement to be the official supplier of uniforms, performance apparel, and connected fitness products, but retained its rights to supply performance footwear and be an MLB sponsor as an Official Performance Footwear Supplier and Sponsor of MLB. In 2018, Under Armour worked with a manufacturing and distribution partner to sell MLB-licensed fan wear at retail.

Internationally, Under Armour sponsored and sold its products to several Canadian, European, and Latin American soccer and rugby teams to help drive brand awareness in various countries and regions across the world. In Canada, it was an official supplier of performance apparel to Rugby Canada and Hockey Canada, had advertising rights at many locations in the Air Canada Center during the NHL Toronto Maple Leafs' home games, and was the official supplier of performance products to the Maple Leafs. In Europe, Under Armour was the official supplier of performance apparel to two professional soccer teams and the Welsh Rugby Union. In 2014 and 2015, Under Armour became the official match-day and training wear supplier for the Colo-Colo soccer club in Chile, the Cruz Azul soccer team in Mexico, and the São Paulo soccer team in Brazil.

In addition to sponsoring teams and events, Under Armour's brand-building strategy in the United States was to secure the endorsement of individual athletes. One facet of this strategy was to sign endorsement contracts with newly emerging sports stars—examples included Jacksonville Jaguars running back Leonard Fournette, Milwaukee Bucks point guard Brandon Jennings, Philadelphia 76ers center Joel Embiid, Charlotte Bobcats point guard Kemba Walker, 2012 National League (baseball) Most Valuable Player Buster Posey, 2012 National League Rookie of the Year Bryce Harper, tennis phenom Sloane Stephens, WBC super-welterweight boxing champion Camelo Alvarez, and PGA golfer Jordan Spieth. But the company's endorsement roster also included established stars: NFL football players Tom Brady, Julio Jones, and Anquan Boldin; Golden State Warriors point guard Stephen Curry; professional baseball players Ryan Zimmerman, Jose Reyes, and Clayton Kershaw; tennis star Andy Murray; U.S. Women's National Soccer Team players Heather Mitts and Lauren Cheney; U.S. Olympic and professional volleyball player Nicole Branagh; and U.S. Olympic swimmer Michael Phelps. In 2015, Under Armour negotiated 10-year extensions of its endorsement contracts with Stephen Curry and Jordan Spieth; both deals included grants of stock in the company. Recently, Under Armour had signed celebrities outside the sports world to multiyear contracts, including ballerina soloist Misty Copeland and fashion model Giselle Bündchen; wrestler, actor, and producer Dwayne "The Rock" Johnson; and rapper A$AP Rocky (Rakim Mayers). Copeland was featured in one of Under Armour's largest advertising campaigns for women's apparel offerings. Johnson was playing an integral role in promoting UA's connected fitness, apparel, footwear, and accessory products. Mayers was expected to have his own line of premium clothing in a forthcoming Under Armour Sportswear collection. In addition to signing endorsement agreements with prominent sports figures and celebrities in the United States, Under Armour had become increasingly active in using endorsement agreements with well-known athletes to help build public awareness of the Under Armour brand in those foreign countries where it was striving to build a strong market presence. As of early 2019, Under Armour had signed endorsement agreements with several hundred international athletes in a wide variety of sports.

Under Armour's strategy of signing high-profile sports figures to endorsement contracts, sponsoring a variety of sports events, and supplying products to sports teams emblazoned with the company's logo had long been used by Nike and The adidas Group. Both rivals had far larger rosters of sports figure endorsements than Under Armour and supplied their products to more collegiate and professional sports teams than Under Armour.

Nonetheless, Under Armour's aggressive entry into the market for securing such endorsement agreements had spawned intense competition among the three rivals to win the endorsement of athletes, and teams with high profiles and high perceived public appeal had caused the costs of winning such agreements to spiral upward. In 2014, Under Armour reportedly offered between $265 million and $285 million to entice NBA star Kevin Durant, who plays for the Golden State Warriors, away from Nike; Nike matched the offer and Durant elected to stay with Nike.[11] In 2015, adidas bested Nike in a bidding war to sign Houston Rockets star and runner-up NBA Most Valuable Player James Harden to a 13-year endorsement deal, when Nike opted not to match adidas' offer of $200 million. The deal with Harden was said to be a move by adidas to reclaim its number-two spot in sports apparel sales in North America behind Nike, months after being surpassed by Under Armour.[12] In 2017, it took $200 million—nearly $12.8 million per year—for Under Armour to secure a 16-year deal with UCLA to outfit all of UCLA's men's and women's athletic teams. In 2018 Under Armour enticed Joel Embiid to switch from adidas to Under Armour for a five-year apparel and footwear endorsement deal that made him the highest-earning center in the NBA (the exact terms were not disclosed).

Under Armour spent approximately $126.2 million in 2018 for athlete and superstar endorsements, various team and league sponsorships, athletic events, and other marketing commitments, compared to about $150.4 million in 2017, $176.1 million in 2016, $126.5 million in 2015, $90.1 million in 2014, $53.0 million in 2012, and $29.4 million in 2010.[13] The company was contractually obligated to spend a minimum of $208.3 million for endorsements, sponsorships, events, and other marketing commitments from 2020 to 2023.[14] Under Armour did not know precisely what its future endorsement and sponsorship costs would be because its contractual agreements with most athletes were subject to certain performance-based variables and because it was actively engaged in efforts to sign additional endorsement contracts and sponsor additional sports teams and athletic events.

Retail Marketing and Product Presentation

The primary thrust of Under Armour's retail marketing strategy was to increase the floor space *exclusively* dedicated to Under Armour products in the stores of its major retail accounts. The key initiative here was to design and fund Under Armour "concept shops"—including flooring, lighting, walls, fixtures and product displays, and images—within the stores of its major retail customers. This shop-in-shop approach was seen as an effective way to gain the placement of Under Armour products in prime floor space and create a more engaging and sales-producing way for consumers to shop for Under Armour products.

In stores that did not have Under Armour concept shops, Under Armour worked with retailers to establish sales-enhancing placement of its products and various point-of-sale displays. In "big-box" sporting goods stores, it was important to be sure that Under Armour's growing variety of products gained visibility in all of the various departments (hunting apparel in the hunting goods department, footwear and socks in the footwear department, and so on). Except for the retail stores with Under Armour concept shops, company personnel worked with retailers to employ in-store fixtures, life-size mannequins, and displays that highlighted the UA logo and conveyed a performance-oriented, athletic look. The merchandising strategy was not only to enhance the visibility of Under Armour products and drive sales but also grow consumer awareness that Under Armour products delivered performance-enhancing advantages.

Media and Promotion   Under Armour advertised in a variety of national digital, broadcast, and print media outlets, as well as social and mobile media. Its advertising campaigns were of varying lengths and formats and frequently included prominent athletes and personalities. Advertising and promotional campaigns from 2015 to 2017 featured Michael Phelps, Stephen Curry, Jordan Spieth, Tom Brady, Lindsey Vonn, Misty Copeland, and Dwayne Johnson. In 2018, UA had a digitally led marketing approach for the launch of its UA HOVR™ running shoe models, which included a variety of content on various social media platforms.

Distribution Strategy

Under Armour products were available in roughly 17,000 retail store locations worldwide in 2018. In many foreign countries, Under Armour relied on independent marketing and sales agents, instead of its own marketing staff, to recruit retail accounts and solicit orders from retailers for UA merchandise. Under Armour also sold its products directly to consumers through its own Brand House stores, factory outlet stores, and various geographic websites.

Wholesale Distribution In 2018, Under Armour had about 13,500 points of distribution in North America, just under 40 percent of the 35,000 places that consumers could buy athletic apparel and footwear.[15] The company's biggest retail account was Dick's Sporting Goods, which in 2018 accounted for 10 percent of the company's net revenues. Until its bankruptcy and subsequent store liquidation in 2016, The Sports Authority had been UA's second largest retail account; the loss of this account was a principal factor in Under Armour's struggle to grow wholesale sales to retailers in North America. Other important retail accounts included Academy Sports and Outdoors, Hibbett Sporting Goods, Modell's Sporting Goods, Bass Pro Shops, Cabela's, Footlocker, The Army and Air Force Exchange Service, and such well-known department store chains as Macy's, Nordstrom, Belk, Dillard's, and Kohl's. In Canada, the company's important retail accounts included Sport Chek and Hudson's Bay. Roughly 75 percent of all sales made to retailers were to large-format national and regional retail chains. The remaining 25 percent of wholesale sales were to lesser-sized outdoor and specialty retailers, institutional athletic departments, leagues, teams, and fitness specialists. Independent and specialty retailers were serviced by a combination of in-house sales personnel and third-party commissioned manufacturer's representatives.

Direct-to-Consumer Sales In 2018, about 38 percent of Under Armour's net revenues were generated through direct-to-consumer sales, versus 23 percent in 2010 and 6 percent in 2005; the direct-to-consumer channel included sales of discounted merchandise at Under Armour's factory outlet stores and full-price sales at Under Armour Brand Houses, and various country websites. The factory outlet stores gave Under Armour added brand exposure and helped familiarize consumers with Under Armour's product lineup while also functioning as an important channel for selling discontinued, out-of-season, and/or overstocked products at discount prices without undermining the prices of Under Armour merchandise being sold at retail stores, Brand Houses, and company websites. As of March 31, 2019, Under Armour was operating 162 stores in factory outlet malls in North America; these stores attracted about 75 million shoppers in 2018.

During the past several years, Under Armour had begun opening company-owned Brand House stores in high-traffic retail locations in the United States to showcase its branded apparel and sell its products direct-to-consumers at retail prices. As of March 31, 2019, the company was operating 16 Under Armour Brand House stores in North America.

UA management's e-commerce strategy called for sales at www.underarmour.com (and 26 other in-country websites as of 2016) to be one of the company's principal vehicles for sales growth in upcoming years. To help spur e-commerce sales, the company was enhancing its efforts to drive traffic to its websites, improve its online merchandising techniques and storytelling about the many different Under Armour products sold on its sites, and use promotions to attract online buyers. From time-to-time, its websites offered free limited-time shipping on specified items. Starting in 2017, to better compete with Amazon, the company had begun offering free 4 to 6 business day shipping on orders over $60 and free 3 business day shipping on orders over $150. Free shipping on returns within 60 days was standard.

Product Licensing In 2017, 2.3 percent of the company's net revenues ($116.6 million) came from licensing arrangements to manufacture and distribute Under Armour branded products. Under Armour preapproved all products manufactured and sold by its licensees, and the company's quality assurance team strived to ensure that licensed products met the same quality and compliance standards as company-sold products. Under Armour had relationships with several licensees for team uniforms, eyewear, and custom-molded mouth guards, as well as the distribution of Under Armour products to college bookstores and golf pro shops.

Distribution Outside North America Under Armour's first strategic move to gain international distribution occurred in 2002 when it established a relationship with a Japanese licensee, Dome Corporation, to be the exclusive distributor of Under Armour products in Japan. The relationship evolved, with Under Armour making a minority equity investment in Dome Corporation in 2011 and Dome gaining distribution rights for South Korea. Dome sold Under Armour branded apparel, footwear, and accessories to professional sports teams, large sporting goods retailers, and several thousand independent retailers of sports apparel in Japan and South Korea. Under Armour worked closely with Dome to develop variations of Under Armour products to better accommodate the different sports interests and preferences of Japanese and Korean consumers.

A European headquarters was opened in 2006 in Amsterdam, The Netherlands, to conduct and oversee sales, marketing, and logistics activities across Europe. The strategy was to first sell Under Armour products directly to teams and athletes and then leverage visibility in the sports segment to access broader audiences of potential consumers. By 2011, Under Armour had succeeded in selling products to Premier League Football clubs and multiple running, golf, and cricket clubs in the United Kingdom; soccer teams in France, Germany, Greece, Ireland, Italy, Spain, and Sweden; as well as First Division Rugby clubs in France, Ireland, Italy, and the United Kingdom. Sales to European retailers quickly followed on the heels of gains being made in the sports team segment. By year-end 2012, Under Armour had 4,000 retail customers in Austria, France, Germany, Ireland, and the United Kingdom and was generating revenues from sales to independent distributors who resold Under Armour products to retailers in Italy, Greece, Scandinavia, and Spain. From 2014 to 2017, sales continued to expand at a rapid clip in countries in Europe, the Middle East, and Africa; sales in EMEA countries surpassed $1 billion in 2017 (see

Exhibit 3B). In 2018, Under Armour had sales totaling $588.6 million in 57 of the 100 countries constituting the EMEA region. However, operating profits in this region were elusive, dropping to a loss of $9.4 million in 2018 after reporting operating income of $18.0 million in 2017 (see Exhibit 3C). Adidas strongly defended its industry-leading position with European retailers, and Under Armour frequently found itself embroiled in hotly contested price-cutting battles with adidas and Nike to win orders from retailers in many EMEA locations.

In 2010 and 2011, Under Armour began selling its products in parts of Latin America and Asia. In Latin America, Under Armour sold directly to retailers in some countries and in other countries sold its products to independent distributors who then were responsible for securing sales to retailers. In 2014, Under Armour launched efforts to make Under Armour products available in over 70 of Brazil's premium points of sale and e-commerce hubs; expanded sales efforts were also initiated in Chile and Mexico. While sales were trending upward in Latin America, the company's operating losses in the region had increased every year since 2015 (see Exhibit 3C).

In 2011, Under Armour opened a retail showroom in Shanghai, China—the first of a series of steps to begin the long-term process of introducing Chinese athletes and consumers to the Under Armour brand, showcase Under Armour products, and learn about Chinese consumers. Additional retail locations in Shanghai and Beijing soon followed (some operated by local partners). By April 2014, there were five company-owned and franchised retail locations in mainland China that merchandised Under Armour products; additionally, the Under Armour brand had been recently introduced in Hong Kong through a partnership with leading retail chain GigaSports.

Under Armour began selling its branded apparel, footwear, and accessories to independent distributors in Australia, New Zealand, and Taiwan in 2014; these distributors were responsible for securing retail accounts to merchandise Under Armour products to consumers. The distribution of Under Armour products to retail accounts across Asia was handled by a third-party logistics provider based in Hong Kong.

In 2013, Under Armour organized its international activities into four geographic regions—North America (the United States and Canada), Latin

America, Asia-Pacific, and Europe/Middle East/ Africa (EMEA). In the company's 2013 Annual Report, Kevin Plank said, "We are committed to being a global brand with global stories to tell, and we are on our way."[16] Sales of Under Armour products in EMEA, the Asia-Pacific, and Latin America accounted for 25.8 percent of Under Armour's total net revenues in 2018, up from 11.5 percent in 2015, and 8.7 percent in 2014. Under Armour saw growth in foreign sales as the company's biggest market opportunity in upcoming years, chiefly because of the sheer number of people residing outside the United States who could be attracted to patronize the Under Armour brand. In 2017 Nike generated about 53 percent of its revenues outside North America, and adidas got about 70 percent of its sales outside its home market of Western Europe and 80 percent outside of North America—these big international sales percentages for Nike and adidas were a big reason why Under Armour executives were confident that growing UA's international sales represented an enormous market opportunity for the company, despite the stiff competition it could expect from its two bigger global rivals.

One of Under Armour's chief initiatives to build international awareness of the Under Armour brand and rapidly grow its sales internationally was to open growing numbers of stores in popular factory outlet malls and to locate Brand Houses in visible, high-traffic locations in major cities. UA had 37 factory outlet stores and 35 Brand Houses at year-end 2016, 57 factory outlet stores and 57 Brand House stores in international locations as of year-end 2017, and a total of 76 factory outlet and 76 Brand House stores in various locations in Canada, China, Chile, and Mexico as of March 31, 2019. In October 2018, UA sold its Brazilian subsidiary and entered into a license and distribution agreement with a third party to continue to sell UA products in Brazil.

Product Design and Development

Top executives believed that product innovation—as concerns both technical design and aesthetic design— was the key to driving Under Armour's sales growth and building a stronger brand name.

UA products were manufactured with technically advanced specialty fabrics produced by third parties.

The company's product development team collaborated closely with fabric suppliers to ensure that the fabrics and materials used in UA's products had the desired performance and fit attributes. Under Armour regularly upgraded its products as next-generation fabrics with better performance characteristics became available and as the needs of athletes changed. Product development efforts also aimed at broadening the company's product offerings in both new and existing product categories and market segments. An effort was made to design products with "visible technology," utilizing color, texture, and fabrication that would enhance customers' perception and understanding of the use and benefits of Under Armour products.

Under Armour's product development team had significant prior industry experience at leading fabric and other raw material suppliers and branded athletic apparel and footwear companies throughout the world. The team worked closely with Under Armour's sports marketing and sales teams as well as professional and collegiate athletes to identify product trends and determine market needs. Collaboration among the company's product development, sales, and sports marketing team had proved important in identifying the opportunity and market for five recently launched product lines and fabric technologies:

- CHARGED COTTON™ products, which were made from natural cotton but performed like the products made from technically advanced synthetic fabrics, drying faster and wicking moisture away from the body.
- STORM Fleece products, which had a unique, water-resistant finish that repelled water without stifling airflow.
- Products with a COLDBLACK® technology fabric that repelled heat from the sun and kept the wearer cooler outside.
- ColdGear® Infrared, a ceramic print technology applied to the inside of garments that provided wearers with lightweight warmth.
- UA HOVR™, a proprietary underfoot cushioning wrapped in a mesh web, equipped with a MapMyRun powered sensor designed to deliver energy return and real-time coaching.

In 2017 Under Armour opened its newest center for footwear performance innovation located in Portland, Oregon, bringing together footwear design and development teams in a centralized location.

Sourcing, Manufacturing, and Quality Assurance

Many of the high-tech specialty fabrics and other raw materials used in UA products were developed by third parties and sourced from a limited number of preapproved specialty fabric manufacturers; no fabrics were manufactured in-house. Under Armour executives believed outsourcing fabric production enabled the company to seek out and utilize whichever fabric suppliers were able to produce the latest and best performance-oriented fabrics to Under Armour's specifications, while also freeing more time for UA's product development staff to concentrate on upgrading the performance, styling, and overall appeal of existing products and expanding the company's overall lineup of product offerings.

In 2018, approximately 49 percent of the fabric used in UA products came from five suppliers, with primary locations in Malaysia, Taiwan, Vietnam, Turkey, and Mexico. Because a big fraction of the materials used in UA products were petroleum-based synthetics, fabric costs were subject to crude oil price fluctuations. The cotton fabrics used in the CHARGED COTTON™ products were also subject to price fluctuations and varying availability based on cotton harvests.

In 2017, substantially all UA products were made by 44 primary contract manufacturers, operating in 16 countries; 10 manufacturers produced approximately 55 percent of UA's products. Approximately 58 percent of UA's apparel and accessories products were manufactured in Jordan, Vietnam, China, and Malaysia. Under Armour's footwear products were made by five primary contract manufacturers operating primarily in Vietnam, China, and Indonesia; these five manufacturers produced approximately 87 percent of the company's footwear products.

All contract manufacturers making Under Armour apparel products purchased the fabrics they needed from the five fabric suppliers preapproved by Under Armour. All of the makers of UA products across all divisions were evaluated for quality systems, social compliance, and financial strength by Under Armour's quality assurance team, prior to being selected and also on an ongoing basis. The company strived to qualify multiple manufacturers for particular product types and fabrications and to seek out contractors that could perform multiple manufacturing stages, such as procuring raw materials and providing finished products, which helped UA control its cost of goods sold. All contract manufacturers were required to adhere to a code of conduct regarding quality of manufacturing, working conditions, and other social concerns. However, the company had no long-term agreements requiring it to continue to use the services of any manufacturer, and no manufacturer was obligated to make products for UA on a long-term basis. UA had subsidiaries strategically located near its manufacturing partners to support its manufacturing, quality assurance, and sourcing efforts for its products.

Under Armour had a 17,000-square-foot Special Make-Up Shop located at one of its distribution facilities in Maryland where it had the capability to make and ship customized apparel products on tight deadlines for high-profile athletes and teams. While these apparel products represented a tiny fraction of Under Armour's revenues, management believed the facility helped provide superior service to select customers.

Inventory Management

Under Armour based the amount of inventory it needed to have on hand for each item in its product line on existing orders, anticipated sales, and the rapid delivery requirements of customers. Its inventory strategy was focused on (1) having sufficient inventory to fill incoming orders promptly and (2) putting strong systems and procedures in place to improve the efficiency with which it managed its inventories of individual products and total inventory. The amounts of seasonal products it ordered from manufacturers were based on current bookings, the need to ship seasonal items at the start of the shipping window in order to maximize the floor space productivity of retail customers, the need to adequately stock its Factory House and Brand House stores, and the need to fill customer orders. Excess inventories of particular products were either shipped to its Factory House stores or earmarked for sale to third-party liquidators.

However, the growing number of individual items in UA's product line and uncertainties surrounding upcoming consumer demand for individual items made it difficult to accurately forecast how many units to order from manufacturers and what the appropriate stocking requirements were for many items. New inventory management practices were instituted in 2012 to better cope with stocking requirements for individual items and avoid excessive inventory buildups. Year-end inventories of $1.16 billion in 2017 equated to 154.6 days of inventory and inventory turnover of 2.36 turns per year. UA's description of its restructuring plans in 2017 signaled that inventory reduction initiatives were included. Year-end inventories of $1.02 billion in 2018 equated to 130.4 days of inventory and inventory turnover of 2.80 turns per year.

Competition

The $280 billion global market for sports apparel, athletic footwear, and related accessories was fragmented among some 25 brand-name competitors with diverse product lines and varying geographic coverage and numerous small competitors with specialized-use apparel lines that usually operated within a single country or geographic region. Industry participants included athletic and leisure shoe companies, athletic and leisure apparel companies, sports equipment companies, and large companies having diversified lines of athletic and leisure shoes, apparel, and equipment. The global market for athletic footwear was projected to reach $114.8 billion by 2022, growing at a CAGR of 2.1 percent during the period 2016 to 2022.[17] The global market for athletic and fitness apparel was forecast to grow about 4.3 percent annually from 2015 to 2020 and reach about $185

EXHIBIT 4

Major Competitors and Brands in Selected Segments of the Sports Apparel, Athletic Footwear, and Accessory Industry, 2019

Performance Apparel for Sports (baseball, football, basketball, softball, volleyball, hockey, lacrosse, soccer, track & field, and other action sports)
- Nike
- Under Armour
- Adidas
- Eastbay
- Russell

Performance Activewear and Sports-Inspired Lifestyle Apparel
- Polo Ralph Lauren
- Lacoste
- Izod
- Cutter & Buck
- Timberland
- Columbia
- Puma
- Li Ning
- Many others

Performance-Driven Athletic Footwear
- Nike
- Adidas
- New Balance
- Reebok
- Saucony
- Puma
- Rockport
- Converse
- Ryka
- Asics
- Li Ning

Performance Skiwear
- Salomon
- North Face
- Descente
- Columbia
- Patagonia
- Marmot
- Helly Hansen
- Bogner
- Spyder
- Many others

Training/Fitness Clothing
- Nike
- Under Armour
- Adidas
- Puma
- Fila
- Lululemon athletica
- Champion
- Asics
- Eastbay
- SUGOI
- Li Ning

Performance Golf Apparel
- Footjoy
- Nike
- Adidas
- Under Armour
- Polo Golf
- Ashworth
- Cutter & Buck
- Greg Norman
- Puma
- Many others

billion by 2020.[18] Exhibit 4 shows a representative sample of the best-known companies and brands in selected segments of the sports apparel, athletic footwear, and sports equipment industry.

From 2017 to 2019, consumers across the world shopped for the industry's products digitally (online) or physically in stores. And they shopped either for a favorite brand or for multibrand. The trend was for more consumers to shop digitally and for a brand deemed to be the best or their favorite. Multibrand shoppers typically wanted to explore and compare the options, either through a dot-com experience or in stores where they could view the products firsthand, get advice or personalized assistance, and/or get the product immediately.

As Exhibit 4 indicates, the sporting goods industry consisted of many distinct product categories and market segments. Because the product mixes of different companies varied considerably, it was common for the product offerings of industry participants to be extensive in some segments, moderate in others, and limited to nonexistent in still others. Consequently, the leading competitors and the intensity of competition varied significantly from market segment to market segment. Nonetheless, competition tended to be intense in most every segment with substantial sales volume and typically revolved around performance and reliability, the breadth of product selection, new product development, price, brand name strength and identity through marketing and promotion, the ability of companies to convince retailers to stock and effectively merchandise their brands, and the capabilities of the various industry participants to sell directly to consumers through their own retail/factory outlet stores and/or at their company websites. It was common for the leading companies selling athletic footwear, sports uniforms, and sports equipment to actively sponsor sporting events and clinics and to contract with prominent and influential athletes, coaches, professional sports teams, colleges, and sports leagues to endorse their brands and use their products.

Nike was the clear global market leader in the sporting goods industry, with a global market share in athletic footwear of about 25 percent and a sports apparel share of 5 percent. The adidas Group, with businesses that produced athletic footwear, sports uniforms, fitness apparel, sportswear, and a variety of sports equipment and marketed them across the world, was the second largest global competitor. These two major competitors of Under Armour are profiled as follows.

Nike, Inc.

Incorporated in 1968, Nike was the dominant global leader in the design, development, and worldwide marketing and selling of footwear, sports apparel, sports equipment, and accessory products. Nike was a truly global brand, with a broader and deeper portfolio of products, models, and styles than any other industry participant. The company had 2018 global sales of $36.4 billion and net income of $1.9 billion in fiscal year ending May 31, 2018; 2018 net income was 55 percent below the $4.2 billion in net income reported in fiscal year 2017. Nike was the world's largest seller of footwear with Nike-branded sales of $22.3 billion and Converse-branded sales of $1.9 billion; it held the number-one market share in all markets and in all categories of athletic footwear (its running shoe business alone had sales of $5.3 billion). Nike's footwear line included some 1,500 models/styles. Nike was also the world's largest sports apparel brand, with 2018 sales of $10.7 billion. Sales of Nike products to women reached $7 billion in 2017 and approached $7.5 billion in 2018.

Nike's strategy in 2017 and 2018 was driven by three core beliefs. One was that the growing popularity of sports and active lifestyles reflected a desire to lead healthier lives. As a result, companies like Nike were becoming more relevant for more moments in people's lives because of their growing participation in calorie-burning, wellness, and fitness activities and because active lifestyles stimulated greater interest in sports-related activities and sports events. Moreover, streaming of sports events and social media were changing the ways people consumed sports content. The NBA, for example, had over 1.3 billion social media followers across the league, teams, and player pages. The growth of watching streamed events on mobile phones was exploding. Second, in a connected, mobile-led world, consumers had become infinitely better informed and, thus, more powerful because of the information they could access in seconds and the options this opened up—"powered consumers" were prone to consult their phones (or conduct Internet searches on other devices) for price comparisons and availability before deciding where to shop or what to purchase online. Third, the world was operating at faster speeds and the numbers of powered consumers was about to explode. Nike's CEO expected over 2 billion digitally connected people in markets in China, India, and Latin America would join the middle class by 2030. In North America, Nike estimated that its primary consumer base was 50 million people, but that if population trends in China continued at the expected rate, Nike's projected consumer base in China would be more than 500 million people by 2030.

For years, the heart and soul of Nike's strategy had been creating innovative products and powerful storytelling that produced an emotional connection with consumers and caused them to gravitate to purchase Nike products. But at the same time Nike executives understood that brand strength had to be earned every day by satisfying consumer needs and meeting, if not exceeding, their expectations. Exhibit 5 shows Nike's worldwide retail and distribution network at the end of fiscal 2018.

In October 2017, Nike CEO Mark Parker provided a brief overview of the company's "Triple Double" strategy that had three components: 2X Innovation, 2X Speed, and 2X Direct:

> In 2X Innovation, we will lead with more distinct platforms, moving from seeding to scaling a lot

faster. We'll . . . give consumers better choices to match their preferences. And we'll set a new expectation for style, creating a new aesthetic to wear in all moments of their lives. To the consumer, there is no trade-off between sport and style. We know that more than half of the athletic footwear and apparel is bought for nonsport activities, and we have even more room to grow in this market.

In 2X Speed, we're investing in digital end to end to serve this insatiable consumer demand for new and fresh products. To use a sports analogy, you can't run an up-tempo offense if only half your plays are designed for speed. So we're building new capabilities and analytics to deliver personalized products in real time, and we're engaging with more partners companywide to move faster against our goals. In our supply chain, we've joined forces with leading robotics and automation companies, and we're serving millions of athletes and sports fans faster through manufacturing bases that are closer to our North American consumer. 2X Speed is really all about delivering the right product in the moment, 100 percent of the time.

We never ever take the strength of our brand and premium product for granted. They are indeed our most valuable assets. With 2X Direct [to Consumer], we want as many Nike touch points as possible to live up to those expectations, and that's why we are investing heavily in our own channel and leading with digital. And with our strategic partners, we'll move resources away from undifferentiated retail and toward environments where we can better control with distinct consumer experiences.[19]

Nike's Worldwide Retail and Distribution Network, 2018

United States	Foreign Countries
• ~15,000 retail accounts	• ~15,000 retail accounts
• 220 Nike factory outlet stores	• 664 Nike factory outlet stores
• 31 Nike and NIKETOWN stores	• 65 Nike and NIKETOWN stores
• 112 Converse retail and factory outlet stores	• 61 Converse retail and factory outlet stores
• 29 Hurley stores	• 62 Distribution centers
• 8 Primary distribution centers	• Independent distributors and licensees in over 190 countries
• Company website (www.nike.com)	• 5 websites

Principal Products Nike's 1,500 athletic footwear models and styles were designed primarily for specific athletic use, although many were worn for casual or leisure purposes. Running, training, basketball, soccer, sport-inspired casual shoes, and kids' shoes were the company's top-selling footwear categories. It also marketed footwear designed for baseball, football, golf, lacrosse, cricket, outdoor activities, tennis, volleyball, walking, and wrestling. The company designed and marketed Nike-branded sports apparel and accessories for most all of these same sports categories, as well as sports-inspired lifestyle apparel, athletic bags, and accessory items. Footwear, apparel, and accessories were often marketed in "collections" of similar design or for specific

purposes. It also marketed apparel with licensed college and professional team and league logos. Nike-brand offerings in sports equipment included bags, socks, sport balls, eyewear, timepieces, electronic devices, bats, gloves, protective equipment, and golf clubs. Nike was also the owner of the Converse brand of athletic footwear and the Hurley brand of swimwear, assorted other apparel items, and surfing gear.

Exhibit 6 shows a breakdown of Nike's sales of footwear, apparel, and equipment by geographic region for fiscal years 2015 to 2017.

Marketing, Promotions, and Endorsements
Nike responded to trends and shifts in consumer preferences by (1) adjusting the mix of existing product

EXHIBIT 6

Nike's Sales of Nike Brand Footwear, Apparel, and Equipment, by Geographic Region and by Wholesale and Nike Direct, Fiscal Years 2016–2018

	FISCAL YEAR ENDING MAY 31		
Sales Revenues and Earnings (in millions)	2018	2017	2016
North America			
Revenues—Nike Brand footwear	$ 9,322	$ 9,684	$ 9,299
Nike Brand apparel	4,938	4,866	4,746
Nike Brand equipment	595	646	719
Total Nike Brand revenues	$14,855	$15,216	$14,764
Sales to wholesale customers	10,159	10,756	10,674
Sales through Nike Direct	4,696	4,460	4,090
Earnings before interest and taxes	$3,600	$ 3,875	$ 3,763
Profit margin	24.2%	25.6%	25.5%
Europe, Middle East, and Africa			
Revenues—Nike Brand footwear	$ 5,875	$ 5,192	$ 5,043
Nike Brand apparel	2,940	2,395	2,149
Nike Brand equipment	427	383	376
Total Nike Brand revenues	9,242	$ 7,970	$ 7,568
Sales to wholesale customers	6,765	5,917	5,869
Sales through Nike Direct	2,477	2,053	1,699
Earnings before interest and taxes	1,587	$ 1,507	$ 1,787
Profit margin	17.2%	18.9%	23.6%
Greater China			
Revenues—Nike Brand footwear	$ 3,496	$ 2,920	$ 2,599
Nike Brand apparel	1,508	1,188	1,055
Nike Brand equipment	130	129	131
Total Nike Brand revenues	$ 5,134	$ 4,237	$ 3,785
Sales to wholesale customers	3,216	2,774	2,623
Sales through Nike Direct	1,918	1,463	1,162
Earnings before interest and taxes	$ 1,807	$ 1,507	$ 1,372
Profit margin	35.2%	35.6%	36.2%

Sales Revenues and Earnings (in millions)	FISCAL YEAR ENDING MAY 31		
	2018	2017	2016
Asia Pacific and Latin America			
Revenues—Nike Brand footwear	$ 3,575	$ 3,285	$ 2,930
Nike Brand apparel	1,347	1,185	1,117
Nike Brand equipment	244	267	270
Total Nike Brand revenues	$ 5,166	$ 4,737	$ 4,317
Sales to wholesale customers	3,829	3,631	3,411
Sales through Nike Direct	1,337	1,106	906
Earnings before interest and taxes	$ 1,189	$ 980	$ 1,022
Profit margin	23.0%	19.8%	23.7%
All Regions			
Revenues—Nike Brand footwear	$22,268	$21,081	$19,871
Nike Brand apparel	10,733	9,654	9,067
Nike Brand equipment	1,396	1,425	1,496
Global Brand Divisions	88	73	73
Total Nike Brand revenues	$34,485	$32,233	$30,507
Sales to wholesale customers	23,969	23,078	22,577
Sales through Nike Direct	6,332	9,082	7,857
Corporate expenses	(1,456)	(724)	(1,173)
Total Nike earnings before interest and taxes	$ 4,379	$ 4,945	$ 4,642
Profit margin	12.7%	15.3%	15.2%
Converse			
Revenues	$ 1,886	$ 2,042	$ 1,955
Earnings before interest and taxes	310	477	487
Profit margin	16.4%	23.4%	24.9%

Note: The revenue and earnings figures for all geographic regions include the effects of currency exchange fluctuations. The Nike Brand revenues for equipment include the Hurley brand, and the Nike Brand revenues for footwear include the Jordan brand. The earnings before interest and taxes figures associated with Total Nike Brand Revenues include those for the Hurley and Jordan brands.

Source: Nike, Inc., 2018 Annual Report and Notice of Annual Meeting, accessed August 2, 2019, https://s1.q4cdn.com/806093406/files/doc_financials/2018/ar/docs/nike-2018-form-10K.pdf.

offerings, (2) developing new products, styles, and categories, and (3) striving to influence sports and fitness preferences through aggressive marketing, promotional activities, sponsorships, and athlete endorsements. Nike spent $3.34 billion in fiscal 2017 (as compared to $2.75 billion in 2013) for what it termed "demand creation expense" that included the costs of advertising, promotional activities, and endorsement contracts. Well over 500 professional, collegiate, club, and Olympic sports teams in football, basketball, baseball, ice hockey, soccer, rugby, speed skating, tennis, swimming, and other sports wore Nike uniforms with the Nike swoosh prominently visible. There were over 1,000 prominent professional athletes with Nike endorsement

contracts in 2011–2017, including former basketball great Michael Jordan; NFL player Drew Brees; NBA players LeBron James, Kobe Bryant, Kevin Durant, and Dwayne Wade; professional golfers Tiger Woods and Michelle Wie; soccer player Cristiano Ronaldo; and professional tennis players Venus and Serena Williams, Roger Federer, and Rafael Nadal. When Tiger Woods turned pro, Nike signed him to a five-year $100 million endorsement contract and made him the centerpiece of its campaign to make Nike a factor in the golf equipment and golf apparel marketplace. Nike's long-standing endorsement relationship with Michael Jordan led to the introduction of the highly popular line of Air Jordan footwear and, more recently, to the launch of the Jordan brand of athletic shoes, clothing, and gear. In 2003 LeBron James signed an endorsement deal with Nike worth $90 million over seven years, and in 2015 he signed a lifetime deal with Nike. Because soccer was such a popular sport globally, Nike had more endorsement contracts with soccer athletes than with athletes in any other sport; track and field athletes had the second largest number of endorsement contracts.

Resources and Capabilities Nike had an incredibly deep pool of valuable resources and capabilities that enhanced its competitive power in the marketplace and helped spur product innovation, shorten speed-to-market, enable customers to use digital tools to customize the colors and styling of growing numbers of Nike products, and thereby drive strong brand attachment and sales growth. Examples of these included the following:

- The company's Nike APP and the SNKRS app were in more than 20 countries across North America and Europe, plus China and Japan, countries that drove close to 90 percent of Nike's growth. These apps provided easy access to Nike products and were becoming a popular way for customers to shop Nike products and make online purchases. The Nike App was the number-one mono-brand retail app in the United States. Nike's apps and growing digital product ecosystem were key components of the company's 2X Speed strategy to operate faster and get innovative products in the hands of consumers faster.

- The creation and ongoing enhancement of the NikePlus membership program which in 2017 connected 100 million consumers to Nike—NikePlus members who used the company's mobile apps spent more than three times as much time on nike.com as other site visitors. Starting in 2018, NikePlus members were entitled to "reserved-for-you service" that used machine learning-powered algorithms to set aside products in a member's size that the algorithms predicted members would like. Members could also use a "reserved-by-you" service to gain guaranteed access to products they wanted; this newly developed capability was deemed especially valuable to members wanting a recently

introduced product in high demand. In 2018, Nike began accelerating invitations to NikePlus members to personalized events and experiences and extending benefits and offers from NikePlus partners like Apple Music, Headspace, and Class Pass. Special Nike Unlock offers were sent to members once a month. Nike expected that NikePlus membership would triple over the next five years. Nike executives anticipated that converting consumers into NikePlus members would heighten their relationship to and connection with Nike.

- The establishment of an Advanced Product Creation Center charged with keeping the pipeline flowing with product innovations, new digital products, and manufacturing innovations to make 2X Speed a reality. Nike was aggressively investing in 3D modeling and other related technology to quickly create prototypes of new products; with traditional technology, it often took 4 to 6 months to go from new idea-to-design-to-product prototype. So far, Nike had been able to go from design, to prototyping, to manufacturing, to delivery in less than 6 months, as compared to 9 to 12 months. Nike's goal was to improve its rapid prototyping capabilities to the point where 100 percent of new product innovations could be rapid-prototyped at the Advanced Product Creation Center in Portland, Oregon. Employee athletes, athletes engaged under sports marketing contracts, and other athletes wear-tested and evaluated products during the development and prototyping process.

- A relaunch of all 40+ nike.com websites in late 2017 that featured a new design with better visual appeal and functionality, more storytelling, eye-catching product displays, and better product descriptions—all aimed at generating more visitor traffic, longer shopping times, increased online sales, and achieving 2X Direct.

- Implementing robot-assisted manufacturing capabilities and other recently developed manufacturing innovations (such as oscillating knives, laser cutting and trimming, phylon mold transfer, and computerized stitching) on a broad scale. In one instance, the use of advanced robotics and digitization techniques was generating a continuous, automated flow of the upper portion of a footwear model with 30 percent fewer steps, 50 percent less labor, and less waste in just 30 seconds per shoe—a total of 1,200 automated robots had been installed to perform an assortment of activities at various manufacturing facilities in 2017. In another instance, Nike had made manufacturing breakthroughs in producing the bottoms of its footwear (the midsoles and outsoles) using innovative techniques capable of delivering a pair of midsoles and outsoles, on average, in 2.5 minutes, compared to more than 50 minutes with previously used techniques. This new process used 75 percent less energy, entailed 50 percent less tooling cost, and enabled a 60 percent reduction in labor.

- Revamped supply chain practices that had shortened the lead times from manufacturing to market availability from 60 days to 10 days in one instance and from six to nine months to three months in other instances.

- Creating a digital technology called Nike iD, whereby customers could go to Nike iD, design their own customized version of a product (say a pair of Free Run Flyknit shoes), view a prototype in an hour or so, have the shoes knitted to order, and get them delivered in 10 days or less.[20]

All of Nike's competitively valuable resources and capabilities were being dynamically managed; enhancements were made as fast as ways to improve could be developed and instituted and new capabilities were being added in an effort (1) to provide customers with a better "Nike Experience" and (2) to respond faster to ongoing changes in consumer preferences and expectations. Collaborative efforts were under way in Nike's organizational units to transfer new or enhanced resources and capabilities to all seven of the company's product categories and also extend them to all geographic regions and countries where Nike had a market presence. The goal was to mobilize Nike's resources and capabilities to produce an enduring competitive advantage over rivals and give customers the best possible experience in purchasing and using Nike products.

Manufacturing   In fiscal year 2018, Nike sourced its athletic footwear from 124 factories in 13 countries. About 94 percent of Nike's footwear was produced by independent contract manufacturers in Vietnam, China, and Indonesia but the company had manufacturing agreements with independent factories in Argentina, Brazil, India, Italy, and Mexico to manufacture footwear for sale primarily within those countries. Nike-branded apparel was manufactured outside of the United States by 328 independent contract manufacturers located in 37 countries; most of the apparel production occurred in China, Vietnam, Thailand, Indonesia, Sri Lanka, Malaysia, and Cambodia. The top five contract manufacturers accounted for approximately 47 percent of NIKE Brand apparel production.

The adidas Group

The mission of The adidas Group was to be the best sports company in the world. Headquartered in Germany, its businesses and brands in 2018 consisted of:

- Adidas—a designer and marketer of active sportswear, uniforms, footwear, and sports products in football, basketball, soccer, running, training, outdoor, and six other categories (90.6 percent of Group sales in 2018). The mission at adidas was to be the best sports brand in the world.

- Reebok—a well-known global provider of athletic footwear for multiple uses, sports and fitness apparel, and accessories (7.7 percent of Group sales in 2018). The mission at Reebok was to be the best fitness brand in the world.

- Other businesses (1.7 percent of Group sales in 2018)—these sales represented 2018 sales of businesses whose earlier divestitures were not fully completed until early 2018.

Exhibit 7 shows the company's financial highlights for 2016 to 2017. In 2016–2017, the company divested five businesses—TaylorMade Golf, Adams Golf, Ashworth brand sports apparel, CCR Hockey, and Rockport brand shoes—to focus all of its resources on achieving faster and more profitable sales growth in both its adidas and Reebok businesses.

The company sold products in virtually every country of the world. In 2018, its extensive product

EXHIBIT 7

Financial Highlights for The adidas Group, 2016–2018 (in millions of €)

Income Statement Data	2018	2017	2016
Net sales	€21,915	€21,218	€18,483
Gross profit	11,363	10,703	9,100
Gross profit margin	51.8%	50.4%	49.2%
Operating profit	2,882	2,070	1,582
Operating profit margin	10.8%	9.8%	8.6%
Net income	€1,702	€1,173	€1,017
Net profit margin	7.8%	5.5%	5.5%
Balance Sheet Data			
Inventories	€3,445	€3,692	€3,763
Working capital	3,563	4,033	3,468
Net sales by brand			
adidas	€19,851	€18,993	€16,334
Reebok	1,687	1,843	1,770
Net sales by product			
Footwear	€12,783	€12,427	€10,132
Apparel	8,223	7,747	7,352
Equipment*	910	1,044	999
Net sales by region			
Western Europe	€5,885	€5,932	€4,275
North America	4,689	4,275	3,412
Asia Pacific**	7,161	6,403	Not reported
Latin America	1,634	1,907	1,731
Emerging Markets***	1,144	1,300	Not reported
Russia and Commonwealth of Independent States	595	660	679

* In 2017, the company completed the previously announced divestitures of its TaylorMade Golf, Adams Golf, Ashworth, and CCM Hockey businesses. In 2016, the company completed its divestiture of its Rockport brand shoe business.

** The company redefined the countries included in the Asia Pacific Region in 2018 and did not report sales data for this region prior to 2017.

***Consists mainly of countries in the Middle East and Africa. Data for this region (which was newly defined in 2018) was not reported for years prior to 2017.

Source: "Annual Report 2018," Adidas, https://report.adidas-group.com/fileadmin/user_upload/adidas_Annual_Report_GB-2018-EN.pdf.

offerings were marketed through thousands of third-party retailers (sporting goods chains, department stores, independent sporting goods retailer buying groups, and lifestyle retailing chains—with a combined total of 150,000 locations worldwide, and Internet retailers), 2,395 company-owned retail stores, 13,000 franchised adidas and Reebok branded stores with varying formats, and company websites (www.adidas.com and www.reebok.com) in 40 countries.

Like Under Armour and Nike, both adidas and Reebok were actively engaged in sponsoring major sporting events, teams, and leagues and in using athlete endorsements to promote their products. Recent high-profile sponsorships and promotional partnerships included numerous professional soccer and rugby teams, sports teams at the University of Miami, Arizona State University, and Texas A&M University; FIFA World Cup events; the Summer and Winter Olympics; the Boston Marathon and London

Marathon; and official outfitters of items for assorted professional sports leagues (NBA, NHL, NFL, and MLB) and teams. High-profile athletes that were under contract to endorse adidas and Reebok products included NBA players James Harden, Derrick Rose, and Damian Lillard; soccer players David Beckham and Lionel Messi; NFL players Aaron Rodgers, C.J. Spiller, Robert Griffin III, Demarco Murray, Landon Collins, and Von Miller; MLB players Chase Utley, brothers B.J. and Justin Upton, Carlos Correa, Josh Harrison, and Chris Bryant; and tennis star Naomi Osaka. It had also signed non-sports celebrities Kanye West and Pharrell. In 2003, soccer star David Beckham, who had been wearing adidas products since the age of 12, signed a $160 million lifetime endorsement deal with adidas that called for an immediate payment of $80 million and subsequent payments said to be worth an average of $2 million annually for the next 40 years.[21] Adidas was anxious to sign Beckham to a lifetime deal not only to prevent Nike from trying to sign him but also because soccer was considered the world's most lucrative sport and adidas management believed that Beckham's endorsement of adidas products resulted in more sales than all of the company's other athlete endorsements combined. Companywide expenditures for marketing, advertising, event sponsorships, athlete endorsements, public relations, and point-of-sale activities were €3.00 billion in 2018 (13.7 percent of net sales) versus €2.72 billion in 2017 (12.8 percent of net sales).

In 2015–2017, adidas launched a number of initiatives to become more America-centric and regain its number-two market position lost to Under Armour in 2015. This included a campaign to sign up to 250 National Football League players and 250 Major League Baseball players over the next three years. It had secured 1,100 new retail accounts that involved prominent displays of freshly styled adidas products and newly introduced running shoes with high-tech features. The adidas brand regained its number-two position in the United States in 2017.

Research and development activities commanded considerable emphasis at The adidas Group. Management had long stressed the critical importance of innovation in improving the performance characteristics of its products. New apparel and footwear collections featuring new fabrics, colors, and the latest fashion were introduced on an ongoing basis to heighten consumer interest, as well as to provide performance enhancements—indeed, in 2018, 74 percent of sales at adidas came from products launched in 2018 (versus 79 percent in 2017); at Reebok, 67 percent of sales came from products launched in 2018 (versus 69 percent in 2017).

Some 1,041 people (1.8 percent of total employees) were engaged in research and development (R&D) activities in 2018; in addition, the company drew upon the services of well-regarded researchers at universities in Canada, the United States, England, and Germany. R&D expenditures in 2018 were €153 million versus €187 million in 2017, €149 million in 2016, €139 million in 2015, and €126 million in 2014.

Over 95 percent of production was outsourced to 130 independent contract manufacturers that produced in 289 manufacturing facilities; these manufacturing sites were located in China and other Asian countries (71 percent), Europe (5 percent), the Americas (18 percent), and Africa (6 percent). The Group operated 10 relatively small production and assembly sites of its own in Germany (1), Sweden (1), Finland (1), the United States (4), and Canada (3). In 2018, 97 percent of the Group's production of footwear was performed in Asia (Vietnam was the largest sourcing country with 42 percent); annual volume sourced from footwear suppliers had ranged from a low of 256 million pairs to a high of 409 million pairs during 2013–2018. In 2018, 91 percent of total apparel volume was produced in Asia, with Cambodia being the largest sourcing country (24 percent) followed by China with 19 percent and Vietnam with 18 percent. The remaining 9 percent came from the Americas (4 percent), Europe (4 percent), and Africa (1 percent). During 2013–2018, apparel production ranged from 292 million to 457 million units and the production of hardware products ranged from 94 million to 113 million units. In all three categories, the largest production volumes occurred in 2018.

The company was stepping up its investments in company-owned, robot-intensive micro-factories to speed certain products to key geographic markets in Europe and the United States much faster and to also lower production costs and boost gross profit margins. At the same time, the company had begun reengineering its existing supply chain and production processes to enable the company to respond quicker to shifts in buyer preferences, be able to reorder seasonal products and sell them to buyers within the season, and to reduce the time it took to get freshly designed products manufactured and into the marketplace.

Executives at The adidas Group expected that the Group's global sales would increase between 5 and 8 percent in 2019; management also wanted to achieve a 2019 operating margin of 11 percent, and grow 2019 net income to about €1.9 billion. Financial highlights for 2016–2018 are shown in Exhibit 7.

ENDNOTES

1 "Under Armour Reports Third Quarter Net Revenues Growth of 22%; Reiterates Full Year Net Revenues Outlook of $4.925 Billion," Press Release, Under Armour, Inc., October 25, 2016, http://investor.underarmour.com/news-releases/news-release-details/under-armour-reports-third-quarter-net-revenues-growth-22.

2 Company press release, January 31, 2017.

3 "Under Armour Reports Fourth Quarter and Full Year Results; Announces Outlook for 2017," Press Release, Under Armour, Inc., January 31, 2019, http://investor.underarmour.com/news-releases/news-release-details/under-armour-reports-fourth-quarter-and-full-year-results.

4 Douglas A. McIntyre and Jon C. Ogg, "20 Worst CEOs in America 2017," December 26, 2017, https://247wallst.com (accessed February 22, 2017).

5 Nike's fiscal year runs from June 1 to May 31, so Nike's reported sales from December 1, 2016, through November 30, 2017 (its last two quarters of fiscal 2017 and first two quarters of fiscal 2018), represent a reasonable approximation of its sales in North America and its sales globally during the months of 2017.

6 Sara Germano, "Under Armour Overtakes Adidas in the U.S. Sportswear Market," Wall Street Journal, January 8, 2015, www.wsj.com (accessed April 19, 2016).

7 "Mission Statement: About Under Armour," Under Armour, Inc., https://www.underarmour.co.uk/en-gb/about-under-armour.html.

8 "Under Armour, Inc. (UAA) CEO Kevin Plank on Q4 2018 Results - Earnings Call Transcript," Seeking Alpha, February 12, 2019, https://seekingalpha.com/article/4240252-armour-inc-uaa-ceo-kevin-plank-q4-2018-results-earnings-call-transcript.

9 "Under Armour, Inc. (UAA) CEO Kevin Plank on Q4 2018 Results - Earnings Call Transcript." Seeking Alpha, February 12, 2019. https://seekingalpha.com/article/4240252-armour-inc-uaa-ceo-kevin-plank-q4-2018-results-earnings-call-transcript.

10 Presentation by Paul Phipps, UA's Chief Technology and Digital Officer, at Under Armour's Investor Day, December 12, 2018.

11 Dennis Green, "Kevin Durant: 'No One Wants to Play in Under Armour' Shoes," Business Insider, August 30, 2017, www.businessinsider.com (accessed February 22, 2018).

12 Nate Scott, "James Harden Signs 13-year, $200 Million Deal with adidas after Nike Opts Not to Match," USA Today, August 13, 2015, www.usatoday.com (accessed February 21, 2018).

13 Company 10-K Reports, 2014, 2015, 2016, 2017, and 2018.

14 Company 10-K report for 2018.

15 Presentation by Jason LaRose, UA's President-North America Region, at Under Armour's Investor Day, December 12, 2018.

16 "2013 Under Armour Annual Report," Under Armour, Inc. 2013, http://investor.underarmour.com/static-files/57b70adf-cb2c-498c-a95b-b099b6a7d8f9.

17 According to Allied Market Research, "Athletic Footwear Market—Report," published June 2016, www.alliedmarketresearch.com.

18 Allied Market Research, "Sports Apparel Market—Report," published October 2015, www.alliedmarketresearch.com.

19 "Q114 Earning Transcript," Nike Investor Day 2017, Nike, Inc, https://s1.q4cdn.com/806093406/files/doc_events/2017/10/updtd/NIKE-Inc.-2017-Investor-Day-Transcript-With-Q-A-FINAL.pdf.

20 Transcript of presentations by Nike's top executives at "Nike Investor Day 2017," October 25, 2017, posted in the Investor Relations section of www.nike.com (accessed February 24, 2018).

21 Steve Seepersaud, "5 of the Biggest Athlete Endorsement Deals," www.askmen.com (accessed February 5, 2012).

IROBOT IN 2019: CAN THE COMPANY KEEP THE MAGIC?

DAVID L. TURNIPSEED *University of South Alabama*
JOHN E. GAMBLE *Texas A&M University–Corpus Christi*

Having the largest market share in a rapidly growing industry, controlling over 75 percent of global revenue, and experiencing record growth and sales in the latest fiscal year was a situation that most companies would find calming. In 2018, its second year as a consumer-focused company, iRobot reported a 24 percent increase in revenue and a 10 percent increase in operating profit over the prior year, after absorbing the impact of tariffs imposed in the fourth quarter 2018, and announced expectations for about 17 to 20 percent revenue growth in 2019, which would push revenue to $1.28 to $1.31 billion. The company's stock reached $130.57 on April 23, 2019, which was a 118 percent increase over the same date in 2018. Despite these successes, iRobot lost market share as the robotic vacuum industry moved from startup to mainstream. A summary of the company's financial performance between fiscal 2014 and fiscal 2018 is presented in Exhibit 1.

However, for the management team at iRobot, those metrics only served to help fine-tune and develop strategy to improve the company's performance and defend against several looming competitive threats. The company's focus was the design and manufacture of robots that empowered people to do more both inside and outside of the home. The iRobot consumer robots helped people find smarter ways to clean and accomplish more in their daily lives. iRobot's portfolio of robotic solutions featured proprietary technologies for the connected home and advanced concepts in cleaning, lawn mowing, mapping and navigation, human-robot interaction,

and physical solutions that moved the company beyond simple robotic vacuums. The company had announced a relationship with Amazon Web Services (AWS) that was believed to enable iRobot to address significant opportunities within the consumer business and the connected home. The AWS Cloud would allow devices to interact easily and securely and enable iRobot to scale the number of connected robots it supported globally and allow for increased capabilities in the smart home.

Although iRobot's recent past had been magical, the company faced significant headwinds. Global penetration of robotic vacuums was about 10 percent, and iRobot had about 60 percent market share in 2017, but several serious competitors had emerged, and in many cases, offered similar products at much lower prices, resulting in a loss of market share for the company of about 3 percent. iRobot had divested its military and industrial robots and had become a consumer company with two product lines—robotic floor cleaners and robotic lawn mowers. Also, customer privacy issues and the threat of data leaks from the company's robots' cameras and mapping feature had caused negative publicity. The company's CEO had ignited a furor when he announced that iRobot "could" reach an agreement to share data with Apple, Amazon, or Alphabet. Equally problematic, as the company moved into mid-2019, were unpredictable spikes in tariffs due to the U.S.-China trade problems, as well as market weaknesses including rising labor costs and weak protections for intellectual property.

EXHIBIT 1

Financial Summary for iRobot, Fiscal Year 2014–Fiscal Year 2018 (In thousands of $, except per share amounts)

	YEAR ENDED				
	December 29, 2018	December 30, 2017	December 31, 2016	January 2, 2016	December 27, 2014
Consolidated Statements of Income:					
Total revenue	$1,092,584	$883,911	$660,604	$616,778	$556,846
Gross profit	555,428	433,159	319,315	288,926	258,055
Operating income	105,822	72,690	57,557	60,618	53,117
Income tax expense	20,630	25,402	19,422	18,841	14,606
Net income	87,992	50,964	41,939	44,130	37,803
Net Income Per Share:					
Basic	$3.18	$1.85	$1.51	$1.49	$1.28
Diluted	$3.07	$1.77	$1.48	$1.47	$1.25
Shares Used in Per Share Calculations:					
Basic	27,692	27,611	27,698	29,550	29,485
Diluted	28,640	28,753	28,292	30,107	30,210
Consolidated Balance Sheet Data:					
Cash and cash equivalents	$130,373	$128,635	$214,523	$179,915	$185,957
Short term investments	31,605	37,225	39,930	33,124	36,166
Total assets	766,961	691,522	507,912	521,743	493,213
Total liabilities	231,639	221,195	118,956	104,332	102,777
Total stockholders' equity	535,322	470,327	388,956	417,411	390,436

Source: iRobot Corporation, 2018 Annual Report, April 8, 2019, https://investor.irobot.com/static-files/afe34f92-c23f-4b64-b377-fb37788c0648.

The iRobot management team had an incredible track record on which to build—the task moving into the second half of 2019 was to avoid or overcome the external competitive threats and leverage prior achievements into future successes that would keep iRobot number one in its industry.

Company History

iRobot, the leading global consumer robot company, was founded in 1990 by MIT roboticists Colin Angle, Helen Greiner, and Rodney Brooks, who shared the vision of making practical robots a reality. The company's first robot was the Genghis, designed for space exploration. Five years later, the Ariel was developed to detect mines, and two years later in 1998, iRobot won a DARPA (Defense Advanced Research Projects Agency) contract to build tactical robots. The company's PackBot robot was used in the United States to search the World Trade Center after the 9/11 attacks and deployed with U.S. troops in Afghanistan and Iraq.

Also in 2002, the company developed a robot that was used to search the Great Pyramid of Egypt (and it found a "secret room"). Perhaps the most notable event in 2002 was the development of the first iRobot Robotic Vacuum Cleaner (RVC) named Roomba. Two years later in 2004, iRobot won a U.S. Army contract to build the 312 SUGV (Small Unmanned Ground Vehicle) that was used by soldiers and combat engineers for ordinance disposal. Also in 2004, the company entered into an agreement with the Japanese distribution company Sales On Demand Corporation (SODC) to promote and distribute iRobot products in Japan, the largest consumer robotics market outside of North America.

In November 2005, iRobot became the first robot manufacturer to have a successful public stock offering. The company sold 4.3 million shares of stock at $24.00 and raised $103 million. Also in 2005, the Scooba—a floor washing robot—was launched, followed in 2007 by the Looj gutter cleaning robot, the Verro pool cleaning robot, and the Create—a programmable mobile robot. The company continued its internationalization, and partnered with Robopolis, a French distribution company, to sell its products in Germany, Spain, Portugal, the Netherlands, Austria, France, and Belgium. iRobot continued a prolific trend of products, and in 2008 introduced the Roomba pet series and a professional series of RVCs. The company also expanded into maritime robots and won a contract from DARPA to build a LANdroid communication robot, which served as a mobile signal repeater.

In 2010, iRobot's Seaglider maritime robot helped monitor the oil leakage following the BP Deepwater Horizon oil spill in the Gulf of Mexico. The next year, 2011, the company introduced an improved Scooba floor washing robot, a new series of Roomba dry vacuum robots, and the 110 FirstLook, which was a small lightweight robot that could be thrown. The FirstLook was designed for use by infantry forces to locate and identify hazards while keeping personnel safe. In 2012, the company purchased a rival firm, Evolution Robotics, Inc., for $74 million. Evolution Robotics produced a hard floor cleaner that used Swiffer pads to clean wooden floors, which was different from iRobot's products. iRobot's home robot sales exceeded 10 million units in 2013.

A new floor scrubbing robot and a vacuuming robot that included intelligent visual mapping and cloud connected app control were launched in 2015. In 2016, the Braava jet mopping robot was introduced, and the company opened an office in Shanghai, China, which significantly expanded its global footprint. iRobot made the decision to focus exclusively on consumer robots, divesting its defense and security robot business in mid-2016. There was increased investment in advancing mapping and navigation, and user interaction including cloud and app development.

iRobot continued its globalization strategy in 2017, and in April of that year, the company acquired SODC, its distribution partner in Japan, and Robopolis, its French distribution partner that served Western Europe. Wi-Fi connectivity was included on two new Roomba vacuum models (690 and 890), which extended Wi-Fi connectivity to the full line of Roombas. The company introduced two new connected products to its product portfolio to bring the advantages of cloud connectivity to its consumers. The iRobot HOME App transmitted the robots' maps directly to customers through "post-mission" cleaning maps. iRobot believed that the data sourced from the robots' maps would accelerate new product development as well as digital partnerships for the smart home.

iRobot introduced a new direction in 2019, when it introduced its newest line of consumer robot, the Terra.

The iRobot Product Line in 2019

i7 and e5   iRobot debuted new Roomba vacuums in 2019 including the i7 and e5. The Roomba i7 is the only robotic vacuum that can empty its own dirt bin, and with its Imprint Smart Mapping, the only smart vacuum that can be scheduled to clean rooms by name. The i7, which sold for $799.00 (vacuum only) or $999.00 with the dirt disposal base, could be verbally controlled with Alexa or Google Assistant. *Digital Trends* named the Roomba i7 "Best Overall" in February, 2019, and in March 2019, *PC Magazine* rated it "Editor's Choice." The new Roomba e5 Wi-Fi controlled robovac had five times the suction of the Roomba 600 series vacuums, was WiFi connected, and was compatible with Alexa and Google Assistant. The Roomba e5, had intelligent navigation, could be controlled with the iRobot HOME app, and sold for $399.00.

900 Series Roomba Vacuums   iRobot's newest Roomba in 2018 was the 960, a lower cost alternative to the 980. The 960 won second place and Editor's Choice in *PC Magazine*'s "Best Robot Vacuums of 2018." The 960 helped keep floors cleaner throughout an entire house via intelligent visual navigation, the iRobot HOME App control with Wi-Fi connectivity. The Roomba 960 had five times the suction power of the previous generation of Roomba RVCs, and extended mapping, visual navigation, and cloud connectivity to a wider range of customers. The Roomba 960 sold for $699.99, compared to $899.00 for the 980. The Roomba 960 was named Editor's Choice in March 2019 by *PC Magazine,* and the Roomba 980 received *PC Magazine*'s seventh place for best RVC. The greatest difference between the two models was longer battery life and deeper carpet cleaning for the 980. The greatest difference between the two models was longer battery life and deeper carpet cleaning for the 980.

800 Series Roomba Vacuums

The Roomba 800 series robots had an EROForce technology, which included brushless, counter-rotating extractors that increase suction for better performance than bristle brushes, while requiring less maintenance than previous Roomba models. The Roomba 890, which sold for $499.99 in February 2018, was selected "Runner-Up" Best Robotoc Vacuum by *Consumer Reports.*

600 Series Roomba Vacuums

600 series robots had a three-stage cleaning system that vacuumed every section of a floor multiple times as well as AeroVac technology and improved brush design, which enabled the robot to better handle fibers like hair, pet fur, lint, and carpet fuzz. The Roomba 690 sold for $279.00 and was Wi-Fi connected. The 690 received *PC Magazine*'s third place choice for Best Robotic Vacuum of 2018, "Editor's Choice" by *PC Magazine* in March 2019, and *Toptenreveiws* named it "Best Overall" in April 2019. The bottom-line Roomba 614, which sold for $299.99 in February 2018, was not Wi-Fi capable.

Braava Automatic Floor Mopping Robots

The Braava robots were designed for hard surface floors and used a different cleaning approach than did Roomba models. The Braava 380t robot, priced at $299 in February 2018, automatically dusted and damp-mopped hard-surface floors using popular cleaning cloths or iRobot-designed reusable microfiber cloths. The Braava robot included a special reservoir to dispense liquid throughout the cleaning cycle to keep the cloth damp. The 380t could use iAdapt navigation to map where it had cleaned and where it needed to go.

The Braava 240 was designed for smaller spaces than the 380t, and could wet mop, damp-sweep, or dry-sweep hard floors. The iRobot HOME App was compatible with the Braava Jet 240 and helped users get the most out of their robot by enabling them to choose the desired cleaning options for their unique home. *PC Review* gave the Brava Jet 4/5 (tied for highest) in its May 2019 Best Robot Mops Reviews. The Braava 240 sold for $169.00 in April 2019.

Mirra Pool Cleaning Robot

iRobot's Mirra 530 pool-cleaning robot was designed to clean any type of in-ground residential pools. It could remove debris as small as two microns from pool floors, walls, and stairs. The robot had a scrubbing brush to clean leaves, hair, dirt, algae, and bacteria off pool walls and floor, and a pump and filter that cleaned 70 gallons of water per minute. In April 2019 the Heavy.com reviews rated the Mirra 530 "best for deep cleaning in-ground pools." The Mirra sold for $999.00 in May 2019.

Terra Lawn Mowing Robot

iRobot unveiled its lawn mower robot, Terra, in January 2019. The robotic lawn mower would be launched in Germany during 2019, and introduced to the United States in 2020, although some U.S consumers would be allowed in a beta test program. Pricing would be announced later in 2019.

The Terra can be controlled from the company's iRobot Home app, and the owner can adjust the mower deck height to cut grass to the desired length. CEO Angle said that the robotic lawn mower had been in design for over 10 years, and the company gave up twice because of issues with the satellite-based GPS and the lasers that direct the robot's movements. The Terra has Imprint Smart Mapping that enables the robot to know exactly where it is on the lawn and cut in straight lines without boundary wires.

Three iRobot products—the Roomba 960, Roomba 690, and Roomba 980—were listed among the 10 Best Robot Vacuums by *PC Magazine* in 2018; however, the Eufy RoboVac 11, selling for $219, was chosen number one, ahead of iRobot's Roomba 960, selling for $699, over three times the price of the Eufy RoboVac 11. The iRobot Roomba e5 was chosen fourth-best robovac in January 2019 by *Consumer Reports*.

The Robotic Vacuum Industry

According to a market report by Persistence Market Research, the residential robotic vacuum cleaner (RVC) market was estimated at $1.3 billion at year-end 2015 and was expected to increase at an annual rate of 12 percent to reach $2.5 billion by 2021. Production of residential RVCs was about 1.9 million units at the end of 2015 and was forecasted to increase at an annual rate of 16.5 percent to reach 4.8 million units by 2021. The market penetration was quite low for robotic vacuums, and in 2018 was approximately 10 percent of the total households in the United States. In March 2019, MarketWatch forecast global demand for RVCs to grow at a compound average growth rate of 18.6 percent over the next five years. iRobot believed that the immediately addressable market in the United States was double the current base of about 13 million households, with a long-term potential of 86 million households.

Improved functionality and superior performance were among the key factors driving adoption of robotic vacuum cleaners in households. Product innovation was paramount for key companies in the RVC industry. A majority of leading companies were increasingly concentrating on research and development (R&D) of unconventional products in order to gain a competitive edge.

There was a trend of bagless vacuum cleaners that could accelerate market growth. New product launches of RVCs included advanced features such as vacuum cleaners with UV sterilization, spinning brushes, security cameras, Internet connectivity, voice response, app features, and mapping features. Such advancements were expected to drive the market further. Innovation of a novel technology stair-climbing robotic vacuum cleaner was expected to present lucrative opportunities in the near future.

The industry was not without challenges, as the huge market size and low penetration attracted new entrants and resulted in price-based competition. There was also a trend toward new and low-volume products. All these combined to put pressure on gross margins.

iRobot's Strategy

The company's offensive strategy going into 2019 was to maintain Roomba's leadership in the consumer robotic industry while positioning the company as a strategic player in the emerging smart home. iRobot believed that it was critical that the company protect its design, marketing, and branding lead with respect to floor care, while extending it into new areas like lawn mowing over the next few years, even at the expense of reduced short-term profitability. CEO Angle set out the company's 2019 strategy, designed to protect iRobot's market share as the global industry matured, as:

- Diversification of the manufacturing and supply base from China.
- Aggressive competitive pricing to fend off competitors.
- Driving higher top-line growth and maintaining dominant market share.
- Increasing investment in research and development to extend iRobot's technology and product leadership.
- Aggressive spending on advertising and marketing.

iRobot's strategy had provided market-leading positions in the robotic segment of the global vacuum cleaner industry—see Exhibit 2. In 2017, iRobot had 88 percent of the North American market, 76 percent of the European/Middle East/African market, and 34 percent of the Asia/Pacific market; however, increasing competition had resulted in a 3 percent loss of market share in 2018.

CEO Angle warned that the new strategy of diversifying the manufacturing and supply base, plus the increasing industry challenges, would reduce profitability in 2019 and 2020. Mr. Angle estimated that the company's gross profit margin would decline from about 51 percent of sales in fiscal 2018 to about 48 percent in 2019.

EXHIBIT 2

Geographic Market Size and Vendor Shares of the Robotic Vacuum Cleaner Industry, 2016

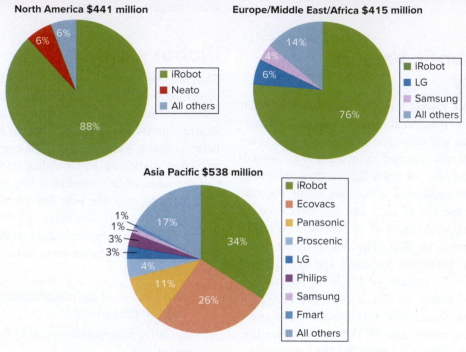

Source: Steve Auger, iRobot: Wiping The Floor With Its Competitors, Seeking Alpha, https://seekingalpha.com.

iRobot's Technology Focus

iRobot believed that a better robot lives in the world by moving around and acting more intelligently in its environment, by cooperating with the people it serves more compellingly, and by physically interacting more effectively with its surroundings. As the number-one global consumer robotics company, iRobot strived to develop best-in-class technology in mapping and navigation, human-robot interaction, and physical solutions.

Mapping and Navigation   iRobot was focused on mapping and navigation technology development to make its robots smarter and simpler to use, and to provide valuable spatial context to the broader ecosystem of connected devices in the home. Robot-built and -maintained home maps were core to the company's long-term strategy, providing important spatial context by capturing the physical space of

the home. Maps provided the information needed to enable robots to purposefully navigate throughout their environment and accomplish meaningful tasks.

User Experience and Digital Features   iRobot invested in the development of interfaces for its robots to provide its customers with rich and convenient ways to interact with the entire iRobot family of products. iRobot's customer interaction and experience with its products was intended to be enriched as a result of connecting the company's robots and integrating them with connected devices in the home, and with other cloud resources and services.

Physical Solutions   iRobot was dedicated to designing and producing robot solutions with market-leading cleaning mission performance that provided convincing value to its customers. The company's robots' core value from the customer's perspective was the ability to effectively and efficiently perform the physical mission—cleaning. iRobot believed that it produced the best mission performance solutions on the market, whether it was vacuuming, mopping, or any other cleaning tasks.

The Smart Home: An Ecosystem of Robots Working Together

iRobot imagined a home that maintained itself and miraculously did just the right things, anticipating its owners' needs. The smart home would be built on an ecosystem of connected and coordinated robots, sensors, and devices that provided homeowners with a high quality of life by seamlessly responding to the needs of daily living—from comfort to convenience to security to efficiency. iRobot was working to build an ecosystem of robots and the data required to enable the smart home.

Robots and other devices in the smart home need to understand the environment so they can figure out what they should do. Angle explained that there was no point to being able to understand the sentence "Go to the kitchen and get me a beer" if the robot doesn't know where the kitchen is.[1] You could also have smart thermostats, lights, blinds, door locks, humidity sensors, TVs, radios, and speakers that sit in this ecosystem. Those would be the building blocks of the smart home. The unifying intelligence tying everything together and what enabled the home to be smart could come from iRobot or a different company.

Guy Hoffman, a robotics professor at Cornell University, said detailed spatial mapping technology would be a major breakthrough for the smart home. With regularly updated maps, Hoffman said, sound systems could match home acoustics, air conditioners could schedule airflow by room, and smart lighting could adjust according to the position of windows and time of day. If a customer bought a Roomba, owned a smartphone, and had connected devices, the Roomba could build a map of the home, place the connected devices on the map, and share that information with all other devices. Then the ecosystem or interconnected system could give the owner a choice of preferences based on the included devices, and have the room start behaving intelligently. If the homeowner did not like how the home behaved, he or she could change preferences and the system would learn. The Amazon Alexa and Google Home devices could also supplement that behavior by providing a voice interface to the system, extending the smart home's reach to things to which they are connected.

iRobot CEO Colin Angle explained the smart home concept to *MIT Technology Review* in December 2017:

> What we're seeing today is a collection of devices that are all controlled by their own apps. The promise of enhanced utility is actually being reduced by the complexity we're introducing. A successful smart home should be built on the idea that nobody programs anything; the basic services in your home would just work. So you would walk up to your front door, which would unlock if you were authorized to enter. You would go in and the light would turn on, the temperature would adjust, and if you started watching TV and moved to another room, the TV show would follow you. When you're no longer using various services, they could shut down automatically to save energy, or be set to respond to the weather or the time of day.
>
> That might sound like an idealized vision of a smart home, but it's completely reasonable to do if you have a robot in the mix that is actively going out and discovering what rooms exist and what the different devices in them are, and you have a way of figuring out what room people are in. iRobot currently has an app that can analyze Wi-Fi coverage in homes using its Wi-Fi connected Roombas. It can provide a map showing where wireless signals are strongest and weakest.
>
> The positioning for iRobot is we're going to be the spatial-understanding people. . . .We're trying to make the home sufficiently self-aware to be self-configuring and useful. . . . The emerging AI home dimension is going to play out in a big way over the next two years.[2]

iRobot Ventures

As part of iRobot's Corporate Development team, the iRobot Ventures group fostered engagement with the entrepreneurs and early-stage companies driving innovation in consumer robotics and in the connected hardware ecosystem. iRobot understood how difficult it was to bring a product to market, and to build a company. The company believed that investors should provide more than just capital and validation of an idea. iRobot Ventures delivered value by facilitating access to the company's engineering and operations resources, as well as a network of external service providers, investors, and partners. iRobot Ventures:

- Sought strategic investments that generated attractive financial returns.
- Syndicated with top-tier VC firms, strategic and angel investors.
- Provided access to internal and external resources.
- Embraced standard terms.
- Made informed investment decisions rapidly.
- Did not seek special treatment or control.

iRobot Ventures supported teams that were passionate about using technology to solve hard problems. The company invested in applications that were consistent with its core business or represented new market opportunities, and participated in the early stages of the innovation lifecycle, where iRobot had the most to add, focusing on the following:

- Consumer technology
- Service-based business models
- Recurring revenue streams
- Cloud services and infrastructure

- Computer vision
- Localization and mapping
- Machine learning and artificial intelligence
- Robotic mobility and manipulation

iRobot's Financial Performance

iRobot enjoyed a meteoric ascent in its financial performance between fiscal year 2016 and fiscal year 2018. Revenue had grown from about $661 million in fiscal 2016 to approximately $1.1 billion in fiscal 2018. The company's gross margin had improved from 48 percent of net revenue to 51 percent between fiscal 2016 and fiscal 2018. Operating income increased from 8.7 percent of net revenue in 2016 to 9.7 percent in 2018, and net income grew from 6.3 percent to 8.1 percent during that time period. iRobot stock also had an impressive gain, increasing from $20.00 in January 2005 to $125.06 in February 2019. The company's financial performance for fiscal year 2016 through fiscal year 2018 is presented in Exhibit 3. The company's balance sheets for fiscal year 2017

EXHIBIT 3

iRobot Corporation's Consolidated Statements of Income, Fiscal Year 2016 – Fiscal Year 2018 (in thousands of $, except per share amounts)

Consolidated Statements of Income	12 MONTHS ENDED		
	Dec. 29, 2018	Dec. 30, 2017	Dec. 31, 2016
Revenue	$1,092,584	$883,911	$660,604
Cost of product revenue	518,612	438,114	337,832
Amortization of acquired intangible assets	18,544	12,638	3,457
Total cost of revenue	537,156	450,752	341,289
Gross profit	555,428	433,159	319,315
Operating expenses:			
Research and development	140,629	113,149	79,805
Selling and marketing	210,411	162,110	115,125
General and administrative	97,501	84,771	66,828
Amortization of acquired intangible assets	1,065	439	0
Total operating expenses	449,606	360,469	261,758
Operating income	105,822	72,690	57,557
Other income, net	2,800	3,676	3,804
Income before income taxes	108,622	76,366	61,361
Income tax expense	20,630	25,402	19,422
Net income	$ 87,992	$ 50,964	$ 41,939

Consolidated Statements of Income	12 MONTHS ENDED		
	Dec. 29, 2018	Dec. 30, 2017	Dec. 31, 2016
Net income per share:			
Basic	$3.18	$1.85	$1.51
Diluted	$3.07	$1.77	$1.48
Number of shares used in per share calculations:			
Basic	27,692	27,611	27,698
Diluted	28,640	28,753	28,292

Source: iRobot Corporation, 2018 Annual Report, April 8, 2019, https://investor.irobot.com/static-files/afe34f92-c23f-4b64-b377-fb37788c0648.

and fiscal year 2018 are presented in Exhibit 4. The 10-year performance of its common shares between June 2009 and May 2019 is shown in Exhibit 5.

iRobot's Rivals in the Floor Care Market

The floor care market was crowded with big-name competitors. However, the iRobot Roomba models placed numbers two, three, six, and seven in the NPD Retail Tracking Service poll in 2017. The iRobot Roombas were the only robotic floor cleaners to place in the top 10—see Exhibit 6. Shark's upright replaced Dyson at number one in the February 1, 2017, *Consumer Reports* reviews, and Shark entered the robotic vacuum market in 2017.

Eufy RoboVac In January 2019, *Consumer Reports* selected the Eufy RoboVac11S, which sold

EXHIBIT 4

iRobot Corporation's Consolidated Balance Sheets, Fiscal Year 2017 – Fiscal Year 2018 (in thousands of $)

Consolidated Balance Sheets	Dec. 29, 2018	Dec. 30, 2017
Current assets:		
Cash and cash equivalents	$130,373	$128,635
Short-term investments	31,605	37,225
Accounts receivable, net	162,166	142,829
Inventory	164,633	106,932
Other current assets	25,660	19,105
Total current assets	514,437	434,726
Property and equipment, net	57,026	44,579
Deferred tax assets	36,979	31,531
Goodwill	118,896	121,440
Intangible assets, net	24,273	44,712
Other assets	15,350	14,534
Total assets	766,961	691,522
Current liabilities:		
Accounts payable	136,742	116,316
Accrued expenses	71,259	73,647
Deferred revenue and customer advances	5,756	7,761
Total current liabilities	213,757	197,724
Deferred tax liabilities	4,005	9,539
Other long-term liabilities	13,877	13,932
Total long-term liabilities	17,882	23,471
Total liabilities	231,639	221,195

Consolidated Balance Sheets	Dec. 29, 2018	Dec. 30, 2017
Commitments and contingencies:		
Preferred stock, 5,000 shares authorized and none outstanding	0	0
Common stock, $0.01 par value, 100,000 shares authorized; 27,788 and 27,945 shares issued and outstanding, respectively	278	279
Additional paid-in capital	172,771	190,067
Retained earnings	367,021	277,989
Accumulated other comprehensive (loss) income	(4,748)	1,992
Total stockholders' equity	535,322	470,327
Total liabilities and stockholders' equity	$766,961	$691,522

Source: iRobot Corporation, 2018 Annual Report, April 8, 2019, https://investor.irobot.com/static-files/afe34f92-c23f-4b64-b377-fb37788c0648.

EXHIBIT 5

Monthly Performance of iRobot Corporation's Stock Price, May 2009 – May 2019

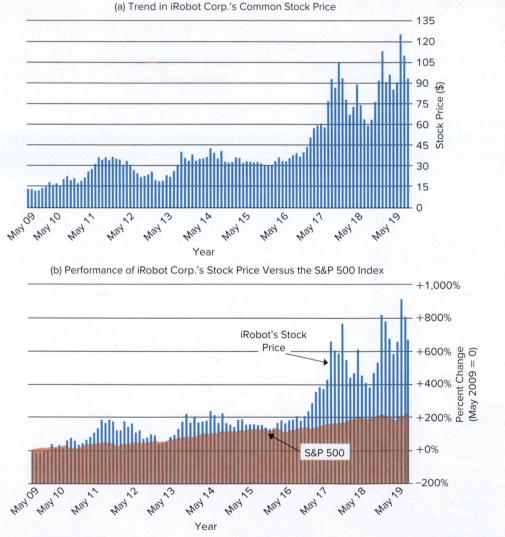

(a) Trend in iRobot Corp.'s Common Stock Price

(b) Performance of iRobot Corp.'s Stock Price Versus the S&P 500 Index

Adapted from bigcharts.marketwatch.com.

EXHIBIT 6

Top 10 Floor Cleaner Vacuums, 2017

Rank	Floor Cleaner Name
1	Dyson V8 Stick Cordless
2	iRobot Roomba 690 Robotic
3	iRobot Roomba 650
4	Shark Rotator Professional Upright
5	Bissell Bare Floor
6	iRobot Roomba 980
7	iRobot Roomba 960
8	Hoover Deep Carpet
9	Dyson V7 Stick
10	Shark Navigator Upright

Source: "Retail: We Help You Win Across Channels," The NPD Group, Inc., https://www.npd.com/wps/portal/npd/us/industry-expertise/retail/.

for $224.99 on Amazon in January 2019, as the Second Best Robovac, and the Eufy 30C, which sold for $299.00 on Amazon, as the third best. In January 2018, *PC Magazine* selected the RoboVac 11 as Editor's Choice and first place among eight in "Best Robotic Vacuums of 2018." In February 2018, the RoboVac 11 sold for $219.00 on Amazon. The Eufy Robotic mop was picked number one in *Atopdaily'*s 2018 Robotic Mop Review.

Neato Robotics   The Neato Botvac D5, which sold for $500 on Amazon in late 2017, was chosen fourth best RVC by *Consumer Reports* in November 2017. The Dyson Botvac Connected and Botvac Connected D were chosen fourth and fifth best, respectively, by *PC Magazine* in January 2018. Neato's Botvac Connected was compatible with smart home devices and platforms, synched with 2.4GHz Wi-Fi networks, and had an app for Android and iOS that enabled owners to interact and control the vacuum from Amazon Alexa, Google Home, the Neato Chatbot for Facebook, and from a tablet or smartphone. The app notified the owner about the vacuum status, enabling the homeowner to easily schedule the vacuum and keep the home clean.

Dyson   Dyson Technology, an established British manufacturer of consumer electronics, lighting, and traditional vacuum cleaners, entered the RVC market with the Dyson 360Eye, which was the result of 17 years of RVC development by the company. The new Dyson robot was introduced in Tokyo. The 360Eye had twice the suction of any other RVC, was controlled by the Dyson Link app, and would respond to voice commands. It was equipped with a camera and could map the rooms in which it was used.

Dyson's 360 EYE, which sold for $999.99 on Amazon in early 2018, was selected sixth best RVC by *PC Magazine* in January 2018.

LG   LG is a South Korean multinational conglomerate that had begun manufacturing robotic vacuums in 2001 with the Robotking. The LG Hom-Bot CR5765GD automatically adjusts suction based on the floor that it is cleaning, and is operated by a manufacturer's app downloaded to the owner's smartphone. If the Hom-Bot detects movement in the home, it can take photos and videos of the intruder and send it to the homeowner's phone. The Hom-Bot was selected as the fifth best robovac by *Consumer Reports* in January 2019, and sold for $1,448 on Amazon.

Shark   Shark was one of several brands developed by SharkNinja Operating, LLC, a Massachusetts-based developer of cleaning solutions and household appliances. The Shark ION ROBOT 750 was Wi-Fi capable and could be controlled with a mobile app or by voice command. All Home Robotics, in March 2018, did a comparison of the Shark ION 750 and the Roomba 890 and concluded that unless the home had deep shag carpet, the Shark 750 would be the one to buy. Also, BestReviews Guide scored the Shark Ion 750 8.3/10 in its May 2019 reviews. In May 2019, the Shark ION 750 sold for $215.99 on Amazon, compared to $499.99 for the Roomba 890 at Best Buy, Target, and Bed Bath & Beyond.

Samsung   Samsung, the South Korean multinational electronics and appliance manufacturer, was a late entrant into the RVC market. The newest Samsung robot models—POWERbot—are Wi-Fi capable and map the house in which they are used. The POWERbot can be controlled by a smartphone app, Amazon's Alexa, or Google Assistant. The Samsung line of POWERbot Robotic Vacuum cleaners ranged from the R9000, which sold for $399, to the R7090, which sold for $699.00.

The Samsung POWERbot SR20H9051 RVC was voted "Best in Class" by *Consumer Reports* in November 2017. The POWERbot R7040, which sold for $393 on Amazon, was chosen sixth best by *Consumer Reports* in January 2019, and the Samsung POWERbot R7065, which sold for $449.00 on Amazon, received the seventh best award.

Ecovacs Ecovacs, founded in 1998, is a global consumer robotics company based in China, whose focus is helping consumers "Live Smart, Enjoy Life" with their line of products to help with daily household chores. The company's product line comprises DEEBOT floor cleaner, the WINBOT window cleaner, ATMBOT air cleaner, and FAMIBOT entertainment and security robot. Several Ecovacs products include Wi-Fi connectivity. Ecovacs is one of the top three brands of in-home robots worldwide, and has 65 percent of the market share in China, where it is the #1 brand. Ecovacs currently has operations in Mainland China, North America, Europe, Malaysia, and Australia. Ecovacs' DEEBOT floor cleaner line of robots are sold in the United States at major big box retailers such as Best Buy, Target, Macy's, Home Depot, and Staples.

Prices in April 2019 ranged from $379.99 for the DEEBOT M88 to $189.00 for the NEO Robot on Amazon. The Ecovacs DEEBOT M88 was voted best RVC by *Consumer Reports* in January 2019, and the DEEBOT N79 was the best-selling robotic vacuum on Amazon for Black Friday in 2017. The *New York Times'* Wirecutter review in March 2018 selected the DEEBOT N79 as the best choice RVC. *Digital Trends* cited the Ecovas DEEBOT 901, which sold for $224 from Amazon, as "Best for Pets" in its February 2019 Best RVC review. The Ecovacs DEEBOT 80 Pro Robotic Vacuum with Mop was picked first place by Offers.com in April 2018, and number two by *ATOPDAILY's* Best Robot Mop Reviews in 2018.

Competitive Risks

A significant risk for Roomba was that competitors' cheaper cleaning products were what consumers really wanted. In May 2016, the *New York Times'* Sweethome blog ousted the $375 Roomba 690 as its most-recommended robovac in favor of the $220 Eufy RoboVac 11. The Sweethome blog said that the Roomba's Internet connectivity and other advanced features would not justify the greater cost for most users. Short-seller Axler's June 2016 report caused concern with the prediction that value-priced appliance maker SharkNinja Operating LLC could launch a robovac by the end of 2016. In September 2017, *Investor's Business Daily* reported that iRobot stock fell 16 percent over concerns about Shark entering the robotic vacuum market, and Spruce Point Capital Management remarked that "SharkNinja has entered the robotic vacuum market with a 'functionality at a reasonable price' strategy to compete directly with the Roomba. Given Shark's historical success, we assume that their entry into the market will translate into sales and margin pressure for iRobot beginning with Q4 2017."[3]

One potential iRobot defense against these new competitors was iRobot's portfolio of 1,000 patents worldwide that covered the very concept of a self-navigating household robot vacuum as well as basic technologies like object avoidance. A handful of those patents were being tested in a series of patent infringement lawsuits iRobot filed in April against Bissell, Stanley, Black & Decker, Hoover Inc., Chinese outsourced manufacturers, and other robovac makers. That litigation was the most significant in iRobot's history.

Privacy Concerns

iRobot's higher-end Roomba robotic vacuums collected data that identified the walls of rooms and furniture locations as they cleaned. This data enabled the Roomba to avoid collisions with furniture, but it also created a map of the home that iRobot could share with Google, Apple, or Amazon. iRobot had made the Roomba compatible with Amazon's Alexa voice assistant in March 2017, and according to the company's CEO Angle, iRobot could extract value from that by data sharing agreements and connecting for free with as many companies as possible to make the device more useful in the home.

However, the idea of iRobot's data sharing caused investor concern when *Reuters* reported in July 2017 that iRobot's chief executive, Colin Angle, announced that a deal could come within two years to share its maps for free with customer consent to one or more of the Big Three. Albert Gidari, director of privacy at the Stanford Center for Internet and Society, said that if iRobot did share the data, it would raise a variety of legal questions. Guy Hoffmann, a robotics professor at Cornell University, said that companies such as Apple, Amazon, and Google could use the data obtained by the iRobot devices to recommend home goods for customers to buy. A potential problem with sharing data about users' homes is that it raises clear privacy issues, said Ben Rose, an analyst for Battle Road Research who covers iRobot.

Homeowners were able to opt out of Roomba's cloud-sharing functions, using the iRobot Home app, but technically the iRobot terms of service and privacy policy indicated that the company had the right to share users' personal information, according to *The Verge* in a June 24, 2017, article. The potential sale of personal information was disclosed in the company's privacy policy, but was unlikely to be discovered by most consumers.

In a written response in *Consumer Reports* reported by the *New York Times* on July 25, 2017, iRobot management stated that it was "committed to the absolute privacy of our customer-related data." Consumers can use a Roomba without connecting it to the Internet, or "opt out of sending map data to the cloud through a switch in the mobile app." "No data is sold to third parties," the statement added. "No data will be shared with third parties without the informed consent of our customers." CEO Angle reinforced iRobot's position in an April 10, 2018, interview with *The Verge,* saying, "iRobot will never sell your data. It's your data, and if you would like that data to be used to do something beyond helping your robot perform its job better [like mapping your home for IoT devices], then you'll need to give permission. We're committed to [EU data privacy legislation] GDPR and are ensuring that if you want to be forgotten, then we'll be able to forget you."[4] Angle stressed that iRobot did not intend to build its future around selling data, however; the company wanted to be a "trusted aggregator of spatial information" that could help with the smart home. Data collected by iRobot devices would be protected by iRobot.

iRobot was proactive in addressing the privacy issue and placed the following on their irobot.com website:

> iRobot does not sell data as our customers always come first. We will never violate their trust by selling or misusing customer-related data, including data collected by our connected products. Right now, the data Roomba collects enables it to effectively clean the home and provides customers with information about cleaning performance. iRobot believes that in the future, this information could provide even more value for our customers by enabling the smart home and the devices within it to work better, but always with their knowledge and control.[5]

Smart home lighting, thermostats, and security cameras were already on the market, but Colin Angle, chief executive of Roomba maker iRobot Corp., said they were still dumb when it came to understanding their physical environment. He thought the mapping technology currently guiding top-end Roomba models could change that and he was basing the company's strategy on it. "There's an entire ecosystem of things and services that the smart home can deliver once you have a rich map of the home that the user has allowed to be shared," said Angle.[6] The iRobot Roomba was already linked to Google Assistant and Amazon's Alexa, which enabled customers to control their Roomba with voice commands.

Looking ahead, the company believed robots and the mapping capabilities they provide would be key to enabling the smart home. For context, the concept of rooms as an organizing concept is often used. Rooms have lighting, heating, TVs, stereos, blinds, and other appliances. If one thought about "what is supposed to happen when I enter a room," everything depended on the room at a foundational level knowing what is in it. In order to "do the right thing," when you enter a room and say "turn on the lights," the room must know what lights are available to turn on. The same for robotic pets, music, TV, heat, blinds, the stove, coffee machines, fans, gaming consoles, or smart picture frames. Understanding spatial context is the required foundation for the true smart home, and maps can provide this.

However, the question of whether the market is ready for a data gathering robot or will be content with just a floor cleaner remains to be answered.

The increasing sales of mapping and data gathering robots (those connected to the Internet) appears to answer that question in the affirmative.

iRobot in 2019

In February 2019, iRobot's Chairman and Chief Executive Officer Colin Angle announced the company's fourth quarter financial results, stating, "We had a phenomenal finish to 2018, exceeding both our fourth-quarter and full-year expectations for revenue growth and profitability after raising our expectations twice during the year."[7] Revenue for the fourth quarter of 2018 was $384.7 million, compared with $326.9 million for the fourth quarter of 2017. Revenue for the full year 2018 was $1,092.6 million, compared with $883.9 million for the full year 2017.

Operating income in the fourth quarter of 2018 was $29.8 million, compared with $23.1 million in the fourth quarter of 2017. Operating income for the full year 2018 was $105.8 million, compared with $72.7 million for the full year 2017. iRobot's revenue grew 24 percent in an increasingly competitive market, and the company was able to earn an operating margin of about 10 percent after absorbing the negative impact of tariffs in the fourth quarter. There was substantial demand for the new Roomba i7 and i7+ robots, which drove strong domestic holiday sales. Internationally, unexpected high revenue in Japan was driven by robust fourth-quarter demand supported by the company's sales and marketing programs in that region. The company launched a Braava national television program in Japan, which helped drive Q4 2018 Braava family revenue growth of 25 percent year-over-year in Japan.

Chairman Angle also set out iRobot's plans and financial expectations for 2019. The company expected full-year 2019 revenue of $1.28 to $1.31 billion (which would be a year-over-year growth of 17 percent to 20 percent), operating income of $108 to $118 million, and EPS of $3.00 to $3.25. According to Angle, the company would continue on a growth by diversification strategy, and focus on supply chair and manufacturing diversification to achieve long-term production stability, as well as driving growth of non-Roomba products.

Angle also pointed out several challenges as well as growth opportunities for the company. He stated, "We are very excited about our 2018 performance and the opportunities that lie ahead. While we are navigating uncharted waters with the current tariff uncertainty, we expect our global business to deliver strong financial performance in 2019 that will in turn fund critical investments in future technologies and marketing, to further solidify our position as the unambiguous leader in robotic floor care. In 2019, we will also definitively establish a diversified revenue stream, introduce a new robotic category with lawn mowing and demonstrate our increasing importance as a strategic player in the smart home to drive enhanced long-term shareholder value."[8]

ENDNOTES

[1] Evan Ackerman, "Interview: iRobot CEO Colin Angle on Data Privacy and Robots in the Home," IEEE Spectrum, September 7, 2017, https://spectrum.ieee.org/automaton/robotics/home-robots/interview-irobot-ceo-colin-angle-on-privacy-and-robots-in-the-home.

[2] Elizabeth Woyke, "Roomba to Rule the Smart Home," MIT Technology Review, December 15, 2017, https://www.technologyreview.com/s/609764/roomba-to-rule-the-smart-home/.

[3] Patrick Seitz, "IRobot Stock Attacked by Home Appliance Vendor SharkNinja," Investors Business Daily, September 13, 2017, https://www.investors.com/news/technology/click/irobot-stock-attacked-by-home-appliance-vendor-sharkninja/.

[4] James Vincent, "iRobot CEO says the future of the smart home is going to mean making friends with robots," Vox Media, Inc., April 19, 2018, https://www.theverge.com/2018/4/19/17256074/roomba-irobot-ceo-colin-angle.

[5] "iRobot Roomba Privacy and Data Sharing," iRobot, http://irobot-homesupport-pl-pl.custhelp.com/app/answers/detail/a_id/964/~/irobot-roomba-privacy-and-data-sharing.

[6] Hamza Shaban, "As Your Roomba Cleans Your floors, It's Gathering Maps of Your House," Los Angeles Times, July 25, 2017, https://www.latimes.com/business/technology/la-fi-tn-roomba-map-20170725-story.html.

[7] Bedford Mass, "iRobot Reports Record Fourth-Quarter and Full-Year Revenue," iRobot, February 06, 2019, http://media.irobot.com/2019-02-06-iRobot-Reports-Record-Fourth-Quarter-and-Full-Year-Revenue.

[8] Bedford Mass, "iRobot Reports Record Fourth-Quarter and Full-Year Revenue," iRobot, February 06, 2019, http://media.irobot.com/2019-02-06-iRobot-Reports-Record-Fourth-Quarter-and-Full-Year-Revenue.

TWITTER, INC. IN 2019: ARE THE GROWTH AND PROFIT SUSTAINABLE?

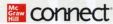

DAVID L. TURNIPSEED *University of South Alabama*

Jack Dorsey, CEO of Twitter Inc., had breathed a slight sigh of relief when the fourth-quarter 2017 financial results showed the first profitable quarter since the company went public in 2013. One year later, the company's 2018 annual report showed net income of $1.2 billion, which was 40 percent of its revenue. Twitter had experienced rapid growth since its founding, and by January 2018 there were more than 330 million active monthly users. Notables with Twitter accounts included U.S. President Donald Trump, Taylor Swift, Justin Timberlake, Ellen DeGeneres, Pope Francis, Katy Perry, and Turkish President Recep Erdogan. However, despite the number of users and the volume of use, Twitter had failed to provide any financial gains until the fourth quarter of 2017, and this profit had come as a result of cutting costs, not growing the business. Research and development, and sales and marketing expenses, had been cut by 24 and 25 percent, respectively, and the company's annual net revenue for fiscal 2017 was down over 3 percent from 2016. Twitter discovered in the third quarter of 2017 that it had been miscalculating monthly user numbers since the fourth quarter of 2014, and consequently was forced to lower the previously reported numbers. Even more problematic was an accumulated deficit of over $2.6 billion.

Although Twitter showed its first full-year profit in fiscal 2018, it was due largely to maintaining low costs, and the impact of the Tax Act. Revenue of $3.0 billion in 2018 was an increase of 24 percent over 2017, but costs for research and development, sales and marketing, and total costs and expenses were below 2016 levels, as a percentage of revenue.

Total costs and expenses were 11 percent lower than 2016, and research and development costs were 20 percent below 2014 levels. The accumulated deficit, which at the end of fiscal 2017 was over $2.6 billion, had been reduced to $1.5 billion.

Twitter Inc.'s consolidated income statements for 2014 through 2018 are presented in Exhibit 1. The company's consolidated balance sheets for 2014 through 2018 are presented in Exhibit 2.

Twitter was a giant in the industry; however, it faced serious competition from companies such as Facebook (including Instagram and WhatsApp), Snap, TikTok, Alphabet (including Google and YouTube), Microsoft (including LinkedIn), and Verizon Media Group. There are also foreign competitors that are regional social media and messaging companies, with strong positions in particular countries, including WeChat, Kakao, and Line, which pose competitive challenges. Many of these competitors were growing at a multiple of Twitter's growth—over the two-year period 2017 to 2018, Facebook had an increase of 296 million monthly active users (+15.8 percent), WhatsApp increased by 300 million (+30 percent), and Instagram had increases of 200 million (+33 percent). Over the same period, Twitter increased only 13 million monthly users (+4.1 percent): In 2018 its share of worldwide digital ad revenue dropped to 0.8 percent in 2018 (compared to Google's 38.2 percent and Facebook's 21.8 percent).

Although Twitter had made a good profit in fiscal 2018, was it due largely to keeping costs at unsustainably low levels? Could the company continue to grow revenue and operate without allowing

EXHIBIT 1

Consolidated Statements of Operations for Twitter, Inc., 2014–2018 (in thousands of $, except per share amounts)

	YEAR ENDED DECEMBER 31,				
	2018	2017	2016	2015	2014
Consolidated Statement of Operations Data:					
Revenue	$3,042,359	$2,443,299	$2,529,619	$2,218,032	$1,403,002
Costs and expenses					
Cost of revenue	964,997	861,242	932,240	729,256	446,309
Research and development	553,858	542,010	713,482	806,648	691,543
Sales and marketing	771,361	717,419	957,829	871,491	614,110
General and administrative	298,818	283,888	293,276	260,673	189,906
Total costs and expenses	2,589,034	2,404,559	2,896,827	2,668,068	1,941,868
Income (loss) from operations	453,325	38,740	(367,208)	(450,036)	(538,866)
Interest expense	(132,606)	(105,237)	(99,968)	(98,178)	(35,918)
Interest income	111,221	44,383	24,277	9,073	1,933
Other income (expense), net	(8,396)	(73,304)	2,065	5,836	(5,500)
Income (loss) before income taxes	423,544	(95,418)	(440,834)	(533,305)	(578,351)
Provision (benefit) for income taxes	(782,052)	12,645	16,039	(12,274)	(531)
Net income (loss)	$1,205,596	$ (108,063)	$ (456,873)	$ (521,031)	$ (577,820)
Net income (loss) per share attributable to common stockholders:					
Basic	$1.60	$(0.15)	$(0.65)	$(0.79)	$(0.96)
Diluted	$1.56	$(0.15)	$(0.65)	$(0.79)	$(0.96)
Weighted-average shares used to compute net income (loss) per share attributable to common stockholders:					
Basic	754,326	732,702	702,135	662,424	604,990
Diluted	772,686	732,702	702,135	662,424	604,990
Other Financial Information:					
Adjusted EBITDA	$1,200,796	$ 862,986	$ 751,493	$ 557,807	$ 300,896
Non-GAAP net income	663,804	328,859	264,406	180,486	68,438
Cost of revenue	17,289	23,849	29,502	40,705	50,536
Research and development	183,799	240,833	335,498	401,537	360,726
Sales and marketing	71,305	94,135	160,935	156,904	157,263
General and administrative	53,835	74,989	89,298	82,972	63,072
Total stock-based compensation	326,228	433,806	615,233	682,118	631,597

Source: Twitter, Inc., 2019 Annual Report, accessed August 2, 2019, http://www.annualreports.com/HostedData/AnnualReports/PDF/NYSE_TWTR_2018.pdf.

EXHIBIT 2

Consolidated Balance Sheets for Twitter, Inc., 2014-2018 (in thousands of $)

	AS OF DECEMBER 31,				
	2018	2017	2016	2015	2014
Consolidated Balance Sheet Data:					
Cash and cash equivalents	$ 1,894,444	$ 1,638,413	$ 988,598	$ 911,471	$ 1,510,724
Short-term investments	4,314,957	2,764,689	2,785,981	2,583,877	2,111,154
Property and equipment, net	885,078	773,715	783,901	735,299	557,019
Total assets	10,162,572	7,412,477	6,870,365	6,442,439	5,583,082
Convertible notes	2,628,250	1,627,460	1,538,967	1,455,095	1,376,020
Total liabilities	3,356,978	2,365,259	2,265,430	2,074,392	1,956,679
Total stockholders' equity	6,805,594	5,047,218	4,604,935	4,368,047	3,626,403

Source: Twitter, Inc., 2019 Annual Report, accessed August 2, 2019, http://www.annualreports.com/HostedData/AnnualReports/PDF/NYSE_TWTR_2018.pdf.

costs and expenses to drift up and erode income? Twitter's CEO and its Board were faced with two daunting questions: (1) what could they do to assure Twitter's continued growth and profitability, and (2) was the company an increasingly attractive take-over candidate?

History of Twitter

Founded in 2006 by Jack Dorsey, Noah Glass, Biz Stone, and Evan Williams, Twitter was an online microblogging and social networking service that allowed users to post text-based messages, known as tweets, and status updates up to 40 characters long. Jack Dorsey sent the first tweet on March 21, 2006: "just setting up my twttr"- Jack(@jack) 21 March, 2006. By the first of January 2018, Twitter had more than 330 million monthly active users.

The history of Twitter began with an entrepreneur named Noah Glass who started a company named Odeo in 2005. Odeo had a product that would turn a phone message into an MP3 hosted on the Internet. One of Odeo's early investors was a former Google employee, Evan Williams, who got very involved with the company. As Odeo grew, more employees were hired including a Web designer, Jack Dorsey, and Christopher "Biz" Stone, a friend of Odeo's new CEO, Evan Williams.

Williams decided that Odeo's future was not in podcasting, and directed the company's employees to develop ideas for a new direction. Jack Dorsey, who had been doing cleanup work on Odeo, proposed a product that was based on people's present status, or what they were doing at a given time. In February 2006, Glass, Dorsey, and a German contract developer proposed Dorsey's idea to others in Odeo, and over time, a group of employees gravitated to Twitter while others focused on Odeo. At one point, the entire Twitter service was run from Glass's laptop.

Noah Glass presented the Twitter idea to Odeo's Board in summer of 2006; the Board was not enthused. Williams proposed to repurchase the Odeo stock held by investors to prevent them from taking a loss, and they agreed. Five years later, the assets of Odeo that the original investors sold for about $5 million were worth $5 billion.

After Williams repurchased Odeo, he changed the name to Obvious Corp. and fired Odeo's founder and the biggest supporter of Twitter, Noah Glass.

Christopher "Biz" Stone left Twitter in 2011 and pursued an entrepreneurial venture with Obvious Corp. for six years. In mid-2017, he returned to Twitter full time. As of the second quarter, 2018, only three of the original Twitter founders remained active in the company: Biz Stone, Jack Dorsey as the company's CEO, and Evan Williams who was on the Board.

Twitter provided an almost-immediate access channel to global celebrities. The majority of the top 10 most-followed Twitter accounts were entertainers who used the service to communicate with their fans, spread news, or build a public image. The near-instant gratification through direct updates from celebrities such as Rihanna, Jimmy Fallon, Lady Gaga, and Taylor Swift and the feeling of inclusion in a specific group of fans was a major reason for social media users to use Twitter. The accounts of high-interest people such as entertainers, politicians, or others at risk of impersonation were verified by Twitter to authenticate their identity. A badge of verification was placed on confirmed accounts to indicate legitimacy. Major sporting events and industry award shows such as the Super Bowl or Academy Awards generated significant online action. The online discussion enabled users to participate in the success of celebrities who often posted behind-the-scenes photo tweets or commentaries. On-set or in-concert tweets were other methods utilized by celebrities to enhance their appeal and fan interaction.

Twitter was quite simple: Tweets were limited to 140 characters until late 2017 when the limit was raised to 280. The character constraint made it easy for users to create, distribute, and discover content that was consistent across the Twitter platform as well as optimized for mobile devices. Consequently, the large volume of Tweets drove high velocity information exchange. Twitter's aim was to become an indispensable daily companion to live human experiences. The company did not have restrictions on whom a user could follow, which greatly enhanced the breadth and depth of available content and allowed users to find the content they cared about most. Also, users could be followed by hundreds of thousands, or millions of other users without requiring a reciprocal relationship, enhancing the ability of users to reach a broad audience. Twitter's public platform allowed both the company and others to extend the reach of Twitter content: Media outlets distributed Tweets to complement their content by making it more timely, relevant, and comprehensive. Tweets had appeared on over one million third-party websites, and in the second quarter of 2013, there were approximately 30 billion online impressions of Tweets.

The Twitter Brand Image

Twitter had a powerful brand image. Its mascot bird was not chosen because birds make tweeting sounds, but rather because "whether soaring high above the earth to take in a broad view, or flocking with other birds to achieve a common purpose, a bird in flight is the ultimate representation of freedom, hope and limitless possibility."[1]

Twitter was initially named "Jitter" and "Twitch," because that is what a phone would do when it received a tweet. However, neither name evoked the image that the founders wanted. Noah Glass got a dictionary and went to "Twitch," then to subsequent words starting with "Tw." He found the word "Twitter," which in the Oxford English dictionary means a short inconsequential burst of information, and chirps from birds. Dorsey and Glass thought that "twitter" described exactly what they were doing, so they decided on that name. The name was already owned, but not being used, and the company was able to buy it very cheaply.

In 2012, the old Twitter bird was redesigned, slightly resized, changed from red to blue, and named Larry the Bird (named after NBA star Larry Bird). The lowercase "t" icon and the text "twitter" were removed; the company name was no longer on the logo. The blue bird alone communicated the Twitter brand. "Twitter achieved in less than six years what Nike, Apple, and Target took decades to do: To be recognizable without a name, just an icon."[2]

According to a Twitter survey conducted to help understand the company's brand legacy, 90 percent of Twitter users worldwide recognized the Twitter brand. Twitter's 2018 ad campaign "What's happening" used only the Twitter logo and hashtag symbol. The Twitter brand was called "minimalization at its finest"[3]—an advertising campaign that did not have one word, but yet delivered a powerful message from the brand.

Twitter's Global High Profile

Twitter had become very well-known because of several high-profile users. Several of the world's leaders had millions of followers, as shown in Exhibit 3. From May 2017 to May, 2019, U.S. President Donald Trump's follow count increased to 60.3 million. President Trump regularly used Twitter to break news, praise his friends, campaign for supporters, and feud with his enemies; consequently, Twitter was in the daily news almost constantly in 2019.

Although the world's leaders had millions of followers, others have far more. As of May 2019, Katy Perry had over 107,400,000 followers, Justin Bieber 105.5 million, former U.S. President Barack Obama 106.1 million, Rihanna 90.9 million, Ellen DeGeneres 77.6 million, Lady Gaga 78.6 million, and Justin Timberlake 64.9 million.

The miraculous plane crash on New York's Hudson River in 2009 was broken on Twitter, and on May 1, 2011, an IT consultant in Pakistan unknowingly live-tweeted the U.S. Navy Seal raid that killed Osama Bin Laden over nine hours before the raid was on the news. Prince William announced his engagement to Catherine Middleton in 2010 on Twitter. Whitney Houston's death and the bombing at the Boston marathon were broken on Twitter. President Obama used Twitter to declare victory in the 2012 U.S. presidential election, with a Tweet that was viewed about 25 million times on the Twitter platform and widely distributed offline in print and broadcast media.

Twitter Services, Products, and Revenue Streams

Twitter's primary service was the Twitter global platform for real-time public self-expression and conversation, which allowed people to create, consume, discover, and distribute content. Some of the most trusted media outlets in the world, such as CNN, Bloomberg, the Associated Press, and BBC used Twitter to distribute content. Periscope was a mobile app launched by Twitter in 2015 that enabled people to broadcast and watch live video with others. Periscope broadcasts could be viewed through Twitter and mobile or desktop web browsers.

Twitter Inc. generated advertising and data licensing revenue as shown in Exhibit 4 by providing mobile advertising exchange services through the Twitter MoPub exchange, and offering data products and data licenses that allowed their data partners to search and analyze historical and real-time data on the Twitter platform, which consisted of public tweets and their content. Also, Twitter's data partners usually purchased licenses to access all or a portion of the company's data for a fixed period. The company operated a mobile ad exchange and received service fees from transactions completed on the exchange. The Twitter mobile ad exchange allowed buyers and sellers to purchase and sell advertising inventory, and it matched buyers and sellers.

EXHIBIT 3

World Leaders with the Most Twitter Followers as of May 2018

	Millions of Followers
Pope Francis, Vatican @Pontifex	33.7
Donald Trump, U.S. @RealDonaldTrump	30.1
Narendra Modi, India @NarendraModi	30.1
Prime Minister, India @PMOIndia	18.0
President, U.S. @POTUS	17.8
The White House, U.S. @WhiteHouse	14.4
Recep Erdogan, Turkey @RT_Erdogan	10.3
HH Sheikh Mohammed, UAE @Jokowi	7.9
Joko Widodo, Indonesia @jokowi	7.4

Source: Statista, "World Leaders with the Most Twitter Followers as of May 2018," accessed July 23, 2019, https://www.statista.com/statistics/281375/heads-of-state-with-the-most-twitter-followers/.

Twitter Restructures

On June 29, 2018, Dorsey announced that he was restructuring Twitter to make the company quicker and more creative, as Ed Ho, VP of product and

EXHIBIT 4

Twitter Inc. Advertising and Data Licensing Revenue, 2016–2018 (in thousands of $)

	YEAR ENDED DECEMBER 31,			2017 to 2018	2016 to 2017
	2018	**2017**	**2016**	**% Change**	**% Change**
Advertising services	$2,617,397	$2,109,987	$2,248,052	24%	(6)%
Data licensing and other	424,962	333,312	281,567	27%	18%
Total revenue	$3,042,359	$2,443,299	$2,529,619	25%	(3)%

2018 Compared to 2017. Revenue in 2018 increased by $599.1 million compared to 2017.

Source: Twitter, Inc., 2019 Annual Report, accessed August 2, 2019, http://www.annualreports.com/HostedData/AnnualReports/PDF/NYSE_TWTR_2018.pdf.

engineering, stepped down to a part-time position. Twitter employees would be organized in functional groups such as engineering, as opposed to the present product teams. Dorsey decided on the structural change to simplify the way the company worked and to make the organization "more straightforward." He believed that a "pure end-to-end functional organization" would help make decision making clearer, allow the company to build a stronger culture, and prepare the company for increased creativity and innovation. Dorsey believed that Twitter must enter a creativity phase to be relevant and important to the world.

Twitter's Stock Performance

Twitter went public on November 7, 2013, with an IPO price of $26.00, and the stock closed up 73 percent ($44.94) on its first trading day. The stock hit its all-time high of $69.00 on January 3, 2014, and began a long down-trend, lasting *until mid-April 2017.* On August 21, 2015, Twitter shares dropped below the IPO price to $25.87, rebounded slightly, and then slid to $14.10 on May 13, 2016. The stock did not get above the IPO price of $26.00 until early February 2018. After a year's climb, Twitter stock hit a three-year high of $47.79 in early July 2018, and then began to slide again, trading in the $28.00 to $32.00 range until rebounding to $40.80 in early May 2019. Exhibit 5 tracks Twitter's market performance between May 2014 and April 2019.

Twitter, Inc. joined the S&P 500 index on June 7, 2018, replacing Monsanto. The addition of Twitter was unusual because the S&P regulations required that the sum of a member company's four most recent quarters, as well as the last quarter, were positive. In April of 2018, Twitter reported its second consecutive profitable quarter, which followed 16 consecutive quarters of losses. The addition of Twitter to the S&P 500 Index would increase the number of individual investors who owned the stock through index funds that track the large company stock gauge. Twitter's addition to the index fueled a rally that pushed the company's stock to more than $40.00/share, which was its highest price since March of 2015.

Twitter's Major Competitors
Facebook

Facebook was the world's largest online social networking and social media company. It was founded in February 2004 by Mark Zuckerberg, Eduardo Saverin, Dustin Moskivitz, Chris Hughes, and Andrew McCollum. As was common among online social networking companies, Facebook was not immediately profitable; however, after becoming profitable in 2010, it had its IPO in 2012 at $38/share. Although the stock price dropped to under $20 in August 2012, it rebounded and was selling at $217.50/share in mid-July 2018, and then began a slide down to $124.95 in December 2018. In late

EXHIBIT 5

EXHIBIT 5

Monthly Performance of Twitter, Inc.'s Stock Price, May 2014 – May 2019

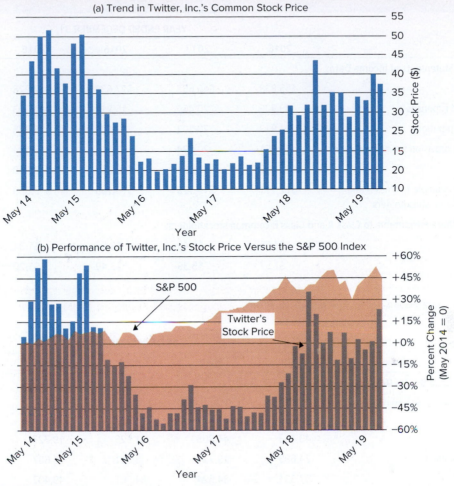

Adapted from bigcharts.marketwatch.com.

December 2018, Facebook stock began a recovery, and in May 2019, was trading at $195.47. In the fourth quarter of 2018, Facebook had 2.32 billion users worldwide—India had the largest number of users at 270 million, the United States was second with 240 million, and Indonesia was third with 140 million.

In January 2019, Facebook had 2.23 billion average monthly users, and 83 percent of the total users were from outside the United States. Facebook's year-over-year revenue growth rate in the first quarter of 2019 was 26 percent. A financial summary for Facebook, Inc. for 2014 to 2018 is presented in Exhibit 6.

WhatsApp

WhatsApp was a freeware and cross-platform messaging and IP service owned by Facebook. The company was founded in 2009 by ex-Yahoo employees Jan Koum and Brian Acton. WhatsApp used the Internet to send messages, audio, video, and images, and was similar to a text messaging service. However, because WhatsApp sent messages over the Internet, the cost for users was much less than texting. The company

EXHIBIT 6

Selected Financial Data for Facebook, Inc., 2014–2018 (in millions of $, except per share data)

	YEAR ENDED DECEMBER 31,				
	2018	2017	2016	2015	2014
Consolidated Statements of Income Data:					
Revenue	$55,838	$40,653	$27,638	$17,928	$12,466
Total costs and expenses	30,925	20,450	15,211	11,703	7,472
Income from operations	24,913	20,203	12,427	6,225	4,994
Income before provision for income taxes	25,361	20,594	12,518	6,194	4,910
Net income	$22,112	$15,934	$10,217	$ 3,688	$ 2,940
Net income attributable to Class A and Class B common stockholders	$22,111	$15,920	$10,188	$ 3,669	$ 2,925
Earnings per share attributable to Class A and Class B common stockholders:					
Basic	$7.65	$5.49	$3.56	$1.31	$1.12
Diluted	$7.57	$5.39	$3.49	$1.29	$1.10

Source: Facebook Inc., 2018 Annual Report, accessed August 2, 2019, http://d18rn0p25nwr6d.cloudfront.net/CIK-0001326801/a109a501-ed16-4962-a3af-9cd16521806a.pdf.

	AS OF DECEMBER 31,				
	2018	2017	2016	2015	2014
Consolidated Balance Sheets Data:					
Cash, cash equivalents, and marketable securities	$41,114	$41,711	$29,449	$18,434	$11,199
Working capital	43,463	44,803	31,526	19,727	11,966
Property and equipment, net	24,683	13,721	8,591	5,687	3,967
Total assets	97,334	84,524	64,961	49,407	39,966
Capital lease obligations	–	–	–	114	233
Total liabilities	13,207	10,177	5,767	5,189	3,870
Additional paid-in capital	42,906	40,584	38,227	34,886	30,225
Total stockholders' equity	84,127	74,347	59,194	44,218	36,096

Source: Facebook Annual Report, 2018.

grew quickly and within a few months of startup, WhatsApp added a service charge to slow down its growth rate. In 2014, WhatsApp was acquired by Facebook for $21.94 billion.

In early 2018, after a long feud with Facebook founder and CEO Mark Zuckerberg about how to get additional revenue from WhatsApp, Koum and Acton resigned from Facebook. Zuckerberg was focused on using targeted ads to WhatsApp's large user base; Koum and Acton were believers in privacy and had no interest in the potential commercial applications. When WhatsApp was sold to Facebook, the founders pledged privacy of WhatsApp. Four years later, Facebook pushed WhatsApp to change its terms of service and give Facebook access to WhatsApp users' phone numbers. Facebook also wanted a unified profile that could be used for ad targeting and data mining, and a recommendation system that would suggest Facebook friends based on WhatsApp contacts. WhatsApp had 1.5 billion users in 180 countries in 2019, with 1 billion daily active WhatsApp users and 65 billion messages sent each day.

Snapchat

Snap Inc. was a camera company that believed that reinventing the camera was a great opportunity to improve the way that people communicated and lived. Snap, Inc.'s products empowered people to express themselves, live in the moment, learn about

the world, and have fun together. The company's flagship product, Snapchat, was a camera application that helped people communicate visually with friends and family through short videos and images called snaps. Snaps were deleted by default, so there was less pressure to look good when creating and sending images on Snapchat. By reducing the friction typically associated with creating and sharing content, Snapchat became one of the most-used cameras in the world.

Snapchat had 300 million users in February 2019 and, on average, 186 million people used Snapchat daily, creating over 3.5 billion snaps every day; however, its users were declining. A financial summary for Snap Inc. for 2015 through 2017 is presented in Exhibit 7.

EXHIBIT 7

Snap, Inc.: Selected Financial Data (in thousands, except per share amounts)

	YEAR ENDED DECEMBER 31,		
	2018	2017	2016
Consolidated Statements of Operations Data:			
Revenue	$ 1,180,446	$ 824,949	$ 404,482
Costs and expenses:			
Cost of revenue	798,865	717,462	451,660
Research and development	772,185	1,534,863	183,676
Sales and marketing	400,824	522,605	124,371
General and administrative	477,022	1,535,595	165,160
Total costs and expenses	2,448,896	4,310,525	924,867
Operating loss	(1,268,450)	(3,485,576)	(520,385)
Interest income	27,228	21,096	4,654
Interest expense	(3,894)	(3,456)	(1,424)
Other income (expense), net	(8,248)	4,528	(4,568)
Loss before income taxes	(1,253,364)	(3,463,408)	(521,723)
Income tax benefit (expense)	(2,547)	18,342	7,080
Net loss	$(1,255,911)	$(3,445,066)	$ (514,643)
Net loss per share attributable to Class A, Class B, and Class C common stockholders			
Basic	$(0.97)	$(2.95)	$(0.64)
Diluted	$(0.97)	$(2.95)	$(0.64)
Adjusted EBITDA	$(575,637)	$(720,056)	$(459,243)

Source: Snap Inc., 2018 Annual Report, accessed August 2, 2019, https://investor.snap.com/~/media/Files/S/Snap-IR/reports-and-presentations/2018-annual-report.pdf.

Instagram

Instagram was a video- and photo-sharing social network service created by Kevin Systrom and Mike Krieger in 2010. Facebook acquired the company in 2012. The agreed price was $1 billion (a mixture of cash and Facebook stock); however, the final price was $715 million because Facebook's share process tumbled before the deal was finalized. If Instagram was a standalone company, it would be worth more than $100 billion, which would be a 100-fold return for Facebook.

In March 2019, Instagram reached 1.1 billion monthly active users, 88 percent of which were outside the United States, and expected revenues of over $8 billion in the next 12 months. Instagram attracted new users at a faster rate than Facebook's main site. At its present rate of growth, it would have over 2 billion users by 2023.

LinkedIn

LinkedIn was a social media service that operated through websites and mobile apps, and focused primarily on professional networking, which enabled members to create, manage, and share their professional identities online, create professional networks, share insights and knowledge, and find jobs and business opportunities. The company was founded in December 2002 by Allen Blue, Reid G. Hoffman, Jean-Luc Vaillant, Konstantin Guericke, and Eric Ly. LinkedIn was named by *Forbes* as one of America's Best Employers in 2016. LinkedIn was acquired by Microsoft for $26.2 billion in June 2016.

In March 2019, LinkedIn had 575 million users in more than 200 countries and territories worldwide.[4]

Further Signs of Encouragement in First Quarter 2019

Twitter's first-quarter 2019 financial results were positive and unexpectedly robust, with revenue growth up 18 percent year-over-year, from $665 million to $787 million. The company's revenues enjoyed growth across all major product and geographic areas. Twitter's largest growth in income was from the United States, which increased by 25 percent, year-over-year, from $347 million to $432 million. Also, international revenue increased 11 percent, year-over-year, from $318 million to $355 million.

Year-over-year advertising revenue increased by 18 percent during the first quarter of 2019, from $575 million to $679 million, and data licensing revenue increased from $90 million to $107 million, year-over-year, which was a 20 percent increase. Cost of revenue increased 18 percent, and stayed steady at 34 percent of revenue, as in the same period, 2018. Research and development and general and administrative expenses were unchanged, as a percentage of revenue year-over-year, at 34 percent and 19 percent, respectively. Sales and marketing expense dropped to 26 percent in the first quarter of 2019 from 27 percent in the same period in the prior year. Income from operations increased to $93.6 million (12 percent of revenue), up from $74.9 million (11 percent), and net income for the first quarter of 2019 increased to $190 million (24 percent of revenue), up from $60.9 million (9 percent of revenue) in the same period in the prior year.

Twitter announced expectations for fiscal 2019, but did not provide a revenue expectation. The company expected operating expenses to increase by about 20 percent year-over-year due to growth and support for the company's investment priorities. Going into the second quarter of fiscal 2019, Twitter was focused on:

1. Health as the top priority. To help people find credible information and feel safe participating in the conversation on Twitter.

2. Conversation as Twitter's superpower. Promoting more conversation on Twitter to ensure that it is the place where people all around the world go to see and talk.

3. Revenue product and sales to support the growth of Twitter customers around the world. The company will continue to invest in revenue product and work to improve its ad platform and ad formats to help its ad partners launch new products and services and connect with what's happening on Twitter. Also Twitter plans to grow its sales

teams in the United States and internationally to better serve large and medium advertisers.

4. Platform investments to ensure long-term success, in the data centers that host Twitter,

customer data security, and the technology to support and improve the service.

ENDNOTES

1 Twitter, Inc.? "Taking Flight: #Twitterbird," accessed June 09, 2019, https://blog.twitter.com/en_us/a/2012/taking-flight-twitterbird.html

2 Armin Vit, "Twitter Gives You the Bird," Under Consideration, accessed June 09, 2019, https://www.underconsideration.com/brandnew/archives/twitter_gives_you_the_bird.php.

3 Sunil Singh, "How a Logo Personified the Twitter Brand," February 15, 2018, https://gulfmarketingreview.com/brands/how-a-logo-personified-the-twitter-brand/.

4 As stated at about.linkedin.com.

NETFLIX IN 2019: STRIVING TO SOLIDIFY ITS POSITION AS THE GLOBAL LEADER

ARTHUR A. THOMPSON *The University of Alabama*

Throughout 2018 and the first three months of 2019, Netflix was on a roll. Movie and TV show enthusiasts across the world were flocking to become Netflix subscribers in unprecedented numbers, and shareholders were exceptionally pleased with Netflix's fast-rising stock price. Over the past eight years, the company had successfully transformed its business model from one where subscribers paid a monthly fee to receive an unlimited number of DVDs each month (delivered and returned by mail with one title out at a time) to a model where subscribers paid a monthly fee to watch an unlimited number of movies and TV episodes streamed over the Internet. In April 2019, Netflix was the world's leading Internet television network with 149 million paid streaming memberships in over 190 countries enjoying more than 165 million hours of TV shows and movies per day, including original series, documentaries, and feature films. Netflix members not only could watch as much streamed content as they wanted—anytime, anywhere, on nearly any Internet-connected screen— but could also play, pause, and resume watching, all without commercials. In the United States, Netflix still had nearly 2.5 million members in May 2019 who, because of limited Internet service or just personal preference, continued to receive DVDs solely by mail (but the numbers of mail-only subscribers were declining monthly).

Netflix's swift growth to 60 million paid subscribers in the United States and its promising potential for rapidly growing its base of international subscribers past 90 million pushed the company's stock price to $360 per share in mid-May 2019 (and an all-time high of $423 in July 2018). Already solidly entrenched as the world's biggest and best-known Internet subscription service for watching TV shows and movies, the only two questions for Netflix in 2019 seemed to be how big Netflix's service might one day become in the world market for on-demand streaming of movies and TV episodes and whether the company had the competitive and financial strength to combat the efforts of larger, resource-rich rivals looking to steal subscribers away from Netflix.

Financial statement data for Netflix for 2005 through 2018 are shown in Exhibits 1 and 2. Netflix had never paid a dividend to its shareholders and the company had declared it had no present intention of paying any cash dividends in the foreseeable future.

Netflix's Drive to Globalize Its Operations

Exhibit 3 shows the remarkably short time frame it took for Netflix to expand its operations from a U.S.-only subscriber base to a global subscriber base. But in 2019, Netflix was still struggling to surmount the barriers erected by the Chinese government in allowing Netflix to enter the People's Republic of China, the world's most massive market for entertainment. The Chinese government had for several years refused to issue Netflix a license to operate in China, preferring instead to control the content its citizens were allowed to see—government censors required that an entire series of a TV show had to

EXHIBIT 1

Netflix's Consolidated Statements of Operations, 2005–2018 (in millions of $, except per share data)

	2018	2017	2016	2010	2005
Revenues	$15,794.3	$11,692.7	$8,830.7	$2,162.6	$682.2
Cost of revenues (almost all of which relates to amortization of content assets)	9,967.5	8,033.0	6,257.5	1,357.4	465.8
Gross profit	5,836.8	3,659.7	2,800.8	805.3	216.4
Operating expenses					
Technology and development	1,221.8	953.7	780.2	163.3	35.4
Marketing	2,369.5	1,436.3	1,097.5	293.8	144.6
General and administrative	630.3	431.1	315.7	64.5	35.5
Other	–	–	–	–	(2.0)
Total operating expenses	4,221.6	3,194.4	2,421.0	521.6	213.4
Operating income	1,605.2	838.7	379.8	283.6	3.0
Interest and other income (expense)	41,725	(115.2)	30.8	(15.9)	5.3
Income before income taxes	1,226.5	485.3	260.5	267.7	8.3
Provision for (benefit from) income taxes	15.2	(73.6)	73.8	106.8	(33.7)
Net income	$ 1,211.2	$ 558.9	$ 186.7	$ 160.8	$ 42.0
Net income per share:					
Basic	$2.78	$1.29	$0.44	$0.44	$0.11
Diluted	$2.68	$1.25	$0.43	$0.40	$0.09
Weighted average common shares outstanding (in millions)					
Basic	435.4	431.9	428.8	365.5	374.5
Diluted	451.2	446.8	438.7	380.1	458.5

Note 1: Some totals may not add due to rounding.

Note 2: The company's board of directors declared a seven-for-one split of its common stock in the form of a stock dividend that was paid in July 2015. Outstanding share and per-share amounts disclosed for all periods prior to 2015 have been retroactively adjusted to reflect the effects of the stock split.

Source: Netflix, Inc., 2006, 2010, and 2018 Annual Report, accessed August 5, 2019.

be approved before it could begin to be shown on an online platform. Aside from the censorship issue, most observers believed the Chinese government also wished to protect aspiring local providers of Internet-based entertainment content from foreign competitors. As a consequence of its dim prospects for getting an operating license from the Chinese government any time soon, in 2017 Netflix had negotiated a licensing arrangement to exclusively provide some of its original content to a fast-growing Chinese company named iQiyi (pronounced Q wee), the leading provider of online entertainment services in China with some 90 million subscribers (as of early 2019). Use of a licensing strategy was attractive to Netflix because it provided a means of gaining content distribution in China and building awareness of the Netflix brand and Netflix content, but the licensing arrangement was expected to generate only small revenues for some years to come.

The U.S. government had instituted restrictions precluding all U.S.-based companies from having operations in North Korea, Syria, and Crimea.

EXHIBIT 2

Selected Balance Sheet and Cash Flow Data for Netflix, 2005–2018 (in millions of $)

	2018	2017	2016	2010	2005
Selected Balance Sheet Data					
Cash, cash equivalents, and short-term investments	$ 3,794.5	$ 2,822.8	$ 1,773.8	$350.4	$212.3
Current assets	9,694.1	7,670.0	5,720.3	637.2	243.7
Total content assets	20,112.1	14,682.0	11,008.8	362.0	57.0
Total assets	25,974.4	19,012.7	13,586.6	982.1	364.7
Current liabilities	6,487.3	5,466.3	4,586.7	388.6	137.6
Long-term debt*	10,360.1	6,499.4	3,364.3	200.0	–
Stockholders' equity	5,238.8	3,582.0	2,679.8	290.2	226.3
Cash Flow Data					
Net cash (used in) provided by operating activities	$(2,680.5)	$(1,785.9)	$(1,474.0)	$276.4	$157.5
Net cash provided by (used in) investing activities	(339.1)	34.3	49.8	(116.1)	(133.2)
Net cash provided by (used in) financing activities	4,048.5	3,077.0	1,091.3	(100.0)	13.3

*All of Netflix's long-term debt consisted of senior unsecured notes that were issued at various points in time and had various maturity dates and various fixed rates of interest.

Source: Netflix, Inc., 2005, 2011, and 2018 Annual Report, accessed August 5, 2019.

EXHIBIT 3

Netflix's Expansion into New Geographic Areas

Date	Entry into New Geographical Areas
September 2010	Canada
September 2011	42 countries in Central America, South America, and the Caribbean
January 2012	United Kingdom, Ireland
October 2012	Denmark, Sweden, Norway, Finland
September 2013	Netherlands
September 2014	Austria, Belgium, France, Germany, Luxembourg, Switzerland
March 2015	Australia, New Zealand
September 2015	Japan
October 2015	Spain, Portugal, Italy
January 2016	Rest of the world—some 130 countries (but excluding the People's Republic of China, North Korea, Syria, and Crimea)

Source: Netflix, Inc., 2017 Annual Report, accessed August 5, 2019, https://s22.q4cdn.com/959853165/files/doc_financials/annual_reports/0001065280-18-000069.pdf.

Netflix estimated that it usually took about two years after the initial launch in a new country or geographic region to attract sufficient subscribers to generate a positive "contribution profit"—Netflix defined "contribution profit (loss)" as revenues less cost of revenues (which consisted of amortization of content assets and expenses directly related to the acquisition, licensing, and production/delivery of such content) and marketing expenses associated with its domestic streaming and international streaming business segments (the company had ceased all marketing activities related to its domestic DVD business).

The Fast-Changing Market for Entertainment Video

In 2018, the world market for entertainment video (movies, TV episodes, and live-streamed events) was undergoing rapid and disruptive change being driven by (1) increasingly pervasive consumer access to high-speed Internet connections, (2) the variety of devices and downloadable apps that consumers could use to access both broadcast and streamed entertainment programs, and (3) the mounting intensity with which well-known, resource-rich companies were competing for viewers of entertainment programs. As of March 31, 2019, almost 4.4 billion of the world's population of 7.7 billion people (56.8 percent) used the Internet; the number of people with broadband Internet access was moving rapidly toward 1 billion—a number that Netflix viewed as its near-term market opportunity.[1] YouTube and Facebook already had 2 billion monthly active users, a number that Netflix viewed as its long-term market opportunity for accessing and attracting more subscribers. Surveys conducted in December 2018 indicated that the average amount of time individuals spent using the Internet on any device was 6 hours and 42 minutes, equal to more than 100 days of online time per year. The worldwide average *fixed* Internet connection speed was 54.3 million bits per second (mbps) and the worldwide average *mobile* Internet connection speed was 25.1 mbps.[2] These speeds were expected to climb steadily toward 75 mbps (or more) by 2025.

People could watch streamed entertainment on smartphones, all types of computers (tablets, laptops, and desktops), in-home TVs with either built-in Internet connections or connected to a digital video disc (DVD) player with built-in Internet access, and recent versions of video game consoles. During the past five to eight years, most households with high-speed Internet service and/or Internet-connected TVs or DVD players had shifted from renting or buying physical DVDs with the desired content to almost exclusively watching streamed movies and TV episodes. This was because streaming had the advantage of allowing household members to order and instantly watch the movies and TV programs they wanted to see and was much more convenient than patronizing a nearby rent-or-purchase location. This shift had permanently undercut the once-thriving businesses of selling movie and music DVDs and/or renting DVDs at local brick-and-mortar locations and standalone rental kiosks (like Redbox in the United States) or delivering/returning DVDs by mail (as at Netflix) and unleashed a fierce battle among the providers of streamed content in countries across the world to become the preferred streamed content provider (or, at worst, a frequently used content provider).

Consumers could view streamed entertainment from growing numbers and types of providers, and the options included:

- Using a TV remote to order movies and popular TV shows instantly streamed directly to a TV (or other connected device) on a pay-per-view basis (generally referred to as "video-on-demand" or VOD). Most all traditional cable and satellite providers of multichannel TV packages were promoting a library of several hundred movie titles (and often prior episodes of top TV shows, as well as other content, most recently including live sports) available on-demand to regular subscribers having a cable or satellite box; the rental prices for pay-per-view and VOD movies from such providers ranged from $1 to $6, but the rental price for popular recently released movies was usually $3.99 to $5.99. However, most every traditional cable and satellite provider had recently begun offering a growing variety of content-viewing options that were streamed directly to a single location (and viewable simultaneously on up to as many as eight compatible WiFi enabled devices) via a special downloadable streaming application that eliminated the need for a cable/satellite box. These streaming options allowed subscribers to customize their own service package (number of channels, Internet speed, telephone service, and home security service). Recently, in the United States, wireless phone providers like AT&T and Verizon had also begun installing thousands of miles of fiber-optic cable annually in their service areas that enabled them to simultaneously provide residences and apartments with multiple content-viewing options (including VOD), perhaps bundled with telephone service, ultra-high-speed Internet service, and/or home security at an attractive monthly price (for a specified period, usually one or two years).

- There were many subscription-based providers of streamed video content across the world in 2019, and more new entrants were expected in upcoming years. In the United States, in early 2019, the clear market leader was Netflix, followed by Amazon Prime and Hulu; others included Vudu, Sling TV, HBO NOW, Starz, MAX GO® (Cinemax), Showtime, Direct TV Now, and Play Station Vue. Disney had announced it would initiate a streaming serve in late 2019. An estimated 37 percent of TV viewers in the United States used subscription-based streaming services in 2017 to watch digital video content on their TVs. However, YouTube ranked first as the market leader among video and entertainment websites, with almost 10 times as many site visits to view videos as Netflix; of course, most all YouTube videos could be accessed for free, and many were videos uploaded by people or brands. The number of video viewers using mobile devices, such as smartphones and tablets, was exploding all across the world. In the United States alone, the number using mobile devices to watch videos was projected to reach 179 million by 2020, and an additional 57 million were expected to watch videos on computers and Internet-connected TVs. Exhibit 4 shows the percentage of Internet users, by country, who watched online video content on any device as of January 2018.

EXHIBIT 4

The Percentage of Internet Users in Selected Countries Who Watched Online Video Content on Any Device as of January 2018

Country	Percentage of Internet Users Watching Online Video Content on Any Device
Saudi Arabia	95%
China	92%
New Zealand	91%
Mexico	88%
Australia	88%
Spain	86%
India	85%
Brazil	85%
United States	85%
Canada	83%
France	81%
Germany	76%
South Korea	71%
Japan	69%

Source: Statista, "Percentage of internet users who watch online video content on any device as of January 2018, by country," accessed June 09, 2019, https://www.statista.com/statistics/272835/share-of-internet-users-who-watch-online-videos/.

Competitors offering pay-per-view and VOD rentals were popular options for households and individuals who rented movies occasionally (once or maybe twice per month), since the rental costs tended to be less than the monthly subscription prices for unlimited streaming from the various streaming providers. However, competitors offering unlimited Internet streaming plans tended to be the most economical and convenient choice for individuals and households who watched an average of three or more titles per month and for individuals who wanted to be able to watch movies or TV shows or special live events streaming on mobile devices.

Netflix was by far the global leader in Internet streaming. It faced numerous competitors of varying competitive strength, geographic coverage, and content offerings; currently, none could match Netflix's global scope or the size of its content library. In North America, Netflix's four biggest Internet streaming competitors in 2019 were Amazon Prime, Hulu, HBO (with its HBO NOW and HBO GO service options), and Walt Disney (beginning in late 2019 and going forward):

- *Amazon Prime Video*—Amazon competed with Netflix via its Amazon Prime membership service. Individuals and households could become an Amazon Prime member for a fee of $119 per year or $11.99 per month (after a one-month free trial); there was a discounted price for students. In April 2018, Amazon announced that it had over 100 million Amazon Prime members globally. In January 2019, Amazon announced that it had over 100 million members in the United States alone. While Amazon had originally created its Amazon Prime membership program as a means of providing unlimited two-day shipping to customers who frequently ordered merchandise from Amazon and liked to receive their orders quickly, in 2012 Amazon began including movie and music streaming as a standard benefit of Prime membership— Amazon's video streaming service was called "Prime Video." Amazon's Prime Video content library contained thousands of movies that could be streamed to members, over 40 original series and movies, and some two million songs.

  In 2017 and 2018, Amazon made Prime Video more attractive to Prime members by (1) adding Prime Originals to its offerings, like *The Marvelous Mrs. Maisel* and the Oscar-nominated movie *The Big Sick;* (2) debuting *NFL Thursday Night Football* on Prime Video (which attracted more than 18 million total viewers over 11 games); and (3) expanding its slate of programming across the globe—launching new seasons of *Bosch, Sneaky Pete,* and *The Man in the High Castle* from the United States, *The Grand Tour* from the United Kingdom, *You Are Wanted* from Germany, while adding new *Sentosha* shows from Japan, along with *Breathe* and the award-winning *Inside Edge* from India. In April 2018, Amazon announced it had agreed to pay the National Football League $65 million a year to stream *NFL Thursday Night Football* globally

to its Amazon Prime members in 2018 and 2019. Also in 2018, Prime Channels offerings were expanded to include CBS All Access in the United States and newly launched channels in the United Kingdom and Germany. In 2017, Prime Video Direct secured subscription video rights for more than 3,000 feature films and committed over $18 million in royalties to independent filmmakers and other rights holders. Going forward, the Prime original series pipeline included Tom Clancy's *Jack Ryan* starring John Krasinski; *The Romanoffs,* starring Aaron Ekhart and Diane Lane; *Carnival Row* starring Orlando Bloom and Cara Delevingne; *Good Omens* starring Jon Hamm; and *Homecoming,* starring Julia Roberts in her first television series. In addition, Prime Video had acquired the global television rights for a multi-season production of *The Lord of the Rings,* as well as *Cortés,* a miniseries based on the epic saga of Hernán Cortés from executive producer Steven Spielberg and starring Javier Bardem. Amazon's budget for Prime Video original content additions and enhancement was reportedly $5 billion in 2018 and $7 billion in 2019.[3]

  Other 2019 benefits of becoming an Amazon Prime member included discounted prices on Kindle eBooks, free reading of designated digital editions of books and magazines, special deals/coupons on purchases of selected products that Amazon sold, one-click ordering via a "dash button," shopping with Alexa, cloud storage and sharing of personal photos and videos, and an opt-in DVD rental service (for an extra fee). In addition, Amazon competed with Netflix's DVDs-by-mail subscription service by allowing people to rent any streamed or downloadable movie, TV program, or other digital content for a limited time (for viewing on a personal computer, portable media player or other compatible device), or to purchase such content in the form of a downloadable file.

- *Hulu*—Hulu had 28 million subscribers as of May 2019, up from 12 million in May 2017. The subscription fee for Hulu was $6 per month for regular streaming (interspersed with ads) and $12 per month for commercial-free streaming, and new subscribers got a one-month free trial. The regular streaming option included advertisements as a means of helping keep the monthly subscription price low. Hulu also offered plans that included not only its video streaming service, but also packages that included 60+ live TV and cable channels (that included sports, news, and entertainment) for a monthly fee of $44.95 and options to add on HBO®, Showtime®, Starz®, and Cinemax®. The Hulu library of offerings included all current season episodes of popular TV shows (available for next-day airing of network TV shows from ABC, NBC, and Fox), over 15,000 back season episodes of 380+ TV shows, over 2,300 movies, most in high-definition, and a growing selection of Hulu-produced original content.

Going into 2018, Hulu was a joint venture co-owned by Walt Disney (30 percent), Fox (30 percent), Comcast (30 percent), and Time Warner (10 percent), but in late 2018 Disney put a deal in place to buy Fox's 30 percent share of Hulu and then, months later, AT&T sold its 10 percent of Hulu to the Disney-Comcast owners of the Hulu joint venture for $1.43 billion. In May 2019, Comcast and Disney announced an agreement whereby Disney would have full 100-percent control of Hulu, starting immediately; the agreement also specified that Comcast would continue to allow Hulu to carry all NBCUniversal content as well as live-stream NBCUniversal channels for Hulu's live TV service until late 2024 (Comcast was the 100-percent owner of NBCUniversal). The deal called for Comcast's ownership stake in Hulu to be officially sold to Disney starting in January 2024.

- *HBO NOW* and *HBO GO*—HBO NOW was an option to receive unlimited streaming of content in HBO's library that included movies, documentaries, sports programs, and original series (*Game of Thrones, Westworld, Silicon Valley, True Detective, Big Little Lies, Sharp Objects*) for a cancel-anytime monthly subscription price of $14.99 (as of 2019). HBO NOW content was viewable on mobile phones, tablets, computers, and Internet-connected TVs. HBO NOW, offered only in the United States and a few

territories, had a reported 8 million subscribers as of February 2019, but it was expected to be hit with thousands of cancellations when its flagship *Game of Thrones* series ended in May 2019. A 2019 study found that HBO subscribers were far less loyal than those subscribing to other streaming services; only 26 percent of HBO subscribers who made their first payment during season 7 of *Game of Thrones* were still subscribers six months later.[4] HBO GO was a bonus offering only for people who subscribed to HBO through a cable or satellite provider; such subscribers used a downloadable app to access the HBO GO website, entered their user name and password of their cable provider to authenticate their subscription, and then clicked on the desired HBO content that was viewable on mobile phones, laptops, and computers. HBO had no interest in offering its HBO GO option to people who were not cable subscribers because its principal revenue source was a percentage of the monthly fees that some 142 million cable subscribers across the world paid their cable company for HBO as part of their cable package—HBO was typically the most expensive of the premium cable channels offered by cable/satellite providers. However, as of 2018, HBO was offering a direct streaming service akin to HBO NOW in several countries that had low cable subscriber rates (namely Spain, Colombia, and the four Nordic countries—Norway, Denmark, Sweden, and Finland). HBO was a division of Time Warner, which had recently merged with AT&T.

- *Walt Disney*— In early 2019 Disney announced it would initiate a streaming service on November 12, 2019, at a monthly subscription price of $6.99. The service included content from all of Disney's library of previously released Disney movies, the content of all of 21st Century Fox's media library (purchased from Fox for $71.3 billion in early 2019), and the licensed content of Hulu, which Disney gained full control over in May 2019. Disney had licensing deals with AT&T and Comcast for Hulu's current content to appear on their services until the time the existing licenses for this content expired.

In April 2018, Comcast, one of the largest cable operators in the United States, announced it had expanded its partnership with Netflix and would begin including a Netflix subscription in new and existing packages offered to its cable subscribers. In July 2018, *The Wall Street Journal* reported that Walmart was likely to enter the video streaming market and establish a subscription service with programming that targeted "Middle America" and that would likely involve a subscription price below what Netflix charged.[5] Walmart was working with a veteran television executive with experience in pay-television on plans for the service. However, in 2019 AT&T, Apple, and Comcast announced plans for launching their own video-streaming services. AT&T planned to use the content of its WarnerMedia division as the core of its streaming service—WarnerMedia consisted of HBO, Turner Broadcasting (which consisted of cable channels CNN, TBS, and TNT), and Warner Bros. Studio and came under AT&T's ownership when its $85.4 billion merger with Time Warner was finalized in 2019 (HBO NOW was to continue as a standalone service to interested consumers). In 2019 AT&T had over 153 million wireless phone subscribers and was also the owner of satellite TV service DirecTV. Disney, in preparation for launching its streaming service in late 2019, had notified Netflix of its intent to withdraw its movies and shows from Netflix as existing licenses expired. In June 2019, it was unclear what bundle of content Apple would use to underpin its streaming service.

Netflix's Business Model and Strategy

Since launching the company's online movie rental service in 1999, Reed Hastings, founder and CEO of Netflix, had been the chief architect of Netflix's subscription-based business model and strategy that had transformed Netflix into the world's largest online entertainment subscription service. Hastings's goals for Netflix were simple—build the world's best Internet service for entertainment content, keep improving Netflix's content offerings and services faster than rivals, attract growing numbers of subscribers every year, and grow long-term earnings per share. Hastings was a strong believer in moving early and fast to initiate strategic changes that would help Netflix outcompete rivals, strengthen its brand image and reputation, and fortify its position as the industry leader.

Netflix's Subscription-Based Business Model

Netflix employed a subscription-based business model. Members could choose from a variety of subscription plans whose prices and terms had varied over the years. Originally, all of the subscription plans were based on obtaining and returning DVDs by mail, with monthly prices dependent on the number of titles out at a time. But as more and more households began to have high-speed Internet connections, Netflix began bundling unlimited streaming with each of its DVD-by-mail subscription options, with the long-term intent of encouraging subscribers to switch to watching instantly streamed content rather than using DVD discs delivered and returned by mail. The DVDs-by-mail part of the business had order fulfillment costs and postage costs that were bypassed when members opted for an instant streaming membership subscription.

In 2018, Netflix offered three types of streaming membership plans. Its basic plan, currently priced at $8.99 per month in the United States, included access to standard definition quality streaming on a single screen at a time. Its standard plan, currently priced at $12.99 per month, was the most popular streaming plan and included access to high-definition quality streaming on two screens concurrently. The company's premium plan, currently priced at $15.99 per month, included access to high-definition and ultra-high definition quality content on four screens concurrently (subject to Internet service and device capabilities). As of April 2019, international pricing for the three plans ranged from approximately $3 to $20 per month per U.S. dollar equivalent; in many countries, the monthly prices of popular international plans were in the range of $7 to $10 per U.S. dollar equivalent.[6] Netflix executives expected that the prices of the various subscription plans in each country would likely rise over time, thereby helping boost the global monthly average revenue the company received per paying subscriber above the 2018 average of $10.31 ($11.40 per month in the United States and $9.43 per month internationally).

Netflix had organized its operations into three business segments: domestic streaming, international streaming, and domestic DVD. The domestic streaming segment derived revenues from monthly membership fees for services consisting solely of streaming content to members in the United States. The international streaming segment derived revenues from monthly membership fees for services consisting solely of streaming content to members outside the United States; the sizes of the title libraries (movies + episodes of TV shows) offered in each country were typically in the 2,000 to 6,000 range, but offerings in the native languages of countries like Sweden, Norway, Poland, Italy, and most Arab-speaking countries were more limited (2,200 to 3,700).[7] The domestic DVD segment derived revenues from monthly membership fees for services consisting solely of DVD-by-mail. Recent performance of Netflix's three business segments is shown in Exhibit 5.

EXHIBIT 5

Netflix's Performance by Business Segment, 2015–2018 (in millions, except for average monthly revenues per paying member and percentages)

Domestic Streaming Segment	2018	2017	2016	2015
Memberships				
Paid memberships at year-end	58.5	52.8	47.9	43.4
Trial memberships at year-end	2.1	2.0	1.5	1.3
Total	60.6	54.8	49.4	44.7
Net membership additions	5.8	5.55	4.7	5.6
Average monthly revenue per paying membership	$11.40	$10.18	$9.21	$8.50
Revenues	$7,646.6	$6,153.0	$5,077.3	$4,180.3
Cost of Revenues (Note 1)	4,038.4	3,319.2	2,855.8	2,487.2
Marketing costs	1,025.4	603.7	412.9	313.6
Contribution profit (Note 2)	$2,582.9	$2,078.5	$1,712.4	$1,375.5
Contribution margin	34%	34%	34%	33%
International Streaming Segment				
Memberships				
Paid memberships at year-end	80.8	57.8	41.2	27.4
Trial memberships at year-end	7.1	5.0	3.2	2.6
Total	87.9	62.8	44.4	30.0
Net membership additions	25.1	18.5	14.3	11.7
Average monthly revenue per paying membership	$9.43	$8.66	$7.81	$7.48
Revenues	$7,782.1	$5,089.2	$3,211.1	$1,953.4
Cost of Revenues (Note 1)	5,776.0	4,359.6	3,042.7	1,780.4
Marketing costs	1,334.1	832.5	684.6	506.4
Contribution profit (Note 2)	$ 672.0	$ (102.9)	$ (516.2)	$ (333.4)
Contribution margin	9%	(2)%	(16)%	(17)%

Domestic Streaming Segment	2018	2017	2016	2015
Domestic DVD Segment				
Memberships				
Paid memberships at year-end	2.7	3.3	4.0	4.8
Trial memberships at year-end	.0	.1	.1	.1
Total	2.7	3.4	4.1	4.9
Net membership losses		.7	.8	.9
Average monthly revenue per paying membership	$10.19	$10.17	$10.22	$10.30
Revenues	$ 365.6	$ 450.5	$ 542.3	$ 645.7
Cost of Revenues (Note 1)	153.1	202.5	262.7	323.9
Marketing costs	—	—	—	—
Contribution profit (Note 2)	$ 212.5	$ 248.0	$ 279.5	$ 321.8
Contribution margin	58%	55%	52%	50%
Global Totals				
Global streaming memberships at year end, including free trials	148.5	117.6	93.8	74.8
Global streaming average monthly revenue per paying membership	$10.31	$9.43	$8.61	$8.15
Revenues	$15,794.3	$11,692.7	$8,830.7	$6,779.5
Operating income	1,605.2	838.7	379.8	305.8
Operating margin	10%	7%	4%	5%
Net income	$ 1,221.2	$ 558.9	$ 186.7	$ 122.6

Note 1: Cost of revenues for the domestic and international streaming segments consist mainly of the amortization of streaming content assets, with the remainder relating to the expenses associated with the acquisition, licensing, and production of such content. Cost of revenues in the domestic DVD segment consist primarily of delivery expenses such as packaging and postage costs, content expenses, and other expenses associated with the company's DVD processing and customer service centers.

Note 2: The company defined contribution margin as revenues less cost of revenues and marketing expenses incurred by segment.

Source: Netflix, Inc., 2017 and 2018 Annual Report, accessed August 5, 2019.

The DVD-by-Mail Option

Subscribers who opted to receive movie and TV episode DVDs by mail went to Netflix's website, selected one or more movies from its DVD library, and received the movie DVDs by first-class mail generally within one business day. Subscribers could keep a DVD for as long as they wished, with no due dates, no late fees, no shipping fees, and no pay-per-view fees. Subscribers returned DVDs via the U.S. Postal Service in a prepaid return envelope that came with each movie order.

The Domestic and International Streaming Options

Netflix launched its Internet streaming service in January 2007, with instant-watching capability for 2,000 titles on personal computers. Very quickly, Netflix invested aggressively to enable its software to instantly stream content to a growing number of "Netflix-ready" devices, including video game consoles (made by Sony, Microsoft, and Nintendo), Internet-connected DVD and Blu-ray players, Internet-connected TVs, TiVo DVRs, and special

Netflix players made by Roku and several other electronics manufacturers. At the same time, it began licensing increasing amounts of digital content that could be instantly streamed to subscribers. Initially, Netflix took a "metered" approach to streaming, in essence offering an hour per month of instant watching on a PC for every dollar of a subscriber's monthly subscription plan. In 2010, Netflix switched to an unlimited streaming option on all of its monthly subscription plans. According to one source, Netflix had an estimated 6,800 movie titles and 530 TV shows available for streaming as of 2010.[8]

In recent years, however, Netflix had gradually shrunk the number of movie titles in its streaming library to approximately 4,000 as of early 2019 and dramatically increased the number of *episodes* of TV shows to approximately 4,700 in early 2019. Netflix had increased the number of new original content offerings in each of the past six years. There were two reasons for the shift in the makeup of Netflix's streaming content. One reason was internal data showing that subscribers spent only about one-third of their time on Netflix watching movies; the second reason was a conviction on the part of Netflix's content executives that if viewers were passionate about a movie, they would have already seen it in theaters by the time it ended up on Netflix. To make the company's movie library more valuable for its subscribers, Netflix had begun releasing a progressively larger number of original movies (80 movies were released in 2018—the number for 2019 had not been announced as of May 2019) and creating more multi-episode original TV series like past hits *House of Cards, The Crown, Orange Is the New Black,* and *Stranger Things.* Going forward, Netflix was expected to continue to place greater emphasis on its own original content—both movies and original TV series—chiefly as a way to more strongly differentiate itself from competitors; top management had announced its intention to spend $9.1 billion on original content in 2019, up from $6 billion in 2017. Netflix spent more than $12 billion on original content production and licenses to show content produced by outside sources; according to a report by *Variety* magazine, Netflix's budget for new content (original production plus licenses) was expected to hit $15 billion in 2019 and $17.8 billion in 2020.

Netflix's Strategy

Netflix's strategy in 2019 was focused squarely on:

- Growing the number of domestic and international streaming subscribers.
- Enhancing the appeal of its library of streaming content, with an increasing emphasis on exclusive original movies and TV series produced in-house.
- Spending aggressively on marketing and advertising in all of the countries and geographic regions the company had recently entered to broaden awareness of the Netflix brand and service and thereby support the company's strategic objective to rapidly grow its base of streaming subscribers.
- Expanding the number of titles that members could download for offline viewing.
- Continuously enhancing its user interface.

Subscriber Growth

Netflix executives were keenly aware that rapid subscriber growth was the key to boosting the company's profitability and justifying the company's lofty stock price of $360 (as of May 22, 2019), which was 134 times the company's 2018 diluted earnings per share of $2.68 and 61 times the consensus EPS of $5.88 that Wall Street analysts and Netflix investors were anticipating the company would earn in 2019. Netflix executives expected that close to 80 percent of the gains in subscriber growth in 2019 and beyond would come in the international arena—in 2018 the growth in international subscribers was 81.2 percent of total subscriber growth (including free trials).

New Content Acquisition

Over the years, Netflix had spent considerable time and energy establishing strong ties with various entertainment video providers to both expand its content library and gain access to new releases as soon as possible after they were released for first-run showing in movie theaters. Prior to the recent push by Amazon Prime and Hulu to attract streaming subscribers, Netflix had successfully negotiated *exclusive* rights to show titles produced by a few studios.

In August 2011, Netflix introduced a new "Just for Kids" section on its website that contained a large selection of kid-friendly movies and TV shows. By March 2012, over one billion hours of Just for Kids programming had been streamed to Netflix members.

New content was acquired from movie studios and distributors through direct purchases, revenue-sharing agreements, and licensing agreements to stream content. Netflix acquired many of its new-release movie DVDs from studios for a low upfront fee in exchange for a commitment for a defined period of time either to share a percentage of subscription revenues or to pay a fee based on content utilization. After the revenue-sharing period expired for a title, Netflix generally had the option of returning the title to the studio, purchasing the title, or destroying its copies of the title. On occasion, Netflix also purchased DVDs for a fixed fee per disc from various studios, distributors, and other suppliers.

In the case of movie titles and TV episodes that were streamed to subscribers via the Internet for instant viewing, Netflix generally paid a fee to license the content for a defined period of time, with the total fees spread out over the term of the license agreement (so as to better match up content payments with the stream of subscription revenues coming in for that content). Following the expiration of the license term, Netflix either removed the content from its library of streamed offerings or negotiated an extension or renewal of the license agreement when management believed there was still enough subscriber interest in the content to justify the renewal fees.

Over the past five years, Netflix's rapidly growing subscriber base (as well as the streaming subscriber growth at Amazon Prime Video, Hulu, and other providers) gave movie studios and the network broadcasters of popular TV shows considerably more bargaining power to command higher prices for their content. Netflix management was acutely aware of its diminishing bargaining power in acquiring content that would be especially appealing to subscribers, and the substantial negative impact that paying higher prices for streaming content had on the company's current and future profit margins. Nonetheless, Netflix executives believed there was still room for the company to earn attractive profits on streaming if it could grow its subscriber base fast enough to more than cover the rising costs of content acquisition.

As indicated earlier, Netflix had recently begun devoting the majority of its new content acquisition budget to producing its own original movies and TV series in-house. Several of these shows were being launched in local languages with local producers to appeal directly, if not exclusively, to subscribers in a particular country or region. A new 2017 Brazilian science-fiction show had scored well with audiences around the world, even though it had been produced in Portuguese for Brazil—Netflix's first instance of a local-language program working well in locations where other languages dominated. In the second half of 2018, Netflix introduced a new original series produced in Denmark, called *The Rain,* that Netflix executives believed would have broad global appeal, along with the second season of the Brazilian program (called *3%*). Other new original content scheduled for 2018 included the second season of *13 Reasons Why* (one of Netflix's most watched television shows around the world in 2017), returning seasons of hits like *Luke Cage, GLOW, Dear White People, Unbreakable Kimmy Schmidt, Santa Clarita Diet, Series of Unfortunate Events,* and a comedy feature film with Adam Sandler and Chris Rock, called *The Week Of.*

Marketing and Advertising

Netflix used multiple marketing approaches to attract subscribers, but especially online advertising (paid search listings, banner ads on social media sites, and permission-based e-mails) and ads on regional and national television. To spur subscriber growth, Netflix had boosted marketing expenditures of all kinds from $25.7 million in 2000 (16.8 percent of revenues) to $142.0 million in 2005 (20.8 percent of revenues) to $298.8 million in 2010 (13.8 percent of revenues) to $1.1 billion in 2016 (12.4 percent of revenues) to $1.44 billion in 2017 (12.3 percent of revenues) and to $2.37 billion in 2018 (15.0 percent of revenues). These expenditures related to:

- Online and television advertising in the United States and newly entered countries. Advertising campaigns of one type or another were under way more or less continuously, with the lure of one-month free trials and announcements of new and forthcoming original titles usually being the prominent ad features. Netflix's expenditures for digital and television advertising were $1.8 billion in 2018, $1.09 billion in 2017, $842.4 million in 2016, and $714.3 million in 2015.

- Costs pertaining to free trial subscriptions.
- Payments to the company's partners. These partners consisted mainly of (1) consumer products manufacturers who produced and distributed devices (particularly remote controls) that facilitated connecting TVs and other media equipment to Netflix, and (2) certain cable providers and other multichannel video programming distributors, mobile operators, and Internet service providers who had begun collaborating with Netflix to make it easy for their customers to connect to Netflix. For example, most all brands of Internet-connected TVs now came with a preinstalled Netflix app that was easily accessed via the TV remote; some TV remotes even had Netflix buttons that provided Netflix subscribers with a one-click connection to their watchlist.

In 2018, multi-channel TV providers like Comcast and Sky were offering customers the option to bundle a subscription to Netflix in with their preferred channel packages. Netflix believed collaboration with a host of cable and mobile phone operators across all geographic markets would likely become common practice very quickly. Management was particularly interested in partnering with mobile operators to create quick and easy-to-use procedures for mobile phone users across the world to access Netflix streamed or downloadable programming. Netflix believed it was particularly important to make mobile streaming from Netflix instantly accessible to those people who basically only wanted to have their relationship with Netflix on a mobile device.

In 2019, Netflix expected its growth in marketing expenditures to outpace revenue growth, partly because it had started investing in more extensive marketing campaigns for new original titles to create more density of viewing and conversation around each title. Netflix CEO Reed Hastings explained the

logic behind trying to make certain new titles a bigger hit in a particular nation or among a particular demographic segment:

> We believe this density of viewing helps on both retention and acquisition, because it makes our original titles even less substitutable. Because we operate in so many countries, we are able to try different [marketing] approaches in different markets and continue to learn [how best to market Netflix's original content and differentiate Netflix from rival streaming providers].[9]

Netflix's Title Selection Software and Efforts to Enhance Its Interface with Users

Netflix had developed proprietary software technology that allowed members to easily scan a movie's length, appropriateness for various types of audiences (G, PG, or R), primary cast members, genre, and an average of the ratings submitted by other subscribers (based on 1 to 5 stars). With one click, members could watch a short preview of a movie or TV show if they wished. Most importantly, perhaps, were algorithms that created a personalized 1- to 5-star recommendation for each title that was a composite of a subscribers' own ratings of movies/TV shows previously viewed, movies/TV shows that the member had placed on a "watchlist" for future viewing and/or mail delivery, and the overall or average rating of all subscribers (several billion ratings had been provided by subscribers over the years).

Subscribers often began their search for titles by viewing a list of several hundred personalized movie/TV show recommendations that Netflix's software automatically generated for each member. Each member's list of recommended movies was the product of Netflix-created algorithms that organized the company's entire content library into clusters of similar movies/TV shows and then sorted the titles in each cluster from most liked to least liked based on subscriber ratings. Those subscribers who favorably or unfavorably rated similar movies/TV shows in similar clusters were categorized as like-minded viewers. When a subscriber was online and browsing through the selections, the software was programmed to check the clusters the subscriber had previously viewed, determine which selections in each cluster the customer had yet to view or place on watchlist, and then display those titles in each cluster in an order that started with the title that Netflix's algorithms predicted the subscriber was most likely to enjoy down to the title the subscriber was predicted to least enjoy. In other words, the subscriber's ratings of titles viewed, the titles on the subscriber's watchlist, and the title ratings of all Netflix subscribers determined the order in which the available titles in each cluster or genre were displayed to a subscriber—with one click, subscribers could see a brief profile of each title and Netflix's predicted rating (from 1 to 5 stars) for the subscriber. When subscribers came upon a title they wanted to view, that title could be watch-listed for future viewing with a single click. A member's complete watchlist of titles was immediately viewable with one click whenever the member went to Netflix's website. With one additional click, any title on a member's watchlist could be activated for immediate viewing. Netflix management saw its title recommendation software as a quick and personalized means of helping subscribers identify and then watch titles they were likely to enjoy.

In 2018, Netflix's strategic initiatives in the user interface arena were focused on enhancing the accessibility of Netflix content for subscribers by (1) offering more programs in local languages and (2) improving the streaming and download speeds for subscribers with suboptimal Internet connections—by making program encoding much more efficient so content selections would load more quickly and provide mobile users with a "really incredible video experience."[10] More efficient encoding also enabled subscribers with spotty Internet connections to quickly download some programs for later viewing when offline.

The Financial Strain of Netflix's Growing Expenditures for Original Content and Other Content Acquisitions

The company's heightened strategic emphasis on original content produced in-house had resulted in multibillion-dollar annual increases in Netflix's financial obligations to pay for streaming content and sharply higher negative cash flows from operations (see Exhibit 6). Netflix was covering these obligations with new issues of common stock and new issues of senior notes (Exhibit 6); details of Netflix's outstanding senior notes are shown in Exhibit 7.

EXHIBIT 6

The Growing Financial Strain of Netflix's Strategic Emphasis on Producing Original Content In-House, 2014–2018 (in millions of dollars)

	2018	2017	2016	2015	2014
Streaming content obligations at year-end	$19,285.9	$17,694.6	$14,479.5	$10,902.2	$9,451.1
Additions to streaming content assets	13,043.4	9,805.8	8,653.3	5,771.6	3,773.0
Additions to DVD content assets	38.6	53.7	77.2	78.0	74.8
Amortization of streaming content assets	7,532.1	6,197.8	4,788.5	3,405.4	2,656.3
Amortization of DVD content assets	41.2	60.7	79.0	79.4	71.9
Net cash used in operating activities	(2,680.5)	(1,785.9)	(1,474.0)	(749.4)	16.4
Proceeds from issuance of debt	3,921.8	3,020.5	1,000.0	1,500.0	400.0
Proceeds from issuance of common stock	124.5	88.4	37.0	78.0	60.5
Outstanding senior notes	10,360.0	6,499.4	3,364.3	2,371.4	885.8

Source: Netflix, Inc., 2018, 2016, and 2014 Annual Report, accessed August 5, 2019.

EXHIBIT 7

Netflix's Outstanding Long-Term Debt as of May 2019

Debt Issues	Principal Amount at Par	Issue Date	Maturity Date	Interest Due Dates
5.375% Senior Notes	$1.34 billion	April 2019	November 2029	May 15 and November 15
3.875% Senior Notes	$900 million	April 2019	November 2029	May 15 and November 15
6.375% Senior Notes	$800 million	October 2018	May 2029	May 15 and November 15
4.625% Senior Notes	$1,260 million	October 2018	May 2029	May 15 and November 15
5.875% Senior Notes	$1.9 billion	April 2018	November 2028	April 15 and November 15
4.875% Senior Notes	$1.6 billion	October 2017	April 2028	April 15 and October 15
3.625% Senior Notes	$1.561 billion	May 2017	May 2027	May 15 and November 15
4.375% Senior Notes	$1.0 billion	October 2016	November 2026	May 15 and November 15
5.50% Senior Notes	$700 million	February 2015	February 2022	April 15 and October 15
5.875% Senior Notes	$800 million	February 2015	February 2025	April 15 and October 15
5.750% Senior Notes	$400 million	February 2014	March 2024	March 1 and September 1
5.50% Senior Notes	$700 million	February 2015	February 2022	April 1 and October 1
5.375% Senior Notes	$500 million	February 2013	February 2021	February 1 and August 1

Sources: Company 2018 10-K Report, p. 52; Company press release, April 24, 2019; and Alex Weprin, "Netflix Issues $2.2 billion in Junk Bonds in Debt-Fueled Content Push," Digital News Daily, April 25, 2019, posted at www.mediapost.com, access May 23, 2019.

Netflix management forecasted that the company would have a negative free cash flow deficit of about $3.5 billion in 2019 and that the company would continue to experience negative, but progressively smaller, cash flow deficits, for several more years due to growing expenditures for original content. However, executive management was confident that the company's expected growth in subscribers, subscription revenues, and operating profit margins would in the near future result in positive and growing cash flows from operations, enabling the company to reduce borrowing and begin to pay down its long-term debt. In April 2018, CEO Reed Hastings said:

> We will continue to raise debt as needed to fund our increase in original content. Our debt levels are quite modest as a percentage of our enterprise value, and we believe [issuing] debt is [a] lower cost of capital compared to equity.[11]

ENDNOTES

[1] Transcript of remarks by David Wells, Netflix's Chief Financial Officer, at Morgan Stanley, Technology, Media & Telecom Conference, February 27, 2018, www.netflix.com (accessed April 5, 2018).

[2] Posted at www.thenextweb.com on January 30, 2019 (accessed May 17, 2019).

[3] Adam Levy, "Here's Exactly How Much Amazon Is Spending on Video and Music Content," The Motley Fool LLC, posted at www.fool.com on April 30, 2019 (accessed May 17, 2019).

[4] Sarah Perez, "Winter Is Coming for HBO NOW Subscriber Growth," posted May 17, 2019 at www.techcrunch.com (accessed May 22, 2019).

[5] Joe Flint, Erich Schwartzel, and Sara Nassauer, "Walmart Explores Its Own Streaming Service," Wall Street Journal, July 28, 2018, posted at www.wsj.com (accessed July 31, 2018).

[6] Netflix 2018 10-K Report, p. 19; Rebecca Moody, "Which Countries Pay the Most and Least for Netflix?" posted April 9, 2019 at www.comparitech.com (accessed May 22, 2019).

[7] Netflix 2018 10-K Report, p. 19; Rebecca Moody, "Which Countries Pay the Most and Least for Netflix?" posted April 9, 2019 at www.comparitech.com (accessed May 22, 2019).

[8] Travis Clark, "New Data Shows Netflix's Number of Movies Has Gone Down by Thousands of Titles since 2010 — But Its TV Catalog Size Has Soared," Business Insider, February 20, 2018, www.businessinsider.com (accessed April 16, 2018).

[9] Netflix, Inc., "Q1 Results and Q2 Forecast," April 16, 2018, https://s22.q4cdn.com/959853165/files/doc_financials/quarterly_reports/2018/q1/FINAL-Q1-18-Shareholder-Letter.pdf.

[10] Netflix, Inc., "Q1 Results and Q2 Forecast," April 16, 2018, https://s22.q4cdn.com/959853165/files/doc_financials/quarterly_reports/2018/q1/FINAL-Q1-18-Shareholder-Letter.pdf.

[11] Netflix, Inc. "Netflix CEO Reed Hastings: We Spend Money More Like a Media Company Than a Tech Company," accessed June 09, 2019, https://www.cnbc.com/2018/04/16/netflix-ceo-reed-hastings-were-more-media-than-tech-on-budget.html.

MATTEL INCORPORATED IN 2019: HARD TIMES IN THE TOY INDUSTRY

RANDALL D. HARRIS *Texas A&M University-Corpus Christi*
JEFFREY WYLIE *MBA Student, Texas A&M University-Corpus Christi*

Speaking to investment analysts on February 7, 2019, Ynon Kreiz, the Chief Executive Officer (CEO) of Mattel Incorporated, said: "We're happy to announce our fourth quarter 2018 results, which demonstrate meaningful progress in executing our strategy and significant improvement over last year."[1] Beneath the confident tone, however, were some sobering results: a sales decline of $300 million for the company from 2017–2018, a $500 million net loss in 2018, and a messy bankruptcy and liquidation for one of the company's key sales outlets, Toys "R" Us. These issues, combined with a global downturn for toy sales in 2018, gave a lot of urgency to Kreiz's turnaround efforts at Mattel. Still, there were some bright spots in the CEO's report to analysts: Fourth-quarter results for the company had shown improvement during the critical 2018 holiday season, restructuring efforts inside Mattel were beginning to show results, and sales for the company's flagship products, Barbie and Hot Wheels, had rebounded in the fourth quarter. But was it enough to reverse the slide at Mattel?

Kreiz had been named Chairman and CEO of Mattel on April 19, 2018, and was succeeding Margo Georgiadis in the job. Ms. Georgiadis, hired away from Alphabet Inc.'s Google division, had been appointed as Mattel CEO in February 2017. Unfortunately, Georgiadis had been unable to reverse a sharp drop in Mattel's revenues, earnings, and stock price.[2] The slide in Mattel's fortunes had been sharpened by the bankruptcy of Toys "R" Us, a key customer for Mattel's products, in September 2017. Toys "R" Us had closed all of their stores in the United States on June 29, 2018. Kreiz, appointed while the Toys "R" Us bankruptcy was under way, was now the fourth CEO for Mattel in the last five years.

As he sat listening to his Chief Financial Officer (CFO) discuss the company's earnings in detail with the investment analysts, Ynon Kreiz's mind wandered for a moment and he pondered his next move as CEO of Mattel. Where to begin? In the last several years, Mattel had been involved in off-and-on merger negotiations with Hasbro, their closest competitor in the toy industry. Central to these merger discussions was a painful reality: Children around the world were growing up faster and were increasingly drawn to online content, movies, smartphones and videogames. Competition for store space, sales, and market share in the toy industry was intense. Making matters worse, Mattel's traditional sales channel, physical retail stores, were increasingly under strain and consolidating. The bankruptcy of Toys "R" Us was symptomatic of this retail consolidation. Online retail competition, notably Amazon.com, was increasingly making inroads into the sales of traditional brick-and-mortar retailers. Mattel had also stumbled in their competition with Hasbro, losing out to Hasbro on key contracts with major companies like Disney.

Kreiz had taken the reins of the company with a mandate from investors to streamline Mattel operations, improve the company's focus on technology and entertainment, and deliver a recovery in Mattel's struggling stock price. Central to Kreiz's turnaround plan was a focus on Mattel's power brands, such as

Barbie and Hot Wheels, as well as a push to develop the company's intellectual property (IP) with a move into movies and television programming. However, from a peak stock price of $47.82 per share in 2013, Mattel was now trading between $10 and $15 per share in early 2019. The company had reported losses in both 2017 and 2018. The fourth quarter of 2018, however, showed a glimmer of hope. There were signs that Mattel was beginning to reverse the slide in their fortunes. Was Ynon Kreiz on the right track? What more could be done? Further, what should Kreiz and Mattel do next?

Mattel Incorporated History

Mattel was founded by Ruth and Elliott Handler out of a garage in Southern California in 1945.[3] Their first two products were picture frames and dollhouse furniture crafted from scraps of picture frame. Their first hit toy was the "Uke-A-Doodle," a toy ukulele, released in 1947. Mattel was formally incorporated in 1948 with their headquarters based in Los Angeles, California.[4]

In 1955, Mattel began advertising their toys on a popular television show, the Mickey Mouse Club, which revolutionized the way in which toys were marketed to children. Mattel released a number of new toys on the television show. In 1959, Ruth Handler created an innovative design for a new type of doll, and named it after her own daughter, Barbara. The introduction of the Barbie Doll became a smash hit and propelled Mattel to the top of the toy industry. Mattel would go on to sell over 1 billion Barbie Dolls, making Barbie the largest selling and most profitable toy in Mattel's toy lineup. The Barbie Doll was followed in 1960 with the Chatty Cathy, a talking doll that would change the toy industry and lead to many imitators.

Hot Wheels die-cast vehicles were rolled out in 1968. Hot Wheels toys influenced the lives of several generations of children, leading the company to estimate that at least 41 million children had grown up alongside the Hot Wheels brand. After a long and successful career with Mattel, Ruth and Elliott Handler left Mattel in 1975.

Mattel was an early entrant into the electronic games market, introducing an electronic handheld game in 1977. Initial success with the handheld game led to the IntelliVision home video entertainment system and a spin-off corporation, Mattel Electronics. This early venture into electronics did not last, however, as declining sales and mounting losses forced Mattel into abandoning the electronics initiative. Mattel took a $394 million loss in 1983 and debated a bankruptcy filing. Mattel reevaluated their diversification strategy as a result and closed or divested all non-toy related subsidiaries in the wake of the losses.

The He-Man and the Masters of the Universe line of action figures was the next best seller for the company beginning in 1982. The company estimated sales of the He-Man line at $400 million in 1985.[5] However, the success was short lived and sales dropped, contributing to a loss of $115 million in 1987. Mattel began a revived working relationship with the Disney Company in 1988. This combination revived Mattel, leading to hit products based on Disney characters like Mickey Mouse and characters from the top-grossing Disney animated movie *Toy Story*.

Mattel purchased Fisher-Price in 1993, merged with Tyco Toys in 1997, and acquired the parent company for the American Girl Brand in 1998. The company also acquired the Learning Company, a U.S. based educational software company, in the fall of 1998. The Learning Company, a merger financed with Mattel stock, was acquired for $3.5 billion.[6] One of the Learning Company's more popular software offerings was the "Where in the World is Carmen Sandiego?" series.

Losses from The Learning Company acquisition were almost immediate. In addition to inflated sales forecasts for the unit, Mattel had bought the Learning Company just as children were switching from games and learning toys on CD-ROM to downloading them from the Internet. Unfortunately, The Learning Company was delivering their products primarily on CD-ROM at that time.[7] In addition to the ouster of then CEO Jill Barad, Mattel booked a $430 million loss in 2000.

New CEO Robert Eckert moved swiftly in 2000 to restructure Mattel. He dumped The Learning Company along with other software-related assets and began a restructuring plan for the company, with the goal of achieving $200 million in immediate cost savings. Eckert also reduced the company's dividend and cut about 10 percent of the workforce.[8] Although painful, the company had better luck that year with licensing agreements. In 2000, Mattel retained the master licensing rights to market and sell Harry Potter toys, collectibles and games, and also agreed with Disney to market Disney Princess dolls.

As part of CEO Eckert's restructuring efforts, the company announced in April 2001 that Mattel would close its last U.S. manufacturing site and move the operations to Mexico.[9] This plant closure was part of the continuing cost-cutting efforts at the company, and closed Mattel's final U.S. plant in Murray, Kentucky. The plant had been operational since 1973 and employed 980 manufacturing and distribution workers. Mattel had been an early adopter of overseas manufacturing, and had been making toys in Mexico for 25 years and in Asia for 30 years at the time of this final U.S. plant closure.[10]

By 2007, approximately 65 percent of Mattel's toys were made in China. This included five wholly owned Mattel factories as well as numerous contractor and subcontractor facilities. Mattel had also developed, over time, a reputation for quality and safety in their manufacturing practices.[11] Nevertheless, in May to June 2007, Mattel discovered toys manufactured with lead-tainted paint during routine safety checks at a number of contractor facilities in China. The subsequent investigation into the tainted toys led to a crisis for Mattel, with a large public outcry, regulatory scrutiny, and the recall of over 19 million Mattel-branded toys.[12] While a major setback for the company, Mattel was noted for handling the recalls swiftly and effectively.[13] Mattel also moved swiftly to diversify their manufacturing facilities to other countries in order to avoid supply disruptions and other risks.

Mattel gradually recovered from the lead paint crisis, and revenue growth for the company resumed in 2010. Then, in 2012, sales of Barbie Dolls began to drop.[14] Gross sales for the Barbie Doll line exceeded $1.2 billion in 2012, and the drop in Barbie sales was balanced by strong sales in other Mattel toy lines, particularly the Disney Princess Doll line. The release of the Disney movie *Frozen* provided a sharp boost to Mattel's Disney line of dolls and related products in 2013, and this somewhat countered the slump in the core Barbie brand. Net sales for Mattel Inc. overall peaked in 2013 at $6.48 billion, despite the Barbie sales slump.

By the third quarter of 2014, however, sales of the Barbie brand had dropped 21 percent from the previous year.[15] What was wrong with Barbie? Analysts acknowledged that Barbie was still one of the top doll brands in the world, but noted that girls were increasingly drawn to other, more innovative dolls and games that ran on tablets, computers, and smartphones.[16] Further, while Barbie's core demographic used to be between the ages of 3 and 9, the market for Barbie now appeared to be between the ages of 3 and 6. Children were maturing faster than ever in the 21st century. There had also been long-standing complaints about a lack of diversity in the Barbie Doll line, particularly given the changing demographics of the U.S. child population.[17]

Other Mattel lines then began to join the Barbie sales slump, including the popular American Girl brand, Hot Wheels, and Fisher-Price infant toys. Overall net sales for Mattel dropped by $400 million in 2014. In January 2015, Mattel CEO Bryan Stockton was replaced by Christopher Sinclair, a long-standing director on Mattel's board of directors. In 2016, Disney moved their license to the Princess line of dolls, including their blockbuster *Frozen* toys, to Mattel rival Hasbro. The loss of the Disney license had a negative impact on Mattel. Making matters worse, sales during the fourth quarter of 2016 failed to meet expectations, and Mattel had to cut prices to salvage the all-important holiday season.[18]

In the wake of the holiday 2016 debacle, Margo Georgiadis was named CEO of Mattel in February of 2017. From February 2017 to April 2018, Mattel's stock price dropped by 50 percent, and Ms. Georgiadis was unable to reverse the continued slide in Mattel's sales and earnings.[19] In November of 2017, Hasbro made a takeover offer for Mattel, an offer that Mattel's board rejected.[20] Ms. Georgiadis then left Mattel abruptly in April 2018. Former studio executive Ynon Kreiz, a member of Mattel's board of directors since June of 2017, was named the incoming CEO. Kreiz began his tenure as CEO of Mattel on April 26, 2018. Since becoming CEO, Kreiz had been trying to shift the focus of Mattel to intellectual property (IP) instead of tangible products.[21] Kreiz began to move Mattel into films, television, and franchise management of the major Mattel brands, such as Barbie. He had had some initial success, but more time was needed to see if he could successfully change the focus of the company.[22]

Vision, Mission, and Strategic Goals

Mattel Inc. had no formal mission or vision statement. The company stated that the Mattel Incorporated family of companies was "a worldwide leader in the design, manufacture and marketing of toys and family products.[23] The company also emphasized the power of play, stating that play was essential for creating future generations of thinkers, makers, and doers. Mattel had been named one of the world's most ethical companies by *Ethnisphere Magazine* in 2013, and was also ranked Number 2 on *Corporate Responsibility Magazine*'s "100 Best Corporate Citizens" list.[24]

In her report to Mattel shareholders in early 2018, CEO Margo Georgiadis had outlined five strategic pillars to transform the company and return it to growth:

1. Building Mattel's core brands into connected 360-degree play systems and experiences.

2. Accelerating emerging markets growth with digital first solutions.

3. Focusing and strengthening the company's innovation pipeline.

4. Reshaping the company's operations.

5. Reigniting Mattel's culture and team.[25]

Ms. Georgiadis noted a number of changes in Mattel's executive ranks in her report, including the appointment of Ynon Kreiz to Mattel's Board of Directors in June 2017. Georgiadis also noted that the organizational structure of Mattel had been flattened and simplified to accelerate decision making within the company. The changes had accelerated under Kreiz, who had initiated significant layoffs within the Mattel organization.

Ms. Georgiadis introduced incoming CEO Kreiz on Mattel's April 26, 2018, call with analysts. On the call, CEO Kreiz said:

We have a lot to do to reach our objectives. But I'm very confident that we have the right plan and the right team in place. . . . We are already making strong progress against our strategic pillars. My immediate focus (for Mattel) includes the following priorities: implementing our Structural Simplification to restore profitability, stabilizing revenue, reinvigorating our concept to drive creativity, which I believe is essential to our success; and strengthening our collaboration with our partners.[26]

Incoming CEO Kreiz also articulated his longer range vision for Mattel during the call with analysts:

The big picture opportunity is to transform Mattel to an IT (information technology) driven high-performing toy company, that is more efficient, more profitable and has a higher growth trajectory. We have very strong assets, including some of the world's best and greatest toy brands. We have a very good team and a very good strategy that I feel very good about. So our focus now is to deliver on our transformation plan and maximize value for the company and for our shareholders. This is not going to be easy. There's no denying that we faced significant challenges over the last few years and there are still headwinds in certain key areas of the business. But I feel confident about where we sit and what we have to do to take it on.[27]

Company Operations

Mattel Inc. had their worldwide headquarters in El Segundo, California, just south of the Los Angeles International Airport (LAX). As of December 2018, the company employed 27,000 people on a worldwide basis. The corporate headquarters consisted of two main buildings in El Segundo, with additional leased buildings in the immediate area for company operations. Mattel also had another major facility in East Aurora, New York, which was used for North American operations and support.

Mattel's American Girl operations were based in Middleton, Wisconsin, with a headquarters facility, a warehouse and distribution facilities in the immediate Middleton, Wisconsin, area. Mattel also had retail and related office space in 20 additional cities around the United States, and 40 countries around the world.[28] Mattel sold their products in 150 nations.

Manufacturing for the company was conducted through both company-owned facilities and by contract through third-party manufacturers. Mattel had company-owned manufacturing facilities in Canada, China, Indonesia, Malaysia, Mexico, and Thailand. Manufacture of core products for the company was generally conducted by company-owned facilities in order to improve flexibility and to lower manufacturing costs.[29] However, under Kreiz, the company was reviewing all of their manufacturing operations on a worldwide basis. Non-core toy products were produced by third-party contract manufacturers. Mattel also purchased some toys from unrelated companies for resale through Mattel sales channels.

Creativity and innovation was a critical issue for companies like Mattel in the toy industry. Mattel invested heavily in refreshing, redesigning, and extending their existing toy lines, as well as developing brand new toy product lines for their company. Product design and development was conducted in-house by a group of professional toy designers and engineers. In 2018, the company spent approximately $76 million on product design and development.

Mattel's toy business was highly seasonal. A significant portion of purchasing by Mattel's customers occurred during the third and fourth quarters of the year.[30] It was critical that Mattel manufacture enough of the right toys in advance of the fourth quarter to meet this surge in demand. Conversely, not manufacturing unpopular toys was also important to avoid stocking unpopular items. It was difficult for the company to match supply and demand with significant lead times for production early in the year. This seasonality in demand also meant increased need by Mattel for working capital earlier in the year in order to meet the anticipated surge in production to meet year-end demand for toys.

Mattel Products

Mattel's brands and products were organized into two main categories: (1) Power Brands and (2) Toy Box. Each category had a multitude of products as part of their portfolio:

1. Power Brands. This category included the Barbie Doll and related accessories, Hot Wheels,

Fisher-Price and Thomas & Friends, and American girl brands.

2. Toy Box. The category includes owned brands such as MEGA, Polly Pocket, Uno, Enchantimals, Fireman Sam, and Matchbox as well as partner brands such as Disney, WWE Wrestling, Nickelodeon, Warner Bros., NBC Universal, and Mojang. These companies typically partner with Mattel to produce products for one or more of its digital content creations such as CARS, Jurassic World, Minecraft, and many more.

Mattel had plans to update and expand many of these brands including the following:

Barbie: 2019 was the 60th birthday of Barbie, and Mattel continued to introduce diversity to the Barbie line as well as increasing animated content.

Hot Wheels: Mattel had many new and continued initiatives with Hot Wheels for 2019, including a world tour and a partnership with Nintendo's Mario Kart.

Fisher-Price: The Fisher-Price product line was focused on being a partner with parents as well as increasing diversity and representation in its animated content.

Toy Box: Mattel was planning to continue its many partnerships with companies such as Disney, NBC Universal, and many others. In addition, the company had plans to enhance their products offerings and introduce a Pokémon product line.

Mattel Marketing

Marketing toys to children and their parents was an advertising intensive activity. Mattel spent heavily on marketing and promotional activities. Marketing activity was seasonal, with a peak during the fourth quarter of the year. Mattel advertised through TV and radio commercials, magazines, and newspapers. Promotional activity for the company included in-store displays, major events focusing on Mattel-branded products, and marketing tie-ins with various consumer products companies. During 2018, Mattel spent $526.4 million, or 11.7 percent of company net sales, on advertising and promotion.

Of particular importance to Mattel was the rise of social media and the Internet as a marketing and promotional channel. Children and their parents were increasingly accessing information about toys on social media websites. Mattel had carefully developed their Facebook presence, and had cultivated 14 million followers for their Barbie page. Mattel also had a strong presence on YouTube for Barbie, with 6 million subscribers.

Mattel Customers

Mattel sold their products throughout the world. Mattel toys and related products were sold directly to discount retailers, free-standing toy stores, department stores, chain stores, and wholesalers. Mattel also had several small retail stores near to their corporate headquarters and distribution centers. American Girl products were sold directly to consumers through their own retail stores and also to retailers. Mattel also sold some of their products online through company subsidiaries.

In 2018, two customers of Mattel accounted for 34 percent of company sales. These two customers were Walmart and Target. Exhibit 1 presents a sales breakdown of Mattel's major customers for 2016 through 2018. The retailer Toys "R" Us had been a major customer for Mattel, and its bankruptcy and closure in 2018 had a major impact on both Mattel and the entire toy industry.

Key Executives

Ynon Kreiz was the Chairman and CEO of Mattel. Kreiz, 54, was born and raised in Israel. He earned a BA in Economics and Management in 1991 from Tel Aviv University. After moving to Los Angeles, Kreiz earned an MBA from UCLA in 1993.

In 1996, Kreiz moved to London to launch Fox Kids Europe, a Pay-TV children's television network. He served as Chairman and CEO of Fox Kids Europe from 1997 to 2002. Fox Kids Europe was acquired by the Walt Disney Company in 2001.

After a stint at a venture capital firm, Kreiz served as Chairman and CEO of Endemol from 2008 to 2011. Endemol was a European-based global television and digital production company. Then in 2013, Kreiz became Chairman and CEO of Maker Studios in Los Angeles. Maker Studios produced short-form videos for YouTube and other platforms. Maker was sold to the Walt Disney Company in 2014. Kreiz stepped down as CEO of Maker Studios in January 2016. Kreiz then joined Mattel's board of directors in 2017, and became Mattel CEO in April 2018.

CEO Kreiz was joined by Richard Dickson as Mattel's President and Chief Operating Officer (COO). Dickson, 51, had been President and COO since April 2015. Mr. Dickson had extensive retail experience, including almost a decade at Bloomingdale's. Mattel's Chief Legal Officer, Robert Normile, was the longest serving executive at Mattel. Normile had been Chief Legal Officer at Mattel since February 2011, and had an extensive legal background.

All of the remaining members of Kreiz's top management team, including Chief Financial Officer Joseph Euteneuer, had served two years or less in their current roles. There had also been key departures from Mattel's leadership team in 2018. Roberto Isaias had replaced Michael Eilola as Executive Vice President and Chief Supply Chain Officer in February 2019. The Chief Communications Officer

EXHIBIT 1

Mattel Incorporated Major Customers (dollars in thousands)			
Major Customer	2016	2017	2018
Wal-Mart	$1,100,000	$1,000,000	$1,020,000
Toys "R" Us	$600,000	$600,000	–
Target	$400,000	$400,000	$370,000

Source: Mattel, Inc., 2018 Annual Report, accessed August 5, 2019, https://mattel.gcs-web.com/static-files/d231da34-60d7-44f0-83df-933c52b5d688.

and Chief Technology Officer had also departed in 2018, and both of those positions were unfilled as of February 2019. Exhibit 2 provides a brief summary of Mattel's top leadership team in 2019.

Financial Status

Net sales for Mattel decreased from $6.02 billion in 2014 to $4.51 billion in 2018. Variable expenses remained relatively stable during the 2014–2017 time period, resulting in a sharp drop in gross profit as well. However, variable expenses decreased by approximately $300 million in 2018, suggesting that restructuring efforts were beginning to stabilize the company. The company reported a negative operating income and a $530 million net loss in 2018. Exhibit 3 presents Mattel's consolidated income statements for 2014–2018.

Steep losses in 2017 and 2018 resulted in retained earnings write-downs on Mattel's balance sheet of $1.2 billion and $588 million in 2017 and 2018, respectively. Total stockholder's equity decreased from $2.9 billion in 2014 to $669 million in 2018. In an effort to solidify the company's short-term debt position, Mattel entered into a credit agreement in December 2017 to provide seasonal financing for their company operations. This credit facility consisted of $1.3 billion in an asset-based lending facility and $294 million in a revolving credit facility.[31] Also in December 2017, Mattel issued $1.00 billion in 6.75% senior unsecured notes, due December 2020. The net result of these moves was total debt for Mattel reaching $2.8 billion at year-end 2017. The debt load, although heavy, stabilized for the company in 2018. Exhibit 4 presents Mattel's consolidated balance sheets for 2014–2018.

Cash flow from operations had been positive since 2014, but turned negative in 2017 and 2018. Mattel continued to invest cash flows into the

EXHIBIT 2

Mattel Inc. Leadership in 2019

Name	Brief Biography
Ynon Kreiz *Chairman and Chief Executive Officer* Age: 54 Tenure: 1 Year	Ynon Kreiz has served as Chairman of Mattel Inc. since May 17, 2018, and as its Chief Executive Officer since April 26, 2018. Mr. Kreiz holds a B.A. in Economics and Management from Tel Aviv University and an M.B.A. from UCLA's Anderson School of Management.
Richard Dickson *President and Chief Operating Officer* Age: 51 Tenure: 5 Years	Richard Dickson has been the President and Chief Operating Officer of Mattel, Inc. since April 2, 2015. Mr. Dickson started his career and spent nearly a decade with Bloomingdale's, a leading U.S. fashion retailer.
Roberto Isaias *Executive Vice President, Chief Supply Chain Officer* Age: 51 Tenure: 0 Years	Roberto Isaias has been Executive Vice President and Chief Supply Chain Officer of Mattel, Inc. since February 2019. Prior to joining Mattel, Inc., Mr. Isaias came to Mattel Incorporated from Proctor & Gamble Mexico in 2002.
Joseph Euteneuer *Chief Financial Officer* Age: 63 Tenure: 2 Years	Joe Euteneuer has been the Chief Financial Officer of Mattel Inc. since September 25, 2017. Mr. Euteneuer holds a Bachelor's degree from Arizona State University and is a certified public accountant.
Robert Normile *Executive Vice President, Chief Legal Officer, Secretary* Age: 59 Tenure: 21 Years	Robert Normile has served as Executive Vice President, Chief Legal Officer and Secretary of Mattel, Inc. since February 2011. Mr. Normile was previously associated with the law firms of Latham & Watkins LLP and Sullivan & Cromwell LLP.
Amanda Thompson *Executive Vice President, Chief People Officer* Age: 43 Tenure: 2 Years	Amanda J. Thompson has been Executive Vice President and Chief People Officer of Mattel, Inc. since September 2017. From 2012 to 2017, Ms. Thompson served as Chief People Officer of TOMS Shoes. Ms. Thompson held several executive and leadership roles at Starbucks Coffee Company from 2006 to 2012.

Source: "Mattel Leadership," Mattel, Inc., https://corporate.mattel.com/about-us/.

EXHIBIT 3

Mattel Inc. Consolidated Income Statements 2014–2018 (amounts in thousands of $, except per share, employee, and stockholder data)

	2018	2017	2016	2015	2014
Net Sales	$4,510,852	$4,881,951	$5,456,650	$5,702,613	$6,023,819
Cost of sales	2,716,127	3,061,122	2,902,259	2,896,255	3,022,797
Gross profit (loss)	1,794,725	1,820,829	2,554,391	2,806,358	3,001,022
Advertising & promotion expenses	526,436	642,286	634,947	717,852	733,243
Other selling & administrative expenses	1,504,796	1,521,366	1,400,211	1,547,584	1,614,065
Operating income (loss)	(236,507)	(342,823)	519,233	540,922	653,714
Interest expense	181,886	10,5214	95,118	85,270	79,271
Interest income	6,463	7,777	9,144	7,230	7,382
Other non-operating income (expense), net	7,331	(64,727)	(23,517)	1,033	5,085
Income (loss) before income taxes	(419,261)	(504,987)	409,742	463,915	586,910
Total deferred income tax provision (benefit)	14,527	436,802	1,236	4,133	8,142
Provision (benefit) for income taxes	111,732	548,849	91,720	94,499	88,036
Net income (loss)	(530,993)	(1,053,836)	318,022	369,416	498,874
Less net income allocable to participating restricted stock units	–	–	1,377	3,179	4,028
Net income (loss) applicable to common shares	($530,993)	($1,053,836)	$316,645	$366,237	$494,846
Weighted average shares outstanding-basic	345,012	343,564	341,480	339,172	339,016
Weighted average shares outstanding-diluted	345,012	343,564	344,233	339,748	340,768
Year End shares outstanding	345,300	343,800	342,400	339,700	338,100
Net income (loss) per share-basic	($1.54)	($3.07)	$0.93	$1.08	$1.46
Net income (loss) per share-diluted	($1.54)	($3.07)	$0.92	$1.08	$1.45
Dividends declared per common share	-	$0.91	$1.52	$1.52	$1.52
Total number of employees	27,000	28,000	32,000	31,000	31,000
Number of common stockholders	26,000	27,000	28,000	29,000	30,000

Note: Mattel Inc. Fiscal Year ends on December 31.

Source: Mattel, Inc., 2018 Annual Report, accessed August 5, 2019, https://mattel.gcs-web.com/static-files/d231da34-60d7-44f0-83df-933c52b5d688.

EXHIBIT 4

Mattel Inc. Consolidated Balance Sheets 2014–2018 (amounts in thousands of $)

	2018	2017	2016	2015	2014
Cash & equivalents	$ 594,481	$1,079,221	$ 869,531	$ 892,814	$ 971,650
Accounts receivable, net	970,083	1,128,610	1,115,217	1,145,099	1,093,180
Inventories	542,889	600,704	613,798	587,521	562,047
Prepaid expenses & other current assets	244,987	303,053	341,518	571,429	559,074
Total current assets	2,352,440	3,111,588	2,940,064	3,196,863	3,185,951

	2018	2017	2016	2015	2014
Property, plant & equipment, gross	2,691,352	2,740,997	2,645,539	2,507,861	2,395,244
Less: accumulated depreciation	2,033,757	1,955,712	1,871,574	1,766,714	1,657,375
Property, plant & equipment, net	657,595	785,285	773,965	741,147	737,869
Goodwill	1,386,424	1,396,669	138,7628	1,384,520	1,393,968
Deferred income taxes	49,937	76,750	508,363	317,391	385,434
Total assets	5,243,465	6,238,503	6,493,794	6,552,689	6,722,046
Accounts payable	537,965	5,721,66	664,857	651,681	430,259
Accrued royalties	108,109	111,669	107,077	122,153	112,886
Other accrued liabilities	363,974	420,054	350,248	340,512	360,106
Accrued liabilities	700,421	792,139	628,826	658,225	639,907
Income taxes payable	10,046	9,498	19,722	18,752	18,783
Total current liabilities	1,252,608	1,623,803	1,505,573	1,645,572	1,088,949
Long-term debt	2,851,723	2,873,119	2,134,271	1,800,000	2,100,000
Benefit plan liabilities	166,289	168,539	192,466	195,916	229,963
Total noncurrent liabilities	3,321,392	3,357,245	2,580,439	2,273,863	2,684,026
Common stock	441,369	441,369	441,369	441,369	441,369
Additional paid-in capital	1,812,682	1,808,391	1,790,832	1,789,870	1,767,096
Treasury stock at cost	2,354,617	2,389,877	2,426,749	2,494,901	2,533,566
Retained earnings (accumulated deficit)	1,629,527	2,179,358	3,545,359	3,745,815	3,896,261
Total stockholders' equity (deficit)	669,465	1,257,455	2,407,782	2,633,254	2,949,071
Total liabilities and stockholders' equity	5,243,465	6,238,503	6,493,794	6,552,689	6,722,046

Note: Mattel Inc. Fiscal Year Ends December 31.

Source: Mattel, Inc., 2014, 2016, and 2018 Annual Report, accessed August 5, 2019.

company as well, with net cash flows from investment activities reaching ($160 million) in 2018. Cash flows from financing activities turned negative again for the company in 2018, mostly from early debt repayments. Cash and equivalents at year-end 2018 dropped sharply to $594 million. Exhibit 5 presents Mattel's consolidated cash flow statements for 2014–2018.

Mattel Revenues by Category and Region

While overall revenues for Mattel were down approximately $300 million in 2018, there were hints of a recovery, particularly in the all important fourth quarter. Mattel's two strongest brands, Barbie and Hot Wheels, both had sales increases in 2018. Barbie revenues increased 12.5 percent in 2018 and returned Barbie to billion-dollar brand status. Hot Wheels revenues increased 7 percent and exceeded $800 million in sales. The rest of Mattel's brand portfolio, however, continued to struggle. The American Girl product line, in particular, was down sharply in 2018. Fisher-Price sales were also soft, although some of this line's weakness may have been attributable to the closure of Toys "R" Us retailers in the United States. Exhibit 6 presents Mattel's revenues by major brand category for 2016 through 2018.

Geographically, the revenue downturn for Mattel was most pronounced in the North American region. Sales in North America declined from $3.01 billion in 2017 to $2.76 billion in 2018. International regions for Mattel, while declining, were not declining as

EXHIBIT 5

Mattel Inc. Cash Flow Statements 2014–2018 (amounts in thousands of $)

	2018	2017	2016	2015	2014
Net income (loss)	($530,993)	($1,053,836)	$318,022	$369,416	$498,874
Depreciation	232,837	240,818	235,797	233,025	207,701
Amortization	39,095	33,949	26,543	32,402	41,000
Accounts receivable	76,373	13,626	(24,033)	(136,259)	90,285
Valuation allowance on US deferred tax assets	–	456,642	–	–	–
Inventories	(53,840)	(91,644)	(37,195)	(74,262)	43,392
Prepaid expenses & other current assets	56,378	33,681	34,754	(36,865)	(25,319)
Accounts payable & accrued liabilities	(54,819)	98,044	9,006	248,047	(34,653)
Other assets & liabilities, net	(5,968)	(49,062)	(23,571)	38,229	(28,336)
Net cash flows from operating activities	(27,317)	(27,614)	594,509	734,557	888,564
Purchases of tools, dies & molds	(74,662)	(128,940)	(140,124)	(142,363)	(147,236)
Purchases of other property, plant & equipment	(77,752)	(168,219)	(122,069)	(111,818)	(113,221)
Foreign currency forward exchange contracts	(18,615)	60,993	(6,103)	(61,509)	(19,933)
Net cash flows from investing activities	(160,758)	(235,663)	(311,910)	(282,495)	(708,552)
Payments of short-term borrowings, net	–	(1,611,586)	(83,914)	–	(4,278)
Proceeds from short-term borrowings, net	4,176	1,419,418	259,168	16,914	–
Payments of long-term borrowings	(750,000)	–	(300,000)	–	(44,587)
Proceeds from long-term borrowings, net	471,797	988,622	350,000	–	(495,459)
Share repurchases	–	–	–	–	(177,162)
Payment of dividends on common stock	–	(311,973)	(518,529)	(515,073)	(514,813)
Net cash flows from financing activities	(285,157)	458,450	(281,471)	(500,222)	(227,319)
Effect of currency exchange rate changes	(11,508)	14,517	(24,411)	(30,676)	(20,259)
Increase (decrease) in cash & equivalents	(484,740)	209,690	(23,283)	(78,836)	(67,566)
Cash & equivalents at beginning of year	1,079,221	869,531	892,814	971,650	1,039,216
Cash & equivalents at end of year	$594,481	$1,079,221	$869,531	$892,814	$971,650

Note: Mattel Inc. Fiscal Year Ends on December 31.

Source: Mattel, Inc., 2016, and 2018 Annual Report, accessed August 5, 2019.

sharply. Total international sales declined from $2.50 billion in 2017 to $2.31 billion in 2018. Sales in the Emerging Markets category actually increased from 2017 to 2018, an unusual bright spot for the company, and a possible harbinger for future growth. Overall, international sales appeared to be more resilient to the current downturn in Mattel sales. Exhibit 7 presents Mattel's revenues by geography for 2016 through 2018.

Stock Performance

Mattel's stock price peaked at an all-time high of $47.82 on December 30, 2013. Sales and earnings for the company also peaked in 2013, and the company's stock price closely tracked these trends in revenues and earnings. Exhibit 8 tracks Mattel Incorporated's stock price performance from April 2014 to April 2019.

EXHIBIT 6

Mattel Revenues by Major Brand Category, 2016–2018 ($ in thousands)

Brand Category	2018	2017	2016
Barbie	$1,088,953	$ 952,894	$ 971,795
Hot Wheels	834,058	777,341	796,969
Fisher-Price and Thomas & Friends	1,185,669	1,370,543	1,546,111
American Girl	342,442	473,302	592,118
Toy Box	1,624,408	1,938,047	2,166,722
Gross Sales	5,075,529	5,514,125	6,073,714
Sales Adjustments	(564,677)	(632,174)	(617,064)
Net Sales	$4,510,852	$4,881,951	$5,456,650

Source: Mattel, Inc., 2018 Annual Report, accessed August 5, 2019, https://mattel.gcs-web.com/static-files/d231da34-60d7-44f0-83df-933c52b5d688.

EXHIBIT 7

Mattel Revenues by Geography, 2016–2018 ($ in thousands)

Geographic Region	2018	2017	2016
North American Region	$2,763,299	$3,010,598	$3,626,099
International Region			
Europe	1,013,983	1,281,672	1,293,302
Latin America	653,992	675,286	636,535
Global Emerging Markets	644,255	546,569	744,817
Total International Region	2,312,230	2,503,527	2,447,615
Gross Sales	5,075,529	5,514,125	6,073,714
Sales Adjustments	(564,677)	(632,174)	(617,064)
Net Sales	$4,510,852	$4,881,951	$5,456,650

Source: Mattel, Inc., 2018 Annual Report, accessed August 5, 2019, https://mattel.gcs-web.com/static-files/d231da34-60d7-44f0-83df-933c52b5d688.

From a peak in December 2013, Mattel's stock price had drifted lower in fits and starts. The Year 2016 saw a brief rebound in the company's fortunes, but a continual stream of weakening revenues and earnings had fed the weakening price action for the stock price as well. This culminated with a major sell-off in October of 2017 following the release of negative third-quarter 2017 earnings for the company.

In early 2019, the company had been trading in the $10 to $15 price range. Given this price range, the market capitalization of the company was approximately $4.50 billion. It was not possible to calculate a trailing Price/Earnings ratio for the company, given the negative earnings for the company beginning in 2017. Dividends for the company had been suspended beginning in the fourth quarter of 2017.

EXHIBIT 8

Mattel Incorporated's Stock Performance, April 2014–April 2019

(a) Trend in Mattel Incorporated's Common Stock Price

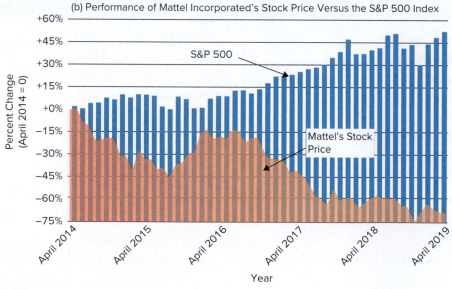

(b) Performance of Mattel Incorporated's Stock Price Versus the S&P 500 Index

Source: Mattel Inc. Stock Performance, April 2014–April 2019. MarketWatch, Inc.

Mattel did not repurchase any shares of its common stock in 2016, 2017, or 2018.

U.S. Toy and Craft Supplies Wholesaling Industry

Mattel participated in the U.S. Toy and Craft Supplies Wholesaling Industry (Toy Industry). The toy industry consisted of U.S.-based companies that were wholesalers of toys and craft supplies, as well as various miscellaneous items.[32] Toy and craft supplies were purchased from both U.S. and international manufacturers and then sold to U.S. retailers, including discount department stores, big-box retailers, and independent specialty retail outlets.

While industry revenues were $28.70 billion in 2018, the toy industry faced an increasingly difficult market environment in the United States. With only occasional reversals, revenue for the industry had fallen every year since 2013. Toy industry participants were squeezed on all sides. On the manufacturing side, large and mostly international manufacturers were increasingly integrating vertically and bypassing the toy industry wholesalers to sell directly to large retail chains in the United States. On the retail side, there was increasing consolidation of industry players, leaving only a few very large retailers with which to negotiate. These conditions, combined with falling demand for toys and falling prices, resulted in fierce competition for toy industry participants. Revenue for the toy industry was projected to fall by 0.7 percent in 2019.[33]

Products and Services

The toy industry was composed of four major segments: (1) traditional toys, including children's vehicles, (2) video games, (3) hobby and craft supplies and (4) other items. Demand for toys was seasonal, with sales peaking in the fourth quarter of the year, and closely tied to consumer confidence and spending. However, while consumer confidence in the United States had been rising, consumers had also become increasingly frugal and thrifty, particularly with toy purchases. Consumers were tending to buy less expensive toys in order save money.[34]

Traditional toys made up 53.50 percent of industry revenue in 2018. This segment included action figures, dolls, sporting goods, building sets, board games, and plush toys for children. Demand for traditional toys was under pressure in the United States. Children were increasingly demanding electronic toys and video games. Further, children appeared to be outgrowing toys at a faster rate, particularly as they entered the 8 to 12 age range. Traditional toys continued to decline as a percentage of industry revenue. Exhibit 9 illustrates the relative sizes of the toy industry products and services segments in 2018.

Demand for video games, as a result, continued to grow into 2018. Major manufacturers such as Sony and Microsoft continued to introduce new gaming consoles, spurring new game introduction and passionate usage by teenagers. Demand for video games was also increasingly penetrating younger and younger age groups. Sales of video games represented 26.50 percent of industry sales in 2018, and

was anticipated to rise as a percentage of industry revenue.[35]

The hobby and craft supplies segment included items such as scrapbooking supplies, needlework kits, and craft kits. Demand in this segment had remained relatively stable, and was closely tied to consumer discretionary spending. Hobby and craft supplies represented 4.4 percent of industry revenue in 2018.

The other category in the industry consisted of various other product categories not classified elsewhere. This included items such as playing cards, fireworks, and coloring books. Revenues in this segment had remained fairly consistent at 15.6 percent of industry revenue.[36]

Major Markets

The bulk of toy industry sales were conducted through major retailers in the United States. Market share of major retailers had increased, however, allowing them to source toys directly from manufacturers. Wholesale toy companies, as a result, faced a difficult and increasingly competitive environment for sales, with significant pricing pressure from retailers. This had pressured pricing on toys downward. Toy companies had also begun to focus their sales efforts on retailers and retail chains with less purchasing power (smaller retailers) and also had begun to focus more on direct sales of toys to consumers. Exhibit 10 illustrates a percentage breakdown of the major market segments of the U.S. toy industry in 2018.

Discount department stores, such as Walmart and Target, made up 28.6 percent of toy industry sales in 2018. These large retailers purchased toys in large volumes in an attempt to drive down prices for the end consumer. Retailers had also begun to bypass toy wholesalers, such as Mattel and Hasbro, and had begun to increasingly purchase toys directly from international manufacturers. The net combination of these conditions continued to pressure the margins of toy industry wholesalers. The volume of toys supplied to discount department stores was expected to continue a gradual decline.

Big-box retailers, such as Michaels and Jo-Ann, represented 27 percent of toy industry revenues in 2018.[37] The bankruptcy of Toys "R" Us in 2017 and

U.S. Toy & Craft Supplies Wholesaling Industry: Product and Services Segments 2018

Products & Services

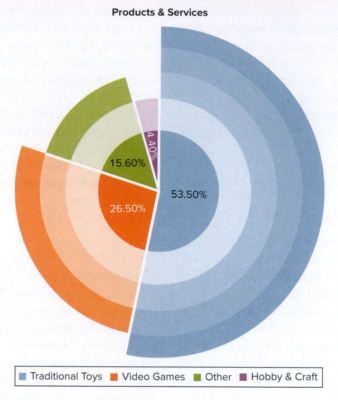

53.50%

26.50%

15.60%

4.40%

■ Traditional Toys ■ Video Games ■ Other ■ Hobby & Craft

Note: U.S Toys & Supplies Wholesaling: $28.70 Billion.

Source: IBISWorld, Toy & Craft Supplies Wholesaling Industry in the US. https://www.ibisworld.com.

United States closure in 2018 disrupted toy sales in the fourth quarter of 2018. Major toy wholesalers were negatively affected, and attempted to compensate for the Toys "R" Us closure by moving their sales initiatives to discount department stores and other retail outlets.

Independent specialty stores represented 21 percent of toy industry revenues in 2018. Independent specialty stores were smaller than other retail outlets, and relied more heavily on toy industry wholesalers for shipments of toys and related items. Independent retailers were under considerable pressure from discount department stores and big-box retailers due to intense price competition from their larger competitors. Sales to independent specialty stores was anticipated to remain stable, although a number of smaller

independents were expected to be acquired or leave the industry.[38]

The heavy competition in retail had led many toy industry participants to attempt direct sales to consumers through company websites. Consumers rarely purchased toys in large volumes, however, making online sales generally unprofitable. Direct sales accounted for 3.0 percent of industry revenues in 2018.

The remaining sales in the industry were either trade between wholesalers in the industry (19 percent of industry revenue) or directly to other businesses (1.3 percent of industry revenue). Both sales channels were relatively stable, and generally represented trade among industry participants for various reasons.

EXHIBIT 10

EXHIBIT 10

U.S. Toy & Craft Supplies Wholesaling Industry: Major Market Segments 2018

Major Markets

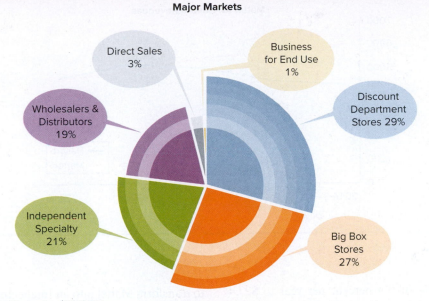

Direct Sales 3%

Business for End Use 1%

Wholesalers & Distributors 19%

Discount Department Stores 29%

Independent Specialty 21%

Big Box Stores 27%

Note: U.S Toys & Supplies Wholesaling: $28.70 Billion.

Source: IBISWorld, Toy & Craft Supplies Wholesaling Industry in the US. https://www.ibisworld.com.

Competition

The two main competitors in the U.S. toy industry were Mattel and Hasbro. Combined, the two companies controlled approximately 18.40 percent of the U.S. market for toys.[39] The remaining 81.60 percent of companies were predominately small, privately owned competitors with five or less employees that typically competed for consumers in their local communities. Mattel had been the undisputed industry leader in the U.S. toy industry for many years, but Hasbro's sales had exceeded Mattel beginning in 2017. Hasbro had seen sharp sales gains when it had been awarded a license from Walt Disney Company to market dolls and other products tied to Disney's smash hit movie *Frozen* in 2016. Exhibit 11 presents a revenue comparison for Mattel and Hasbro.

Notable competitors in the U.S. toy industry included Mattel, Hasbro, Jakks Pacific, Just Play Products, Lego, Mega Entertainment, Moose Toys, Spin Master and VTech. Notable competitors in the international market included Mattel, Hasbro, Famosa, Giochi Preziosi, Lego, MGA Entertainment, Playmobil, Ravensburger, Simba, Spin Master, and VTech.[40]

Competition in both the United States and worldwide was very strong, and was intensifying. Individual toys faced shorter and shorter life cycles as children would discard older toys in favor of the latest fashion or Hollywood movie release. Technology was also increasingly in use by children at an earlier and earlier age. A phenomenon also increasingly observed was the trend of "children getting older younger" as children outgrew toys at an earlier age.[41] Competition for retailer shelf space was fierce, and was increasingly concentrated in the hands of companies like Walmart and Target. Competition was also intensifying due to the entry of online retailers, such as Amazon.com, who would promote toys from a wide variety of toy companies and compete aggressively on price.

The Outlook for the U.S. Toy and Crafts Industry

Looking ahead in the U.S. toys and crafts industry, revenues for the industry were forecasted to continue a downward trend from 2019 to 2023, according to IBIS World. Industry revenue was forecasted to

EXHIBIT 11

Mattel versus Hasbro Revenue Comparison 2014–2018 (dollars in millions)

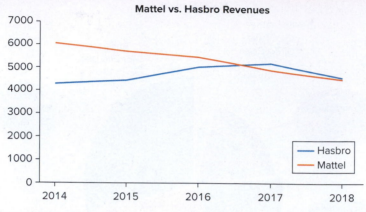

Source: Mergent, Inc., Mergent Online. https://www.mergent.com/.

decrease at a rate of 0.9 percent per year to $27.4 billion in 2023. The retail price of toys was also forecasted to continue to decline, as softening demand, retailer consolidation, and pricing pressure from international toy manufacturers continued to pressure pricing in the industry. Industry participants were also forecasted to decline through 2023 as margin pressures continued to force the exit of smaller and weaker industry participants in the toy industry.

Mattel's Outlook Going into Mid-2019

Wrapping up the February 7 conference call, financial analysts were very interested in Mattel's outlook going ahead into 2019. Mattel CEO Kreiz commented:

> Toys are a strategic category for many retailers. This is not just another product that they sell from the aisles. It drives traffic, engagement and obviously there is a product that has emotional connection to the consumer. So the toy industry is in a good place. We see demand, we see retailers leaning in, and we're seeing consumers looking to continue to be entertained, inspired and wanting to play with our products. So we remain very positive about our relationships and collaboration with the different retailers to step in and optimize for results.[42]

Analysts also wanted to know more about Mattel's content strategy, and the efforts of Kreiz and others

to transform Mattel into an Intellectual Property (IP) driven, high-performing toy company. Kreiz said:

> The fundamental advantage that we have is that we are the owner of one of the strongest portfolios of children's and family entertainment franchises in the world. And the opportunities that we see are to expand our IP and franchises into highly accretive business areas in and of themselves. So we do expect incremental transformative upside potential from these initiatives. And of course, at the same time there will be a halo effect on the core toy business. So we would expect to see uplift in the toy space as well.[43]

After the conference call ended, Kreiz reflected on the call and on the future of Mattel. While Kreiz's initial efforts had yielded good results, more remained to be done. Was there enough time to effect a turnaround?

CEO Kreiz was also aware of discussions that previous Mattel CEO Margo Georgiadis had undertaken with rival company Hasbro regarding a possible takeover in 2017. Those discussions had stalled without resolution.[44] There was a time in Mattel's history when Mattel had discussed taking over Hasbro, but that was not the situation today.

Ynon Kreiz had been tasked with leading the way forward for Mattel. What were his options for consideration? Should he consider a merger with Hasbro, or perhaps another company? Perhaps now was the time to reevaluate the takeover proposal from Hasbro. Would a bid by Hasbro for Mattel spark a bidding war, and possibly other bids for Kreiz's company? What would Mattel's Board of Directors say if Kreiz undertook either merger or acquisition negotiations? Was a merger or an acquisition the way forward?

Kreiz, having been a member of Mattel's Board of Directors before becoming CEO, was very familiar with Mattel's IP transformation plan. Was the way forward an excellent execution of the company's transformation plan? What were the elements of the plan that required action, and what other steps should Kreiz undertake in order to restore Mattel to market success and profitability? What were the defensive actions that needed to be undertaken to defend Mattel's core products and brands, and what offensive actions should he undertake to move the company forward in the toy industry?

Kreiz felt a deep sense of urgency as he picked up his smartphone and headed back to the office.

Copyright ©2019 by Randall D. Harris

ENDNOTES

[1]El Segundo, " Mattel Reports Full Year and Fourth Quarter 2018 Financial Results," Mattel, Inc., February 07, 2019, https://mattel.gcs-web.com/news-releases/news-release-details/mattel-reports-full-year-and-fourth-quarter-2018-financial.

[2]D. Cimilluca and P. Ziobro, "Mattel Names New CEO as It Seeks Answer to Sales Slump,"*The Wall Street Journal,* April 19, 2018, www.wsj.com.

[3]A third partner, Harold Matson, dropped out early in the company's history.

[4]Mattel, Inc., corporate.mattel.com.

[5]Ibid.

[6]A. Goldman, "Mattel Cuts Its Losses by Giving Learning Co. Away," *Los Angeles Times,* September 20, 2000, articles.latimes.com.

[7]Ibid.

[8]A. Goldman, "Mattel Will Shut Last U.S. Manufacturing Site," *Los Angeles Times,* April 4, 2001, articles.latimes.com.

[9]Ibid.

[10]Ibid.

[11]L. Story and D. Barboza, "Mattel Recalls 19 Million Toys Sent from China," *New York Times,* August 15, 2007, www.nytimes.com.

[12]Ibid.

[13]Ibid.

[14]J. Kell, "Mattel's Barbie Sales Down for a Third Consecutive Year," *Fortune,* January 30, 2015, fortune.com.

[15]S. Halzak, "Barbie Sales Are Nosediving, and That's Just One of Mattel's Problems," *Washington Post,* October 16, 2014, www.washingtonpost.com.

[16]Ibid.

[17]P. Ziebro, "Mattel to Add Curvy, Petite, Tall Barbies," *Wall Street Journal,* January 28, 2018, www.wsj.com.

[18]D. Cimilluca and P. Ziobro, "Mattel Names New CEO as It Seeks Answer to Sales Slump," *Wall Street Journal,* April 19, 2018, www.wsj.com.

[19]Ibid.

[20]P. Ziebro and D. Mattioli, "Hasbro Sets Its Sights on Mattel," *Wall Street Journal,* November 10, 2017, www.wsj.com.

[21]Mattel 2018 Annual Report, www.mattel.com.

[22]S. Mallas, "Mattel: From Plastic Producer to Producing Content," April 1, 2019, https://seekingalpha.com/article/4252112-mattel-plastic-producer-producing-content.

[23]Mattel, Inc.

[24]Ibid.

[25]"2017 Annual Report," Mattel, Inc., https://mattel.gcs-web.com/static-files/3ad8db55-3088-419d-b83c-2a4b20999156.

[26]"MAT – Q1 2018 Mattel Inc. Earnings Call," Thomson Reuters Markets, LLC, April 26, 2018, https://mattel.gcs-web.com/static-files/3ad8db55-3088-419d-b83c-2a4b20999156.

[27]Ibid.

[28]Mattel 2017 Annual Report, www.mattel.com.

[29]Ibid.

[30]Ibid.

[31]Mattel 2017 Annual Report, www.mattel.com.

[32]IBIS World, "Toys & Crafts Supplies Wholesaling in the U.S.," October 2018, www.ibisworld.com.

[33]Ibid.

[34]Ibid.

[35]Ibid.

[36]Ibid.

[37]Ibid.

[38]Ibid.

[39]Ibid.

[40]Ibid.

[41]Mattel 2017 Annual Report, www.mattel.com.

[42]"Q4 2018 Mattel Inc. Earnings Call," Thomson Reuters Markets, LLC, February 07, 2019, https://mattel.gcs-web.com/static-files/dd4d5984-d723-41f0-bac8-2a17de381044.

[43]Ibid.

[44]D. Cimilluca and P. Ziobro, "Mattel Names New CEO as It Seeks Answer to Sales Slump," *Wall Street Journal,* April 19, 2018, www.wsj.com.

TESLA'S STRATEGY IN 2019: IS SUSTAINED PROFITABILITY A REALISTIC PROSPECT?

ARTHUR A. THOMPSON *The University of Alabama*

After reporting a net profit of $311.5 million in the third quarter of 2018 and a net profit of $139.5 million in the fourth quarter of 2018, Tesla shocked shareholders and Wall Street by reporting an operating loss of $521.8 million and a net loss of $702.1 million for the first quarter of 2019. According to CEO Elon Musk, multiple factors accounted for the losses:

- Deliveries of the premium-priced Model S and Model X fell over 50 percent to 12,091 units compared to the quarterly average of about 25,000 units for the previous two years.

- Pull-forward sales of the Model S and Model X into Q4 of 2018 to escape the scheduled reduction in Q1 2019 of the $7,500 federal tax credit for purchases of Tesla's electric vehicles.

- Discontinuation of the lower-cost 75kWh battery pack option for both Model S and Model X vehicles.

- A mismatch between orders for high-performance versions of the Model S and Model X and the number of deliverable cars (due to a need to update the production lines for the next-generation powertrains installed in the Model S and Model X).

- A need to ship thousands of newly produced Model 3 vehicles to China and Europe to meet international buyer demand (which involved longer shipping times and increases in the number of vehicles in transit, and thus delivery times that deferred sales of many Model 3 vehicles in these markets until Q2 of 2019) and which also limited the production and sales of the Model 3 for customers in the United States. So while the company produced 62,975 Model 3 vehicles in Q1 (approximately 3 percent more than in Q4 of 2018), customer deliveries of the Model 3 amounted to only 50,928 vehicles in Q1 of 2019.

- A net $121 million loss for unexpected costs incurred for higher return rates for cars sold under the company's "residual value guarantee" for leased vehicles and "buy back guarantee" on prior sales of Model S and Model X vehicles.

- Restructuring costs of $43.5 million and other nonrecurring charges of $23.5 million.

Following the April 22 earnings announcement, Tesla's stock price, which had already slumped from $346 per share in mid-January to $263 just before the earnings report was released, continued its downward trend, reaching $188 on May 30, 2019. Exhibit 1 shows sales of Tesla's three models from 2012 when the Model S was first introduced through the first quarter of 2019.

Tesla's Deliveries of the Model S, Model X, and Model 3 to Customers, 2012 through the First Quarter of 2019

Period	Model S Deliveries	Model S plus Model X Deliveries	Model 3 Deliveries
2012	2,653		
2013	22,477		
2014	31,655		
2015	50,332		
2016		76,230	
2017		101,420	1,734
2018		99,475	146,055
Q1 2019		12,091	50,928

Source: Company 10K reports, 2012-2018 and Tesla First Quarter 2019 Update, April 24, 2019.

Company Background

Tesla Motors was incorporated in July 2003 by Martin Eberhard and Marc Tarpenning, two Silicon Valley engineers who believed it was feasible to produce an "awesome" electric vehicle. Tesla's namesake was the genius Nikola Tesla (1856–1943), an electrical engineer and scientist known for his impressive inventions (of which more than 700 were patented) and his contributions to the design of modern alternating-current (AC) power transmission systems and electric motors. Tesla's first vehicle, the Tesla Roadster (an all-electric sports car) introduced in early 2008, was powered by an AC motor that descended directly from Nikola Tesla's original 1882 design.

Financing Early Operations

Eberhard and Tarpenning financed the company until Tesla's first round of investor funding in February 2004. Elon Musk contributed $6.35 million of the $6.5 million in initial funding and, as the company's majority investor, assumed the position of Chairman of the company's board of directors. Martin Eberhard put up $75,000 of the initial $6.5 million, with two private equity investment groups and a number of private investors contributing the remainder.[1] Several rounds of investor funding ensued, with Elon Musk emerging as the company's biggest shareholder. Other notable investors included Google co-founders Sergey Brin and Larry Page, former eBay President Jeff Skoll, and Hyatt heir Nick Pritzker. In 2009, Germany's Daimler AG, the maker of Mercedes vehicles, acquired an equity stake of almost 10 percent in Tesla for a reported $50 million.[2] Daimler's investment was motivated by a desire to partner with Tesla to accelerate the development of Tesla's lithium-ion battery technology and electric drive train technology and to collaborate on electric cars being developed at Mercedes. Later in 2009, Tesla was awarded a $465 million low-interest loan by the U.S. Department of Energy to accelerate the production of affordable, fuel-efficient electric vehicles; Tesla used $365 million for production engineering and assembly of its forthcoming Model S and $100 million for a powertrain manufacturing plant employing about 650 people that would supply all-electric powertrain solutions to other automakers and help accelerate the availability of relatively low-cost, mass-market electric vehicles.

In June 2010, Tesla Motors became a public company, raising $226 million with an initial public offering of common stock. It was the first American car company to go public since Ford Motor Company in 1956.

Management Changes at Tesla

In August 2007, with the company plagued by delays in getting its first model—the Tesla Roadster—into production, co-founder Martin Eberhard was ousted as Tesla's chief executive officer (CEO). While his successor managed to get the Tesla Roadster into production in March 2008 and begin delivering Roadsters to customers in October 2008, internal turmoil in the executive ranks prompted Elon Musk to decide it made more sense for him to take on the role as Tesla's chief executive officer—while continuing to serve as chairman of the board—because he was making all the major decisions anyway.

Elon Musk

Elon Musk was born in South Africa, taught himself computer programming and, at age 12, made $500 by selling the computer code for a video game he invented.[3] In 1992, after spending two years at Queen's University in Ontario, Canada, Musk transferred to the University of Pennsylvania where he earned an undergraduate degree in business and a second degree in physics. During his college days, Musk spent some time thinking about two important matters that he thought merited his time and attention later in his career: one was that the world needed an environmentally clean method of transportation; the other was that it would be good if humans could colonize another planet.[4] After graduating from the University of Pennsylvania, he decided to move to California and pursue a PhD in applied physics at Stanford; however, he left the program after two days to pursue his entrepreneurial aspirations instead.

Musk's first entrepreneurial venture was to join up with his brother, Kimbal, and establish Zip2, an Internet software company that developed, hosted, and maintained some 200 websites involving "city guides" for media companies. In 1999 Zip2 was sold to a wholly owned subsidiary of Compaq Computer for $307 million in cash and $34 million in stock options—Musk received a reported $22 million from the sale.[5]

In March 1999, Musk co-founded X.com, a Silicon Valley online financial services and e-mail payment company. One year later, X.com acquired Confinity, which operated a subsidiary called PayPal. Musk was instrumental in the development of the person-to-person payment platform and, seeing big market opportunity for such an online payment platform, decided to rename X.com as PayPal. Musk pocketed about $150 million in eBay shares when PayPal was acquired by eBay for $1.5 billion in eBay stock in October 2002.

In June 2002, Elon Musk with an investment of $100 million of his own money founded his third company, Space Exploration Technologies (SpaceX), to develop and manufacture space launch vehicles, with a goal of revolutionizing the state of rocket technology and ultimately enabling people to live on other planets. Upon hearing of Musk's new venture into the space flight business, David Sacks, one of Musk's former colleagues at PayPal, said, "Elon thinks bigger than just about anyone else I've ever met. He sets lofty goals and sets out to achieve them with great speed."[6] In 2011, Musk vowed to put a man on Mars in 10 years.[7] In May 2012, a SpaceX Dragon cargo capsule powered by a SpaceX Falcon Rocket completed a near flawless test flight to and from the International Space Station; since then, under contracts with NASA, the SpaceX Dragon had delivered cargo to and from the Space Station multiple times. Going into 2018, SpaceX secured contracts of over $12 billion to conduct over 100 missions. Currently, SpaceX was working toward developing fully and rapidly reusable rockets and test launching its new Falcon Heavy rocket, said to be the world's most powerful rocket. The company was said to be both profitable and cash-flow positive in 2013 to 2017. Headquartered in Hawthorne, California, SpaceX had 5,000 employees and was owned by management, employees, and private equity firms; Elon Musk was the company's CEO and largest stockholder.

Another of Elon Musk's business ventures was SolarCity Inc., a full-service provider of solar system design, financing, solar panel installation, and ongoing system monitoring for homeowners, municipalities, businesses (including Intel, Walmart, Walgreens, and eBay), universities, nonprofit organizations, and military bases. Initially, investors were generally bullish on SolarCity's future prospects, and the company's stock price rose from about $10.50 in late December 2012 to an all-time high of $85 in March 2013. But when the company's losses continued to grow, investor sentiment cooled and SolarCity's stock price dropped to the $16 to $20 range in February 2016. While Solar City had installed many solar energy systems and managed more solar systems for homes than any other solar company in the United States, its business model of recovering the capital and operating costs of the installed systems through leasing fees and power purchase agreements had resulted in negative cash flows and ever-larger net losses. In November 2016, to rescue SolarCity from probable bankruptcy, Tesla acquired the company for $2.6 billion (the deal was approved by an 85 percent shareholder vote); SolarCity's operations were folded into a new division named Tesla Energy. However, the business model was changed to one where customers financed their new solar power installations with cash and loans, thus producing a healthier mix of upfront and recurring revenue; moreover, the costs of installing solar-powered installations were expected to decline, partly because of improvements in solar technology, greater efficiencies in manufacturing solar-generation systems, and cost savings achieved by operating Tesla's automotive and energy divisions as sister companies.

From 2008 to 2015, many business articles had been written about Musk's brilliant entrepreneurship in creating companies with revolutionary products that either spawned new industries or disruptively transformed existing industries. In a 2012 *Success* magazine article, Musk indicated that his commitments to his spacecraft, electric car, and solar panel businesses were long term and deeply felt.[8] The author quoted Musk as saying, "I never expect to sort of sell them off and do something else. I expect to be with those companies as far into the future as I can imagine." Musk indicated he was involved in both Tesla's motor vehicle and energy businesses "because I'm concerned about the environment," while "SpaceX is about trying to help us work toward extending life beyond Earth on a permanent basis and becoming a multiplanetary species." The same writer described Musk's approach to a business as one of rallying employees and investors without creating false hope.[9] The article quoted Musk as saying:

> You've got to communicate, particularly within the company, the true state of the company. When people really understand it's do or die but if we work hard and pull through, there's going to be a great outcome, people will give it everything they've got.

Asked if he relied more on information or instinct in making key decisions, Musk said he made no bright-line distinction between the two.

> Data informs the instinct. Generally, I wait until the data and my instincts are in alignment. And if either the data or my instincts are out of alignment, then I sort of keep working the issue until they are in alignment, either positive or negative.[10]

Musk was widely regarded as being an inspiring and visionary entrepreneur with astronomical ambition and willingness to invest his own money in risky and highly problematic business ventures. He set stretch performance targets and high product quality standards, and he pushed hard for their achievement. He exhibited perseverance, dedication, and an exceptionally strong work ethic. He typically worked 85 to 90 hours a week. Most weeks, Musk split his time between SpaceX and Tesla.

In 2019, Elon Musk's base salary as Tesla's CEO was $62,400, an amount required by California's minimum wage law; however, he was accepting only $1 in salary. The company's Board of Directors in 2017 established an executive compensation plan for Musk tied to Tesla's performance on various metrics; compensation was in the form of stock option awards subject to various vesting conditions. As of April 30, 2019, Musk controlled 38.6 million shares of Tesla common stock (worth some $9.2 billion); his shareholdings gave him 21.7 percent of total shareholder voting power in Tesla.

Musk's Vision and Strategy for Tesla Elon Musk's strategic vision for the automotive segment of Tesla's operations featured three major elements:

1. Bring a full-range of affordable electric-powered vehicles to market and become the world's foremost manufacturer of premium quality, high-performance electric vehicles.

2. Convince motor vehicle owners worldwide that electric-powered motor vehicles were an appealing alternative to gasoline-powered vehicles.

3. Accelerate the world's transition from carbon-producing, gasoline-powered motor vehicles to zero emission electric vehicles.

In 2016, Musk's stated near-term strategic objective was for Tesla to achieve sales of about 500,000 electric vehicles annually by year-end 2018, but this sales target soon was pushed out to the end of 2019 at the earliest and more probably the end of 2020, assuming sales of the Model 3 took off as expected. In 2018, Musk envisioned that Tesla would introduce an SUV version of the Model 3 sedan (called Model Y) in 2019, also perhaps begin deliveries of the Tesla Semi in late 2019 to spur the switch to electric-powered vehicles in the freight transportation industry, and then a new version of the Tesla Roadster in 2020 to 2021. His strategic intent was for Tesla to be the world's biggest and most highly regarded producer of electric-powered motor vehicles, dramatically increasing the share of electric vehicles on roads across the world and causing global use of gasoline-powered motor vehicles to fall into permanent long-term decline.

At its core, therefore, Tesla's strategy was aimed squarely at utilizing the company's battery and electric drivetrain technology to disrupt the world automotive industry in ways that were sweeping and transformative. If Tesla's strategy proved to be as successful as Elon Musk believed it would be, industry observers expected that Tesla's competitive position and market standing vis-à-vis the world's best-known automotive manufacturers would be vastly stronger in 2025 than it was in 2018 and 2019.

Tesla's Early Sales Successes with the Model S and Model X, 2012 to 2018

In 2017 and 2018 production and sales of the company's trailblazing Model S sedan (introduced in 2012) and Model X sports utility vehicle (introduced in late 2015) were proceeding largely on plan. Combined sales of these two models were almost 101,500 units in 2017 and just under 100,000 units in 2018 (see Exhibit 1). The Model S was a fully electric, four-door, five-passenger luxury sedan with an all-glass panoramic roof, high definition backup camera, a 17-inch touchscreen that controlled most of the car's functions, keyless entry, xenon headlights, dual USB ports, tire pressure monitoring, and numerous other features that were standard in most luxury vehicles. The cheapest Model S had a base price of $75,700 in 2018 and, when equipped with options frequently selected by customers, carried a retail sticker price ranging from $95,000 to $136,000. The Model X was the longest range all-electric production sport utility vehicle in the world; it could seat up to seven adults and incorporated a unique falcon wing door system for easy access to the second and third seating rows. The Model X had an all-wheel drive dual motor system and autopilot capabilities, along with a full assortment of standard and optional features. Retail sticker prices in 2018 ranged from a base price

of $80,700 to $97,000 for a well-equipped Model X to $140,000 for a fully loaded model. Both the Model S and Model X were being sold in North America, Europe, and Asia in 2017 and 2018.

The Model S was the most-awarded car of 2013, including *Motor Trend*'s 2013 Car of the Year award and *Automobile* magazine's 2013 Car of the Year award. The National Highway Traffic Safety Administration (NTSHA) in 2013, 2014, and 2015 awarded the Tesla Model S a 5-star safety rating, both overall and in every subcategory (a score achieved by approximately 1 percent of all cars tested by the NHTSA). *Consumer Reports* gave the Model S a score of 99 out of 100 points in 2013, 2014, and 2015, saying it was "better than anything we've ever tested." However, the Tesla Model S did not make the *Consumer Reports* list of the "10 Top Picks" in 2016, 2017, and 2018, but the Model S did earn a perfect 100 score on the 2018 road test drive.

The sleek styling and politically correct power source of Tesla's Model S and Model X were thought to explain why thousands of wealthy individuals in countries where the two models were being sold—anxious to be a part of the migration from gasoline-powered vehicles to electric-powered vehicles and to publicly display support for a cleaner environment—had become early purchasers and advocates for Tesla's vehicles. Indeed, word-of-mouth praise among current owners and glowing articles in the media were so pervasive that Tesla had not yet spent any money on advertising to boost customer traffic in its showrooms. In a presentation to investors, a Tesla officer said, "Tesla owners are our best salespeople."[11]

Tesla's Excruciating Struggle to Boost Production Volumes of the Model 3

Tesla Motors began assembling the first models of its new "affordably-priced" entry-level Model 3 electric car in May 2017 and delivered the first units the last week of July, with a goal of gradually ramping up production to a total of 1,500 units by the end of September. The first production vehicles, delivered to employees who had placed preproduction reservations over a year earlier, were preconfigured with rear-wheel drive and a long-range battery; had a range of 310 miles and 0 to 60 mph acceleration time of 5.1 seconds; and a sticker price starting at $44,000 with premium upgrades available for an additional $5,000. Deliveries of the standard Model 3, with a base price of $35,000, 220 miles of range, and a 0 to 60 mph acceleration time of 5.6 seconds, were expected to begin in the United States in November 2017. Dual motor all-wheel drive configurations were scheduled to be available in early 2018. Plans called for international deliveries of the Model 3 to begin in late 2018, contingent upon regulatory approvals, starting with left-hand drive markets and followed by right-hand drive markets in 2019.

Tesla unveiled six drivable prototypes of the Model 3 for public viewing and a limited number of test drives on the evening of March 31, 2016. Buyer reaction was overwhelmingly positive. Over the next two weeks, some 350,000 individuals paid a $1,000 deposit to reserve a place in line to obtain a Model 3; reportedly, the number of reservations grew to nearly 400,000 units over the next several months. Because of the tremendous amount of interest in the Model 3, Elon Musk announced in May 2016 that Tesla was advancing its schedule to begin producing the Model 3 from late 2017 to mid-2017 and further that it was going to accelerate its efforts to expand production capacity of the Model 3, with a goal of getting to a production run rate of 500,000 units annually by year-end 2018 instead of year-end 2020.

In early August 2017, in a letter updating shareholders on the company's second-quarter 2017 results, Musk said:

> Based on our preparedness at this time, we are confident we can produce just over 1,500 [Model 3] vehicles in Q3 and achieve a run rate of 5,000 vehicles per week by the end of 2017. We also continue to plan on increasing Model 3 production to 10,000 vehicles per week at some point in 2018.[12]

But in his third-quarter 2017 update on November 1, 2017, Musk related a host of production bottlenecks and challenges that were blocking the ramp-up of Model 3 production and delaying deliveries, saying, "this makes it difficult to predict exactly how long it will take for all bottlenecks to be cleared or when new ones will appear. Based on what we know now, we currently expect to achieve a production rate of 5,000 Model 3 vehicles per week by late Q1 2018."[13]

However, Tesla's "production hell" with the Model 3 continued to haunt the company in early 2018. Many analysts believed Tesla's problems stemmed from having taken huge shortcuts in the parts approval process, production line validation, and full beta testing of the Model 3 in order to begin early assembly and production ramp-up. There were other reasons, including ongoing parts bottlenecks and inconsistent manufacturing quality. Production line employees interviewed by reporters indicated significant numbers of units coming off the assembly line had quality problems involving malfunctioning parts/components and/or faulty installation issues that required reworking. A big parking lot just outside the assembly plant in Fremont, California, was said to be full of Model 3s awaiting corrective attention; a few were even being junked because of the high cost of restoring them to a condition that would pass final predelivery inspection. On February 7, 2018, Musk reported:

> We continue to target weekly Model 3 production rates of 2,500 by the end of Q1 and 5,000 by the end of Q2. It is important to note that while these are the levels we are focused on hitting and we have plans in place to achieve them, our prior experience on the Model 3 ramp has demonstrated the difficulty of accurately forecasting specific production rates at specific points in time. What we can say with confidence is that we are taking many actions to systematically address bottlenecks and add capacity in places like the battery module line where we have experienced constraints, and these actions should result in our production rate significantly increasing during the rest of Q1 and through Q2.
>
> Despite the delays that we experienced in our production ramp, Model 3 net reservations remained stable in Q4. In recent weeks, they have continued to grow as Model 3 has arrived in select Tesla stores and received numerous positive reviews, including *Automobile* magazine's 2018 Design of the Year award.[14]

A week or so later, Tesla shut down the Model 3 assembly line for four days to address some of the problems being encountered. Nonetheless, in early March 2018, there were reports from multiple sources that Tesla had not been able to consistently achieve a production run rate of 800 units per week. Musk's target of a weekly production rate of 2,500 Model 3s by the end of March proved unachievable.

In addition, there were accumulating reports from the owners of Model 3s relating to touchscreen issues—one related to the audio system volume suddenly blasting higher without the screen having been touched; another related to drivers returning to their parked Model 3 and discovering the touchscreen on and the audio sound blaring; still another related to "phantom" inputs along the edges of the touchscreen when certain apps were opened. In some instances, Tesla had replaced the touchscreens; in others, it promised a software solution would soon be forthcoming. A second reported problem, in which the battery capacity decreased noticeably while the car was parked in the sun on a hot day for several hours, had been reported by a number of Model 3 owners and, to a lesser extent, by a few Model S and Model X owners. It appeared that battery drain problems often occurred in Model 3 vehicles experiencing touchscreen issues. A couple of Model 3 owners with technical backgrounds had speculated the problem related to touchscreens being mounted on a large metal pedestal such that large temperature differentials between a vehicle's hot interior and its cooler exterior caused the touchscreen and plastic touchpad to warp and produce other anomalies as the metal pedestal absorbed heat from inside the vehicle. In late March 2018, the cause had not been pinpointed, but the problem turned out to be related to only a few vehicles rather than faulty design that would drive up warranty costs for Model 3s already delivered. During the last week of March, Elon Musk tweeted that he had taken over the role of supervising Model 3 production for the time being.

The first week of April 2018, Tesla reported that it produced 34,494 vehicles in the first quarter of 2018 and delivered 29,980 vehicles, of which 11,730 were Model S; 10,070 were Model X; and 8,180 were Model 3; as of March 31, 4,060 Model S and Model X vehicles and 2,040 Model 3 vehicles were in transit to customers. Tesla also reported that after shifting some production resources away from Model S and Model X production over to production and assembly of the Model 3 during the last week of March, it was able to produce 2,020 Models 3s in the last seven days leading up to April 3. In its production and delivery announcement, the company further said:

> Given the progress made thus far and upcoming actions for further capacity improvement, we expect that the Model 3 production rate will

climb rapidly through Q2. Tesla continues to target a production rate of approximately 5,000 units per week in about three months.

Finally, we would like to share two additional points about Model 3:

- The quality of Model 3 coming out of production is at the highest level we have seen across all our products. This is reflected in the overwhelming delight experienced by our customers with their Model 3s. Our initial customer satisfaction score for Model 3 quality is above 93 percent, which is the highest score in Tesla's history.

- Net Model 3 reservations remained stable through Q1. The reasons for order cancellation are almost entirely due to delays in production in general and delays in availability of certain planned options, particularly dual motor AWD and the smaller battery pack.[15]

While progress was finally being made in boosting Model 3 production volumes, Tesla still had to prove it could overcome three challenges with the potential to imperil Musk's vision for the company:

1. Gasoline prices across much of the world had dropped significantly from 2015 to early 2018 and were expected by many knowledgeable observers to remain permanently "low" because crude oil prices worldwide were expected to stay below $80 per barrel, in part due to the growing abundance of shale oil and the sharply lower costs of extracting oil from shale deposits. Affordable gasoline prices made the purchase of electric vehicles less attractive, given that (1) electric vehicles were higher priced than vehicles with gasoline engines, (2) electric vehicles so far were limited to an upper range of about 300 miles on a single battery charge, and (3) new vehicles powered by gasoline engines were getting more miles per gallon (due to government-mandated mileage-efficiency requirements).

2. Tesla was facing the prospect of much more formidable competition from virtually all of the world's major motor vehicle manufacturers (BMW, Mercedes-Benz, Jaguar, Volkswagen-Audi, Toyota, Honda, Nissan, General Motors, and Ford) that were rushing to introduce affordable and high-end electric vehicles with features

and engine configurations that would enable them to compete head-on with the Model S, Model X, and Model 3. Several vehicle makers were also pursuing the development of electric-powered semitrucks for commercial uses.

3. Tesla had yet to prove it could boost operating efficiency and lower costs enough to be both price competitive and attractively profitable in producing and marketing its vehicle models. It reported both a loss from operations and a net loss during 2013–2017, despite growing its automotive sales and leasing revenues from $2.61 billion in 2013 to $9.64 billion in 2017. In February 2018, the company did say it expected to generate a positive *quarterly* operating income before the end of 2018 (but not a positive operating income for the *year*). While Tesla's ongoing operating losses and net losses were partly, or perhaps largely, due to the sizable new product development costs associated with the Model X and Model 3 and to the required accounting treatments for both leased vehicles and Tesla's generous stock compensation plan, it was nonetheless disconcerting that Tesla's operating loss of $1.63 billion in 2017 was the largest in the company's history and its 2017 operating profit per vehicle sold was a negative $15,855.[16]

A possible fourth challenge seemed to be gathering steam on the Tesla message boards in the first four months of 2018. People with Model 3 reservations, because of all the production problems and delivery delays they had been hearing about, had posted concerns about taking delivery of the Model 3 they had ordered. In one anecdotal case, a poster told of when he went to the Tesla delivery location to take delivery of a black Model 3, he could clearly see paint swirls on the hood; when told by the delivery person that the service department had done the best job it could to buff out the swirls and that the car would be sold "as is," the poster refused delivery. But after further conversation with the delivery person the poster said he then agreed to pay an extra $1,000 for a red Model 3 after being promised by the delivery person it would be ready for pickup in one week—after 10 days, the poster said he had received no notification to come pick up the red Model 3. There were also message

board posts from some Model S and Model X owners about the repair problems they were experiencing with their vehicles. There was one extreme example where an unhappy Model S owner reported having to take his vehicle to the Tesla service center for repairs six times in the past five months. In late March 2018 Tesla announced it was recalling about 123,000 Model S sedans globally after discovering that certain corroding bolts in cold weather climates could lead to a power-steering failure.

When Tesla announced its financial and operating results for the first quarter of 2018 ending March 31, Elon Musk said that after numerous adjustments in assembly methods and correcting problems with faulty and improperly designed parts, Tesla was now able to sustain a production rate of 3,000 Model 3s per week. He also said that continued refinements of the assembly process and improved operational uptime of the associated machinery should lead to a production rate of "well over 5,000" vehicles per week by the end of June or beginning of July. Musk admitted that he had been wrong in mandating use of so many robots along the assembly line, and that now the assembly line had been and was still being greatly simplified, with more use being made of semi-automated and manual assembly to perform certain tasks until the company had enough time to perfect the use of robots and enable full automation to resume. Musk confidently predicted that the Model 3 would become the best-selling medium-sized premium sedan in the United States before year-end and that if Tesla executed according to plan the company would achieve positive cash flows and positive net income (excluding noncash stock-based compensation) in both the third and fourth quarters of 2018.[17] During the May 2, 2018, conference call with analysts to discuss Tesla's Q1 2018 financial results, Musk expressed his appreciation to the Chinese government for its announcement that foreign companies would henceforth be allowed to have 100 percent ownership of manufacturing facilities in China and said Tesla could have a Gigafactory capable of vehicle production in China "not later than the fourth quarter" of 2018.[18]

Exhibit 2 presents selected financial statement data for Tesla for 2015 through the first quarter of 2019.

EXHIBIT 2

Selected Financial Data for Tesla, Inc., Years Ended December 31, 2015–2018 plus Q1 of 2019 (in millions of $, except share and per share data)

		YEARS ENDED DECEMBER 31			
	Quarter 1 2019	2018	2017	2016	2015
Income Statement Data:					
Revenues:					
Automotive sales	$3,508.7	17,631.5	$ 8,534.8	$5,589.0	$3,431.6
Automotive leasing	215.1	883.5	1,106.5	761.8	309.4
Total automotive revenues	3,723.9	18,515.0	9,641.3	6,350.8	3,741.0
Energy generation and storage	324.7	1,555.2	1,116.3	181.4	14.5
Services and other	492.9	1,391.00	1,001.2	468.0	290.6
Total revenues	4,541.5	21,461.3	11,758.8	7,000.1	4,046.0
Cost of revenues:					
Automotive sales	2,856.2	13,685.6	6,724.5	4,268.1	2,639.9
Automotive leasing	117.1	488.4	708.2	482.0	183.4
Total automotive cost of revenues	2,973.3	14,174.0	7,432.7	4,750.1	2,823.3
Energy generation and storage	316.9	1,364.9	874.5	178.3	12.3
Services and other	685.5	1,880.4	1,229.0	472.5	286.9
Total cost of revenues	3,975.7	17,419.2	9,536.3	5,400.9	3,122.5
Gross profit (loss)	565.7	4,042.0	2,222.5	1,599.3	923.5
Operating expenses:					
Research and development	340.2	1,460.4	1,378.1	834.4	717.9
Selling, general and administrative	703.9	2,834.5	2,476.5	1,432.2	922.2
Restructuring and other	43.5	—	—	—	—
Total operating expenses	1,087.6	4,430.1	3.854.6	2,266.6	1,640.1
Loss from operations	(521.8)	(388.1)	(1,632.1)	(667.3)	(716.6)
Interest income	8.8	24.5	19.7	8.5	1.5
Interest expense	(157.5)	(663.1)	(471.3)	(198.8)	(118.9)
Other income (expense), net	25.7	21.9	(125.4)	111.3	(41.7)
Loss before income taxes	(644.8)	(1,004.7)	(2,209.0)	(875,624)	(875.6)
Provision for income taxes	22.9	57.8	31.5	13,039	13.3
Net loss	$ (667.6)	$ (1,062.6)	$ (2,240.6)	$ (773.0)	$ (888.7)
Net loss attributable to noncontrolling interests and subsidiaries	(34.5)	(86.5)	(279.2)	(98.1)	—
Net loss attributable to common shareholders	$(702.1)	(976.1)	$(1,961.4)	(674.9)	$(888.7)
Net loss per share of common stock, basic and diluted	$(4.10)	$(5.72)	$(11.83)	$(4.68)	$(6.93)
Weighted average shares used in computing net loss per share of common stock, basic and diluted	173.0	170.5	165.8	144.2	128.2

		YEARS ENDED DECEMBER 31			
	Quarter 1 2019	2018	2017	2016	2015
Selected Balance Sheet Data:					
Cash and cash equivalents	$2,198.2	$ 3,685.6	$ 3,367.9	$1,196,908	$1,196.9
Inventory	3,836.8	3,113.4	2,263.5	2,067.5	1,277.8
Total current assets	7,677.8	8,306.3	6,570.5	6,259.8	2,791.4
Property, plant, and equipment, net	9,850.9	11,330.1	10,027.5	5,983.0	3,403.3
Total assets	28,912.5	29,739.6	28,655.4	22,644.1	8,092.5
Total current liabilities	9,242.8	9,992.1	7,674.7	5,827.0	2,816.3
Long-term debt and capital leases, net of current portion	9,7887.9	9,403.7	9,418.3	5,860.0	2,040.4
Total stockholders' equity	4,605.6	4,923.2	4,237.2	4,752.9	1,088.9
Selected Cash Flow Data:					
Cash flows used in operating activities	$ (639.6)	$ (1,062.6)	$(2,240.6)	$ (773.0)	$ (888.7)
Proceeds from issuance of common stock in public offerings	—	6,176.27	400.2	1,701.7	730.0
Purchases of property and equipment excluding capital leases	(279.9)	(2,100.78)	(3,414.8)	(1,280.8)	(1,634.9
Net cash used in investing activities	(305.8)	(2,337.4)	(4,419.0)	(1,416.4)	(1,673.6)
Net cash provided by financing activities	(653.0)	573.8	4,414.9	3,744.0	1,523.5

Source: Company 10-K reports for 2015 and 2018; Company 10Q Report for period ended March 31, 2019.

Tesla in 2018–2019

Following the acquisition of Solar City in late 2016, Tesla described its business in the following way:

> We design, develop, manufacture and sell high-performance fully electric vehicles, and energy generation and storage systems, and also install and maintain such systems and sell solar electricity. We are the world's only vertically integrated sustainable energy company, offering end-to-end clean energy products, including generation, storage and consumption. We have established and continue to grow a global network of stores, vehicle service centers and Supercharger stations to accelerate[19] the widespread adoption of our products, and we continue to develop self-driving capability in order to improve vehicle safety. Our sustainable energy products, engineering expertise, intense focus to accelerate the world's transition to sustainable energy, and business model differentiate us from other companies.

> We currently produce and sell three fully electric vehicles, the Model S sedan, the Model X sport utility vehicle ("SUV") and the Model 3 sedan. . . . We also intend to bring additional vehicles to market in the future, including trucks and an all-new sports car. . . . We sell our vehicles through our own sales and service network which we are continuing to grow globally. The benefits we receive from distribution ownership enable us to improve the overall customer experience, the speed of product development, and the capital efficiency of our business. We are also continuing to build our network of Superchargers and Destination Chargers in North America, Europe, and Asia to provide fast charging that enables convenient long distance travel.

> . . . In addition, we are leveraging our technological expertise in batteries, power electronics, and integrated systems to manufacture and sell energy storage products. In late 2016, we began production and deliveries of our latest generation energy storage products, Powerwall 2 and

Powerpack 2. Powerwall 2 is a home battery. . . . Powerpack 2 is an energy storage system for commercial, industrial, and utility applications.

Finally, we sell and lease solar systems (with or without accompanying energy storage systems) to residential and commercial customers and sell renewable energy to residential and commercial customers at prices that are typically below utility rates. Since 2006, we have installed solar energy systems for hundreds of thousands of customers. Our long-term lease and power purchase agreements with our customers generate recurring payments and create a portfolio of high-quality receivables that we leverage to further reduce the cost of making the switch to solar energy. The electricity produced by our solar installations represents a very small fraction of total U.S. electricity generation. With tens of millions of single-family homes and businesses in our primary service territories, and many more in other locations, we have a large opportunity to expand and grow this business. [Revenues and cost of goods sold from the energy generation and storage activities of SolarCity/Tesla Energy are shown in Exhibit 2.]

We manufacture our vehicle products primarily at our facilities in Fremont, California, Lathrop, California, Tilburg, Netherlands, and at our Gigafactory 1 near Reno, Nevada. We manufacture our energy storage products at Gigafactory 1 and our solar products at our factories in Fremont, California, and Buffalo, New York (Gigafactory 2).[20]

During 2014–2017, Tesla raised billions of dollars via the sale of senior notes convertible into common stock, other types of long-term debt, and issues of new common stock to provide funding for research and development (R&D), the development of new models, expanded production capabilities, an ever-growing network of recharging stations, and opening retail showrooms and Tesla service centers. Tesla's long-term debt and contractual capital lease obligations grew from $600 million at year-end 2013 to $9.8 billion as of March 31, 2019; and the number of shares of common stock outstanding rose from 119 million to nearly 173 million during the same period. In recent years, Tesla had burned through cash at a torrid pace because of the heavy expenses it was incurring for design and engineering, gearing up to produce certain parts and component systems internally, constructing new facilities,

equipping vehicle assembly lines with robotics technology, tools, and other machinery, and boosting its employee count from almost 6,000 employees at year-end 2013 to over 48,800 at year-end 2018.

Tesla ended Q1 2019 with $2.2 billion in cash and cash equivalents, down from $3.7 billion on December 31, 2018; this was due to a $920 million bond repayment and increases in the number of vehicles in transit. Executive management expected that the company's capital expenditures in 2019 would be about $2.0 to $2.5 billion. The new Gigafactory in Shanghai, China, was being almost fully funded with local debt; as of March 31, 2019, a $522 million credit line had been secured with local banks. In May 2019, Tesla announced offerings of $650 million of common stock and $1,350 million in convertible senior notes due in 2024; underwriters were granted a 30-day option to purchase up to an additional 15 percent of each offering. Elon Musk participated by purchasing $10 million of common stock. Aggregate gross proceeds of the offering, given exercise of the 30-day option, were approximately $2.3 billion before discounts and expenses.

Tesla's Strategy to Become the World's Biggest and Most Highly Regarded Producer of Electric Vehicles

In 2019, Tesla's strategy was focused on continuing to gear up production of the Model 3, continuing the development of the new Model Y SUV and the Tesla Semi, continuing to add production capabilities at Gigafactory 1 near Reno, Nevada, getting the new Gigafactory in China ready to produce Model 3 vehicles in late 2019, and adding service centers and Supercharger stations in the United States, much of Europe, China, and Australia. At the Tesla Energy division, efforts were under way to (1) standardize the product offering, (2) simplify the customer buying experience, (3) concentrate sales and marketing efforts on the markets with the strongest economics, and (4) implement a new pricing and product deployment strategy aimed at combatting mounting competition from established companies with a similar portfolio of energy storage products and more competitively priced solar products. Tesla fell far short of its goal of tripling sales of energy storage products in 2018.

Product Line Strategy

A key element of Tesla's long-term strategy was to offer vehicle buyers a full line of electric vehicle options. So far Tesla had introduced four models—the Tesla Roadster, Model S, Model X, and Model 3. Aggressive efforts were under way to get the Model Y into the marketplace in late 2019–2020 along with the Tesla Semi truck. These were scheduled to be followed by a new Roadster 2 model and a pickup truck.

Tesla's First Vehicle—The Tesla Roadster

Following Tesla's initial funding in 2004, Musk took an active role within the company. Although he was not involved in day-to-day business operations, he nonetheless exerted strong influence in the design of the Tesla Roadster, a two-seat convertible that could accelerate from 0 to 60 miles per hour in as little as 3.7 seconds, had a maximum speed of about 120 miles per hour, could travel about 245 miles on a single charge, and had a base price of $109,000. Musk insisted from the beginning that the Roadster have a lightweight, high-strength carbon fiber body, and he influenced the design of components of the Roadster ranging from the power electronics module to the headlamps and other styling features.[21] Prototypes of the Roadster were introduced to the public in July 2006. The first "Signature One Hundred" set of fully equipped Roadsters sold out in less than three weeks; the second hundred sold out by October 2007. General production began in March 2008. New models of the Roadster were introduced in July 2009 (including the Roadster Sport with a base price of $128,500) and in July 2010. Sales of Roadster models to countries in Europe and Asia began in 2010. From 2008 through 2012, Tesla sold more than 2,450 Roadsters in 31 countries.[22] Sales of Roadster models ended in December 2012 so that the company could concentrate exclusively on producing and marketing the Model S. However, Tesla announced in early

2015 that Roadster owners would be able to obtain a Roadster 3.0 package that enabled a 40 to 50 percent improvement in driving range to as much as 400 miles on a single charge; management indicated additional updates for Roadsters would be forthcoming. In 2017, Tesla announced it would reintroduce a new version of the Roadster in 2020 (after it began deliveries of the Tesla Semi truck and Model Y).

Tesla's Second Vehicle—The Model S

Customer deliveries of Tesla's second vehicle—the sleek, eye-catching Model S sedan—began in July 2012. Tesla introduced several new options for the Model S in 2013, including a subzero weather package, parking sensors, upgraded leather interior, several new wheel options, and a yacht-style center console. Xenon headlights and a high-definition backup camera were made standard equipment on all Model S cars. In 2014 an all-wheel drive powertrain was introduced to provide buyers with four powertrain options. The Model S powertrain options were further modified several times. In May 2019, the Model S was being offered with two powertrain options:

- 100D—all-wheel drive, 100-kWh battery pack, 335-mile driving range, 0 to 60 mph in 4.1 seconds, with a standard price of $94,000 (which included Smart Air Suspension)

- P100D—maximum performance all-wheel drive with dual front and rear motors (mounted on the front and rear axles), 100-kWh battery pack, 315-mile driving range, 0 to 60 mph in 2.5 seconds, with a standard price of $135,000 (which included the best interior and other premium upgrades)

Popular options included enhanced autopilot software ($5,000); full self-driving capability—subject to further software validation and regulatory approval ($3,000); and third-row, rear-facing seating ($4,000). From time to time, Tesla sent software updates to all Model S vehicles previously delivered to customers that included new and updated features. In 2018–2019, all Model S vehicles had a standard software feature called "Range Assurance," an always-running application within the car's navigation system that kept tabs on the vehicle's battery charge-level and the locations of

Tesla Supercharging stations and parking-spot chargers in the vicinity. When the vehicle's battery began running low, an alert appeared on the navigation screen, along with a list of nearby Tesla Supercharger stations and public charging facilities; a second warning appeared when the vehicle was about to go beyond the radius of nearby chargers without enough juice to get to the next facility, at which point drivers were directed to the nearest charge point. There was also a Trip Planner feature that enabled drivers to plan long-distance trips based on the best locations for recharging both en route and at the destination; during travel, the software was programmed to pull in new data about every 30 seconds, updating to show which charging facilities had vacancies or were full. Autopilot software features were updated and upgraded as fast as they were developed and tested.

In the United States, customers who purchased a Model S (or any other Tesla model) before 2019 were eligible for a federal tax credit of up to $7,500. A number of states also offered rebates on electric vehicle purchases, with states like California and New York offering rebates as high as $7,500. Customers who leased a Model S were not entitled to rebates. Legislation authorizing the federal tax credit called for the tax credits on a manufacturer's electric vehicles to expire once the manufacturer's cumulative sales of electric vehicles reached 200,000 units. Bills had been introduced in Congress to extend the credits past a cumulative sales volume of 200,000 units, but none of these had passed as of June 3, 2019.

Tesla's Third Vehicle—The Model X Crossover SUV

To reduce the development costs of the Model X, Tesla had designed the Model X so that it could share about 60 percent of the Model S platform. The Model X had seating for seven adults, dual electric motors that powered an all-wheel drive system, and a driving range of about 260 miles per charge. The Model X's distinctive "falcon-wing doors" provided easy access to the second and third seating rows, resulting in a profile that resembled a sedan more than an SUV. The three drive train options for the Model X in 2018 were the same as for the Model S, but the driving ranges and acceleration times for the Model X were different from those of the Model S.

In 2018, the standard price for the Model X with a 75D drive train was $79,500; the standard price for a 100D Model X was $96,000 (which included Smart Air Suspension); and the standard price for a P100D Model X was $140,000 (which included the best interior and other premium upgrades). The Model X was the first SUV ever to achieve a 5-star safety rating in every category and subcategory; it had both the lowest probability of occupant injury and a rollover risk half that of any SUV on the road. Over-the-Internet software updates were standard.

Tesla's Fourth Vehicle—The Model 3

The idea behind the Model 3 was to incorporate all the company had learned from the development and production of the Roadster, Model S, and Model X to create the world's first mass-market electric vehicle priced on par with its gasoline-powered equivalents. The Model 3 was attractively styled, with seating for five adults, a driving range of 210 to 310 miles depending on drive train selection, and 0 to 60 mph acceleration capability of less than six seconds. While the stated base price was $35,000, the range of available upgrades and options could up the price to $55,000 or more. The average selling price of the Model 3 in 2018 exceeded $45,000 and as of June 2019 Tesla had produced very few of the $35,000 base-price Model 3 versions (since it was far more profitable to sell more fully equipped Model 3s).

Going into 2018, at least 300,000 people had paid $1,000 to reserve a Model 3 and were waiting in line for delivery. From the outset, the Model 3 had been designed to enable efficient, high-volume production. However, the Model 3 posed a much tougher production cost challenge than Tesla's three previous models, all of which had prices in the $80,000 to $130,000 range. The Model 3's profitability hinged on being able to drive production costs per unit down more than 50 percent below what had been achieved with prior models. Of particular concern was the lithium-ion battery pack, the single biggest cost component in the Model S and Model X, which had an estimated cost of $209 per kilowatt-hour as of December 2017.[23] Part of the solution was equipping the Model 3 with less powerful electric motors, but a host of other cost-saving efficiencies had to be achieved as well for Tesla to make a profit on Model 3s equipped with minimal options.

One factor likely to prove problematic for many prospective Model 3 buyers in the United States in 2019 (as well as for the buyers of Model S and Model X) was a provision in the federal legislation stating that once the *cumulative* sales volume of a manufacturer's zero emission vehicles in the United States reached 200,000 vehicles, the size of the $7,500 federal tax credit entered a one-year phase-out period where buyers of qualifying vehicles were "eligible for 50 percent of the credit if acquired in the first two quarters of the phase-out period and 25 percent of the credit if acquired in the third or fourth quarter of the phase-out period."[24] Purchasers of that manufacturer's vehicles were not eligible for any federal tax credit after the phase-out period. Tesla's cumulative sales in the United States would almost certainly exceed 200,000 vehicles sometime in 2018 (probably sometime before July 1), meaning that a hefty percentage of people with Model 3 reservations would qualify for only some or none of the $7,500 tax credit. Buyers who leased a Tesla were not eligible for the tax credit (the credit went to the company offering the lease; the tax credits were also based on the size of the battery). Some states also offered tax credits for the purchases of plug-in electric vehicles. There were also a variety of other tax credits offered by states. The governments of China, Japan, Norway, United Kingdom, and several other European countries offered tax incentives for electric vehicle purchases as well. In 2018, Canada discontinued the use of incentives for electric vehicles with a manufacturer's suggested list price of price greater than C$75,000 (US$58,500) and Norway had phased out tax credits as well.

Tesla's Model Y Crossover SUV

In 2017, Elon Musk announced that Tesla had launched plans for the development and production of an all-electric crossover SUV that would be built on the same platform as the Model 3. The Model Y SUV was to be a smaller version of the Model X SUV and carry price tags comparable to the Model 3. In May 2018, while Tesla was struggling with all of its Model 3 production problems, Musk said he was planning for the production of the Model Y to be a "manufacturing revolution," with a simplified manufacturing process and greater use of robots.[25] Tesla unveiled a prototype of its Model Y SUV in March 2019 and announced a target volume production date of late 2020 for North America and early 2021 for beginning deliveries to Europe and China. Elon Musk in May 2019 said that Tesla's current "default plan" was to produce the Model Y SUV at the Tesla Factory in Fremont, with a target volume production date of late 2020 for North America and early 2021 for deliveries to Europe and China. Industry observers speculated that Tesla would show prototypes of the Model Y in the second half of 2018, after hearing Musk say in May 2018 that the company would announce no later than the fourth quarter of 2018 where a production facility for the Model Y SUV would be located. Because Musk was aiming for production of one million Model Ys annually, industry observers speculated that Tesla would need to establish a second manufacturing facility in the United States and that Tesla might purchase an existing plant from an automaker, since sedan production in the United States was dropping rapidly due to an accelerating shift in buyer preferences away from sedans and toward SUVs and light trucks. Ford Motor had announced it would cease production of four of its slow-selling traditional passenger cars (Taurus, Fusion, Focus, and Fiesta) by 2020; General Motors was expected to cease production of its Chevrolet Cruze compact and possibly its Chevrolet Sonic and Impala sedans at the end of their current product cycles. Fiat Chrysler had already killed its Dodge Dart and Chrysler 200 sedan models.

The 300-mile range version of the Model Y was scheduled to be priced at $48,000, roughly $20,000 less than other all-electric SUVs. Plans called for it to have well-appointed standard equipment, superior acceleration and handling, a roomy interior, and an assortment of optional extras. Because the Model Y was expected to appeal to a large market segment, Elon Musk expected that the Model Y would ultimately have higher annual sales than Model S, Model X, and Model 3 combined.

The Tesla Semi Truck

Mention was made of a semi truck in Tesla's 2016 master plan. But behind the scenes Tesla had moved swiftly to come up with not only a design but also prototypes. The Semi was unveiled with much fanfare at a press conference on November 16, 2017. The company described the Semi as a Class 8 semi-trailer truck prototype that would be powered by four electric motors of the type used in the Model 3; have Tesla Autopilot, which permitted semi-autonomous driving, as standard equipment; and have a driving range of up to a range of 500 miles (805 km) on a full charge. Elon Musk said the 500-mile version, equipped with Tesla's latest battery design, would be able to run for 400 miles (640 km) after an 80 percent charge in 30 minutes using a solar-powered Tesla Megacharger charging station. He also said the Semi would be able to accelerate from 0 to 60 mph in 5 seconds unloaded and in 20 seconds fully loaded. Tesla expected to offer a warranty for a million miles and said maintenance would be simpler than for a diesel truck. A week later, Musk said that the regular production versions for the 300-mile range version of the Semi would be priced at $150,000 and the 500-mile range version would be priced at $180,000; the company also said it planned to offer a Founder's Series Semi at $200,000. Scores of companies, including Walmart, United Parcel Service, Anheuser-Busch, J.B. Hunt Trucking Co, and PepsiCo, immediately lined up to place pre-orders for 5 to 150 Semis (at an initial reservation price of $5,000, which was quickly raised to $20,000 per reservation) so they could conduct tests of how well the Semi would perform in their operations. In March 2018, Tesla began testing the Semi with real cargo, hauling battery packs from Gigafactory 1 in Nevada to the Tesla Factory in Fremont, California. Pictures of the Semi being loaded with cargo at the Nevada Gigafactory and traveling on the highways were immediately publicized in the media and posted on the Internet and social media. Production of the Semi was originally scheduled to begin in 2019 but it appeared the schedule would likely be pushed back until 2020.

In Elon Musk's Q1 2018 Update Letter to Shareholders on May 2, 2018, no mention was made of the Tesla Semi; however, in a later conference call with Wall Street analysts that same day, Musk did say the company had about 2,000 reservations for the Semi. Observers speculated that near-term plans for the Semi had moved to the back burner temporarily due to the company's decision to accelerate production of the Model Y and Tesla's lack of capital to fund further development and build a new production facility for the Semi.

The Tesla Pickup Truck

While Elon Musk began talking about Tesla making an all-electric pickup truck (and an all-electric cargo van on the same chassis) in 2016, the company was still in the early stages of designing the vehicle and settling on its features as of June 2019. Elon Musk confirmed in a podcast in early June that Tesla wanted to keep the starting price below $50,000 and make sure the truck was highly functional from a load-carrying standpoint, saying:

> "It's going to be a truck that is more capable than other trucks. The goal is to be a better truck than a [Ford] F-150 in terms of truck-like functionality and be a better sports car than a standard [Porsche] 911. That's the aspiration."[26]

Musk went on to say that the truck's appearance would be pretty sci-fi and not be for everyone. Further, buyers of the truck would have a range of optional extras that could push the price up close to $70,000 (on a par with current roomy, luxurious pickups with powerful engines). He indicated the truck would be unveiled in late 2019.

Distribution Strategy: A Company-Owned and -Operated Network of Retail Stores and Service Centers

Tesla sold its vehicles directly to buyers and also provided them with after-sale service through a network of company-owned sales galleries and service centers. This contrasted sharply with the strategy of rival motor vehicle manufacturers, all of whom sold vehicles and replacement parts at wholesale prices to their networks of franchised dealerships that in turn handled retail sales, maintenance and service, and warranty repairs. Management believed that integrating forward into the business of traditional automobile dealers and operating its own retail sales and service network had three important advantages:

1. *The ability to create and control its own version of a compelling buying customer experience,* one that was differentiated from the buying experience consumers had with sales and service locations of franchised automobile dealers. Having customers deal directly with Tesla-employed sales and service personnel enabled Tesla to (a) engage and inform potential customers about electric vehicles in general and the advantages of owning a Tesla in particular and (b) build a more personal relationship with customers and, hopefully, instill a lasting and favorable impression of Tesla Motors, its mission, and the caliber and performance of its vehicles.

2. *The ability to achieve greater operating economies in performing sales and service activities.* Management believed that a company-operated sales and service network offered substantial opportunities to better control inventory costs of both vehicles and replacement parts, manage warranty service and pricing, maintain and strengthen the Tesla brand, and obtain rapid customer feedback.

3. *The opportunity to capture the sales and service revenues of traditional automobile dealerships.* Rival motor vehicle manufacturers sold vehicles and replacement parts at wholesale prices to their networks of franchised dealerships that in turn handled retail sales, maintenance and service, and warranty repairs. But when Tesla buyers purchased a vehicle at a Tesla-owned sales gallery, Tesla captured the full retail sales price, roughly 10 percent greater than the wholesale price realized by vehicle manufacturers selling through franchised dealers. And, by operating its own service centers, it captured service revenues not available to vehicle manufacturers who relied upon their franchised dealers to provide needed maintenance and repairs. Furthermore, Tesla management believed that company-owned service centers avoided the conflict of interest between vehicle manufacturers and their franchised dealers where the sale of warranty parts and repairs by a dealer were a key source of revenue and profit for the dealer but where warranty-related costs were typically a substantial expense for the vehicle manufacturer.

Tesla Sales Galleries and Showrooms

Going into 2019, all of Tesla's sales galleries and showrooms were in or near major metropolitan areas; some were in prominent regional shopping malls and others were on highly visible sites along busy thoroughfares. Most sales locations had only several vehicles in stock that were available for immediate sale. The vast majority of Tesla buyers, however, preferred to customize their vehicle by placing an order via the Internet, either while in a sales gallery or at home.

In years past, Tesla had aggressively expanded its network of sales galleries and service centers to broaden its geographical presence and to provide better maintenance and repair service in areas with a high concentration of Tesla owners. In 2013, Tesla began combining its sales and service activities at a single location (rather than having separate locations, as earlier had been the case); experience indicated that combination sales and service locations were more cost-efficient and facilitated faster expansion of the company's retail footprint. At the end of 2018, Tesla had over 350 sales and service locations around the world. Tesla's goal was to have sufficient service locations to ensure that after-sale services were available to owners when and where needed.

However, in the United States, there was a lurking threat to Tesla's strategy to bypass distributing through franchised Tesla dealers and sell directly to consumers. Going back many years, franchised automobile dealers in the United States had feared that automotive manufacturers might one day decide to integrate forward into selling and servicing the vehicles they produced. To foreclose any attempts by manufacturers to compete directly against their franchised dealers, automobile dealers in every state in the United States had formed statewide franchised dealer associations to lobby for legislation blocking motor vehicle manufacturers from becoming retailers of new and used cars and providing maintenance and repair services to vehicle owners. Legislation either forbidding or severely restricting the ability of automakers to sell vehicles directly to the public had been passed in 48 states; these laws had been in effect for many years, and franchised dealer associations were diligent in pushing for strict enforcement of these laws.

As sales of the Model S rose briskly from 2013 to 2015 and Tesla continued opening more sales galleries and service centers, both franchised dealers and statewide dealer associations became increasingly anxious about "the Tesla problem" and what actions to take to block Tesla's sell-direct strategy. Dealers and dealer trade associations in a number of states were openly vocal about their concerns and actively began lobbying state legislatures to consider either enforcement actions against Tesla or amendments to existing legislation that would bring a halt to Tesla's efforts to sell vehicles at company-owned showrooms. A host of skirmishes ensued in 12 states. In several cases, settlements were reached that allowed Tesla to open a select few sales locations, but the numbers were capped. In states where manufacturer-direct sales to consumers were expressly prohibited, Tesla was allowed to have sales galleries, service centers, and Supercharger locations—but was prevented from using its sales galleries to take orders, conduct test drives, deliver cars, or discuss pricing with potential buyers. Buyers in these states could place an order via the Internet, specify when they would like the car to arrive, and then either have it delivered to a nearby Tesla service center for pickup or have it delivered directly to their home or business location.

Tesla Announces Sales Gallery Closures and Shift to Online Sales In February 2019 Tesla unexpectedly announced it was closing most of its 120 sales galleries in malls and shopping centers and would begin to sell its cars only online. The shift was made partly to reduce employee headcount and operating expenses and partly to relax lobbying efforts in states that did not permit manufacturers to own and operate their own dealerships. As part of the shift, new owners were granted up to a week to return their newly purchased Tesla vehicle if they were not satisfied. In the same announcement, Tesla said it would be shifting resources to improve its repair service systems, with the goal of providing same-day service to Tesla owners. However, auto dealers in several states, along with the National Automobile Dealers Association, remained dissatisfied with Tesla's online sales approach, noting that franchise laws in some states required dealers to have a physical presence in their state to sell online and that one of the main purposes of local franchising and licensing laws

was to promote investment in an extensive network of independent, neighborhood new-car dealers.

Tesla Service Centers

Tesla Roadster owners could upload data from their vehicle and send it to a service center on a memory card; all other Tesla owners had an on-board system that could communicate directly with a service center, allowing service technicians to diagnose and remedy many problems before ever looking at the vehicle. When maintenance or service was required, a customer could schedule service by contacting a Tesla service center. Some service locations offered valet service, where the owner's car was picked up, replaced with a well-equipped loaner car, and then returned when the service was completed—there was no additional charge for valet service. In some locations, owners could opt to have service performed at their home, office, or other remote location by a Tesla Mobile Service technician who had the capability to perform a variety of services that did not require a vehicle lift. Mobile service technicians could perform most warranty repairs, but the cost of their visit was not covered under the New Vehicle Limited Warranty. Mobile service pricing was based on a per visit, per vehicle basis; there was a $100 minimum charge per visit. Tesla's mobile service fleet consisted of 411 vehicles at year-end 2018, with coverage of all of North America. As of early 2018, the company's mobile service fleet in North America was completing 30 percent of all service jobs at a cost below the average fees charged at its service centers.

Prepaid Maintenance Program

Tesla recommended that Model S, Model X, and Model 3 owners have an inspection every 12 months or 12,500 miles, whichever came first. Owners could purchase plans covering prepaid maintenance for three years or four years; these involved simply prepaying for service inspections at a discounted rate. All Model S, Model X, and Model 3 vehicles were protected by a 4-year or 50,000 miles (whichever came first) New Vehicle Limited Warranty and an 8-year or unlimited miles Battery and Drive Unit Limited Warranty. These warranties covered the repair or replacement necessary to correct defects in materials or workmanship of any parts manufactured or supplied by Tesla. Owners could also purchase an Extended Service Agreement for two years (or 25,000 miles) or four years (or 50,000 miles), whichever came first.

Tesla's Supercharger Network: Providing Recharging Services to Owners on Long-Distance Trips

A major component of Tesla's strategy to build rapidly growing long-term demand for its vehicles was to make battery recharging while driving long distances convenient and worry-free for all Tesla vehicle owners. Tesla's solution to providing owners with ample and convenient recharging opportunities was to establish an extensive geographic network of recharging stations. Tesla's Supercharger stations were strategically placed along major highways connecting city centers, usually at locations with such nearby amenities as roadside diners, cafes, and shopping centers that enabled owners to have a brief rest stop or get a quick meal during the recharging process—about 90 percent of Model S and Model X buyers opted to have their vehicle equipped with supercharging capability when they ordered their vehicle. All Model S and Model X owners were entitled to *free* supercharging service at any of Tesla's Supercharging stations; Model 3 owners had to pay a recharging fee. In March 2018, Tesla announced price increases for its Supercharging stations to about $0.25 per kwh. Tesla owners charged their vehicles at home more than 90 percent of the time and used Supercharger stations mainly for trips or when they needed extra range. A 50 percent recharge took 20 minutes, an 80 percent recharge took 40 minutes, and a 100 percent recharge took 75 minutes. As of year-end 2018, Tesla had a total of 1,421 Supercharger stations globally; most Tesla stations had between 6 and 30 charging spaces, but newer stations in high-traffic corridors had as many as 50 spaces, a customer lounge, and a café. About 300 new Supercharger locations were planned for 2019.

Tesla executives never expected that Supercharger stations would become a profit center for the company; rather, they believed that the benefits of rapidly growing the size of the company's Supercharger network came from (1) relieving the "range anxiety" electric vehicle owners suffered when driving on a long-distance trip and (2) reducing the inconvenience to travelers of having to deviate from the shortest direct route and detour to the closest Supercharger station for needed recharging.

Technology and Product Development Strategy

Headed into the second quarter of 2019, Tesla had spent over $5.9 billion on R&D activities to design, develop, test, and refine the components and systems needed to produce top quality electric vehicles and, further, to design and develop prototypes of the Tesla Roadster, Model S, Model X, Model 3, Model Y, and Tesla Semi vehicles. Tesla executives believed its R&D activities had produced core competencies in powertrain and vehicle engineering and innovative manufacturing techniques. The company's core intellectual property was contained in its electric powertrain technology—the battery pack, power electronics, induction motor, gearbox, and control software that enabled these key components to operate as a system. Tesla personnel had designed each of these major elements for the Tesla Roadster and Model S; much of this technology had been used in the powertrain systems that Tesla previously had built for other manufacturers (mainly Toyota and Mercedes) and had been further improved and refined in the powertrain systems being used in the Model X, Model 3, and the prototypes for the Tesla Semi.

The powertrain used in Tesla vehicles in 2019 was a compact, modular system with far fewer moving parts than the powertrains of traditional gasoline-powered vehicles, a feature that enabled Tesla to implement powertrain enhancements and improvements as fast as they could be identified, designed, and tested. Tesla had incorporated its latest powertrain technology into its three current models and was planning to use much of this technology in producing its forthcoming electric vehicles.

Although Tesla had more than 500 patents and pending patent applications domestically and internationally in a broad range of areas, in 2014, Tesla announced a patent policy whereby it irrevocably pledged the company would not initiate a lawsuit against any party for infringing Tesla's patents through activity relating to electric vehicles or related equipment so long as the party was acting in good faith. Elon Musk said the company made this pledge in order to encourage the advancement of a common, rapidly evolving platform for electric vehicles, thereby benefiting itself, other companies making electric vehicles, and the world. Investor reaction to this announcement was largely negative on grounds that it would negate any technology-based competitive advantage over rival manufacturers of electric vehicles.

Battery Pack

In prior years, Tesla had tested hundreds of battery cells of different chemistries and performance features. It had an internal battery cell testing lab and had assembled an extensive performance database of the many available lithium-ion cell vendors and chemistry types. Based on this evaluation, it had elected to use "18650 form factor" lithium-ion battery cells, chiefly because a battery pack containing 18650 cells offered two to three times the driving range of the lithium-ion cells used by other makers of electric vehicles. Management believed that the company's accumulated experience and expertise had produced a core competence in designing battery packs that were safe, reliable, and had long lives. At the same time, it had pioneered the development of advanced manufacturing techniques that enabled mass production of high-quality battery packs at low cost. Ongoing improvement of its production methods had allowed the Tesla to reduce the costs and improve the performance of its batteries over time. Management believed Tesla's current battery pack design gave it the ability to change battery cell chemistries and form factor if needed and, also, to capitalize on the advancements in battery cell technology being made globally. Going forward, Tesla believed it had the capabilities to quickly incorporate the latest advancements in battery technology and continue to optimize battery pack system performance and cost for its future vehicles.

Power Electronics

The power electronics in Tesla's powertrain system had two primary functions—the control of torque generation in the motor while driving and the control of energy delivery back into the battery pack while charging. The first function was accomplished through the drive inverter, which converted direct current from the battery pack into alternating current to drive the induction motors, provide acceleration, and enhance the overall driving performance of the vehicle. The second function was to capture kinetic energy from the wheels being in motion but being slowed down by applying the brakes and reverse the flow of energy to help recharge the battery pack—a technology called "regenerative braking." (When brakes are applied in gasoline-powered vehicles, the brake pads clamp down on the wheels to slow the vehicle, letting the kinetic energy escape as heat; but in electric vehicles, and most hybrid vehicles, the regenerative braking systems slow the vehicle by reversing the flow of electricity to the electric motors powering the wheels, while also capturing the heat from the kinetic energy to generate electrical energy for partially recharging the battery pack.) When the electric vehicle was parked, battery recharging was accomplished by the vehicle's charger, which converted alternating current (usually from a wall outlet or other electricity source) into direct current which could be accepted by the battery.

Owners could use any available source of power to charge a Tesla's battery pack. A standard 12-amp/110-volt wall outlet could recharge a mostly discharged battery pack to full capacity in about 21 hours. Tesla recommended that owners install *at least* a 24-amp/240-volt outlet in their garage or carport (the same voltage used by many electric ovens and clothes dryers), which permitted charging at the rate of 34 miles of range per hour of charging time. But owners who installed a more powerful 60-amp/240-volt wall connector outlet could charge a 75-kWh battery that had been driven 300 miles in 8 hours and 42 minutes; installation of a 90-amp/240-volt circuit breaker enabled charging a 100-kWh battery in 5 hours and 47 minutes. On a road trip, a 120-kW Supercharger could recharge a battery driven 300 miles in 75 minutes.

Control Software

The battery pack and the performance and safety systems of Tesla vehicles required the use of numerous microprocessors and sophisticated software. For example, computer-driven software monitored the charge state of each of the cells of the battery pack and managed all of the safety systems. The flow of electricity between the battery pack and the motor had to be tightly controlled in order to deliver the best possible performance and driving experience. There were software algorithms that enabled the vehicle to mimic the "creep" feeling that drivers expected from an internal combustion engine vehicle without having to apply pressure on the accelerator. Other algorithms were used to control traction, vehicle stability, acceleration, and regenerative braking. Drivers used the vehicle's information systems to optimize performance and charging modes and times. In addition to the vehicle control software, Tesla had developed software for the infotainment systems of the Model S, Model X, and Model 3. Almost all of the software programs had been developed and written by Tesla personnel. Starting in 2014, Tesla began devoting progressively larger fractions of its programming resources and expertise to developing and enhancing its software for vehicle autopilot functionality, including such features as auto-steering, traffic-aware cruise control, automated lane changing, automated parking, driver warning systems, automated braking, object detection, and self-driving. In October 2016, Tesla began equipping all models with hardware needed for full self-driving capability, including cameras that provided 360-degree visibility, updated ultrasonic sensors for object detection, a forward-facing radar with enhanced processing, and a powerful onboard computer. Wireless software updates periodically sent to the microprocessors on board each Tesla owner's vehicle, together with field data feedback loops from the onboard camera, radar, ultrasonic sensors, and GPS, enabled the autopilot system in Tesla vehicles to continually learn and improve its performance. In early 2019, Elon Musk said he expected Tesla's autopilot software to be able to handle all modes of driving by the end of 2019 and that Tesla's autopilot system would be safer than human drivers within two years.

Vehicle Design and Engineering

Tesla had devoted considerable effort to creating significant in-house capabilities related to designing and engineering portions of its vehicles, and it had become knowledgeable about the design and engineering of those parts, components, and systems that it purchased from suppliers. Tesla personnel had designed and engineered the body, chassis, and interior of its current models. As a matter of necessity, Tesla was forced to redesign the heating, cooling, and ventilation system for its electric vehicles to operate without the energy generated from an internal combustion engine and to integrate with its own battery-powered thermal management system. In addition, the low-voltage electric system that powered the radio, power windows, and heated seats had to be designed specifically for use in an electric vehicle. Tesla had developed expertise in integrating these components with the high-voltage power source in its vehicles and in designing components that significantly reduced their load on the vehicle's battery pack, so as to maximize the available driving range. All Tesla vehicles incorporated the latest advances in mobile computing, sensing, displays, and connectivity.

Tesla personnel had accumulated considerable expertise in lightweight materials, since an electric vehicle's driving range was heavily impacted by the vehicle's weight and mass. The Tesla Roadster had been built with an in-house designed carbon fiber body to provide a good balance of strength and mass. The Model S and Model X had a lightweight aluminum body and a chassis that incorporated a variety of materials and production methods to help optimize vehicle weight, strength, safety, and performance. Weight reduction was an important factor in the design of the Model 3. In addition, top management believed that the company's design and engineering team had core competencies in computer-aided design and crash test simulations; this expertise had reduced the development time for the Model 3 and the Tesla Semi prototypes.

Manufacturing Strategy

Tesla had contracted with Lotus Cars, Ltd., to produce Tesla Roadster "gliders" (a complete vehicle minus the electric powertrain) at a Lotus factory in Hethel, England. The Tesla gliders were then shipped to a Tesla facility in Menlo Park, California, where the battery pack, induction motors, and other powertrain components were installed as part of the final assembly process. The production of Roadster gliders ceased in January 2012.

In May 2010, Tesla purchased the major portion of a recently closed automobile plant in Fremont, California, for $42 million; months later, Tesla purchased some of the plant's equipment for $17 million. The facility—formerly a General Motors manufacturing plant (1960–1982), then operated as a joint venture between General Motors and Toyota (1984–2010)—was closed in 2010. Tesla executives viewed the facility as one of the largest, most advanced, and cleanest automotive production plants in the world. The 5.3 million square feet of manufacturing and office space was deemed sufficient for Tesla to produce about 500,000 vehicles annually (approximately 1 percent of the total worldwide car production), thus giving Tesla room to grow its output of electric vehicles to 500,000 or more vehicles annually. The Fremont plant's location in the northern section of Silicon Valley facilitated hiring talented engineers already residing nearby and because the short distance between Fremont and Tesla's Palo Alto headquarters ensured "a tight feedback loop between vehicle engineering, manufacturing, and other divisions within the company."[27] Tesla officially took possession of the 370-acre site in October 2010, renamed it the Tesla Factory, and immediately launched efforts to get a portion of the massive facility ready to begin manufacturing components and assembling the Model S in 2012. In late 2015, Tesla completed construction of a new high-volume paint shop and a new body shop line capable of turning out 3,500 Model S and Model X bodies per week (enough for 175,000 vehicles annually). In 2016 and 2017, Tesla made significant additional investments at the Tesla Factory, including a new body shop with space and equipment for Model 3 final assembly. Tesla expected the Fremont facility, together with a neighboring 500,000-square-foot building that Tesla had leased, would be expanded to 10 million square feet in the coming years. However, in 2018 rumors began surfacing that Tesla was actively looking for additional production sites—one in the United States, one in China, and one in Europe.

In December 2012, Tesla opened a new 60,000-square-foot facility in Tilburg, Netherlands, about 50 miles from the port of Rotterdam, to serve as the final assembly and distribution point for all Tesla vehicles sold in Europe and Scandinavia. The facility, called the Tilburg Assembly Plant, received nearly complete vehicles shipped from the Tesla Factory, performed certain final assembly activities, conducted final vehicle testing, and handled the delivery to customers across Europe. It also functioned as Tesla's European service and parts headquarters. Tilburg's central location and its excellent rail and highway network to all major markets on the European continent allowed Tesla to distribute to anywhere across the continent in about 12 hours. The Tilburg operation had been expanded to over 200,000 square feet in order to accommodate a parts distribution warehouse for service centers throughout Europe, a center for remanufacturing work, and a customer service center. A nearby facility in Amsterdam provided corporate oversight for European sales, service, and administrative functions.

Tesla's manufacturing strategy was to source a number of parts and components from outside suppliers but to design, develop, and manufacture in-house those key components where it had considerable intellectual property and core competencies (namely lithium-ion battery packs, electric motors, gearboxes, and other powertrain components) and to perform all assembly-related activities itself. In 2018, the Tesla Factory contained several production-related activities, including stamping, machining, casting, plastics molding, drive unit production, robotics-assisted body assembly, paint operations, final vehicle assembly, and end-of-line quality testing. In addition, Tesla manufactured lithium-ion battery packs, electric motors, gearboxes, and components for Model S and Model X at the Tesla Factory.

While some major vehicle component systems were purchased from suppliers, there was a high level of vertical integration in the manufacturing processes at the Tesla Factory in 2018 and 2019. From 2016 to 2019, efforts to expand production capacity at the Tesla Factory were ongoing to accommodate growing sales of the Model S and Model X and to enable production of the Model 3 to reach 10,000 units per week.

In 2014, Tesla began producing and machining various aluminum components at a 431,000-square-foot facility in Lathrop, California; an aluminum castings operation was added in 2016. Aluminum parts and components were used extensively to help reduce the weight of Tesla vehicles.

Initially, production costs for the Model S were adversely impacted by an assortment of startup costs at the Tesla Factory, manufacturing inefficiencies associated with inexperience and low-volume production, higher prices for component parts during the first several months of production runs, and higher logistics costs associated with the immaturity of Tesla's supply chain. However, as Tesla engineers redesigned various elements of the Model S for greater ease of manufacturing, supply chain improvements were instituted, and manufacturing efficiency rose, the costs of some parts decreased, and overall production costs for the Model S trended downward.

Tesla had encountered a number of unexpected quality problems in the first two to three months of manufacturing the Model X. Getting the complicated hinges on the falcon-wing doors to function properly proved to be particularly troublesome. Customers who received the first wave of Model X deliveries also reported problems with the front doors and windows and with the 17-inch dashboard touchscreen freezing (a major problem because so many functions were controlled from this screen). Most of these problems were largely resolved by mid-2016, although Model X owners rated the reliability of their vehicles significantly lower than Model S owners—the chief culprit was the falcon-wing doors, which reportedly had generated significant warranty claims and warranty costs. Weekly production volumes of the Model X rose steadily in the second half of 2016.

Musk believed Tesla had learned valuable manufacturing lessons in ramping up the production volume of the Model 3 at the Fremont plant. These lessons were being incorporated into producing the Model S, Model X, and Model 3 during the first quarter of 2019 at Fremont and to an even greater extent in designing and equipping the new Shanghai plant that began construction in early 2019. The first-generation production line for the Model 3 in Shanghai was Tesla's first step in building a manufacturing platform that could be replicated quickly and cost efficiently across all vehicle types and in different geographic locations. Designs for a second production line in Shanghai were already under way, and expectations were that the second production line would be at least 50 percent cheaper per unit of capacity than the current Model 3-related assembly lines in Fremont.[28] Major gains in production efficiency and approximately 50 percent lower unit costs for the Model 3 were expected when production of the Model 3 ramped up in the new production facility in Shanghai where Tesla was installing a much-simplified production process and increasing use of robot-assisted assembly.

Tesla's "Gigafactory 1"

In February 2014, Tesla announced that it and various partners, principally Panasonic—Tesla's supplier of lithium-ion batteries since 2010—would invest $4 to $5 billion through 2020 in a "gigafactory" capable of producing enough lithium-ion batteries to make battery packs for 500,000 vehicles (plus Tesla's recently developed energy storage products for both businesses and homeowners). The planned output of the battery factory in 2020 exceeded the total global production of lithium batteries in 2013. Tesla's direct investment in the project was scheduled to be $2 billion. Tesla expected the new plant (named the Tesla Gigafactory, later changed to Gigafactory 1) to reduce the company's battery pack cost by more than 30 percent—to around $200 per kWh by some estimates (from the 2017 level of about $300 per kWh).

Tesla opted to locate Gigafactory 1 on a site in an industrial park east of Reno, Nevada, partly because the state of Nevada offered Tesla a lucrative incentive package said to be worth $1.25 billion over 20 years and partly because the only commercially active lithium mining operation in the United States was in a nearby Nevada county (this county was reputed to have the fifth-largest deposits of lithium in the world). Construction began immediately. The facility was being built in phases. Tesla's plan in 2019 was to continue expanding Gigafactory 1 over the next few years so that its battery-making capacity would significantly exceed the volume needed for 500,000 vehicles per year when construction first started. Tesla had already added space at Gigafactory 1 to enable the manufacture of Tesla Energy's two primary energy storage products (Powerwall and Powerpack) and the manufacture of Model 3 drive units. As many as 10,000 workers were expected to be employed at Gigafactory 1 in 2020.

Because Tesla had in 2015 to 2017 discovered ways to build an improved lithium-ion battery that would be larger and safer, and require fewer individual batteries per battery pack, Tesla executives in 2018 expected the unit cost of producing battery packs at Gigafactory 1 to decline to around $200 per kWh sometime in the second half of 2018. In March 2018 Volkswagen indicated it had just signed agreements with battery makers to supply it with batteries for its forthcoming electric vehicles at a cost of about $115 kWh, significantly below Tesla's $200 cost target. Nonetheless, in 2019 Tesla reiterated its confidence that Gigafactory 1 would be the world's highest-volume and lowest-cost source of lithium-ion batteries as production of the Model 3 expanded toward 10,000 units per week.

Less than a month after announcing its intent to build the Gigafactory, Tesla sold $920 million of convertible senior notes due 2019 carrying an interest rate of 0.25 percent and $1.38 billion in convertible senior notes due 2021 carrying an interest rate of 1.25 percent. The senior notes due 2019 were convertible into cash, shares of Tesla's common stock, or a combination thereof, at Tesla's election. The convertible senior notes due 2021 were convertible into cash and, if applicable, shares of Tesla's common stock (subject to Tesla's right to deliver cash in lieu of shares of common stock). To protect existing shareholders against ownership dilution that might result from the senior notes being converted into additional shares of Tesla stock, Tesla immediately entered into convertible note hedge transactions and warrant transactions at an approximate cost of $186 million that management expected would reduce potential dilution of existing shareholder interests and/or offset cash payments that Tesla was required to make in excess of the principal amounts of the 2019 notes and 2021 notes. The senior notes due in 2019 were paid in cash in early 2019.

Supply Chain Strategy

Tesla's Model S, Model X, and Model 3 used thousands of purchased parts and components sourced globally from hundreds of suppliers. Components were obtained from multiple sources in some cases, but in most cases the components were purchased from a single source. Tesla had been trying to secure alternate sources of supply for many single-sourced components but, so far, success had been limited, which had prompted the company to begin producing more parts and components internally.

While Tesla had developed close relationships with the suppliers of lithium-ion battery cells and certain other key system parts, it typically did not have long-term agreements with them with the exception of the relationship it had with Panasonic, which had become Tesla's sole lithium-cell battery supply partner from the outset.

Marketing Strategy

From 2014 through 2018, Tesla's principal marketing goals and functions were to:

- Generate demand for the company's vehicles and drive sales leads to personnel in the Tesla's showrooms and sales galleries.

- Build long-term brand awareness and manage the company's image and reputation.

- Manage the existing customer base to create brand loyalty and generate customer referrals.

- Obtain feedback from the owners of Tesla vehicles and make sure their experiences and suggestions for improvement were communicated to Tesla personnel engaged in designing, developing, and/or improving the company's current and future vehicles.

As the first company to commercially produce a federally compliant, fully electric vehicle that achieved market-leading range on a single charge, Tesla had been able to generate significant media coverage of the company and its vehicles. Management expected this would continue to be the case for some time to come. So far, the extensive media coverage, largely favorable reviews in motor vehicle publications and *Consumer Reports,* praise from owners of Tesla vehicles and admiring car enthusiasts (which enlarged Tesla's sales force at zero cost), and the decisions of many green-minded affluent individuals to help lead the movement away from gasoline-powered vehicles had all combined to drive good traffic flows at Tesla's sales galleries and create a flow of orders and preproduction reservations. As a consequence, during the period 2012 to 2018, Tesla had achieved a growing volume of sales without traditional advertising and at relatively low marketing costs. Nonetheless, Tesla did make use of pay-per-click advertisements on websites and mobile applications relevant to its target clientele. It also displayed and demonstrated its vehicles at such widely attended public events as the Detroit, Los Angeles, and Frankfurt auto shows.

Marketing at Tesla Energy   In early 2018, Tesla negotiated marketing agreements with both Home Depot and Lowe's to stock and help promote its innovative Solar Roof tiles for residential and commercial roof applications. But these agreements were discontinued when sales proved negligible and solar cell marketing was transitioned to Tesla's sales galleries and showrooms.

In the United States, Tesla Energy sold residential energy storage products through a network of channel partners. Outside of the United States, it used its own international sales organization and a network of channel partners to market and sell residential energy storage products, and it had recently launched pilot programs for the sale of residential solar panels in certain countries. Powerwall 2 products were sold directly to utilities, who then deployed the product in customer homes. Powerpack 2 systems were sold to commercial and utility customers through Tesla Energy's international sales organization comprised of experienced energy industry professionals; in some locations sales were made through channel partners. In the United States and Mexico, Tesla Energy marketed installed solar energy systems (with or without energy storage) to commercial customers, with sales being transacted with cash, leases, and purchased power agreements.

Tesla's Leasing Activities

Tesla, in partnership with various financial institutions, began leasing vehicles to customers in 2014; the number and percentage of customers opting to lease Model S vehicles increased substantially in 2015. By year-end 2015, Tesla was not only offering loans and leases in North America, Europe, and Asia through its various partner financial institutions, but also offering loans and leases directly through its own captive finance subsidiaries in certain areas of the United States, Germany, Canada, and Great Britain.

Some of Tesla's financing programs outside of North America in 2015–2017 provided customers with a resale value guarantee under which those customers had the option of selling their vehicle back to Tesla at a preset future date, generally at the end of the term of the applicable loan or financing program, for a predetermined resale value. In certain markets, Tesla also offered vehicle buyback guarantees to financial institutions that could obligate Tesla to repurchase the vehicles for a predetermined price. These programs, when first introduced in 2015 and 2016, had been widely publicized and attracted numerous buyers, but Tesla determined in late 2016 and 2017 to back away from these offers in most countries because they were proving unprofitable, had unattractive accounting requirements, and exposed Tesla to the risk that the vehicles' resale value could be lower than its estimates and also to the risk that the volume of vehicles sold back to Tesla at the guaranteed resale price might be higher than the company's estimates—such risks had to be accounted for by establishing a contingent liability (in the current liabilities section of the balance sheet) deemed sufficient to cover these risks.

Sales of Regulatory Credits to Other Automotive Manufacturers

Because Tesla's electric vehicles had no tailpipe emissions of greenhouse gases or other pollutants, Tesla earned zero emission vehicle (ZEV) and greenhouse gas (GHG) credits on each vehicle sold in the United States. Moreover, it also earned corporate average fuel economy (CAFE) credits on its sales of vehicles because of their high equivalent miles per gallon ratings. All three of these types of regulatory credits had significant market value because the manufacturers of traditional gasoline-powered vehicles were subject to assorted emission and mileage requirements set by the U.S. Environmental Protection Agency (EPA) and by certain state agencies charged with protecting the environment within their borders; automotive manufacturers whose vehicle sales did not meet prevailing emission and mileage requirements were allowed to achieve compliance by purchasing credits earned by other automotive manufacturers. Tesla had entered into contracts for the sale of ZEV and GHG credits with several automotive manufacturers, and it also routinely sold its CAFE credits. Tesla's sales of ZEV, GHG, and CAFE credits produced revenues of $418.6 million in 2018, $360.3 million in 2017, $302.3 million in 2016, $168.7 million in 2015, $216.3 million in 2014, and $194.4 million in 2013. In Exhibit 2, these amounts were included on Tesla's income statement in the revenue category labeled "Automotive sales"; without these revenues, as frequently noted by Wall Street analysts, Tesla's losses in 2013 through 2018 would have been significantly higher. Tesla's sales of ZEV credits amounted to $15.4 million in Q1 2019 (versus $50.3 million in Q1 2018).

Tesla Energy in 2018

In 2015, Tesla formed Tesla Energy, a new subsidiary that would begin producing and selling two energy storage products in 2016—Powerwall for homeowners and Powerpack for industrial, commercial, and utility customers. Powerwall was a lithium-ion battery charged either by electricity generated from a home's solar panels or from power company sources when electric rates were low. Tesla saw Powerwall as principally a product that energy-conscious homeowners with a rooftop solar system could use to lower their monthly electric bills by programming Powerwall to power their homes during certain hours when local power company rates were high and then recharging the battery during the late-night hours when rates were low. However, Powerwall home batteries could also be used as a backup power source in case of unexpected power outages. Powerpack models were 100 kW lithium-ion batteries that industrial, commercial, and utility enterprises could use for energy storage or backup power.

In the first week after announcing its new Powerwall and Powerpack products, Tesla received 38,000 reservations for Powerwall (residential buyers

could place a reservation with no money down) and requests from 2,500 companies indicating interest in installing or distributing Powerpack batteries. Tesla moved swiftly to prepare its supply chain and production teams to begin volume builds on both products. Production began at the Tesla Factory in Fremont and then shifted to the Gigafactory in the last part of 2015. In early 2016, both Powerwall and Powerpack production was operating smoothly and expanding at the Gigafactory. Production and deliveries of Powerwall 2 and Powerpack 2 began in late 2016. Both products had the capability to receive over-the-air firmware and software updates that enabled additional features. In 2018, these two energy storage products were being used for backup power, independence from utility grids, peak demand reduction, demand response, reducing intermittency of renewable generation, and wholesale electric market services.

When Solar Energy was merged into Tesla, the company arranged to lease a facility, called Gigafactory 2, in Buffalo, New York, to produce (1) solar energy systems sold to residential and commercial customers and (2) its freshly developed Solar Roof, which used aesthetically pleasing and durable glass roofing tiles designed to complement the architecture of homes and commercial buildings to turn sunlight into electricity, which was being marketed in 2018 with distribution partners Home Depot and Lowe's.

Tesla Energy's solar energy systems included solar panels that converted sunlight into electrical current, inverters that converted the electrical output from the panels to a usable current compatible with the electric grid, racking that attached the solar panels to the roof or ground, electrical hardware that connected the solar energy system to the electric grid, and a monitoring device. The majority of the components were purchased from vendors; the company maintained multiple sources for each major component to ensure competitive pricing and adequate supplies.

Tesla Energy had an in-house engineering team that designed its energy storage products and created customized energy storage solutions and solar energy systems for customers. In the United States, it used its national sales organization, channel partner network, and customer referral program to market and sell its residential solar and energy storage systems. Outside the United States, Tesla Energy used its international sales organization and a network of channel partners to market and sell Powerwall 2, and it had recently launched pilot programs for the sale of residential solar products in certain countries. It also sold Powerwall 2 directly to utilities, who then installed the product in customer homes.

In December 2017, Tesla completed installation of a 100-megawatt lithium-ion battery hooked into the electricity grid in South Australia to relieve power shortages created by a tornado in 2016. Elon Musk had promised that once the contract was signed, Tesla would complete the project in 100 days or it would be furnished free of charge—Tesla completed the installation in 60 days. According to Musk, the battery was three times more powerful than the world's next biggest battery.

Tesla's revenues from energy generation and storage products were $1.1 billion in 2017 and $1.6 billion in 2018 (refer to Exhibit 2), resulting in gross profits of $241.7 million in 2017 and $190.3 million in 2018. Elon Musk was very optimistic about the growth opportunities for Tesla Energy, but Tesla's financial reporting did not reveal whether Tesla Energy's operations were generating positive or negative operating profit margins.

The Electric Vehicle Segment of the Global Automotive Industry

Global sales of passenger cars and SUVs in 2017 were roughly 81 million. Sales of other types of vehicles (light or pickup trucks, heavy or cargo-carrying trucks, recreational vehicles, buses, and minibuses) totaled just over 26 million. In 2017, global sales of plug-in electric vehicles totaled 1.22 million units—plug-in vehicles included both battery-only vehicles and so-called plug-in hybrid electric vehicles equipped with a gasoline or diesel engine for use when the vehicle's battery pack (rechargeable only from an external plug-in source) was depleted,

usually after a distance of 20 to 50 miles. Hybrid vehicles were jointly powered by an internal combustion engine and an electric motor that ran on batteries charged by regenerative braking and the internal combustion engine; the batteries in a hybrid vehicle could not be restored to a full charge by connecting a plug to an external power source. Exhibit 3 shows the best-selling plug-in electric vehicles in the United States from 2013 through 2018.

There was no question in 2018 and beyond that Tesla was faced with intensifying competition in the global marketplace for electric-powered vehicles. Virtually every motor vehicle manufacturer in the world was introducing new battery-powered electric vehicles, most with driving ranges of 200 miles or more. In 2018 and 2019, models with 200+ mile driving ranges had been introduced by Audi, Jaguar, Mercedes, Kia, Volvo, General Motors, and Hyundai. Fresh models from Porsche, Aston Martin, Nissan, Audi, Volkswagen, BMW, General Motors, and Ford were scheduled for 2020. Sales of a second-generation Nissan Leaf with a driving range of up to 150 miles began in January 2018. At year-end 2018, there were 43 models of electric-powered vehicles being sold in the United States, with annual sales totaling just over 361,000 units. Through May 2019, there were 45 models being sold in the United States, with sales in the first five months totaling 109,500 units, more than 10,000 units higher than sales for the first five months of 2018; 16 of these models were all-electric (battery-operated) vehicles.

In 2018 Volkswagen announced plans to equip 16 factories to produce electric vehicles by the end of 2022, compared with 3 currently, and to build as many as 3 million electric cars per year by 2025. In December 2017, Toyota said by around 2025, every Toyota and Lexus model sold around the world would be available either as a dedicated electrified model or have an electrified option. Additionally, Toyota expected to have annual sales of more than 5.5 million electrified vehicles by 2030 (including more than one million zero-emission vehicles totally powered by either batteries or fuel cells) and to halt all production of gasoline-powered vehicles by 2040. In 2018, the government of Germany launched a

Sales of Best-Selling Plug-in Electric Vehicles in the United States, 2013–2018

Best-Selling Models	2013	2014	2015	2016	2017	2018
Tesla Model 3*	—	—	—	—	1,764	139,782
Toyota Prius PHV/Prime	12,088	13,264	4,191	2,474	20,963	27,595
Tesla Model X*	—	—	214	18,223	21,315	26,100
Tesla Model S*	17,650	17,300	25,202	28,896	27,060	25,745
Honda Clarity PHEV	—	—	—	—	—	18,602
Chevrolet Volt	23,094	18,805	15,393	24,739	20,349	18,306
Chevrolet Bolt EV*	—	—	—	579	23,297	18,019
Nissan Leaf*	22,610	30,200	17,269	14,006	11,230	14,715
BMW 530e	—	—	—	—	3,772	8,664
Ford Fusion Energi	6,089	11,550	9,750	15,938	9,632	8,074
Chrysler Pacifica Hybrid	—	—	—	—	4,597	7,062
BMW i3	—	6,092	11,024	7,625	6,276	6,117
Ford C-Max Energi	7,154	8,433	7,591	7,957	8,140	582
All Others	4,260	12,243	19,532	32,847	41,701	41,994
United States Total	95,642	123,049	116,099	158,614	199,826	361,307
Worldwide	Not available	320,713	550,297	777,497	1,227,117	2,018,247

*Battery-operated.

Source: Inside EVs, "Monthly Plug-in Sales Scorecard," https://insideevs.com, accessed March 5, 2018 and June 4, 2019.

campaign to put one million electric cars on its roads by 2020 and to have 40 percent electric cars on its roads by 2035.

Hydrogen Fuel Cells: An Alternative to Electric Batteries

Many of the world's major automotive manufacturers, while actively working on next-generation battery-powered electric vehicles, were nonetheless hedging their bets by also pursuing the development of hydrogen fuel cells as an alternative means of powering future vehicles. Toyota was considered the leader in developing hydrogen fuel cells and was sharing some of its fuel-cell technology patents for free with other automotive companies in an effort to spur an answer to whether there was merit in installing fuel cells

and building out a hydrogen charging network. Audi, Honda, Toyota, Mercedes-Benz, and Hyundai had recently introduced first-generation models powered by hydrogen fuel cells.[29]

Hydrogen fuel cells could be refueled with hydrogen in three to five minutes. California and several states in the northeastern United States already had a number of hydrogen refueling stations. Existing gasoline stations could add hydrogen refueling capability at a cost of about $1.5 million. A full tank of hydrogen provided vehicles with a driving range of about 310 miles. While battery-powered vehicles were currently cheaper than fuel-cell-powered vehicles, experts expected that cheaper materials, more efficient fuel cells, and scale economies would in upcoming years enable producers of fuel-cell vehicles to match the prices of battery-powered electric vehicles.

ENDNOTES

[1] John Reed, "Elon Musk's Groundbreaking Electric Car," *FT Magazine,* July 24, 2009, www.ft.com (accessed September 26, 2013).

[2] Tesla press release, and Michael Arrington, "Tesla Worth More Than Half a Billion After Daimler Investment," May 19, 2009, www.techcrunch.com (accessed September 30, 2013).

[3] Josh Friedman, "Entrepreneur Tries His Midas Touch in Space*," Los Angeles Times,* April 23, 2003, www.latimes.com (accessed on September 16, 2013).

[4] David Kestenbaum, "Making a Mark with Rockets and Roadsters," National Public Radio, August 9, 2007, www.npr.org (accessed on September 17, 2013).

[5] David Kestenbaum, "Making a Mark with Rockets and Roadsters," National Public Radio, August 9, 2007, www.npr.org (accessed on September 17, 2013).

[6] Josh Friedman, "Entrepreneur Tries His Midas Touch in Space," *Los Angeles Times,* April 22, 2003, https://www.latimes.com/archives/la-xpm-2003-apr-22-fi-spacex22-story.html.

[7] Video interview with Alan Murray, "Elon Musk: I'll Put a Man on Mars in 10 Years," *Market Watch* (New York: *The Wall Street Journal*), December 1, 2011 (accessed on September 16, 2013).

[8] Mike Seemuth, "From the Corner Office—Elon Musk," *Success,* April 10, 2011, www.success.com (accessed September 25, 2013).

[9] Mike Seemuth, "From the Corner Office --Elon Musk," Success, April 10, 2011, www.success.com (accessed September 25, 2013).

[10] Mike Seemuth, April 10, 2011, "From the Corner Office—Elon Musk," *Success.*

[11] Jeff Evanson, Tesla Motors Investor Presentation, September 14, 2013, www.teslamotors.com (accessed November 29, 2013).

[12] Tesla Second Quarter 2017 Shareholder Letter, August 2, 2017.

[13] Tesla, Inc., "Tesla Third Quarter 2017 Update," accessed August 05, 2019, https://ir.tesla.com/static-files/d68bddfe-6f2b-4f8f-bed0-94dd7a49cc0f

[14] Tesla Fourth Quarter 2017 Shareholder Letter, February 7, 2018.

[15] Tesla, Inc., "Tesla Q1 2018 Vehicle Production and Deliveries," accessed August 05, 2019, https://ir.tesla.com/static-files/f3536958-0d36-45ae-9240-56afce77a114.

[16] As reported in *Autoweek,* "Tesla Has to Turn Potential into Real Profits," May 5, 2017, www.autoweek.com (accessed March 7, 2018).

[17] Tesla First Quarter 2018 Shareholder Letter, May 2, 2018.

[18] "Tesla Q1 2018 Results—Earnings Call Transcript," May 2, 2018, www.seekingalpha.com (accessed May 9, 2018).

[19] Tesla, Inc., 2017 Annual Report, accessed August 5, 2019, https://tesla.gcs-web.com/static-files/c5818f93-accd-4102-9f79-66363f716fea.

[20] Company 10-K report for 2017, pp 1–2.

[21] According to information in Martin Eberhard's blog titled "Lotus Position," July 25, 2006, www.teslamotors.com/blog/lotus-position (accessed September 17, 2013).

[22] 2013 10-K Report, p. 4.

[23] Mark Stevenson, "Lithium-ion Battery Packs Now $209 per kwh, Will Fall to $100 by 2025: Bloomberg Analysis," *Green Car Reports,* December 11, 2017, www.greencarreports.com (accessed March 7, 2018).

[24] Internal Revenue Service, "Plug-In Electric Drive Vehicle Credit (IRC 30D)," accessed June 14, 2019, https://www.irs.gov/businesses/plug-in-electric-vehicle-credit-irc-30-and-irc-30d

[25] Tesla First Quarter 2018 Shareholder Letter, May 2, 2018.

[26] Fred Lambert, "Tesla Pickup Truck to Cost Less Than $50,000, 'be better than F150,' Says Elon Musk," June 2, 2019, https://electrek.co/2019/06/02/tesla-pickup-truck-price-f150-elon-musk/.

[27] Company press release May 20, 2010.

[28] Tesla First Quarter 2019 Shareholder Letter, April 23, 2019.

[29] George Ghanem, "Avoid Tesla Because Hydrogen Is the New Electric," March 6, 2016, www.seekingalpha.com (accessed March 7, 2016).

THE WALT DISNEY COMPANY: ITS DIVERSIFICATION STRATEGY IN 2018

JOHN E. GAMBLE *Texas A&M University–Corpus Christi*

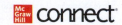

The Walt Disney Company was a broadly diversified media and entertainment company with a business lineup that included theme parks and resorts, motion picture production and distribution, cable television networks, the ABC broadcast television network, eight local television stations, and a variety of other businesses that exploited the company's intellectual property. The company's revenues had increased from $45 billion in fiscal year 2013 to $55 billion in fiscal 2017 and its share price had regularly outperformed the S&P 500. While struggling somewhat in the mid-1980s, the company's performance had been commendable in almost every year since Walt Disney created Mickey Mouse in 1928.

The company ended 2017 with a modest 1 percent increase in revenues and 4 percent increase in net income over the year prior. However, its announcement in December 2017 that it would acquire 21st Century Fox for $71.3 billion in cash and stock had the potential to radically improve its future financial performance. The transaction was approved by the U.S. Department of Justice (DOJ) Antitrust Division in June 2018 and was expected to be finalized by year-end 2018. The acquisition of 21st Century Fox would extend Disney's impressive collection of media franchises to include Fox, FX, Fox News Channel, Fox Business Network, Fox Sports Network, National Geographic Channel, Star India, 28 local television stations in the United States and more than 350 international channels, Twentieth Century Fox Film, and Twentieth Century Fox television production studios. Twenty-First Century Fox also held a 39.1 percent stake in Sky, Europe's leading entertainment company that served nearly 23 million households in five countries.

Disney CEO Robert Iger commented on the ability of the acquisition to further boost shareholder value during an investors' conference shortly after the DOJ consent decree announcement in June 2018.

> The acquisition of 21st Century Fox will bring significant financial value to Disney and the shareholders of both companies, and after six months of integration planning we're even more enthusiastic and confident in the strategic fit of these complementary assets and the talent at Fox.
>
> Just to remind you of the incredibly valuable assets that we're acquiring—our deal includes such premier entertainment properties as Twentieth Century Fox Film and Twentieth Century Fox Television, FX and National Geographic, Fox's regional sports networks, Fox Networks Group International, and Star India, as well as Fox's interests in Hulu and Sky. Since we first announced our deal in December, the intrinsic value of these assets has increased—thanks, in part, to the benefits of tax reform and certain operating improvements.
>
> As we've said before, the combination of Disney and 21st Century Fox is an extremely compelling proposition for consumers. It will allow us to create even more appealing high-quality content, expand our direct-to-consumer offerings and international presence, and deliver more exciting and personalized entertainment experiences to meet the growing demands of consumers worldwide.[1]

As the company entered the third quarter of 2018, it was coming off an impressive second quarter, but faced several strategic issues. The company's core Parks and Resorts business continued to grow and record healthy profit margins, but its larger Media Networks business had seen minimal revenue growth in recent years and was experiencing declining operating profits as media consumers turned from cable to direct-to-consumer (DTC) programming. The company's Studio Entertainment business unit had also struggled to develop stable revenue and earnings growth and its Consumer Products & Interactive Media business unit had seen a decline in revenues and operating profits in the past year. Going into 2019, Iger and Disney's management team would have to evaluate the corporation's strategy to bolster the performance of its existing business units and develop new media delivery capabilities while preparing for the integration of the probable acquisition of 21st Century Fox.

Company History

Walt Disney's venture into animation began in 1919 when he returned to the United States from France, where he had volunteered to be an ambulance driver for the American Red Cross during World War I. Disney volunteered for the American Red Cross only after being told he was too young to enlist for the United States Army. Upon returning after the war, Disney settled in Kansas City, Missouri, and found work as an animator for Pesman Art Studio. Disney, and fellow Pesman animator, Ub Iwerks, soon left the company to found Iwerks-Disney Commercial Artists in 1920. The company lasted only briefly, but Iwerks and Disney were both able to find employment with a Kansas City company that produced short animated advertisements for local movie theaters. Disney left his job again in 1922 to found Laugh-O-Grams, where he employed Iwerks and three other animators to produce short animated cartoons. Laugh-O-Grams was able to sell its short cartoons to local Kansas City movie theaters, but its costs far exceeded its revenues—forcing Disney to declare bankruptcy in 1923. Having exhausted his savings, Disney had only enough cash to purchase a one-way train ticket to Hollywood, California, where his brother, Roy, had offered a temporary room. Once in California, Disney

began to look for buyers for a finished animated-live action film he retained from Laugh-O-Grams. The film was never distributed, but New York distributors Margaret Winkler and Charles Mintz were impressed enough with the short film that they granted Disney a contract in October 1923 to produce a series of short films that blended cartoon animation with live action motion picture photography. Disney brought Ub Iwerks from Kansas City to Hollywood to work with Disney Brothers Studio (later to be named Walt Disney Productions) to produce the Alice Comedies series that would number 50-plus films by the series end in 1927. Disney followed the Alice Comedies series with a new animated cartoon for Universal Studios. After Disney's *Oswald the Lucky Rabbit* cartoons quickly became a hit, Universal terminated Disney Brothers Studio and hired most of Disney's animators to continue producing the cartoon.

In 1928, Disney and Iwerks created Mickey Mouse to replace Oswald as the feature character in Walt Disney Studios cartoons. Unlike with Oswald, Disney retained all rights over Mickey Mouse and all subsequent Disney characters. Mickey Mouse and his girlfriend, Minnie Mouse, made their cartoon debuts later in 1928 in the cartoons, *Plane Crazy, The Gallopin' Gaucho,* and *Steamboat Willie. Steamboat Willie* was the first cartoon with synchronized sound and became one of the most famous short films of all time. The animated film's historical importance was recognized in 1998 when it was added to the National Film Registry by the United States Library of Congress. Mickey Mouse's popularity exploded over the next few decades with a Mickey Mouse Club being created in 1929, new accompanying characters such as Pluto, Goofy, Donald Duck, and Daisy Duck being added to Mickey Mouse cartoon storylines, and Mickey Mouse appearing in Walt Disney's 1940 feature length film, *Fantasia.* Mickey Mouse's universal appeal reversed Walt Disney's series of failures in the animated film industry and became known as the mascot of Disney Studios, Walt Disney Productions, and The Walt Disney Company.

The success of The Walt Disney Company was sparked by Mickey Mouse, but Disney Studios also produced several other highly successful animated feature films including *Snow White and the Seven Dwarfs* in 1937, *Pinocchio* in 1940, *Dumbo* in 1941, *Bambi* in 1942, *Song of the South* in 1946, *Cinderella* in 1950, *Treasure Island* in 1950, *Peter Pan* in 1953, *Sleeping Beauty* in 1959, and *One Hundred-One Dalmatians* in 1961. What would prove to be Disney's greatest achievement began to emerge in 1954 when construction began on his Disneyland Park in Anaheim, California. Walt Disney's Disneyland resulted from an idea that Disney had many years earlier while sitting on an amusement park bench watching his young daughters play. Walt Disney thought that there should be a clean and safe park that had attractions that both parents and children alike would find entertaining. Walt Disney spent years planning the park and announced the construction of the new park to America on his *Disneyland* television show that was launched to promote the new $17 million park. The park was an instant success when it opened in 1955 and recorded revenues of more than $10 million during its first year of operation. After the success of Disneyland, Walt Disney began looking for a site in the eastern United States for a second Disney park. He settled on an area near Orlando, Florida, in 1963 and acquired more than 27,000 acres for the new park by 1965.

Walt Disney died of lung cancer in 1966, but upon his death, Roy O. Disney postponed retirement to become president and CEO of Walt Disney Productions and oversee the development of Walt Disney World Resort. Walt Disney World Resort opened in October 1971—only two months before Roy O. Disney's death in December. The company was led by Donn Tatum from 1971 to 1976. Tatum had been with Walt Disney Productions since 1956 and led the further development of Walt Disney World Resort and began the planning of EPCOT in Orlando and Tokyo Disneyland. Those two parks were opened during the tenure of Esmond Cardon Walker, who had been an executive at the company since 1956 and chief operating officer since Walt Disney's death in 1966. Walker also launched The Disney Channel before his retirement in 1983. Walt Disney Productions was briefly led by Ronald Miller, who was the son-in-law of Walt Disney. Miller was ineffective as Disney chief executive officer and was replaced by Michael Eisner in 1984.

Eisner formulated and oversaw the implementation of a bold strategy for Walt Disney Studios, which included the acquisitions of ABC, ESPN, Miramax Films, and the Anaheim Angels, and the Fox Family

Channel; the development of Disneyland Paris, Disney-MGM Studios in Orlando, Disney California Adventure Park, Walt Disney Studios theme park in France, and Hong Kong Disneyland; and the launch of the Disney Cruise Line, the Disney Interactive game division, and the Disney Store retail chain. Eisner also restored the company's reputation for blockbuster animated feature films with the creation of *The Little Mermaid* in 1989, and *Beauty and the Beast* and *The Lion King* in 1994. Despite Eisner's successes, his tendencies toward micromanagement and skirting board approval for many of his initiatives and his involvement in a long-running derivatives suit led to his removal as chairman in 2004 and his resignation in 2005.

The Walt Disney Company's CEO in 2018, Robert (Bob) Iger, became a Disney employee in 1996 when the company acquired ABC. Iger was president and CEO of ABC at the time of its acquisition by The Walt Disney Company and remained in that position until made president of Walt Disney International by Alan Eisner in 1999. Bob Iger was promoted to president and chief operating officer of The Walt Disney Company in 2000 and was named as Eisner's replacement as CEO in 2005. Iger's first strategic moves in 2006 included the $7.4 billion acquisition of Pixar animation studios and the purchase of the rights to Disney's first cartoon character, Oswald the Lucky Rabbit, from NBCUniversal. In 2007, Robert Iger commissioned two new 340-meter ships for the Disney Cruise Lines that would double its fleet size from two ships to four. The new ships ordered by Iger were 40 percent larger than Disney's two older vessels and entered service in 2011 and 2012. Iger also engineered the acquisition of Marvel Entertainment in 2009 that would enable the Disney production motion pictures featuring Marvel comic book characters such as Iron Man, Incredible Hulk, Thor, Spider-Man, and Captain America. In 2012, Walt Disney acquired Lucasfilm in a $4 billion cash and stock transaction. Lucasfilm was founded by George Lucas and was best known for its *Star Wars* motion picture franchise.

A financial summary for The Walt Disney Company for 2013 through 2017 is provided in Exhibit 1. Exhibit 2 tracks the performance of The Walt Disney Company's common shares between July 2013 and July 2018.

EXHIBIT 1

Financial Summary for The Walt Disney Company, Fiscal Years 2013–2017 (in millions of $, except per share amounts)

	2017	2016	2015	2014	2013
Revenues	$55,137	$55,632	$52,465	$48,813	$45,041
Net income	9,366	9,790	8,852	8,004	6,636
Net income attributable to Disney	8,980	9,391	8,382	7,501	6,136
Per common share					
Earnings attributable to Disney					
Diluted	$5.69	$5.73	$4.90	$4.26	$3.38
Basic	$5.73	$5.76	$4.95	$4.31	$3.42
Dividends	$1.56	$1.42	$1.81	$0.86	$0.75
Balance sheets					
Total assets	$95,789	$92,033	$88,182	$84,141	$81,197
Long-term obligations	26,710	24,189	19,142	18,537	17,293
Disney shareholders' equity	41,315	43,265	44,525	44,958	45,429
Statements of cash flows					
Cash provided by operations	$12,343	$13,136	$11,385	$10,148	$9,495
Investing activities	4,111	5,758	4,245	3,345	4,676
Financing activities	8,959	7,220	5,801	6,981	4,458

Source: The Walt Disney Company, 2017 Annual Report, accessed August 5, 2019, http://www.annualreports.com/HostedData/AnnualReportArchive/w/NYSE_DIS_2017.pdf.

The Walt Disney Company's Corporate Strategy and Business Operations in 2018

In 2018, The Walt Disney Company was broadly diversified into theme parks, hotels and resorts, cruise ships, cable networks, broadcast television networks, television production, television station operations, live action and animated motion picture production and distribution, music publishing, live theatrical productions, children's book publishing, interactive media, and consumer products retailing. The company's corporate strategy was centered on (1) creating high-quality content, (2) exploiting technological innovations to make entertainment experiences more memorable, and (3) international expansion. The company's 2006 acquisition of Pixar and 2009 acquisition of Marvel were executed to enhance the resources and capabilities of its core animation business with the addition of new animation skills and characters. The company's 2011 acquisition of UTV was engineered to facilitate its international expansion efforts. The acquisition of Lucasfilm's *Star Wars* franchise in 2012 not only allowed the company to produce new films in the series, but integrate *Star Wars* into its other business units, including theme park attractions. When asked about the company's planned acquisition of 21st Century Fox and Walt Disney Company's strategic priorities during a media, cable, and telecommunications conference in February 2018, Bob Iger made the following comments:

> We've been a company that has emphasized the value of high-quality, branded entertainment. And the acquisitions of Pixar, Marvel, and Lucasfilm/*Star Wars,* obviously were a reflection of that core strategy.

EXHIBIT 2

Performance of The Walt Disney Company's Stock Price, July 2013 to July 2018

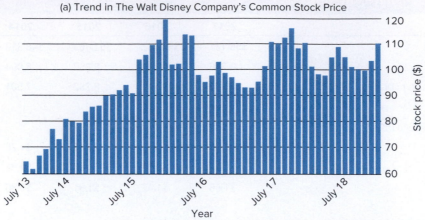

(a) Trend in The Walt Disney Company's Common Stock Price

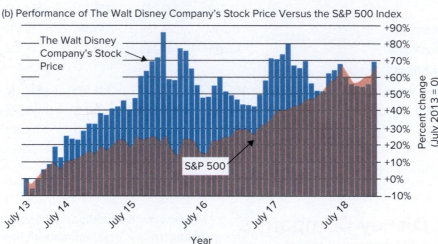

(b) Performance of The Walt Disney Company's Stock Price Versus the S&P 500 Index

The Walt Disney Company's Stock Price

S&P 500

Source: "Form 10-K, The Walt Disney Company," United States Securities and Exchange Commission, September 30, 2017, https://www.sec.gov/Archives/edgar/data/1001039/000100103917000198/fy2017_q4x10k.htm.

This gives us a larger portfolio of high-quality branded content. When you think about FX, when you think about National Geographic, when you think about a number of the franchises that Fox has created, including their Marvel franchises and *Avatar* and other product, we believe that this fits beautifully into a strategy to continue to invest in entertainment, particularly in a world that seems to be growing in terms of its appetite to consume entertainment.

Secondly, we've been talking a lot about using technology to reach consumers in more modern, more efficient, and effective ways. That certainly has changed significantly. When I talk about a dynamic marketplace, I think it's most evident in

how people access entertainment, how they consume entertainment, and this acquisition gives us the ability not only to have essentially more product, more intellectual property, but to bring it to the consumer in more compelling ways and ways we think the consumer wants their entertainment more and more. The Star and Sky assets and the Hulu assets give us an opportunity to do that.

And then lastly, we've talked a lot about wanting to grow our company globally. The Walt Disney Company has been a global company for a long time, but in many of the markets that we operate in our penetration was relatively superficial. We spent a fair amount of time over the last decade deepening that penetration in markets. You mentioned Shanghai Disneyland, which would be an example of how we've done that in China. This gives us the ability to have a far more global footprint and to diversify the company's interest from a geographic perspective.[2]

Disney's corporate strategy also called for sufficient capital to be allocated to its core theme parks and resorts business to sustain its advantage in the industry. The company expanded the range of attractions at its theme parks with billion-dollar plus additions such as its new Toy Story Land attractions opened in 2018 at Shanghai Disneyland and Disney's Hollywood Studios and its Star Wars Land scheduled to open in Disney's Hollywood Studios and Anaheim's Disneyland in 2019. Expansions were also under way in 2018 at Tokyo Disney Resort and Hong Kong Disneyland.

The Walt Disney Company's corporate strategy also attempted to capture synergies existing between its business units. Two of the company's highest grossing films, *Pirates of the Caribbean: On Stranger Tides* and *Cars 2* were also featured at the company's Florida and California theme parks. The company had leveraged ESPN's reputation in sports by building 230-acre ESPN Wide World of Sports Complex in Orlando that could host amateur and professional events and boost occupancy in its 18 resort hotels and vacation clubs located at the Walt Disney World resort.

In 2018, the company's business units were organized into four divisions: Media Networks, Parks and Resorts, Studio Entertainment, and Consumer Products & Interactive Media.

Media Networks

The Walt Disney Company's media networks business unit included its domestic and international cable networks, the ABC television network, television production, and U.S. domestic television stations. The company's television production was limited to television programming for ABC, and its eight local television stations were all ABC affiliates. Six of Disney's eight domestic television stations were located in the 10 largest U.S. television markets. In all, ABC had 244 affiliates in the United States.

When asked about the decline in cable television viewership, Bob Iger suggested that the content delivery method was less important than the quality and appeal of content.

> Well, for the most part, we've looked at channels less as channels and more as brands. And it's less important to us how people get those channels—obviously, it's important in terms of how they are monetized in today's world—but what's more important to us is the quality of the brand and intellectual property that fits under that brand umbrella. And our intention is to—as the world shifts in terms of distribution and consumption we talked about earlier—is to migrate those brands and those products in the more modern direction from a distribution and consumption perspective.[3]

Exhibit 3 provides the market ranking for Disney's local stations and its number of subscribers and ownership percentage of its cable networks. The exhibit also provides a brief description of its ABC broadcasting and television production operations. The division also included Radio Disney, which aired family-oriented radio programming on 34 terrestrial radio stations (31 of which were owned by Disney) in the United States. Radio Disney was also available on SiriusXM satellite radio, iTunes Radio Tuner and Music Store, XM/DIRECTV, and on mobile phones. Radio Disney was also broadcasted throughout most of South America on Spanish language terrestrial radio stations. The company's 2011 acquisition of UTV would expand the division's television broadcasting and production capabilities to India.

Among the most significant challenges to Disney's media networks division was the competition for viewers, which impacted advertising rates and revenues. Not only did the company compete against other broadcasters and cable networks for viewers, but it also competed against other types of entertainment and delivery platforms. For example, consumers might prefer to watch videos, movies, or other content on the Internet or Internet streaming services rather than watch cable or broadcast television. The effect of the Internet on broadcast news had been significant and the growth of streaming services had the potential to affect the advertising revenue potential of all of Disney's media businesses.

To combat competing streaming content providers and capitalize on such opportunities, Disney launched two direct-to-consumer (DTC) streaming

EXHIBIT 3

The Walt Disney Company's Media Network Subscribers, 2013 and 2017 (in millions)

	Estimated Subscribers (in millions)[1]	Estimated Subscribers (in millions)[1]
Cable Networks	2013	2017
ESPN[2]		
ESPN	99	88
ESPN–International	n.a.	146
ESPN2	99	87
ESPNU	72	67
ESPNEWS	73	66
SEC Network	n.a.	60
Disney Channels Worldwide		
Disney Channel–Domestic	99	92
Disney Channels–International[3]	141	221
Disney Junior–Domestic	58	72
Disney Junior–International[3]	n.a.	151
Disney XD–Domestic	78	74
Disney XD–International[3]	91	127
Freeform	n.a.	90
A + E and Vice		
A&E[2]	99	91
Lifetime	99	91
HISTORY	99	92
Lifetime Movie Network	82	73
Lifetime Real Women[3]	18	n.a.
FYI	n.a.	58
Viceland	n.a.	70

Broadcasting

ABC Television Network (244 local affiliates reaching nearly 100 percent of U.S. television households)

Television Production

ABC Studios and ABC Media Productions (Daytime, primetime, late night and news television programming)

Domestic Television Stations

Market	TV Station	Television Market Ranking[4]
New York, NY	WABC-TV	1
Los Angeles, CA	KABC-TV	2
Chicago, IL	WLS-TV	3
Philadelphia, PA	WPVI-TV	4
San Francisco, CA	KGO-TV	6
Houston, TX	KTRK-TV	8
Raleigh-Durham, NC	WTVD-TV	24
Fresno, CA	KFSN-TV	54

(1) Estimated U.S. subscriber counts according to Nielsen Media Research as of September 2017, except as noted below.

(2) ESPN and A&E programming is distributed internationally through other networks discussed below.

(3) Subscriber counts are not rated by Nielsen and are based on internal management report.

(4) Based on Nielsen Media Research, U.S. Television Household Estimates, January 1, 2017.

Source: The Walt Disney Company, 2017 Annual Report, accessed August 5, 2019, http://www.annualreports.com/HostedData/AnnualReportArchive/w/NYSE_DIS_2017.pdf.

services and Over-the-Top (OTT) services that delivered content without a distributor. Disney's ESPN-branded multisports content was planned for DTC distribution in 2018 and a Disney-branded DTC service that featured the company's film and television content was planned for 2019. Bob Iger discussed the company's DTC and OTT strategy in a 2017 interview.

> Direct-to-consumer really is still a relatively nascent business, although obviously Netflix probably wouldn't look at it that way. But what we were doing was creating really, two different OTT or DTC products. One was sports, and the other one I'll call family, which was going to include Disney, Marvel, Pixar, and Star Wars. And what we saw doing was bringing them both out reasonably priced. We have not announced price but I did suggest they would both be substantially below what Netflix currently charges for a few reasons.[4]

Bob Iger discussed during an analysts' conference how the development of ESPN + and its family-oriented DTC services would allow the company to catch up with emerging media trends that it had missed.

> It's no secret that we have seen the development and the growth of an entirely new media marketplace, and so we start with the premise that we want to participate in this new marketplace or this new market. Right now, we're only doing so at the tip of the iceberg, so to speak, with Hulu—that would be an example of that, and we have a relatively small stake in Hulu, about 30 percent. So our OTT interests are essentially designed to be part of this new marketplace, first. And I talked about it earlier, if you look at how the consumer today wants their media, first of all, they're far more interested in mobile, mobile first, in many cases. The user interface is particularly critical; this is really true for millennials and younger, where the user interface that exists in the sort of traditional television platform is not as compelling to them. It is essential for us to provide our content on platforms and with user interfaces that are serving today's consumer better.[5]

Operating results for Disney's media networks division for fiscal 2015 through fiscal 2017 are presented in Exhibit 4.

Parks and Resorts

The Walt Disney Company's parks and resorts division included the Walt Disney World Resort in Orlando, the Disneyland Resort in California, Disneyland Paris, the Aulani Disney Resort and Spa in Hawaii, the Disney Vacation Club, the Disney Cruise Line, and Adventures by Disney. The company also owned a 47 percent interest in Hong Kong Disneyland Resort and a 43 percent interest

---

EXHIBIT 4

Operating Results for Walt Disney's Media Networks Business Unit, Fiscal Years 2015–2017 (in millions of $)

Revenues	2017	2016	2015
Affiliate fees	$ 12,659	$ 12,259	$ 12,029
Advertising	8,129	8,509	8,361
TV/SVOD distribution and other	2,722	2,921	2,874
Total revenues	23,510	23,689	23,264
Operating expenses	14,068	13,571	13,150
Selling, general, administrative and other	2,647	2,705	2,869
Depreciation and amortization	237	255	266
Equity in the income of investees	(344)	(597)	(814)
Operating Income	$ 6,902	$ 7,755	$ 7,793

Source: The Walt Disney Company, 2017 Annual Report, accessed August 5, 2019, http://www.annualreports.com/HostedData/AnnualReportArchive/w/NYSE_DIS_2017.pdf.

in Shanghai Disney Resort. Disney also licensed the operation of Tokyo Disney Resort in Japan. Revenue for the division was primarily generated through park admission fees, hotel room charges, merchandise sales, food and beverage sales, sales and rentals of vacation club properties, and fees charged for cruise vacations.

Revenues from hotel lodgings and food and beverage sales were a sizable portion of the division's revenues. For example, at the 25,000-acre Walt Disney World Resort alone, the company operated 18 resort hotels with approximately 22,000 rooms. Walt Disney World Resort also included the 127-acre Disney Springs retail, dining, and entertainment complex where visitors could dine and shop during or after park hours. Walt Disney World Resort in Orlando also included four championship golf courses, full-service spas, tennis, sailing, water skiing, two water parks, and a 230-acre sports complex that was host to over 200 amateur and professional events each year.

Walt Disney's 486-acre resort in California included two theme parks—Disneyland and Disney California Adventure—along with three hotels and its Downtown Disney retail, dining, and entertainment complex. Disney California Adventure was opened in 2001 adjacent to the Disneyland property and included four lands—Golden State, Hollywood Pictures Backlot, Paradise Pier, and Bug's Land. The park was initially built to alleviate overcrowding at Disneyland and was expanded with the addition of World of Color in 2010 and Cars Land in 2012 to strengthen its appeal with guests.

Aulani was a 21-acre oceanfront family resort located in Oahu, Hawaii. Disneyland Paris included two theme parks, seven resort hotels, two convention centers, a 27-hole golf course, and a shopping, dining, and entertainment complex. The company's Hong Kong Disneyland, Shanghai Disney Resort, and Tokyo Disney Resort theme parks were highly popular with ambitious expansion plans.

The company also offered timeshare sales and rentals in 14 resort facilities through its Disney Vacation Club. The Disney Cruise Line operated four ships out of North America and Europe. Disney's cruise activities were developed to appeal to the interests of children and families. Its Port Canaveral cruises included a visit to Disney's Castaway Cay, a 1,000-acre private island in the Bahamas. The popularity of Disney's cruise vacations allowed its fleet to be booked to full capacity year-round.

The division's operating results for fiscal years 2015 through 2017 are presented in Exhibit 5.

Studio Entertainment

The Walt Disney Company's studio entertainment division produced live-action and animated motion pictures, direct-to-video content, musical recordings,

EXHIBIT 5

Operating Results for Walt Disney's Parks and Resorts Business Unit, Fiscal Years 2015–2017 (in millions of $)

Revenues	2017	2016	2015
Domestic	$ 14,812	$ 14,242	$ 13,611
International	3,603	2,732	2,551
Total revenues	18,415	16,974	16,162
Operating expenses	10,667	10,039	9,760
Selling, general, administrative and other	1,950	1,913	1,884
Depreciation and amortization	1,999	1,721	1,517
Equity in the loss of investees	25	3	—
Operating Income	$ 3,774	$ 3,298	$ 3,031

Source: The Walt Disney Company, 2017 Annual Report, accessed August 5, 2019, http://www.annualreports.com/HostedData/AnnualReportArchive/w/NYSE_DIS_2017.pdf.

and *Disney on Ice* and *Disney Live!* live performances. The division's motion pictures were produced and distributed under the Walt Disney Pictures, Pixar, Marvel, Lucasfilm, and Touchstone banners. The division also distributed Dreamworks Studios motion pictures that were released from 2010 to 2016.

Most motion pictures typically incurred losses during the theatrical distribution of the film because of production costs and the cost of extensive advertising campaigns accompanying the launch of the film. Profits for many films did not occur until the movie became available on DVD or Blu-Ray disks for home entertainment, which usually began three to six months after the film's theatrical release. Revenue was also generated when a movie moved to pay-per-view (PPV)/video-on-demand (VOD) two months after the release of the DVD and when the motion picture became available on subscription premium cable channels such as HBO about 16 months after PPV/VOD availability. Broadcast networks such as ABC could purchase telecast rights to movies later as could basic cable channels such as Lifetime or the Hallmark Channel. Premium cable channels such as Showtime and Starz might also purchase telecast rights to movies long after its theatrical release. Similarly, subscription video on demand (SVOD) services such as Netflix might acquire distribution rights to a film for a 12- to 19-month window.

Telecast right fees decreased as the length of time from initial release increased. Operating results for the Walt Disney Company's Studio Entertainment division for fiscal 2015 through fiscal 2017 are reproduced in Exhibit 6.

Consumer Products & Interactive Media

The company's consumer products division included the company's Disney Store retail chain and businesses specializing in merchandise licensing and children's book and magazine publishing. In 2018, the company owned and operated 221 Disney Stores in North America, 87 stores in Europe, 55 stores in Japan, and 2 stores in China. Its publishing business included comic books, various children's book magazine titles available in print and eBook format, and smartphone and tablet computer apps designed for children. The division's sales were primarily affected by seasonal shopping trends and changes in consumer disposable income.

Operating results for Disney's Consumer Products & Interactive Media division for fiscal year 2015 through 2017 are presented in Exhibit 7. The company's consolidated statements of income for fiscal 2015 through fiscal 2017 are presented in Exhibit 8. The Walt Disney Company's balance sheets for fiscal 2016 and fiscal 2017 are presented in Exhibit 9.

EXHIBIT 6

Operating Results for Walt Disney's Studio Entertainment Business Unit, Fiscal Years 2015–2017 (in millions of $)

	2017	2016	2015
Revenues			
Theatrical distribution	$ 2,903	$ 3,672	$ 2,321
Home entertainment	1,798	2,108	1,799
TV/SVOD distribution and other	3,678	3,661	3,246
Total revenues	8,379	9,441	7,366
Operating expenses	3,667	3,991	3,050
Selling, general, administrative and other	2,242	2,622	2,204
Depreciation and amortization	115	125	139
Operating Income	$ 2,355	$ 2,703	$ 1,973

Source: The Walt Disney Company, 2017 Annual Report, accessed August 5, 2019, http://www.annualreports.com/HostedData/AnnualReportArchive/w/NYSE_DIS_2017.pdf.

Operating Results for Walt Disney's Consumer Products & Interactive Media Business Unit, Fiscal Years 2015–2017 (in millions of $)

	2017	2016	2015
Revenues			
Licensing, publishing and games	$ 3,256	$ 3,819	$ 3,850
Retail and other	1,577	1,709	1,823
Total revenues	4,833	5,528	5,673
Operating expenses	1,904	2,263	2,434
Selling, general, administrative and other	1,007	1,125	1,172
Depreciation and amortization	179	175	183
Equity in the income of investees	1	—	—
Operating Income	$ 1,744	$ 1,965	$ 1,884

Source: The Walt Disney Company, 2017 Annual Report, accessed August 5, 2019, http://www.annualreports.com/HostedData/AnnualReportArchive/w/NYSE_DIS_2017.pdf.

EXHIBIT 8

Consolidated Statements of Income for The Walt Disney Company, Fiscal Years 2015–2017 (in millions of $, except per share data)

	2017	2016	2015
Revenues	$55,137	$55,632	$52,465
Costs and expenses	41,264	41,274	39,241
Restructuring and impairment charges	98	156	53
Add: Other income	78	—	—
Net interest expense	385	260	117
Add: Equity in the income of investees	(320)	(926)	(814)
Income before income taxes	13,788	14,868	13,868
Income taxes	4,422	5,078	5,016
Net Income	9,366	9,790	8,852
Less: Net Income attributable to noncontrolling interests	386	399	470
Net Income attributable to The Walt Disney Company (Disney)	$ 8,980	$ 9,391	$ 8,382
Earnings per share attributable to Disney:			
Diluted	$5.69	$5.73	$4.90
Basic	$5.73	$5.76	$4.95
Weighted average number of common and common equivalent shares outstanding:			
Diluted	1,578	1,639	1,709
Basic	1,568	1,629	1,694

Source: The Walt Disney Company, 2017 Annual Report, accessed August 5, 2019, http://www.annualreports.com/HostedData/AnnualReportArchive/w/NYSE_DIS_2017.pdf.

EXHIBIT 9

Consolidated Balance Sheets for The Walt Disney Company, Fiscal Years 2016 and 2017 (in millions, except per share data)

	September 30, 2017	October 1, 2016
CURRENT ASSETS		
Cash and cash equivalents	$ 4,017	$ 4,610
Receivables	8,633	9,065
Inventories	1,373	1,390
Television costs and advances	1,278	1,208
Other current assets	588	693
Total current assets	15,889	16,966
Film and television costs	7,481	6,339
Investments	3,202	4,280
Parks, resorts and other property, at cost		
Attractions, buildings and equipment	54,043	50,270
Accumulated depreciation	29,037	26,849
	25,006	23,421
Projects in progress	2,145	2,684
Land	1,255	1,244
	22,380	21,512
Intangible assets, net	6,995	6,949
Goodwill	31,426	27,810
Other assets	2,390	2,340
Total assets	$95,789	$92,033
LIABILITIES AND EQUITY		
Current liabilities		
Accounts payable and other accrued liabilities	$8,855	$9,130
Current portion of borrowings	6,172	3,687
Deferred revenue and other	4,568	4,025
Total current liabilities	19,595	16,842
Borrowings	19,119	16,483
Deferred income taxes	4,480	3,679
Other long-term liabilities	6,443	7,706
Commitments and contingencies		
Redeemable noncontrolling interests	1,148	—
Equity		
Preferred stock, $0.01 par value		
Authorized — 100 million shares, Issued — none	—	—

(Continued)

	September 30, 2017	October 1, 2016
Authorized — 4.6 billion shares, Issued — 2.9 billion shares	36,248	35,859
Retained earnings	72,606	66,088
Accumulated other comprehensive loss	(3,528)	(3,979)
	105,326	97,968
Treasury stock, at cost, 937.8 million shares at October 1, 2011 and 803.1 million shares at October 2, 2010	(64,011)	(54,703)
Total Disney Shareholder's equity	41,315	43,265
Noncontrolling interests	3,689	4,058
Total Equity	45,004	47,323
Total liabilities and equity	$95,789	$92,033

Source: The Walt Disney Company, 2017 Annual Report, accessed August 5, 2019, http://www.annualreports.com/HostedData/AnnualReportArchive/w/NYSE_DIS_2017.pdf.

The Walt Disney Company's Second Quarter 2018 Performance and Its Future Prospects

The Walt Disney Company reported revenues and earnings per share increases during its first six months of fiscal 2018 of 6 percent and 59 percent, respectively, from the first six months of the year prior. The company's strong financial performance during the first six months of 2018 was led by its Parks and Resorts business unit, which saw year-over-year revenue and operating income increases of 13 percent and 24 percent, respectively; and its Studio business unit, which recorded a year-over-year revenue increase of 9 percent and a year-over-year operating income increase of 12 percent. Disney's Media Networks and Consumer Products & Interactive Media divisions suffered 9 percent and 4 percent operating income decreases, respectively, with neither achieving meaningful revenue growth.

Chairman Iger summarized Disney's strong second quarter performance and summarized the company's position at mid-2018.

> We're very pleased with our results in Q2, especially in our Parks and Resorts and Studio businesses.

Our parks continue to drive growth through operational excellence and by effectively leveraging our extraordinary content. As an example, I just got back from opening our new Toy Story Land in Shanghai Disneyland and I'm happy to report that our first major addition to the park was met with strong reviews and great excitement. We're thrilled with the reaction and the enthusiasm generated by the new land bodes well for future expansion.

Turning to our Studio . . . It's clear from the recent results—as well as from the slate ahead—that our Studio has and will continue to raise the bar in terms of both creative and commercial success.

The incredible performance of Marvel's *Black Panther* is just one of many examples. We're proud of this movie on so many levels—it speaks volumes about great, innovative storytelling, the power of new perspectives and unbridled creativity.

We followed the phenomenal success of *Black Panther* with another Marvel masterpiece, *Avengers: Infinity War,* which broke domestic and global records to become the largest movie opening in history. With this latest success, our Studio has delivered nine of the top ten biggest domestic box office openings of all time—all of them released in the last six years.

On the sports front, we're very encouraged by the reaction to our ESPN + service, which launched just about a month ago. The reviews have been strong, and the response from sports fans has been enthusiastic.

We're also merging Consumer Products and Parks and Resorts together—combining strategy and resources to create extraordinary experiences and products that bring our stories and characters to life for consumers inside our parks, at home, and beyond.[6]

As the company moved closer to the consummation of its acquisition of 21st Century Fox, it had several pressing strategy decisions related to its existing lineup of businesses. Failure to adequately resolve competitive disadvantages in its core and historical businesses would make the integration of one of the world's largest media companies even more complex and difficult.

ENDNOTES

[1] Bob Iger, Christine McCarthy, and Singer Lowell, "The Walt Disney Company Investor Conference Call," Walt Disney Company, June 20, 2018, https://www.thewaltdisneycompany.com/wp-content/uploads/2018/06/investor-call-transcript-2018-0620.pdf.

[2] Bob Iger, "The Walt Disney Company at the Morgan Stanley Technology, Media & Telecom Conference," Walt Disney Company, February 26, 2018, https://www.thewaltdisneycompany.com/wp-content/uploads/rai-ms-2018-0226-transcript-1.pdf.

[3] Bob Iger, "The Walt Disney Company at the Morgan Stanley Technology, Media & Telecom Conference," Walt Disney Company, February 26, 2018, https://www.thewaltdisneycompany.com/wp-content/uploads/rai-ms-2018-0226-transcript-1.pdf.

[4] Bob Iger, Christine McCarthy, and Singer Lowell, "Q&A with Senior Management," Walt Disney Company, December 14, 2017, https://www.thewaltdisneycompany.com/wp-content/uploads/managementqa-2017-12-14.pdf.

[5] Bob Iger, "The Walt Disney Company at the Morgan Stanley Technology, Media & Telecom Conference," Walt Disney Company, February 26, 2018, https://www.thewaltdisneycompany.com/wp-content/uploads/rai-ms-2018-0226-transcript-1.pdf.

[6] Bob Iger, Christine McCarthy, and Singer Lowell, "Q2 FY18 Earnings Conference Call," Walt Disney Company, May 08, 2018, https://www.thewaltdisneycompany.com/wp-content/uploads/2018/03/q2-fy18-earnings-transcript.pdf.

ROBIN HOOD

JOSEPH LAMPEL *Alliance Manchester Business School*

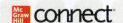

It was in the spring of the second year of his insurrection against the High Sheriff of Nottingham that Robin Hood took a walk in Sherwood Forest. As he walked, he pondered the progress of the campaign, the disposition of his forces, the Sheriff's recent moves, and the options that confronted him.

The revolt against the Sheriff had begun as a personal crusade. It erupted out of Robin's conflict with the Sheriff and his administration. However, alone Robin Hood could do little. He therefore sought allies, men with grievances and a deep sense of justice. Later he welcomed all who came, asking few questions and demanding only a willingness to serve. Strength, he believed, lay in numbers.

He spent the first year forging the group into a disciplined band, united in enmity against the Sheriff and willing to live outside the law. The band's organization was simple. Robin ruled supreme, making all important decisions. He delegated specific tasks to his lieutenants. Will Scarlett was in charge of intelligence and scouting. His main job was to shadow the Sheriff and his men, always alert to their next move. He also collected information on the travel plans of rich merchants and tax collectors. Little John kept discipline among the men and saw to it that their archery was at the high peak that their profession demanded. Scarlett took care of the finances, converting loot to cash, paying shares of the take, and finding suitable hiding places for the surplus. Finally, Much the Miller's son had the difficult task of provisioning the ever-increasing band of Merry Men.

The increasing size of the band was a source of satisfaction for Robin, but also a source of concern. The fame of his Merry Men was spreading, and new recruits were pouring in from every corner of England. As the band grew larger, their small bivouac became a major encampment. Between raids the men milled about, talking and playing games. Vigilance was in decline, and discipline was becoming harder to enforce. "Why," Robin reflected, "I don't know half the men I run into these days."

The growing band was also beginning to exceed the food capacity of the forest. Game was becoming scarce, and supplies had to be obtained from outlying villages. The cost of buying food was beginning to drain the band's financial reserves at the very moment when revenues were in decline. Travelers, especially those with the most to lose, were now giving the forest a wide berth. This was costly and inconvenient to them, but it was preferable to having all their goods confiscated.

Robin believed that the time had come for the Merry Men to change their policy of outright confiscation of goods to one of a fixed transit tax. His lieutenants strongly resisted this idea. They were proud of the Merry Men's famous motto: "Rob the rich and give to the poor." "The farmers and the townspeople," they argued, "are our most important allies. How can we tax them, and still hope for their help in our fight against the Sheriff?"

Robin wondered how long the Merry Men could keep to the ways and methods of their early days.

The Sheriff was growing stronger and becoming better organized. He now had the money and the men and was beginning to harass the band, probing for its weaknesses. The tide of events was beginning to turn against the Merry Men. Robin felt that the campaign must be decisively concluded before the Sheriff had a chance to deliver a mortal blow. "But how," he wondered, "could this be done?"

Robin had often entertained the possibility of killing the Sheriff, but the chances for this seemed increasingly remote. Besides, killing the Sheriff might satisfy his personal thirst for revenge, but it would not improve the situation. Robin had hoped that the perpetual state of unrest and the Sheriff's failure to collect taxes would lead to his removal from office. Instead, the Sheriff used his political connections to obtain reinforcement. He had powerful friends at court and was well regarded by the regent, Prince John.

Prince John was vicious and volatile. He was consumed by his unpopularity among the people, who wanted the imprisoned King Richard back. He also lived in constant fear of the barons, who had first given him the regency but were now beginning to dispute his claim to the throne. Several of these barons had set out to collect the ransom that would release King Richard the Lionheart from his jail in Austria. Robin was invited to join the conspiracy in return for future amnesty. It was a dangerous proposition. Provincial banditry was one thing, court intrigue another. Prince John had spies everywhere, and he was known for his vindictiveness. If the conspirators' plan failed, the pursuit would be relentless and retributions swift.

The sound of the supper horn startled Robin from his thoughts. There was the smell of roasting venison in the air. Nothing was resolved or settled. Robin headed for camp promising himself that he would give these problems his utmost attention after tomorrow's raid.

STARBUCKS IN 2019: IS THE COMPANY ON TRACK TO ACHIEVE OPERATIONAL EXCELLENCE AND ATTRACTIVE GROWTH?

ARTHUR A. THOMPSON *The University of Alabama*

Since its founding in 1987 as a modest nine-store operation in Seattle, Washington, Starbucks had become the premier roaster, marketer, and retailer of specialty coffees in the world, with over 30,100 store locations in 78 countries as of April 2019 and expected annual sales of more than $26 billion in fiscal year 2019, ending September 30, 2019. In addition to its flagship Starbucks brand coffees and coffee beverages, Starbucks' other brands included Teavana teas, Seattle's Best Coffee, Evolution Fresh juices and smoothies, Ethos bottled waters, and Princi and LaBoulange pastries, breads, and snack foods. Starbucks stores also sold snack foods, pastries, and sandwiches purchased from a variety of local, regional, and national suppliers. In January 2017, Starbucks launched a new strategic initiative to:

- Open 20 to 30 Starbucks Reserve™ Roasteries and Tasting Rooms, which would bring to life the theater of coffee roasting, brewing, and packaging for customers, include a coffee bar with a full menu of coffee beverages, space for a mixology bar serving traditional Italian cocktails, and an upscale Princi bakery, a newly created Starbucks subsidiary that featured fresh-baked

artisanal Italian breads, sandwiches, and pastries. The Starbucks Roaster and Tasting Room stores were designed in an open, marketplace style to (a) showcase the theater of roasting Starbucks Reserve™ coffees and the baking and other food preparation activities ongoing in the Princi kitchen, (b) enable customers to engage with store personnel at the Reserve coffee bar and Princi counter, and (c) gather with friends either at community tables or in lounge areas around two fireplaces.

- Open 1,000 Starbucks Reserve stores worldwide to bring premium experiences to customers and promote the company's recently introduced Starbucks Reserve™ coffees; these locations offered a more intimate small-lot coffee experience and gave customers a chance to chat with a barista about all things coffee. The menu at Starbucks Reserve stores included handcrafted hot and cold Starbucks Reserve™ coffee beverages, hot and cold teas, ice cream/coffee beverages, packages of Starbucks Reserve™ whole bean coffees, and an assortment of small plates, sandwiches and wraps, desserts, wines, and beer.

There were four types of brewing methods for the coffees and teas.

- Transform about 20 percent of the company's existing portfolio of Starbucks stores into Starbucks Reserve coffee bars.

Exhibit 1 provides an overview of Starbucks' performance during fiscal years 2010–2018.

Company Background
Starbucks Coffee, Tea, and Spice

Starbucks got its start in 1971 when three academics, English teacher Jerry Baldwin, history teacher Zev Siegel, and writer Gordon Bowker—all coffee aficionados—opened Starbucks Coffee, Tea, and Spice in touristy Pikes Place Market in Seattle. The three partners shared a love for fine coffees and exotic teas and believed they could build a clientele in Seattle that would appreciate the best coffees and teas. By the early 1980s, the company had four Starbucks stores in the Seattle area and had been profitable every year since opening its doors.

Howard Schultz Enters the Picture

In 1981, Howard Schultz, vice president and general manager of U.S. operations for a Swedish maker of stylish kitchen equipment and coffeemakers based in New York City, decided to pay Starbucks a visit. He was curious why Starbucks was selling so many of his company's products. When he arrived at the Pikes Place store, a solo violinist was playing Mozart at the

---

EXHIBIT 1

Financial and Operating Summary for Starbucks Corporation, Fiscal Years 2010–2018 ($ in millions, except for per-share amounts)

	Sept. 30 2018	Oct. 1 2017	Oct. 2, 2016	Oct. 3, 2010
INCOME STATEMENT DATA				
Net revenues:				
Company-operated stores	$19,690.3	$17,650.7	$16,844.1	$ 8,963.5
Licensed stores	2,652.2	2,355.0	2,154.2	875.2
Consumer packaged goods, foodservice, and other	2,377.0	2,381.1	2.317.6	868.7
Total net revenues	$24,719.5	$22,386.8	$21,315.9	$10,707.4
Cost of sales, including occupancy costs	$10,174.5	$ 9,038.2	$ 8,511.1	$ 4,458.6
Store operating expenses	7,193.2	6,493.3	6,064.3	3,551.4
Other operating expenses	539.3	553.8	545.4	293.2
Depreciation and amortization expenses	1,247.0	1,011.4	980.8	510.4
General and administrative expenses	1,759.0	1,393.3	1,360.6	569.5
Restructuring and impairments	224.4	153.5	—	53.0
Total operating expenses	21,137.4	18,643.5	17,462.2	9,436.1
Income from equity investees and other	301.2	391.4	318.2	148.1
Operating income	3,883.3	4,134.7	4,171.9	1,419.4
Gain resulting from acquisition of joint venture	1,376.4	—	—	—
Net gain resulting from divestiture of certain operations	499.2	93.5	5.4	—
Net earnings attributable to Starbucks	$4,518.0	$2,884.97	$2,818.9	$945.6
Net earnings per common share—diluted	$3.24	$1.97	$1.90	$0.62

(Continued)

(Continued)

	Sept. 30	Oct. 1	Oct. 2,	Oct. 3,
	2018	**2017**	**2016**	**2010**
BALANCE SHEET DATA				
Current assets	$12,494.2	$ 5,283.4	$ 4,757.9	$2,756.5
Current liabilities	5,684.2	4,220.7	4,546.8	2,703.6
Total assets	24,156.4	14,365.6	14,312.5	6,385.9
Long-term debt (including current portion)	9,090.2	3,932.6	3,585.2	549.4
Shareholders' equity	1,175.8	5,457.0	5,890.7	3,674.7
OTHER FINANCIAL DATA				
Net cash provided by operating activities	$11,937.8	$ 4,251.8	$ 4,697.9	$1,704.9
Capital expenditures (additions to property, plant, and equipment)	1,976.4	1,519.4	1,440.3	440.7
STORE INFORMATION				
Stores open at year-end				
United States				
Company-operated stores	9,684	8,222	7,880	6,707
Licensed stores	7,770	5,708	6,588	4,424
International				
Company-operated stores	5,657	5,053	4,831	2,182
Licensed stores	8,356	8,356	7,082	3,545
Worldwide	29,324	27,339	25,085	16,858
Worldwide percentage change in sales at company-operated stores open 13 months or longer	2%	3%	5%	7%

Starbucks' fiscal year ends on the Sunday closest to September 30.

Sources: Company 10-K Reports, 2018, 2017, and 2011.

door (his violin case open for donations). Schultz was immediately taken by the powerful and pleasing aroma of the coffees, the wall displaying coffee beans, and the rows of coffeemakers on the shelves. As he talked with the clerk behind the counter, the clerk scooped out some Sumatran coffee beans, ground them, put the grounds in a cone filter, poured hot water over the cone, and shortly handed Schultz a porcelain mug filled with freshly brewed coffee. After only taking three sips of the brew, Schultz was hooked. He began asking questions about the company, the coffees from different parts of the world, and the different ways of roasting coffee.

Later, when he met with two of the owners, Schultz was struck by their knowledge about coffee, their commitment to providing customers with quality coffees, and their passion for educating customers about the merits and quality of dark-roasted, fine coffees. One of the owners told Schultz, "We don't manage the business to maximize anything other than the quality of the coffee."[1] Schultz was also struck by the business philosophy of the two partners. It was clear that Starbucks stood not just for good coffee, but also for the dark-roasted flavor profiles that the founders were passionate about. Top quality, fresh-roasted, whole-bean coffee was the company's differentiating feature and a bedrock value. The company depended mainly on word-of-mouth to get more people into its stores, then built customer loyalty cup by cup as buyers gained a sense of discovery and excitement about the taste of fine coffee.

On his return trip to New York, Howard Schultz could not stop thinking about Starbucks and what it would be like to be a part of the enterprise. Schultz recalled, "There was something magic about it, a passion and authenticity I had never experienced in business."[2] By the time he landed at Kennedy Airport, he knew in his heart he wanted to go to work for Starbucks. But it took over a year and multiple meetings and discussions to convince the owners to bring in a high-powered New Yorker who had not grown up with the values of the company. In Spring 1982, Schultz was offered the job of heading marketing and overseeing Starbucks' retail stores; he assumed his new responsibilities at Starbucks in September 1982.

Starbucks and Howard Schultz: The 1982–1985 Period

In his first few months at Starbucks, Schultz spent most of his time in the four Seattle stores—working behind the counters, tasting different kinds of coffee, talking with customers, getting to know store personnel, and learning the retail aspects of the coffee business. In December, he began the final part of his training, that of actually roasting the coffee. Schultz spent a week getting an education about the colors of different coffee beans, listening for the telltale second pop of the beans during the roasting process, learning to taste the subtle differences among the various roasts, and familiarizing himself with the roasting techniques for different beans.

Schultz overflowed with ideas for the company. However, his biggest inspiration and vision for Starbucks' future came during the spring of 1983 when the company sent him to Milan, Italy, to attend an international housewares show. While walking from his hotel to the convention center, he spotted an espresso bar and went inside to look around. The cashier beside the door nodded and smiled. The "barista" behind the counter greeted Schultz cheerfully and began pulling a shot of espresso for one customer and handcrafting a foamy cappuccino for another, all the while conversing merrily with patrons standing at the counter. Schultz thought the barista's performance was "great theater." Just down the way on a side street, he went into an even more crowded espresso bar where the barista, whom he surmised to be the owner, was greeting customers by name; people were laughing and talking in an atmosphere that plainly was comfortable and familiar. In the next few blocks, he saw two more espresso bars. That afternoon, Schultz walked the streets of Milan to explore more espresso bars. Some were stylish and upscale; others attracted a blue-collar clientele. Most had few chairs and it was common for Italian opera to be playing in the background. What struck Schultz was how popular and vibrant the Italian coffee bars were. Energy levels were typically high and they seemed to function as an integral community gathering place. Each one had its own unique character, but they all had a barista that performed with flair and there was camaraderie between the barista and the customers.

Schultz remained in Milan for a week, exploring coffee bars and learning as much as he could about the Italian passion for coffee drinks. Schultz was particularly struck by the fact that there were 1,500 coffee bars in Milan, a city about the size of Philadelphia, and a total of 200,000 in all of Italy. In one bar, he heard a customer order a "caffe latte" and decided to try one himself—the barista made a shot of espresso, steamed a frothy pitcher of milk, poured the two together in a cup, and put a dollop of foam on the top. Schultz liked it immediately, concluding that lattes should be a feature item on any coffee bar menu even though none of the coffee experts he had talked to had ever mentioned coffee lattes.

Schultz's 1983 trip to Milan produced a revelation: The Starbucks stores in Seattle completely missed the point. There was much more to the coffee business than just selling beans and getting people to appreciate grinding their own beans and brewing fine coffee in their homes. What Starbucks needed to do was serve fresh-brewed coffee, espressos, and cappuccinos in its stores (in addition to beans and coffee equipment) and try to create an American version of the Italian coffee bar culture. Going to Starbucks should be an experience, a special treat, a place to meet friends and visit. Re-creating the authentic Italian coffee bar culture in the United States could be Starbucks' differentiating factor.

Schultz Becomes Frustrated

On Schultz's return from Italy, he shared his revelation and ideas for modifying the format of Starbucks' stores, but the owners strongly resisted, contending that Starbucks was a retailer, not a restaurant or coffee bar. They feared serving drinks would put them in the beverage business and diminish the integrity of Starbucks' mission as a purveyor of fine coffees. They pointed out that Starbucks had been profitable every year and there was no reason to rock the boat in a small, private company like Starbucks. It took Howard Schultz nearly a year to convince them to let him test an espresso bar when Starbucks opened its sixth store in April 1984. It was the first store designed to sell beverages and it was the first store located in downtown Seattle. Schultz asked for a 1,500-square-foot space to set up a full-scale Italian-style espresso bar, but he was allocated only 300 square feet in a corner of the new store. The store opened with no fanfare as a deliberate experiment to see what happened. By closing time on the first day, some 400 customers had been served, well above the 250-customer average of Starbucks' best performing stores. Within two months the store was serving 800 customers per day. The two baristas could not keep up with orders during the early morning hours, resulting in lines outside the door onto the sidewalk. Most of the business was at the espresso counter, while sales at the regular retail counter were only adequate.

Schultz was elated at the test results, expecting that the owners' doubts about entering the beverage side of the business would be dispelled and that he would gain approval to pursue the opportunity to take Starbucks to a new level. Every day he shared the sales figures and customer counts at the new downtown store. But the lead owner was not comfortable with the success of the new store, believing that it felt wrong and that espresso drinks were a distraction from the core business of marketing fine Arabica coffees at retail.[3] While he didn't deny that the experiment was succeeding, he would not agree to go forward with introducing beverages in other Starbucks stores.

Over the next several months, Schultz made up his mind to leave Starbucks and start his own company. His plan was to open espresso bars in high-traffic downtown locations, serve espresso drinks and coffee by the cup, and try to emulate the friendly, energetic atmosphere he had encountered in Italian espresso bars. The two owners, knowing how frustrated Schultz had become, supported his efforts to go out on his own and agreed to let him stay in his current job and office until definitive plans were in place. Schultz left Starbucks in late 1985.

Schultz's Il Giornale Venture

With the aid of a lawyer friend who helped companies raise venture capital and go public, Schultz began seeking out investors for the kind of company he had in mind. Ironically, one of the owners committed to investing $150,000 of Starbucks' money in Schultz's coffee bar enterprise and became Schultz's first investor. The other owner proposed that the new company be named Il Giornale Coffee Company (pronounced il-jor-nahl'-ee), a suggestion that Howard accepted. In December 1985, Schultz and one of the Starbucks owners made a trip to Italy where they visited some 500 espresso bars in Milan and Verona, observing local habits, taking notes about décor and menus, snapping photographs, and videotaping baristas in action.

By the end of January 1986, Schultz had raised about $400,000 in seed capital, enough to rent an office, hire a couple of key employees, develop a store design, and open the first store. But it took until the end of 1986 to raise the remaining $1.25 million needed to launch at least eight espresso bars and prove that Schultz's strategy and business model were viable. Schultz made presentations to 242 potential investors, 217 of which said "no." Many who heard Schultz's hour-long presentation saw coffee as a commodity business and thought that Schultz's espresso bar concept lacked any basis for sustainable competitive advantage (no patent on dark roast, no advantage in purchasing coffee beans, no way to bar the entry of imitative competitors). Some noted that coffee couldn't be turned into a growth business— consumption of coffee had been declining since the mid-1960s. Others were skeptical that people would pay $1.50 or more for a cup of coffee, and the company's unpronounceable name turned some off. Nonetheless, Schultz maintained an upbeat attitude and displayed passion and enthusiasm in making his pitch. He ended up raising $1.65 million from about 30 investors; most of the money came from nine people, five of whom became directors.

The first II Giornale store opened in April 1986. It measured 700 square feet and was located near the entrance of Seattle's tallest building. The décor was Italian and there were Italian words on the menu. Italian opera music played in the background. The baristas wore white shirts and bow ties. All service was stand-up—there were no chairs. National and international papers were hung on rods on the wall. By closing time on the first day, 300 customers had been served—mostly in the morning hours. But while the core idea worked well, it soon became apparent that several aspects of the format were not appropriate for Seattle. Some customers objected to the incessant opera music, others wanted a place to sit down; many people did not understand the Italian words on the menu. These "mistakes" were quickly fixed, but an effort was made not to compromise the style and elegance of the store. Within six months, the store was serving more than 1,000 customers a day. Regular customers had learned how to pronounce the company's name. Because most customers were in a hurry, it became apparent that speedy service was essential.

Six months after opening the first store, a second store was opened in another downtown building. In April 1987, a third store was opened in Vancouver, British Columbia, to test the transferability of the company's business concept outside Seattle. Schultz's goal was to open 50 stores in five years and he needed to dispel his investors' doubts about geographic expansion early on to achieve his growth objective. By mid-1987, sales at each of the three stores were running at a rate equal to $1.5 million annually.

II Giornale Acquires Starbucks

In March 1987, the Starbucks owners decided to sell the whole Starbucks operation in Seattle—the stores, the roasting plant, and the Starbucks name. Schultz knew immediately that he had to buy Starbucks; his board of directors agreed. Schultz and his newly hired finance and accounting manager drew up a set of financial projections for the combined operations and a financing package that included a stock offering to II Giornale's original investors and a line of credit with local banks. Within weeks, Schultz had raised the $3.8 million needed to buy Starbucks. The

acquisition was completed in August 1987. The new name of the combined companies was Starbucks Corporation. Howard Schultz, at the age of 34, became Starbucks' president and CEO.

Starbucks as a Private Company: 1987–1992

The Monday morning after the deal closed, Howard Schultz returned to the Starbucks offices at the roasting plant, greeted all the familiar faces, and accepted their congratulations. Then, he called the staff together for a meeting on the roasting plant floor:[4]

> All my life I have wanted to be part of a company and a group of people who share a common vision. . . . I'm here today because I love this company. I love what it represents. . . . I know you're concerned. . . . I promise you I will not let you down. I promise you I will not leave anyone behind. . . . In five years, I want you to look back at this day and say "I was there when it started. I helped build this company into something great."[5]

Schultz told the group that his vision was for Starbucks to become a national company with values and guiding principles that employees could be proud of. He aspired for Starbucks to become the most respected brand name in coffee and for the company to be admired for its corporate responsibility. He indicated that he wanted to include people in the decision-making process and that he would be open and honest with them. For Schultz, building a company that valued and respected its people, that inspired them, and that shared the fruits of success with those who contributed to the company's long-term value was essential, not just an intriguing option. He made the establishment of mutual respect between employees and management a priority.

The business plan Schultz had presented investors called for the new 9-store company to open 125 stores in the next five years—15 the first year, 20 the second, 25 the third, 30 the fourth, and 35 the fifth. Revenues were projected to reach $60 million in 1992. But the company lacked experienced management. Schultz had never led a growth effort of such magnitude and was just learning what the job of CEO was all about, having been the president of a small company for barely two years. Dave Olsen, a Seattle coffee bar owner whom Schultz had recruited to direct store operations at Il Giornale, was still learning the ropes in managing a multistore operation. Ron Lawrence, the company's controller, had worked as a controller for several organizations. Other Starbucks employees had only the experience of managing or being a part of a six-store organization.

Schultz instituted a number of changes in the first several months. To symbolize the merging of the two companies and the two cultures, a new logo was created that melded the designs of the Starbucks logo and the Il Giornale logo. The Starbucks stores were equipped with espresso machines and remodeled to look more Italian than old-world nautical. Il Giornale green replaced the traditional Starbucks brown. The result was a new type of store—a cross between a retail coffee bean store and an espresso bar/café—that quickly evolved into Starbucks' signature.

By December 1987, the mood at Starbucks was distinctly upbeat, with most all employees buying into the changes that Schultz was making and trust beginning to build between management and employees. New stores were on the verge of opening in Vancouver and Chicago. One Starbucks store employee, Daryl Moore, who had started working at Starbucks in 1981 and who had voted against unionization in 1985, began to question the need for a union with his fellow employees. Over the next few weeks, Moore began a move to decertify the union. He carried a de-certification letter around to Starbucks' stores, securing the signatures of employees who no longer wished to be represented by the union. He got a majority of store employees to sign the letter and presented it to the National Labor Relations Board. The union representing store employees was decertified. Later, in 1992, the union representing Starbucks' roasting plant and warehouse employees was also decertified.

Market Expansion Outside the Pacific Northwest

The first Chicago store opened in October 1987 and three more stores were opened over the next six months. Initially, customer counts at the stores were substantially below expectations because Chicagoans did not take to dark-roasted coffee as fast as Schultz had anticipated. While it was more expensive to supply fresh coffee to the Chicago stores out of the Seattle warehouse, the company solved the problem of freshness and quality assurance by putting freshly roasted beans in special FlavorLock bags that utilized vacuum packaging techniques with a one-way valve to allow carbon dioxide to escape without allowing air and moisture in. Moreover, rents and wage rates were higher in Chicago. The result was a squeeze on store profit margins. Gradually, customer counts improved, but Starbucks lost money on its Chicago stores until, in 1990, prices were raised to reflect higher rents and labor costs, more experienced store managers were hired, and a critical mass of customers caught on to the taste of Starbucks products.

Portland, Oregon, was the next market entered, and Portland coffee drinkers took to Starbucks products quickly. Store openings in Los Angeles and San Francisco soon followed. L.A. consumers embraced Starbucks quickly and the *Los Angeles Times* named Starbucks the best coffee in America before the first store opened.

Starbucks' store expansion targets proved easier to meet than Schultz had originally anticipated and he upped the numbers to keep challenging the organization. Starbucks opened 15 new stores in fiscal 1988, 20 in 1989, 30 in 1990, 32 in 1991, and 53 in 1992—producing a total of 161 stores, significantly above his original 1992 target of 125 stores.

From the outset, the strategy was to open only company-owned stores; franchising was avoided so as to keep the company in full control of the quality of its products and the character and location of its stores. But company-ownership of all stores required Starbucks to raise new venture capital to cover the cost of new store expansion. In 1988, the company raised $3.9 million; in 1990, venture capitalists provided an additional $13.5 million; and in 1991, another round of venture capital financing generated $15 million. Starbucks was able to raise the needed funds despite posting losses of $330,000 in 1987, $764,000 in 1988, and $1.2 million in 1989. While the losses were troubling to Starbucks' board of directors and investors, Schultz's business plan had forecast losses during the early years of expansion. At a particularly tense board meeting where directors sharply questioned Schultz about the lack of profitability, Schultz said:[6]

Look, we're going to keep losing money until we can do three things. We have to attract a management team well beyond our expansion needs. We have to build a world-class roasting facility. And we need a computer information system sophisticated enough to keep track of sales in hundreds and hundreds of stores.[7]

Schultz argued for patience as the company invested in the infrastructure to support continued growth well into the 1990s. He contended that hiring experienced executives ahead of the growth curve, building facilities far beyond current needs, and installing support systems laid a strong foundation for rapid profitable growth later on down the road. His arguments carried the day with the board and with investors, especially since revenues were growing approximately 80 percent annually and customer traffic at the stores was meeting or exceeding expectations.

Starbucks became profitable in 1990. After-tax profits had increased every year since 1990 except for fiscal year 2000 (because of $58.8 million in investment write-offs in four dot-com enterprises) and for fiscal year 2008 (when the sharp global economic downturn hit the company's bottom line very hard).

Rapid Expansion of the Network of Starbucks Locations

In 1992 and 1993, Starbucks began concentrating its store expansion efforts in the United States on locations with favorable demographic profiles that also could be serviced and supported by the company's operations infrastructure. For each targeted region, Starbucks selected a large city to serve as a "hub"; teams of professionals were located in hub cities to support the goal of opening 20 or more stores in the hub within two years. Once a number of stores were opened in a hub, then additional stores were opened in smaller surrounding "spoke" areas in the region. To oversee the expansion process, Starbucks had zone vice presidents that oversaw the store expansion process in a geographic region and that were also responsible for instilling the Starbucks culture in the newly opened stores. For a time, Starbucks went to extremes to blanket major cities with stores, even if some stores cannibalized a nearby store's business.

While a new store might draw 30 percent of the business of an existing store two or so blocks away, management believed a "Starbucks everywhere" strategy cut down on delivery and management costs, shortened customer lines at individual stores, and increased foot traffic for all the stores in an area. In 2002, new stores generated an average of $1.2 million in first-year revenues, compared to $700,000 in 1995 and only $427,000 in 1990; the increases in new-store revenues were due partly to growing popularity of premium coffee drinks, partly to Starbucks' growing reputation, and partly to expanded product offerings. But by 2008–2009 the strategy of saturating big metropolitan areas with stores began cannibalizing sales of existing stores to such an extent that average annual sales per store in the United States dropped to less than $1,000,000 and pushed store operating margins down from double-digit levels to mid-single-digit levels. As a consequence, Starbucks' management cut the number of metropolitan locations, closing 900 underperforming Starbucks stores in 2008–2009, some 75 percent of which were within three miles of another Starbucks store.

Despite the mistake of oversaturating portions of some large metropolitan areas with stores, Starbucks was regarded as having the best real estate team in the coffee bar industry and a core competence in identifying good retailing sites for its new stores. The company's sophisticated methodology enabled it to identify not only the most attractive individual city blocks but also the exact store location that was best. It also worked hard at building good relationships with local real estate representatives in areas where it was opening multiple store locations.

Licensed Starbucks Stores   In 1995, Starbucks began entering into licensing agreements for store locations in areas in the United States where it did not have the ability to locate company-owned outlets. Two early licensing agreements were with Marriott Host International to operate Starbucks retail stores in airport locations and with Aramark Food and Services to put Starbucks stores on university campuses and other locations operated by Aramark. Very quickly, Starbucks began to make increased use of licensing, both domestically and internationally. Starbucks preferred licensing to franchising because it permitted tighter controls over the operations of licensees, and in the case of many foreign locations licensing was much less risky.

Starbucks received a license fee and a royalty on sales at all licensed locations and supplied the coffee for resale at these locations. All licensed stores had to follow Starbucks' detailed operating procedures and all managers and employees who worked in these stores received the same training given to managers and employees in company-operated Starbucks stores.

International Expansion In markets outside the continental United States, Starbucks had a two-pronged store expansion strategy: either open company-owned-and-operated stores or else license a reputable and capable local company with retailing know-how in the target host country to develop and operate new Starbucks stores. In most countries,

Starbucks utilized a local partner/licensee to help it locate suitable store sites, set up supplier relationships, recruit talented individuals for positions as store managers, and adapt to local market conditions. Starbucks looked for partners/licensees that had strong retail/restaurant experience, had values and a corporate culture compatible with Starbucks, were committed to good customer service, possessed talented management and strong financial resources, and had demonstrated brand-building skills. In those foreign countries where business risks were deemed relatively high, most if not all Starbucks stores were licensed rather than being company-owned and operated.

Exhibit 2 shows the speed with which Starbucks grew its network of company-operated and licensed retail stores.

EXHIBIT 2
Company-Operated and Licensed Starbucks Stores

A. NUMBER OF STARBUCKS STORE LOCATIONS WORLDWIDE, FISCAL 1987–FISCAL 2018, MARCH 2019

End of Fiscal Year*	Company-operated Store Locations		Licensed Store Locations		Worldwide Total
	United States	International	United States	International	
1987	17	0	0	0	17
1990	84	0	0	0	84
1995	627	0	49	0	676
2000	2,446	530	173	352	3,501
2005	4,918	1,263	2,435	1,625	10,241
2010	6,707	2,182	4,424	3,545	16,858
2015	6,764	2,198	4,364	3,309	23,043
2017	8,512	4,763	5,745	6,043	27,339
2018	8,583	6,758	6,043	7,940	29,324
March 31, 2019	15,655 Worldwide		14,529 Worldwide		30,184

B. INTERNATIONAL STARBUCKS STORE LOCATIONS, SEPTEMBER 30, 2018

International Locations of Company-operated Starbucks Stores		International Locations of Licensed Starbucks Stores			
		Americas		Europe/Africa/Middle East	
Canada	1,109	Canada	409	Turkey	453
United Kingdom	335	Mexico	708	United Kingdom	653
China	3,521	16 Others	622	United Arab Emirates	186
Japan	1,286			Spain	142

Thailand	352	China, Asia-Pacific		Saudi Arabia	166
All Others	155	China*	0*	Kuwait	142
		Taiwan	458	Germany	152
		South Korea	1,231	32 Others	936
		Philippines	360		
		Malaysia	268		
		Indonesia	365		
International Company-Operated Total	8,356	Thailand	372	International Licensed Total	7,940
		8 Others	517		

*In the first quarter of fiscal 2018, Starbucks acquired its Chinese licensing partner's share of their joint venture in China, resulting in the transfer of all 1,477 licensed stores in China to company-operated retail stores.

Source: Company records posted in the investor relations section at HYPERLINK "http://www.starbucks.com" www.starbucks.com, accessed May 4, 2012; company 10-K Reports 2014 and 2016; company 2018 10-K Report, pp 4-6; and company press release, April, 25, 2019.

Store Design and Ambience: Key Elements of the "Starbucks Experience"

Store Design

Starting in 1991, Starbucks created its own in-house team of architects and designers to ensure that each store would convey the right image and character. Stores had to be custom-designed because the company didn't buy real estate and build its own free-standing structures. Instead, each space was leased in an existing structure, making each store differ in size and shape. Most stores ranged in size from 1,000 to 1,500 square feet and were located in office buildings, downtown and suburban retail centers, airport terminals, university campus areas, and busy neighborhood shopping areas convenient for pedestrian foot traffic and/or drivers. A few were in suburban malls. Four store templates—each with its own color combinations, lighting scheme, and component materials—were introduced in 1996; all four were adaptable to different store sizes and settings.

But as the number of stores increased rapidly over the next 20-plus years, greater store diversity and layouts quickly became necessary. Some stores were equipped with special seating areas to help make Starbucks a desirable gathering place where customers could meet and chat or simply enjoy a peaceful interlude in their day. Flagship stores in high-traffic, high-visibility locations had fireplaces, leather chairs, newspapers, couches, and lots of ambience. Increasingly, the company began installing drive-through windows at locations where speed and convenience were important to customers and locating kiosks in high-traffic supermarkets, building lobbies, the halls of shopping malls, and other public places where passers-by could quickly and conveniently pick up a Starbucks beverage and/or something to eat.

A new global store design strategy was introduced in 2009. Core design characteristics included the celebration of local materials and craftsmanship, a focus on reused and recycled elements, the exposure of structural integrity and authentic roots, the absence of features that distracted from an emphasis on coffee, seating layouts that facilitated customer gatherings, an atmosphere that sought to engage all five customer senses (sight, smell, sound, hearing, and feel), and flexibility to meet the needs of many customer types.[8] Each new store was to be a reflection of the environment in which it operated and be environmentally friendly. In 2010, Starbucks began an effort to achieve LEED (Leadership in Energy and Environmental Design) Certification for all new company-owned stores (a LEED-certified building had to incorporate green building design, construction, operations, and maintenance solutions).[9]

To better control average store opening costs, the company centralized buying, developed standard contracts and fixed fees for certain items, and consolidated work under those contractors who displayed good cost control practices. The retail operations group outlined exactly the minimum amount of equipment each core store needed, so that standard items could be ordered in volume from vendors at 20 to 30 percent discounts, then delivered just in time to the store site either from company warehouses or the vendor. Modular designs for display cases were developed. The layouts for new and remodeled stores were developed on a computer, with software that allowed the costs to be estimated as the design evolved. All this cut store opening and remodeling costs significantly and shortened the process to about 18 weeks.

Store Ambience

Starbucks management viewed each store as a billboard for the company and as a contributor to building the company's brand and image. The company went to great lengths to make sure the store fixtures, the merchandise displays, the colors, the artwork, the banners, the music, and the aromas all blended to create a consistent, inviting, stimulating environment that evoked the romance of coffee and signaled the company's passion for coffee. To try to keep the coffee aromas in the stores pure, smoking was banned, and employees were asked to refrain from wearing perfumes or colognes. Prepared foods were kept covered so customers would smell coffee only. Colorful banners and posters were used to keep the look of the Starbucks stores fresh and in keeping with seasons and holidays. All these practices reflected a conviction that every detail mattered in making Starbucks stores a welcoming and pleasant "third place" (apart from home and work) where people could meet friends and family, enjoy a quiet moment alone with a newspaper or book, or simply spend quality time relaxing—and most importantly, have a satisfying experience.

Starting in 2002, Starbucks began providing Internet access capability and enhanced digital entertainment to patrons. The objective was to heighten the "third place" Starbucks experience, entice customers into perhaps buying a second latte or espresso while they caught up on e-mail, listened to digital music, put the finishing touches on a presentation, or surfed the Internet. Wireless Internet service and faster Internet speeds were added as fast as they became available.

Starbucks' Strategy to Expand Its Product Offerings and Enter New Market Segments

Starting in the mid-1990s and continuing to the present, Howard Schultz began a long-term strategic campaign to expand Starbucks product offerings beyond its retail stores and to pursue sales of Starbucks products in a wider variety of distribution channels and market segments. The strategic objectives were to capitalize on Starbucks growing brand awareness and brand-name strength and create a broader foundation for sustained long-term growth in revenues and profits.

The first initiative involved the establishment of an in-house specialty sales group to begin marketing Starbucks coffee to restaurants, airlines, hotels, universities, hospitals, business offices, country clubs, and select retailers. Early users of Starbucks coffee included Horizon Airlines, a regional carrier based in Seattle, and United Airlines. The specialty sales group then soon won accounts at Hyatt, Hilton, Sheraton, Radisson, and Westin hotels, resulting in packets of Starbucks coffee being in each room with coffee-making equipment. Later, the specialty sales group began working with leading institutional food-service distributors, including SYSCO Corporation and US Foodservice, to handle the distribution of Starbucks products to hotels, restaurants, office coffee distributors, educational and health care institutions, and other such enterprises. In fiscal 2009, Starbucks generated revenues of $372.2 million from providing whole bean and ground coffees and assorted other Starbucks products to some 21,000 foodservice accounts.

The second initiative came in 1994 when PepsiCo and Starbucks entered into a joint venture arrangement to create new coffee-related products in bottles or cans for mass distribution through Pepsi channels. The joint venture's first new product, a lightly flavored carbonated coffee drink, was a failure. Then, at a meeting with Pepsi executives, Schultz suggested developing a bottled version of Frappuccino, a new cold coffee drink Starbucks began serving at its retail stores in the summer of 1995 that quickly became a big hot weather seller. Pepsi executives were enthusiastic. Sales of Frappuccino ready-to-drink beverages reached $125 million in 1997 and achieved a national supermarket penetration of 80 percent. Sales of ready-to-drink Frappuccino products soon began in Japan, Taiwan, South Korea, and China chiefly through agreements with leading local distributors. In 2010, sales of Frappuccino products worldwide reached $2 billion annually.[10]

In 1995, Starbucks partnered with Dreyer's Grand Ice Cream to supply coffee extracts for a new line of coffee ice cream made and distributed by Dreyer's under the Starbucks brand. Starbucks coffee-flavored ice cream became the number-one-selling super-premium brand in the coffee segment in mid-1996. In 2008, Starbucks discontinued its arrangement with Dreyer's and entered into an exclusive agreement with Unilever to manufacture, market, and distribute Starbucks-branded ice creams in the United States and Canada. Unilever was the global leader in ice cream with annual sales of about $6 billion; its ice cream brands included Ben & Jerry's, Breyers, and Good Humor. There were seven flavors of Starbucks ice cream and two flavors of novelty bars being marketed in 2010, but buyer demand eroded after several years and Starbucks-branded ice cream was discontinued in 2013. However, in 2017, new premium ice cream drinks (a scoop of ice cream drowned in expresso called an "affogato," several other affogato concoctions, and tall cold brew floats and malts) became top-ten menu items at the new Starbucks Roastery and Starbucks Reserve store locations in Seattle and were quickly rolled out to other Reserve locations.

In 1998, Starbucks licensed Kraft Foods to market and distribute Starbucks whole bean and ground coffees in grocery and mass merchandise channels across the United States. Kraft managed all distribution, marketing, advertising, and promotions and paid a royalty to Starbucks based on a percentage of net sales. Product freshness was guaranteed by Starbucks' FlavorLock packaging, and the price per pound paralleled the prices in Starbucks' retail stores. Flavor selections in supermarkets were more limited than the varieties at Starbucks stores. The licensing relationship with Kraft was later expanded to include the marketing and distribution of Starbucks coffees in Canada, the United Kingdom, and other European countries. Going into 2010, Starbucks coffees were available in some 33,500 grocery and warehouse clubs in the United States and 5,500 retail outlets outside the United States; Starbucks' revenues from these sales were approximately $370 million in fiscal 2009.[11] During fiscal 2011, Starbucks discontinued its distribution arrangement with Kraft and instituted its own in-house organization to handle direct sales of packaged coffees to supermarkets and to warehouse club stores (chiefly Costco, Sam's Club, and BJ's Warehouse).

In 1999, Starbucks purchased Tazo Tea for $8.1 million. Tazo Tea, a tea manufacturer and distributor based in Portland, Oregon, was founded in 1994 and marketed its teas to restaurants, food stores, and tea houses. Starbucks proceeded to introduce hot and iced Tazo Tea drinks in its retail stores. As part of a long-term campaign to expand the distribution of its lineup of super-premium Tazo teas, Starbucks expanded its agreement with Kraft to market and distribute Tazo teas worldwide. In August 2008, Starbucks entered into a licensing agreement with a partnership formed by PepsiCo and Unilever (Lipton Tea was one of Unilever's leading brands) to manufacture, market, and distribute Starbucks' super-premium Tazo Tea ready-to-drink beverages (including iced teas, juiced teas, and herbal-infused teas) in the United States and Canada—in 2012, the Pepsi/Lipton Tea partnership was the leading North American distributor of ready-to-drink teas. In fiscal 2011, when Starbucks broke off its packaged coffee distribution arrangement with Kraft, it also broke off its arrangement with Kraft for distribution of Tazo tea and began selling Tazo teas directly to supermarkets (except for Tazo Tea ready-to-drink beverages).

In 2001, Starbucks introduced the Starbucks Card, a reloadable card that allowed customers to pay for their purchases with a quick swipe of their card at the cash register and also to earn "stars" and redeem rewards. Since then, Starbucks Rewards™ had evolved into one of the best retail loyalty programs in existence, aided by the introduction of Starbucks Gift Cards, the Starbucks mobile app, rewards for in-store purchases, and purchases of Starbucks products in grocery stores and other retail locations where Starbucks products were sold. Rewards members earned two stars for every $1 spent on purchases; cardmembers also had the opportunity to take advantage of monthly "Double-Star Day" promotions. In April 2019, Starbucks shifted from a two-tier reward structure (green star and gold star status) to a single-tier rewards structure where the various benefits/perks were linked to having earned 25, 50, 150, 250, and 400 stars. Users of the Starbucks app could easily see how many stars they currently had, place orders and make payments right from their phone, and find the nearest Starbucks location. Members with a Starbucks Rewards™ Visa® Card also earned one star for every $4 purchased with the Starbucks Visa card. When members reloaded a registered Starbucks Card using their Starbucks Rewards™ Visa® Card on the mobile app or Starbucks.com, they received one star for every dollar loaded in addition to the two stars earned for every dollar spent when using a registered Starbucks Card or the Starbucks mobile app for purchases in participating Starbucks stores. As of April 2019, there were 16.3 million active Starbuck Rewards™ members globally. Use of Starbucks Reward cards accounted for 40 percent of transactions in company-operated stores in the United States, and about 75 percent of Starbucks customers in North America either used a Starbucks Card or the Starbuck mobile app to pay for in-store purchases.

In 2003, Starbucks spent $70 million to acquire Seattle's Best Coffee, an operator of 540 Seattle's Best coffee shops and 86 Seattle's Best Coffee Express espresso bars, and marketer of some 30 varieties of Seattle's Best whole bean and ground coffees. The decision was made to operate Seattle's Best as a separate subsidiary. Very quickly, Starbucks expanded its licensing arrangement with Kraft Foods to include marketing, distributing, and promoting the sales of Seattle's Best coffees and by 2009, Seattle's Best coffees were available nationwide in supermarkets and at more than 15,000 foodservice locations (college campuses, restaurants, hotels, airlines, and cruise lines). A new Seattle's Best line of ready-to-drink iced lattes was introduced in April 2010, with

manufacture, marketing, and distribution managed by PepsiCo as part of the long-standing Starbucks–PepsiCo joint venture for ready-to-drink Frappuccino products. In 2010, Starbucks introduced new distinctive red packaging and a red logo for Seattle's Best Coffee, boosted efforts to open more franchised Seattle's Best cafés, and expanded the availability of Seattle's Best coffees to 30,000 distribution points. When Starbucks' licensing agreement with Kraft to handle sales and distribution of Seattle's Best coffee products was terminated in 2011, responsibility for the sales and distribution of Seattle's Best products was transitioned to the same in-house sales force that handled direct sales and distribution of Starbucks-branded coffees and tea products to supermarkets and warehouse clubs.

In 2005, Starbucks Corporation acquired Ethos™ Water, a privately held bottled water company based in Santa Monica, California, whose mission was to help children around the world get clean water by supporting water projects in such developing countries as Bangladesh, the Democratic Republic of Congo, Ethiopia, Honduras, India, and Kenya. One of the terms of the acquisition called for Starbucks to donate $1.25 million in 2005–2006 to support these projects. In the years since the acquisition, a key element of Starbucks' corporate social responsibility effort has been to donate $0.05US ($0.10CN in Canada) for every bottle of Ethos Water sold in Starbucks stores to the Ethos® Water Fund, part of the Starbucks Foundation, to fund ongoing efforts to provide clean water to children in developing countries, and to support water, sanitation, and hygiene education programs in water-stressed countries.

In 2008, Starbucks introduced a new coffee blend called Pike Place™ Roast that would be brewed every day, all day, in every Starbucks store.[12] Before then, Starbucks rotated various coffee blends through its brewed lineup, sometimes switching them weekly, sometimes daily. While some customers liked the ever-changing variety, the feedback from a majority of customers indicated a preference for a consistent brew that customers could count on when they came into a Starbucks store. The Pike Place blend was brewed in small batches at 30-minute intervals so as to provide customers with a freshly brewed coffee. In January 2012, after eight months of testing over 80 different recipe and roast iterations, Starbucks introduced three blends of lighter-bodied and milder-tasting Starbucks Blonde Roast® coffees to better appeal to an estimated 54 million coffee drinkers in the United States who said they liked flavorful, lighter coffees with a gentle finish. The Blonde Roast blends were available as a brewed option in Starbucks stores in the United States and in packaged form in Starbucks stores and supermarkets. Because the majority of coffee sales in supermarkets were in the light and medium roast categories, Starbucks management saw its new Blonde Roast coffee blends as being a $1 billion market opportunity in the United States alone. From time to time, Starbucks introduced new blends of its packaged whole bean and ground coffees—some of these were seasonal, but those that proved popular with buyers became standard offerings.

In fall 2009, Starbucks introduced Starbucks VIA® Ready Brew, packets of roasted coffee in an instant form, in an effort to attract a bigger fraction of on-the-go and at-home coffee drinkers. VIA was made with a proprietary microground technology that produced an instant coffee with a rich, full-bodied taste that closely replicated the taste, quality, and flavor of traditional freshly brewed coffee. Encouraged by favorable customer response, Starbucks expanded the distribution of VIA to some 25,000 grocery, mass merchandise, and drugstore accounts, including Kroger, Safeway, Walmart, Target, Costco, and CVS. Instant coffee made up a significant fraction of coffee purchases in the United Kingdom (80 percent), Japan (53 percent), Russia (85 percent), and several other countries where Starbucks stores were located; globally, the instant and single-serve coffee category was a $23 billion market. By the end of fiscal year 2011, VIA products were available at 70,000 locations and generating annual sales of $250 million.[13]

In fall 2011, Starbucks began selling Starbucks-branded coffee K-Cup® Portion Packs for the Keurig® Single-Cup Brewing system in its retail stores; the Keurig Brewer was produced and sold by Green Mountain Coffee Roasters. Starbucks entered into a strategic partnership with Green Mountain to manufacture the Starbucks-branded portion packs and also to be responsible for marketing, distributing, and selling them to major supermarket chains, drugstore chains, mass merchandisers and wholesale clubs,

department stores, and specialty retailers throughout the United States and Canada. The partnership made good economic sense for both companies. Green Mountain could manufacture the single-cup portion packs in the same plants where it was producing its own brands of single-cup packs and then use its own internal resources and capabilities to market, distribute, and sell Starbucks-branded single-cup packs alongside its own brands of single-cup packs. It was far cheaper for Starbucks to pay Green Mountain to handle these functions than to build its own manufacturing plants and put its own in-house resources in place to market, distribute, and sell Starbucks single-cup coffee packs. Just two months after launch, shipments of Starbucks-branded single-cup portion packs had exceeded 100 million units and the packs were available in about 70 percent of the targeted retailers; company officials estimated that Starbucks had achieved an 11 percent dollar share of the market for single-cup coffee packs in the United States.[14]

In March 2012, Starbucks announced that it would begin selling its first at-home premium single cup espresso and brewed coffee machine, the Verismo™ system by Starbucks, at select Starbucks store locations, online, and in upscale specialty stores. The Verismo brewer was a high-pressure system with the capability to brew both coffee and Starbucks-quality espresso beverages, from lattes to americanos, consistently and conveniently one cup at a time; sales of the Verismo single-cup machine put Starbucks into head-to-head competition with Nestlé's Nespresso machine and, to a lesser extent, Green Mountain's popular lineup of low-pressure Keurig brewers. At the time, the global market for premium at-home espresso/coffee machines was estimated at $8 billion.[15] The Verismo introduction was the last phase of Starbucks' strategic initiative to offer coffee products covering all aspects of the single-cup coffee segment—instant coffees (with its VIA offerings), single portion coffee packs for single-cup brewers, and single-cup brewing machines.

In response to customer requests for more wholesome food and beverage options and also to bring in business from non-coffee drinkers, Starbucks in 2008 altered its menu offerings in stores to include fruit cups, yogurt parfaits, skinny lattes, banana walnut bread, a 300-calorie farmer's market salad with all-natural dressing, and a line of 250-calorie "better-for-you" smoothies.[16] In 2009–2011, the company continued to experiment with healthier, lower-calorie selections and by May 2012, retail store menus included a bigger assortment of hot and cold coffee and tea beverages, pastries and bakery selections, prepared breakfast and lunch sandwiches and wraps, salads, parfaits, smoothies, juices, and bottled water—at most stores in North America, food items could be warmed. A bit later, beer, wine, and other complementary food offerings were added to the menus at some stores to help them become an attractive and relaxing after-work destination. During 2013–2017, it became standard practice for Starbucks to continually tweak its menu offerings, switching out whimsical and limited-edition offerings and adding/dropping certain beverages, flavorings, breakfast items, sandwiches, pastries, and snacks, both to broaden buyer appeal and respond to ongoing shifts in buyer preferences; in 2018–2019, Starbucks began introducing new store menus at the beginning of each season (spring, summer, fall, and winter), along with special holiday menu offerings in November–December. Menu offerings at Starbucks stores were typically adapted to local cultures—for instance, the menu offerings at stores in North America included a selection of muffins, but stores in France had no muffins and instead featured locally made pastries.

Starbucks purchased cold-pressed juice maker Evolution Fresh for $30 million in 2011 to use Starbucks' sales and marketing resources to grow the sales of Evolution Fresh, capture a bigger share of the $3.4 billion super-premium juice segment, and begin a long-term campaign to pursue growth opportunities in the $50 billion health and wellness sector of the U.S. economy. A $70 million juice-making facility in California was opened in 2013 to make Evolution Fresh products. Starbucks also opened four Evolution Fresh juice bars after the acquisition, but in 2017 decided to ditch the standalone juice bar concept, opting to sell Evolution Fresh beverages in Starbucks stores and supermarkets. Evolution Fresh competed with PepsiCo's category leader Naked juice brand, as well as scores of other large and small bottled juice brands. As of 2017, Starbucks had secured 20,000 points of distribution for Evolution Fresh products and the brand was said to be "thriving."

In 2012, Starbuck paid $620 million to acquire Atlanta-based specialty tea retailer Teavana, which sold more than 100 varieties of premium loose-leaf teas and tea-related merchandise through 300 company-owned stores (usually located in upscale shopping malls) and on its website; Teavana teas were used mostly for home consumption. Howard Schultz planned for Starbucks to capitalize on Teavana's world-class tea authority, its passion for tea, and its global sourcing and merchandising capabilities to (a) expand Teavana's domestic and global footprint, (b) bring an elevated tea experience to the patrons of Starbucks domestic and international locations, and (c) increase Starbucks' penetration of the $40 billion world market for tea, especially in the world's high-consumption tea markets where Starbucks had stores. By 2016 and 2017, sales at Teavana stores had eroded to the point where the stores were unprofitable, prompting Starbucks to begin the process of closing all 379 Teavana stores (the majority by spring 2018). However, the sales of Teavana products and beverages in Starbucks stores were popular and contributed to store profitability, accounting for sales of more than $1 billion annually and growing fast enough to double over the next five years. In late 2017, Starbucks sold its Tazo Tea business to Unilever for $384 million, opting to focus its sales of tea products on the Teavana brand. In May 2019, Starbucks began marketing three flavors of Teavana™ Sparkling Craft Iced Teas in all of its stores in the United States; these complemented its other Teavana bottled tea offerings.

Also in 2012, Starbucks bought Bay Bread Group's La Boulange sandwich and coffee shops for $100 million. When Starbucks acquired the San Francisco chain, plans called not only for bringing La Boulange products into its stores to bolster its lineup of pastries and sandwiches but also to open new La Boulange cafes and expand the chain's geographic footprint. Three years later, however, Starbucks concluded that sales at the La Boulange cafes were growing too slowly to support its growth and profitability targets; it closed the 23 existing La Boulange cafes but retained the manufacturing facilities to stock Starbucks stores with La Boulange bakery products. In 2018, the La Boulange brand name was typically not very visible in Starbucks stores but La Boulange–made morning pastries and breakfast sandwiches were still popular sellers during the morning hours when customer traffic at Starbucks stores was high.

Starbucks overall sales mix in its company-owned retail stores in fiscal 2018 was 74 percent beverages, 20 percent food, 2 percent packaged and single-serve coffees and teas, and 4 percent ready-to-drink beverages, coffee-making equipment, and other merchandise.[17] However, the product mix in each Starbucks store varied, depending on the size and location of each outlet. Larger stores carried a greater variety of whole coffee beans, gourmet food items, teas, coffee mugs, coffee grinders, coffee-making equipment, filters, storage containers, and other accessories. Smaller stores and kiosks typically sold a full line of coffee and tea beverages, a limited selection of whole bean and ground coffees and Teavana teas, and a few coffee-drinking accessories.

Starbucks' Consumer Products Group

In 2010, Starbucks formed a new Consumer Products Group (CPG) to be responsible for sales of Starbucks products sold in all channels other than Starbucks' company-operated and licensed retail stores and to manage the company's partnerships and joint ventures with PepsiCo, Unilever, Green Mountain Coffee Roasters, and others. A few years later, CPG was renamed and slightly reorganized into what was called the Channel Development segment. In 2018, management of the Channel Development segment was responsible for sales and distribution of roasted whole bean and ground coffees, Starbucks-branded single-serve products, a variety of ready-to-drink beverages (such as Frappuccino®, Starbucks Doubleshot® and Starbucks Refreshers® beverages), Evolution juices, and other branded products sold worldwide through grocery stores, warehouse clubs, specialty retailers, convenience stores, and U.S. foodservice accounts. This segment accounted for sales of $2.3 billion and operating income of $927.1 million in fiscal year 2018, up from revenues of $707.4 million and operating income of $261.4 million in fiscal year 2010. Starbucks executives considered that the sales opportunities for Starbucks products in distribution channels outside Starbucks retail stores were quite attractive from the standpoint of both long-term growth and profitability. On August 26, 2018, Starbucks' Channel Development segment finalized licensing and distribution agreements with Nestlé S.A. ("Nestlé") to sell and market the company's consumer packaged goods and foodservice products and received an up-front prepaid royalty payment of approximately $7 billion.

Advertising

Starbucks spent sparingly on advertising, preferring instead to build the brand cup by cup with customers and depend on word of mouth and the appeal of its storefronts. However, Starbucks opted to significantly step up its advertising to combat the strategic initiatives of McDonald's and several other fast-food chains in 2008–2009 to begin offering premium coffees and coffee drinks at prices below those charged by Starbucks. In 2009, McDonald's reportedly spent more than $100 million on television, print, radio, billboard, and online ads promoting its new line of McCafé coffee drinks. Starbucks countered with the biggest advertising campaign the company had ever undertaken, spending a total of $176.2 million in fiscal 2010 versus $126.3 million the prior year.[18] The company's advertising expenses totaled $260.3 million in fiscal 2018, $282.6 million in 2017, $248.6 million in fiscal 2016, and $227.9 million in fiscal 2015.

Howard Schultz's Efforts to Make Starbucks a Great Place to Work, 1988–2018

Howard Schultz deeply believed that Starbucks' success was heavily dependent on customers having a very positive experience in its stores. This meant having store employees who were knowledgeable about the company's products, who paid attention to detail in preparing the company's espresso drinks, who eagerly communicated the company's passion for coffee, and who possessed the skills and personality to deliver consistent, pleasing customer service. Many of the baristas were in their 20s and worked part-time, going to college on the side or pursuing other career activities. Schultz viewed the company's challenge as one of attracting, motivating, and rewarding store employees in a manner that would make Starbucks a company that people would want to work for and that would generate enthusiastic commitment and higher levels of customer service. Moreover, Schultz wanted to send all Starbucks employees a message that would cement the trust that had been building between management and the company's workforce.

Instituting Health Care Coverage for All Employees

One of the requests that employees had made to the prior owners of Starbucks back in the 1980s was to extend health care benefits to part-time workers. Their request had been turned down, but Schultz believed that expanding health care coverage to include part-timers was something the company needed to do. He knew from having grown up in a family that struggled to make ends meet how difficult it was to cope with rising medical costs. In 1988, Schultz went to the board of directors with his plan to expand the company's health care coverage to include part-timers who worked at least 20 hours per week. He saw the proposal not as a generous gesture but as a core strategy to win employee loyalty and commitment to the company's mission. Board members resisted because the company was then unprofitable and the added costs of the extended coverage would only worsen the company's bottom line. But Schultz argued passionately that it was the right thing to do and wouldn't be as expensive as it seemed. He observed that if the new benefit reduced turnover, which he believed was likely, then it would reduce the costs of hiring and training—which equaled about $3,000 per new hire. He further pointed out that it cost $1,500 a year to provide an employee with full benefits. Part-timers, he argued, were vital to Starbucks, constituting two-thirds of the company's workforce. Many were baristas who knew the favorite drinks of regular customers; if the barista left, that connection with the customer was broken. Moreover, many part-time employees were called upon to open the stores early, sometimes at 5:30 or 6 a.m.; others had to work until closing, usually 9 p.m. or later. Providing these employees with health care benefits, he argued, would signal that the company honored their value and contribution.

The board approved Schultz's plan and part-timers working 20 or more hours were offered the same health coverage as full-time employees starting in late 1988. Starbucks paid 75 percent of an employee's health care premium; the employee paid 25 percent. Over the years, Starbucks extended its health coverage to include preventive care, prescription drugs, dental care, eye care, mental health, and chemical dependency. Coverage was also offered for unmarried partners in a committed relationship. Since most Starbucks employees were young and comparatively healthy, the company had been able to provide broader coverage while keeping monthly payments relatively low.

A Stock Option Plan for Employees

By 1991, the company's profitability had improved to the point where Schultz could pursue a stock option plan for all employees, a program he believed would have a positive, long-term effect on the success of Starbucks.[19] Schultz wanted to turn every Starbucks employee into a partner, give them a chance to share in the success of the company, and make clear the connection between their contributions and the company's market value. Even though Starbucks was still a private company, the plan that emerged called for granting stock options to every full-time and part-time employee in proportion to their base pay. In May 1991, the plan, dubbed Bean Stock, was presented to the board. Though board members were concerned that increasing the number of shares might unduly dilute the value of the shares of investors who had put up hard cash, the plan received unanimous approval. The first grant was made in October 1991, just after the end of the company's fiscal year in September; each partner was granted stock options worth 12 percent of base pay. When the Bean Stock program was initiated, Starbucks dropped the term "employee" and began referring to all of its people as "partners" because every member of the Starbucks workforce became eligible for stock option awards after six months of employment and 500 paid work hours.

Starbucks went public in June 1992, selling its initial offering at a price of $17 per share. Starting in October 1992 and continuing through October 2004, Starbucks granted each eligible employee a stock option award with a value equal to 14 percent of base pay. Beginning in 2005, the plan was modified to tie the size of each employee's stock option awards to three factors: (1) Starbucks' success and profitability for the fiscal year, (2) the size of an employee's base wages, and (3) the price at which the stock option could be exercised. Since becoming a public company, Starbucks stock had split 2-for-1 on six occasions. Performance-based stock awards to employees totaled about 5 million shares in fiscal 2017; these shares had an average value of $54.30 on the date of the grant and vested in two equal annual installments beginning two years from the grant date.

Starbucks' Stock Purchase Plan for Employees

In 1995, Starbucks implemented an employee stock purchase plan that gave partners who had been employed for at least 90 days an opportunity to purchase company stock through regular payroll deductions. Partners who enrolled could devote anywhere from 1 to 10 percent of their base earnings (up to an annual maximum of $25,000) to purchasing shares of Starbucks stock. After the end of each calendar quarter, each participant's contributions were used to buy Starbucks stock at a discount of 5 percent of the closing price on the last business day of each calendar quarter (until March 2009, the discount was 15 percent). Roughly 30 percent of Starbucks partners participated in the stock purchase plan during the 2000–2011 period. Participation has eroded in the past three fiscal years due to Starbucks' flat stock price performance since October 2015. In fiscal 2018, about 600,000 shares were purchased under this plan.

The Workplace Environment

Starbucks management believed its competitive pay scales and comprehensive benefits for both full-time and part-time partners (employees) allowed it to attract motivated people with above-average skills and good work habits. An employee's base pay was determined by the pay scales prevailing in the geographic region where an employee worked and by the person's job, skills, experience, and job performance. About 90 percent of Starbucks' partners were full-time or part-time baristas, paid on an hourly basis. In 2019, after six months of employment, baristas at company-owned stores in the United States could expect to earn $11–$12 per hour, according to ZipRecruiter;

the national average pay for Starbucks baristas in 2019 was $460 per week.[20] Hourly-paid shift supervisors earned about $13–$14 an hour; store managers earned about $50,000, and salaries for district managers were in the $75,000 to $85,000 range.[21]

Starbucks was named to *Fortune*'s list of the "100 Best Companies to Work For" 14 times during the 1988–2019 period. Surveys of Starbucks partners conducted by *Fortune* magazine in the course of selecting companies for inclusion on its annual list indicated that full-time baristas liked working at Starbucks because of the camaraderie, while part-timers were particularly pleased with the health insurance benefits.[22]

Schultz's approach to offering employees good compensation and a comprehensive benefits package was driven by his belief that sharing the company's success with the people who made it happen helped everyone think and act like an owner, build positive long-term relationships with customers, and do things in an efficient way. Schultz's rationale, based on his father's experience of going from one low-wage, no-benefits job to another, was that if you treat your employees well, that is how they will treat customers.

Exhibit 3 summarizes Starbucks' fringe benefit package.

Employee Training and Recognition

To accommodate its strategy of rapid store expansion, Starbucks put in systems to recruit, hire, and train baristas and store managers. Starbucks' vice president for human resources used some simple guidelines in screening candidates for new positions: "We want passionate people who love coffee. . . .We're looking for a diverse workforce, which reflects our community. We want people who enjoy what they're doing and for whom work is an extension of themselves."[23]

Every partner/barista hired for a retail job in a Starbucks store received at least 24 hours' training in their first two to four weeks. Training topics included coffee history, drink preparation, coffee knowledge, customer service, and retail skills, plus a four-hour workshop on "Brewing the Perfect Cup." Baristas spent considerable time learning about beverage preparation—grinding the beans, steaming milk, learning to pull perfect (18- to 23-second) shots of

EXHIBIT 3

Starbucks' Fringe Benefit Program, 2019

- Medical, dental, and vision coverage.
- Sick pay, up to 40 hours per year.
- Paid vacations (up to 120 hours annually for hourly workers with 5 or more years of service at retail stores and up to 200 hours annually for salaried and non-retail hourly employees with 10 or more years of service).
- Seven paid holidays.
- One paid personal day every six months for salaried and non-retail hourly partners only.
- Mental health and chemical dependency coverage.
- 401(k) retirement savings plan—partners age 18 or older with 90 days of service were eligible to contribute from 1% to 75% of their pay each pay period (up to the annual IRS dollar limit--$18,500 for calendar year 2018). Partners age 50 and older had a higher IRS annual limit ($24,500 for calendar year 2018). Starbucks matched 100% of the first 5% of eligible pay contributed each pay period. Starbucks' matching contributions to the 401(k) plans worldwide totaled $111.7 million in fiscal 2018 and $101.4 million in fiscal 2017.
- Short- and long-term disability.
- Stock purchase plan—eligible employees could buy shares at a 5 percent discount through regular payroll deductions of between 1 and 10 percent of base pay.
- Life insurance coverage equal to annual base pay for salaried and non-retail employees; coverage equal to $5,000 for store employees. Supplemental coverage could be purchased in flat dollar amounts of $10,000, $25,000, and $45,000.
- Short-term disability coverage (partial replacement of lost wages/income for 26 weeks, after a short waiting period); hourly employees can purchase long-term disability coverage.
- Company-paid long-term disability coverage for salaried and non-retail employees.
- Accidental death and dismemberment insurance.
- Adoption assistance. Reimbursement of up to $10,000 to help pay for qualified expenses related to the adoption of an eligible child.
- Financial assistance program for employees that experience a financial crisis.
- Stock option plan (Bean stock). Shares were granted to eligible partners, subject to the company's achievement of specified performance targets and the employee's continued employment through the vesting period. Vesting occurred in two equal annual installments beginning two years from the grant date. The company's board of directors determined how many shares were to be granted each year and also established the specified performance targets. About 9.5 million shares were granted in fiscal year 2018.
- Pre-tax payroll deductions for work-related commuter expenses.
- A free coffee or tea product each week.
- An in-store discount of 30% on purchases of beverages, food, and merchandise.
- A college achievement plan featuring full tuition reimbursement every semester for employees enrolled in Arizona State University's top ranked online degree programs. As of March 2018, some 1,282 Starbucks employees had graduated and over 10,000 were currently working toward their degrees.
- Gift-matching benefits—Starbucks matched up to $1,500 per fiscal year for individual contributions of money or volunteer time to eligible nonprofit organizations.

Source: Information in the Careers section at www.starbucks.com, accessed May 28, 2019; and company 2018 10-K Report, pp. 80–82.

espresso, memorizing the recipes of all the different drinks, practicing making the different drinks, and learning how to customize drinks to customer specifications. There were sessions on cash register operations, how to clean the milk wand on the espresso machine, explaining the Italian drink names to unknowing customers, making eye contact with customers and interacting with them, and taking personal responsibility for the cleanliness of the store. And there were rules to be memorized: Milk must be steamed to at least 150 degrees Fahrenheit but never more than 170 degrees; every espresso shot not pulled within 23 seconds must be tossed; never let coffee sit in the pot more than 20 minutes; always compensate dissatisfied customers with a Starbucks coupon that entitles them to a free drink.

There were also training programs for shift supervisors, assistant store managers, store managers, and district managers that went much deeper, covering not only coffee knowledge and information imparted to baristas but also the details of store operations, practices and procedures as set forth in the company's operating manual, information systems, and the basics of managing people. In addition, there were special career development programs, such as a coffee masters program for store employees and more advanced leadership skills training for shift supervisors and store management personnel. When Starbucks opened stores in a new market, it sent a Star team of experienced managers and baristas to the area to lead the store opening effort and to conduct one-on-one training following the basic orientation and training sessions.

To recognize and reward partner contributions, Starbucks had created a partner recognition program consisting of 18 different awards and programs.[24] Examples included Partner of the Quarter Awards (for one partner per store per quarter) for significant contributions to their store and demonstrating behaviors consistent with the company's mission and values; Spirit of Starbucks awards for making exceptional contributions to partners, customers, and community while embracing the company's mission and values; a Manager of the Quarter for store manager leadership; Green Apron Awards where partners could recognize fellow partners for how they bring to life the company's mission, values, and customer commitment; and Bravo and Team Bravo! awards for above and beyond the call of duty performance and achieving exceptional results.

Starbucks' Mission, Business Principles, and Values

During the early building years, Howard Schultz and other Starbucks senior executives worked to instill some values and guiding principles into the Starbucks culture. The cornerstone value in their effort "to build a company with soul" was that the company would never stop pursuing the perfect cup of coffee by buying the best beans and roasting them to perfection. Schultz was adamant about controlling the quality of Starbucks products and building a culture common to all stores. He was rigidly opposed to selling artificially flavored coffee beans—"we will not pollute our high-quality beans with chemicals"; if a customer wanted hazelnut-flavored coffee, Starbucks would provide it by adding hazelnut syrup to the drink, rather than by adding hazelnut flavoring to the beans during roasting. Running flavored beans through the grinders left chemical residues behind that altered the flavor of beans ground afterward.

Starbucks' management was also emphatic about the importance of employees paying attention to what pleased customers. Employees were trained to go out of their way, and to take heroic measures if necessary, to make sure customers were fully satisfied. The theme was "just say yes" to customer requests. Further, employees were encouraged to speak their minds without fear of retribution from upper management—senior executives wanted employees to be vocal about what Starbucks was doing right, what it was doing wrong, and what changes were needed. The intent was for employees to be involved in and contribute to the process of making Starbucks a better company.

Starbucks' Mission Statement

In early 1990, the senior executive team at Starbucks went to an offsite retreat to debate the company's values and beliefs and draft a mission statement. Schultz wanted the mission statement to convey a strong sense of organizational purpose and to articulate the company's fundamental beliefs and guiding principles. The draft was submitted to all employees for review and several changes were made based on employee comments. The resulting mission statement and guiding principles are shown in Exhibit 4. In 2008, Starbucks partners from all across the company met for several months to refresh the mission statement and rephrase the underlying guiding principles; the revised mission statement and guiding principles are also shown in Exhibit 4.

In 2019, Starbucks' stated values were:

- Creating a culture of warmth and belonging, where everyone is welcome.

- Acting with courage, challenging the status quo and finding new ways to grow our company and each other.

EXHIBIT 4

Starbucks' Mission Statement and Business Principles

Mission Statement, 1990–October 2008

Establish Starbucks as the premier purveyor of the finest coffee in the world while maintaining our uncompromising principles as we grow.

The following six guiding principles will help us measure the appropriateness of our decisions:

- Provide a great work environment and treat each other with respect and dignity.
- Embrace diversity as an essential component in the way we do business.
- Apply the highest standards of excellence to the purchasing, roasting, and fresh delivery of our coffee.
- Develop enthusiastically satisfied customers all of the time.
- Contribute positively to our communities and our environment.
- Recognize that profitability is essential to our future success.*

Mission Statement, October 2008–Present

Our Mission: To inspire and nurture the human spirit—one person, one cup, and one neighborhood at a time.**

Here are the principles of how we live that every day:

Our Coffee

It has always been, and will always be, about quality. We're passionate about ethically sourcing the finest coffee beans, roasting them with great care, and improving the lives of people who grow them. We care deeply about all of this; our work is never done.**

Our Partners

We're called partners, because it's not just a job, it's our passion. Together, we embrace diversity to create a place where each of us can be ourselves. We always treat each other with respect and dignity. And we hold each other to that standard.**

Our Customers

When we are fully engaged, we connect with, laugh with, and uplift the lives of our customers—even if just for a few moments. Sure, it starts with the promise of a perfectly made beverage, but our work goes far beyond that. It's really about human connection.**

Our Stores

When our customers feel this sense of belonging, our stores become a haven, a break from the worries outside, a place where you can meet with friends. It's about enjoyment at the speed of life—sometimes slow and savored, sometimes faster. Always full of humanity.**

Our Neighborhood

Every store is part of a community, and we take our responsibility to be good neighbors seriously. We want to be invited in wherever we do business. We can be a force for positive action—bringing together our partners, customers, and the community to contribute every day. Now we see that our responsibility—and our potential for good—is even larger. The world is looking to Starbucks to set the new standard, yet again. We will lead.**

Our Shareholders

We know that as we deliver in each of these areas, we enjoy the kind of success that rewards our shareholders. We are fully accountable to get each of these elements right so that Starbucks—and everyone it touches—can endure and thrive.**

---

* Starbucks Coffee Company. "Fiscal 2003 Annual Report" Accessed June 19, 2019. https://globalassets.starbucks.com/assets/e31d4604b78141bfb13172aa5fd67cfa.pdf

** Starbucks Coffee Company. "Our Starbucks Mission Statement" Accessed June 09, 2019. http://www.starbucks.in/about-us/company-information/mission-statement.

- Being present, connecting with transparency, dignity, and respect.
- Delivering our best in all we do, holding ourselves accountable for results.
- We are performance-driven, through the lens of humanity.

In addition to being expected to live by the company's values, all Starbucks personnel were expected to conform to the highest standards of ethical conduct and to take all legal and ethical responsibilities seriously.[25]

Starbucks' Coffee Purchasing Strategy

Coffee beans were grown in 70 tropical countries and were the second most traded commodity in the world after petroleum. Most of the world's coffee was grown by some 25 million small farmers, most of whom lived on the edge of poverty. Starbucks personnel traveled regularly to coffee-producing countries, building relationships with growers and exporters, checking on agricultural conditions and crop yields, and searching out varieties and sources that would meet Starbucks' exacting standards of quality and flavor. The coffee-purchasing group, working with Starbucks personnel in roasting operations, tested new varieties and blends of green coffee beans from different sources. The company's supplies of green coffee beans were chiefly grown on about 1 million small family farms (less than 30 acres) located in the coffee-growing communities of countries across the world. Sourcing from multiple geographic areas not only allowed Starbucks to offer a greater range of coffee varieties to customers but also spread its risks regarding weather, price volatility, and changing economic and political conditions in coffee-growing countries.

Starbucks' coffee sourcing strategy had three key elements:

- Make sure that the prices Starbucks paid for green (unroasted) coffee beans was high enough to ensure that small farmers were able to cover their production costs and provide for their families. The company was firmly committed to a goal of "100 percent ethically sourced coffees"— in 2016 management believed it had reached a milestone of 99 percent ethically sourced coffee.[26] Because the company also purchased tea and cocoa for its stores, it was similarly committed to 100 percent ethically sourced tea and cocoa.

- Utilize purchasing arrangements that limited Starbucks exposure to sudden price jumps due to weather, economic and political conditions in the growing countries, new agreements establishing export quotas, and periodic efforts to bolster prices by restricting coffee supplies.

- Work directly with small coffee growers, local coffee-growing cooperatives, and other types of coffee suppliers to promote coffee cultivation methods that were environmentally sustainable. Starbucks' objective was to "make coffee the world's first sustainable agricultural product."[27]

Pricing and Purchasing Arrangements

Commodity-grade coffee was traded in a highly competitive market as an undifferentiated product. However, high-altitude Arabica coffees of the quality purchased by Starbucks were bought on a negotiated basis at a substantial premium above commodity coffee. The prices of the top-quality coffees sourced by Starbucks depended on supply and demand conditions at the time of the purchase and were subject to considerable volatility due to weather, economic and political conditions in the growing countries, new agreements establishing export quotas, and periodic efforts to bolster prices by restricting coffee supplies.

Starbucks bought coffee using fixed-price and price-to-be-fixed purchase commitments, depending on market conditions, to secure an adequate supply of quality green coffee. Price-to-be-fixed contracts were purchase commitments whereby the quality, quantity, delivery period, and other negotiated terms were agreed upon, but the date at which the base price component of commodity-grade coffee was to be fixed was as yet unspecified. For these types of contracts, either Starbucks or the seller had the option to select a date on which to "fix" the base price of commodity-grade coffee prior to the delivery date. As of October 1, 2018, Starbucks had a total of $1.1 billion in purchase commitments, comprised of $996 million under fixed-price contracts and an estimated $166 million under price-to-be-fixed contracts. All of the price-to-be-fixed contracts gave Starbucks the right to fix the base price component of commodity-grade coffee. Management believed that its purchase agreements as of October 2018, together with its existing inventory, would provide an adequate supply of green coffee through fiscal 2019.[28]

Food products, such as pastries, breakfast sandwiches, and lunch items, were purchased from national, regional, and local sources, as were needed paper and plastic products, such as cups and cutlery. Management believed, based on relationships established with these suppliers and manufacturers, that the risk of nondelivery of sufficient amounts of these items to its various store locations was remote.

Starbucks' Ethical Sourcing Practices for Coffee Beans

Starbucks was committed to buying green coffee beans that were grown in accordance with environmentally sustainable agricultural practices and guaranteed that small coffee growers received prices for their green coffee beans sufficiently high enough to allow them to pay fair wages to their workers, earn enough to reinvest in their farms and communities, develop the business skills needed to compete in the global market for coffee, and afford basic health care, education, and home improvements. To promote achievement of these outcomes, Starbucks operated nine farmer support centers staffed with agronomists and sustainability experts who worked with coffee farming communities to promote best practices in coffee production, implement advanced soil-management techniques, improve both coffee quality and yields, and address climate and other impacts.

Since 1998, Starbucks had partnered with Conservation International's Center for Environmental Leadership to develop specific guidelines (called Coffee and Farmer Equity [C.A.F.E.] Practices) covering four areas: product quality, the price received by farmers/growers, safe and humane working conditions (including compliance with minimum wage

requirements and child labor provisions), and environmentally responsible cultivation practices.[29] Top management at Starbucks set a goal that by 2015 all of the green coffee beans purchased from growers would be C.A.F.E. Practice certified, Fair Trade certified, organically certified, or certified by some other equally acceptable third party. By 2011, 86 percent of Starbucks' purchases of green coffee beans were from C.A.F.E. Practices–verified sources and about 8 percent were from Fair Trade–certified sources, making Starbucks among the world's largest purchasers and marketers of Fair Trade–certified coffee beans. Since 2015, Starbucks coffee had been verified as 99 percent ethically sourced, and the company was committed to reaching its goal of 100 percent.

In September 2015, Starbucks launched the One Tree for Every Bag Commitment, an effort to plant 20 million coffee tree seedlings to replace trees declining in productivity due to age and disease such as coffee leaf rust. The goal was exceeded in just over a year. To build on that success, Starbucks committed to providing a total of 100 million coffee tree seedlings to farmers by 2025, particularly in coffee-growing communities being impacted by climate change.

Small Farmer Support Programs   Because many of the small family farms that grew coffees purchased by Starbucks often lacked the money to make farming improvements and/or cover all expenses until they sold their crops, Starbucks provided funding for loans to small coffee growers. In 2010, $14.6 million was loaned to nearly 56,000 farmers who grew green coffee beans for Starbucks in 10 countries; in 2011, $14.7 million was loaned to over 45,000 farmers who grew green coffee beans for Starbucks in 7 countries. Later, the company established the Starbucks Global Farmer Fund to invest $50 million by 2020 in providing loans to coffee farmers to strengthen their farms through coffee tree renovation and infrastructure improvements. Moreover, the Starbucks Foundation began partnering with organizations with local expertise to award grants to support smallholder-farming families in coffee-growing and tea-growing communities, reaching approximately 47,000 direct and indirect beneficiaries. By 2020 the Foundation planned to reach 200,000 people.

Coffee Roasting Operations

Starbucks considered the roasting of its coffee beans to be something of an art form, entailing trial-and-error testing of different combinations of time and temperature to get the most out of each type of bean and blend. Recipes were put together by the coffee department, once all the components had been tested. Computerized roasters guaranteed consistency. Highly trained and experienced roasting personnel monitored the process, using both smell and hearing, to help check when the beans were perfectly done—coffee beans make a popping sound when ready. Roasting standards were exacting. After roasting and cooling, the coffee was immediately vacuum-sealed in bags that preserved freshness for up to 26 weeks. As a matter of policy, however, Starbucks removed coffees on its shelves after three months and, in the case of coffee used to prepare beverages in stores, the shelf life was limited to seven days after the bag was opened.

In 2018, Starbucks had multiple roasting plants in numerous locations, having expanded its roasting operations as its store base expanded to more geographic regions and countries. Roasting plants also had additional space for warehousing and shipping coffees. In keeping with Starbucks' corporate commitment to reduce its environmental footprint, since 2009 all newly built roasting plants had conformed to LEED (Leadership in Energy and Environment Design) standards devised by the United States Green Building Council; LEED standards were the most widely used green building rating system in the world for evaluating the environmental performance of a building and encouraging market transformation toward sustainable design. Starbucks had launched an initiative to achieve LEED certification for all company-operated facilities by the end of 2010, and facilities constructed prior to 2010 were remodeled and/or retrofitted accordingly.[30]

Starbucks' Corporate Social Responsibility Strategy

Howard Schultz's effort to "build a company with soul" included a long history of doing business in ways that were socially and environmentally responsible. A commitment to do the right thing had been central to how Starbucks operated since Howard Schultz first became CEO in 1987, and one of the core beliefs at Starbucks was that "the way to build a great, enduring company is to strike a balance between profitability and a social conscience."[31] The specific actions comprising Starbucks' social responsibility strategy had varied over the years but the intent of the strategy was consistently one of contributing positively to the communities in which Starbucks had stores, being a good environmental steward, and conducting the company's business in ways that earned the trust and respect of customers, partners/employees, suppliers, and the general public.

In 2019, Starbucks' corporate social responsibility (CSR) strategy had five main elements:

1. *Ethically sourcing all of its products*—This CSR element had two main pieces: (a) all of the company's actions and collaborative efforts in purchasing the company's supplies of coffee, tea, and cocoa that were aimed at providing loans and technical assistance to the small family farms that grew these products, paying prices for these products that improved the living standards and economic well-being of the farmers and their communities, and trying to institute better soil-management and sustainable farming practices; and (b) striving to buy the manufactured products and services it needed from suppliers who not only adhered to strict food safety and product quality standards, and certain Starbucks-specified operating practices, but also signed an agreement pledging compliance with the company's global Supplier Code of Conduct. This code of conduct included:[32]

    *   Demonstrating commitment to the welfare, economic improvement, and sustainability of the people and places that produce products and services for Starbucks.

    *   Adherence to local laws and international standards regarding human rights, workplace safety, and worker compensation and treatment.

    *   Meeting or exceeding national laws and international standards for environmental

protection and minimizing negative environmental impacts of the supplier's operations.

- Commitment to measuring, monitoring, reporting, and verification of compliance to this code.
- Pursuing continuous improvement of these social and environmental principles.

Verification of compliance was subjects to audits by Starbucks personnel or acceptable third parties. From time to time, Starbucks had temporarily or permanently discontinued its business relationship with suppliers who failed to comply or failed to work with Starbucks to correct a non-complying situation.

2. *Community involvement and corporate citizenship*—Active engagement in community activities and display of good corporate citizenship had always been core elements in the way Starbucks conducted its business. Starbucks stores and employees regularly volunteered for community improvement projects and initiatives that would have a meaningful impact on the localities in which Starbucks had a presence. In fiscal 2011 Starbucks sponsored a special global month of service in which more than 60,000 employees in 30 countries volunteered for over 150,000 service hours and completed 1,400 community-service projects; every year since, Starbucks has held a Global Month of Service.

The company had a goal of having 100 percent of its stores worldwide participating in community service projects. Recently, through a strategic alliance with Feeding America, Starbucks had instituted a "food share" program to rescue food that would otherwise spoil in its stores to donate to organizations providing meals to needy families and homeless people. Management estimated that when the program was fully operational in all Starbucks stores that the food donations would help provide 50 million meals per year. As of 2017, some 5 million meals from 2,700 stores had been donated.

3. *Environmental stewardship*—Initiatives here included a wide variety of actions to increase recycling, reduce waste, be more energy efficient, use renewable energy sources, conserve water resources, make all company facilities as green as possible by using environmentally friendly building materials and energy-efficient designs, and engage in more efforts to address climate change. Beginning in January 2011, all new company-owned retail stores globally were built to achieve LEED certification; as of 2017 Starbucks had built more than 1,500 LEED-certified stores in 20 countries. The company's goal was to have 10,000 greener retail stores by 2025. In 2008, Starbucks set a goal of reducing water consumption by 25 percent in company-owned stores by 2015, and after two years had implemented proactive measures that had decreased water use by almost 22 percent. Starbucks had invested in renewable energy since 2005, and it achieved a milestone in 2015 by purchasing the equivalent of 100 percent of the electricity consumption of all company-operated stores worldwide from renewable energy sources, primarily utilizing Renewable Energy Credits from the United States and Canada and through green electricity-supply contracts across Europe. Starbucks was the number one purchaser of renewable electricity in its sector on the EPA's Green Power Partnership National Top 100 list. In North Carolina and Washington State, Starbucks had invested in a solar farm and a wind farm that delivered enough energy to power more than 700 Starbucks stores.

By 2011, nearly 80 percent of company-owned Starbucks stores in North America were recycling cardboard boxes and other back-of-store items; there were front-of-store recycling bins in place in all company-owned locations where there were municipal recycling capabilities (50 percent of company-owned stores in the United States as of year-end 2015). Since 1985, Starbucks had given a $0.10 discount to customers who brought reusable cups and tumblers to stores for use in serving the beverages they ordered. In 2018, a program was in place to double the recycled content, recyclability, and reusability of the cups in which beverages were served by 2022, and an initiative had been launched to empower 10,000 Starbucks employees to be "sustainability champions" by 2020. Stores participated in Earth Day activities each year with in-store promotions and volunteer efforts to educate employees and customers about the impacts their actions had on the environment.

4. *Creating opportunities to help people achieve their dreams*– The chief initiatives here included hiring 100,000 young people aged 16–24 who were disconnected from work and school by 2020, hiring at least 25,000 veterans and military spouses by 2025, welcoming and employing 10,000 refugees across the 75 countries in which Starbucks stores were located by 2022, and expanding partner participation in the company's college achievement plan that covered full-tuition reimbursement for admission to one of Arizona State University's online degree programs. Starbucks had initiated a program to make "Youth Opportunity" grants to support mentoring, work placement, and apprenticeship programs for young people, and in 2017, in partnership with 50 other employers, had committed to hiring, training, and advancing the careers of 100,000 youth aged 16–24 by 2020.

5. *Charitable contributions*–The Starbucks Foundation, set up in 1997, oversaw a major portion of the company's philanthropic activities; it received the majority of its funding from Starbucks Coffee Company and private donations. Over the years, the Starbucks Foundation had made close to 200 grants to nonprofit organizations such as the American Red Cross for relief efforts to communities experiencing severe damage from earthquakes, hurricanes, tornadoes, floods, and other natural disasters, Save the Children for efforts to improve education, health, and nutrition, the Global Fund and Product (RED)™ to provide medicine to people in Africa with AIDS, and a wide assortment of community-building efforts. Donations were made in cash and in-kind contributions. In 2017, the foundation made grants ranging from $10,000 to $100,000 to more than 40 nonprofits in 27 U.S. cities, plus others to various communities across the world.[33]

Water, sanitation, and hygiene education programs in water-stressed countries were supported through the Starbucks Foundation's Ethos Water Fund. For each bottle of Ethos water purchased at Starbucks stores, Starbucks donated $0.05 ($0.10 in Canada) to the Ethos© Water Fund. Since 2005, the Fund had made over $15 million in grants, benefiting more than 500,000 people around the world.

Starbucks had been named to *Corporate Responsibility Magazine*'s list of the 100 Best Corporate Citizens on numerous occasions; this list was based on more than 360 data points of publicly available information in seven categories: Environment, Climate Change, Human Rights, Philanthropy, Employee Relations, Financial Performance, and Governance. Over the years, Starbucks had received over 25 awards from a diverse group of organizations for its philanthropic, community service, and environmental activities.

An Embarrassing Incident at a Starbucks Store In April 2018, Starbucks suffered a public relations disaster when a Starbucks manager in Philadelphia called the police a few minutes after two black men arrived at a store and sat waiting for a friend. They had not yet purchased anything when the police were called. After police arrived, they arrested the two men. Social media erupted and the incident was widely covered by the media. After investigating what happened, Starbucks determined that insufficient support and training, bias, and a company policy that defined customers as paying patrons—versus anyone who enters a store—led to the decision to call the police. Starbucks' president met with the two men to express the company's apologies, reconcile, and commit to actions to reaffirm the company's mission and enduring values to create a welcoming environment. The company further decided to close more than 8,000 company stores for three hours on the afternoon of May 29 to conduct bias awareness training for 175,000 Starbucks partners, share life experiences, listen to experts, reflect on the realities of bias in society, and talk about how to create store spaces where everyone would feel like they belong.

Top Management Changes: Changing Roles for Howard Schultz

In 2000, Howard Schultz decided to relinquish his role as CEO, retain his position as chairman of the company's board of directors, and assume the newly created role of chief strategic officer. Orin Smith, a Starbucks executive who had been with the company since its early days, was named CEO. Smith retired in 2005 and was replaced as CEO by Jim Donald who had been president of Starbucks' North American division. In 2006, Donald proceeded to set a long-term objective of having 40,000 stores worldwide and launched a program of rapid store expansion in an effort to achieve that goal.

But investors and members of Starbucks' board of directors (including Howard Schultz) became uneasy about Donald's leadership of the company when the company's stock price drifted downward through much of 2007, customer traffic in Starbucks stores in the United States began to erode in 2007, and Donald kept pressing for increased efficiency in store operations at the expense of good customer service. In January 2008, the Starbucks board asked Howard Schultz to return to his role as CEO and lead a major restructuring and revitalization initiative.

Schultz immediately revamped the company's executive leadership team and changed the roles and responsibilities of several key executives.[34] Believing that Starbucks had become less passionate about customer relationships and the coffee experience that had fueled the company's success, Schultz hired a former Starbucks executive to fill the newly created position of chief creative officer responsible for elevating the in-store experience of customers and achieving new levels of innovation and differentiation. He then proceeded to launch a series of actions to recast Starbucks into the company he envisioned it ought to be, push the company to new plateaus of differentiation and innovation, and prepare for renewed global expansion of Starbucks' retail store network. This transformation effort, which instantly became the centerpiece of his return as company CEO, had three main themes: strengthen the core, elevate the experience, and invest and grow.

In 2010, as part of Schultz's "invest and grow" aspect of transforming Starbucks, the company began formulating plans to open "thousands of new stores" in China over time.[35] Japan had long been Starbucks' biggest foreign market outside North America, but Howard Schultz stated, "Asia clearly represents the most significant growth opportunity on a go-forward basis."[36] Schultz's transformation effort was a resounding success, with more than 10,000 stores being opened during fiscal years 2011–2017 and impressive gains in revenues and profits. During fiscal 2018, Starbucks was opening stores in China at the rate of 1 every 15 hours; headed into June 2018, the company had more than 3,300 stores across 141 cities in China and was serving more than 6.4 million customers a week. Shanghai alone had over 600 Starbucks stores, more than any other city in the world. Starbucks' goal was to have 5,000 stores in China by 2021.

In April 2017, following a December 2016 announcement, Howard Schultz officially stepped down as Starbucks CEO, turning the role over to Kevin Johnson, Starbucks chief operating officer with whom Schultz had worked closely for the past two years–they had adjoining offices connected by a door and usually visited together multiple times a day. Shultz stayed on as chairman of the company's board of directors and focused his time on social initiatives and plans for the upscale Roastery Reserve brand. Schultz exuded confidence that Johnson was the right person to lead Starbucks in the future and that he was well prepared to meet the challenges of continuing to build the Starbucks brand, enhance the consumer experience, and manage its global operations.

Then, in a surprise announcement on June 4, 2018, Schultz at the age of 64 announced that he was resigning as Starbucks executive chairman and member of the board of directors effective June 26, thus ending his career at Starbucks. According to Starbucks, his honorary title would be chairman emeritus. In interviews with the media, Schultz indicated that he would be writing a book and exploring a number of options from philanthropy to public service. There was immediate speculation that he would run for president of the United States in 2020; on numerous occasions, he had expressed his disagreement with many policies of the Trump Administration. In early 2019, Schultz announced his intentions to run for president as an independent.

Luckin Coffee's Sudden Emergence as a Local Competitor to Challenge Starbucks in China

China-based Luckin Coffee began operations in October 2017, and by March 31, 2019, had opened an astonishing 2,370 wholly owned locations in 28 cities—a blitz rarely seen in the retail or restaurant industries. The company's strategic intent was to become the largest network of coffee stores in China by the end of 2019—plans called for opening 2,500 more locations in the remaining months of 2019. Starbucks currently had approximately 3,900 stores in China in April 2019, and planned to add about 375 by the end of the calendar year.

In 2018, its first full year of operation, Luckin Coffee used aggressive promotions and coupons offering price discounts to achieve revenues of $125.3 million on which it reported a loss of $241.3 million. For the three months ending March 31, 2019, Luckin reported revenues of $71.3 million and a net loss of $82.2 million. Revenues during the first three months of 2019 were derived from the sale of freshly brewed drinks (75.4 percent), other products (17.6 percent), and "other" (7.0 percent). The company reported in April 2019 that it had achieved a total of 16.8 million customer ransactions since inception and sold some 90 million items in 2018. Its customer repurchase rate in 2018 was just over 54 percent.

Some 2,163 of Luckin Coffee's stores (91 percent) were "pickup stores" with limited seating and were typically located in areas with high demand for coffee (office buildings, commercial areas, and university campuses); the company also had 109 "relax stores" and 98 delivery kitchens. Luckin had created mobile apps covering the entire customer purchase process, enabling it to offer app users a 100 percent cashier-free option. Luckin Coffee sourced premium Arabica coffee beans from prominent suppliers and engaged World Barista Champion teams to design its coffee recipes. Its coffee had won the Gold Medal in the 2018 IIAC International Coffee Tasting Championship. The company purchased coffee machines, coffee condiments, juices, and assorted food products that were sold in its stores from reputable outside vendors at what Luckin management believed were favorable prices. Luckin had 16,645 employees as of March 31, 2019.

On April 17, 2019, Luckin Coffee filed documents with the Securities and Exchange Commission stating its desire to undertake an initial public offering (IPO) of common stock and become a public company, with its stock trading on the NASDAQ under the symbol LK. In its IPO filing, Luckin Coffee management cited four company strengths as contributing to its initial success:

- Being the leading and fastest growing player driving coffee consumption in China.
- Being the pioneer of a disruptive new retail model.
- Having strong technology capabilities.
- Offering a superior customer proposition underpinned by high quality, high affordability, and high convenience.

In May 2019, the company's IPO application received SEC approval, and Luckin quickly moved forward with its IPO. Luckin priced its IPO issue at $17 per share and raised $561 million on an upsized offering of 33 million shares, making it one of the fastest companies ever to reach a $6 billion valuation (based on all the preferred and common shares outstanding). Its common stock began trading May 17, 2019, with initial trades around $25 per share; however, the share price began a downward trend in the latter stages of the first day's trading session and closed at $20.36. By the fourth trading day, the share price had fallen under the initial offer price of $17 and, during the next five trading days, the share price ranged from $13.71 to $16.32. But the price stabilized over the next five weeks, hovering in the $18 to $19.50 range, as investors waited to see whether and how fast the company could move toward becoming profitable.

ENDNOTES

[1] Howard Schultz and Dori Jones Yang, *Pour Your Heart Into It* (New York: Hyperion, 1997), p. 34.

[2] Ibid., p. 36.

[3] Ibid., pp. 61–62.

[4] Ibid., pp. 101–102.

[5] Howard Schultz, *Pour Your Heart Into It: How Starbucks Built a Company One Cup at a Time*, Hachette UK Limited, 2012.

[6] Ibid., p. 142.

[7] Ibid.

[8] "Starbucks Plans New Global Store Design," *Restaurants and Institutions*, June 25, 2009, accessed at www.rimag.com on December 29, 2009.

[9] Starbucks Global Responsibility Report for 2009, p. 13.

[10] As stated by Howard Schultz in an interview with *Harvard Business Review* editor-in-chief Adi Ignatius; the interview was published in the July–August 2010 issue of the *Harvard Business Review,* pp. 108–115.

[11] 2009 Annual Report, p. 5.

[12] Company press release, April 7, 2008.

[13] Company press release, April 13, 2010.

[14] Company press release, January 26, 2012.

[15] Starbucks management presentation at UBS Global Consumer Conference, March 14, 2012, accessed at www.starbucks.com on May 18, 2012.

[16] Company press release, July 14, 2008.

[17] 2018 10-K Report, p. 4.

[18] Claire Cain Miller, "New Starbucks Ads Seek to Recruit Online Fans," *The New York Times,* May 18, 2009, accessed at www.nytimes.com on January 3, 2010.

[19] As related in Schultz and Yang, *Pour Your Heart Into It,* pp. 131–136.

[20] Information posted at www.ziprecruiter.com, May 28, 2019.

[21] Data posted at www.glassdoor.com, accessed May 28, 2019.

[22] Company news release, May 21, 2009, accessed at www.starbucks.com on June 14, 2010.

[23] Kate Rounds, "Starbucks Coffee," *Incentive*, Vol. 167, No. 7, p. 22.

[24] Information posted at www.sbuxrecognition.com, accessed June 1, 2018.

[25] Posted at https://www.starbucks.com/careers/working-at-starbucks/culture-and-values, accessed June 19, 2019.

[26] *Starbucks 2016 Global Social Impact Performance Report,* p. 4.

[27] Ibid.

[28] 2018 10-K Report, p. 7.

[29] Information posted in the corporate responsibility section at www.starbucks.com, accessed June 18, 2010.

[30] Company press release, February 19, 2009.

[31] Starbucks Coffee Company, "Our Mission," accessed June 09, 2019, https://www.starbucks.com/about-us/company-information/mission-statement.

[32] Information on "Doing Business with Starbucks," posted at www.starbucks.com/business/suppliers, accessed June 5, 2018.

[33] Information posted at www.starbucks.com/responsibility/community/starbucks-foundation, accessed June 5, 2018

[34] Transcript of Starbucks Earnings Conference Call for Quarters 1 and 3 of fiscal year 2008, posted at http://seekingalpha.com and accessed June 16, 2010.

[35] Mariko Sanchanta, "Starbucks Plans Major China Expansion," *The Wall Street Journal,* April 13, 2010, accessed at http://online.wsj.com on June 10, 2010.

[36] Ibid.

PROFITING FROM PAIN: BUSINESS AND THE U.S. OPIOID EPIDEMIC

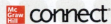

ANNE T. LAWRENCE *San Jose State University*

In 2017, McKesson Corporation, a leading whole-sale drug distributor, agreed to pay $150 million in fines to the U.S. Department of Justice. The charges were that the company had failed to implement effective controls to prevent the diversion of prescription opioids for nonlegitimate uses, in violation of the Controlled Substances Act.[1] For example, McKesson had supplied pharmacies in Mingo County, West Virginia—a poor, rural county with the fourth-highest death rate from opioid overdoses in the nation, with 3.3 million more hydrocodone pills in one year than it had in five consecutive earlier years.[2] At the time, Mingo County had just 25,000 residents. Yet, the company had not flagged these orders to federal drug enforcement officials as out-of-the-ordinary.

McKesson, which at the time was the fifth-largest company in the United States—with almost $200 billion in annual revenue—played a largely unnoticed middleman role in the pharmaceutical industry. The firm's main business was shipping legal, government-approved medicines to pharmacies, hospitals, and health systems. McKesson's unmarked trucks rolled out at midnight from its 28 enormous, highly automated distribution centers, en route to their morning deliveries of one-third of all pharmaceuticals sold in North America. Although distributors like McKesson did not either manufacture or dispense opioids, they were responsible for notifying the federal Drug Enforcement Administration (DEA) and corresponding state regulators if orders suggested that controlled substances were being improperly diverted.[3]

McKesson and other drug distributors were not the only businesses implicated in the nation's burgeoning epidemic of addictive opioids. Drug companies—such as Purdue Pharma, the maker of OxyContin—had developed new prescription opioids and aggressively marketed them to doctors and patients, making vast profits for their owners. Entrepreneurs had opened pain clinics where unscrupulous doctors could write big scripts for the addictive pills, and pharmacies had looked the other way while dispensing drugs to suspicious patients. And illegal businesses, from producers of street drugs like heroin to networks of dealers, had also played their parts. What responsibility did these businesses bear for the tragedy of opioid addiction, disability, and death?

The Opioid Epidemic

At the time of McKesson's settlement with the Justice Department, the United States was deep in the throes of what the Centers for Disease Control and Prevention (CDC) had called "the worst drug overdose epidemic in [U.S.] history."[4]

Fueling the epidemic was addiction to prescription opioids. Opioids were a class of painkillers derived from the opium poppy. Also referred to as narcotics, opioids included legal prescription medications such as morphine, codeine, hydrocodone, oxycodone, and fentanyl, as well as illegal drugs such as heroin. Opioids worked by dulling the sensation of pain. At high doses, they could also cause feelings of intense euphoria. The journalist John Temple, author

of the investigative report *American Pain,* described the "high" experienced by users of oxycodone, a strong opioid, this way:

> To understand oxycodone, imagine everything that makes a man or woman feel good, all the pre-occupations and pastimes we are programmed to enjoy. Sex, love, food. Money, power, health. Synthesize all of that pleasure-seeking potency, and multiply by ten. Then cram it all into a pebble-sized blue pill. That's oxycodone—one of the most irresistible opioid narcotics ever cooked up in the six-thousand-year-old history of dope.[5]

Opioids were highly addictive, and as users developed tolerance, they required larger and larger doses to get high or just to feel normal. Withdrawal from opioids, addiction to which could occur after even a single dose, could be excruciating. Users in withdrawal often experienced intense cravings, fever, sweats, and pain—sensations that addicts referred to as "jonesing." Addiction caused physical changes in the brain, weakening a user's impulse control and making it almost impossible to quit without medical assistance.[6]

Opioids were killers. In high doses, these drugs caused breathing to slow and finally stop, bringing death by respiratory arrest. In 2015, 33,091 Americans died from an opioid overdose.[7] This was just slightly less than the number that died that year in car accidents. Between 1999 and 2015, the rate of death from opioid overdose (number of deaths per 100,000 people) quintupled, that is, it was *five times* higher in 2015 than it was a decade and a half earlier.[8]

Deaths from opioid overdose cut across all geographical regions and demographic groups, but some places and people were harder hit than others. Government data showed that although drug overdose deaths grew for all groups, those in mid-life (aged 45 to 54) had the highest rates. Rates were higher for non-Hispanic whites than for other ethnic groups. The states with the worst opioid problems were West Virginia, New Hampshire, Kentucky, and Ohio, with Rhode Island, Pennsylvania, Massachusetts, and New Mexico not far behind.[9] Opioid use was higher where the economy was bad; as unemployment rates rose, so did overdose deaths.[10] Some researchers called these drug overdoses a "death of despair," part of a broader pattern of rising mortality among middle-aged whites in the United States. "Ultimately, we see our story as about the collapse of the white, high-school educated working class after its heyday in the early 1970s, and the pathologies that accompany that decline" these researchers wrote.[11]

Many opioid overdoses occurred in private, but a startling number occurred in full view of the community. As Margaret Talbot reported in *The New Yorker,* "At this stage of the American opioid epidemic, many addicts are collapsing in public—in gas stations, in restaurant bathrooms, in the aisles of big box stores."[12] She related this story about the experience of two small-town paramedics, who responded to an emergency call from a softball field:

> It was the first practice of the season for the girls' Little League team, and dusk was descending. [The paramedics] . . . stopped near a scrubby set of bleachers, where parents had gathered to watch their daughters bat and field. Two of the parents were lying on the ground, unconscious, several yards apart. As [one of the paramedics] later recalled, the couple's thirteen-year-old daughter was sitting behind a chain-link backstop with her teammates, who were hugging her and comforting her. The couple's younger children, aged ten and seven, were running back and forth between their parents screaming, "Wake up! Wake up!"

The parents survived after the paramedics administered a drug called naloxone, but were later arrested on charges of child neglect.[13]

The pain inflicted by the opioid epidemic went well beyond overdose deaths. People who were addicted to opioids stole from their neighbors to support their habit, ignored their work and family responsibilities, and strained public welfare and law enforcement systems. Some were incarcerated, filling the jails. They made more visits to hospital emergency rooms and drove up health care costs. Babies born to addicted mothers often suffered from neonatal abstinence syndrome, going through painful withdrawal after birth.[14] Grandparents, other relatives, and foster parents were raising the children of addicted parents.

The costs to local governments were often crushing. Ross County, Ohio, for example, saw its child services budget almost double from $1.3 million to $2.4 million from 2009 to 2016. "This has introduced an entirely different metric, an entirely different unpredictability in budgeting," said the top official of Indiana County, Pennsylvania, which had drawn on contingency funds to cover extra costs associated with the opioid crisis.[15]

Some research showed that opioid abuse had hurt the economy by keeping people out of the workforce. A survey of men between the ages of 25 and 54 who were not working or looking for work found that almost half had taken pain medication the previous day, and two-thirds of these had taken a prescription pain medication.[16] Of course, these men may have been out of the workforce because they were ill or injured, not because they were hooked on opioids. But anecdotal evidence was suggestive. The owner of an auto parts supplier in Michigan, for example, reported that she had great difficulty filling jobs at her factory. Part of the problem: When she sent new hires for a routine drug test, 60 percent failed to show up.[17]

Purdue Pharma and the Rise of OxyContin

Many observers traced the modern opioid epidemic to the introduction, in 1996, of a new prescription medication called OxyContin.[18] The company that developed it was Purdue Pharma, a privately held drug maker based in Connecticut.[19] In 1952, three brothers, Andrew, Raymond, and Mortimer Sackler—all physicians—had purchased Purdue Frederick, a small pharmaceutical firm whose main products at that time were earwax removers and laxatives. The company later introduced MS Contin, an extended-release form of morphine used mainly by cancer patients. As the patent for this drug approached expiration, Purdue turned to development of an extended-release form of another opioid, oxycodone, which had long been available as a generic. The firm spent around $40 million to develop and test its new drug, which it named OxyContin. In late 1995, the Food and Drug Administration (FDA) approved the 80-mg dose of the drug (it later approved other doses).

Purdue's introduction of OxyContin coincided with changing attitudes in the medical community toward pain management. For many years, opioids were generally used only for end-stage cancer patients or those suffering from acute traumatic injuries or short-term post-surgical pain. Because of the risk of addiction, opioids were not considered appropriate for the treatment of chronic pain, and they were often mixed with other medicines like acetaminophen to discourage patients from taking larger amounts. In the 1980s, however, some physicians began to advocate for treating chronic pain more aggressively, saying that many patients with conditions like arthritis, back injuries, migraines, and fibromyalgia were suffering needlessly. Some campaigned to have pain recognized as the "fifth vital sign" (the other four were body temperature, pulse rate, respiration rate, and blood pressure). Because clinicians could not measure pain objectively, some adopted a 1-to-10 scale, from "no pain" to "the worst pain" the patient had ever experienced.[20]

Purdue allied itself with this view, cultivating relationships with professional associations, such as the American Pain Society and the American Academy of Pain Medicine, which promoted the idea that pain was undertreated. It sponsored pain-management educational conferences in resort locations for doctors. The company also hired more sales representatives, more than doubling its sales force from 318 to 767 between 1996 and 2000. Purdue sales reps were well compensated, earning an average of $126,500 a year, including bonuses based on sales. In 2001 alone, the company paid $40 million in bonuses. The company's detailers, as its sales representatives were known, used prescriber profiles to target general practitioners and those who were frequent prescribers of opioids. They handed out coupons for a 30-day free supply of OxyContin to doctors, who could pass them along to patients.

Purdue's sales representatives downplayed OxyContin's potential for addiction, claiming the risk was less than 1 percent. This dubious assertion was based on a five-sentence letter to the editor that had appeared in a 1980 issue of the *New England Journal of Medicine,* based on records of hospitalized patients in controlled settings. Sales representatives also argued that OxyContin's extended-release

EXHIBIT 1

Overdose Deaths from Prescription Opioids (per 100,000) and Opioid Prescriptions (Morphine Milligram Equivalents per 100), United States, 1999–2016

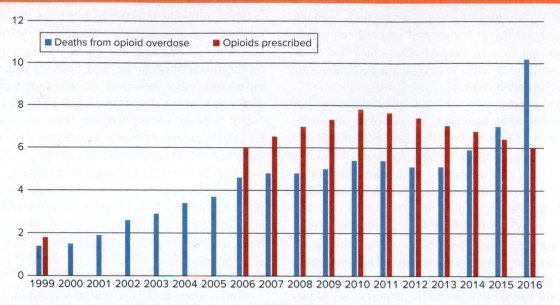

Sources: "Prescription Opioid Overdose Death Rate per 100,000 Population," The Henry J. Kaiser Family Foundation, at www.kff.org; Centers for Disease Control and Prevention, Annual Surveillance Report of Drug-Related Risks and Outcomes, United States, 2017, Table 1B; Gery P. Guy, Jr. et al., "Vital Signs: Changes in Opioid Prescribing in the United States, 2006–2015," Centers for Disease Control and Prevention Weekly, July 7, 2017, and personal correspondence with Dr. Guy. Deaths from legal and illegal fentanyl cannot be distinguished, so both are included in the KFF data base. Data on prescriptions in MMEs for 2000 to 2005 are unavailable, but data on opioid pain reliever sales in kilograms per 10,000 show a steady rise during this period ("Vital Signs: Overdoses of Prescription Opioid Pain Relievers, United States, 1999–2008," Centers for Disease Control and Prevention Morbidity and Mortality Weekly Report, November 4, 2011).

formula made it less susceptible to abuse; although the pill contained a large dose of oxycodone, users would not get a sudden rush because the drug's effects would be spread out over a 12-hour period, they told doctors.

Despite the company's claims that OxyContin's extended-release mechanism made it hard to abuse, addicts quickly discovered that they could crush one of the pills and then swallow, inhale, or inject it to produce an intense high. As the number of prescriptions for opioid medications rose, so did overdose deaths. Exhibit 1 shows the quantity of opioids prescribed from 1999 to 2016, alongside the number of deaths from prescription opioid overdose. (The exhibit reports all opioids prescribed, not just OxyContin.)

As a private company, Purdue had no obligation to file annual reports, and its owners and managers rarely spoke publicly. But the company's senior medical director did tell a reporter in 2001, as awareness of OxyContin's risks began to spread in the public

health community: "A lot of these people [addicts] say, 'Well, I was taking the medicine like my doctor told me to,' and then they start taking more and more and more. I don't see where that's my problem."[21]

Purdue Pharma's marketing campaign for OxyContin was highly effective. In 1996, the company's revenue from OxyContin was $44 million; it continued to rise, peaking at $3.1 billion in 2010. That year, it represented 90 percent of the company's total sales. The private firm's owners profited greatly from the drug's success. In 2015, *Forbes* estimated the Sackler family's net worth at around $14 billion, the 16th largest fortune in the United States.[22]

In 2007, the company settled charges brought by the U.S. Justice Department that it had lied about OxyContin's addiction risks, operating "a corporate culture that allowed this product to be misbranded with the intent to defraud and mislead." The company paid $600 million in fines—$470 million to federal and state governments and $130 million to resolve civil suits. Its top three executives personally paid $34.5 million in fines and were barred from involvement in any government health care program for 12 years.[23]

Government Regulation of Opioids

The federal government strictly regulated the manufacture and distribution of opioid medications like OxyContin under the Controlled Substances Act (CSA) of 1970.

The CSA empowered the Drug Enforcement Administration (DEA) and the FDA to create five lists, or "schedules," of certain controlled substances, ranging from one (Schedule I) to five (Schedule V). Schedule I drugs were those that had no accepted medical use and high potential for abuse; they included heroin, LSD, and MDMA ("Ecstasy"). These drugs were illegal, and physicians could not prescribe them under any circumstances. Schedule II drugs were those that *did* have an accepted medical use, but also had high potential for abuse and could lead to severe psychological and physical dependence. They included most prescription opiates,

such as oxycodone, hydrocodone, codeine, and fentanyl. The DEA registered firms and individuals that handled controlled substances and required them to maintain complete and accurate inventories and records, and to store them securely. It required wholesalers, like McKesson, to maintain a system to detect and prevent the diversion of prescription drugs for nonmedical use. The DEA licensed physicians to prescribe Schedule II painkillers and could revoke a license if a doctor did not provide them for a legitimate medical purpose.

The DEA also established annual production quotas of various controlled substances. It negotiated these quotas with drug manufacturers, based on amounts considered necessary for medical, scientific, research, industrial, and export needs and to maintain sufficient reserves. This system was designed to meet legitimate needs, while preventing diversion. Although each company received its own quota, this information was proprietary, and the DEA published only the aggregate annual quota for each drug.

EXHIBIT 2

Drug Enforcement Agency Aggregate Production Quotas for Oxycodone (for Sale) By Year, in Kilograms, 1994–2017

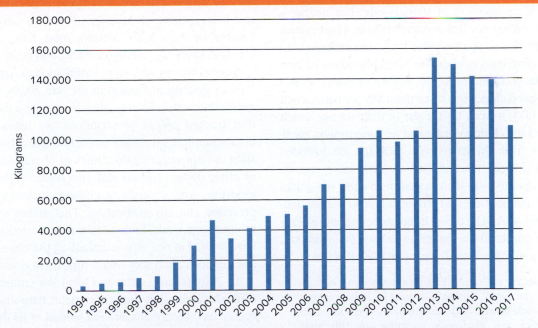

Sources: Federal Register, 1994–1997; U.S. Department of Justice, Drug Enforcement Agency, Diversion Control Division, "Controlled Substances: Final Aggregate Production Quotas," 1998–2006, and "Aggregate Production Quota History for Selected Substances," 2007–2017. This chart includes only oxycodone intended for sale. The DEA maintains a separate quota for oxycodone intended for other uses, such as manufacturing other substances.

After the introduction of OxyContin, the DEA repeatedly raised the aggregate quota for oxycodone (its main component), as shown in Exhibit 2. In 1994, the year before the FDA first approved OxyContin, the DEA limited production to 2,995 kilograms of oxycodone. The agency continued to raise the quota, reaching a peak of 153,750 kilograms in 2013—more than 50 times as high. After 2013, presumably in response to growing concern about the opioid epidemic, the DEA reduced the quota, and by 2017, the amount approved had dropped to 108,510 kilograms.

Pain Clinics and Unscrupulous Physicians

A pivotal role in the opioid epidemic was played by pain clinics—known colloquially as "pill mills"—which dispensed opioids inappropriately for nonmedical uses. Although pill mills sprouted up in many locations in the mid- to late-2000s, the epicenter of the trend was Broward County, Florida, home to Fort Lauderdale.

One of the most notorious was American Pain, which became for a time the largest dispenser of oxycodone in the nation.[24] American Pain was founded in 2008 by a young felon—he had done a short stint in jail for possession of steroids—who had neither a college degree nor any medical training. His business concept was to open a clinic dedicated exclusively to prescribing legal opioids. He hired physicians by running ads on *Craigslist* for doctors with a license to prescribe painkillers. He offered them $75 per patient visit plus $1,000 a week for the use of their license, which enabled the clinic to order and sell prescription medications. The physicians who took the job included retired doctors who wanted to earn more money, young doctors with high student loan debt, and graduates of marginal medical schools who had trouble finding other work. The owner hired his best friend, a beefy former construction worker, to oversee the operation, which journalist John Temple described this way:

> Outside, it looked like a bustling doctor's office, or the DMV. Inside, [a] crew of heavily inked muscle-heads and ex-strippers operated the office and pharmacy, counting out pills and stashing cash in garbage cans. Under their white lab coats, the doctors carried guns.[25]

As business boomed, the clinic moved four times, each time to a larger location with more parking. At its peak, American Pain employed five full-time and several part-time doctors and a staff of about 20. It was raking in $100,000 a day—in cash. In 2009, the young owner's take-home pay was an astonishing $9 million.

Almost 9 out of 10 of American Pain's customers came from out of state, many from the rural counties of Kentucky and Tennessee, which by this time were in the grip of widespread opioid addiction. Patients could see a doctor with no appointment, get a prescription with few questions asked, and then get the script filled in-house. Entrepreneurial "sponsors" drove large groups of people to South Florida, giving them cash for their doctor's visit and prescription and then accepting as compensation a share of their pills, which could be sold back home on the black market. Interstate 75, the main highway connecting Florida to points north in Georgia and Tennessee, became known as "Oxy Alley" or the "blue highway," after the blue 30-mg oxycodone pills manufactured by the drug maker Mallinckrodt.

No one knew exactly how many deaths resulted from American Pain's practices. But drug enforcement officials later estimated that the clinic had prescribed almost 20 million opioids over a two-year period. More than 50 people who died of drug overdoses in Florida had been patients at American Pain. An uncounted number of the clinic's patients must have died in Georgia, Kentucky, Tennessee, Ohio, and other states.

Several factors allowed pill mills such as American Pain to flourish in Florida in the late 2000s. Unlike most other states, Florida did not operate a database that tracked opioid prescriptions, so users could obtain multiple prescriptions without detection. The state did not require pain clinics to obtain a license, or clinic owners to have any specialized training or expertise. And, crucially, it allowed doctors to both prescribe and sell medication. This meant that pill mill patrons could both obtain a prescription, and have it filled in one visit—eliminating the chance that a scrupulous pharmacy would turn them down.

In 2010, federal, state, and local law enforcement officials finally shut down American Pain and prosecuted its owner, manager, and several of its doctors, sending several to prison. The same year, Florida barred convicted felons from operating pain clinics and required pain clinic doctors to have special training. The following year it established a drug database. Other states with concentrations of pill mills made similar moves around this time.

The Crackdown and Turn to Illegal Opioids

Around 2010, several factors converged to slow the diversion of prescription opioids into the hands of abusers. In addition to the crackdown on pill mills, government agencies, medical institutions, and companies all began changing their policies and practices. In 2010, Purdue changed the formulation of OxyContin, so it could not be crushed or dissolved, and it lobbied the government to require hard-to-abuse formulations of opioids. The Centers for Disease Control issued new guidelines on prescription of opioids, as did the Veteran's Administration. States and insurers placed limits on how many pills doctors could prescribe. These moves had their intended effect: data (reported in Exhibit 1) showed that the number of opioid painkillers prescribed peaked in 2010.[26]

As the flow of prescription pills slowed, addicts increasingly turned to illegal street drugs—heroin, fentanyl from criminal sources, and even a powerful animal tranquilizer called carfentanil. A study of patients undergoing treatment for heroin addiction, published in 2014, found that of those who had started using drugs in the 2000s, three-quarters had first used prescription opioids, and had then switched to heroin because it was cheaper and easier to get.[27] "People eventually say, 'Why am I paying $1 per milligram for oxy when for a tenth of the price I can get an equivalent dose of heroin?'" commented one physician at a drug recovery center.[28]

As they made the shift from prescription pills, many addicts turned to so-called black tar heroin, delivered by what *The Washington Post* called a "sophisticated farm-to-arm supply chain fueling America's surging heroin appetite."[29] Relatively inexpensive, with the consistency of a Tootsie roll, black tar heroin was made from poppies grown on the Pacific coast of Mexico. Mexican poppy production rose 160 percent from 2013 to 2015.[30]

According to research by journalist Sam Quinones, most of the black-tar dealers hailed from the area around Xalisco in the state of Nayarit,

Mexico. The "Xalisco Boys," as some law enforcement officers called them, devised a highly effective method of distribution. Managers recruited ambitious young men with few prospects at home and sent them north across the border. The Xalisco Boys avoided big coastal cities, where established gangs controlled the heroin trade, and instead targeted mid-sized communities in the heartland where couriers could blend into the local Latino population—places like Nashville, Columbus, Salt Lake City, Portland, and Denver. The couriers were trained to use rental cars, which could not be seized by authorities, and disposable mobile phones. They did not carry weapons, and they never used the product. The couriers worked on salary and sent most of their earnings to their families in Mexico. If one was arrested, he would be deported, and another would take his place.[31]

Quinones described the operations of the Xalisco Boys this way:

> An addict calls, and an operator directs him to an intersection or parking lot. The operator dispatches a driver, who tools around town, his mouth full of tiny balloons of heroin, with a bottle of water nearby to swig down if the cops stop him. . . The driver meets the addict, spits out the required balloons, takes the money and that's that. It happens every day—from 7 a.m. to 7 p.m., because these guys keep business hours.[32]

A study by the Congressional Research Service found that in 2014, 914,000 Americans had used heroin in the past year.[33] Tragically, many of them died: Heroin-related overdose deaths more than doubled between 2009 and 2014.

A Flood of Lawsuits

As the opioid crisis raged, states, counties, cities and towns, and Indian tribes began bringing lawsuits against various business firms to recoup some of the escalating costs of law enforcement, health care, and child protective services. By 2017, at least 25 government entities had sued the drug companies, distributors, and pharmacy chains that had some hand in the journey of the pain pill from the factory into the addict's hands. These lawsuits relied on a range of legal theories; they variously cited laws related to public nuisance, consumer protection, negligence, and unjust enrichment.

To cite just a few examples:

- McDowell County, West Virginia, sued the three big drug distributors—McKesson, AmerisourceBergen, and Cardinal Health. "In my thinking, they [the distributors] were no different than drug dealers selling on the street," the county sheriff said.[34]

- The state of Ohio sued half-a-dozen drug makers—Purdue Pharma, Teva, Johnson & Johnson, Janssen, Endo, and Allergan—charging them with making false and misleading statements about the risks and benefits of prescription opioids. The state's legal brief stated that these drug companies had "helped unleash a healthcare crisis that has had far-reaching financial, social, and deadly consequences in the state of Ohio."[35]

- The city of Everett, Washington, sued Purdue Pharma for recklessly supplying OxyContin to suspicious physicians and pharmacies in their community, enabling illegal drug diversion and providing a "gateway" to heroin abuse.[36]

- The Cherokee Nation in Oklahoma sued distributors and pharmacies—including Walmart, CVS, and Walgreens—and called for them to reimburse the Cherokees for health care costs. "The resources of the Cherokee Nation are being spent on this crisis that otherwise should be spent on our ordinary, everyday health care needs," said the Cherokee Nation's attorney general.[37]

Some legal experts thought these lawsuits had little chance of success. Prescription opioids had a legitimate medical purpose and had been approved by the government. One expert in product liability law put it this way: "[The distributors] ship a drug that's approved by the FDA, and then a bunch of bad actors intervene—pill mills, doctors who overprescribe, and the addicts themselves. It's a pretty strong argument." Other legal experts, however, thought the companies were in a weaker position. "[The pharmaceutical firms] are big companies that knew their product was doing harm," said an attorney who had been involved in the tobacco lawsuits years earlier. "Instead of helping to solve the problem, they promoted the irresponsible use of their product to improve their bottom line." Added the attorney who represented the Cherokee Nation: "These pharmaceutical companies should be scared as hell."[38]

ENDNOTES

[1] U.S. Department of Justice, "McKesson Agrees to Pay Record $150 Million Settlement for Failure to Report Suspicious Orders of Pharmaceutical Drugs," press release, January 17, 2017.

[2] "Drug Firms Poured 780 Million Painkillers into WV Amid Rise of Overdoses," *Charleston Gazette-Mail,* December 17, 2016.

[3] "As America's Opioid Crisis Spirals, Giant Drug Distributor McKesson Is Feeling the Pain," *Fortune,* June 12, 2017.

[4] Quoted in Andrew Kolodny et al., "The Prescription Opioid and Heroin Crisis: A Public Health Approach to an Epidemic of Addiction," *Annual Review of Public Health,* January 2015, p. 58.

[5] John Temple, *American Pain: How A Young Felon and His Ring of Doctors Unleashed America's Deadliest Drug Epidemic,* Lyons Press, 2016.

[6] Information about opioids and their risks is available from the National Institute of Drug Abuse, www.drugabuse.gov.

[7] Rose A. Rudd et al., "Increases in Drug and Opioid-Involved Overdose Deaths—United States, 2010–2015," *Morbidity and Mortality Weekly Report,* 65(50&51), December 30, 2016. This figure is for drug overdoses due to opioids only; 52,404 Americans died in 2015 from overdoses of all kinds of drugs combined.

[8] Data from the Kaiser Family Foundation, shown in Exhibit 1.

[9] Holly Hedegaard et al., "Drug Overdose Deaths in the United States, 1999–2015," Centers for Disease Control and Prevention, NCHS Data Brief No. 273, February 2017.

[10] "Are Opioid Deaths Affected by Macroeconomic Conditions?" *NBER [National Bureau of Economic Research] Bulletin on Aging and Health,* 2017 #3.

[11] "New Research Identified a 'Sea of Despair' Among White, Working-Class Americans," *The Washington Post,* March 23, 2017. The research cited is Anne Case and Angus Deaton, "Mortality and Morbidity in the 21st Century," *Brookings Papers on Economic Activity,* Spring 2017.

[12] Margaret Talbot, "The Addicts Next Door, a Reporter at Large," *New Yorker,* May 29, 2017, https://www.newyorker.com/magazine/2017/06/05/the-addicts-next-door.

[13] "The Addicts Next Door," *The New Yorker,* June 5 & 12, 2017.

[14] "Study: Rural Areas See Increase in Babies Born with Opioid Addiction," *USA Today,* December 14, 2016.

[15] "How the Opioid Crisis Is Blowing a Hole in the Finances of Small-Town America," *The Epoch Times,* September 21–27, 2017.

[16] Alan B. Krueger, "Where Have All the Workers Gone?" Paper prepared for the Boston Federal Reserve Bank's 60th Economic Conference, October 4, 2016.

[17] "Eager to Create Blue-Collar Jobs, a Small Business Struggles," *The New York Times,* September 3, 2017.

[18] This account of Purdue's development and marketing of OxyContin is based on Barry Meier, *Pain Killer: A 'Wonder' Drug's Trail of Addiction and Death* (Rodale Press, 2003); Art Van Zee MD, "The Promotion and Marketing of OxyContin: Commercial Triumph, Public Health Tragedy," *American Journal of Public Health,* 99(2), February 2009; Mike Mariani, "Poison Pill: How the American Opiate Epidemic was Started by One Pharmaceutical Company," *Pacific Standard,* February 23, 2015; and "The Family that Built an Empire of Pain," *The New Yorker,* October 30, 2017.

[19] Purdue Pharma had no relationship with Purdue University, although they shared a name.

[20] Kolodny et al., "The Prescription Opioid and Heroin Crisis."

[21] Harriet Ryan, Lisa Girion, and Scott Glover, "You Want A Description Of Hell?' Oxycontin's 12-Hour Problem," *Los Angeles Times*, May 5, 2016. https://www.latimes.com/projects/oxycontin-part1/.

[22] "The OxyContin Clan: The Newcomer to Forbes 200 Families," *Forbes,* July 1, 2015.

[23] "U.S. Maker of OxyContin Painkiller to Pay $600 Million in Guilty Plea," *The New York Times,* May 11, 2007; "Ruling Is Upheld Against Executives Tied to OxyContin," *The New York Times,* December 15, 2010.

[24] This description of American Pain is based on John Temple, *American Pain: How A Young Felon and His Ring of Doctors Unleashed America's Deadliest Drug Epidemic* (Rowman & Littlefield: Guilford, CT, 2015).

[25] John Temple, *American Pain: How A Young Felon and His Ring of Doctors Unleashed America's Deadliest Drug Epidemic,* Lyons Press, 2016.

[26] "Opioid Prescriptions Fall After 2010 Peak," CDC Report Finds," *New York Times,* July 6, 2017.

[27] Theodore J. Cicero et al., "The Changing Face of Heroin Use in the United States," *JAMA Psychiatry,* 71(7), 2014.

[28] Benedict Carey, "Prescription Painkillers Seen as a Gateway to Heroin," Quotas - 2006, The New York Times Company, February 10, 2014, https://www.nytimes.com/2014/02/11/health/prescription-painkillers-seen-as-a-gateway-to-heroin.html..

[29] "Pellets, Planes, and the New Frontier: How Mexican Drug Cartels Are Targeting Small-Town America," *The Washington Post,* September 24, 2015.

[30] "Heroin Trafficking in the United States," *Congressional Research Service,* August 23, 2016.

[31] "Heroin Is a White-People Problem: Bad Medicine, Economic Rot, and the Enterprising Mexican Town that Turned the Heartland onto Black Tar," *Salon,* April 18, 2015.

[32] Sam Quinones, "Serving All Your Heroin Needs," The New York Times Company, April 19, 2015, https://www.nytimes.com/2015/04/19/opinion/sunday/serving-all-your-heroin-needs.html

[33] "Heroin Trafficking in the United States." *Congressional Research Service*, February 14, 2019, https://fas.org/sgp/crs/misc/R44599.pdf

[34] "As America's Opioid Crisis Spirals, Giant Drug Distributor McKesson Is Feeling the Pain." Erika Fry, *Fortune*, June 13, 2017, https://fortune.com/2017/06/13/fortune-500-mckesson-opioid-epidemic/

[35] "In the Common Pleas Court of Ross County, Ohio, Civil Division," Court of Common Pleas, May 31, 2017, https://www.ohioattorneygeneral.gov/Files/Briefing-Room/News-Releases/Consumer-Protection/2017-05-31-Final-Complaint-with-Sig-Page.aspx.

[36] "City of Everett v. Purdue Pharma," January 19, 2017, complaint filed in the Superior Court of the State of Washington.

[37] Melissa Locker, "Inside Cherokee Lawsuit to Fight Opioid Epidemic," *Rolling Stone*, May 26, 2017, https://www.rollingstone.com/culture/culture-features/inside-cherokee-lawsuit-to-fight-opioid-epidemic-120666/; and Nate Hegyi, "Cherokee Nation Sues Wal-Mart, CVS, Walgreens Over Tribal Opioid Crisis, " National Public Radio, April 25, 2017, https://www.npr.org/sections/codeswitch/.2017/04/25/485887058/cherokee-nation-sues-wal-mart-cvs-walgreens-over-tribal-opioid-crisis.

[38] Scott Higham, and Lenny Bernstein. "Drugmakers and Distributors Face Barrage of Lawsuits Over Opioid Epidemic," *The Washington Post,* July 4, 2017, https://www.washingtonpost.com/investigations/drugmakers-and-distributors-face-barrage-of-lawsuits-over-opioid-epidemic/2017/07/04/3fc33c64-5794-11e7-b38e-35fd8e0c288f_story.html?noredirect=on&utm_term=.38ce6e990759.

Glossary

adaptive cultures **Adaptive cultures** are characterized by a willingness on the part of organizational members to accept change and take on the challenge of introducing and executing new strategies.

backward integration **Backward integration** involves performing industry value chain activities previously performed by suppliers or other enterprises engaged in earlier stages of the industry value chain.

balanced scorecard The **balanced scorecard** is a widely used method for combining the use of both strategic and financial objectives, tracking their achievement, and giving management a more complete and balanced view of how well an organization is performing.

benchmarking **Benchmarking** is a potent tool for learning which companies are best at performing particular activities and then using their techniques (or "best practices") to improve the cost and effectiveness of a company's own internal activities.

best practice A **best practice** is a method of performing an activity that consistently delivers superior results compared to other approaches.

best-cost provider strategies **Best-cost provider strategies** are a *hybrid* of low-cost provider and differentiation strategies that aim at satisfying buyer expectations on key quality/features/performance/service attributes and beating customer expectations on price.

blue ocean strategies **Blue ocean strategies** offer growth in revenues and profits by discovering or inventing new industry segments that create altogether new demand.

broad differentiation strategy The essence of a **broad differentiation strategy** is to offer unique product or service attributes that a wide range of buyers find appealing and worth paying for.

business ethics **Business ethics** involves the application of general ethical principles to the actions and decisions of businesses and the conduct of their personnel.

business model A company's **business model** sets forth how its strategy and operating approaches will create value for customers, while at the same time generating ample revenues to cover costs and realizing a profit. The two elements of a company's business model are its (1) customer value proposition and (2) its profit formula.

business strategy **Business strategy** is primarily concerned with strengthening the company's market position and building competitive advantage in a single-business company or a single business unit of a diversified multibusiness corporation.

capability **Capability** is the capacity of a company to competently perform some internal activity. Capabilities are developed and enabled through the deployment of a company's resources.

cash cow A **cash cow** generates operating cash flows over and above its internal requirements, thereby providing financial resources that may be used to invest in cash hogs, finance new acquisitions, fund share buyback programs, or pay dividends.

cash hog A **cash hog** generates operating cash flows that are too small to fully fund its operations and growth; a cash hog must receive cash infusions from outside sources to cover its working capital and investment requirements.

competitive strategy A **competitive strategy** concerns the specifics of management's game plan for competing successfully and securing a competitive advantage over rivals in the marketplace.

corporate culture **Corporate culture** is a company's internal work climate and is shaped by its core values, beliefs, and business principles. A company's culture is important because it influences its traditions, work practices, and style of operating.

corporate restructuring **Corporate restructuring** involves radically altering the business lineup by divesting businesses that lack strategic fit or are poor performers and acquiring new businesses that offer better promise for enhancing shareholder value.

corporate social responsibility (CSR) **Corporate social responsibility (CSR)** refers to a company's *duty* to operate in an honorable manner, provide good working conditions for employees, encourage workforce diversity, be a good steward of the environment, and actively work to better the quality of life in the local communities in which it operates and in society at large.

corporate social responsibility strategy   A company's **corporate social responsibility strategy** is defined by the specific combination of socially beneficial activities it opts to support with its contributions of time, money, and other resources.

corporate strategy   Corporate strategy establishes an overall game plan for managing a *set of businesses* in a diversified, multibusiness company.

cost driver   A cost driver is a factor having a strong effect on the cost of a company's value chain activities and cost structure.

D

driving forces   Driving forces are the major underlying causes of change in industry and competitive conditions.

dynamic capability   A dynamic capability is the ability to modify, deepen, or reconfigure the company's existing resources and capabilities in response to its changing environment or market opportunities.

E

economic risks   Economic risks stem from the stability of a country's monetary system, economic and regulatory policies, and the lack of property rights protections.

economies of scope   Economies of scope are cost reductions stemming from strategic fit along the value chains of related businesses (thereby, a larger scope of operations), whereas *economies of scale* accrue from a larger operation.

environmental sustainability strategies   Environmental sustainability strategies involve deliberate actions to protect the environment, provide for the longevity of natural resources, maintain ecological support systems for future generations, and guard against the ultimate endangerment of the planet.

ethical relativism   According to the school of **ethical relativism,** different societal cultures and customs create divergent standards of right and wrong; thus, what is ethical or unethical must be judged in the light of local customs and social mores, and can vary from one culture or nation to another.

ethical universalism   According to the school of **ethical universalism,** the same standards of what is ethical and what is unethical resonate with peoples of most societies, regardless of local traditions and cultural norms; hence, common ethical standards can be used to judge employee conduct in a variety of country markets and cultural circumstances.

F

financial objectives   Financial objectives relate to the financial performance targets management has established for the organization to achieve.

first-mover advantages and disadvantages   Because of **first-mover advantages and disadvantages,** competitive advantage can spring from *when* a move is made as well as from *what* a move is made.

forward integration   Forward integration involves performing industry value chain activities closer to the end user.

G

global strategies   Global strategies employ the same basic competitive approach in all countries where a company operates and are best suited to industries that are globally standardized in terms of customer preferences, buyer purchasing habits, distribution channels, or marketing methods. This is the **think global, act global** strategic theme.

H

horizontal scope   Horizontal scope is the range of product and service segments that a firm serves within its focal market.

I

integrative social contracts theory   According to **integrative social contracts theory,** universal ethical principles based on collective views of multiple cultures combine to form a "social contract" that all employees in all country markets have a duty to observe. Within the boundaries of this social contract, there is room for host-country cultures to exert *some* influence in setting their own moral and ethical standards. However, *"first-order"* universal ethical norms always take precedence over *"second-order"* local ethical norms in circumstances in which local ethical norms are more permissive

internal capital market   A strong **internal capital market** allows a diversified company to add value by shifting capital from business units generating *free cash flow* to those needing additional capital to expand and realize their growth potential.

international strategy   A company's **international strategy** is its strategy for competing in two or more countries simultaneously.

J

joint venture   A joint venture is a type of strategic alliance that involves the establishment of an independent corporate entity that is jointly owned and controlled by the two partners.

K

key success factors   **Key success factors** are the strategy elements, product attributes, competitive capabilities, or intangible assets with the greatest impact on future success in the marketplace.

L

low-cost leader   A **low-cost leader**'s basis for competitive advantage is lower overall costs than competitors'. Success in achieving a low-cost edge over rivals comes from eliminating and/or curbing "nonessential" activities and/or outmanaging rivals in performing essential activities.

M

macro-environment   The **macro-environment** encompasses the broad environmental context in which a company is situated and is comprised of six principal components: political factors, economic conditions, sociocultural forces, technological factors, environmental factors, and legal/regulatory conditions.

matrix organizational structure   A **matrix organizational structure** is a combination structure that overlays one type of structure onto another type, with multiple reporting relationships. It is used to foster cross-unit collaboration. Matrix structures are also called composite structures or combination structures.

mission statement   A well-conceived **mission statement** conveys a company's purpose in language specific enough to give the company its own identity.

multidivisional (or divisional) organizational structure   A **multidivisional (or divisional) organizational structure** is a decentralized structure consisting of a set of operating divisions organized along market, customer, product, or geographic lines, along with a central corporate headquarters, which monitors divisional activities, allocates resources, and exercises overall control.

multidomestic strategy   A **multidomestic strategy** calls for varying a company's product offering and competitive approach from country to country in an effort to be responsive to significant cross-country differences in customer preferences, buyer purchasing habits, distribution channels, or marketing methods.

N

network structure   A **network structure** is the arrangement linking a number of independent organizations involved in some common undertaking.

O

objectives   **Objectives** are an organization's performance targets—the results management wants to achieve.

outsourcing   **Outsourcing** involves contracting out certain value chain activities to outside specialists and strategic allies.

P

PESTEL analysis   **PESTEL analysis** can be used to assess the strategic relevance of the six principal components of the macro-environment: political, economic, sociocultural, technological, environmental, and legal forces.

political risks   **Political risks** stem from instability or weakness in national governments and hostility to foreign business.

R

realized strategy   A company's **realized strategy** is a combination of *deliberate planned elements* and *unplanned emergent elements*. Some components of a company's deliberate strategy will fail in the marketplace and become *abandoned strategy elements*.

related businesses   **Related businesses** possess competitively valuable cross-business value chain and resource matchups.

resource   A **resource** is a competitive asset that is owned or controlled by a company.

resource and capability analysis   **Resource and capability analysis** is a powerful tool for sizing up a company's competitive assets and determining if the assets can support a sustainable competitive advantage over market rivals.

resource bundles   Companies that lack a standalone resource that is competitively powerful may nonetheless develop a competitive advantage through **resource bundles** that enable the superior performance of important cross-functional capabilities.

resource fit   A diversified company exhibits **resource fit** when its businesses add to a company's overall mix of resources and capabilities and when the parent company has sufficient resources to support its entire group of businesses without spreading itself too thin.

S

scope of the firm   The **scope of the firm** refers to the range of activities the firm performs internally, the breadth of its product and service offerings, the extent of its geographic market presence, and its mix of businesses.

self-dealing   **Self-dealing** occurs when managers take advantage of their position to further their own private interests rather than those of the company.

social complexity/causal ambiguity   **Social complexity** and **causal ambiguity** are two factors that inhibit the ability of rivals to imitate a firm's most valuable resources and capabilities. Causal ambiguity makes it very hard to figure out how a complex resource contributes to competitive advantage and therefore exactly what to imitate.

spin-off   A **spin-off** is a business unit divestiture approach that creates an independent company by either selling shares to the public via an initial public offering or distributing shares in the new company to shareholders of the corporate parent.

strategic alliance   A **strategic alliance** is a formal agreement between two or more companies to work cooperatively toward some common objective.

strategic fit   **Strategic fit** exists when value chains of different businesses present opportunities for cross-business skills transfer, cost sharing, or brand sharing.

strategic group   A **strategic group** is a cluster of industry rivals that have similar competitive approaches and market positions.

strategic group mapping   **Strategic group mapping** is a technique for displaying the different market or competitive positions that rival firms occupy in the industry.

strategic intent   A company exhibits **strategic intent** when it relentlessly pursues an ambitious strategic objective, concentrating the full force of its resources and competitive actions on achieving that objective.

strategic objectives   **Strategic objectives** relate to target outcomes that indicate a company is strengthening its market standing, competitive vitality, and future business prospects.

strategic plan   A company's **strategic plan** lays out its future direction, performance targets, and strategy.

strategic vision   A **strategic vision** describes "where we are going"—the course and direction management has charted and the company's future product-customer-market-technology focus.

strategy   A company's **strategy** explains why the company matters in the marketplace by specifying an approach to creating superior value for customers and determining how capabilities and resources will be utilized to deliver the desired value to customers.

sustainable business practices   **Sustainable business practices** are those that meet the needs of the present without compromising the ability to meet the needs of the future.

sustainable competitive advantage   A company achieves **sustainable competitive advantage** when an attractively large number of buyers develop a durable preference for its products or services over the offerings of competitors, despite the efforts of competitors to overcome or erode its advantage.

SWOT analysis   **SWOT analysis** is a simple but powerful tool for sizing up a company's internal strengths and competitive deficiencies, its market opportunities, and the external threats to its future well-being.

T

think global, act global   A **think global, act global** strategic theme employs the same basic competitive approach in all countries where the company operates and puts strategic emphasis on building a global brand name and aggressively pursuing opportunities to transfer ideas, new products, and capabilities from one country to another.

think global, act local   A **think global, act local** strategic approach is emphasized in a transnational strategy intended to accommodate cross-country variations in buyer tastes, local customs, and market conditions while also striving for the benefits of standardization.

think local, act local   **Think local, act local** strategy-making approaches are also essential when host-government regulations or trade policies preclude a uniform, coordinated worldwide market approach.

transnational strategy   A **transnational strategy** is a **think global, act local** approach to strategy making that involves employing essentially the same strategic theme (low-cost, differentiation, focused, best-cost) in all country markets, while allowing some country-to-country customization to fit local market conditions.

U

unrelated businesses   **Unrelated businesses** have dissimilar value chains and resources requirements, with no competitively important cross-business value chain relationships.

V

value chain   A company's **value chain** identifies the primary activities that create customer value and related support activities.

value driver   A **value driver** is a value chain activity or factor that can have a strong effect on customer value and creating differentiation.

values   A company's **values** are the beliefs, traits, and behavioral norms that company personnel are expected to display in conducting the company's business and pursuing its strategic vision and mission.

vertical integration   A **vertically integrated** firm is one that performs value chain activities along more than one stage of an industry's overall value chain.

vertical scope   **Vertical scope** is the extent to which a firm's internal activities encompass one, some, many, or all of the activities that make up an industry's entire value chain system, ranging from raw-material production to final sales and service activities.

VRIN tests for sustainable competitive advantage   The **VRIN tests for sustainable competitive advantage** ask if a resource or capability is *valuable, rare, inimitable,* and *nonsubstitutable.*

Indexes

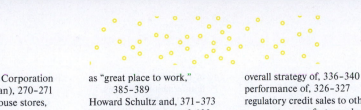